The Advanced Guide to
Microsoft Access 2010
Microsoft Office Specialist Exam 77-885 Study Guide

another Computer Mama Guide

© 2012 Comma Productions, LLC

Front Row Video

Receipt   1

7/22/2012

Deeter Poohbah

Brighton, MI 48116

No of Movies   5

Total Due $17.50

Movies Rented

Harry Potter and the $3.50
Deathly Hallows:
Part 2 (2011)

3-Day Rental

another
**Computer
Mama
Guide**

The Advanced Guide to Microsoft Access 2010

Trademark and Copyright

Limit of Liability/Disclaimer of Warranty:

The Advanced Guide to Microsoft Access 2010

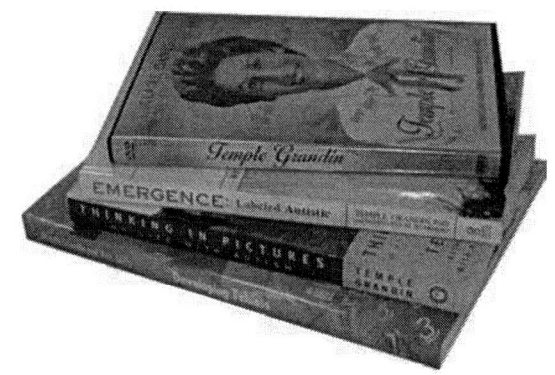

Microsoft Office Specialist Certification

What is the Microsoft Office Specialist Certification?

The Microsoft Office Specialist certification validates through the use of exams that you have obtained specific skill sets within the applicable Microsoft Office programs and other Microsoft programs included in the Microsoft Office Specialist Program. The candidate can choose which exam(s) they want to take according to which skills they want to validate.

CertiPort is the premier provider for validating technology skills.

The **Microsoft Office Specialist** tests are offered at authorized testing centers.

For more information on the MOS exam topics or to find a testing center near you please contact: **www.certiport.com**

What is the Microsoft Office Specialist Certification Program?

The **Microsoft Office Specialist (MOS) Certification Program** enables candidates to show that they have something exceptional to offer – proven expertise in Microsoft Office programs. Recognized by businesses and schools around the world, millions of certifications have been obtained in over 100 different countries. The **Microsoft Office Specialist (MOS) Certification Program** is the only Microsoft-approved certification program of its kind.

The Microsoft Office Specialist Certification Series

Core Certification: Pass any 1 test:
Word 2010 Core: Exam 77-881
Excel® 2010 Core: Exam 77-882
PowerPoint® 2010: Exam 77-883
Access® 2010: Exam 77-885
Outlook® 2010: Exam 77-884

Expert Certification: Pass either test:
Word 2010 Expert: Exam 77-887
Excel® 2010 Expert: Exam 77-888

Master: Pass 3 required and 1 elective test:
Required
Word 2010 Expert: Exam 77-887
Excel® 2010 Expert: Exam 77-888
PowerPoint® 2010: Exam 77-883

Elective
Access® 2010: Exam 77-885 or
Outlook® 2010: Exam 77-884

Please Note: Comma Productions, LLC. is independent from Microsoft Corporation, and not affiliated with Microsoft in any manner. While the Complete Computer Guides may be used in assisting individuals to prepare for a Microsoft Office Specialist Certification exam, Microsoft, its designated program administrator, and Comma Productions, LLC. do not warrant that use of these Complete Computer Guides will ensure passing a Microsoft Office Specialist Certification exam.

The Benefits of Certification

Why Get Certified?

For employers, the certification provides skill-verification tools that not only help assess a person's skills in using Microsoft Office programs but also the ability to quickly complete on-the-job tasks across multiple programs in the Microsoft Office system. (http://www.microsoft.com/learning/en/us/certification/mos.aspx). Certification proves a certain level of advanced competency with the programs in question. Employers don't have to wonder if the skills stated on the resume are honest and without exaggeration. This can lead to further employment opportunities and increased pay.

A person holding Microsoft Office Certification shows not just a level of skill, but an ability to quickly complete tasks, due to familiarity with the program and it's many time-saving features. The hard work that goes into learning Microsoft Office programs to the level of proficiency necessary for successful completion of the Certification Exams also indicates a desire on behalf of the student to learn and succeed.

The Benefits: Earn More, Find Jobs Quicker

Research indicates that employees with Microsoft Certification earn more and find jobs quicker than those employees without certification. Furthermore, employees with certification report a greater feeling of confidence. These things translate into greater job satisfaction. (http://www.microsoft.com/learning/en/us/certification/mos.aspx)

Research also shows that individuals with certification make up to 12% more than those without certification. In addition, 82% of Microsoft Office Specialists report a salary increase after receiving certification. Managers like the skills proven and the ability demonstrated by those with Microsoft Office Certifications.
http://www.certiport.com/Portal/desktopdefault.aspx?page=common/pagelibrary/mos2003.html

For More Information:
www.certiport.com
www.microsoft.com

About Our Certification Program

Books in this Series:
Beginning Guide to
Microsoft® Access 2010

Intermediate Guide to
Microsoft® Access 2010

Advanced Guide to
Microsoft® Access 2010

Microsoft Office Specialist (MOS) Certification for Access 2010

Overview: Our Microsoft Office Specialist certification program for Access 2010 covers all of the exam objectives for the Access certification exam. Microsoft Office Specialist exam 77-85 for Access is an elective exam that demonstrates expert knowledge of database programming and Microsoft Office automation. It is not required for MOS certification.

Our Approach: In designing these Guides, we found that it made more sense to write the lessons based on the Ribbons and Tasks. The beginning of each lesson provides an overview of the Ribbons and Tasks covered.

The Beginning Guide to Microsoft Access 2010 demonstrates the following Ribbons: **Home, Create, Table Tools, Form Layout Tools: Arrange and Format, Query Tools, and Report Layout Tools**. The lesson activities focus on basic database objects: Tables, Forms, Queries and Reports.

The Intermediate Guide to Microsoft Access 2010 demonstrates the following Ribbons: **Table Tools, Form Design Tools: Arrange and Format, Query Tools, Report Design Tools and the Macro Tools**. The programming focuses on representing one-to-many relationships: Form and Subform, Report and Subreport. The lessons show how to design for Real Users that includes creating a Switchboard that opens when the database is launched.

The Advanced Guide to Microsoft Access 2010 begins with a discussion of how to design a database in Third Normal Form to minimize repeat data and reduce errors. The programming focuses on using Key data to create relationships between Tables. The projects include a Receipt Form that calculates the total amount owed and a Receipt Printout formatted for a small Point of Sale (POS) printer.

Course Prerequisites: Students who enroll in the Microsoft Access 2010 program should have strong computer skills including how to use an Internet browser and how to select commands from a menu. Students should know how to save files and send attachments by email as well. In addition, students should have good skills with spreadsheets.

Microsoft Access 2010 Study Guide

Microsoft Office Specialist (MOS): Exam 77-885 for Access 2010

About the Authors

Microsoft Office Specialist (MOS): Exam 77-885 for Access 2010

Elizabeth Ann Nofs
Elizabeth is the Computer Mama. She developed the teaching methodology in the Complete Computer Guide series using breakthrough research in gender balanced training. Elizabeth has taught several thousand men and women from government, manufacturing, small business, and education in both online and hands-on classrooms.

She is the author of the Complete Computer Guides as well as a Microsoft Certified Office Specialist. She earned a BA in Biology from the University of Michigan.

Alex Sergay, Senior Instructional Designer
For more than 20 years, Alex has made complex technology easy to understand. Alex has developed instructional multimedia software for educational websites including the Sounds of English, a linguistics-training tool that earned a ComputerWorld/Smithsonian Laureate.

Alex earned his Masters of Educational Technology from the University of Michigan, Ann Arbor.

Clair Dickson, Student Services
Clair works with adult learners in online, face-to-face and hybrid classroom settings. She is considered "highly qualified" to teach introductory computers, including Microsoft Office.

Clair has a Graduate Certificate in Educational Media and Technology, a program that explored ways to infuse technology into the learning experience so that learning is interactive. She has earned Microsoft Office 2007 Master Certification. She also holds a BS in Secondary English Education from Eastern Michigan University.

Leo Michael Nofs, Technical Writing and Quality Control
Leo is a Microsoft Certified Professional and an Access database designer. He uses his exemplary attention to detail for copy editing the computer instructions for accuracy and clarity.

Traci Nofs, Photography and Photo Editing
Traci has been photographing children and nature since 2000. She works freelance out of her home, including weddings, engagements, and particularly children's photography. She has further enhanced her photos by use of image manipulation, focusing on light and color.

M. Jeanette McCrickard, Office Manager
Jeanette has years of experience as an office manager, including the increasing use of computer-related tasks. Her excellent attention to detail has lead her to work as an Access database administrator and a copy editor.

All of my books

are dedicated to

Fr. Paul Cummings

who taught me

computers.

Love, eBeth

How To Use This Guide
Microsoft Office Specialist Certification Training

The Comma Method
Observation is a perceptual strategy that asks: why am I doing this and which tools would be most effective? Each lesson begins with a discussion of the purpose and the objectives.

Orientation helps students start at the right place. The screen shots in the *Complete Compute Guides* show the entire window as well as a close up of the particular button or command.

Notation There are "breadcrumbs" above each screen image. Like Hansel and Gretel, the breadcrumbs show the pathway to a button or option. Our notation uses the following convention:
Ribbon->Group->Button->Options

Menu Maps
The Comma Method recognizes that there is a difference in how men and women navigate the menus. Men typically have the ability to see the map first. This method of acquiring knowledge is called *Breadth-first.* [1] Women tend to work with the details first. They learn several commands, such as copy, cut, and paste, then they put those concepts under the label, "edit." This method of learning is called *Depth-first*.

The Comma Method uses menu mapping to assist men and women to see both the Breadth and the Depth. An example of the menu map is can be seen here.

[1] Ford, Nigel, Sherry Chen, Matching/mismatching revisited: An Empirical Study of Learning and Teaching Styles. British Journal of Educational Technology v.32 no1 (Jan. 2001)

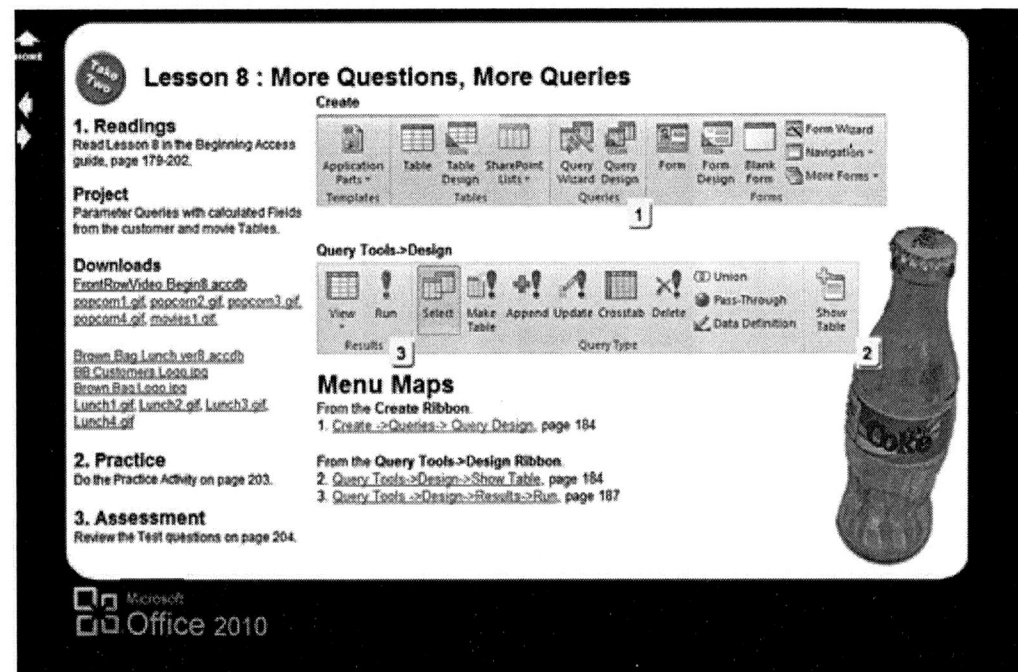

Query Tools->Design

Access 2010: Getting Started

You Say Goodbye, I Say Hello!

Advanced Access Objectives
An overview of the lessons in this book:

1. Representing many-to-many relationship with a Table and Subdatasheet.

2. Using Primary Keys to create Relationships between Tables.

3. Creating a blank Form and adding buttons to open Forms and Reports.

4. Finding common errors in Forms and Queries and correcting the mistakes.

5. Calculating Totals in a Report.

© 2012 Comma Productions, LLC

Lesson 1 : You Say Goodbye, I Say Hello!

1. Readings
Read Lesson 1 in the Advanced Access guide, page 11-27

Project
This overview does not have a demonstration project.

Downloads
There are no downloads for this lesson.

2. Practice
There is no Practice Activity for this lesson.

3. Assessment
There is no test for this lesson.

Advanced Databases

Screenshot of the completed Receipt

Front Row Video

Receipt   1

7/22/2012

Deeter Poohbah

Brighton, MI 48116

No of Movies   5

Total Due $17.50

Movies Rented

Harry Potter and the $3.50
Deathly Hallows:
Part 2 (2011)

3-Day Rental

The Computer Mama Sez: "Advanced" doesn't mean hard. Advanced means this database finally has enough programming to get the work done!

The goal of any successful business is that many customers return many times and buy many things.

So, our Mighty Access database has to represent a many-to-many relationship and document that information in reports. In the Front Row Video business model the customer walks out with many movies and a receipt.

The goal of the Advanced Access programming is to create the Forms and Reports for the customer receipt. This book begins with an important discussion on Tables and Table Relationships. Then, the Advanced Form and Report lessons create the data entry and the Point of Sale (POS) receipt. The last discussions includes strategies for archiving and database administration.

This lesson offers a summary of the goals and objectives for the advanced programming in this Guide.

HOME

 Take One

Goals and Objectives

The *Beginning Guide to Microsoft Access 2010* introduced the database objects: Tables, Queries, Forms and Reports. These lessons showed a one-to-one relationship. The Movies Form has one Record Source: the Movie Table, tblMovies.

The *Intermediate Guide to Microsoft Access 2010* demonstrates several methods of representing one-to-many relationships. For example, there are many movies with the same rating, say "PG,"

The *Advanced Guide to Microsoft Access 2010* creates a link between the customers and the movies: the receipt. The Receipt Form creates a many-to-many relationship. Many customers return many times and rent many movies each time.

What Is The Best Approach? These lessons will create the Receipt Form and Receipt Report using Subforms/Subreports. The information will be related by Key data. The Receipt Report will be formatted to fit a small Point of Sale (POS) printer.

Example of the Completed Receipt Form

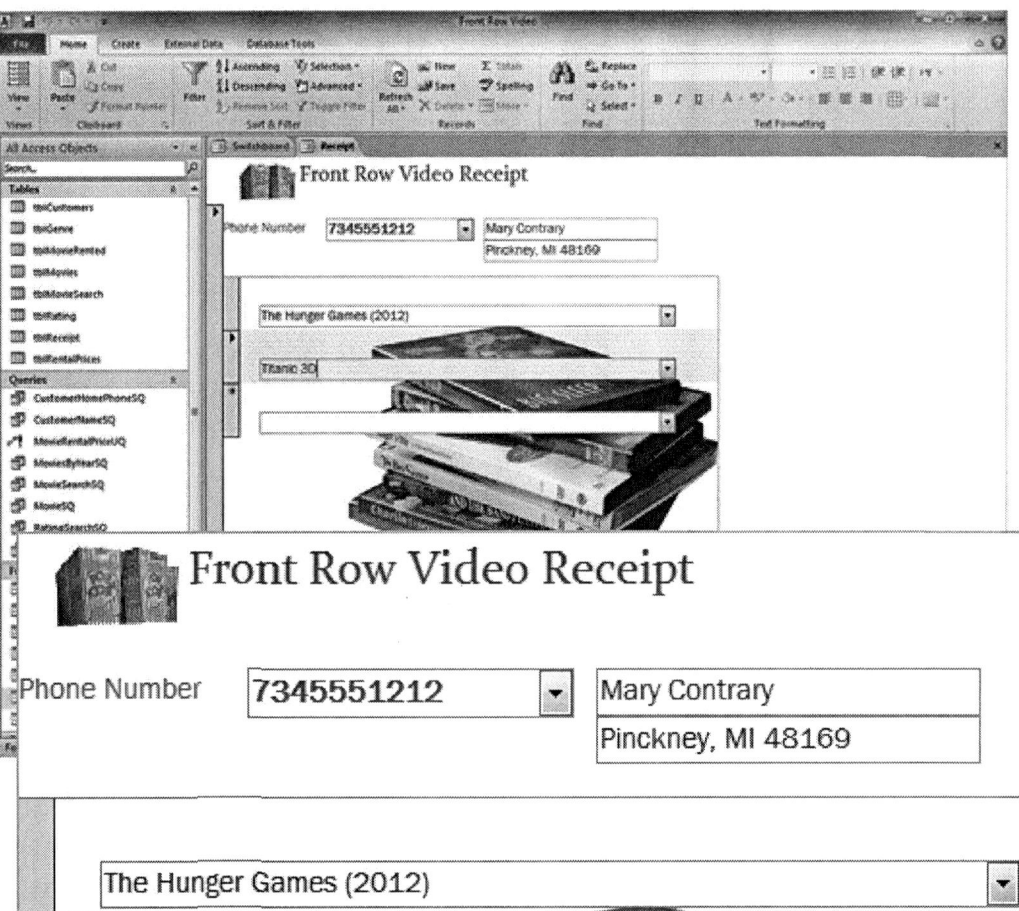

Example of a data diagram for the Receipt Form and Subform
The arrows show the Record Source for the Forms and the Control Source for the Combo Box.

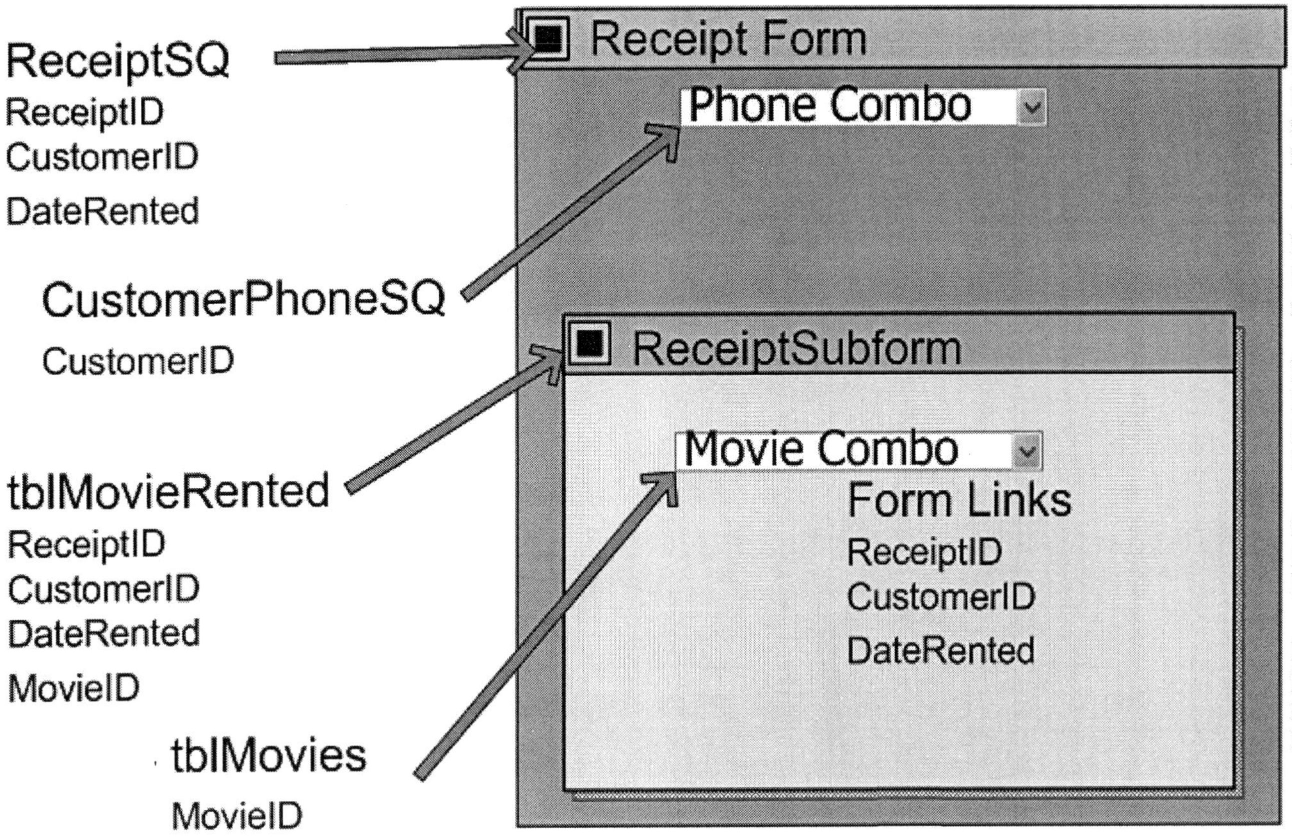

ReceiptSQ
ReceiptID
CustomerID
DateRented

CustomerPhoneSQ
CustomerID

tblMovieRented
ReceiptID
CustomerID
DateRented
MovieID

tblMovies
MovieID

■ Receipt Form

Phone Combo ⌄

■ ReceiptSubform

Movie Combo ⌄

Form Links
ReceiptID
CustomerID
DateRented

Before You Begin:
Draw A Data Diagram
Databases use a Form with a Subform to create a one-to-many relationship.

The Receipt Form has two Forms, two Tables, two Combo Boxes and three links. This is a good place to make a data diagram.

Form: Receipt
Record Source: ReceiptSQ
Default View: Form View
Phone Combo: CustomerPhoneSQ

Form: ReceiptSubform
Record Source: tblMovieRented
Default View: Datasheet

Parent and Child Links:
ReceiptID
CustomerID
DateRented

Relating Tables in a Database

Tables are related by Key Data. The Primary Key is the best Field because it is unique: it is an AutoNumber that is Indexed (no duplicates).

Why Does This Matter? There has to be at least one Field that matches in both Tables to create a relationship. We'll use the Primary Key to create relationships between the Tables.

Plan: This lesson will create a Rental Table that has three prices: new movies cost more than old ones. The Movie Table will be linked to the Rental Prices by a common Field: RentalPriceID, the Primary Key in the Rental Table.

What Are the Steps? Create the Rental Table and Update the Movie Table to add RentalPriceID as a Foreign Key so these Tables can be linked.

Then we'll create an Action Query to update the Rental Prices in the Movie Table. The Update Query will use the Year that a movie was released to determine the Rental Price..

Example of an Update Query

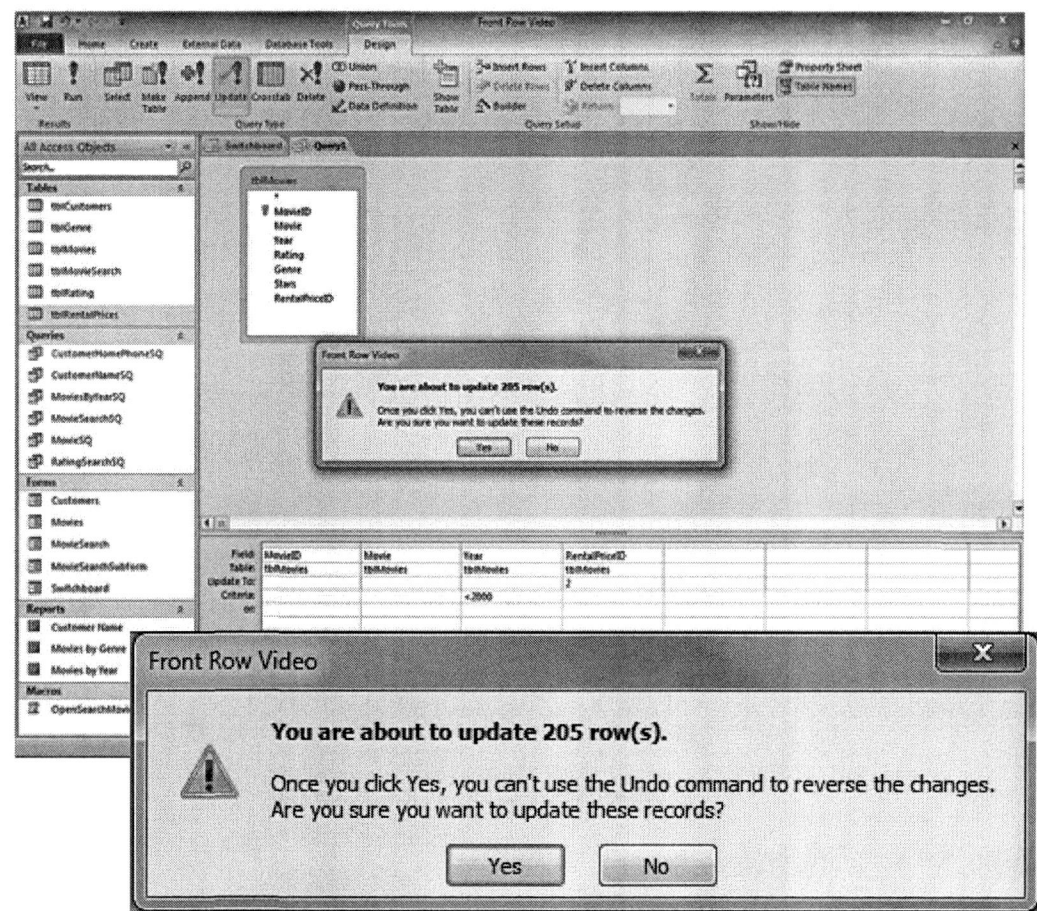

Primary Keys and Relationships

What is a Normalized database? Normalizing a database defines the Table design and how the Tables are related.

Why Does This Matter? Normalizing a database minimizes duplicate data and protects the data integrity. The Tables are small and functional. There should be a separate Table for each collection.

Plan: We will create two new Tables that will be the Record Sources for the Receipt Form and Receipt Subform. The Receipt Subform will inherit three Key Fields from the Receipt Form. So the Table for the Receipt Subform, tblMovieRented, has to be designed with that in mind

What Are the Steps? Create a Table for the Receipt Form and another Table for the Receipt Subform. These Tables will be joined by a matching Key: ReceiptID.

Example of a Table with Key Data: A Primary Key and 3 Foreign Keys

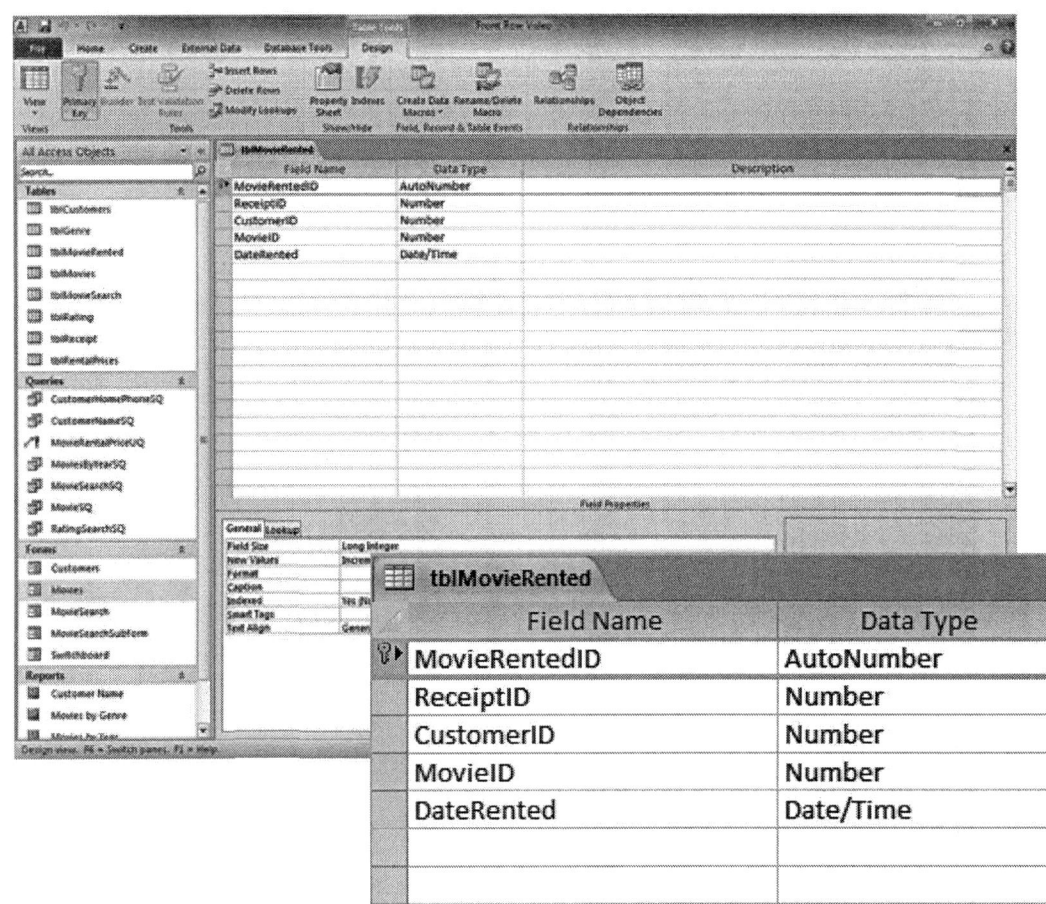

tblMovieRented

Field Name	Data Type
MovieRentedID	AutoNumber
ReceiptID	Number
CustomerID	Number
MovieID	Number
DateRented	Date/Time

Advanced Form Design, part 1: Create the Receipt Subform

Key Concept: The Receipt Form represents a one-to-many relationship: one customer gets many movies. So, there will be a Form and Subform.

Plan: The focus will be on the Receipt Subform. This Form will list the movies rented. It is the "many" part of the one-to-many relationship: many movies. This Subform will be formatted as a Table, which is the way most online forms and web pages are designed.

What Are the Steps? Create a Subform for the movies rented and format the records as a Table.

Worth Noting: You may notice that the Arrange Tools in Microsoft Access are very similar to the Table Tools in Word or Excel.

Example of the MovieRentedSubform in Design View

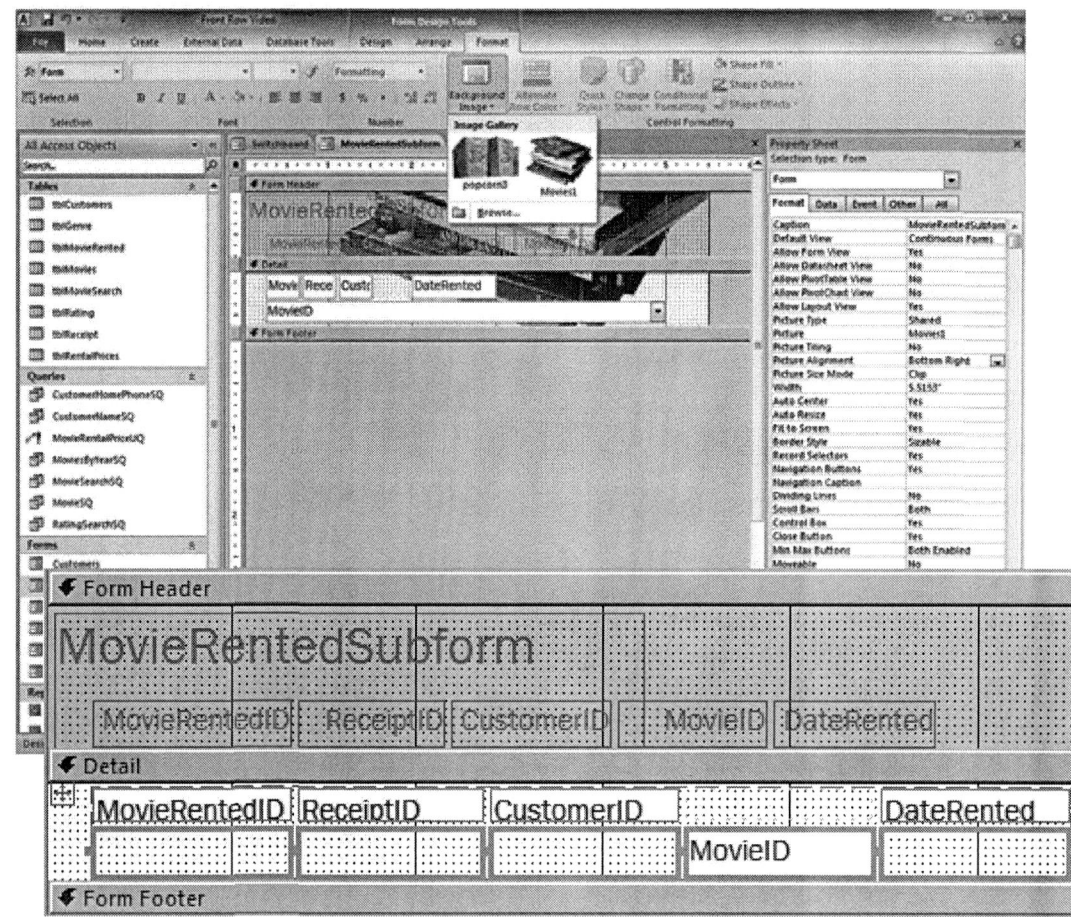

Advanced Form Design, part 2: Create the Receipt Form

Advanced User Interface Design: The Receipt Form will use a Combo Box Control to look up data in one Table and add it to another Table.

Plan: The Receipt Form will enable Users to search for a customer by their phone number and automatically display the customer's information.

What Are the Steps? Create a new Query for the Record Source. The Query will JOIN the Receipt Table with a Query, CustomerNameSQ, that looks up the customer's name and address.

When both Forms are formatted and tested , they will be linked by three Key Fields.

Why Use This Method? A Combo Box Control is an effective way to look up the data. When a User selects a phone number the Form will automatically display the customer's name and address.

Example of the Completed Receipt Form

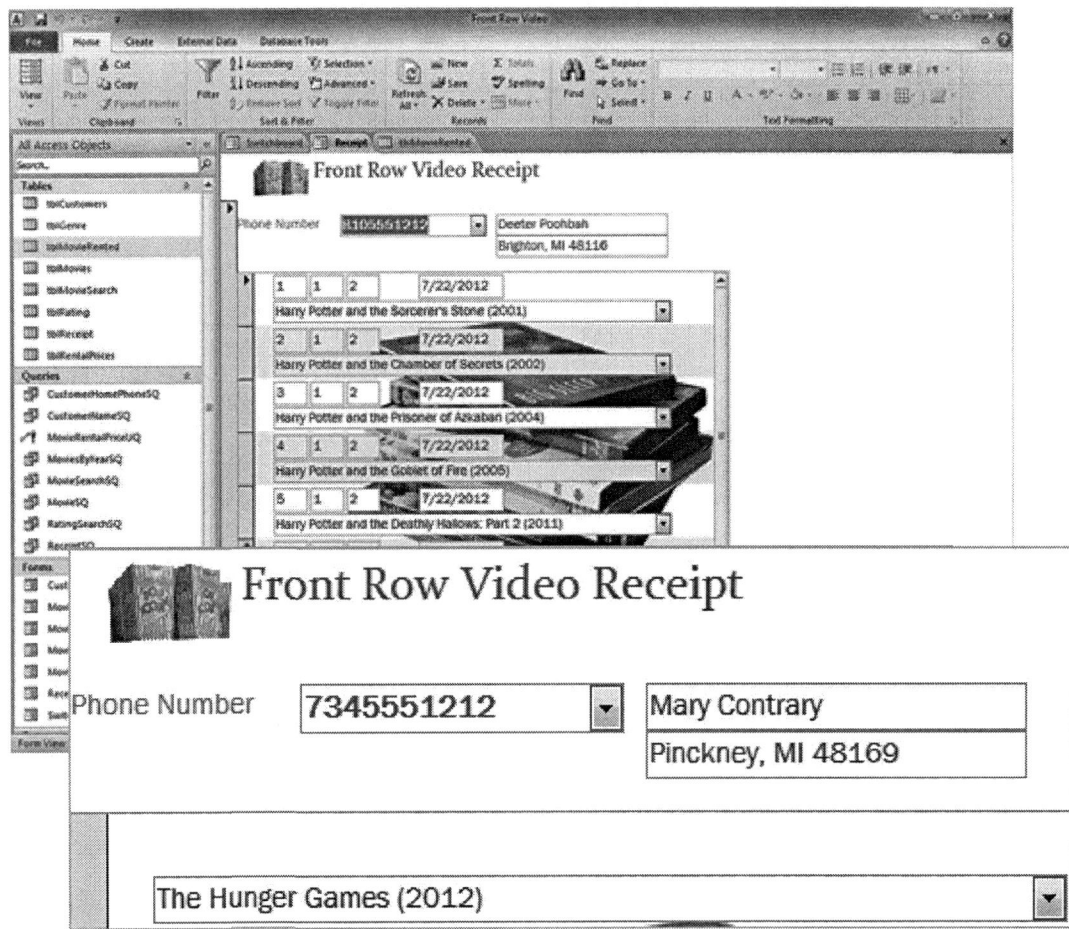

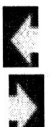
Example of a data diagram for the Receipt Report and Subreport: the arrows show the Record Source

Advanced Report Design: The Report Diagram

The Receipt Report has a Report and a Subreport. Again, this is a good place to draw out the designs.

Both Reports are based on a Query:

The Report uses rptReceiptSQ.
This Query includes:
tblMovieRented
tblMovies
tblRentalPrices
CustomerNameSQ

The Subreport uses rptMovieRentedSQ.
This Query has three Tables:
tblMovieRented
tblMovies
tblRentalPrices

The Receipt Report and Subreport are linked by one Key: ReceiptID

rptReceiptSQ
ReceiptID
CustomerID
DateRented

rptMovieRentedSQ
ReceiptID
DateRented
Movie
Price
Description

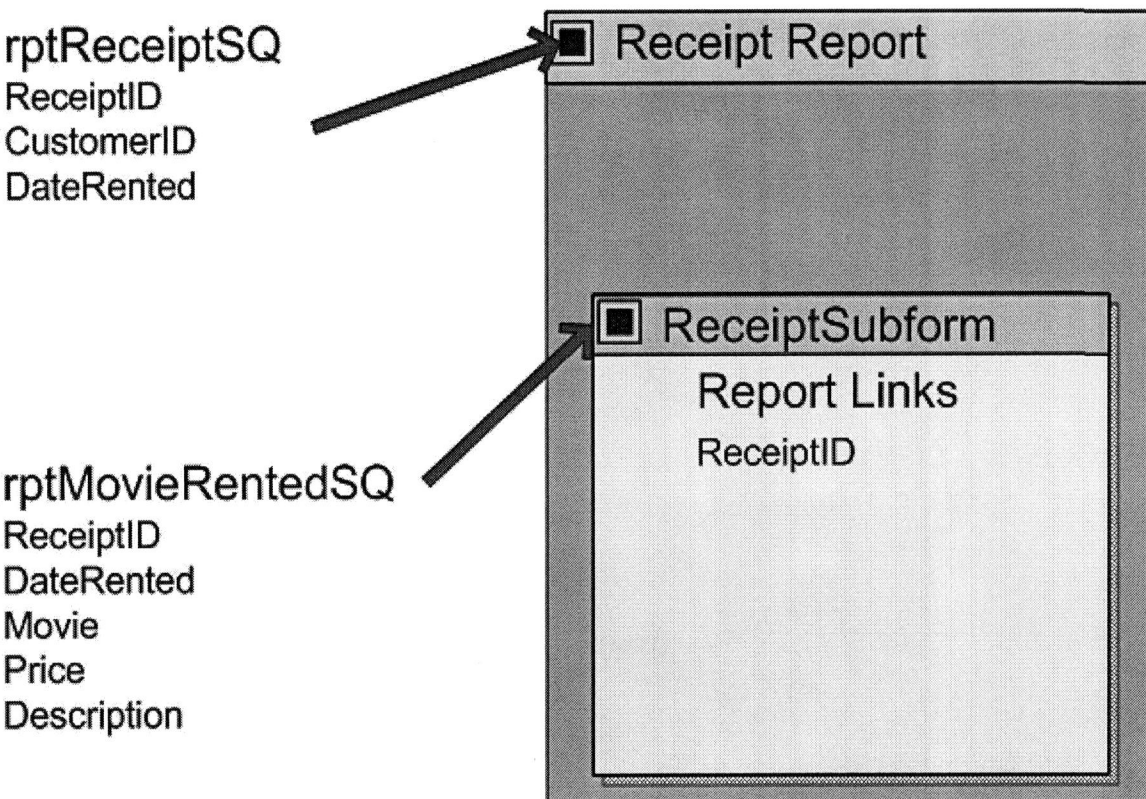

Receipt Report

ReceiptSubform

Report Links

ReceiptID

Advanced Report Design, part 1:

Calculating the Totals: The Receipt Report will use a Select Query that groups the rental prices and calculates the totals for each Receipt.

The Receipt Report represents a many-to-many relationship. It will be designed as a Report and a Subreport linked by matching Keys.

Plan: This lesson will focus on Report Design. The Report Header, the top part of the Receipt, will include the customer's name.

What Are the Steps? The Record Source for the Receipt Report will be a Query, rtpMovieRentedSQ, that uses the same Table that was the Record Source for the Receipt Subform, tblMovieRented.

The Receipt Report will be formatted as a Table and edited to fit a small Point of Sale printer.

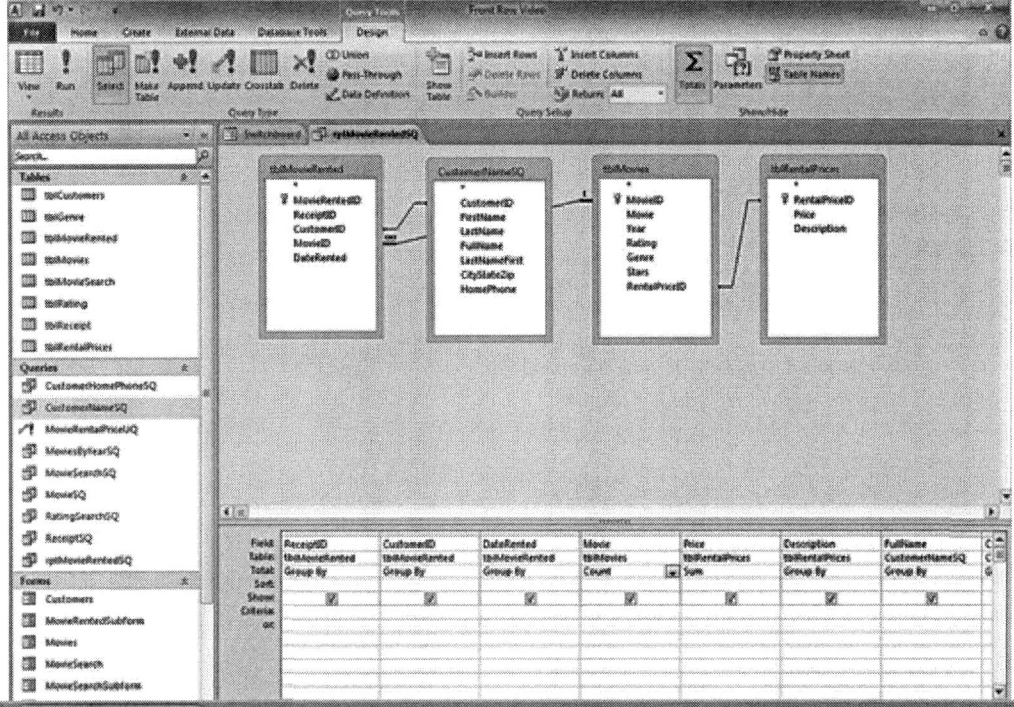

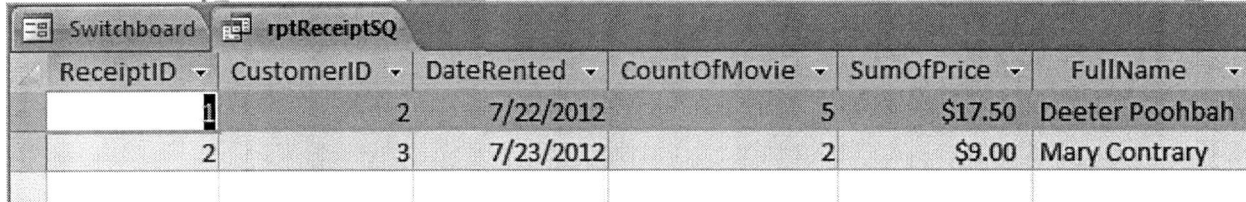

ReceiptID	CustomerID	DateRented	CountOfMovie	SumOfPrice	FullName
1	2	7/22/2012	5	$17.50	Deeter Poohbah
2	3	7/23/2012	2	$9.00	Mary Contrary

Advanced Report Design, part 2:

Finishing the Receipt: The Receipt Subreport represents the "many" side of this relationship. This Subreport will show many movies.

Plan: The Subreport will be a Tabular Report formatted as a Table.

What Are the Steps? Design a new Query to be the Record Source for the Subreport. Create a Receipt Subreport and format the layout with the Table Tools. Add the Subreport to the Receipt Report and confirm the Master and Child Links.

What Are the Issues? The Controls and Headers have to be edited before the Report can be resized for the narrow 2" Point of Sale (POS) printer.

Example of the Completed Receipt Report, formatted for a POS printer

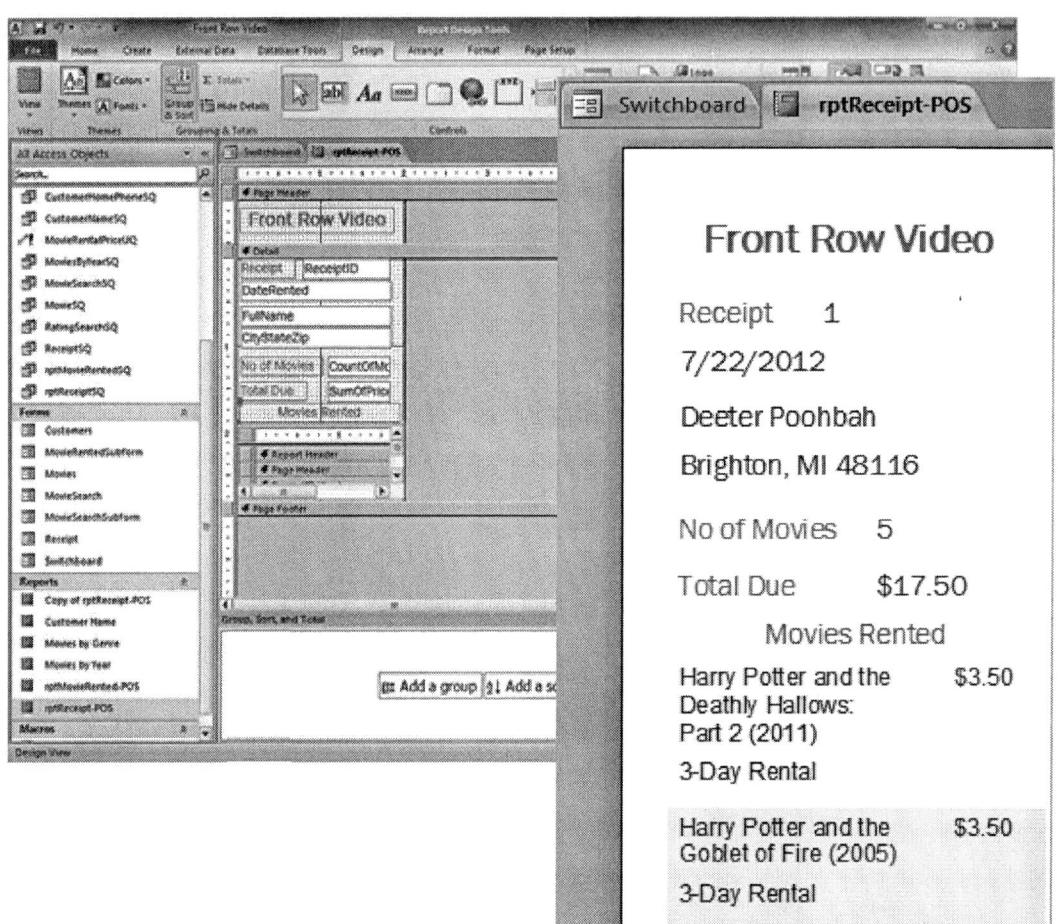

The Producers:
Calculating with Dates

Harvest the Data for Customer Support: Most businesses are date driven. Queries can be used to look for overdue movies.

Plan: Create a new Query as the Record Source for a Report that calculates the numbers of days that each movie is overdue.

The Report will be Grouped by Customer and formatted so that there is only one customer per page. Our customers will get an Overdue Movie Report that is formatted like a letter.

What Are the Steps? Design a Query that Groups the Records by Customer and calculates the Amount Due. Then, create a Report that is formatted like a business letter.

Worth Noting: The new Query will calculate the difference between the DateRented and the current date with the DateDiff() function.

Example of a Query that calculates the differences between two dates

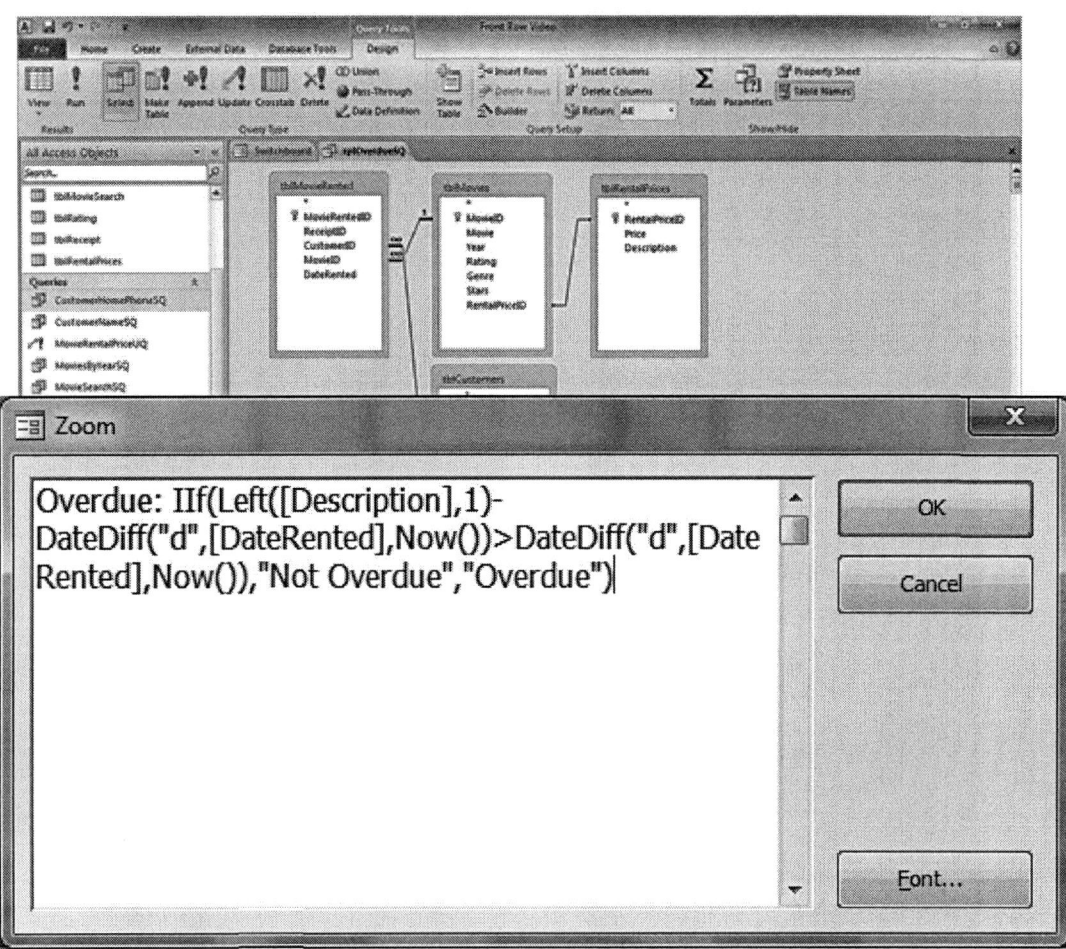

Example of the completed PivotChart after it was added to a Report

Prepare to Share: Show the Data!

Key Concept: Export the data out of Access.

Plan: Analyze the data with two different methods: a Crosstab Query and a PivotChart. The Crosstab Query presents the data in a Table. The PivotChart analyzes data visually.

Then export the data into formats that can be shared by E-mail: Word, Excel, XPS and PDF files

What Are the Steps? Create a Crosstab Query and analyze the results. Also, create a PivotChart Form to display the Movies graphically and add that Form to a Report.

Why Use This Method? When the Report is in Print Preview, the data can be exported in several file formats that can be shared and sent by E-mail.

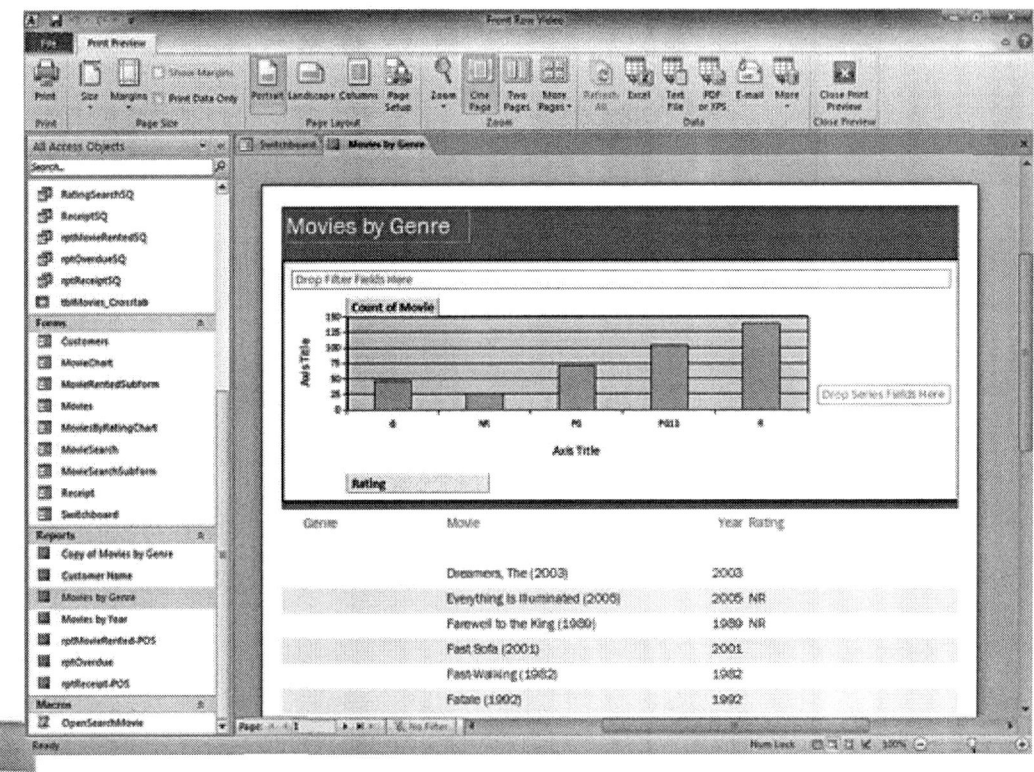

The Administrator:
Strategies for Archiving

Key Concept: Deleting data is not a good idea. The preferred method is to mark the Records as Archive, Done or Obsolete.

Plan: Automate the process of selecting and archiving obsolete Records from a database instead of deleting them.

What Are the Steps? Edit the Table to include a Yes/No Field that indicates if the Movie is Archived. Add two additional Fields to document the status.

Create an Action Query to select, update and copy selected Records to the new Table.

Then, create another Action Query to delete the Records and practice on a COPY of the Table.

Why Use This Method? All businesses need a method for evaluating and archiving the data..

Screenshot of a Make Table Query

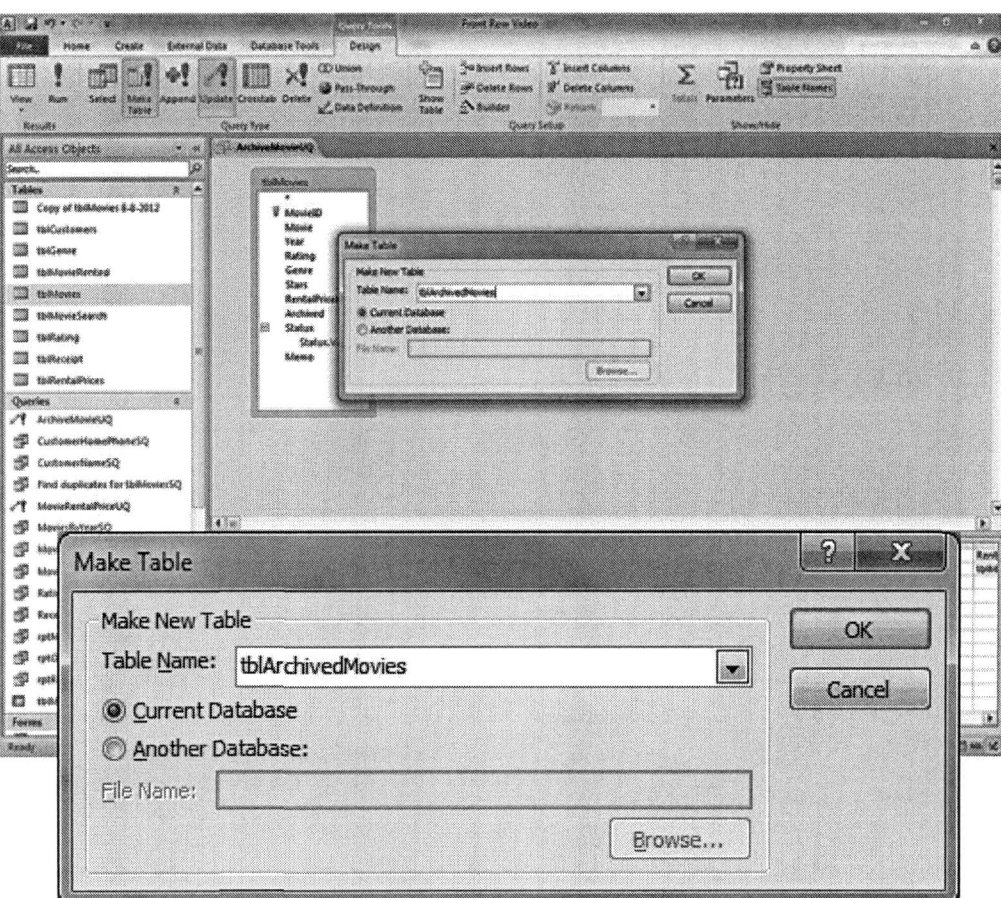

The Administrator:
The Performance Network
Deploying Access in a Multi-User Network:
Split an Access database into two: one that has Tables and another that has everything else.

Plan: Optimize the database so that many Users can access the same data Tables.

What Are the Steps? Create two backup copies of the database: one for Tables, the other for Forms. Open the Form database and delete the Tables.

Open the Tables database and delete all of the Forms, Queries, Reports and Macros.

Finally, link the Tables to the Forms database as External Data and use the Linked Table Manager to refresh the Links.

Worth Noting: This lesson demonstrates how to prepare a database for deployment including Database documentation, Password encryption, and editing the Client Settings.

Screenshot of a Database with Linked Tables

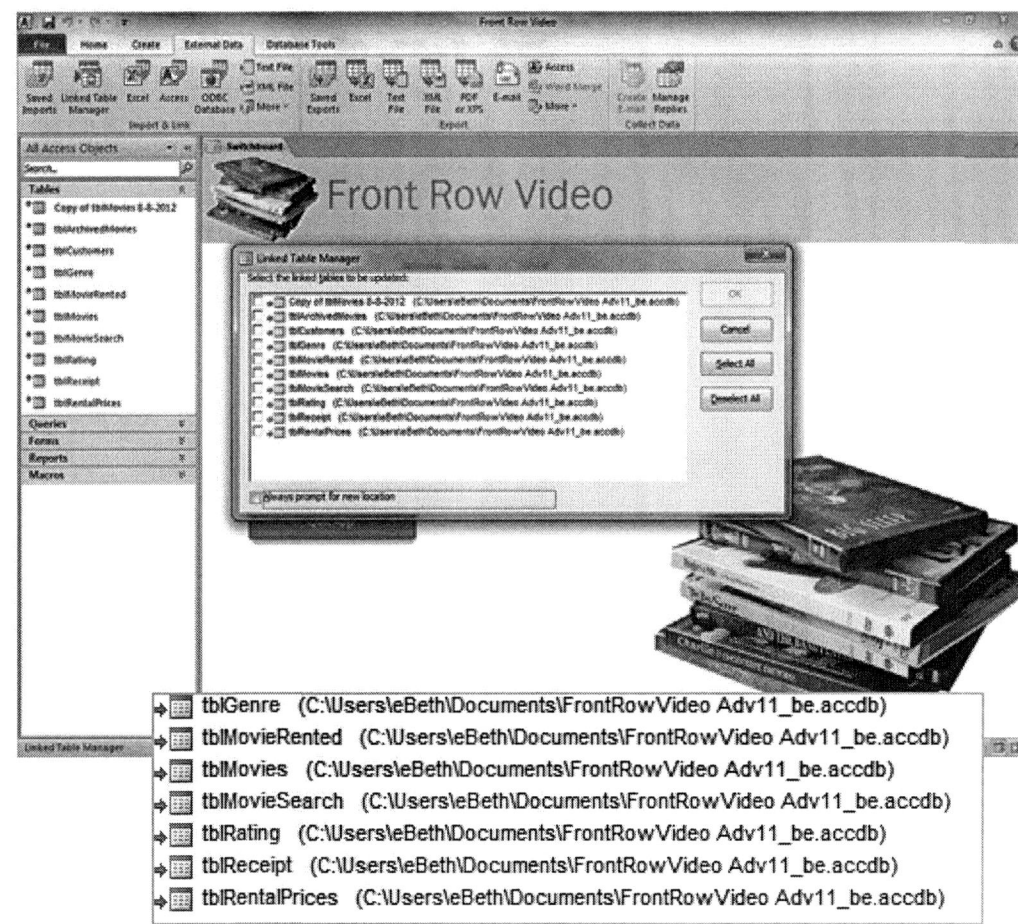

Summary: Advanced Guide to Microsoft Access 2010

So, the Advanced Guide to Access finishes the programming and answers the question: "Who bought what?"

This is a Mighty Access database that can be improved and revised as the business grows.

Well, a good programmer can go for hours on a couple of cookies. Let's get started!

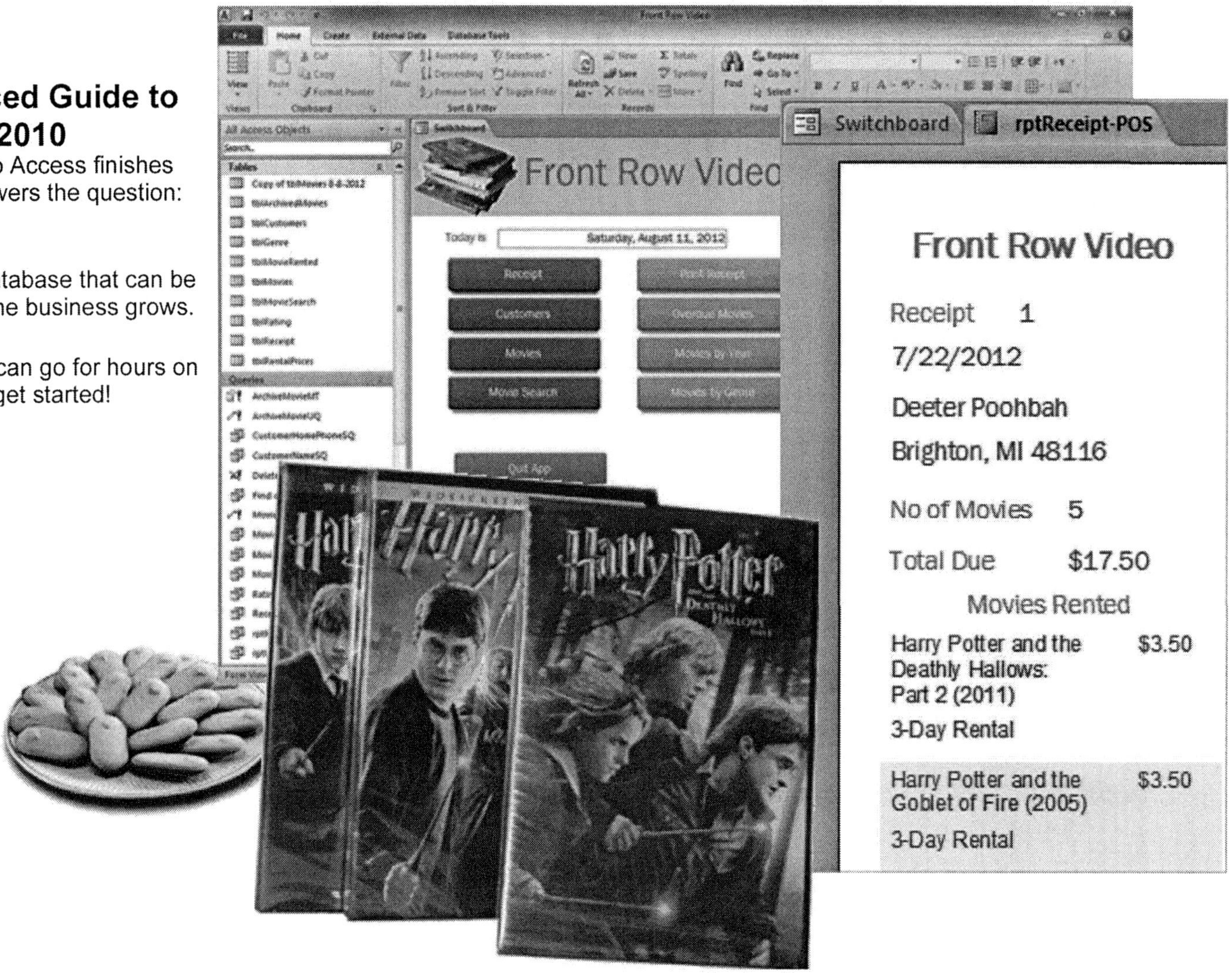

Front Row Video

Receipt   1

7/22/2012

Deeter Poohbah

Brighton, MI 48116

No of Movies   5

Total Due $17.50

Movies Rented

Harry Potter and the $3.50
Deathly Hallows:
Part 2 (2011)
3-Day Rental

Harry Potter and the $3.50
Goblet of Fire (2005)
3-Day Rental

Access 2010: Many to Many in Table Design

Relating Tables in a Relational Database

Advanced Access Objectives
In this lesson, you will learn how to:

1. Define the Primary Key in a new Table

2. Add a Foreign Key to a Table

3. Use the Primary Keys to create Relationships between Tables

4. Add a Subdatasheet and format the Tables to Show/Hide and Freeze the Columns in Datasheet View

© 2012 Comma Productions, LLC

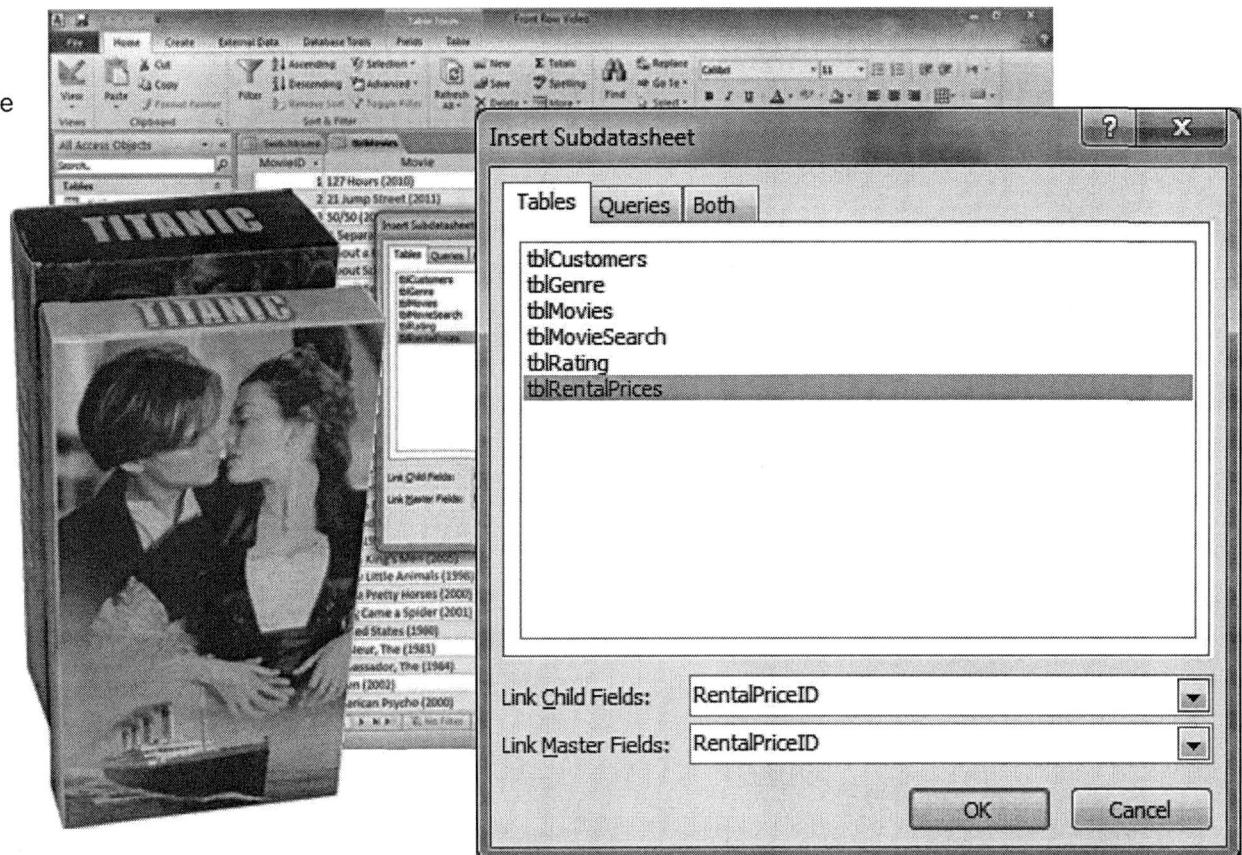

HOME

Lesson 2 : Relating Tables in a Relational Database

Table Tools ->Design->Tools->Primary Key

1. Readings
Read Lesson 2 in the Advanced Access guide, page 29-58.

Project
Create a Table and use the Primary Key to create a relationship to an existing Table.

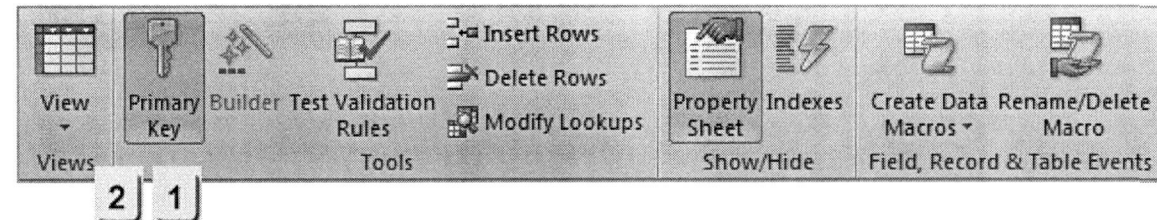

Query Tools->Design Ribbon

Downloads
FrontRowVideo Adv2.accdb
BBL Adv ver2.accdb

2. Practice
Do the Practice Activity on page 59.

3. Assessment
Review the Test questions on page 60.

Menu Maps

From the **Table Tools ->Design Ribbon**
Table Tools ->Design->Tools->Primary Key, page 36
Table Tools ->Views->View->Datasheet, page 37

From the **Query Tools->Design Ribbon**
3. Query Tools ->Design->Results->Run, page 42
4. Query Tools ->Design->Query Type->Update, page 44

More Menu Maps

From the **Home Ribbon**
Home ->Sort & Filter->Descending, page 46
Home ->Records->More->Subdatasheet page 51
Home ->Records->More->Unhide Fields, page 55
Home ->Records->More->Freeze Fields, page 57

Relating Tables in a Relational Database

Field Name	Data Type
MovieID	AutoNumber
Movie	Text
Year	Number
Rating	Text
Genre	Text
Stars	Text
RentalPriceID	Number

Microsoft Access 2010: Example of a Table with a Primary Key, MovieID, as well as a Foreign Key, RentalPriceID

All businesses need to make money. Our Front Row Video database uses a simple business model for the rental prices: new movies cost more, old movies cost less.

Where should this data be stored? The Rental Prices will be stored in a Table: tblRentalPrices.

How will the rental price data be used with the movies? There has to be a Field in tblMovies that matches one in the tblRentalPrices so the two Tables can be joined, or linked. There has to be at least one Field in both Tables to create a relationship.

Tables are related by Key Data. The Primary Key is the best Field because it is unique: It is an AutoNumber that is Indexed (no duplicates). In contrast, last names are not unique: there are many, many customers with the same name.

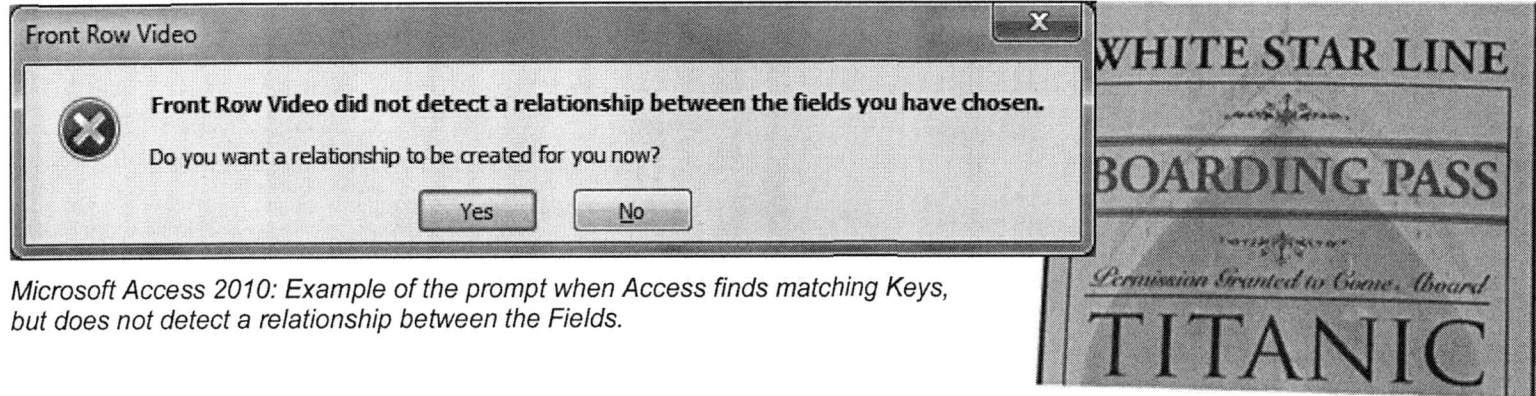

Microsoft Access 2010: Example of the prompt when Access finds matching Keys, but does not detect a relationship between the Fields.

What Are the Objectives?

This lesson will create a Rental Table, tblRental, that has a Primary Key, RentalPriceID and the rental price. The Movie Table will be updated to include the RentalPriceID. The RentalPriceID is the Key that will match in both Tables.

Finally, we will create an Action Query to update the Movie Table with the rental prices.

Create the Rental Table
Create the Rental Table in Design View
Enter the Rental Data

Review and Update the Movie Table
Edit the Movie Table and add a Foreign Key

Update the RentalPriceID in the Movie Table
Create a Select Query to determine the prices
Convert the Select Query to an Update Query
Run the Update Query to modify the movie data

That's the plan.

Microsoft Access 2010: Example of an Update Query

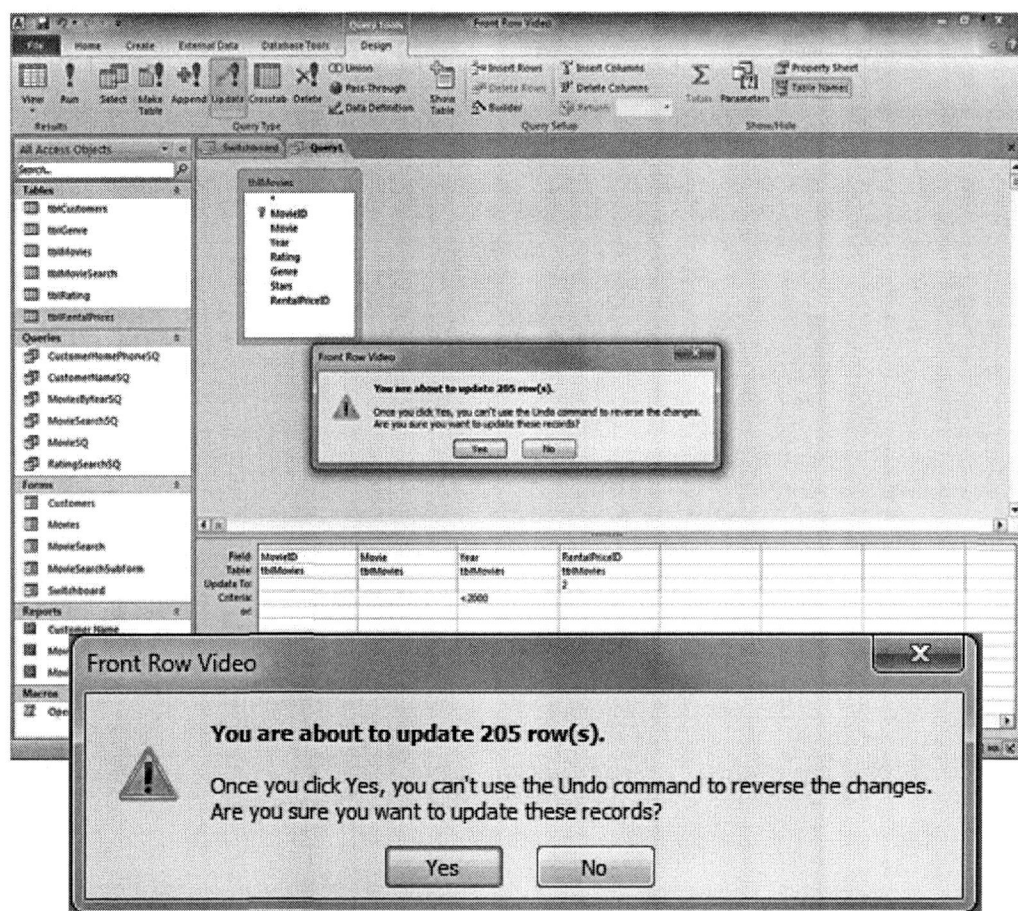

Before You Begin

Before You Begin: Open the Sample Database
Go to **Start -> All Programs ->Microsoft Office.**
Click on **Microsoft Office Access 2010.**
Access will prompt you to open a database.
You can continue with the same database that you
saved or download the sample database if you wish.

The <u>FrontRowVideo Adv2.accdb</u> database has:
Five Tables: tblCustomers, tblGenre, tblMovies,
tblMovieSearch and tblRating.

Six Queries: CustomerHomePhoneSQ,
CustomerNameSQ, MoviesByYearSQ, MovieSQ,
MovieSearchSQ and RatingSearchSQ.

Five Forms: Customers, Movies, MovieSearch,
MovieSearchSubform and the Switchboard.

Three Reports: Customer Name. Movies by Genre,
and Movies by Year.

One Macro: OpenSearchMovie.

Memo to Self: Click **Enable Content** if you see the
Security Warning.

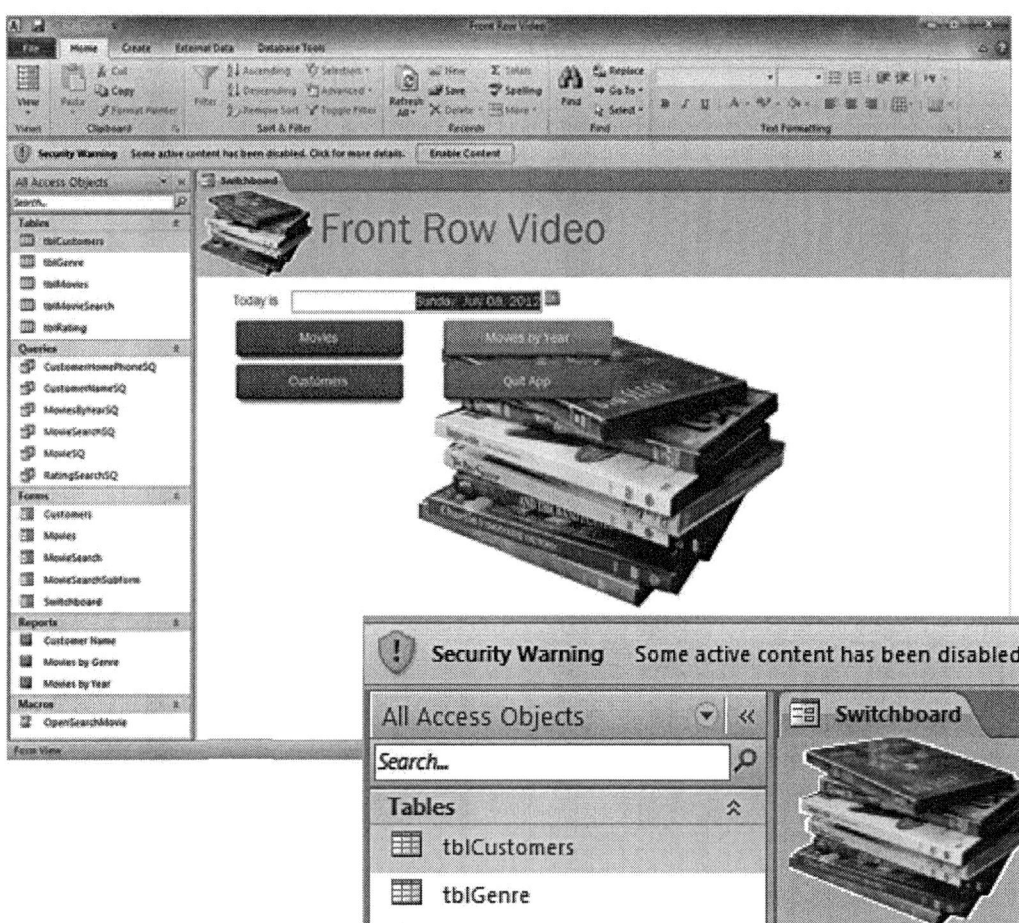

Begin with the Tables...
Try This: Review the Tables
Go to **All Access Objects ->Tables**.

What Do You See? Each Table has its own collection. The Movies Table has movies, the Customers table has customers.

So, the RentalPrices will be a simple collection as well: tblRentalPrices. It will only contain the rental price and the rental description.

Keep going.

All Access Objects ->Tables

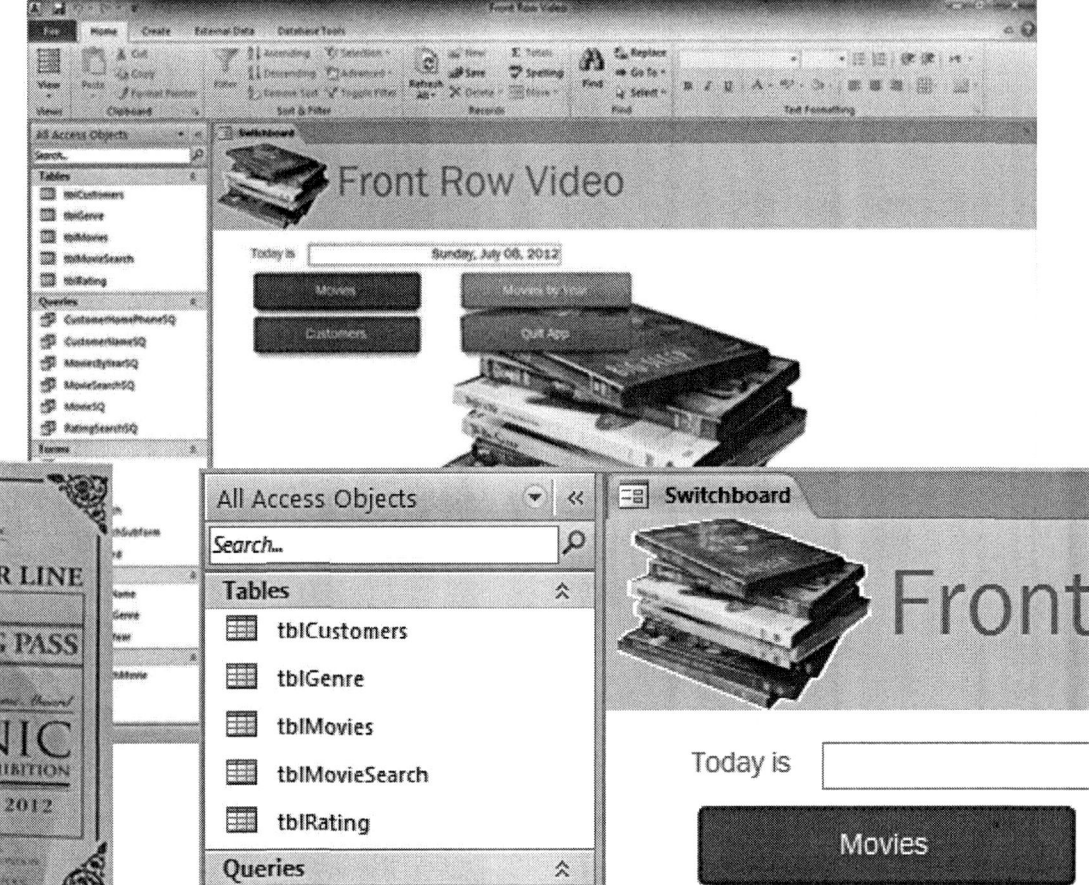

Create a New Table

1. Try This: Create a New Table
Go to **Create ->Tables->Table Design.**
Enter the following, please:

Field Name: RentalPriceID
Data Type: AutoNumber

Field Name: Price
Data Type: Currency

Field Name: Description
Data Type: Memo

Try This, Too: Review the Field Properties
Select a Field Name: Price

Review the **Field Properties** on the bottom:
Format: Currency
Decimal Places: Auto

By default, Currency has two decimal places.
The Field will be formatted with a dollar sign ($)
as well. We're finally working with money in our
Mighty Access database. Keep going.

Create ->Tables->Table Design

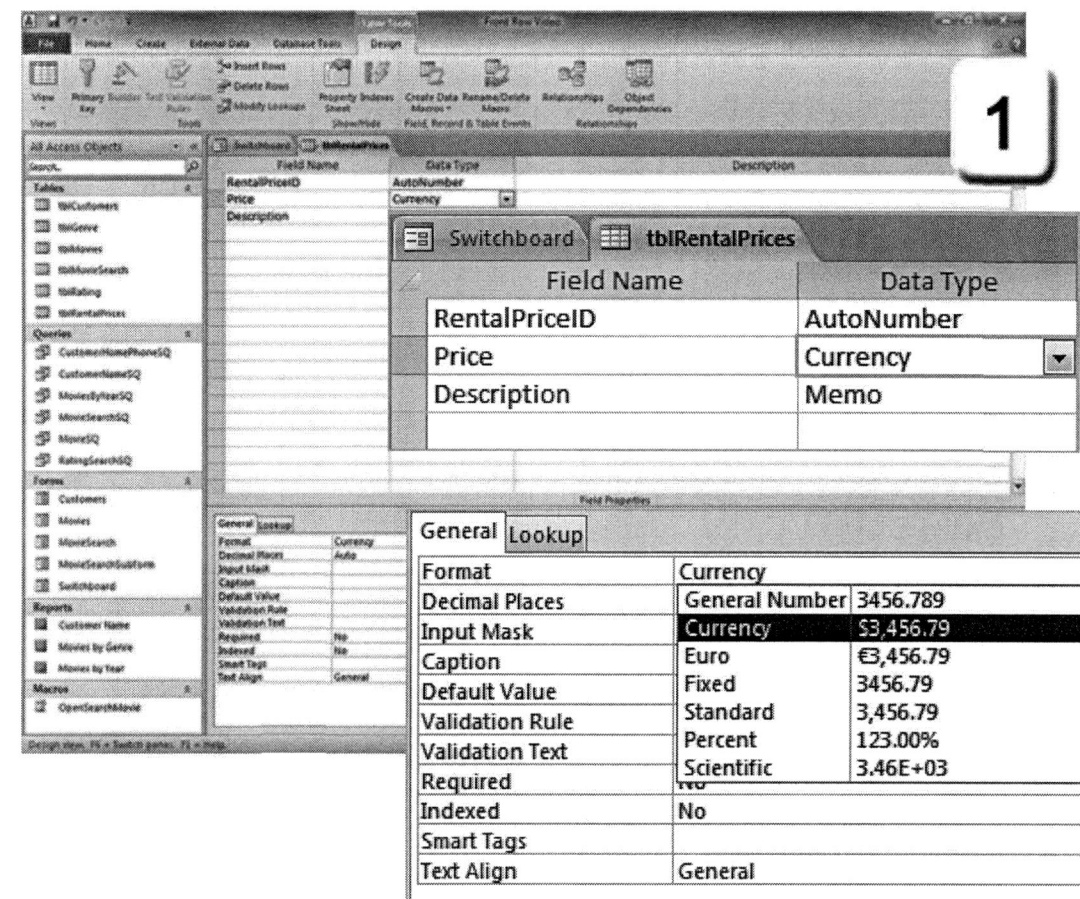

Field Name	Data Type
RentalPriceID	AutoNumber
Price	Currency
Description	Memo

Format	Currency	
Decimal Places	General Number	3456.789
Input Mask	Currency	$3,456.79
Caption	Euro	€3,456.79
Default Value	Fixed	3456.79
Validation Rule	Standard	3,456.79
Validation Text	Percent	123.00%
Required	Scientific	3.46E+03
Indexed	No	
Smart Tags		
Text Align	General	

Exam 77-885: Microsoft Access 2010
2. Building Tables
2.2. Create and Modify Fields: Modify Data Types

Table Tools ->Design->Tools->Primary Key

Define the Primary Key

2. Try This, Too: Create a Primary Key
Select a Field: RentalPriceID
Go to **Table Tools ->Design->Tools.**
Click on **Primary Key.**
What Do You See? The RentalPriceID Field has the symbol for the Key. In the Field Properties, the values are **Indexed** (yes), so that there will be no duplicates.

Do This, Now: Save the Table
Go to **File->Save.**
Enter a Name: tblRentalPrices.

Click **OK**. Keep going.

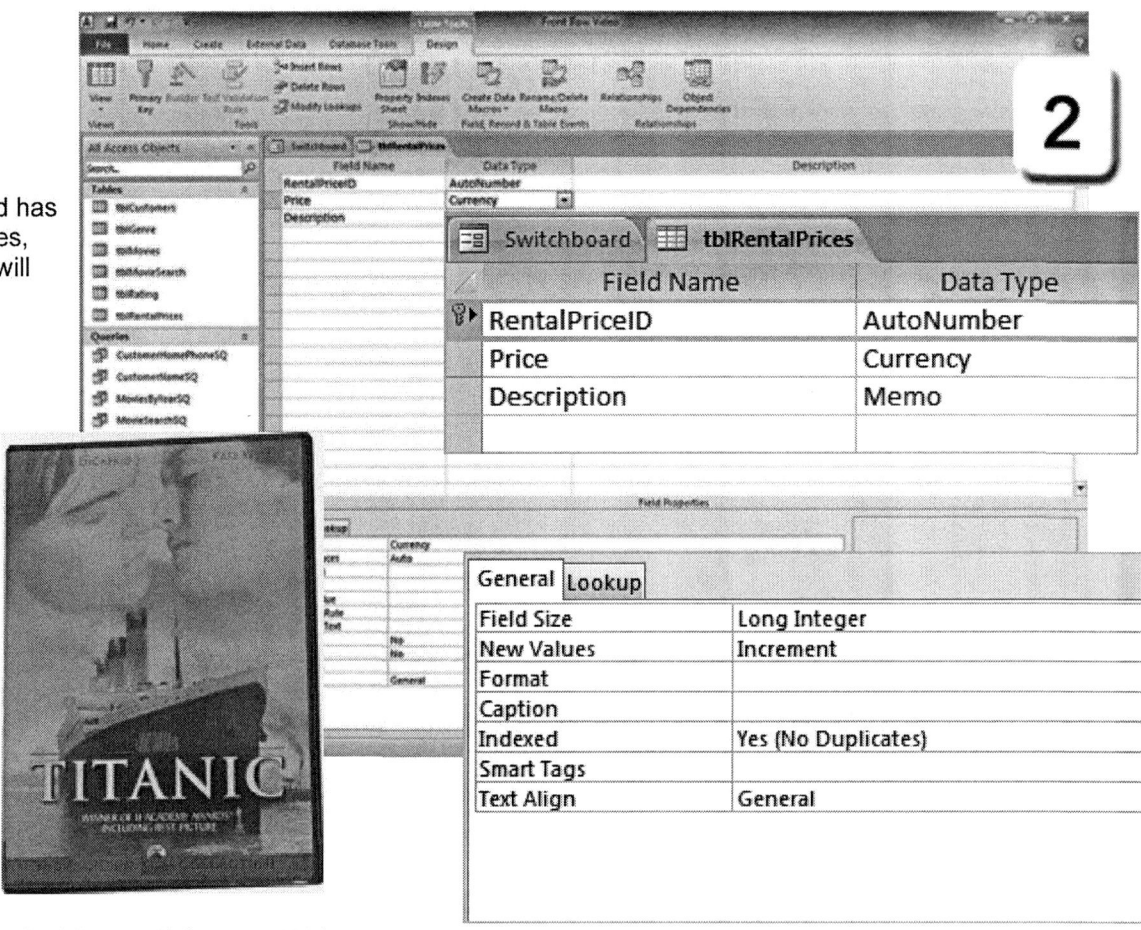

Exam 77-885: Microsoft Access 2010
2. Building Tables
2.4. Set relationships: Define the Primary Key

Add Data to the New Table

This business model has only three rental prices. Please change the View and enter the following:

Before You Begin: Change the View
Go to **Table Tools ->Views->View->Datasheet.**

3. Try This: Enter the Rental Prices
Price $4.50, Description: 1-Day Rental
Price $3.50, Description: 3-Day Rental
Price $2.50, Description: 5-Day Rental

What Do You See? Was the number you entered for the Price formatted for currency?

So that's the Rental Prices in the Rental Table. Please **Close** thblRentalPrices.

The next step is to put a price on the movies.

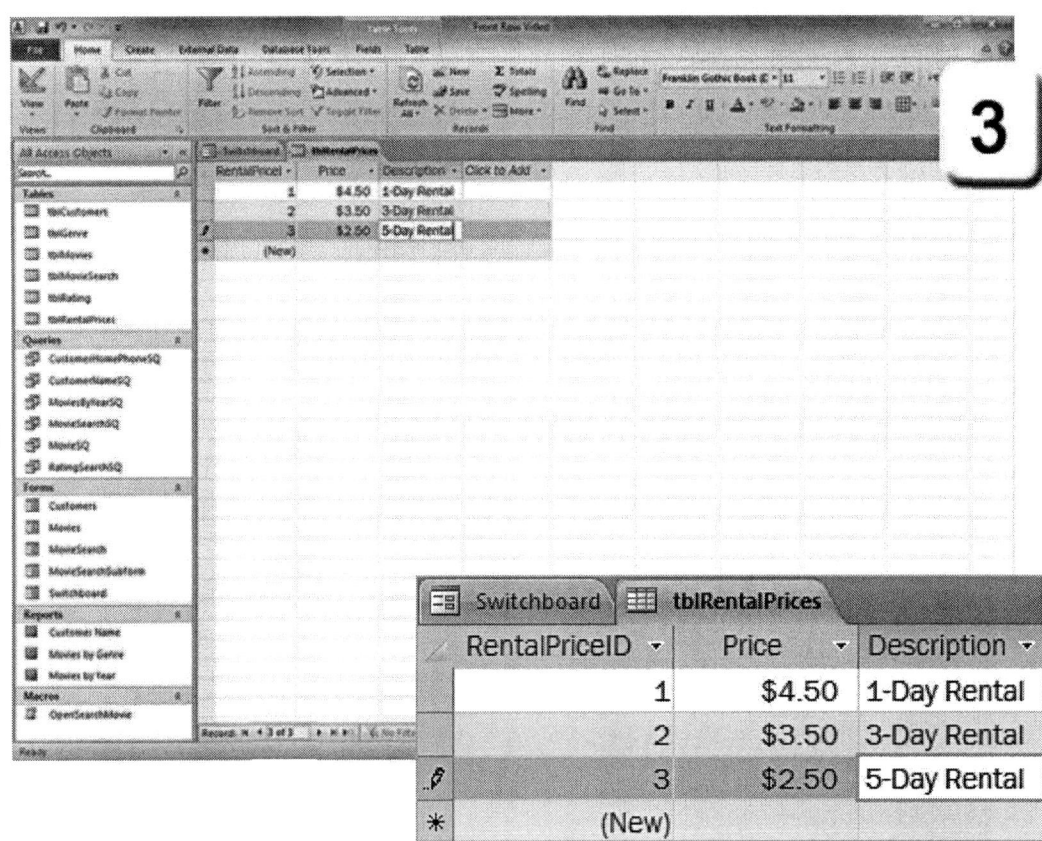

RentalPriceID	Price	Description
1	$4.50	1-Day Rental
2	$3.50	3-Day Rental
3	$2.50	5-Day Rental
* (New)		

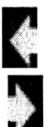

Review the Movie Table

4. Try This: Review the Movie Table
Go to **All Access Objects->Tables**.
Select a Table: tblMovies.
Go to **Home->Views->View->Design View**.

What Do You See? The Movie Table does not have a Field that indicates the rental price. There are Fields for the Movie, Year, Rating, Genre, and even the Stars. No money. No Rental Price.

Sooooo, since most businesses are in business to make money, we should probably do a little more programming in the Front Row Video database, hmmm?

Tables can work together when they share a common Field. The best Field to create a relationship between two Tables is the Primary Key. It is an AutoNumber (each number is unique) and it is Indexed so it is very fast.

Home->Views->View->Design View.

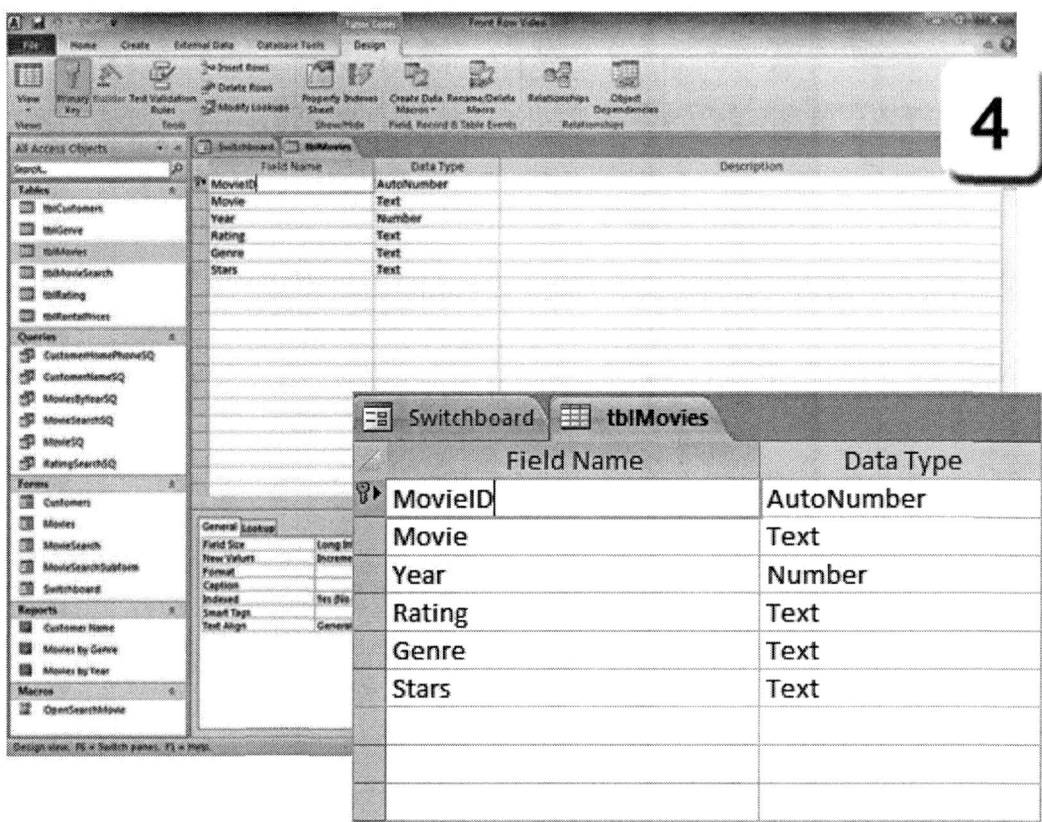

Field Name	Data Type
MovieID	AutoNumber
Movie	Text
Year	Number
Rating	Text
Genre	Text
Stars	Text

Exam 77-885: Microsoft Access 2010
2. Building Tables
2.4. Set relationships: Use Primary Keys to create Relationships

Add the Foreign Key

We want to link the Rental Price to the Movie Table. So, we need to add a Field for the RentalPriceID to the Movie Table.

5. Try This: Add a New Field
Field Name: RentalPriceID
Data Type: Number

What Do You See? Look at the Field Properties.
Field Size: Long Integer (Integers are Whole numbers, "Counting Numbers.")

Indexed: Yes. Duplicates are OK. Many movies will have the same Rental Price.

Do This, Please: Save the Table.
Go to **File->Save.**
Close tblMovies.

Memo to Self: RentalPriceID is still a Key, but it is not the Primary Key for tblMovies. So, RentalPriceID is considered a **Foreign Key**, because it belongs to another Table.

Table Tools ->Design

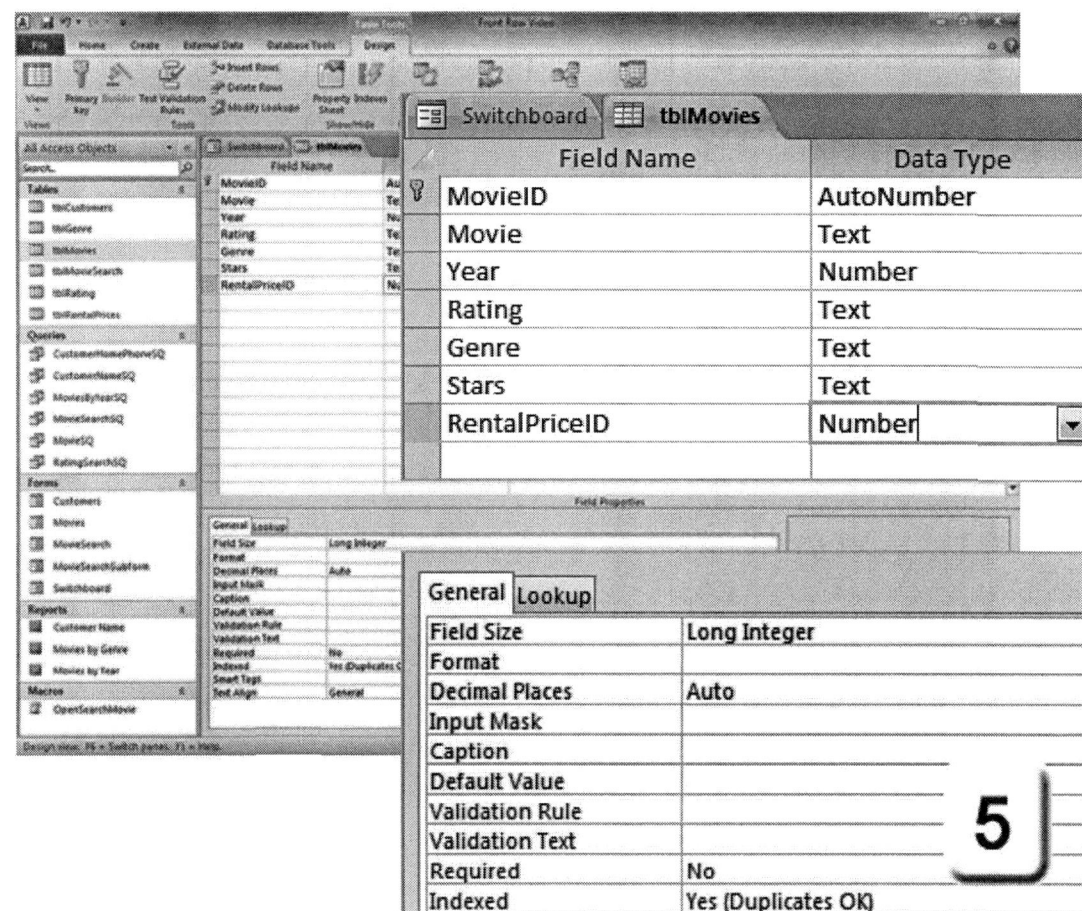

Field Name	Data Type
MovieID	AutoNumber
Movie	Text
Year	Number
Rating	Text
Genre	Text
Stars	Text
RentalPriceID	Number

General	Lookup
Field Size	Long Integer
Format	
Decimal Places	Auto
Input Mask	
Caption	
Default Value	
Validation Rule	
Validation Text	
Required	No
Indexed	Yes (Duplicates OK)

Exam 77-885: Microsoft Access 2010
2. Building Tables
2.4. Set relationships: Use Primary Keys to create Relationships

Create ->Queries->Query Design

Business Rules

In this business model, the Rental Prices are based on a date. New Movies have a higher Rental Price than old ones.

You can use an **Action Query** to add the Rental Prices to the Movie Table. An Action Query selects the Movies based on your Criteria and updates the RentalPriceID in tblMovies.

This lesson begins with a Select Query that has a Criteria for the Year. We'll test the Criteria to see if works: Does the Query select the right Movies?

1. Try This: Create a Select Query
Go to **Create ->Queries->Query Design.**
Select a Table: **tblMovies.**
Click **Add.**
Click **Close.**

Keep going...

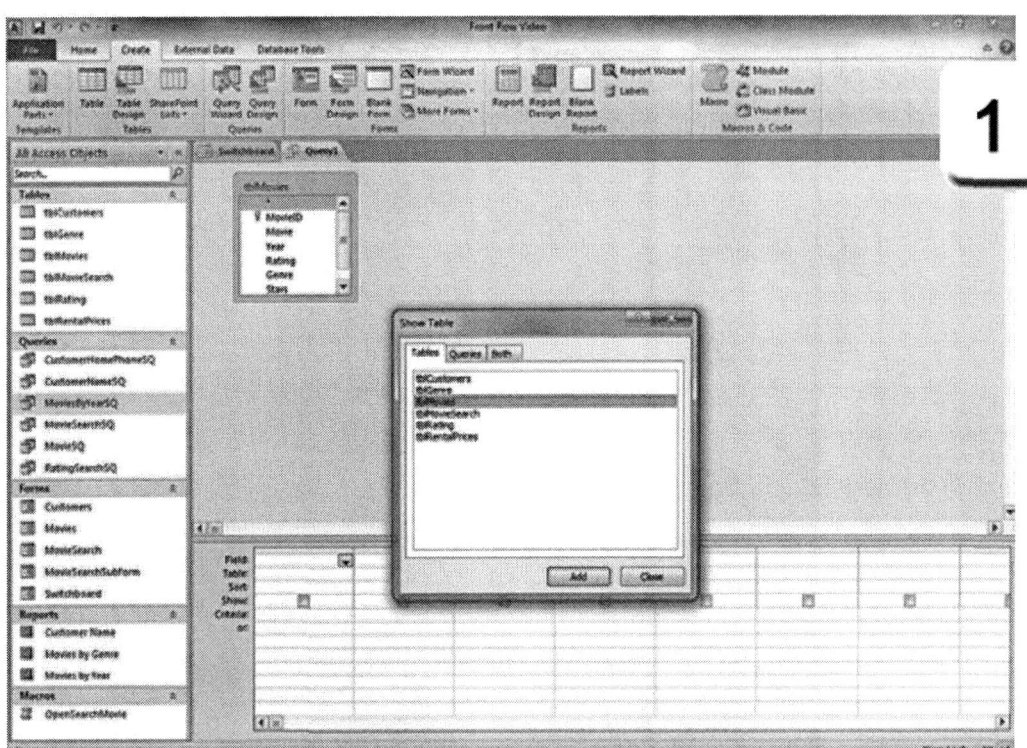

Exam 77-885: Microsoft Access 2010
4. Creating and Managing Queries
4.1. Construct queries: Select Queries

Query Tools ->Design

Edit the Select Query

2. Try it: Add Fields to the Query
Go to tblMovies.
Double click to select the following Fields:
MovieID
Movie
Year
RentalPriceID

Criteria can be used to Filter the Records.
Criteria can be words, phrases or numbers.

Try This, Too: Edit the Criteria
Select a Field: Year
Enter a Criteria: 2012

Keep going.

Field:	MovieID	Movie	Year	RentalPriceID
Table:	tblMovies	tblMovies	tblMovies	tblMovies
Sort:				
Show:	☑	☑	☑	☑
Criteria:			2012	
or:				

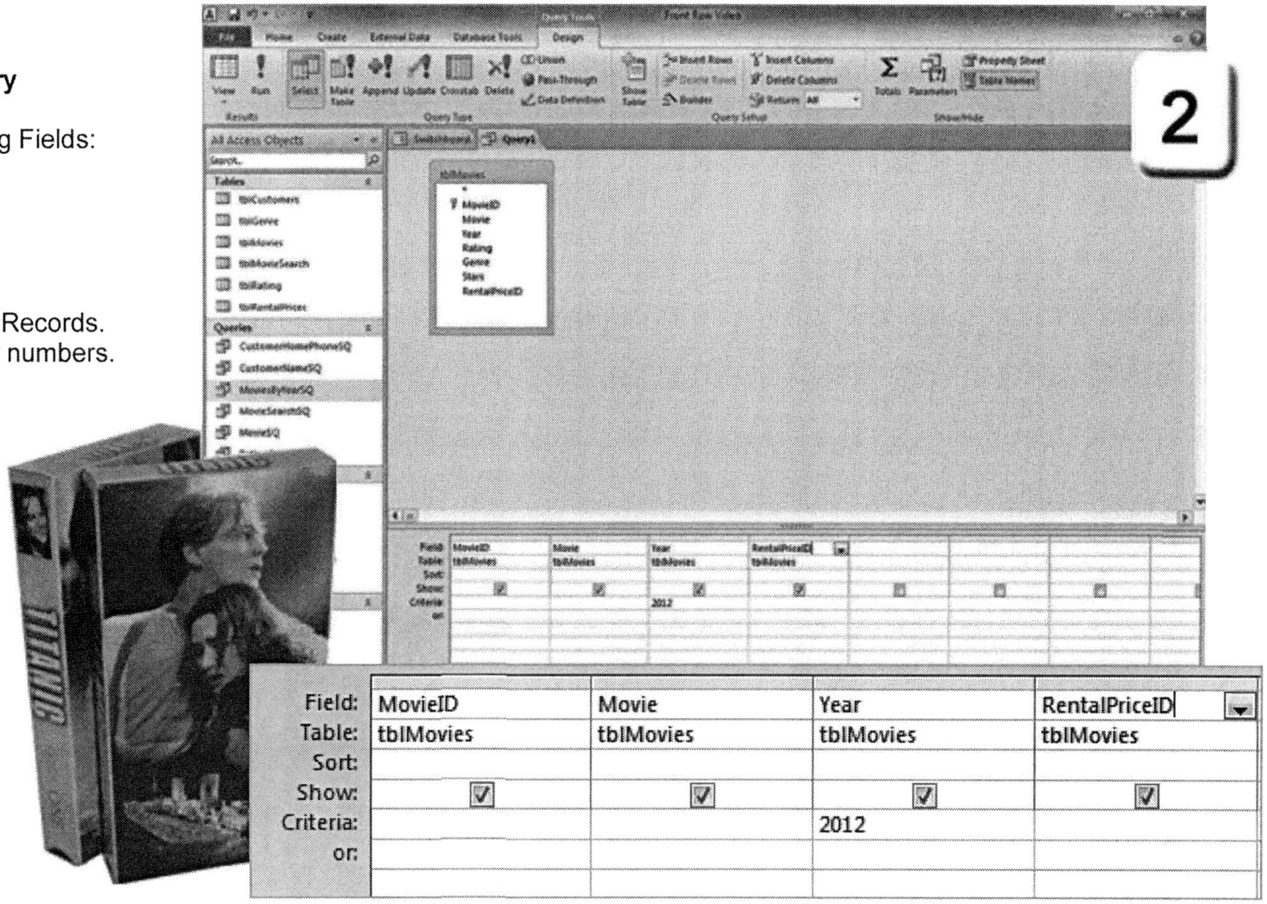

Exam 77-885: Microsoft Access 2010
4. Creating and Managing Queries
4.1. Construct queries: Select Queries

Take Two

Query Tools ->Design->Results->Run

Test the Criteria

3. Try This: Test the Criteria
Go to **Query Tools ->Design->Results->Run.**

What Do You See? There are 4 Movies in this database that were released in the Year 2012.

Then What? The Query selected the Movies we would like to Update to RentalPriceID 1, the premium 1-Day Rental for new Movies.

Do This: Return to Design View
Go to **Home->Views->View.**
Select a **View: Design View.**

Keep going.

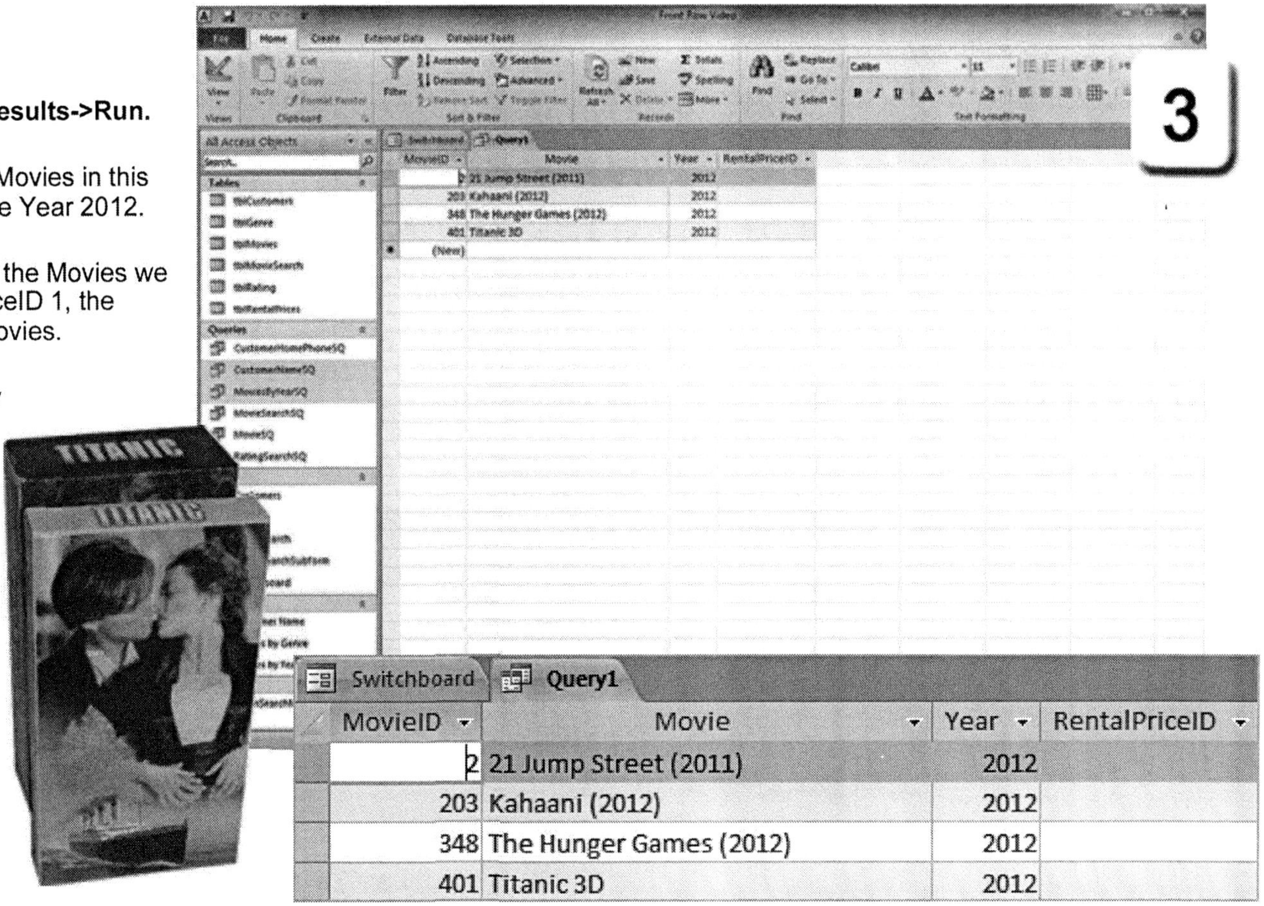

MovieID ▾	Movie ▾	Year ▾	RentalPriceID ▾
2	21 Jump Street (2011)	2012	
203	Kahaani (2012)	2012	
348	The Hunger Games (2012)	2012	
401	Titanic 3D	2012	

Exam 77-885: Microsoft Access 2010
4. Creating and Managing Queries
4.1. Construct queries: Select Queries

Select Query vs. Action Query
4. Try This: Consider the Query Types
Go to **Query Tools ->Design->Query Type.**

What Do You See? We are programming a Select Query. **Select Queries** grab certain Records in a Table. There are several other Query Types we can consider.

Action Queries change the Records. There are three Action Queries: Append, Update and Delete.

An **Append Query** adds more Records to a Table. An **Update Query** changes the data in the Table. A **Delete Query** deletes Records.

So, Here's the Plan: We will use an Update Query that changes the RentalPriceID based on the Criteria for the Year.

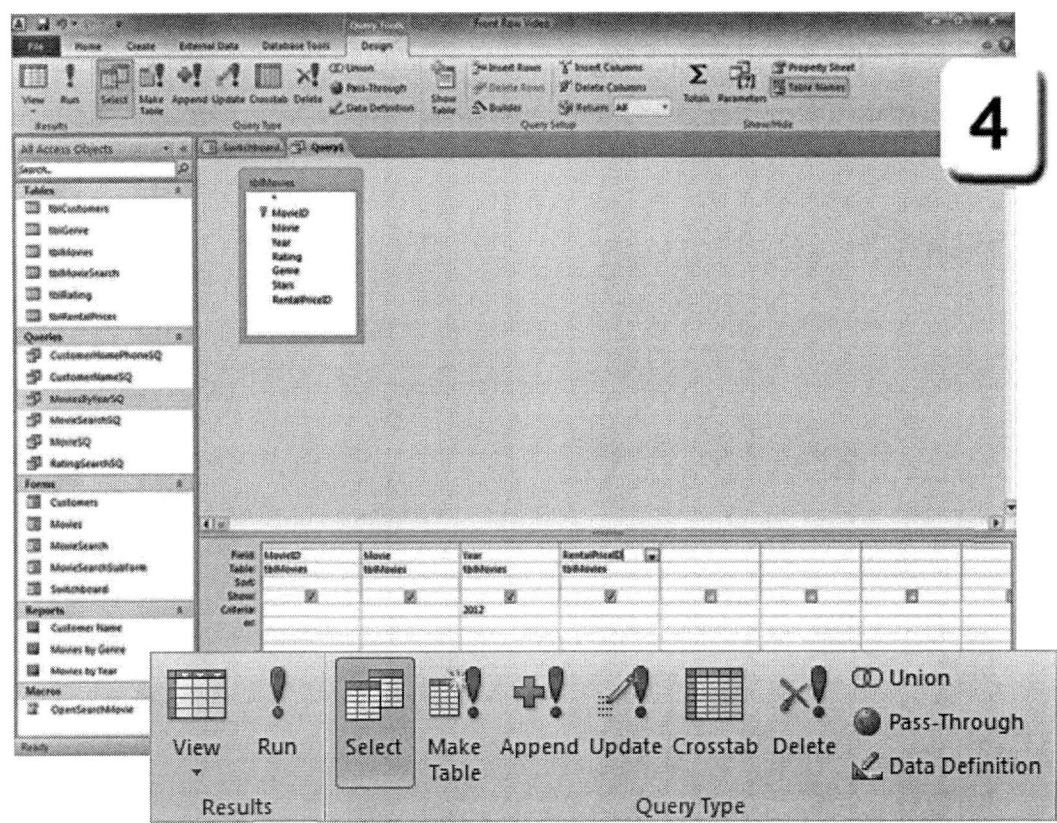

Exam 77-885: Microsoft Access 2010
4. Creating and Managing Queries
4.1. Construct queries: Update Queries

Query Tools ->Design->Query Type->Update

Create an Update Query

5. Try This: Create an Update Query
Go to **Query Tools ->Design->Query Type**.
Select a **Type: Update.**

What Do You See? You should see a new Row
in the QBE grid at the bottom of the Query.

Update to What? The data has to MATCH the
Field it is changing. RentalPriceID is a Number
that refers to a specific price and description.

Try This, Too: Edit the Update Value
Enter the RentalPriceID: 1

RentalPriceID 1 is $4.50 with a 1-Day Rental.

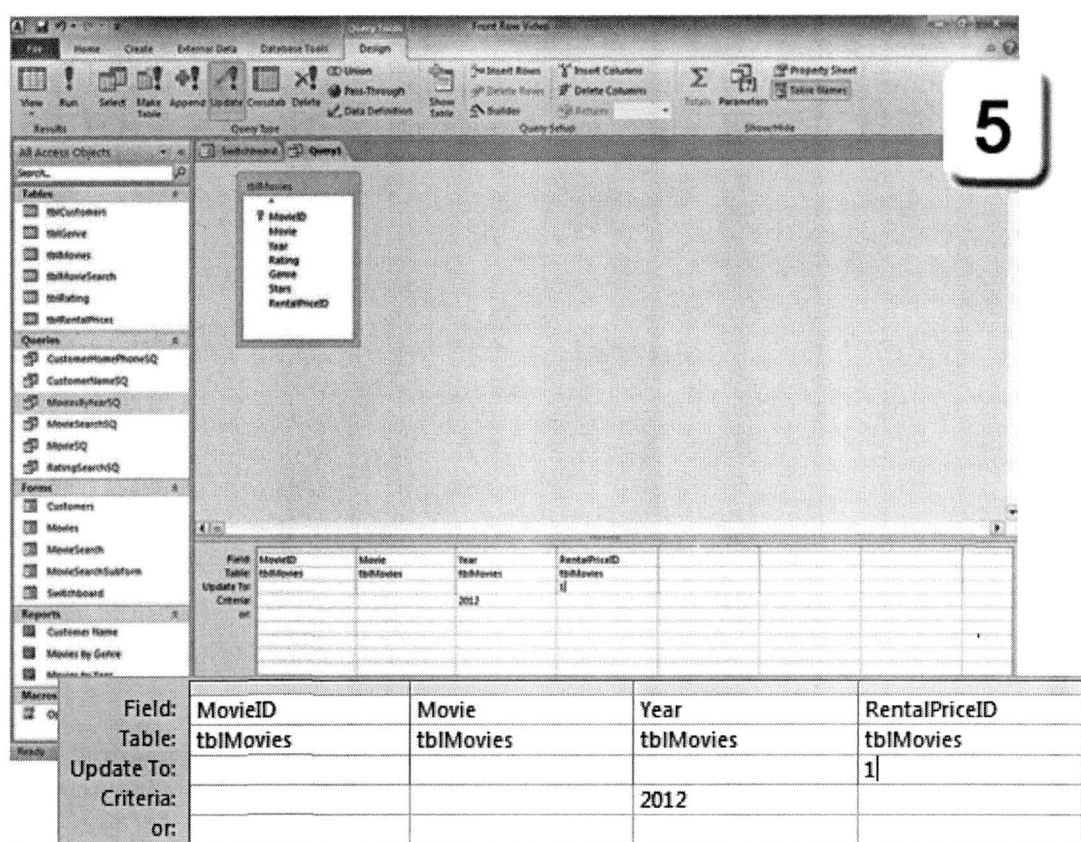

Field:	MovieID	Movie	Year	RentalPriceID
Table:	tblMovies	tblMovies	tblMovies	tblMovies
Update To:				1
Criteria:			2012	
or:				

Exam 77-885: Microsoft Access 2010
4. Creating and Managing Queries
4.1. Construct queries: Update Queries

Run the Action Query

Action Queries alter the data in the Table. It is a one-way step: there is no Undo. You will be prompted to confirm this action.

6. Try This: Run the Action Query
The Update Query is open in Design View.
Go to **Query Tools ->Design->Results->Run.**

What Do You See? When the Query Runs, it will update four rows in tblMovies with the Year: 2012.

You have to confirm this action.
Click **Yes**. Keep going.

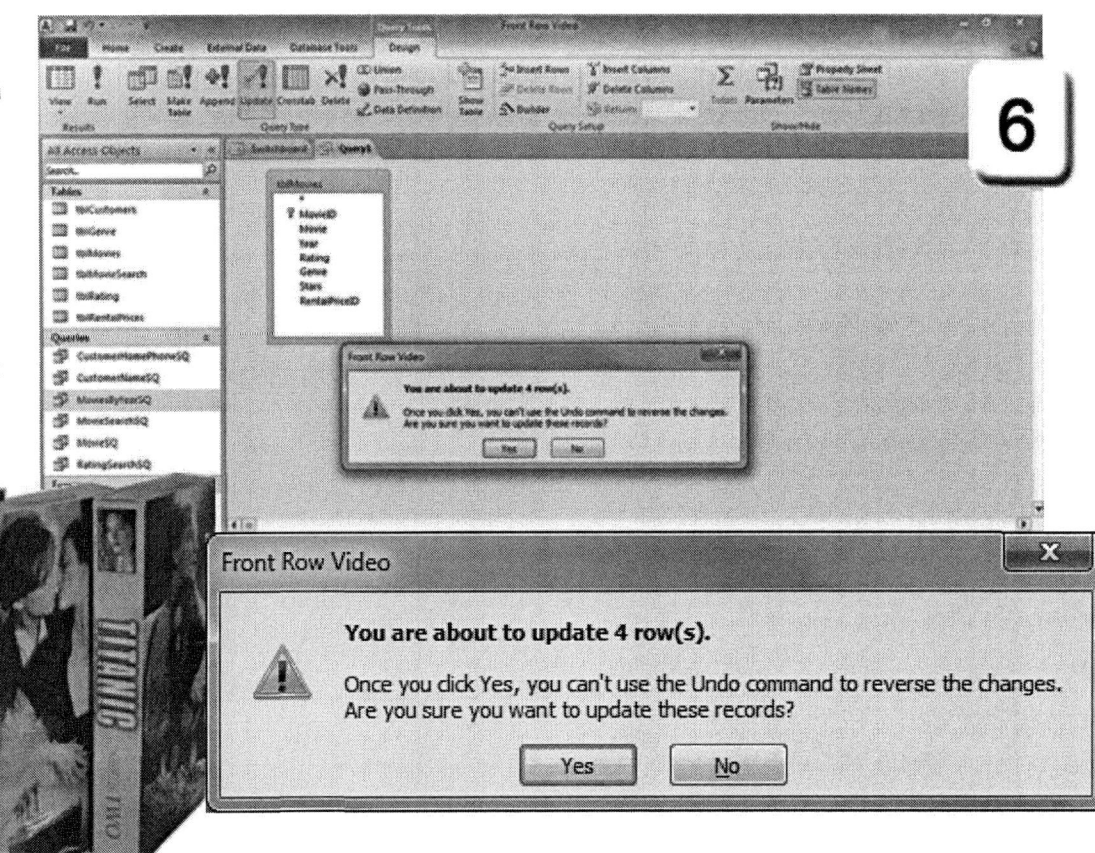

Front Row Video

You are about to update 4 row(s).

Once you click Yes, you can't use the Undo command to reverse the changes. Are you sure you want to update these records?

[Yes]   [No]

Exam 77-885: Microsoft Access 2010
4. Creating and Managing Queries
4.1. Construct queries: Update Queries

Take Two

Review the Results

The Action Query changed the data in tblMovies. Let's open that Table and see what happened.

7. Try This: View the Data in the Table
Go to **All Access Objects->Tables.**
Open a Table: tblMovies.

And This: Sort the Records by Year
Go to **Home ->Sort & Filter->Descending.**

What Do You See? The 2012 Records have been updated with RentalPriceID 1.

So, What Does That Mean? The Movies we selected have an updated RentalPriceID.

This is just one step. We'll run the Update Query a couple more times for the other two Rental Prices, then we'll look at how this all works.

Do This: Close the Table
If you are prompted, please **Save** the changes.

Home ->Sort & Filter->Descending

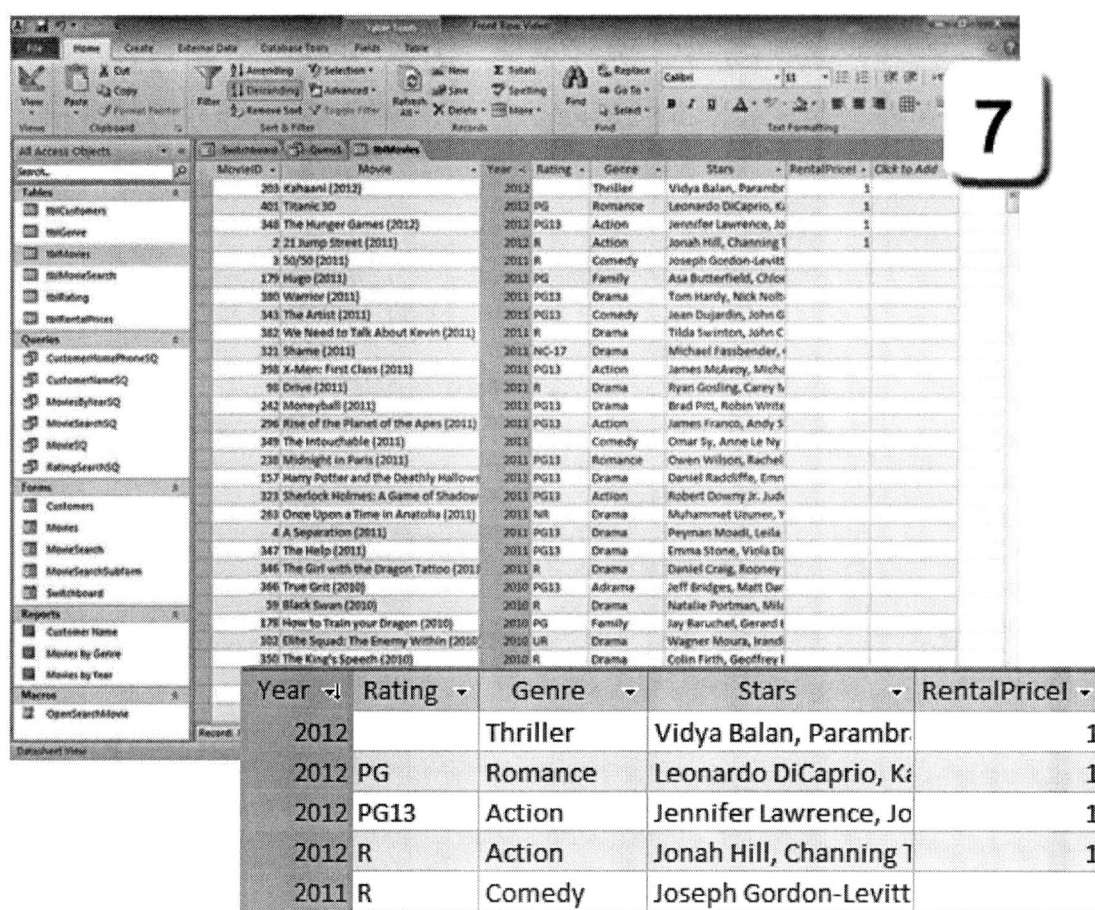

Year	Rating	Genre	Stars	RentalPriceI
2012		Thriller	Vidya Balan, Parambr	1
2012	PG	Romance	Leonardo DiCaprio, Ka	1
2012	PG13	Action	Jennifer Lawrence, Jo	1
2012	R	Action	Jonah Hill, Channing T	1
2011	R	Comedy	Joseph Gordon-Levitt	

Exam 77-885: Microsoft Access 2010
2. Building Tables
2.3. Sort and filter records: Use Sort

Edit the Update Query

You can use the Criteria to select different Years if you wish. We'll go back to the Select Query and test the new Criteria. This Criteria will select all of the Movies that were released before the Year 2000. Then we'll create an Update Query and review the results.

Before You Begin: Change the Query Type
Go to **Query Tools->Query Type->Select**.

What Do You See? The Update Row is gone.

8. Try This: Edit the Criteria
Select a Field: Year
Edit the Criteria: <2000

Keep going.

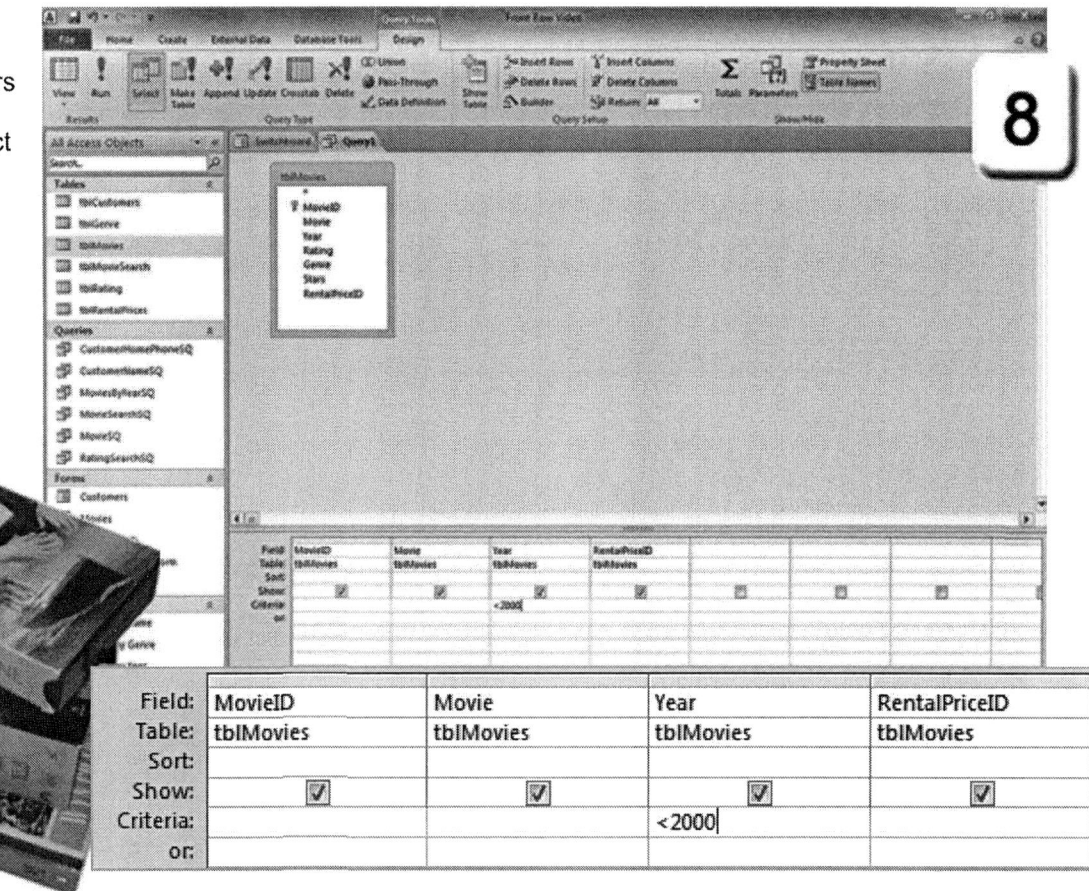

Field:	MovieID	Movie	Year	RentalPriceID
Table:	tblMovies	tblMovies	tblMovies	tblMovies
Sort:				
Show:	☑	☑	☑	☑
Criteria:			<2000	
or:				

Exam 77-885: Microsoft Access 2010
4. Creating and Managing Queries
4.1. Construct queries: Update Queries

Query Tools ->Design->Results->Run

Test and Run the Query

9. Try This: Test the New Query Criteria
The Select Query is open in Design View.
Go to **Query Tools ->Design->Results->Run.**

What Do You See? In this database there are 205
Movies that were released before the Year 2000.

Do This: Return to the Design View
Go to **Home->Views->View->Design View.**

And Do This: Change Back to an Update Query
Go to **Query Tools ->Design->Query Type.**
Select a **Type: Update.**

Try This, Too: Edit the Update Value
Enter the RentalPriceID: 3
RentalPriceID 3 is $2.50 with a 5-Day Rental.

Try This, Now: Run the Update Query
Go to **Query Tools ->Design->Results->Run.**
When it runs, 205 rows in tblMovies will be
updated, You will be asked to confirm this action.

Click **Yes**. Keep going.

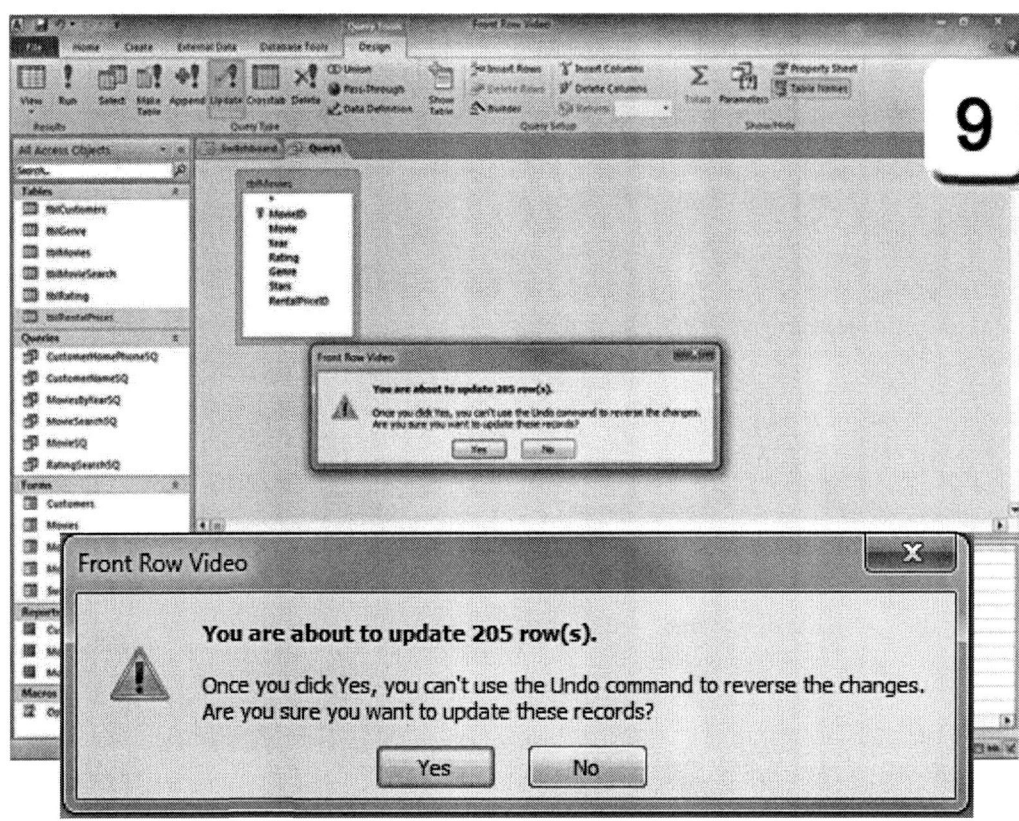

Exam 77-885: Microsoft Access 2010
4. Creating and Managing Queries
4.1. Construct queries: Update Queries

Create Another Update Criteria

Before You Begin: Change the Query Type
Go to **Query Tools->Query Type->Select.**
Try This: Edit the Criteria
Select a Field: Year
Edit the Criteria: >1999 and <2012

And This: Test the New Query Criteria
Go to **Query Tools ->Design->Results->Run.**
This Query returned 192 Movies between the
Year 1999 and 2012.

Finally, Do This: Create an Update Query
Go to **Home->Views->View->Design View.**
Go to **Query Tools ->Design->Query Type.**
Select a **Type: Update.**
Enter the RentalPriceID: 2
RentalPriceID 2 is $3.50 with a 3-Day Rental.

Try This, Now: Run the Update Query
Go to **Query Tools ->Design->Results->Run.**
A total of 192 rows in tblMovies will be updated.
You will be asked to confirm. Click **Yes.**

Query Tools ->Design->Results->Run

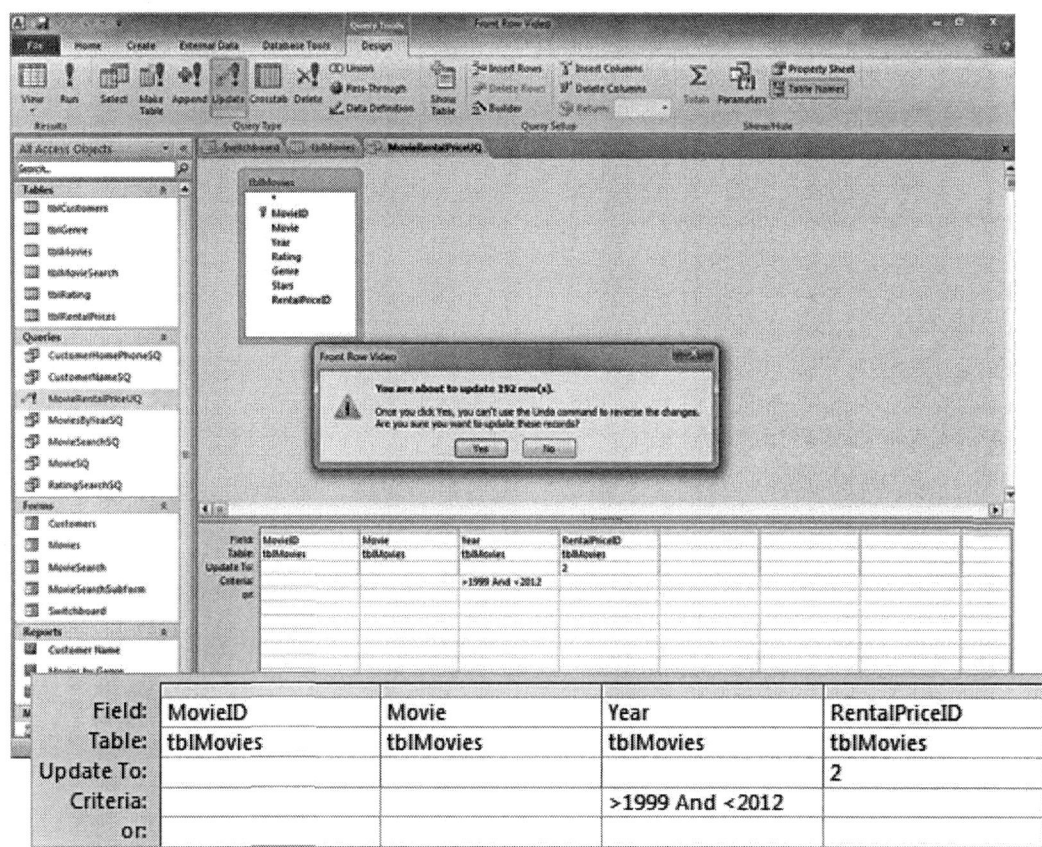

Field:	MovieID	Movie	Year	RentalPriceID
Table:	tblMovies	tblMovies	tblMovies	tblMovies
Update To:				2
Criteria:			>1999 And <2012	
or:				

Exam 77-885: Microsoft Access 2010
4. Creating and Managing Queries
4.1. Construct queries: Update Queries

Did the Data Update?
Before You Forget: Save the Update Query.
Go to **File->Save.**
Enter a Name: MovieRentalPriceUQ
Where UQ means Update Query.
Close the Query.

The Action Query changed the data in tblMovies.
All of the rows should be updated with a
RentalPriceID, based on the Year.

Try This: View the Data in the Table
Go to **All Access Objects->Tables.**
Open a Table: tblMovies.

Try This As Well: Sort the Records by Year
Go to **Home ->Sort & Filter->Descending.**

What Do You See? There are 3 RentalPriceIDs.
2012: RentalPriceID 1.
2000-2011: RentalPriceID 2.
Before 2000: RentalPriceID 3.

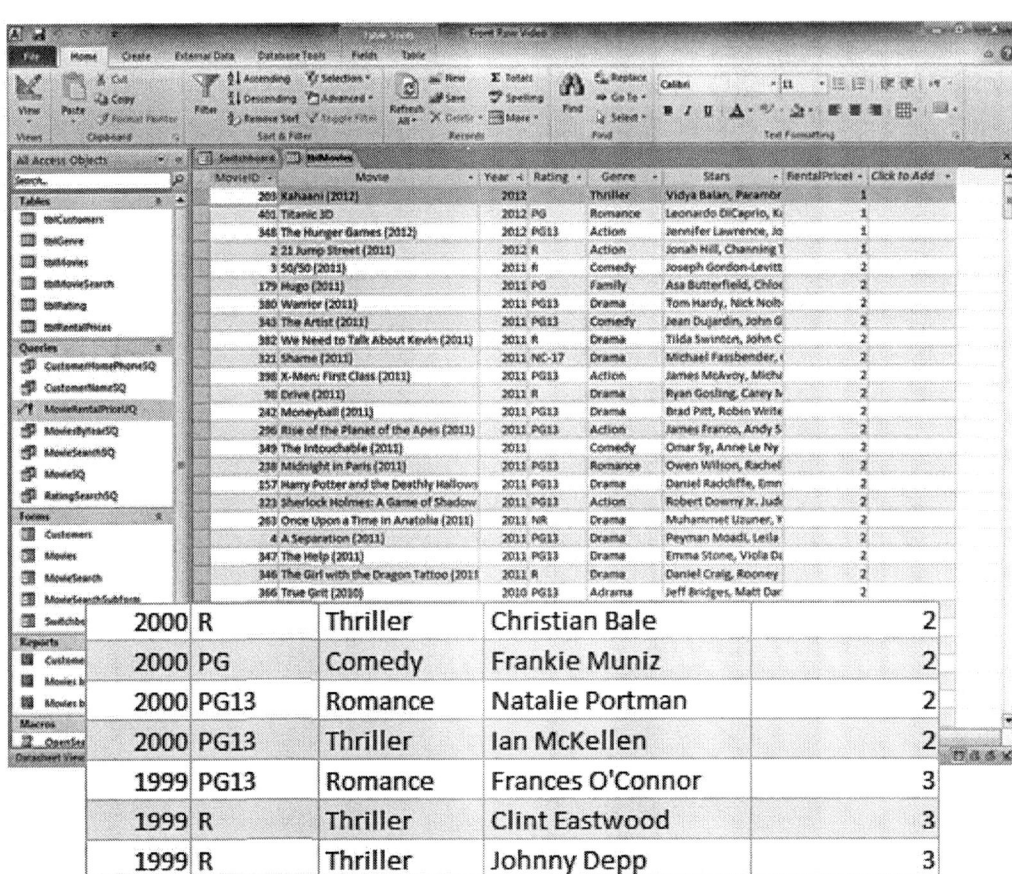

Tables and Subtables

Databases use Forms and Subforms to show a relationship. Tables use Subdatasheets to meet the same goal: create a relationship.

The Form and Subform are linked by a common Field. When you add a Subdatasheet you will be prompted to select a Field that both Tables share.

The following pages will add a Subdatasheet, tblRentalPrices to the tblMovies. Both Tables have the same Field: RentalPriceID.

1. Try This: Add a Subdatasheet
tblMovies is still open in Datasheet View.
Go to **Home ->Records->More->Subdatasheet.**
Select: Subdatasheet.

Keep going.

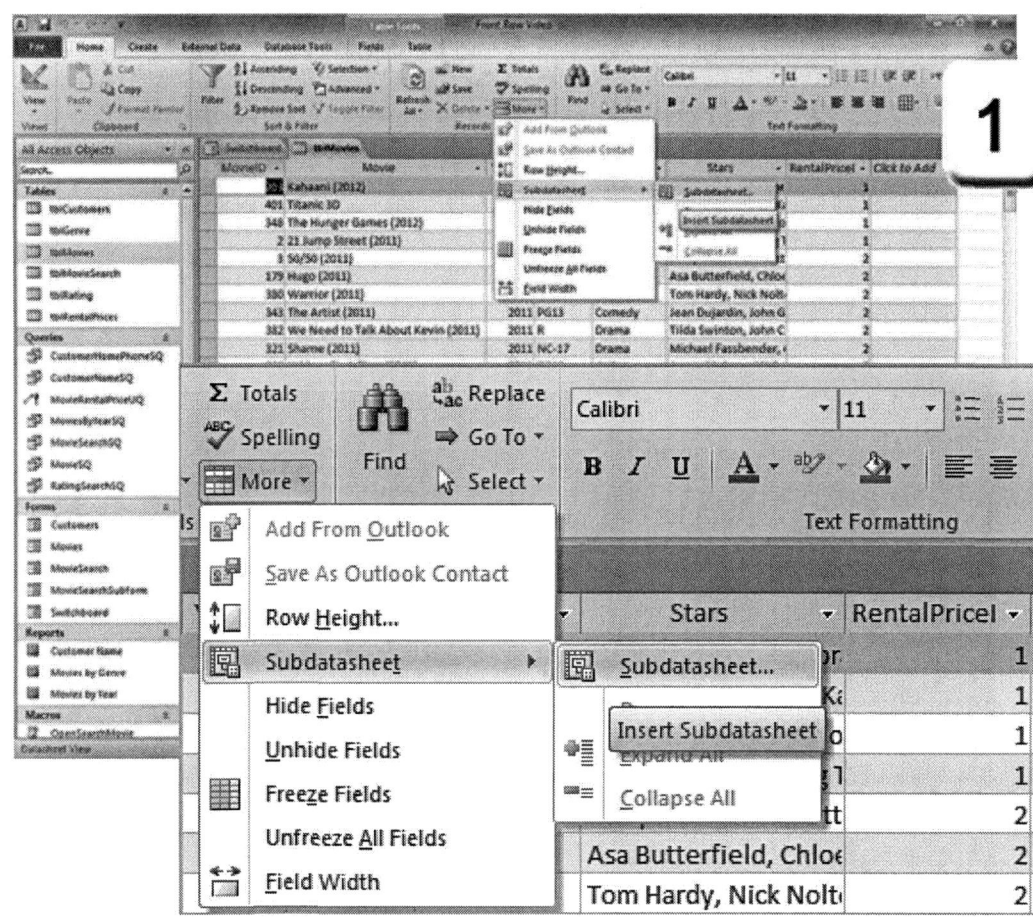

Exam 77-885: Microsoft Access 2010
2. Building Tables
2.4. Set relationships: Use Primary Keys to Create Relationships

Subdatasheet Options

A Subdatasheet can be a Table or a Query. The Subdatasheet will use the Primary Keys to create a one-to-many relationship.

2. Try This: Insert Subdatasheet
Select a Table: tblRentalPrices
Link Child Fields: RentalPriceID
Link Master Fields: RentalPriceID

Click **OK**. Keep going.

Memo to Self: Microsoft Access will immediately look for a relationship between the Fields. A rather large pop-up with a red X may appear-pictured on the next page. This is not a mistake, although it may be startling the first time.

Home ->Records->More->Subdatasheet->Subdatasheet

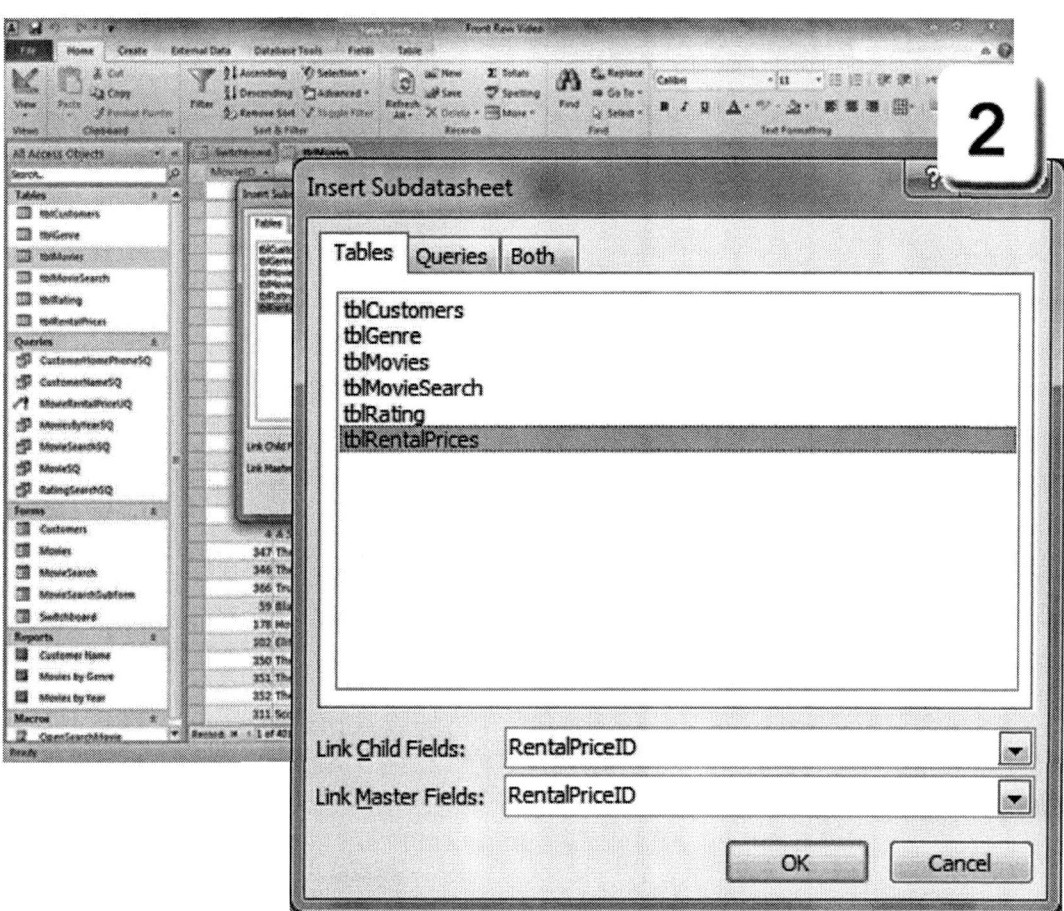

Exam 77-885: Microsoft Access 2010
2. Building Tables
2.4. Set relationships: Use Primary Keys to Create Relationships

Create a Relationship

What Do You See? When you link two Tables by a common Field Microsoft Access will look for a relationship. Are these two Tables related? Yes, we want to link the Movies to the Rental Price.

If Microsoft Access does not detect a relationship between the Fields, you will be asked if you like to create one.

3. Try This: Create a Relationship
Click **Yes**. Keep going.

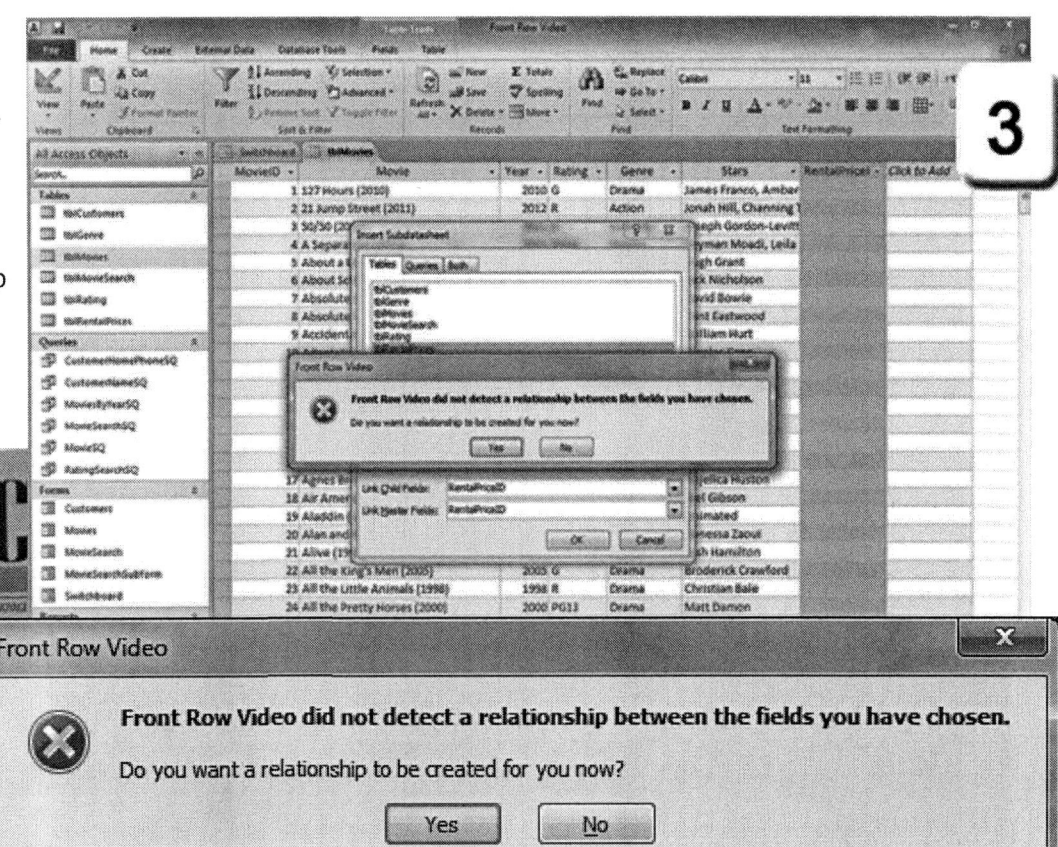

Front Row Video

Front Row Video did not detect a relationship between the fields you have chosen.

Do you want a relationship to be created for you now?

Yes   No

Exam 77-885: Microsoft Access 2010
2. Building Tables
2.4. Set relationships: Use Primary Keys to Create Relationships

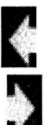

Hello, Table and Subdatasheet
4. Try This: Review the Subdatasheet
The Movie Table, tblMovies, has a Subdatasheet.

What Do You See? There is a plus sign (+) by the Record Selector in each Row. When you click on the plus sign the Subdatasheet will display the Rental Price for that Record, based on the RentalPriceID that matches.

Keep going...

Home ->Records->More->Subdatasheet->Subdatasheet

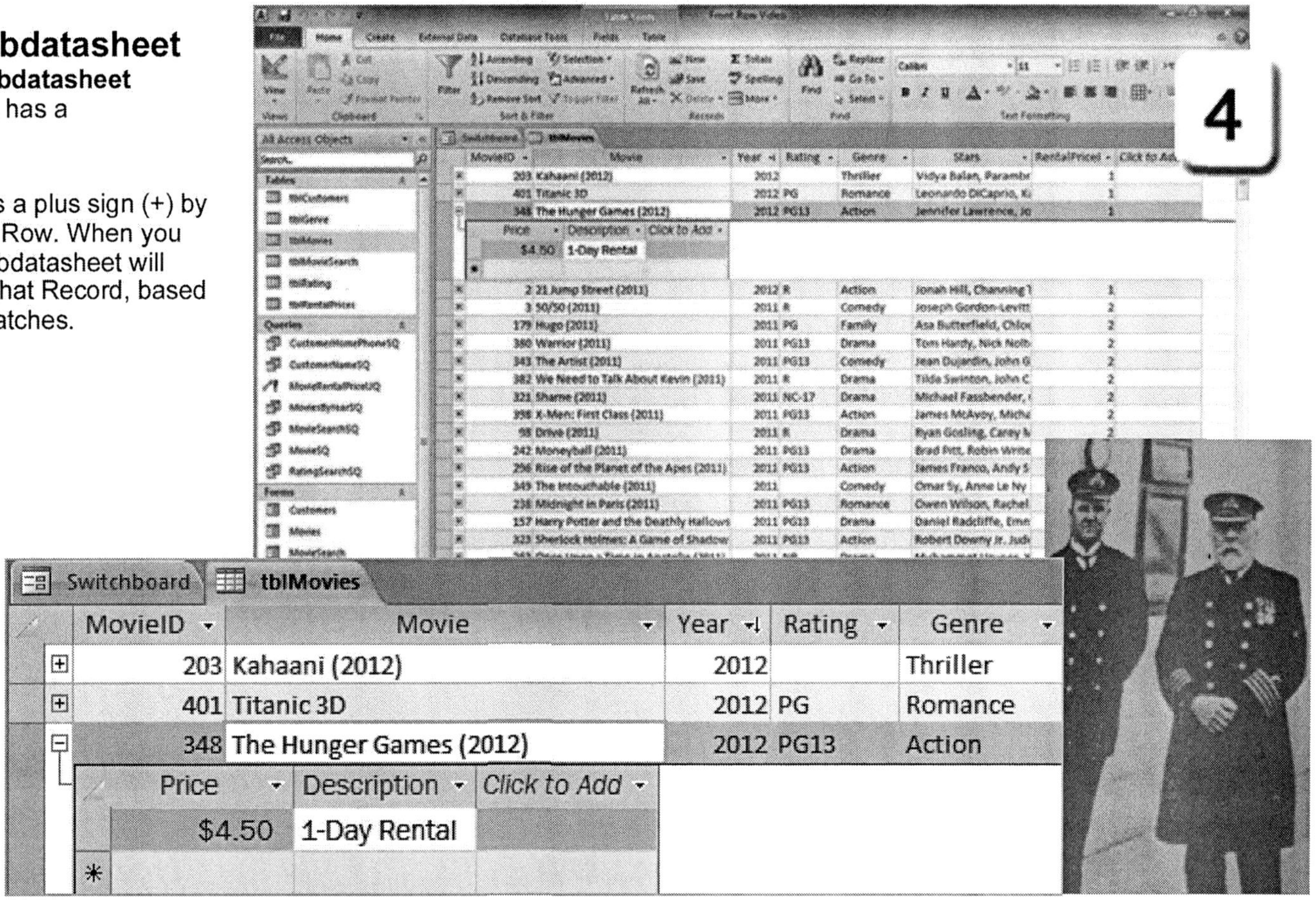

Exam 77-885: Microsoft Access 2010
2. Building Tables
2.1.1. Create tables in Design View

Format the Table: Unhide Fields

What Don't You See? The Primary Key in the Subdatasheet is hidden.

5. Try This: Format the Subdatasheet Fields
Select the Price Column in the Subdatasheet.
Go to **Home ->Records->More->Unhide Fields.**

Keep going.

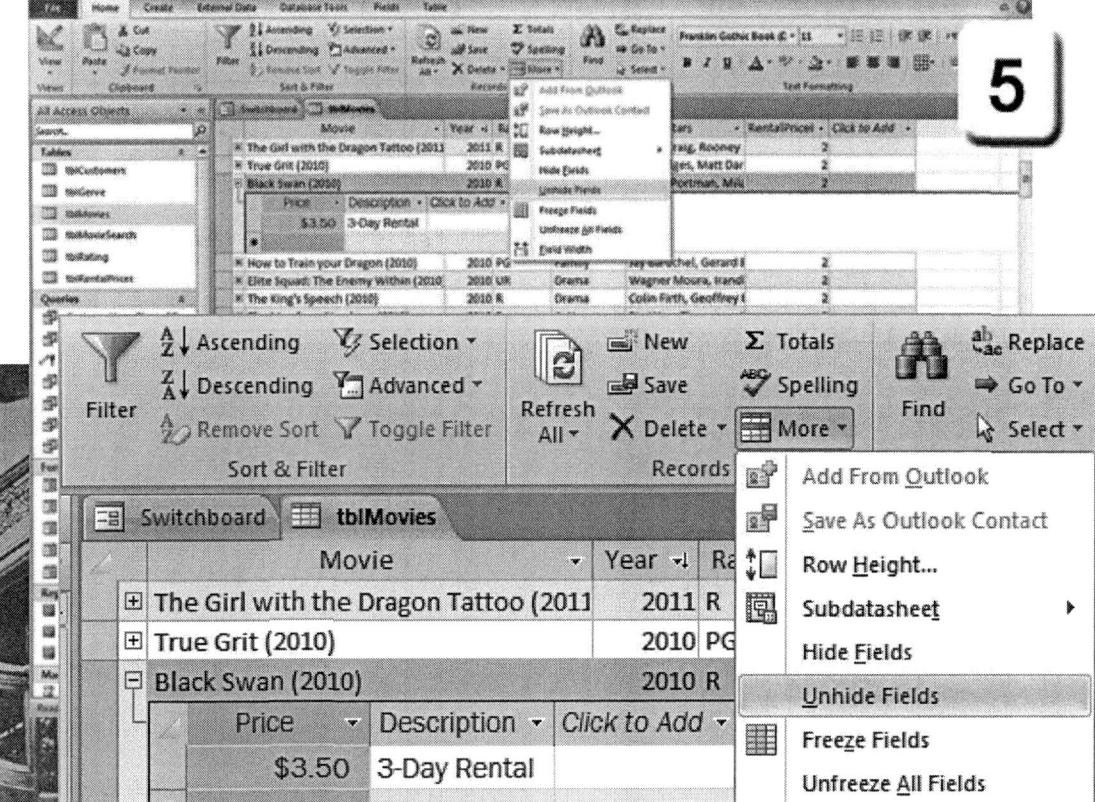

Exam 77-885: Microsoft Access 2010
2. Building Tables
2.2. Create and Modify Fields: Hide or Unhide Fields

Home ->Records->More->Unhide Fields

Format Table: Unhide Fields

What Do You See? The Columns include all of the Fields in tblRentalPrices. There is also a Column for modifying the Table: Click to Add.

6. Try This: Unhide Columns
Select the following Columns:
RentalPriceID
Price
Description

Unselect: Click to Add
Click **Close**.

Now, What Do You See? There should be three Columns in the Subdatasheet: RentalPriceID, Price and Description.

And Try This: Close the Subdatasheet Fields
Click on the minus sign to the left of the name of the Movie to close the Subdatasheet.

Keep going.

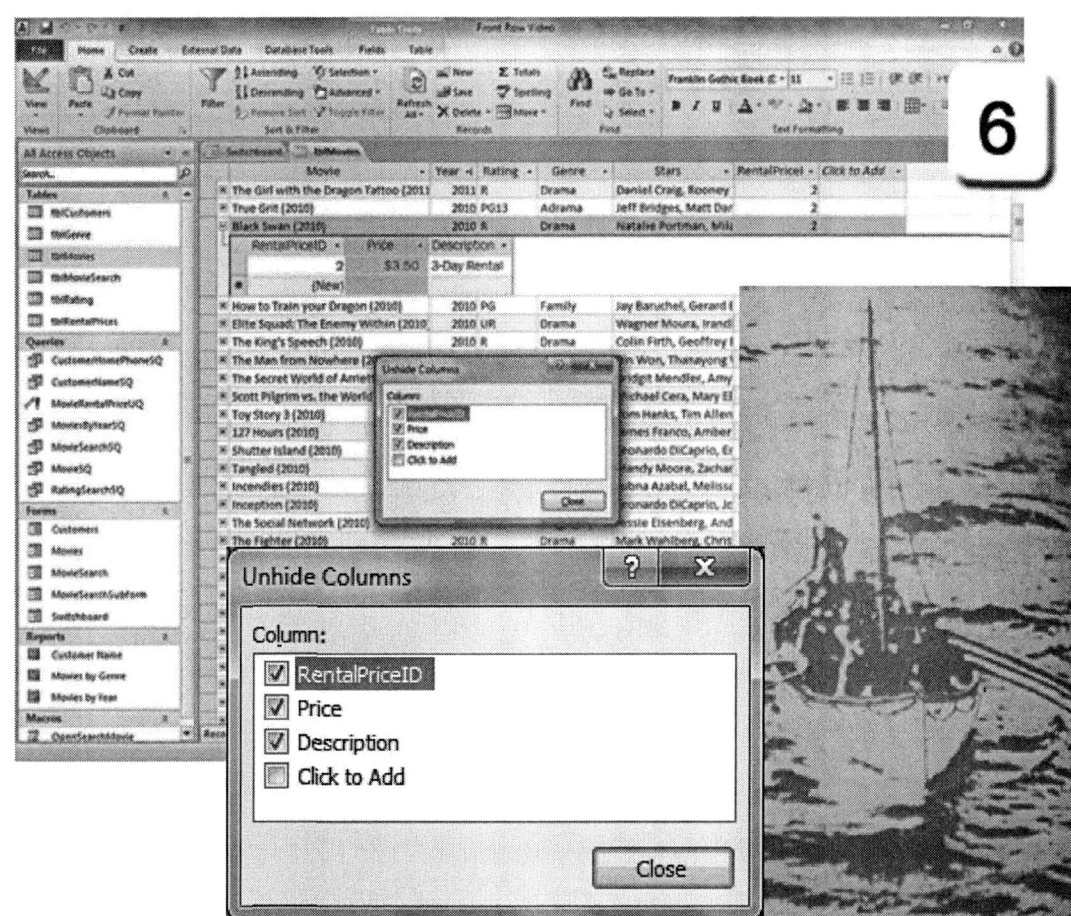

6

Exam 77-885: Microsoft Access 2010
2. Building Tables
2.2. Create and Modify Fields: Hide or Unhide Fields

Format Table: Freeze Fields

When you **Freeze** a Field, you lock that Column into place. The rest of the Datasheet can scroll to the left or right, but the Field that you Freeze will remain fixed.

7. Try This: Freeze a Field in a Table
Select the Movie Column in tblMovies.
Go to **Home ->Records->More->Freeze Fields.**

What Do You See? Use the horizontal Scroll Bar at the bottom of the Table to scroll to the Stars in the far right Column. The Movie Column should remain fixed on the left side of the screen.

Where Have You Seen This Before? You can Resize, Hide and Freeze Columns in Microsoft Excel as well.

OK, Save, Save, Save.

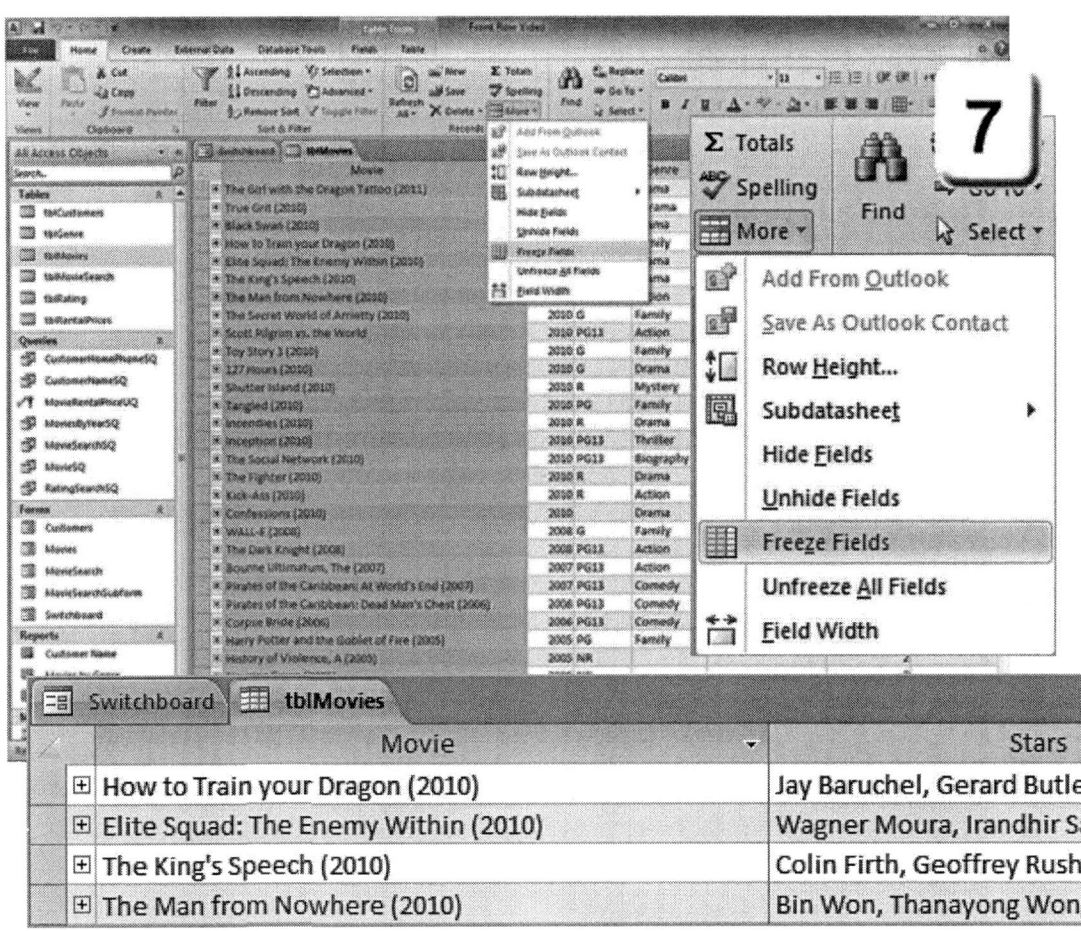

Exam 77-885: Microsoft Access 2010
2. Building Tables
2.2. Create and Modify Fields: Freeze or Unfreeze Fields

Summary

The goal of this lesson was to create a relationship between a Table of Movies and a Table with Rental Prices. The two Tables need a common Field. RentalPriceID was the example used in this programming.

The Primary Key is the best option because it is unique and indexed (fast!).

You done good. Take two cookies if you wish.

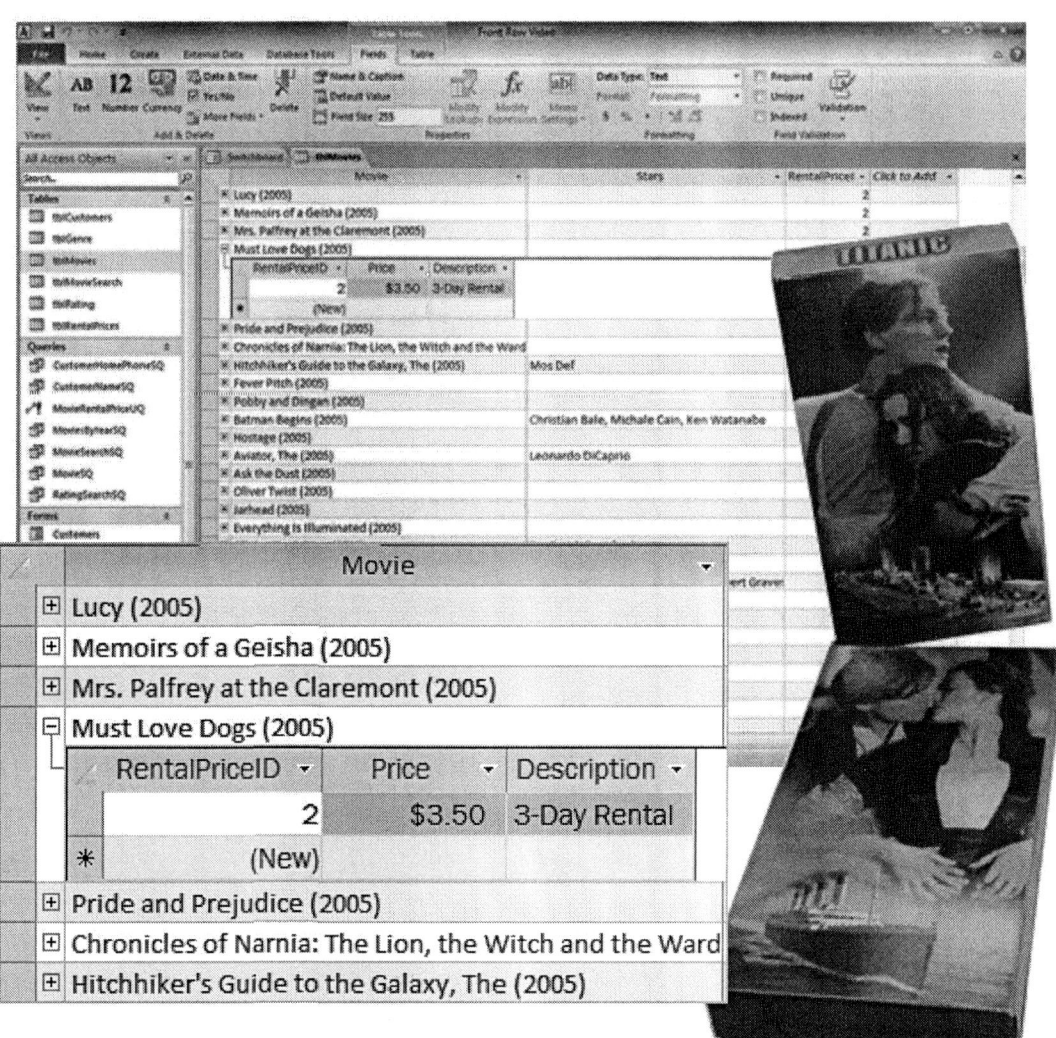

Practice Activities

Lesson 2: Managing Tables

Try This: Do the following steps

1. Open the Brown Bag Lunch database you have been working on.

Or, you may download **BBL Adv ver2.accdb.**

2. Edit the Products Table, tblProducts, in Design View. Add a new Field:
Field Name: Price
Data Type: Currency

Save the Table and close it.

3. Create a Select Query and add tblProducts as the Record Source. Add all Fields to the QBE Grid. Run the Query to test it. Save the Query as ProductPricesUQ.

4. Add a Parameter to the ProductPricesUQ. Select the Type and type the following Criteria: "Sandwich" Run the Query to test it. Note how many Records there are.

5. Change ProductPricesUQ from a Select Query to an Update Query.

6. The Criteria for Type is "Sandwich." In the QBE grid UPDATE the Price to $7.50. Run the Query and update the Records in tblProducts.

7. The Criteria for Type is "Breakfast." In the QBE grid UPDATE the Price to $5.50. Run the Query and update the Records in tblProducts.

8. The Criteria for Type is "Snacks." In the QBE grid UPDATE the Price to $10.50. Run the Query and update the Records in tblProducts.

9. The Criteria for Type is "Tray." In the QBE grid UPDATE the Price to $24.50. Run the Query and update the Records in tblProducts.

10. The Criteria for Type is "Beverages." In the QBE grid UPDATE the Price to $4.50. Run the Query and update the Records in tblProducts. Save and close the Query.

11. Go to All Access Objects and confirm that the Products Table has prices for each Record. Close the Products Table.

12. Open the Specialty Table, tblSpecialty. Add a Subdatasheet to the Specialty Table with the Command Home->Records->More. Add the Products Table: tblProducts.

13. Expand the Subdatasheet and HIDE the ProductID Column.

14. Save and close the Specialty Table.

15. Close the Brown Bag Lunch database.

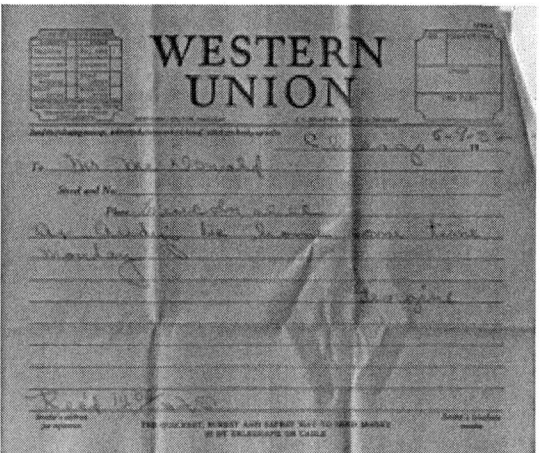

Test Yourself

1. Which would be an Access Table in Third Normal Form?
(Give all correct answers.)
A. tblMovies has only movies
B. tblCustomers has only customer data
C. tblProducts has items and their prices
D. tblPrices has only prices
Tip: Advanced Access, page 34

2. Which are Data Types in an Access Table?
(Give all correct answers.)
A. Auto Number
B. Currency
C. Text
D. Memo
Tip: Advanced Access, page 35

3. Which of the following is true about Key fields?
(Give all correct answers.)
A. A Foreign Key is the Primary Key from another Table
B. A Table can have only one Primary Key
C. A Table can have many Primary Keys
D. A Key Field is a good way to link two Tables
E. A Primary Key can be text or a number
Tip: Advanced Access, page 38-39

4. Which is true about Subdatasheets? (Give all correct answers.)
A. Can be a Table
B. Can be a Query
C. Will use Primary Keys to create relationships
Tip: Advanced Access, page 52

5. Match the Query with its description:

A. Select Query	i. Changes the Record
B. Action Query	ii. Changes the Data in the Table
C. Append Query	iii. Deletes Records
D. Update Query	iv. Displays certain Records
E. Delete Query	v. Adds more Records to a Table

Tip: Advanced Access, page 43

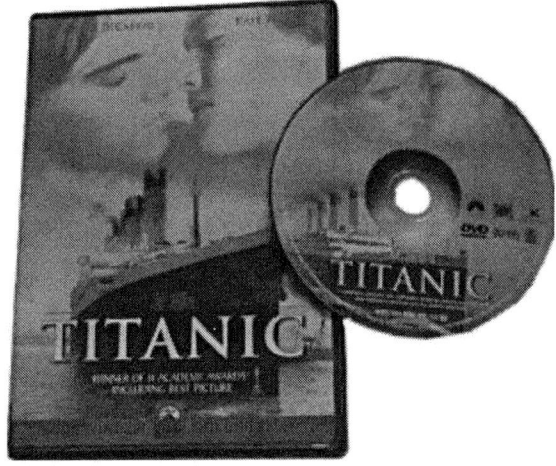

Access 2010: Many-to-Many
Primary Keys and Relationships

Advanced Access Objectives
In this lesson, you will learn how to:

1. Identify the levels of database design: First, Second and Third Normal Form.

2. Create Tables in Design View that have Primary and Foreign Keys.

3. Create Tables that do not have repeating groups: Third Normal Form.

4. Document the Relationships.

5. Edit the Joins between Tables to ensure Data Integrity and Enforce Referential Integrity,

© 2012 Comma Productions, LLC

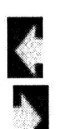

Take Three

Lesson 3 : Primary Keys and Relationships

1. Readings
Read Lesson 3 in the Advanced Access Guide, page 61-86.

Project
Create several Tables with Primary and Foreign Keys.

Downloads
FrontRowVideo Adv3.accdb
BBL Adv ver3.accdb

2. Practice
Do the Practice Activity on page 87.

3. Assessment
Review the Test questions on page 88.

Create Ribbon

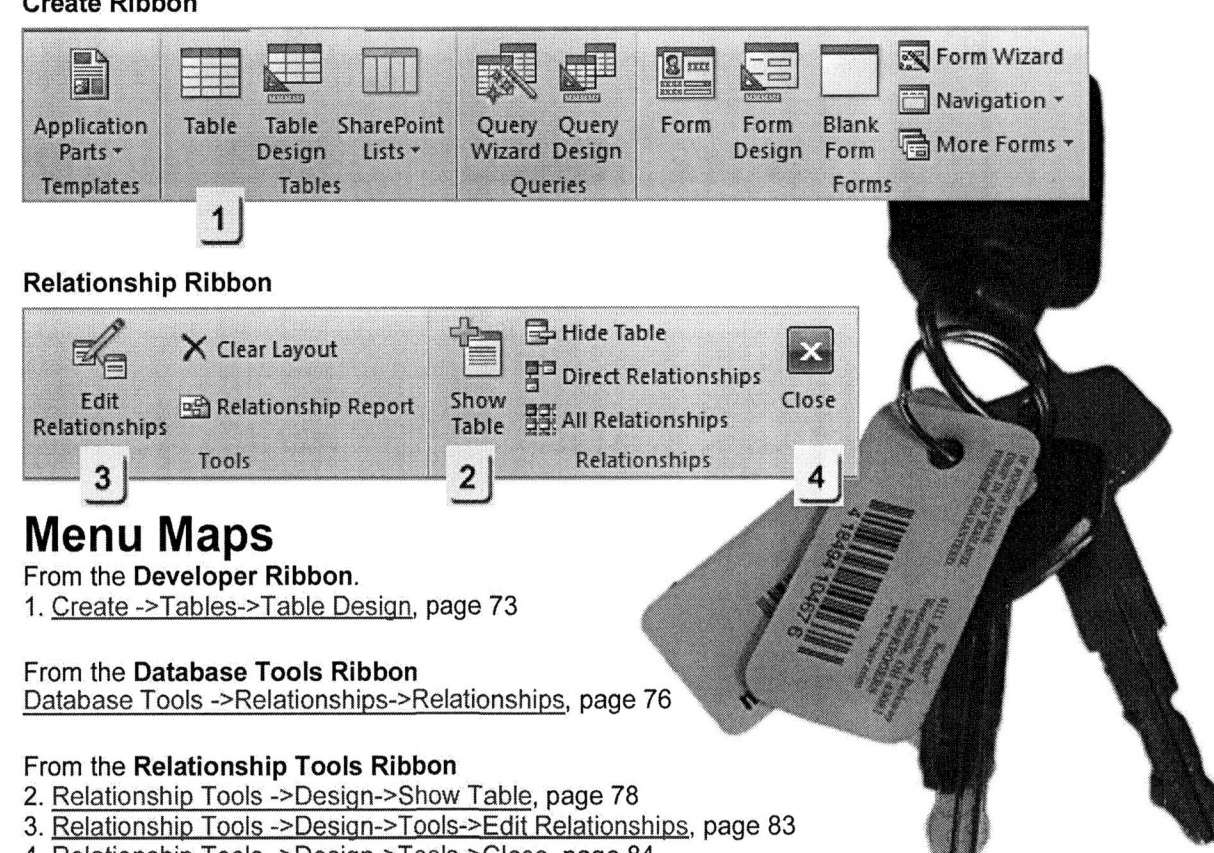

Relationship Ribbon

Menu Maps

From the **Developer Ribbon**.
1. Create ->Tables->Table Design, page 73

From the **Database Tools Ribbon**
Database Tools ->Relationships->Relationships, page 76

From the **Relationship Tools Ribbon**
2. Relationship Tools ->Design->Show Table, page 78
3. Relationship Tools ->Design->Tools->Edit Relationships, page 83
4. Relationship Tools ->Design->Tools->Close, page 84

Table Design, Primary Keys and Relationships

When you begin a database, you need to start backwards--at the end of the process--and analyze the final product. In some databases, the final report may be an insurance claim form. In others, it may be an engineering status report. The Front Row Video database is a simple business model: Who bought what? The final product is a receipt that prints the names of the movies and the rental price. The Receipt Form design will be presented in two lessons: Tables and Forms. In the following lessons, the data captured by the Receipt Form will be queried and formatted for print.

How should the Receipt Tables be designed? What are the relationships?

Microsoft Office Access 2010: Example of the Relationships in a Database

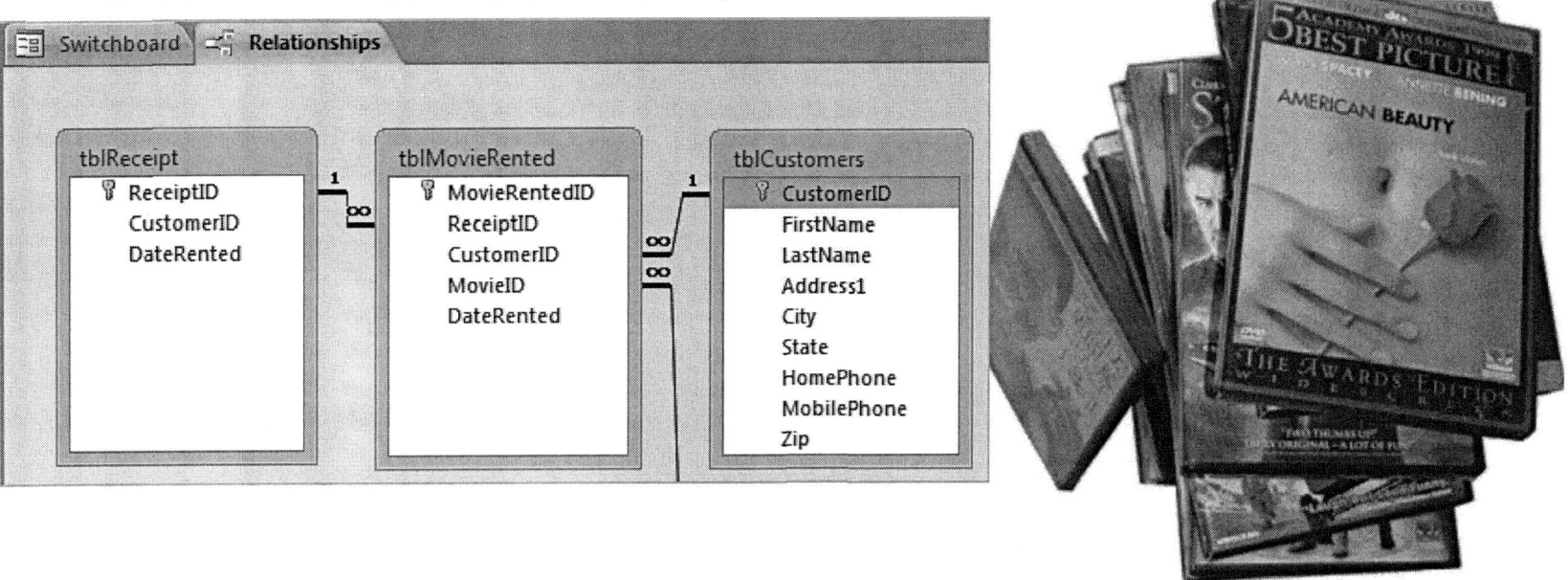

The Receipt Form

The Receipt Form answers the question:
Who bought what?

This Form will combine data from three Tables.
Who: tblCustomers
Bought: tblMovieRented
What: tblMovies

In the following pages, we will create two new Tables that will be the Record Sources for the Receipt Form and ReceiptSubform.

The Receipt Subform will inherit three Key Fields from the Receipt Form. So the Table for the ReceiptSubform, tblMovieRented, has to be designed with that in mind.

Microsoft Office Access 2010: Example of the Completed Receipt Form

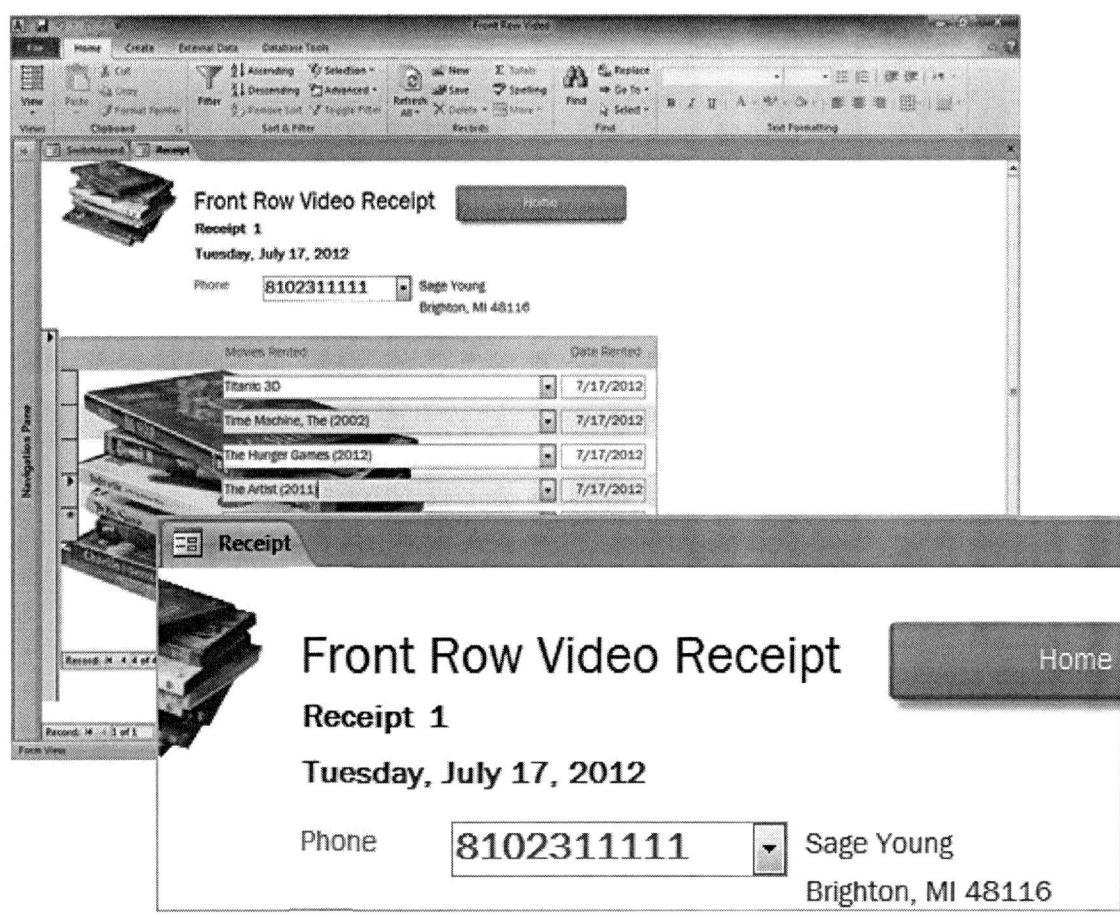

What's the Plan for the Table Design?

The Receipt Form has two Forms, two Tables, two Combo Boxes and three links. Always begin with the Tables. This lesson begins with a short explanation of database design and normalization: There are some really good guidelines for designing Tables.

Create a Table for the Receipt Form

Make a Receipt Table, tblReceipt.
Create a Primary Key, ReceiptID a
Add a Foreign Key (Primary Key to another Table): CustomerID.

The Receipt Table also includes the date, which we will use in several reports.

Create a Table for the MovieRentedSubform

Make a MovieRented Table, tblMovieRented.
Create a Primary Key, ReceiptID
Add the following Foreign Keys:
ReceiptID
CustomerID.
MovieID

This Table will inherit the DateRented from tblReceipt. That's the plan.

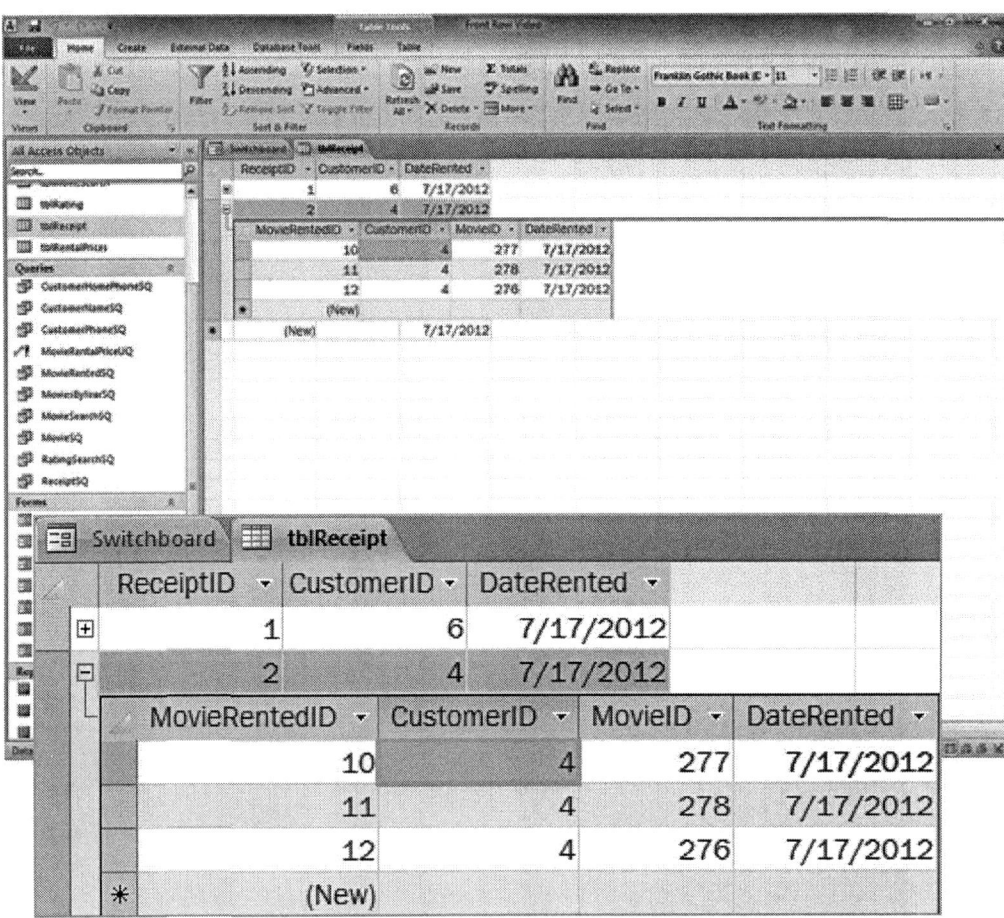

ReceiptID	CustomerID	DateRented
1	6	7/17/2012
2	4	7/17/2012

MovieRentedID	CustomerID	MovieID	DateRented
10	4	277	7/17/2012
11	4	278	7/17/2012
12	4	276	7/17/2012
* (New)			

Before You Begin

Before You Begin: Open the Sample Database
Go to **Start -> All Programs ->Microsoft Office.**
Click on **Microsoft Office Access 2010.**
Access will prompt you to open a database.

This lesson uses the **FrontRowVideo Adv3.accdb**
database that was created in the previous lesson. If
you have been following along with the lessons you
can continue with your own programming or
download the sample database if you wish.

Memo to Self: Click **Enable Content** if you see the
Security Warning.

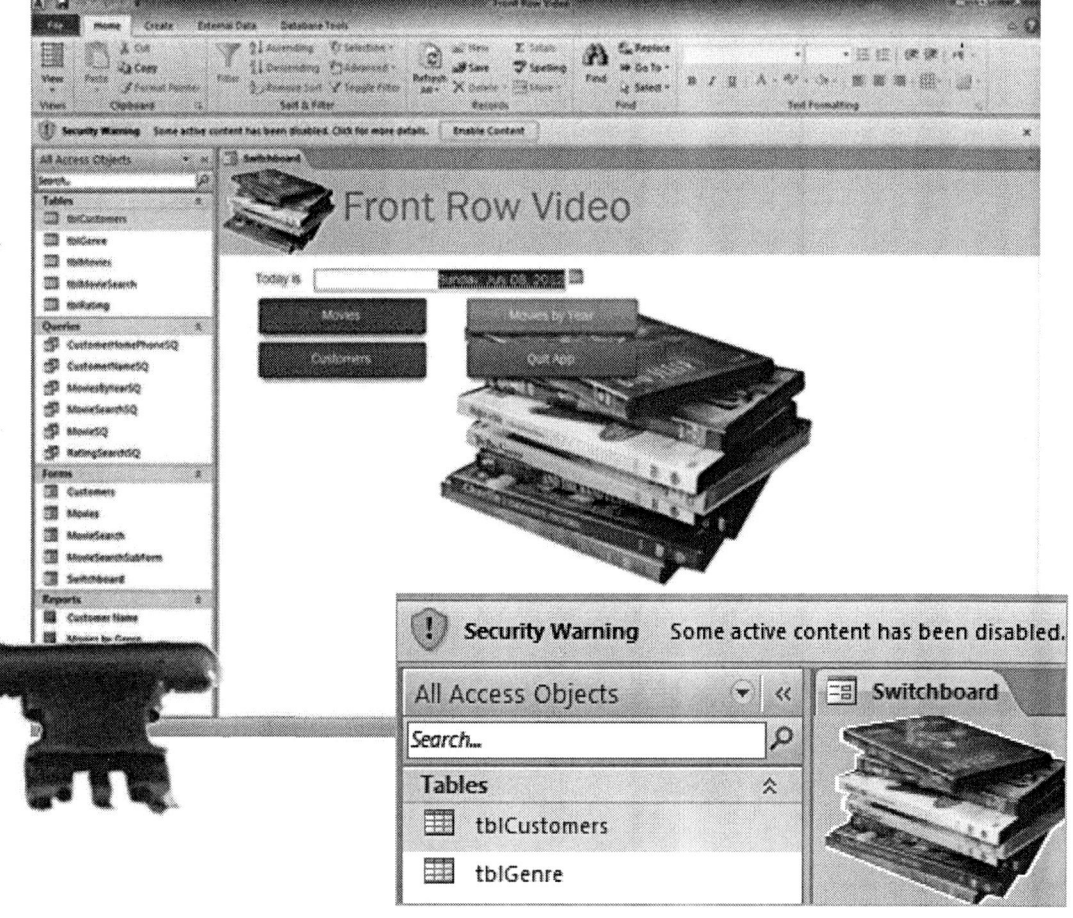

Know Your Data

Try This: Review the Database
Open the **Navigation Pane.**
Go to **All Access Objects.**

The Front Row View has the following:
Six Tables: tblCustomers, tblGenre, tblMovies, tblMovieSearch, tblRating and tblRentalPrices.

Seven Queries:
CustomerHomePhoneSQ, CustomerNameSQ, MovieRentalPriceUQ, MoviesByYearSQ, MovieSearchSQ, MovieSQ and RatingSearchSQ.

Five Forms: Customers, Movies, MovieSearch, MovieSearchSubform and the Switchboard.

Three Reports: Customer Name. Movies by Genre, and Movies by Year.

One Macro: OpenSearchMovie

All Access Objects

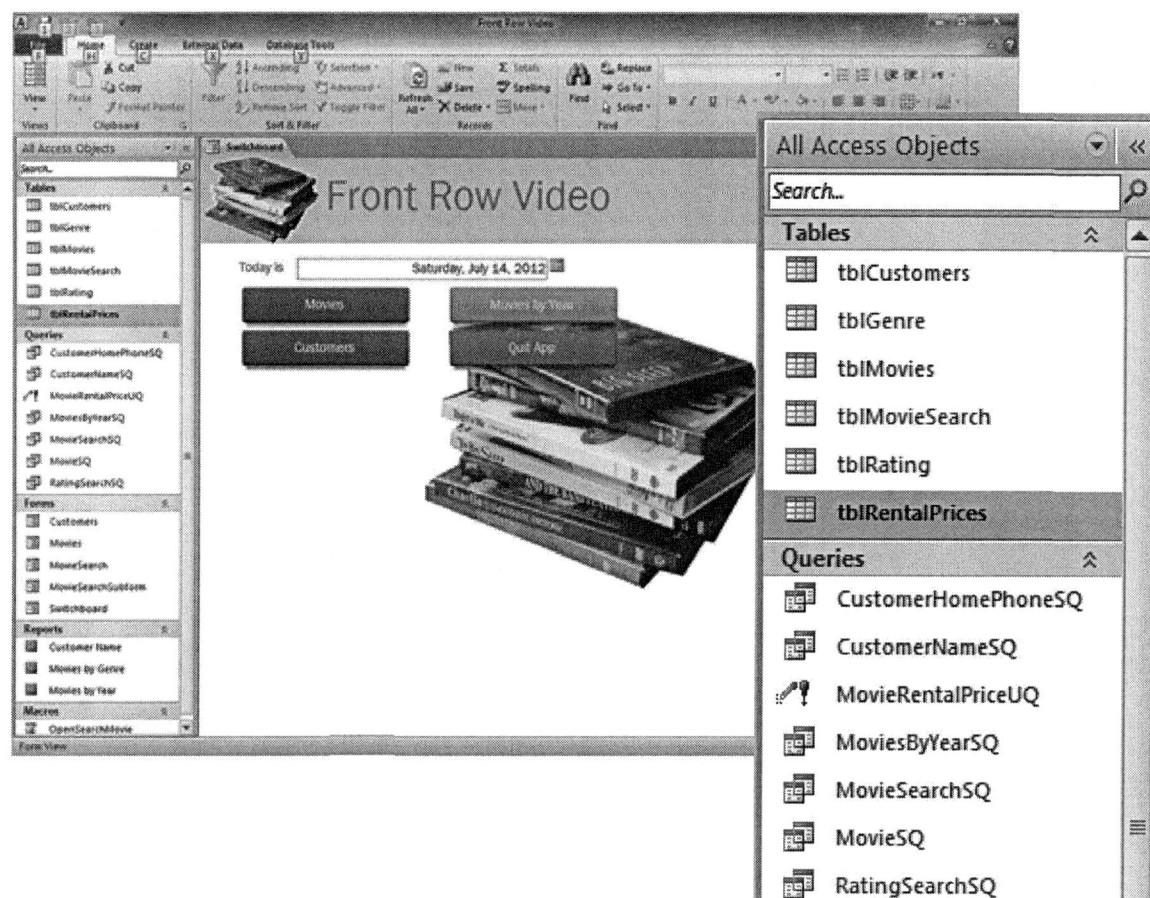

Normalized Table Design

Edgar F. Codd put a lot of thought into how to relate one Table to another. Codd, who received a PhD in 1965 from the University of Michigan, Ann Arbor, defined the concept of **normalization** in 1970. Here is a brief summary of his concepts.

There are a few rules that define a good relational database. Each rule is called a **Normal Form**. Each rule, or form, is more restrictive. There are six Normal Forms.

Normalizing a database defines the Table design and how Tables are related.

The rules are simple:
Minimize duplicate data
Protect the data integrity

Purpose: No repeating groups or redundant data.

Process: Usually, big Tables are reduced to smaller, functional Tables. There should be a separate Table for each collection.

Example of a Table in Microsoft Access

Exam 77-885: Microsoft Access 2010
2. Building Tables
2.1.1. Create tables in Design View: Create Tables that do not have repeating groups

Example of First Normal Form

Definition of First Normal Form:
First Normal Form requires that each Table should have only one value for each Field in a Table.

The Movies Table is a good example of a Table that is in First Normal Form. Each Movie has only one Year, one Rating and one Genre.

Try it: Review the Data
Go to **All Access Objects ->Tables**.
Select a Table: tblMovies
Double-click the Table to open it in Datasheet View.

What Do You See? There are 401 records in tblMovies. There is one Record for each movie. Each movie is indentified by a Primary Key: MovieID.

What Don't You See? There is no information about customers or which customer rented which movie. This Table has data about movies, only movies.

Close tblMovies, please.

Example of a Table from a beginning lesson in First Normal Form

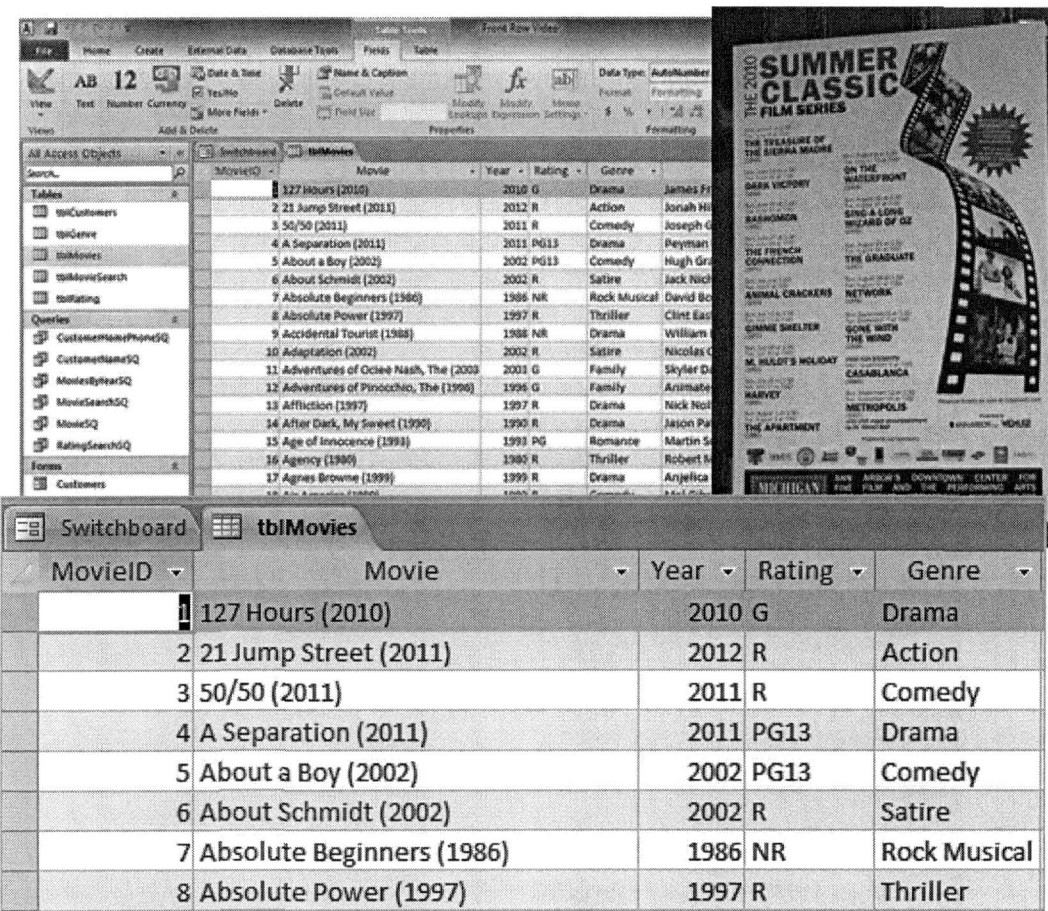

MovieID	Movie	Year	Rating	Genre
1	127 Hours (2010)	2010	G	Drama
2	21 Jump Street (2011)	2012	R	Action
3	50/50 (2011)	2011	R	Comedy
4	A Separation (2011)	2011	PG13	Drama
5	About a Boy (2002)	2002	PG13	Comedy
6	About Schmidt (2002)	2002	R	Satire
7	Absolute Beginners (1986)	1986	NR	Rock Musical
8	Absolute Power (1997)	1997	R	Thriller

Exam 77-885: Microsoft Access 2010
2. Building Tables
2.4. Set relationships: Define Primary Keys

Microsoft Access 2010: Example of Tables in Second Normal Form
The Movie Table gets the Rating from the Rating Table

Second Normal Form (2NF)

Definition of Second Normal Form:
Second Normal Form is a more restricted definition than First Normal Form. Second Normal Form (2NF) requires a separate Table for values that can be used by multiple Tables.

The Rating Table is a good example. The Rating data is limited and static: It doesn't change much.

Users need to look up a Rating in the Rating Table and save it in the Movie Table.

So, tblMovies and tblRating have a common Field, Rating, which is TEXT in both Tables.

Memo to Self: The common Field can be TEXT or NUMBER. However, the Data Type has to MATCH, MATCH, MATCH.

Text goes with Text.
Numbers go with Numbers.

tblMovies

Field Name	Data Type
MovieID	AutoNumber
Movie	Text
Year	Number
Rating	Text
Genre	Text
Stars	Text
RentalPriceID	Number

tblRating

RatingID	Rating
1	G
2	PG
3	PG13
4	PG14
5	PG15
6	R
7	X
8	NR

tblRating

Field Name	Data Type
RatingID	AutoNumber
Rating	Text

Exam 77-885: Microsoft Access 2010
2. Building Tables
2.1.1. Create tables in Design View: Create Tables that do not have repeating groups

Example of Second Normal Form

When you study database normalization, the emphasis is on the Tables. And rightly so: Tables are the bones of the database structure. However, most people only see a database as the Forms they work with.

What would a Second Normal Form look like to a User? A Form with a Combo Box is one good example. The Combo Box on the Movies Form looks up the Rating in tblRating.

Try it: Review the Relationship
Go to **All Access Objects ->Form.**
Select a Form: Movies.
Double-click the Form to open it in Form View.

What Do You See? The Combo Box has a list of Ratings from tblRating.

Memo from the Computer Mama: Feel free to go beyond this simple design and make a more appealing Form! This one is ugggggly!

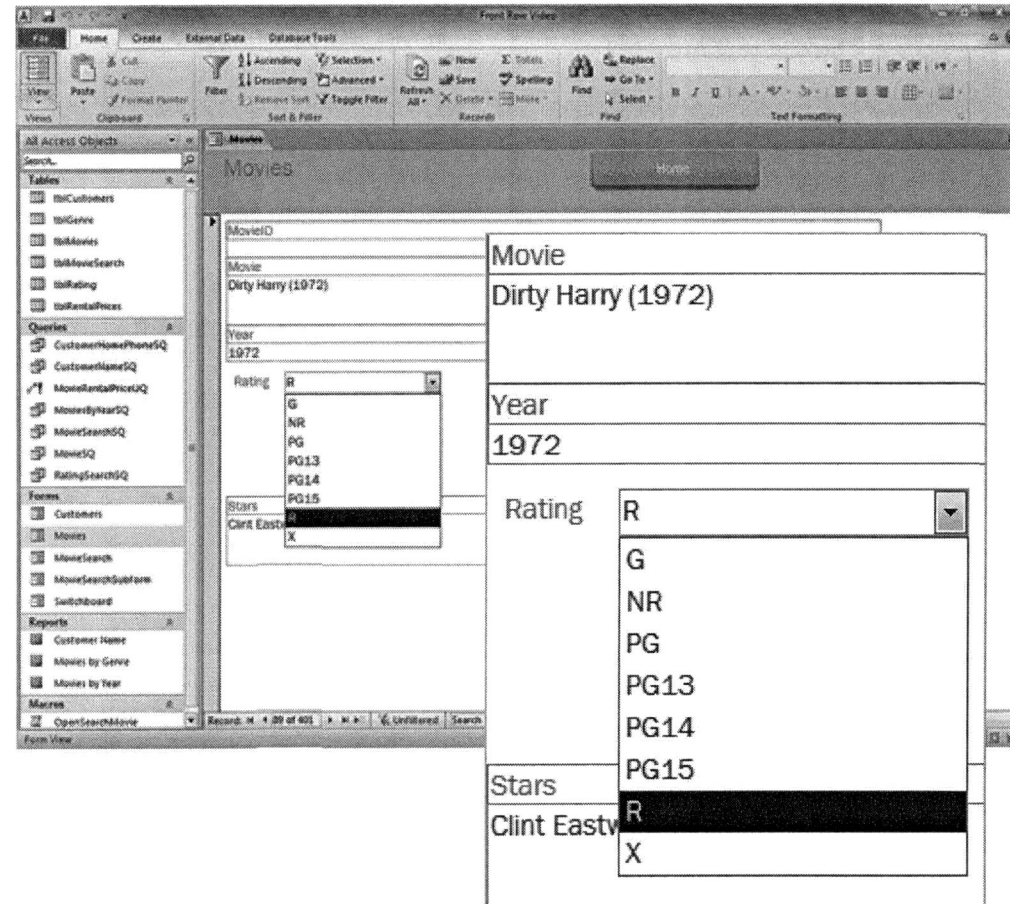

Exam 77-885: Microsoft Access 2010
2. Building Tables
2.1.1. Create tables in Design View: Create Tables that do not have repeating groups

Microsoft Access 2010: Example of Table in Third Normal Form

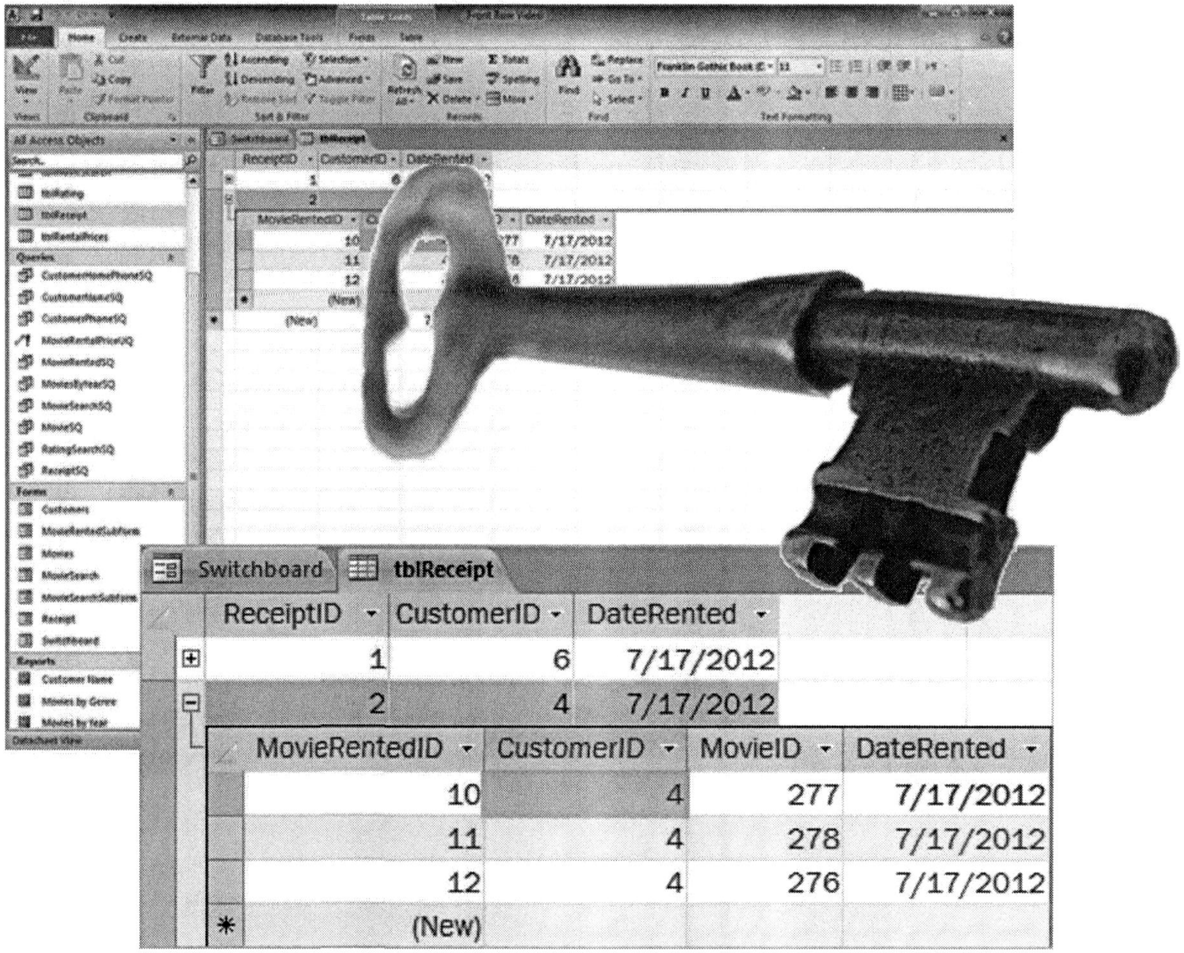

Third Normal Form (3NF)

Definition of Third Normal Form:
Third Normal Form can be summarized by a pun: "the Key, the whole Key and nothing but the Key, so help me Codd!"

A normalized database uses Primary Keys to create Relationships. The Table that is in Third Normal Form has only Keys.

Primary Keys and Foreign Keys, Only
When a database has been designed in Third Normal Form, the Tables that summarize the data should be only Primary Keys.

In this lesson, tblReceipt will be related to tblMovieRented by a common Key: CustomerID.

That's a very, very brief explanation of normalizing a database.

Let's build the Receipt Form, then come back to these concepts again.

ReceiptID	CustomerID	DateRented
1	6	7/17/2012
2	4	7/17/2012

MovieRentedID	CustomerID	MovieID	DateRented
10	4	277	7/17/2012
11	4	278	7/17/2012
12	4	276	7/17/2012
* (New)			

Create ->Tables->Table Design

Create the Receipt Table

1. Try it: Create a Receipt Table
Go to **Create ->Tables->Table Design.**
Add the following Fields and Data Types:

ReceiptID	AutoNumber
CustomerID	Number
DateRented	Date/Time

Try This, Too: Create the Primary Key
Select ReceiptID.
Go to **Table Tools->Design->Tools.**
Click on: **Primary Key.**

Each record in the Receipt Table will be unique: no duplicates.

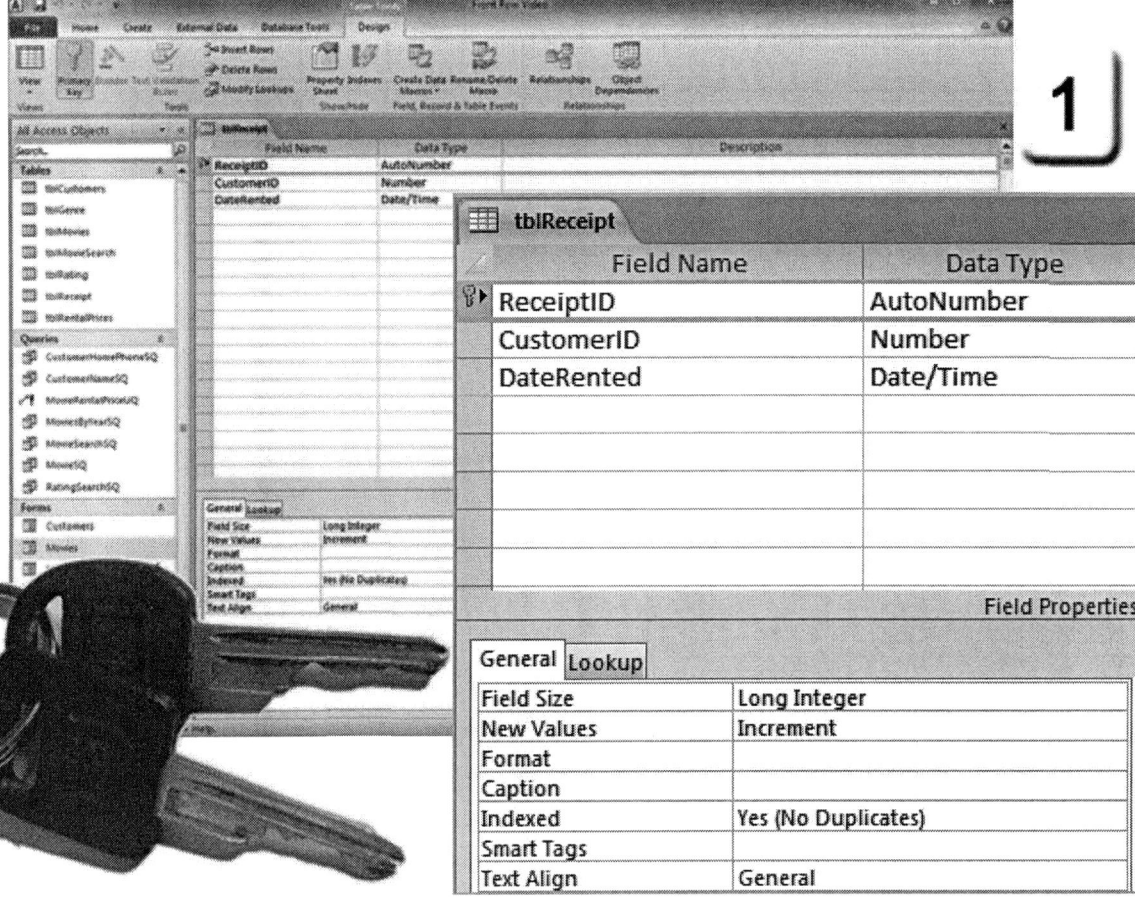

Field Name	Data Type
ReceiptID	AutoNumber
CustomerID	Number
DateRented	Date/Time

Field Properties

General Lookup

Field Size	Long Integer
New Values	Increment
Format	
Caption	
Indexed	Yes (No Duplicates)
Smart Tags	
Text Align	General

Exam 77-885: Microsoft Access 2010
2. Building Tables
2.4. Set relationships: Define Primary Keys

Edit the Date Properties

In this business model, the Receipts are written live, while the customer is standing at the front counter. So, the DateRented can have the current date and time as the **Default Value** for quicker data entry.

2. Try it: Edit the Field Properties
Select a Field: DateRented.
Format: Short Date

Try This, Too: Add an Input Mask
Select a Field Property: Input Mask.
Click on the three-dot builder and walk through the Wizard. You may be asked to **Save** the Table before the Wizard begins.

And This: Enter a Default Value
Select a Field Property: Default Value
Type: =Date()

Finally, Do This: Save the Table
Go to **File->Save**.
Enter a name: tblReceipt.

That's one Table. **Close** tblReceipt.

Table Tools->Design

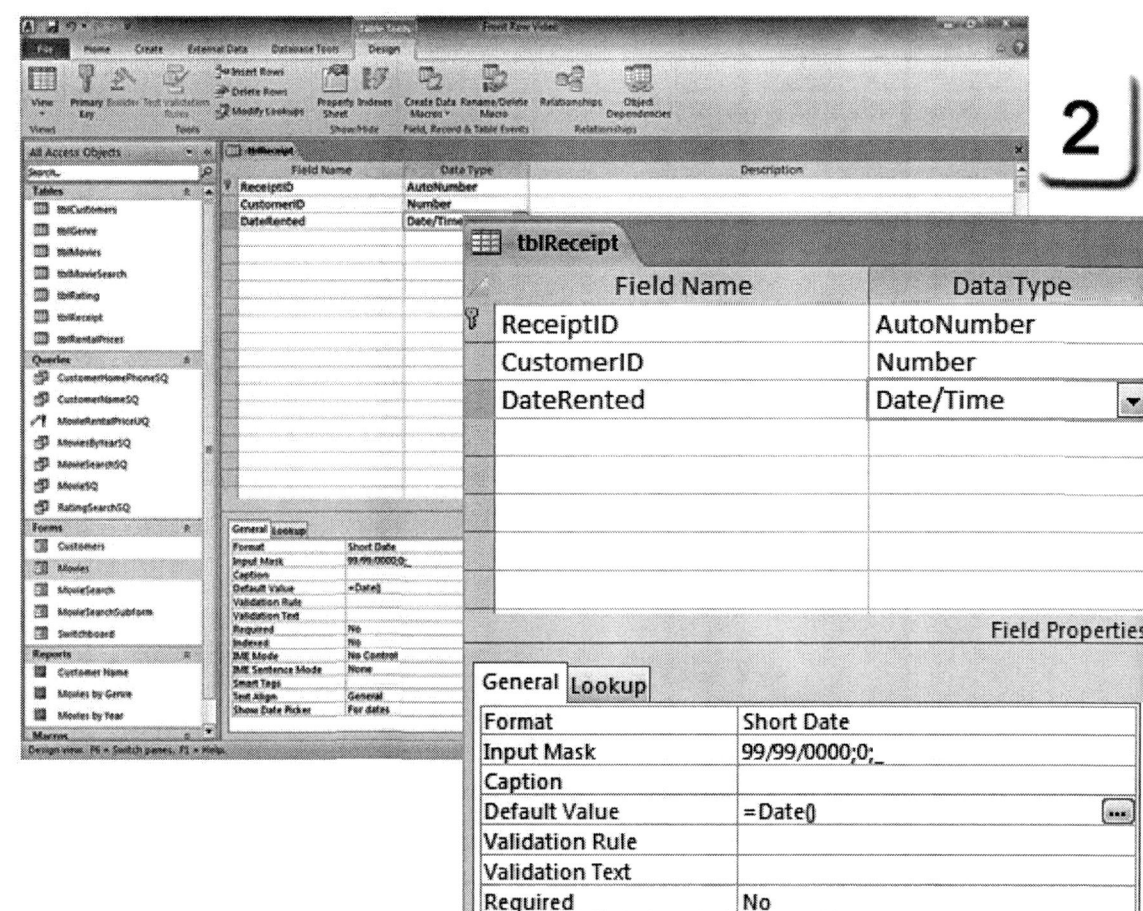

Exam 77-885: Microsoft Access 2010
2. Building Tables
2.2. Create and Modify Fields: Modify Field Properties

Create the MovieRented Table

The MovieRented Table stores all of the numbers (Keys and Dates) that were selected in the Form and Subform.

3. Try it: Create the MovieRented Table
Go to **Create ->Tables->Table Design.**
Add the following Fields and Data Types:

MovieRentedID	AutoNumber
ReceiptID	Number
CustomerID	Number
MovieID	Number
DateRented	Date/Time

Try This, Too: Create the Primary Key
Select MovieRentedID.
Go to **Table Tools->Design->Tools.**
Click on: **Primary Key.**

Please, Do This: Save the Table
Go to **File->Save.**
Enter a name: tblMovieRented.

That's two Tables. **Close** tblMovieRented.

Create ->Tables->Table Design

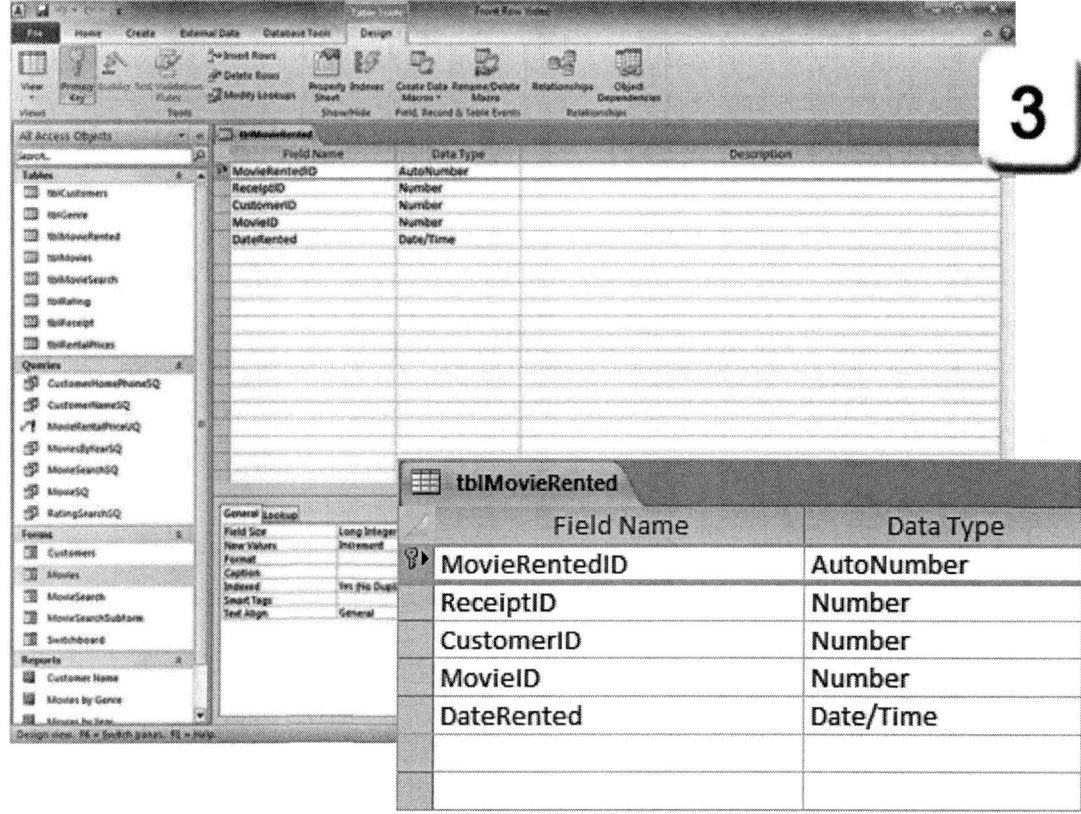

Field Name	Data Type
MovieRentedID	AutoNumber
ReceiptID	Number
CustomerID	Number
MovieID	Number
DateRented	Date/Time

Exam 77-885: Microsoft Access 2010
2. Building Tables
2.1.1. Create tables in Design View

Create Table Relationships

Normalized databases use the Primary Key to create relationships between Tables. The relationship can be ad hoc, such as creating a Join between two Tables in a Query, or it can be explicit as part of the database definitions.

Microsoft Access defines relationships with the **Database Tools**.

1. Try it: Create the Table Relationships
Go to **Database Tools ->Relationships**.
Click on: **Relationships**.

Keep going...

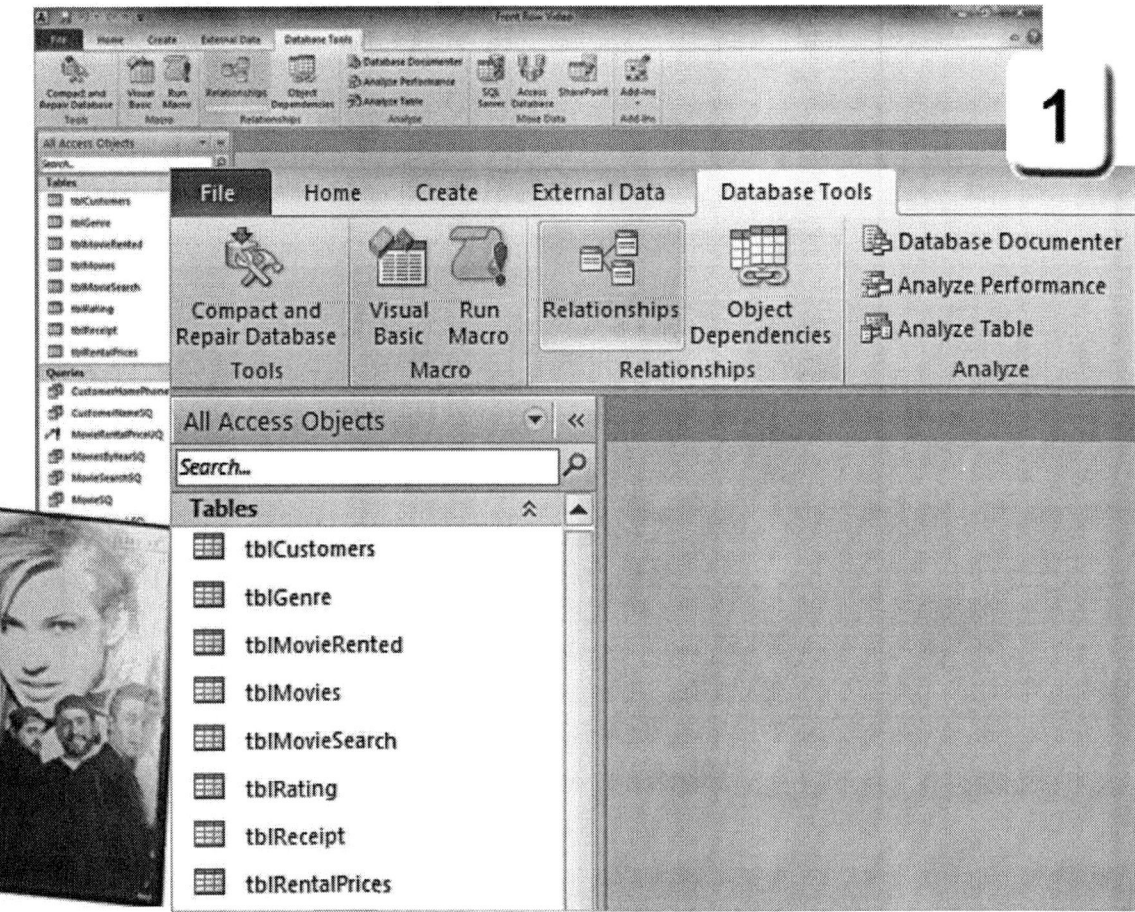

Exam 77-885: Microsoft Access 2010
2. Building Tables
2.4. Set relationships: Edit the Relationships

Joined Tables

2. What Do You See? The Relationships Window has opened. The Relationship Tools are available.

What Else Do You See? Our database has a pair of Tables that are joined by a common Key field: RentalPriceID.

The relationship, or join, is represented by the line from RentalPriceID in the Movie Table to RentalPriceID in the Rental Prices Table.

This relationship was created when we added tblRentalPrices as a Subdatasheet to tblMovies and linked the Parent and Child by RentalPriceID.

Microsoft Access noticed the matching Keys and prompted us to create a relationship between the two Tables.

Keep going...

Database Tools ->Relationships->Relationships

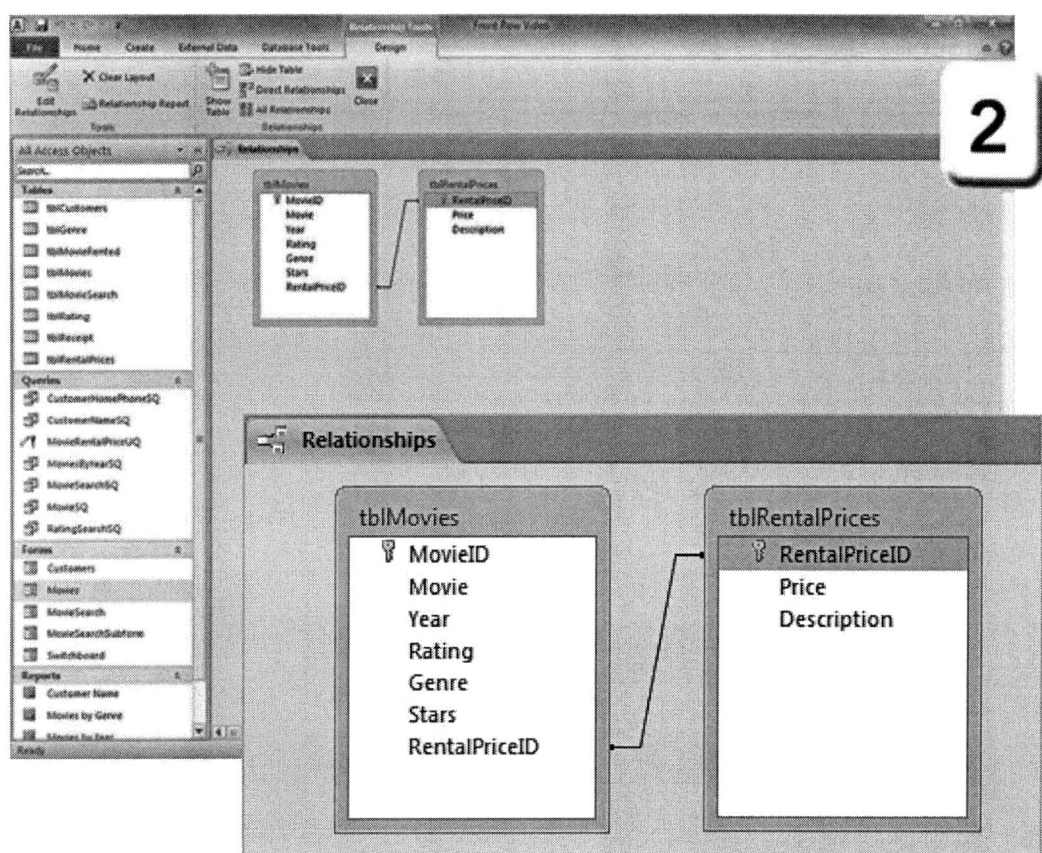

Exam 77-885: Microsoft Access 2010
2. Building Tables
2.4. Set relationships: Edit the Relationships

Add More Tables

Documenting the Table Relationships is quite similar to creating a Query.

3. Try it: Add More Tables
Go to **Relationship Tools ->Design.**
Click on: **Show Table**

What Do You See? The **Show Table** window will prompt you to choose a Table or Query for the Record Source.
Select a Table: tblReceipt. Click **Add**.
Select a Table: tblMovieRented. Click **Add**.
Select a Table: tblCustomers. Click **Add**.

There will be Tables all over the page.
Click **Close** to close the Show Table window. Keep going...

Relationship Tools ->Design->Show Table

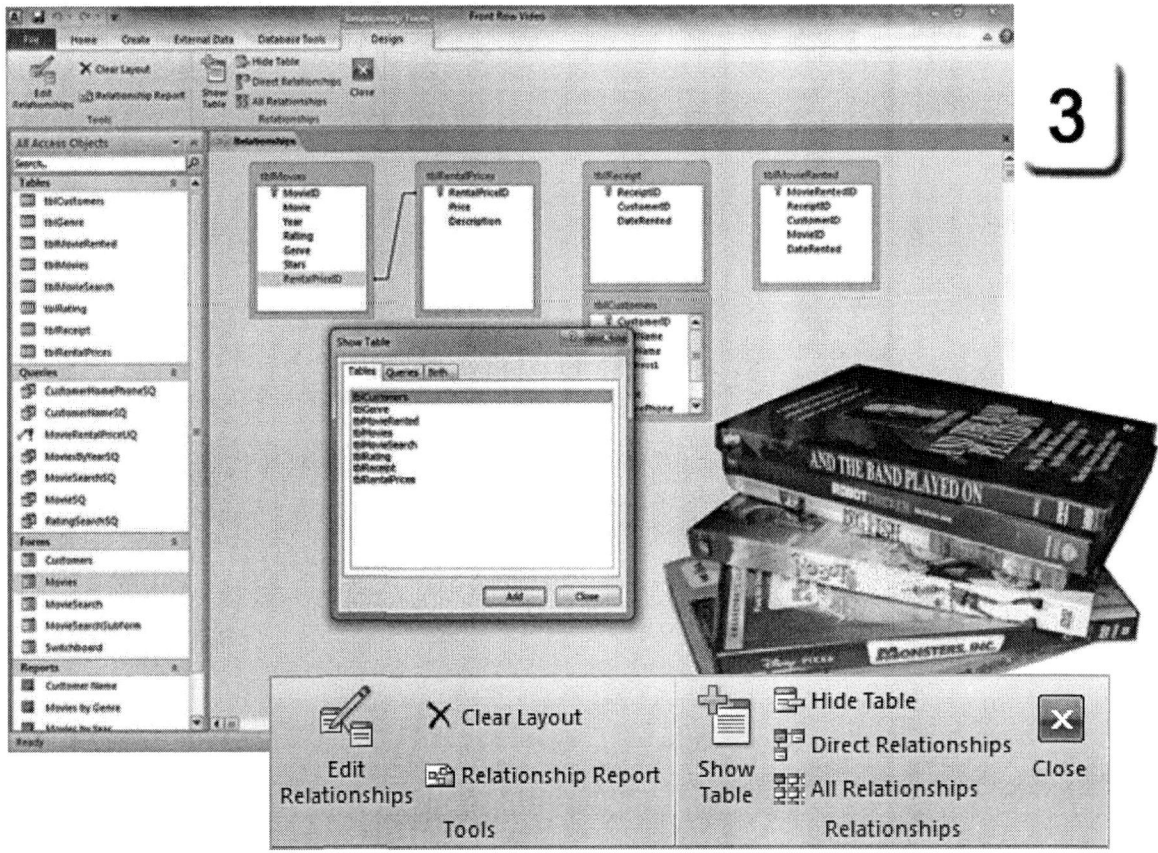

Exam 77-885: Microsoft Access 2010
2. Building Tables
2.4. Set relationships: Edit the Relationships

Edit the Layout

4. Try it: Edit the Layout

Reading from Left to Right, please move the Tables as show in this screen shot.

First Row:
tblReceipt
tblMovieRented
tblCustomers

Second Row:
tblMovies
tblRentalPrices

What is the Goal? The Tables are placed this way to group the Tables by function and create explicit links between them.

Keep going...

Relationship Tools ->Design

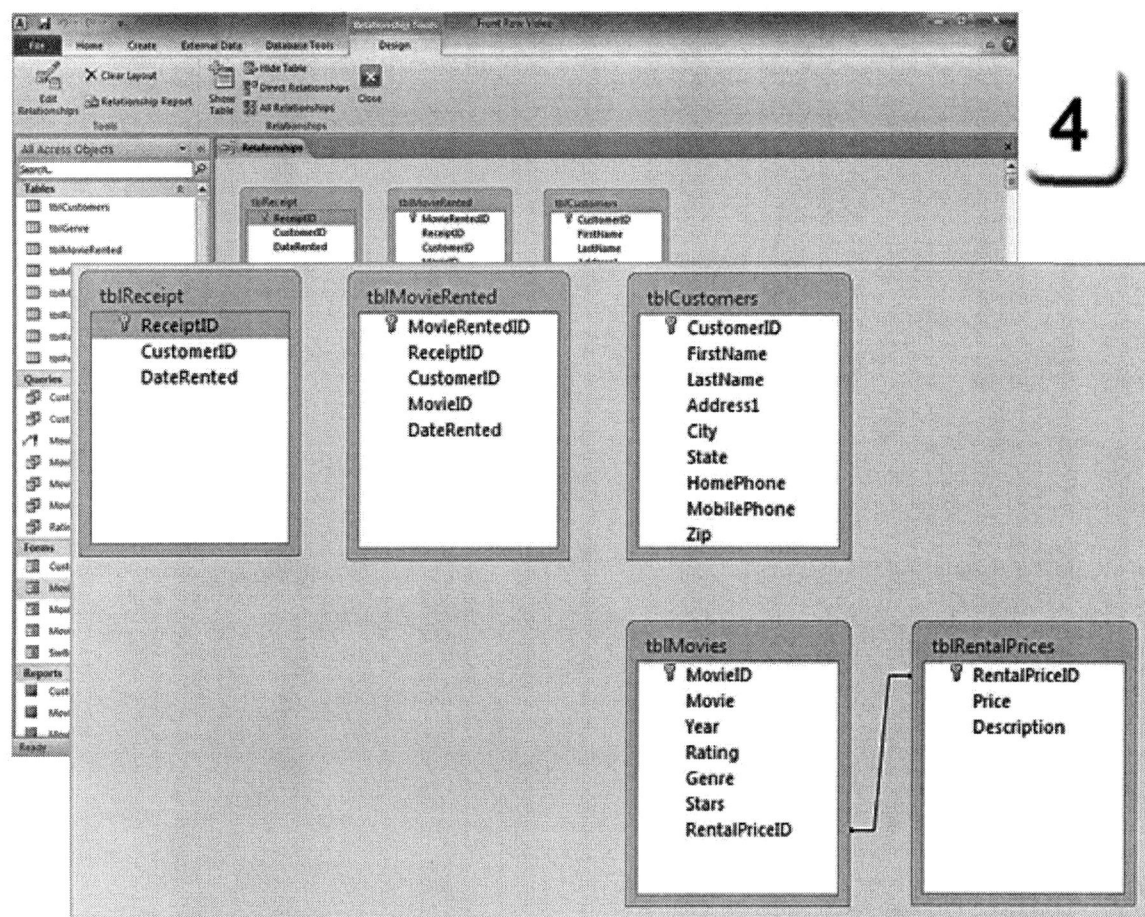

Exam 77-885: Microsoft Access 2010
2. Building Tables
2.4. Set relationships: Edit the Relationships

Join Two Tables

5. Try it: Join Two Tables
Go to tblReceipt.
Select a Field: ReceiptID.
Drag that Field to tblMovieRented and place it
on the one that matches: ReceiptID.

What Do You See? The two Tables will be
JOINED by their common Key: ReceiptID.
There is more to this relationship.

Try This, Too: Edit the Relationship
Double-click the JOIN (the line) between
tblReceipt and tblMovieRented.

What Do You See? The Tables are JOINED
by a matching Key: ReceiptID.

This is a One-to-Many Relationship.
One: tblReceipt
Many: tblMovieRented

Keep going...

Memo to Self: The Edit Relationships window
may pop up by default when you make a join.

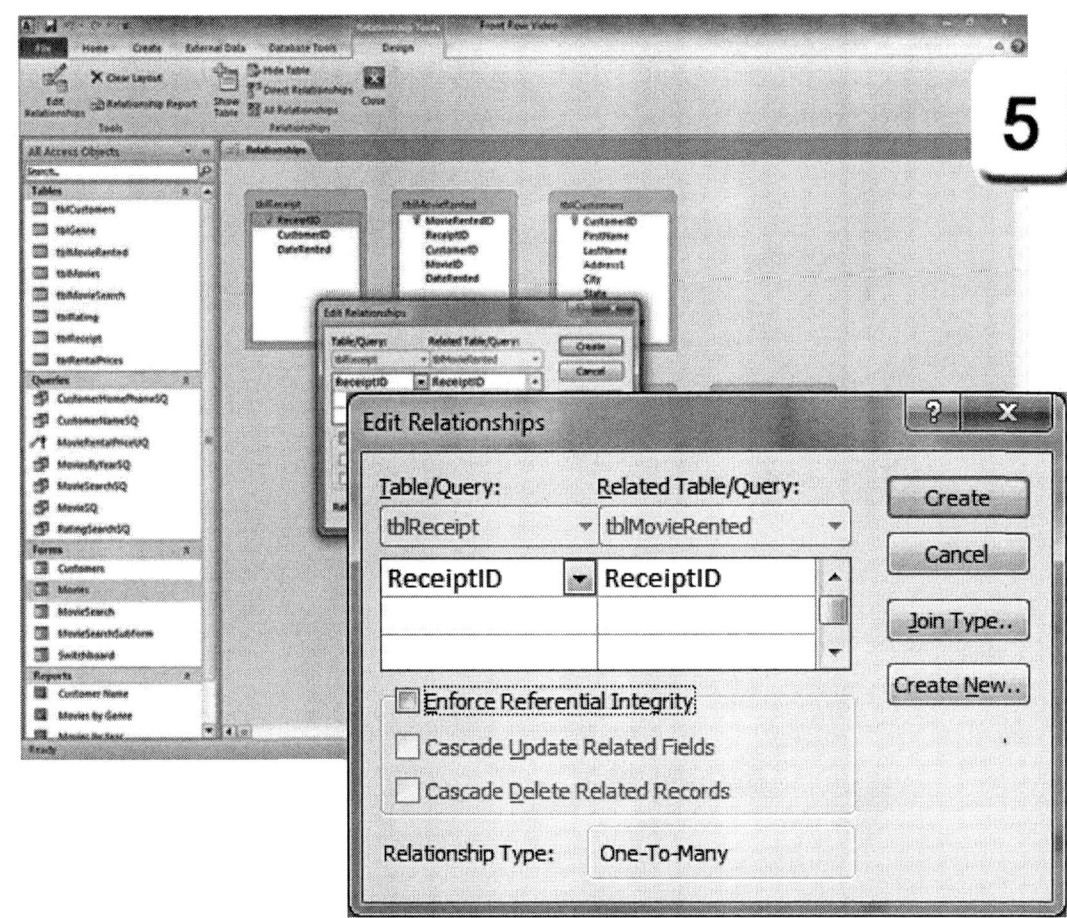

Exam 77-885: Microsoft Access 2010
2. Building Tables
2.4. Set relationships: Edit the Relationships

Enforce Referential Integrity

6. Try it: Enforce Referential Integrity
The goal of referential integrity is to prevent "widows and orphans." The Receipt is a Form with a Subform. The Tables for both the Form and Subform need to be updated.

Cascade Update Related Fields
When you select **Cascade Update Related Fields**, you are editing the "one" side of this One-To-Many relationship. If a Record is edited in tblReceipt, than the matching Record in tblMovieRented will be updated as well.

Cascade Delete Related Fields
When you select **Cascade Delete Related Fields,** you are editing the "many" side of this One-To-Many relationship. If a Record is deleted in tblReceipt, than the matching Record in tblMovieRented will be deleted as well: no widows and orphans.

Try This, Too: Create the Join
Click on **Create**.
Keep going...

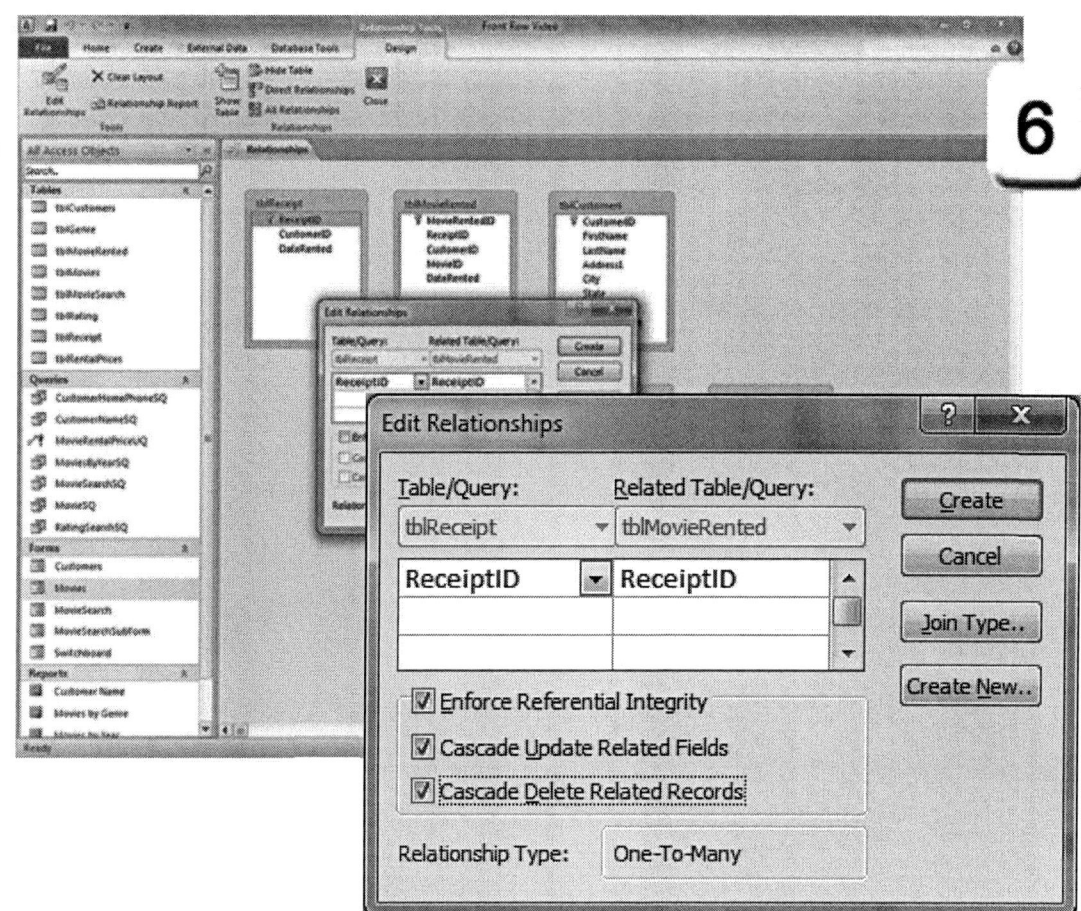

Exam 77-885: Microsoft Access 2010
2. Building Tables
2.4. Set relationships: Edit the Relationships to Enforce Referential Integrity

Review the Join

7. Try it: Review the Join
There should be a line between:
ReceiptID, the Primary Key in tblReceipt.
to ReceiptID, the Foreign Key in tblMovieRented.

Try This, Too: Edit the Join
The Join is more than just a line. It is a
Relationship. Select the Join
Go to **Relationship Tools ->Design->Tools.**
Click on **Edit Relationship.**

The Edit Relationship Window will pop up.
Click on **Join Type.**
Keep going...

Relationship Tools ->Design

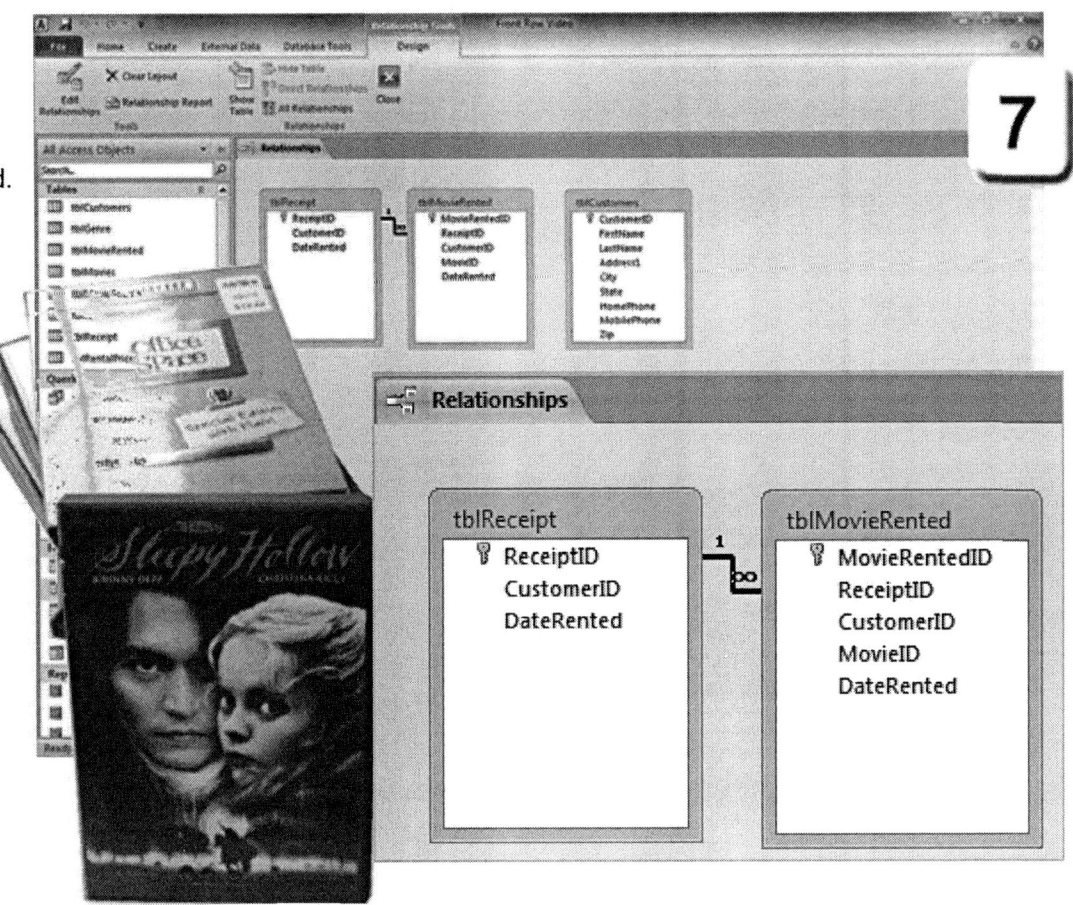

Exam 77-885: Microsoft Access 2010
2. Building Tables
2.4. Set relationships: Edit the Relationships to Enforce Referential Integrity

Define the Join Type

8. What Do You See? There are three ways to define the Join properties: INNER, LEFT Outer and RIGHT Outer Join.

1. Inner join: Only include rows where the joined fields from both Tables are equal.

2. Left outer join: Include ALL records from 'tblReceipt' and only those records from 'tblMovieRented' where the joined fields are equal.

That means "Start with all of the ReceiptIDs in tblReceipt and look up the matching ReceiptIDs in tblMovieRented."

3. Right outer join: Include ALL records from 'tblMovieRented' and only those records from 'tblReceipt' where the joined fields are equal.

That means "Start with the tblMovieRented and look up the ReceiptD that matches in tblReceipt."

We will explore this more when we work with the Action Queries, later. Keep Option 1. Click **OK**.

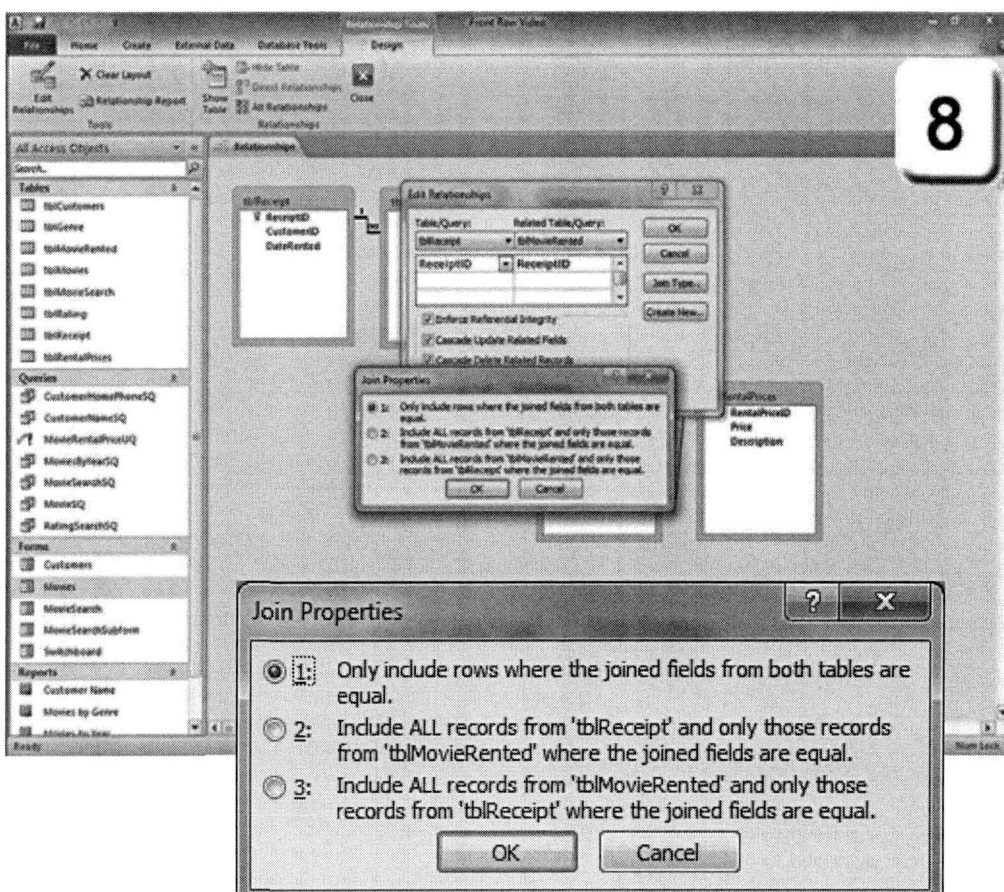

Exam 77-885: Microsoft Access 2010
2. Building Tables
2.4. Set relationships: Define Join Properties

Join the Other Tables

9. Try it: Join the Other Tables
Drag the Keys to create the following Joins. For each link that is created the **Edit Relationship** window will prompt you to confirm that the Keys match. Click **Enforce Referential Integrity** and click **Create**.

From tblMovieRented to tblCustomer:
Link the CustomerID.

From tblMovieRented to tblMovies:
Link the MovieID.

Do This, Too: Close the Relationships
Go to **Relationship Tools ->Design.**
Go to **Relationships->Close.**
When you close the Relationships you will be asked to **Save.**

So....how are these Tables related, now?

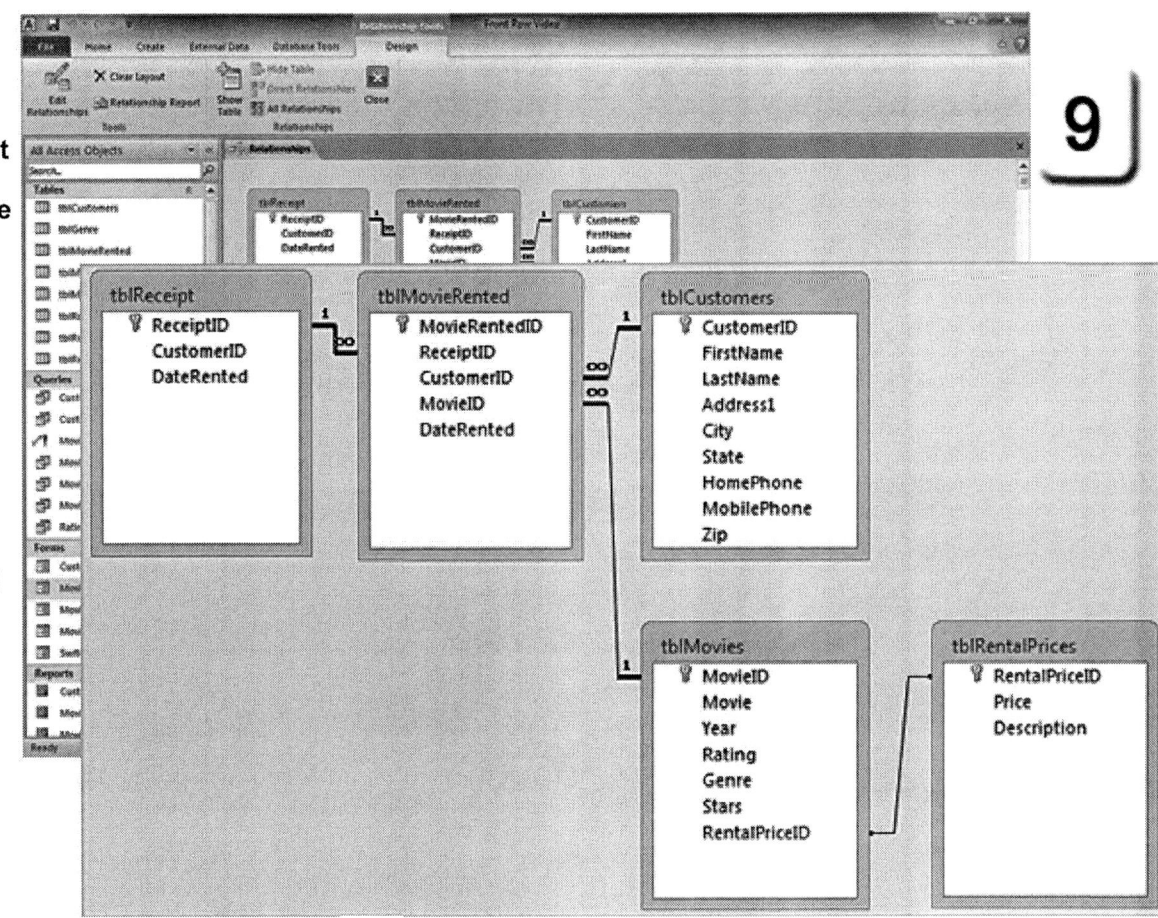

Exam 77-885: Microsoft Access 2010
2. Building Tables
2.4. Set relationships: Define Join Properties

Consider the Relationships

In the previous lesson, we added a Subdatasheet between two Tables and Access prompted us to define a relationship. We also created relationships between the rest of the Tables with the Relationship Tools.

Why Does This Matter? This is a relational database. tblReceipt is related (joined) to tblMovieRented by a common Key: ReceiptID.

Here is a preview of how the data in the Tables will look when we complete the designs:
ReceiptID 2 has one customer: CustomerID 4.

In the Subdatasheet for ReceiptID 2: CustomerID 4, has many movies.

This is an example of a database that is in Third Normal Form.

Preview of the Completed tblReceipt with tblMovieRented as a Subdatasheet

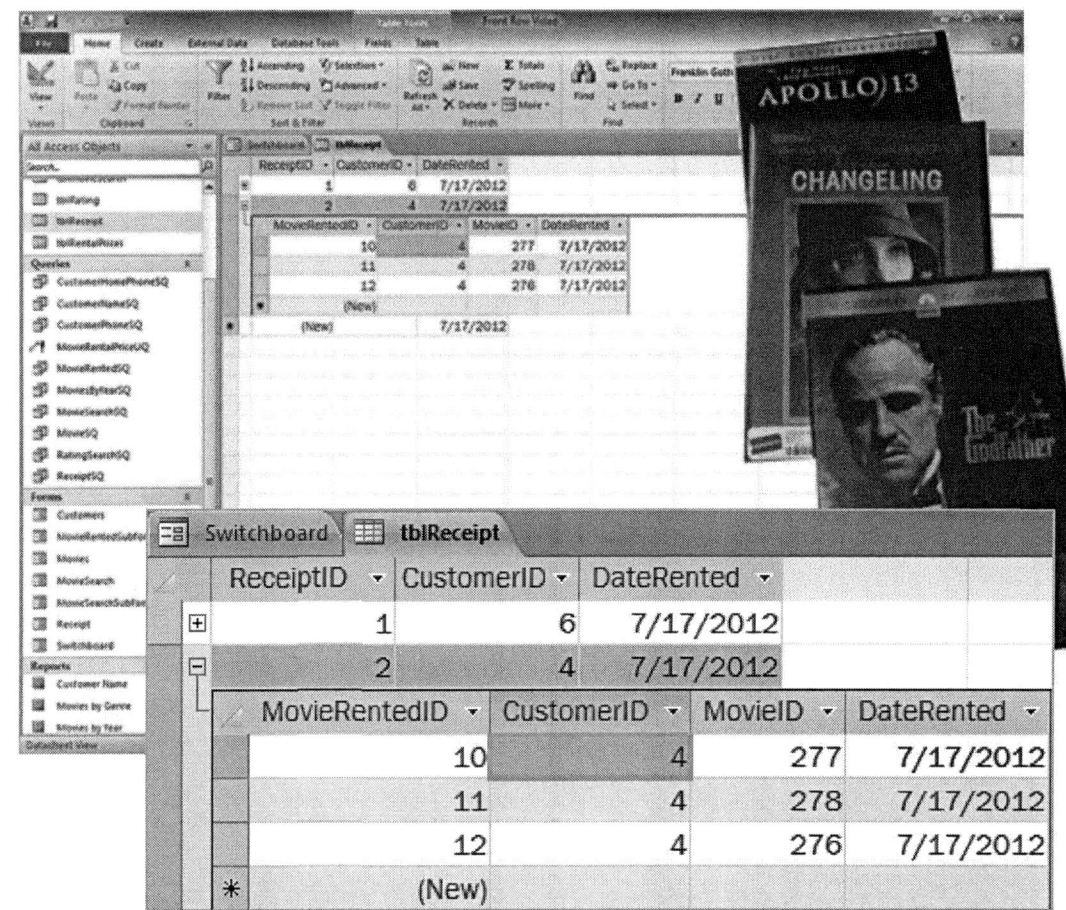

Exam 77-885: Microsoft Access 2010
2. Building Tables
2.1.1. Create tables in Design View: Create Tables that do not have repeating groups

Summary

This discussion began with a brief summary of the rules for designing a database in Third Normal Form. It is a great way to design the Tables.

We created two Tables that have both Primary and Foreign Keys.

Once the Tables are in Third Normal Form, the Queries, Forms and Reports should work, too.

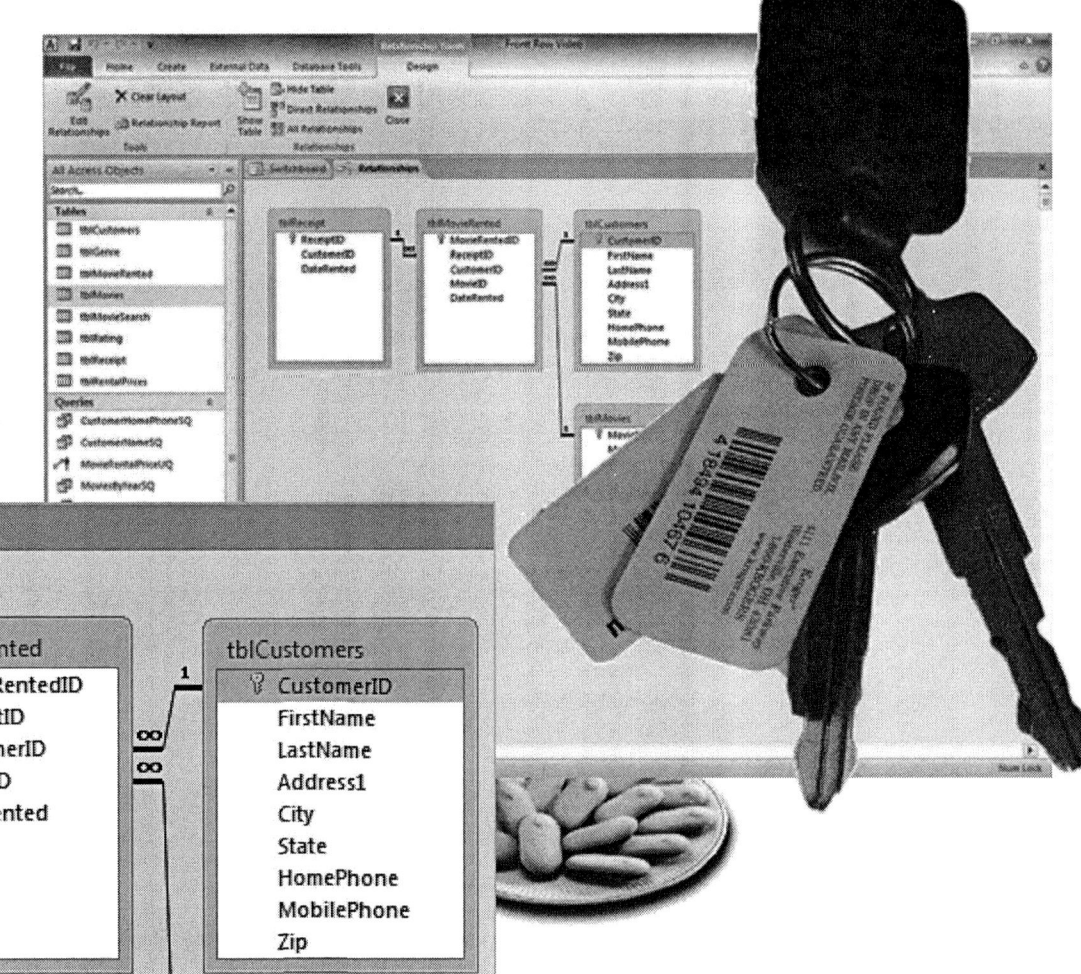

Switchboard   **Relationships**

tblReceipt
- ReceiptID
- CustomerID
- DateRented

tblMovieRented
- MovieRentedID
- ReceiptID
- CustomerID
- MovieID
- DateRented

tblCustomers
- CustomerID
- FirstName
- LastName
- Address1
- City
- State
- HomePhone
- MobilePhone
- Zip

Practice Activities

Lesson 3: Table Design and Key Relationships
Try This: Do the following steps
1. Open the Brown Bag Lunch database you have been working on.

Or, you may download **BBL Adv ver3.accdb**.

2. Create a new Receipt Table, tblReceipt In Design View add the following Fields:
Field Name: ReceiptID, Data Type: AutoNumber.
Field Name: CustomerID, Data Type: Number (Long Integer).

Field Name: Date, Data Type: Date/Time.

Make ReceiptID the Primary Key. Make the Default Value for the Date/Time =Now(). Format the Date as Medium.

Save the Table and name it tblReceipt. Close this Table.

3. Create a new Table for the products sold, tblReceiptProducts. In Design View add the following Fields:
Field Name: ReceiptProductsID, Data Type: AutoNumber.
Field Name: ReceiptD, Data Type: Number (Long Integer).
Field Name: DateReceipt, Data Type: Date/Time.
Field Name: CustomerID, Data Type: Number (Long Integer).
Field Name: ProductID, Data Type: Number (Long Integer).

Field Name: Memo, Data Type: Memo.

Make ReceiptProductsID the Primary Key. Save the Table and name it tblReceiptProducts. Close this Table.

4. Use the command Database Tools->Relationships to document the database with the Relationship Tools. Add the following Tables: tblReceipt, tblReceiptProducts, tblProducts.

5. Create a JOIN from ReceiptID in tblReceipt to ReceiptID in tblReceiptProducts. Enforce Referential Integrity.

6. Create a JOIN from ProductID in tblReceiptProducts to ProductID in tblProducts. Enforce Referential Integrity.

7. Add the Customers Table. Create a JOIN from CustomerID in tblReceipt to CustomerID in tblCustomers. Enforce Referential Integrity.

8. Save and close the Relationship Window.

9. Close the Brown Bag Lunch database.

Test Yourself

1. Which are rules for Normalizing a Database?
(Give all correct answers.)
A. Minimize duplicate data
B. Protect data integrity
Tip: Advanced Access, page 68

2. Second Normal Form is less restrictive than
First Normal Form.
A. True
B. False
Tip: Advanced Access, page 70

3. Third Normal Form uses only Primary and
Foreign Keys to create relationships.
A. True
B. False
Tip: Advanced Access, page 72

4. Which of the following are shown with the
Relationship Command?
(Give all correct answers.)
A. Tables joined by a common Key field
B. Queries that have relationships creating using
the Join command
Tip: Advanced Access, page 76, 77

5. Which is true about Referential Integrity?
(Give all correct answers.)
A. Aims to prevent widow or orphan Records
B. Uses the Cascade Related Fields commands to
update or delete matching records on all Joined
Tables
Tip: Advanced Access, page 81

The Receipt Form, part 1

Advanced Access Objectives
In this lesson, you will learn how to:

1. Use a Table to format a Form.

2. Insert, Merge and Split Rows and Columns in a Tabular Layout.

3. Reposition and Format Control Padding, Margins and Anchoring.

4. Add a Background Image to a Form.

© 2012 Comma Productions, LLC

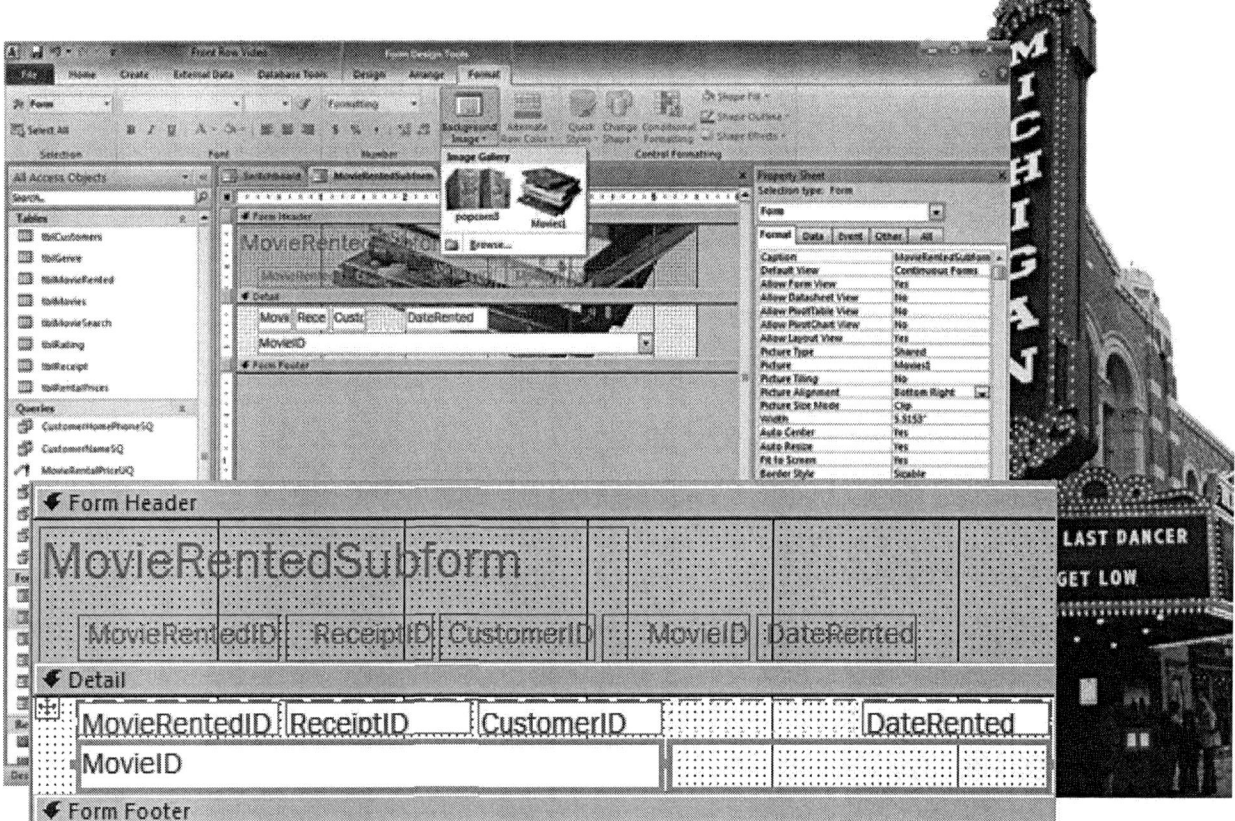

Lesson 4 : The Receipt Form, part 1

1. Readings
Read Lesson 4 in the Advanced Access guide, page 89-117.

Project
Create and format a Tabular Subform and a Receipt Form that looks up customers by their phone number.

Downloads
FrontRowVideo Adv4.accdb
BBL Adv ver4.accdb

2. Practice
Do the Practice Activity on page 118.

3. Assessment
Review the Test questions on page 118.

Form Design Tools->Arrange

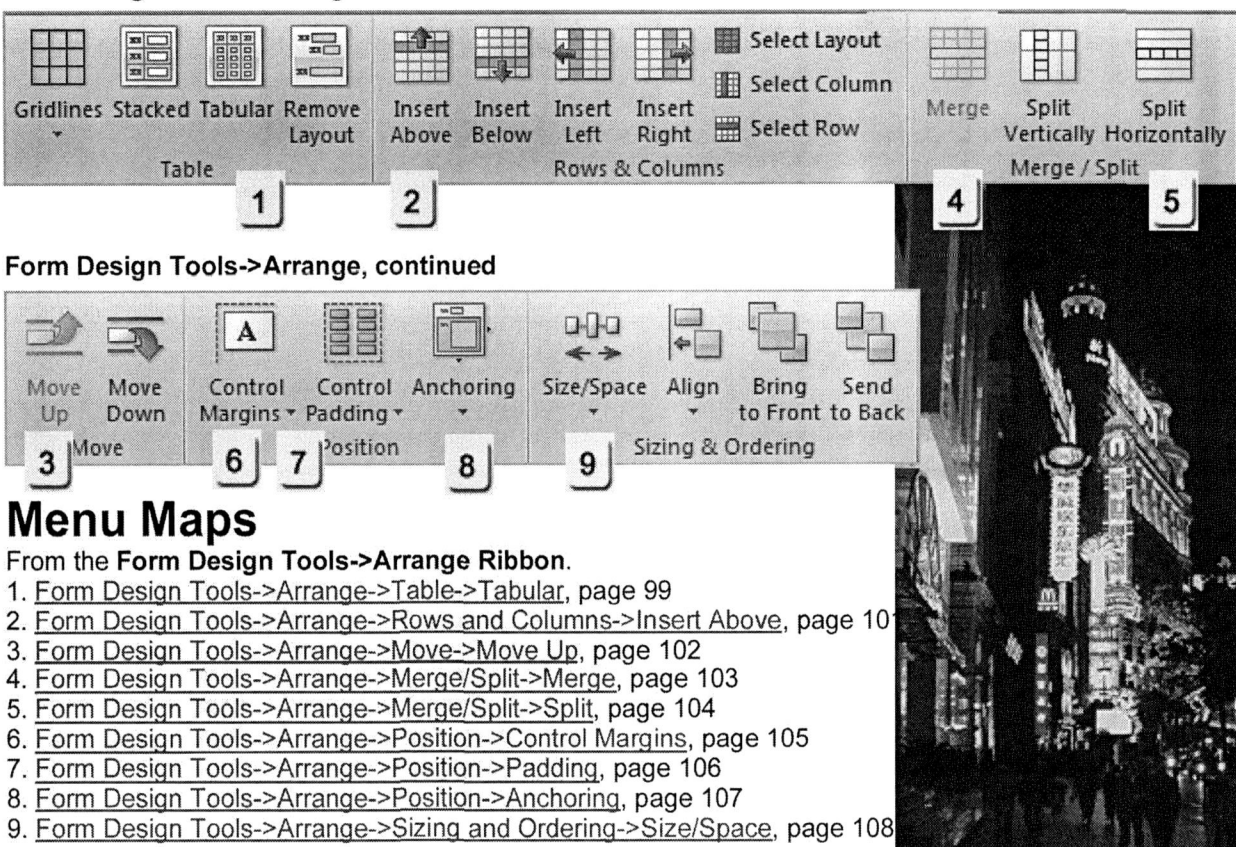

Form Design Tools->Arrange, continued

Menu Maps
From the **Form Design Tools->Arrange Ribbon**.
1. Form Design Tools->Arrange->Table->Tabular, page 99
2. Form Design Tools->Arrange->Rows and Columns->Insert Above, page 10
3. Form Design Tools->Arrange->Move->Move Up, page 102
4. Form Design Tools->Arrange->Merge/Split->Merge, page 103
5. Form Design Tools->Arrange->Merge/Split->Split, page 104
6. Form Design Tools->Arrange->Position->Control Margins, page 105
7. Form Design Tools->Arrange->Position->Padding, page 106
8. Form Design Tools->Arrange->Position->Anchoring, page 107
9. Form Design Tools->Arrange->Sizing and Ordering->Size/Space, page 108

The Receipt Form, part 1

The Receipt Form is an interesting challenge. The Receipt combines most of the Tables in this database: Who (tblCustomer), Bought (tblMovieRented) What (tblMovies). The Receipt Form represents a one-to-many relationship: one customer gets many movies. So, there will be a Form and Subform.

Microsoft Office Access 2010: Example of the completed Receipt Form

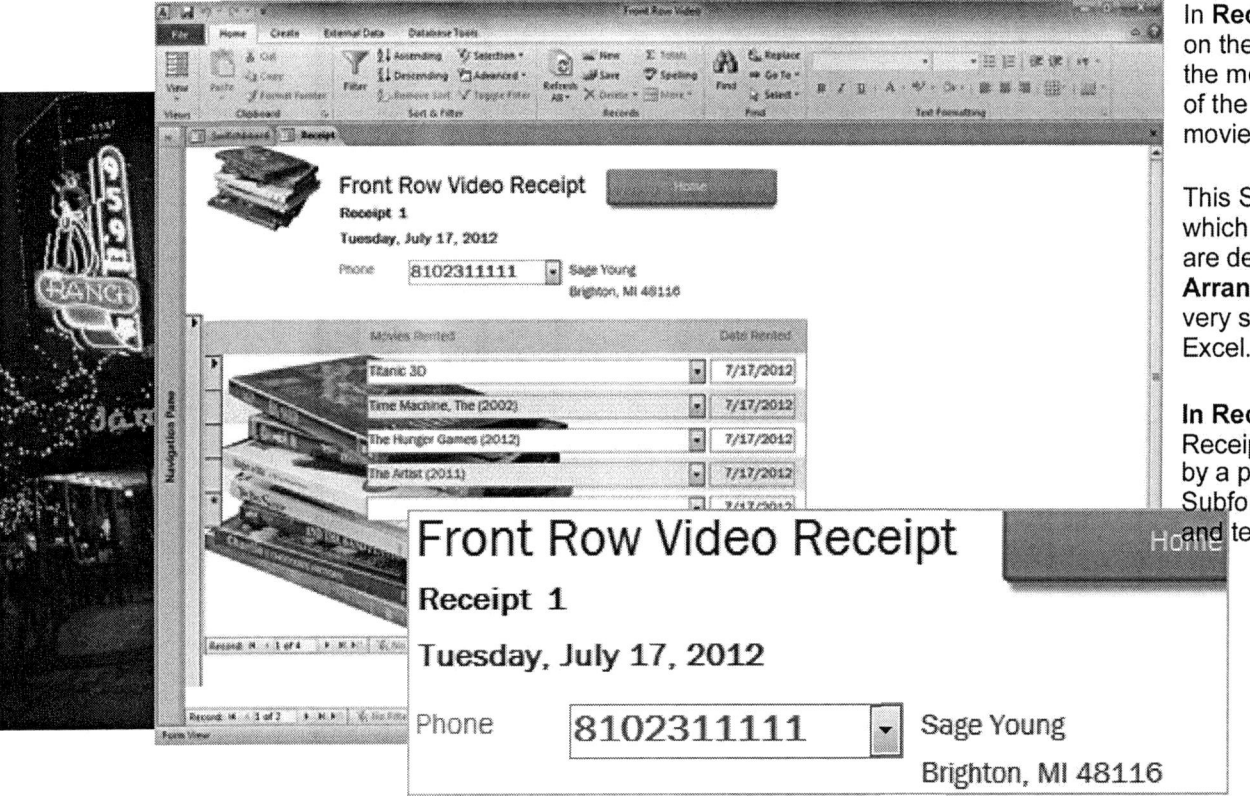

In **Receipt Form, part 1,** the focus will be on the ReceiptSubform. This Form will list the movies rented. This is the "many" part of the one-to-many relationship: many movies.

This Subform will be formatted as a Table, which is the way online forms and webpage are designed. You may notice that the **Arrange Tools** in Microsoft Access are very similar to the Table Tools in Word or Excel.

In Receipt Form, part 2, we will design the Receipt Form so Users can find a customer by a phone number. The Form and Subform will be linked by common Keys and tested.

What is the Plan?

The ReceiptSubform will be based on a Table, tblMovieRented, which was created in the previous lesson. Here is the plan:

Review the Record Source: tblMovieRented
Open tblMovieRented in Design View
Identify the Key Fields

Create the Subform: MovieRentedSubform
The MovieRentedSubform will be a Tabular Form formatted as a Table.

That's a good place to start.

Let's go though the plan, OK?

Example of the MovieRentedSubform in Design View

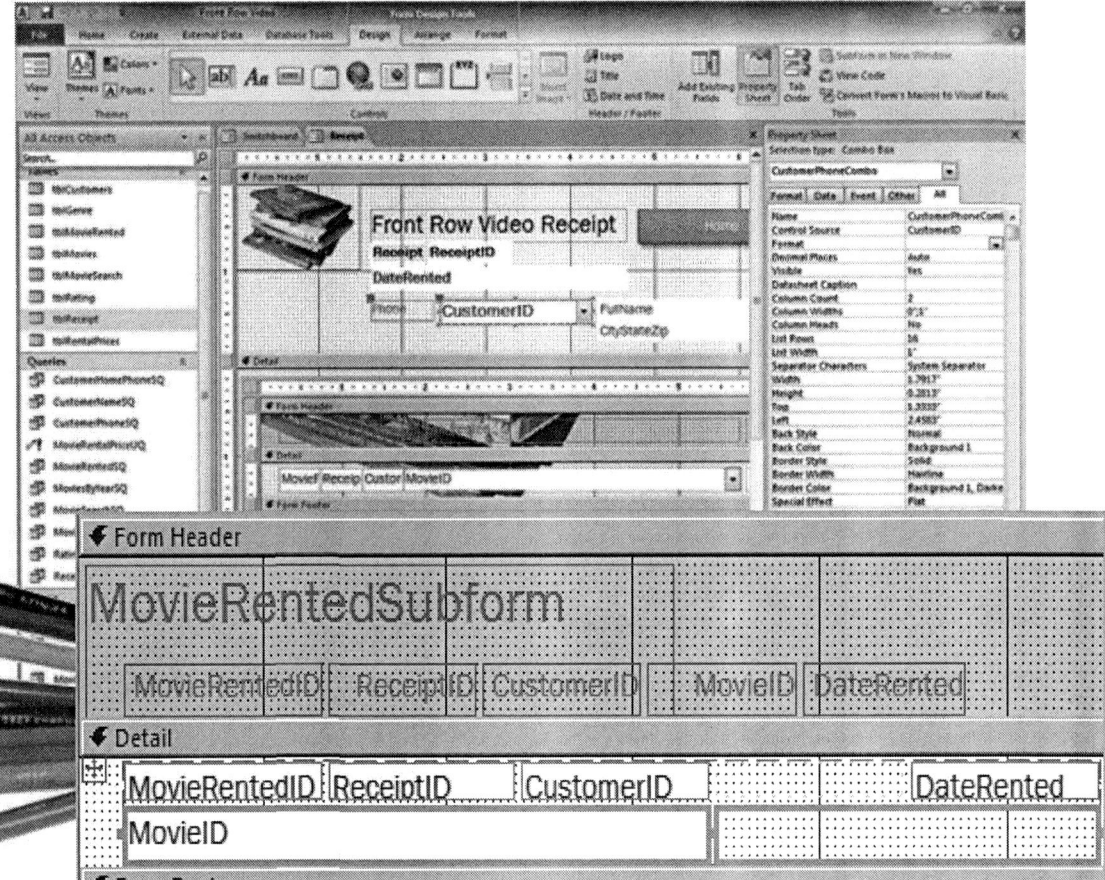

Before You Begin

Before You Begin: Open the Sample Database Go to **Start -> All Programs ->Microsoft Office**.
Click on **Microsoft Office Access 2010.**
Access will prompt you to open a database.
Select: **FrontRowVideo Adv4.accdb**

The sample file, **FrontRowVideo Adv4.accdb,** was developed in the previous lesson. If you have been following along in this book, you can continue with your own database if you wish.

Keep going....

Memo to Self: Databases need to Read and Write. Click **Enable Content** if you see the Security Warning.

Start ->All Programs-> Microsoft Office-> Microsoft Access 2010

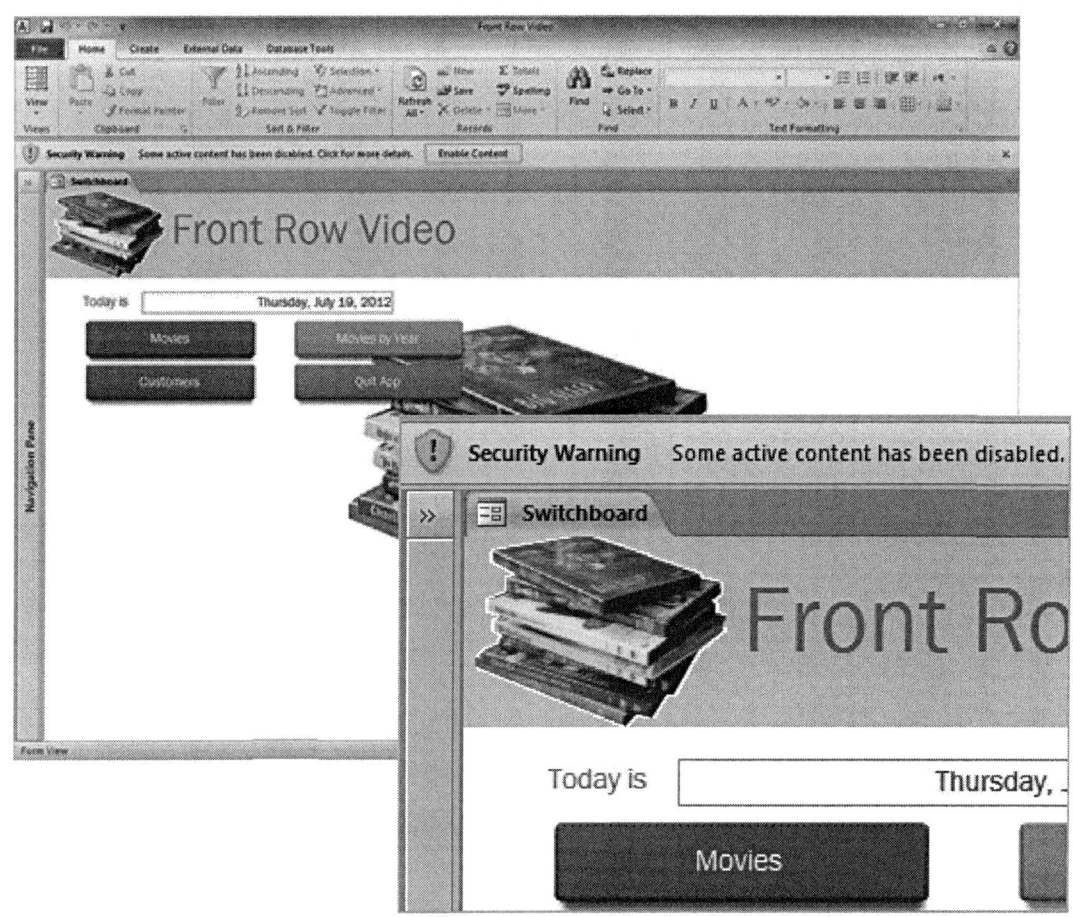

HOME

Know Your Data
Try This: Review the Database
Open the **Navigation Pane.**
Go to **All Access Objects.**

The Front Row View has the following:
Eight Tables: tblCustomers, tblGenre,
tblMovieRented, tblMovies,
tblMovieSearch, tblRating, tblRecipt and
tblRentalPrices.

Seven Queries:
CustomerHomePhoneSQ,
CustomerNameSQ, MovieRentalPriceUQ,
MoviesByYearSQ, MovieSearchSQ,
MovieSQ and RatingSearchSQ.

Five Forms: Customers, Movies,
MovieSearch, MovieSearchSubform and
the Switchboard.

Three Reports: Customer Name. Movies
by Genre, and Movies by Year.

One Macro: OpenSearchMovie

All Access Objects

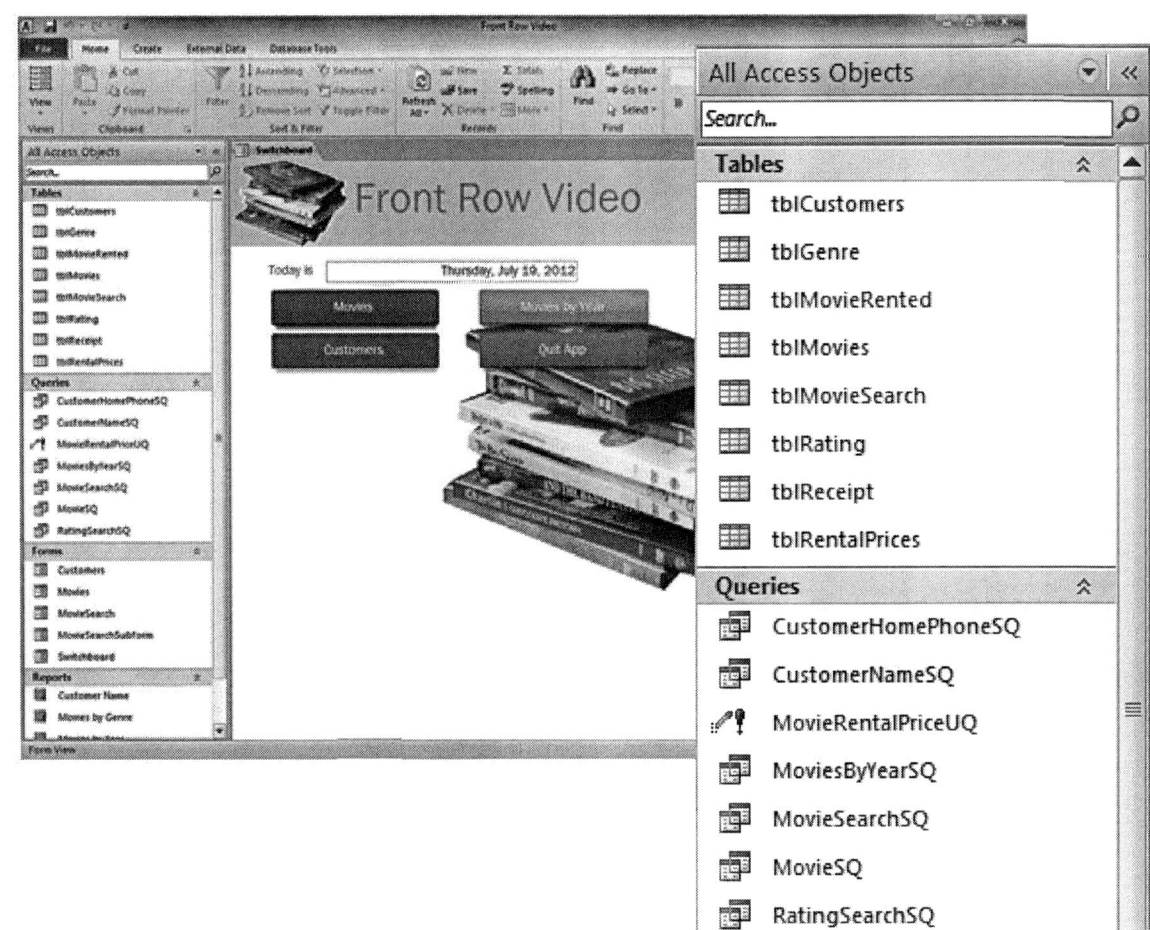

Review the Record Source

The **MovieRentedSubform** will use a Table for the Record Source: tblMovieRented. Please begin this lesson by reviewing the Table Properties.

1. Try it: Review the Record Souce
Go to **All Access Objects->Tables.**
Open a Table: tblMovieRented.
Go to **Home ->Views ->View-> Design View.**

What Do You See? This Table has Keys for:
Who (CustomerID)
Bought (ReceiptID)
What (MovieID)

The **DateRented** is important. Our business model uses the DateRented to calculate how many days since the movie was rented.

Close the Table.
Keep going..

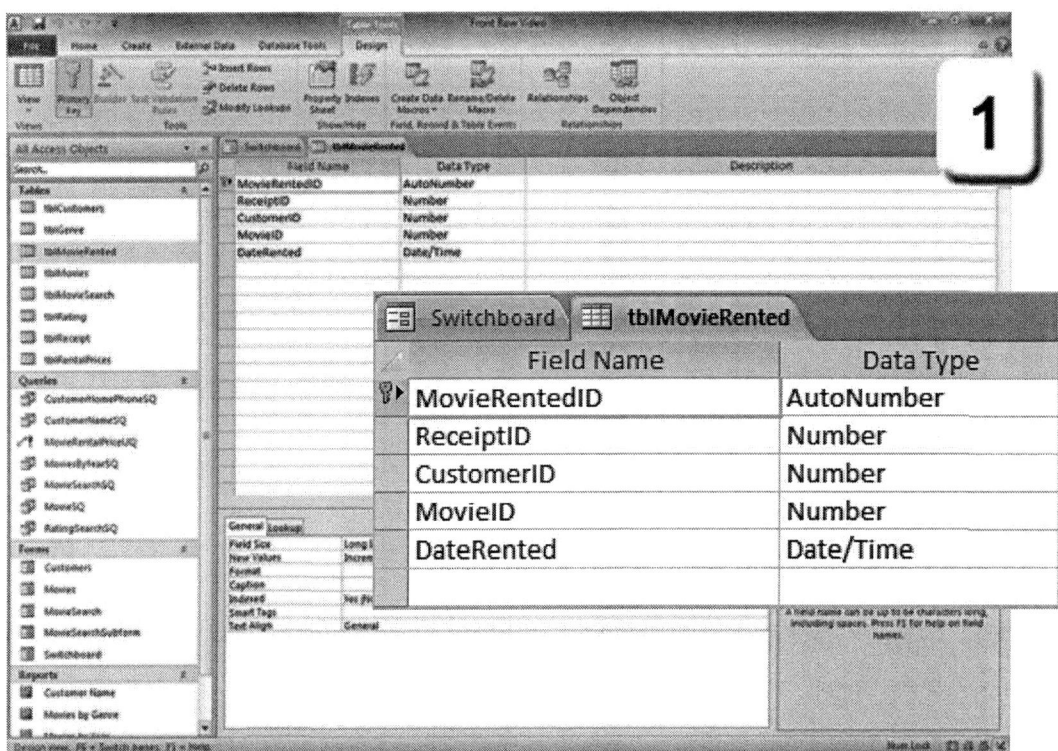

	Field Name	Data Type
🔑▶	MovieRentedID	AutoNumber
	ReceiptID	Number
	CustomerID	Number
	MovieID	Number
	DateRented	Date/Time

HOME

Take One

Create ->Forms ->Form Wizard

Create the Subform

The **MovieRentedSubform** will list the movies that the customer rented. As you go through the Form Wizard please note that this Subform will be **Tabular**.

2. Try it: Create the Receipt Subform
Go to **Create ->Forms ->Form Wizard**.
Select a Record Source: tblMovieRented.
Select all Available Fields.

Click **Next**. Keep going...

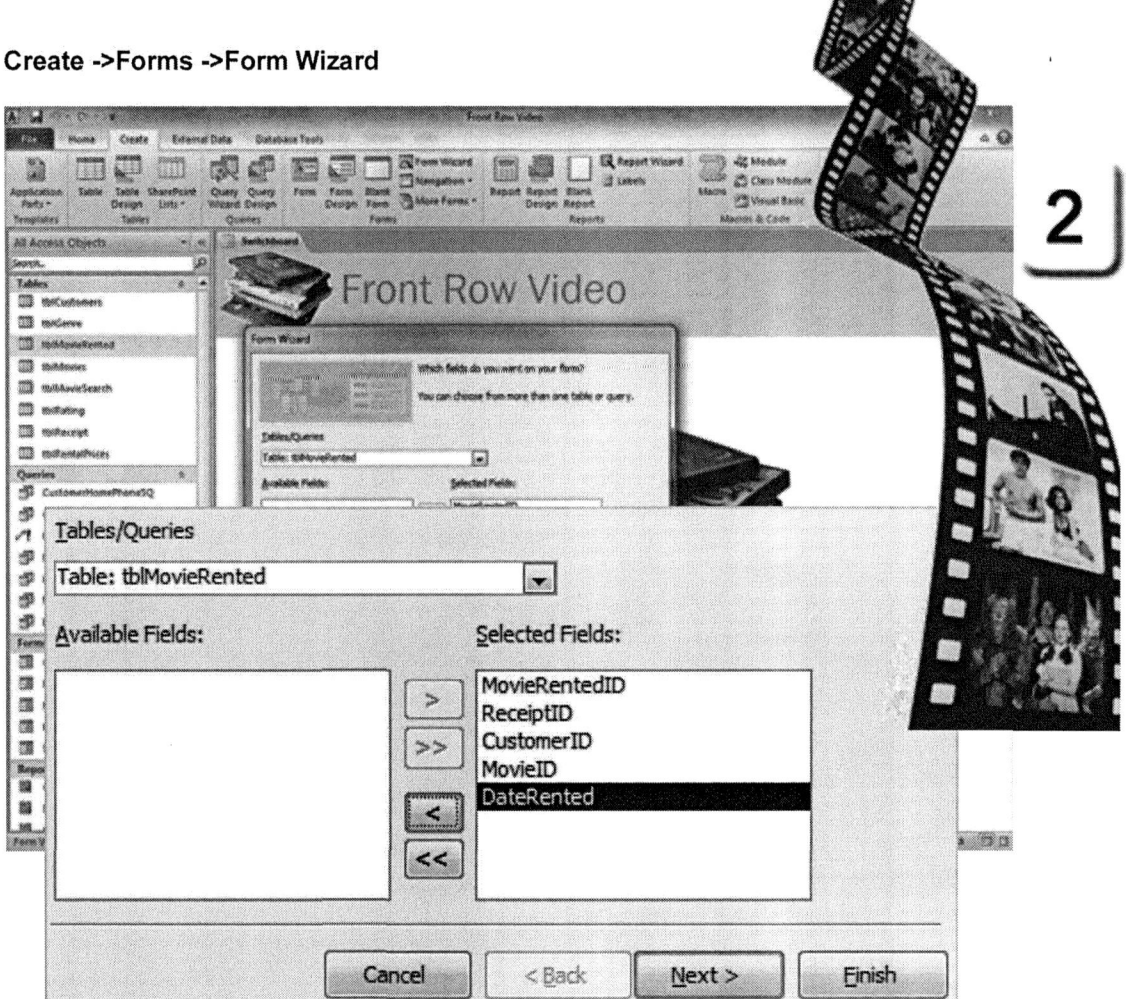

Exam 77-885: Microsoft Access 2010
3. Building Forms
3.1. Create forms: Use the Form Wizard

The Form Wizard

3. Try it: Select a Form Layout
Select a Layout: Tabular.
Click **Next**.

Try This, Too: Finish the Wizard
Name the Form: MovieRentedSubform.
Click **Finish**.
So...what did you get?

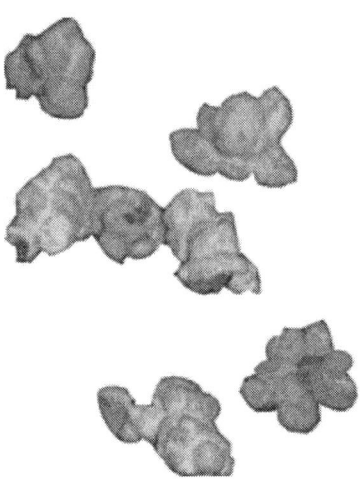

Create ->Forms ->Form Wizard

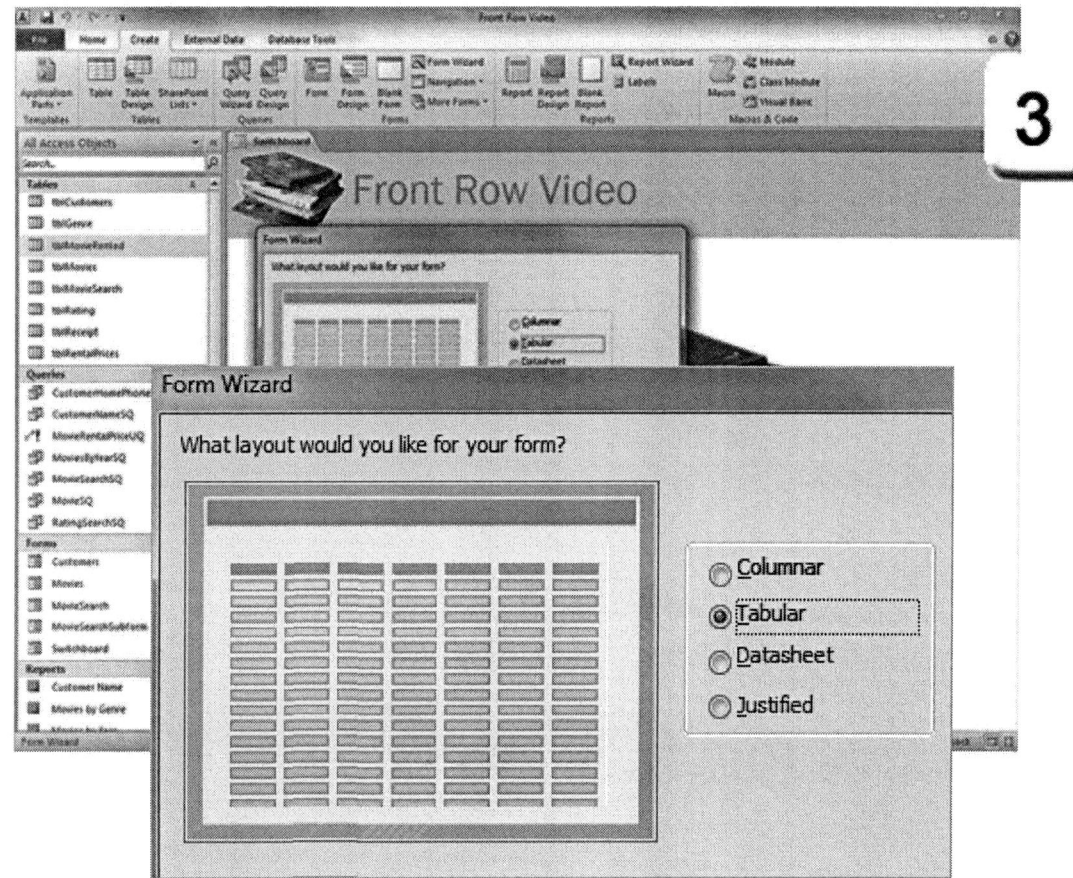

Exam 77-885: Microsoft Access 2010
3. Building Forms
3.1. Create forms: Use the Form Wizard

Hello, Tabular Subform!

The Form Wizard created a new Subform that uses tblMovieRented for the Record Source.

4. Try it: Review the Subform

The MovieRentedSubform has some functions already. Click in the Date Field and try to select a date with the Date Picker.

Not bad...for a start.

Create ->Forms ->Form Wizard

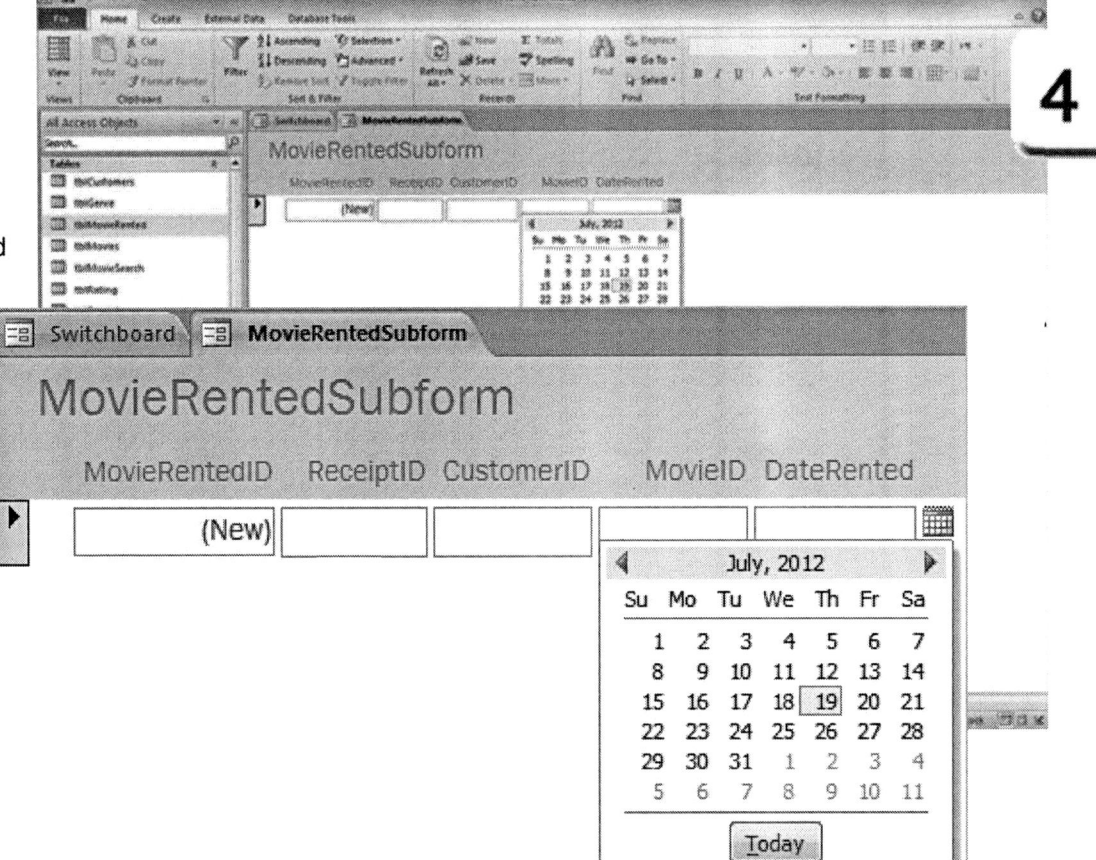

Exam 77-885: Microsoft Access 2010
3. Building Forms
3.3. Apply Form Arrange options: Use Table Functions

Create a Table

We selected a Tabular format when we walked through the Form Wizard. However, this is not a Table, yet. In the following pages we will create and format a Table in Design View.

Before You Begin: Change the View
Go to **Home->Views->View**.
Select a View: Design View.

1. Try it: Create a Table
Select all of the Fields in the Detail Section.
Go to **Form Design Tools->Arrange->Table**.
Select: **Tabular**.

Keep going...

Form Design Tools->Arrange->Table->Tabular

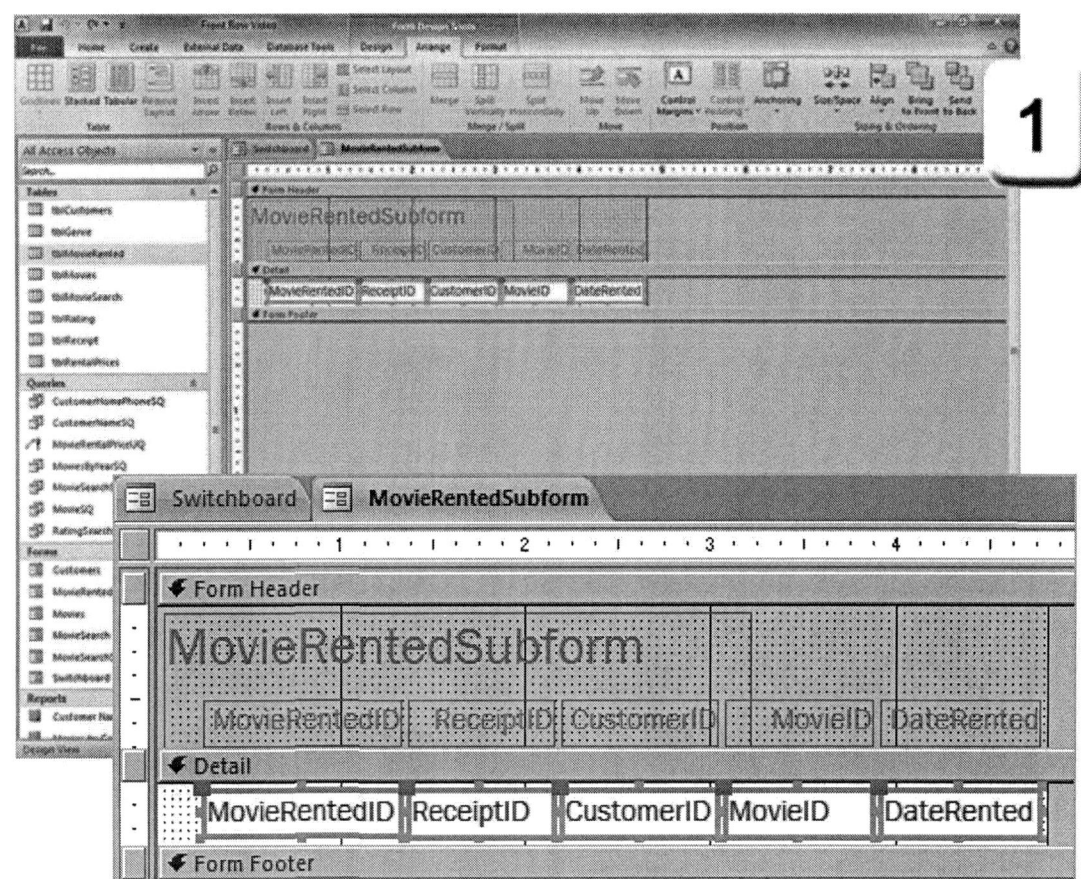

Exam 77-885: Microsoft Access 2010
3. Building Forms
3.3. Apply Form Arrange options: Use Table Functions

Form Design Tools->Arrange

Review the Tools

Microsoft Office 2010 has excellent tools for
formatting Tables in Microsoft Word, Excel,
PowerPoint and Outlook. Microsoft Access
has rich tools as well on the **Arrange** Ribbon.

2. Try it: Review the Arrange Ribbon

When you create a Table, the Arrange
Ribbon Groups become available. The
Groups include:
Table
Rows & Columns
Merge/Split
Move
Position
Sizing and Ordering

Let's see what we can do with this stuff.

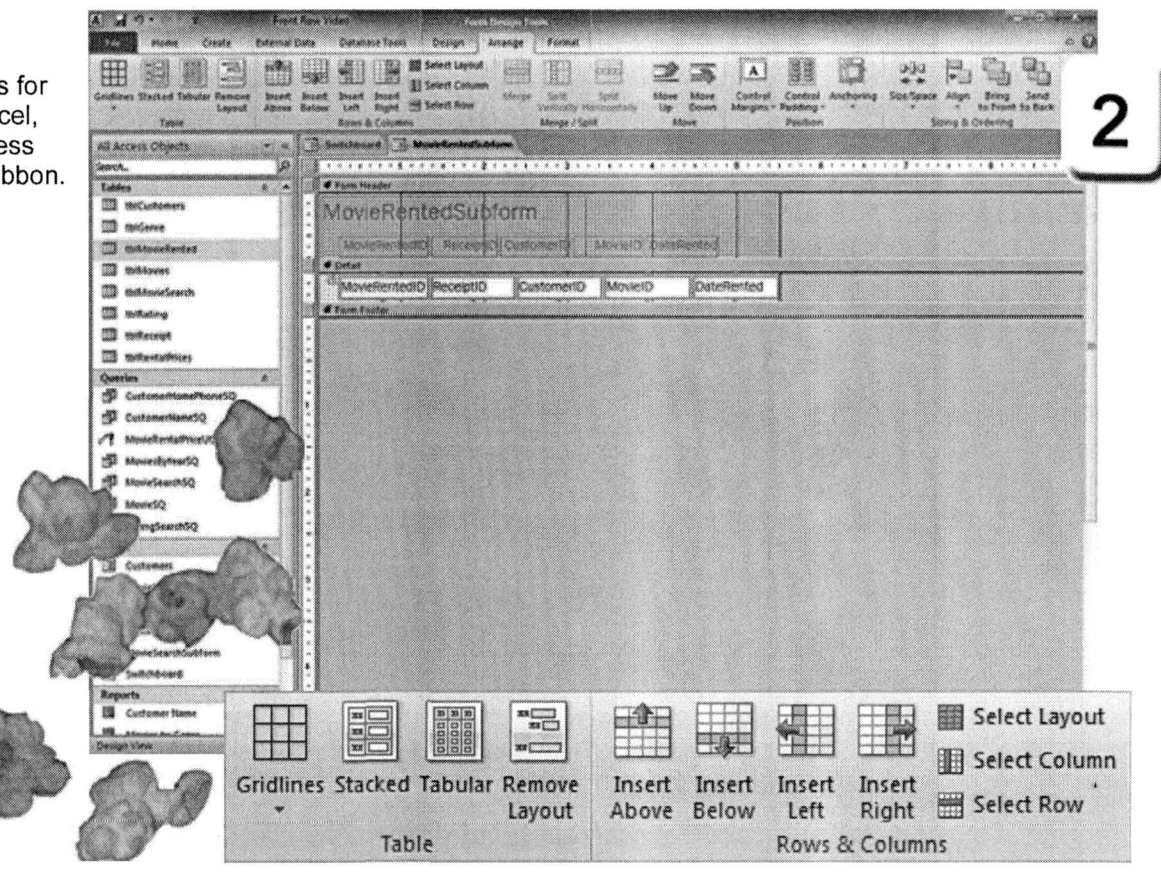

Exam 77-885: Microsoft Access 2010
3. Building Forms
3.3. Apply Form Arrange options: Use Table Functions

Arrange: Insert a New Row

3. Try it: Insert A Row
Go to the **Detail Section**.
Select a **Field**: DateRented.
Go to **Form Design Tools->Arrange**.
Go to **Rows and Columns->Insert Above**.

What Do You See? There should be a new Row above the Fields in the Detail Section.

The next step in this little exercise is to move the DateRented Field up to the new Row.

Keep going...

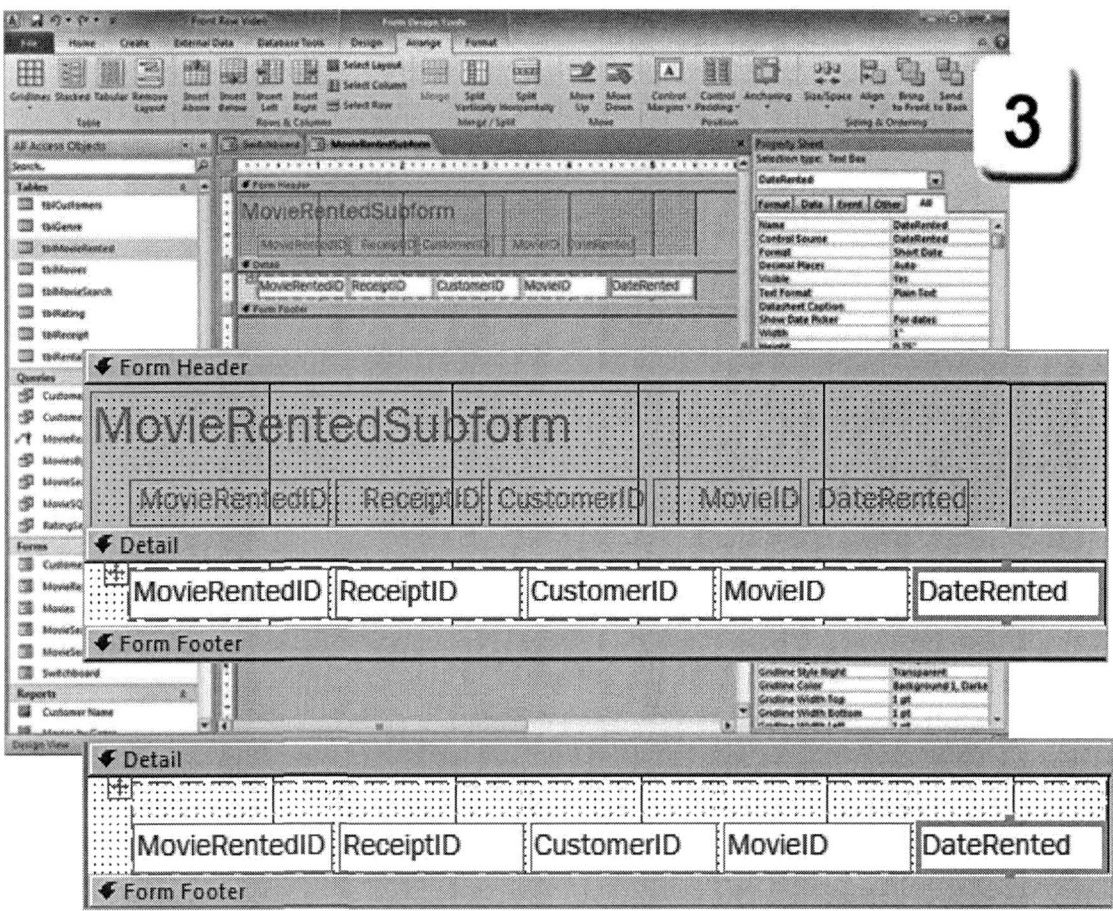

Exam 77-885: Microsoft Access 2010
3. Building Forms
3.3. Apply Form Arrange options: Use Table Functions to Insert Rows and Columns

HOME

Take One

Arrange: Move a Field

Here are the steps to move a Field up to the top Row.

4. Try it: Move a Table Field
Go to the **Detail Section.**
Select a **Field: DateRented.**
Go to **Form Design Tools->Arrange.**
Go to **Move->Move Up.**

What Do You See? The DateRented Field is in the same Column as it was in Row 2.

Try This, Too: Move More Fields Up
Move the following Fields up to Row 1:
MovieRentedID
ReceiptID
CustomerID

Keep going...

Form Design Tools->Arrange->Move->Move Up

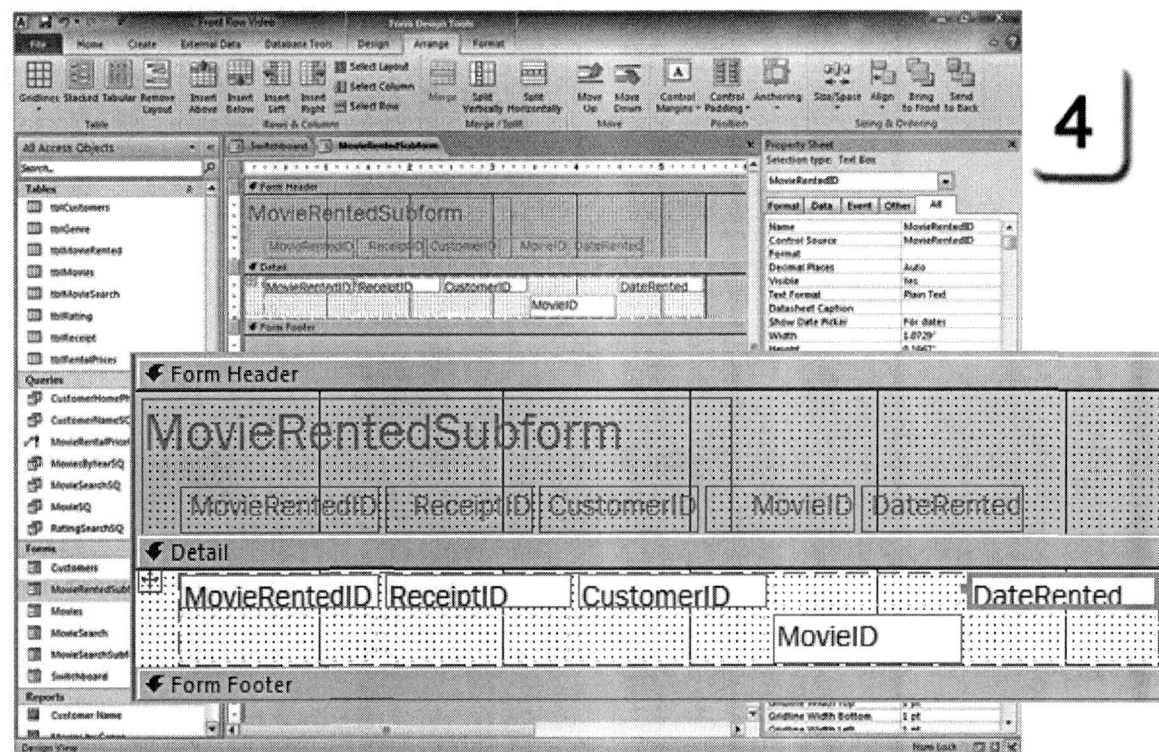

4

Exam 77-885: Microsoft Access 2010
3. Building Forms
3.3. Apply Form Arrange options: Use Table Functions to Move Table Fields

Merge/Split: Merge Cells

Before You Begin: Select a Row
Click on the first Cell in Row 2 to select it.
Go to **Form Design Tools->Arrange.**
Go to **Rows & Columns->Select Row.**

What Do You See? There are really five
Columns in Row 2.

5. Try This: Merge the Cells
Go to **Form Design Tools->Arrange.**
Go to **Merge/Split->Merge.**

Now, What Do You See? There is only one
Column in Row 2, MovieID.

Keep going...

Form Design Tools->Arrange->Merge/Split->Merge

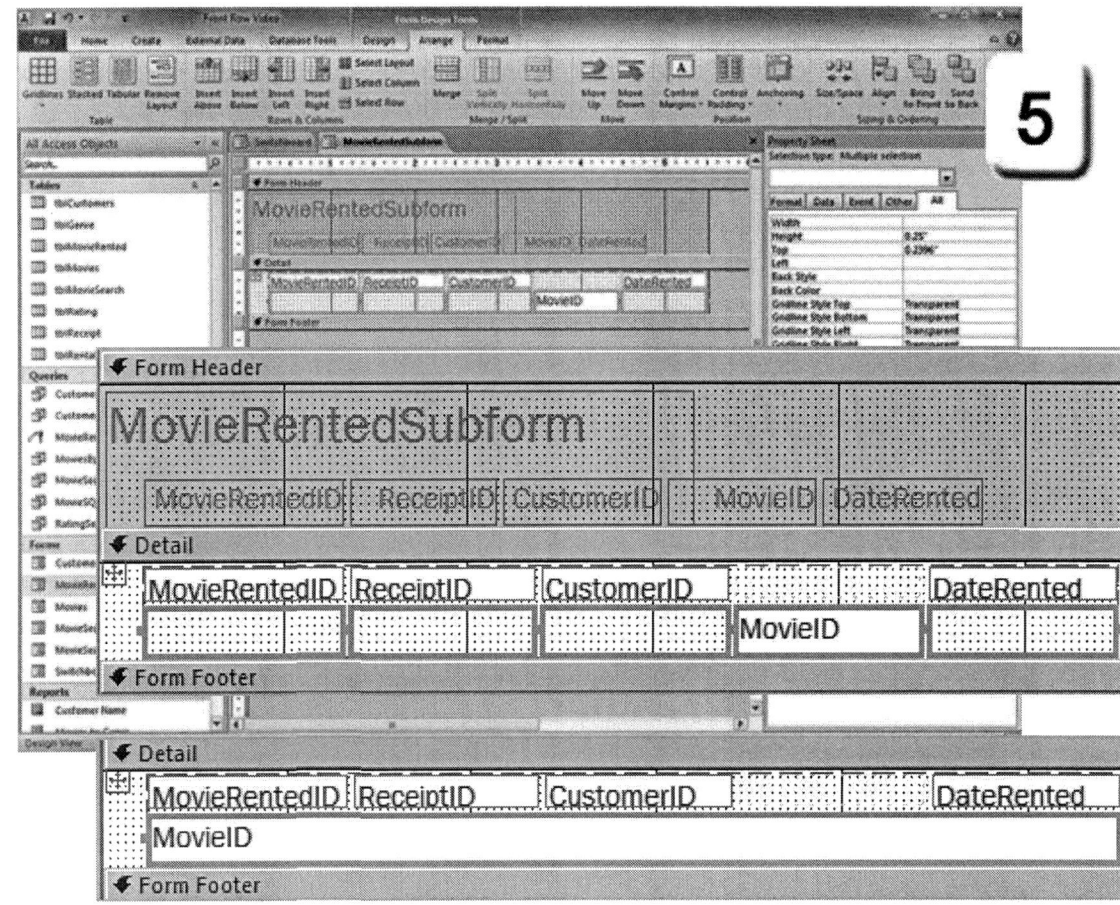

Exam 77-885: Microsoft Access 2010
3. Building Forms
3.3. Apply Form Arrange options: Use Table Functions to Merge Table Fields

Merge/Split: Split Cells

6. Try it: Split the Cells
The second Row in the Detail Section is selected.
Go to **Form Design Tools->Arrange.**
Go to **Merge/Split->Split Horizontally.**

So, What Do You See? No surprises here. The Row was split into two Fields.

Please **UNDO** this Split.

Do This, Please: Save the Subform
Go to **File->Save.**

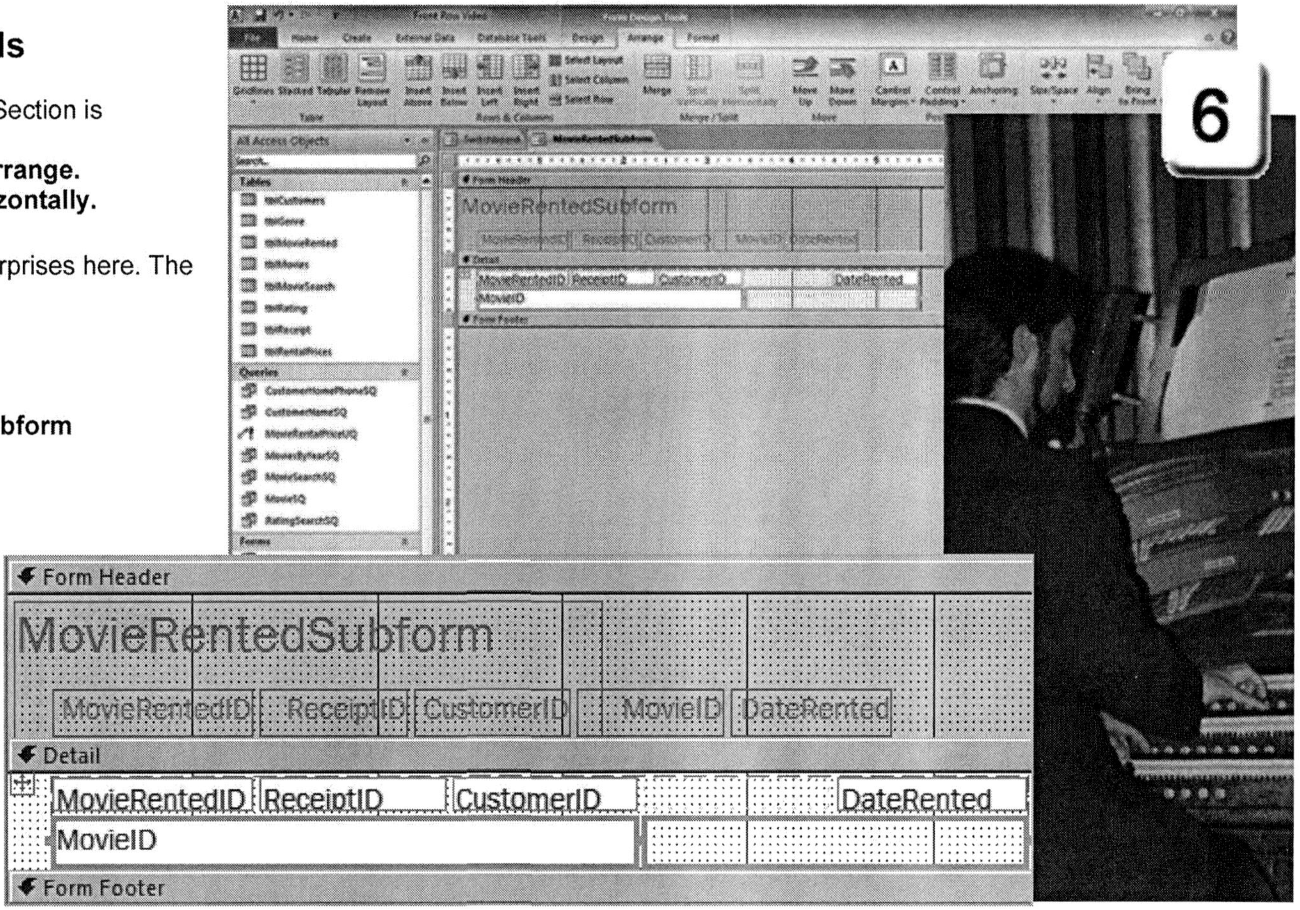

Form Design Tools->Arrange->Merge/Split->Split

Exam 77-885: Microsoft Access 2010
3. Building Forms
3.3. Apply Form Arrange options: Use Table Functions to Split Table Fields

Position: Control Margins

The Cells in a Table have three aspects that can be formatted: Margins, Padding and Anchoring. The **Margin** is the space between the Cell border and the data. The default Margin is None. The other options include Narrow, Medium and Wide.

1. Try it: Control the Cell Margins

The ReceiptSubForm is in Design View.
Row 1 is selected.
Go to **Form Design Tools->Arrange**.
Go to **Position->Control Margins.**
Select a Margin size: Narrow.

Keep going...

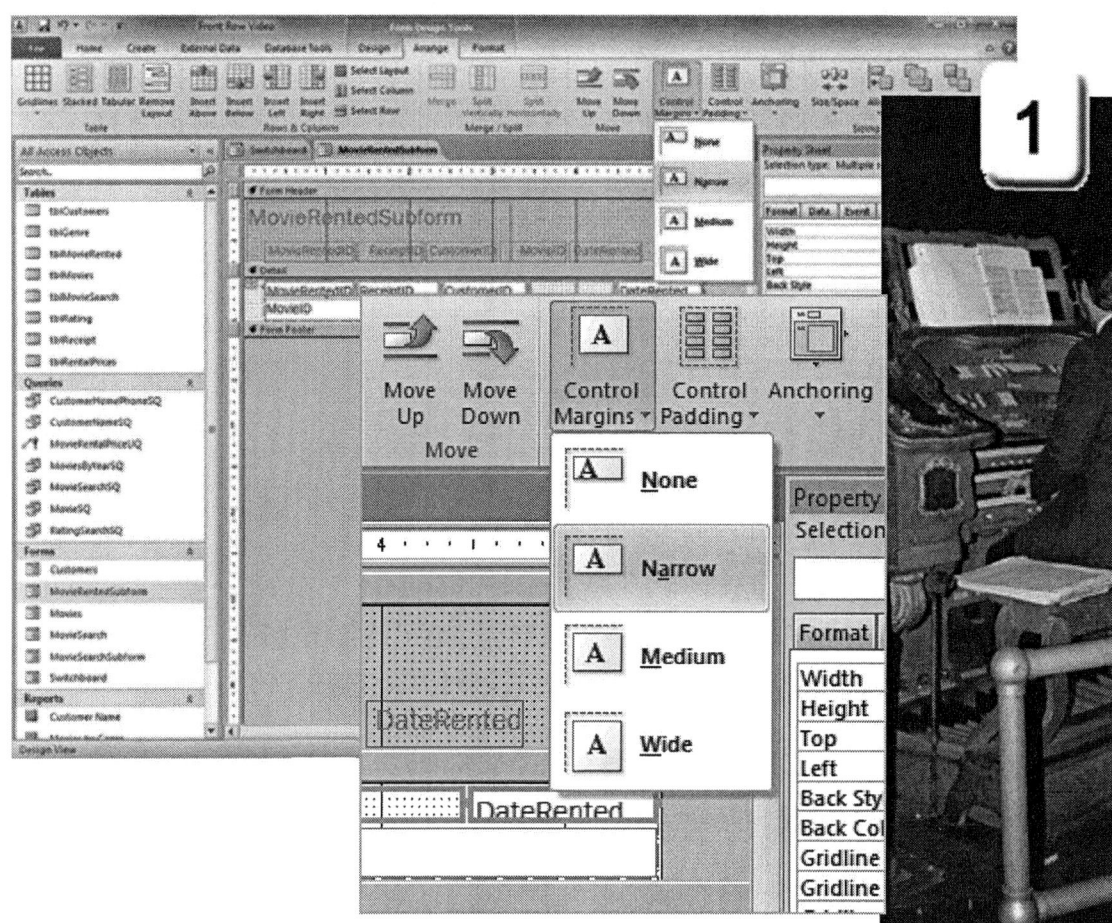

Exam 77-885: Microsoft Access 2010
3. Building Forms
3.3. Apply Form Arrange options: Margins

Take One

Position: Padding

The **Padding** is the space between the Cells.

2. Try it: Edit the Cell Padding
The ReceiptSubForm is still in Design View.
Row 1 is selected.
Go to **Form Design Tools->Arrange.**
Go to **Position->Padding.**
Select a Padding size: Narrow.

Keep going...

Form Design Tools->Arrange->Position->Padding

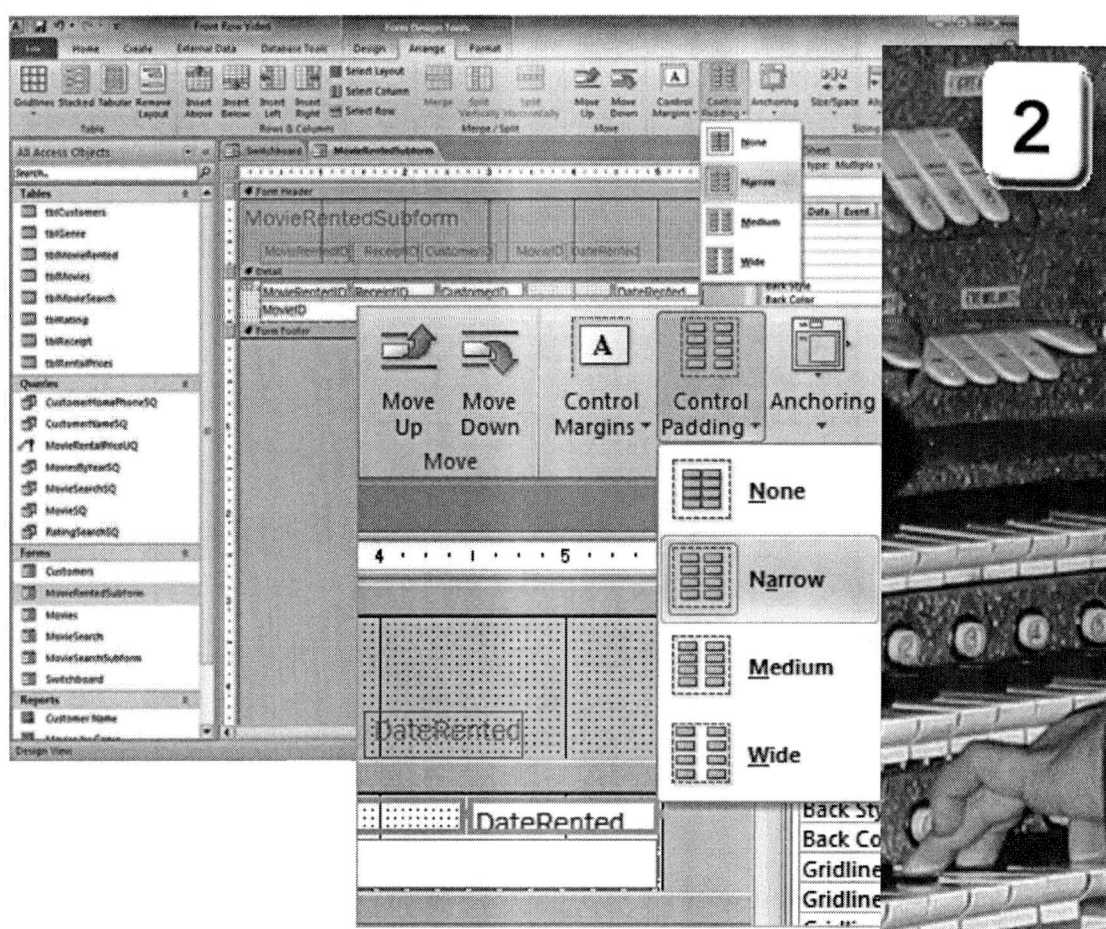

Exam 77-885: Microsoft Access 2010
3. Building Forms
3.3. Apply Form Arrange options: Padding

Position: Anchoring

Anchoring locks a Cell into a place, with respect to the Table or Form. In this example, the Row of Cells is be positioned in the Top Left of the Table, regardless of how the MovieRentedSubform is opened or resized.

3. Try it: Edit the Anchoring
The ReceiptSubForm is open in Design View. Row 1 is still selected.
Go to **Form Design Tools->Arrange.**
Go to **Position->Anchoring.**
Select an option: **Top Left.**

What Do You See? The other options are:
Stretch Across Top
Top Right
Stretch Down
Stretch Down and Across
Stretch Down and Right
Bottom Left
Stretch Across Bottom
Bottom Right

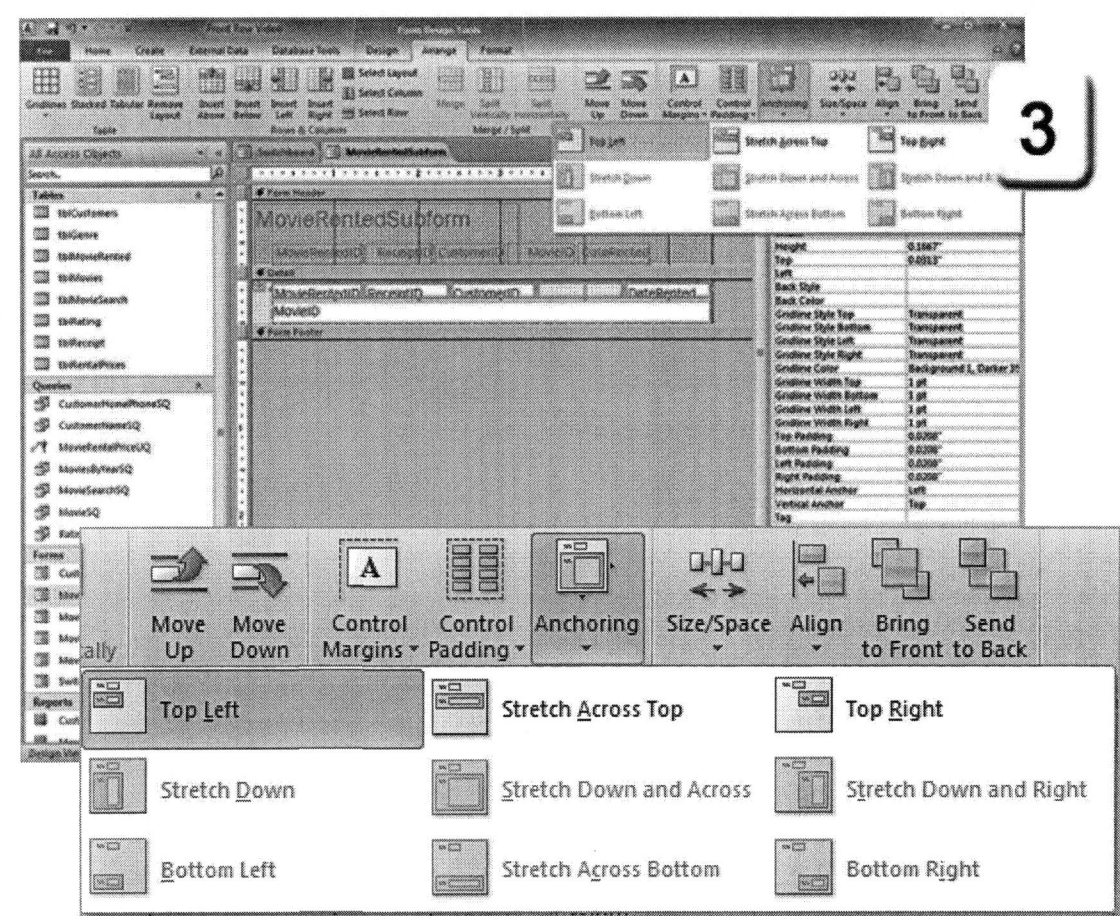

Exam 77-885: Microsoft Access 2010
3. Building Forms
3.3. Apply Form Arrange options: Anchoring

Form Design Tools->Arrange->Sizing and Ordering->Size/Space

Size and Ordering

Let's use the Size/Space options to make the Cells **Size to Fit**, after we changed the Padding.

4. Try it: Edit the Size
The ReceiptSubForm is open in Design View. Row 1 is still selected.
Go to **Form Design Tools->Arrange.**
Go to **Sizing and Ordering->Size/Space.**
Select an option: To Fit.

What Do You See? The Cells in Row 1 were resized to fit after we changed the Padding.

What Else Do You See? In addition to the Size options, you can edit the Spacing, Grid and Grouping.

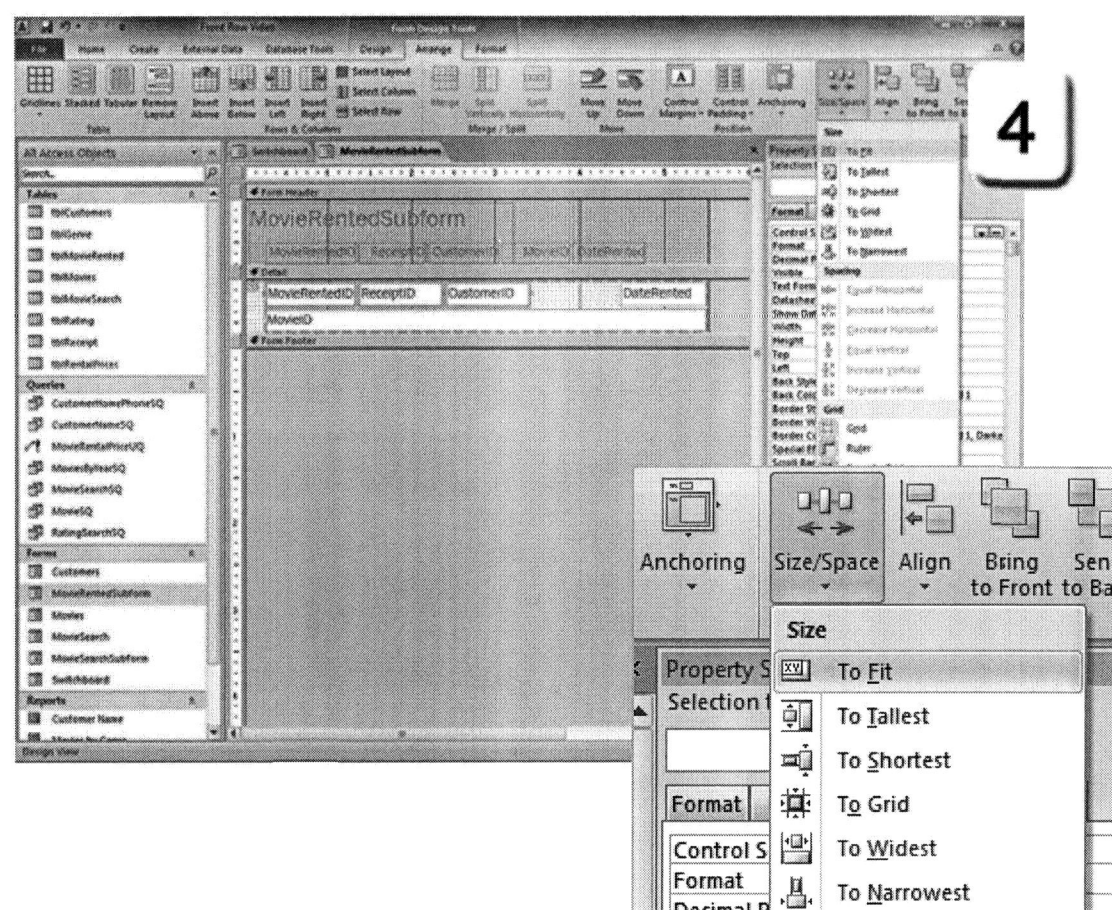

Exam 77-885: Microsoft Access 2010
3. Building Forms
3.3. Apply Form Arrange options: Reposition and Format Controls

Size and Ordering

The Cell size can be edited with the Property Sheet as well.

5. Try it: Resize the Cells
The ReceiptSubForm is open in Design View.
The four Cells in Row 1 are still selected.
Go to **Form Design Tools->Design->Tools.**
Go to **Property Sheet->Format.**
Edit the **Width**: 0.4"

What Do You See? The four Cells in Row 1 were resized. These are Key numbers so they do not have to be as very wide.

Try This, Too: Format the Other Controls
Select a Control: DateRented.
Edit the Width: 1"

Select a Control: MovieID.
Edit the Width: 2.4"
Save. Save. Save.

Memo to Self: If the Cell is formatted **Size to Fit**, the width may default to a different number than the one you entered.

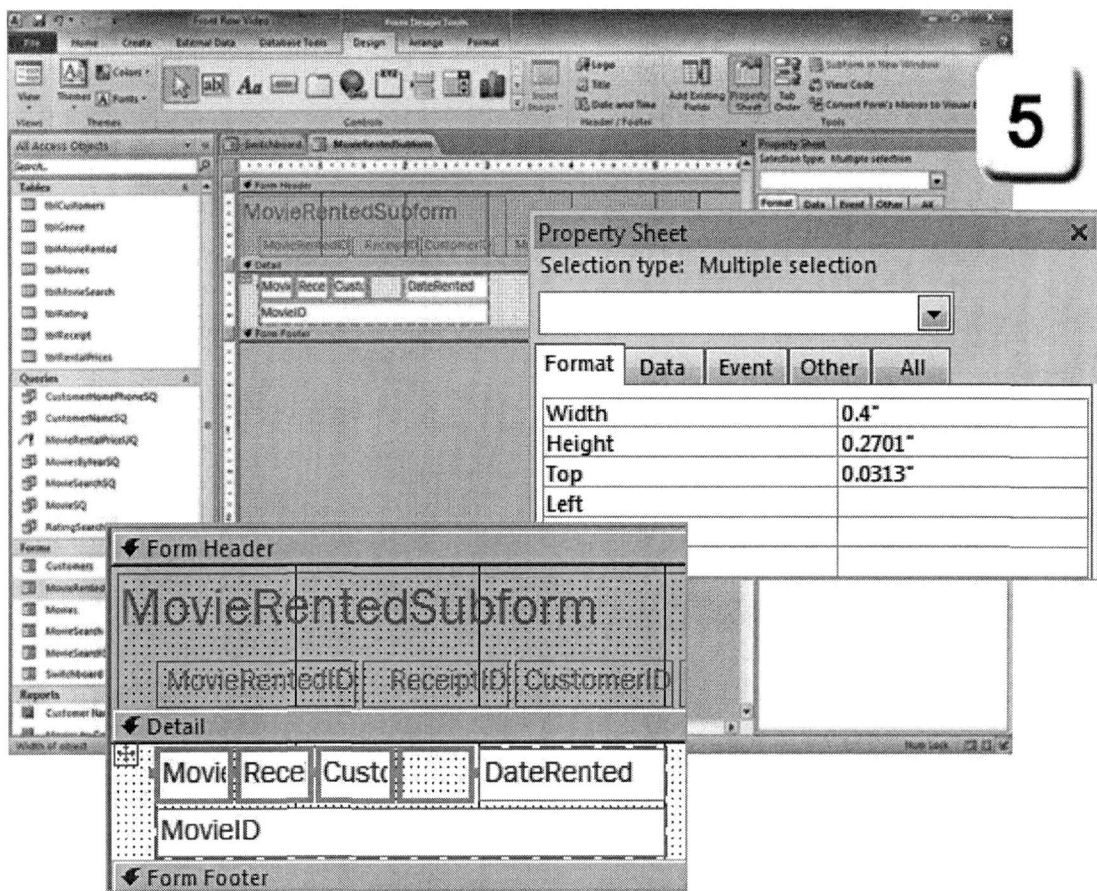

Exam 77-885: Microsoft Access 2010
3. Building Forms
3.2. Apply Form Design options: View Property Sheet

Create a Combo Box

The MovieRentedSubform will use a Combo Box to select a movie. The Combo Box will replace the Text Box for MovieID.

Before You Begin: Delete the Text Box
Go to the Detail Section.
Select a Control: MovieID.
Delete it.

1. Try it: Create a Combo Box
The MovieRentedSubform is in Design View.
Go to **Form Design Tools ->Design.**
Select a **Control: Combo Box.**
Click on the Detail Section to start the Combo Box Wizard.

Select a Record Source: Table or Query.
Click **Next.** Keep going...

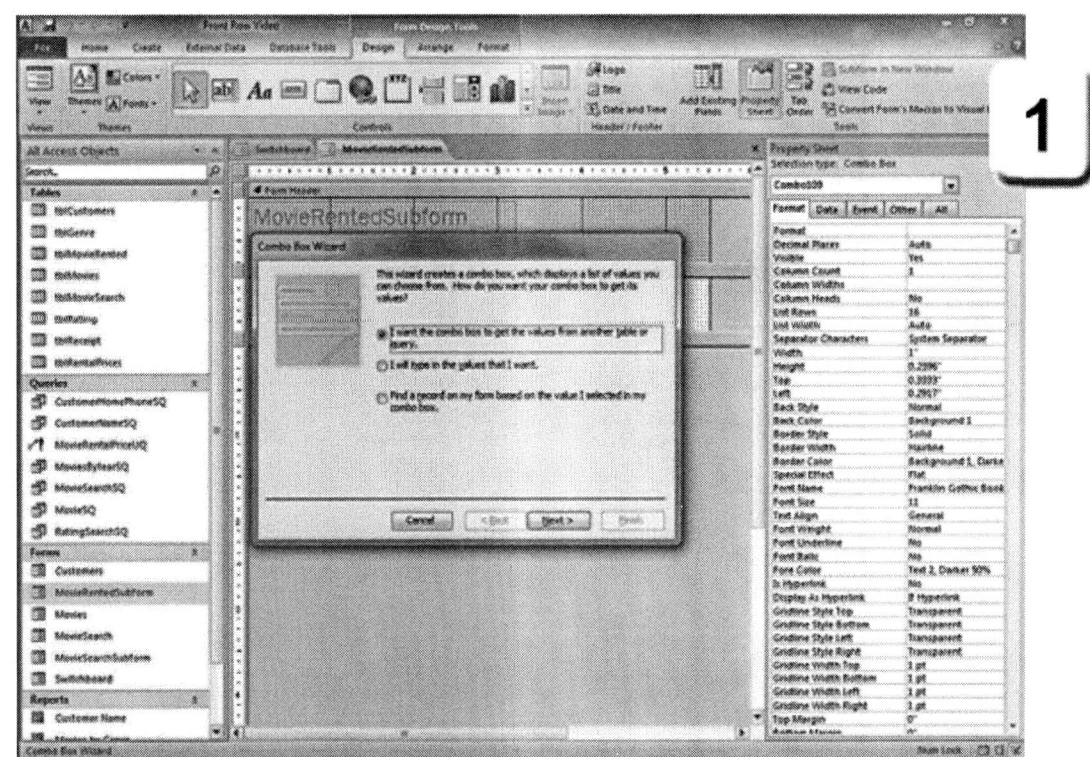

Exam 77-885: Microsoft Access 2010
3. Building Forms
3.2. Apply Form Design options: Add Drop Down Controls

Combo Box: Record Source

2. Try it: Select a Record Source
Select Table: tblMovies.
Click **Next**.

Try This, Too: Select the Fields
Select two of the Available Fields:
MovieID
Movie
Click **Next**.

Try This, Also: Sort the Fields
Select: Movie.
Sort: Ascending.
Click **Next**.

Keep going...

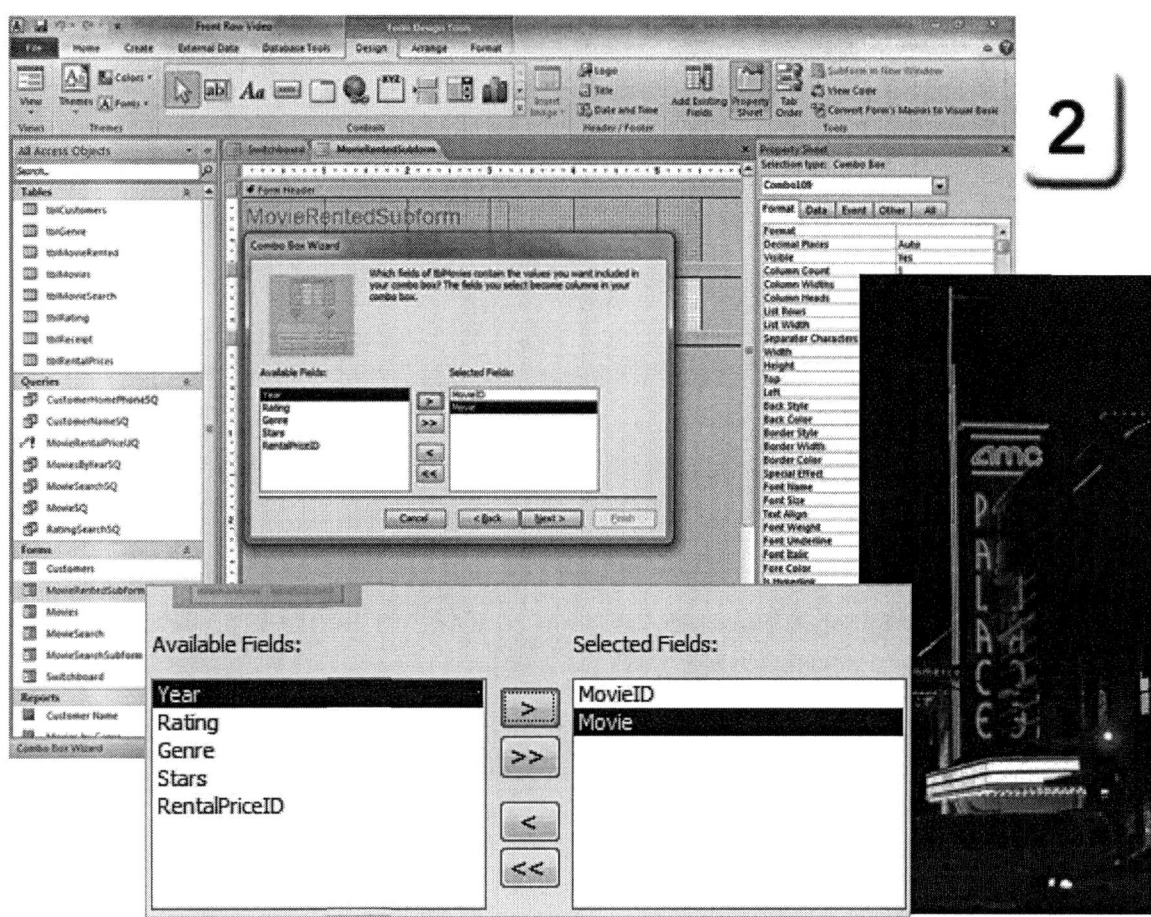

Exam 77-885: Microsoft Access 2010
3. Building Forms
3.2. Apply Form Design options: Add Drop Down Controls

Form Design Tools->Design->Controls->Combo Box

Combo Box: Key Column

There are two Columns in this Combo Box:
Column 1: MovieID
Column 2:Movie

Only one column will be seen in the Drop Down List. If the Key Column is not hidden then Users will see the MovieID, Column 1, and not the name of the Movie, Column 2.

By default, the Combo Wizard hides the Key Column, so Users will see the Movie name.

3. Try it: Hide the Key Column

Hide the key column.
Click **Next**.
Keep going...

You May Have Noticed: This walk through the Combo Box Wizard accepted the default to Hide the Key Column. Why is this so? This Form saves the Primary Key, not the Text, to the Table so it goes with the Default. In a Normalized database there are only Key numbers, not Text, when you get to the final summary (tblMovieRented).

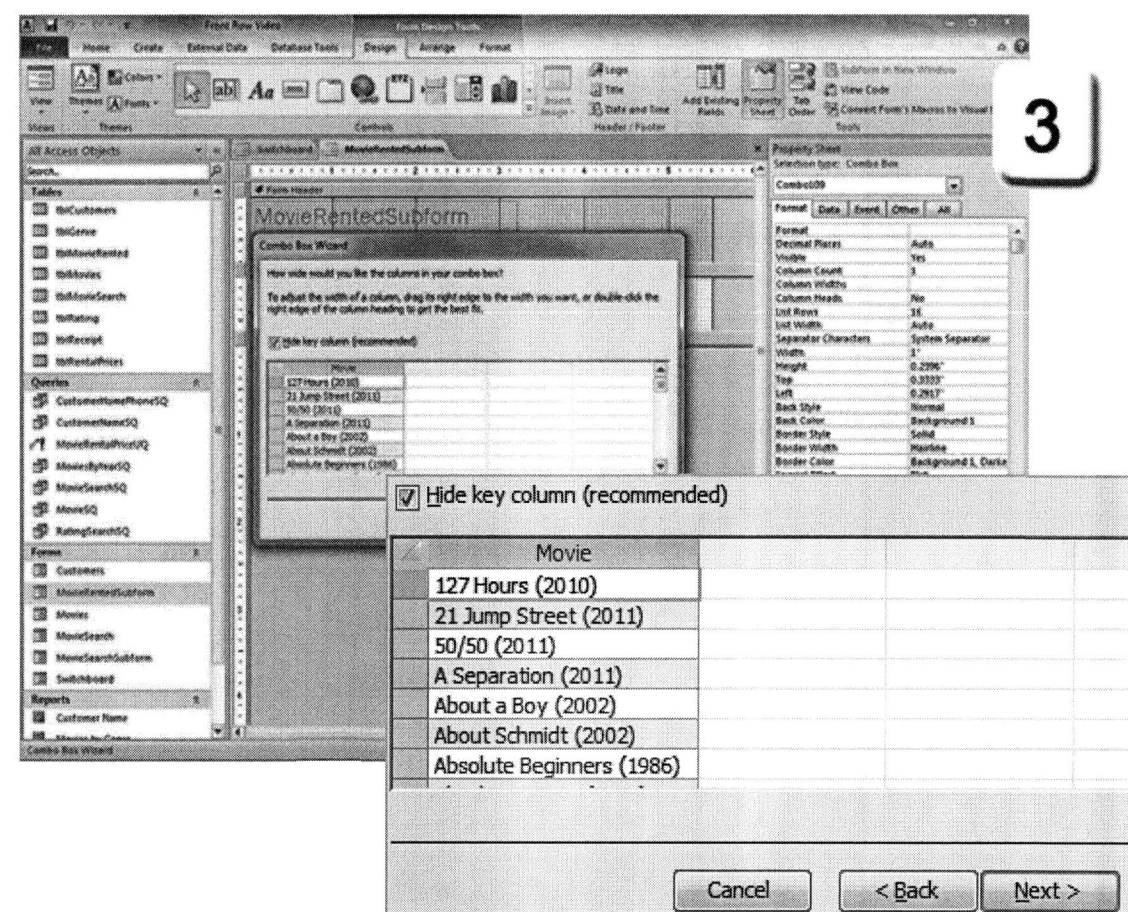

Exam 77-885: Microsoft Access 2010
3. Building Forms
3.2. Apply Form Design options: Add Drop Down Controls

Combo Box: Store Value

The last step of the Combo Box Wizard is to match the value selected by the Combo Box from tblMovies to the value in the Record Source for the Subform, tblMoviesRented.

4. Try it: Store that Value
Select a value to store: MovieID.
Click **Next**.

And Finally: Name the Combo
Enter a name: MovieCombo.
Click **Finish**.

What Do You See? There should be a new Combo Box under Row 1 in the Detail Section of the MovieRentedSubform.

Try This: Edit the Combo Box Properties
The MovieCombo is still selected.
Go to **Form Design Tools->Design->Tools.**
Go to **Property Sheet->Format.**
Width: 4.75"
Top: 0.33"
Left: 0.25"
Keeeeeep going.

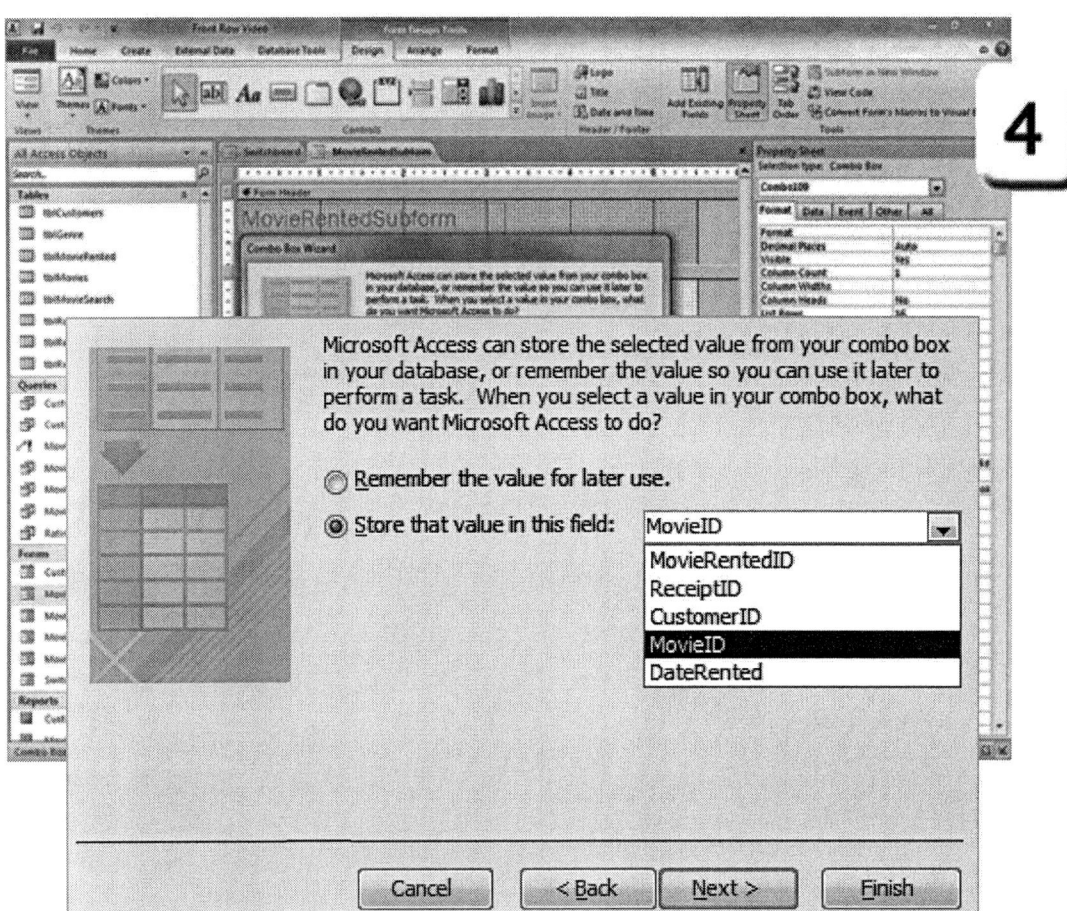

Exam 77-885: Microsoft Access 2010
3. Building Forms
3.2. Apply Form Design options: Add Drop Down Controls

Test the Subform

The only way to know if it works is to use it like a User. Let's see what happens.

Before You Begin: Change the View
Go to **Form Design Tools ->Views.**
Select a **View: Form View**

5. Try it: Test the Combo Box
There are two parts to testing a Combo Box: first, can you see the data from the Table? Second, can you select a Record from the list?

Did it work? **Save** if it does!

Form Design Tools ->Views->View

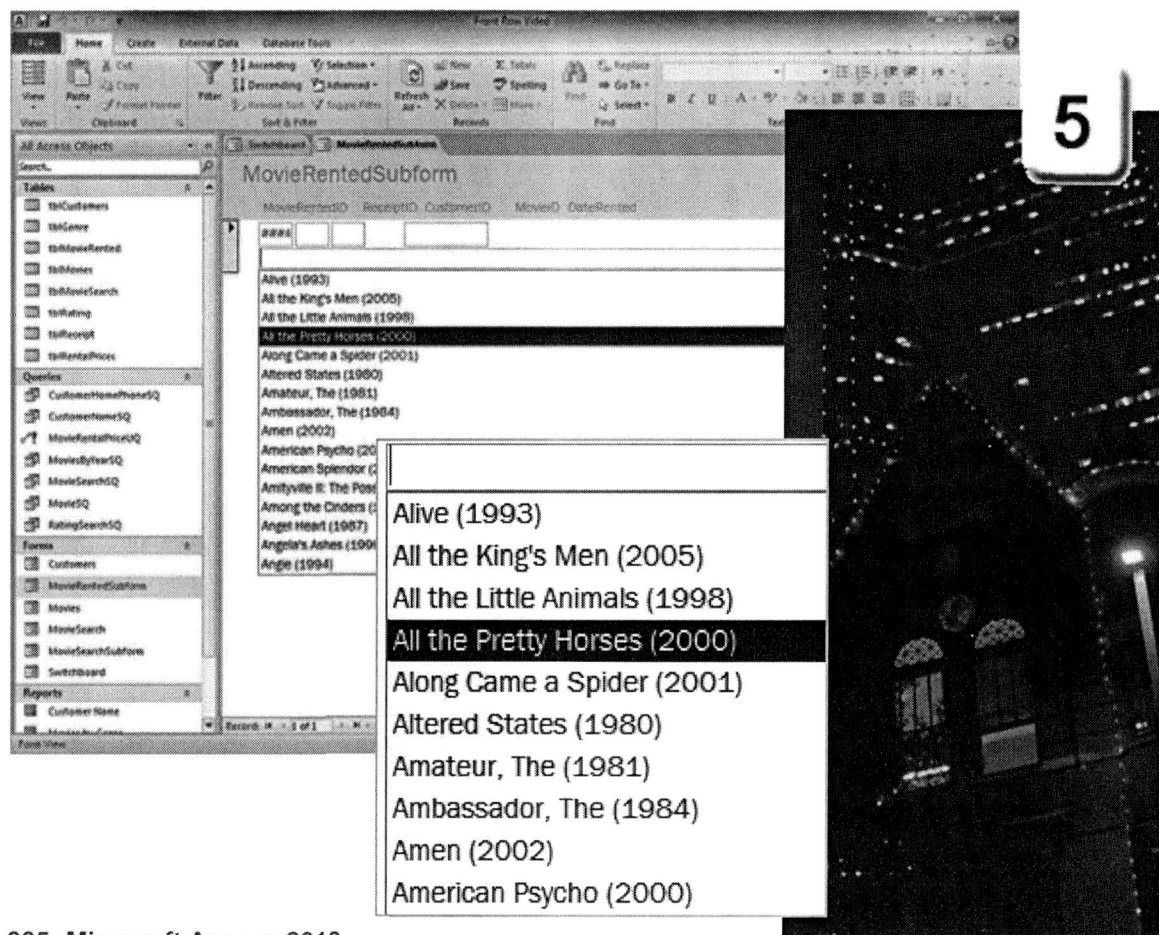

Exam 77-885: Microsoft Access 2010
3. Building Forms
3.2. Apply Form Design options: Add Drop Down Controls

Add a Background Image

6. Try it: Add a Background Image

The MovieRentedSubform is in Design View.
Select the Form.
Go to **Form Design Tools ->Format.**
Go to **Background-> Background Image.**
Choose an Image: Movies1.

Keep going...

Form Design Tools ->Format->Background-> Background Image

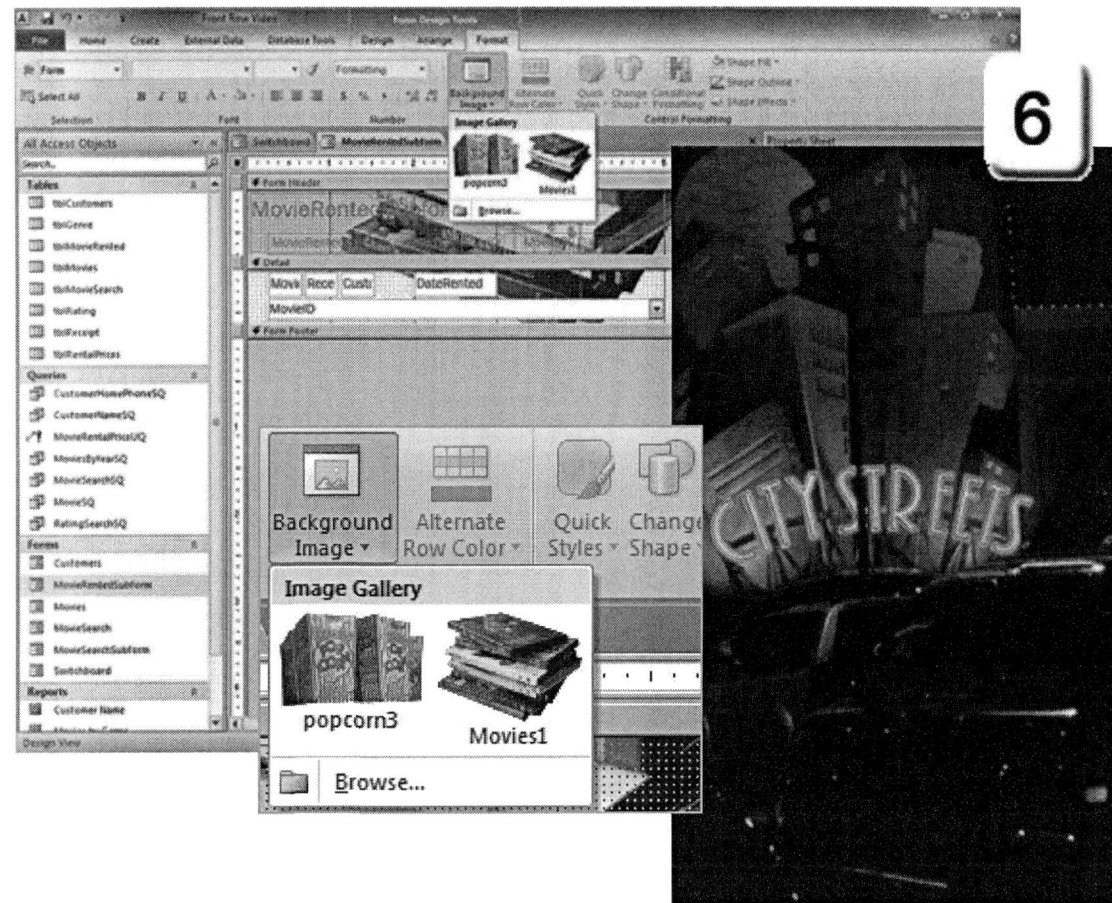

Exam 77-885: Microsoft Access 2010
3. Building Forms
3.4. Apply Form Format options: Apply Background Image to a Form

Property Sheet->Format->Picture Alignment

Edit the Background Image

The Background Image has Properties as that you can edit as well.

7. Try it: Edit the Background Image
The MovieRentedSubform is in Design View and the Property Sheet is still open.

Go to **Property Sheet->Format.**
Go to **Picture Alignment.**
Select an alignment: **Bottom Right.**

Who said Forms had to be beige and gray?

Save. Save. Save.
Close this Form.

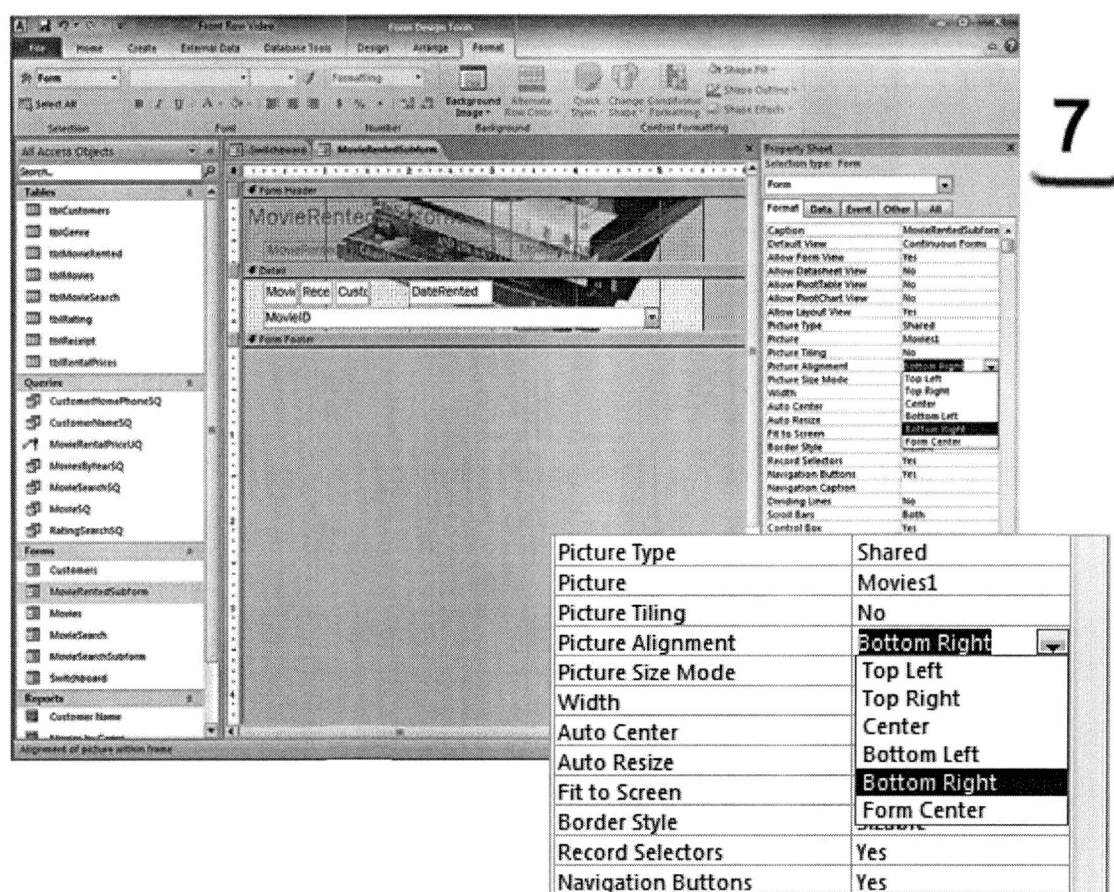

Picture Type	Shared
Picture	Movies1
Picture Tiling	No
Picture Alignment	Bottom Right
Picture Size Mode	Top Left
Width	Top Right
Auto Center	Center
Auto Resize	Bottom Left
Fit to Screen	Bottom Right
Border Style	Form Center
Record Selectors	Yes
Navigation Buttons	Yes

Exam 77-885: Microsoft Access 2010
3. Building Forms
3.4. Apply Form Format options: Apply Background Image to a Form

Summary

The goal of this lesson was to create the MovieRentedSubform.

This Subform was Tabular, so we had a opportunity to work with the Arrange options: Insert, Merge and Split.

We also reviewed the Margins, Padding and Anchoring.

Not bad for a Subform.

Get a cookie! Please come back for seconds. The next lesson creates the Receipt Form.

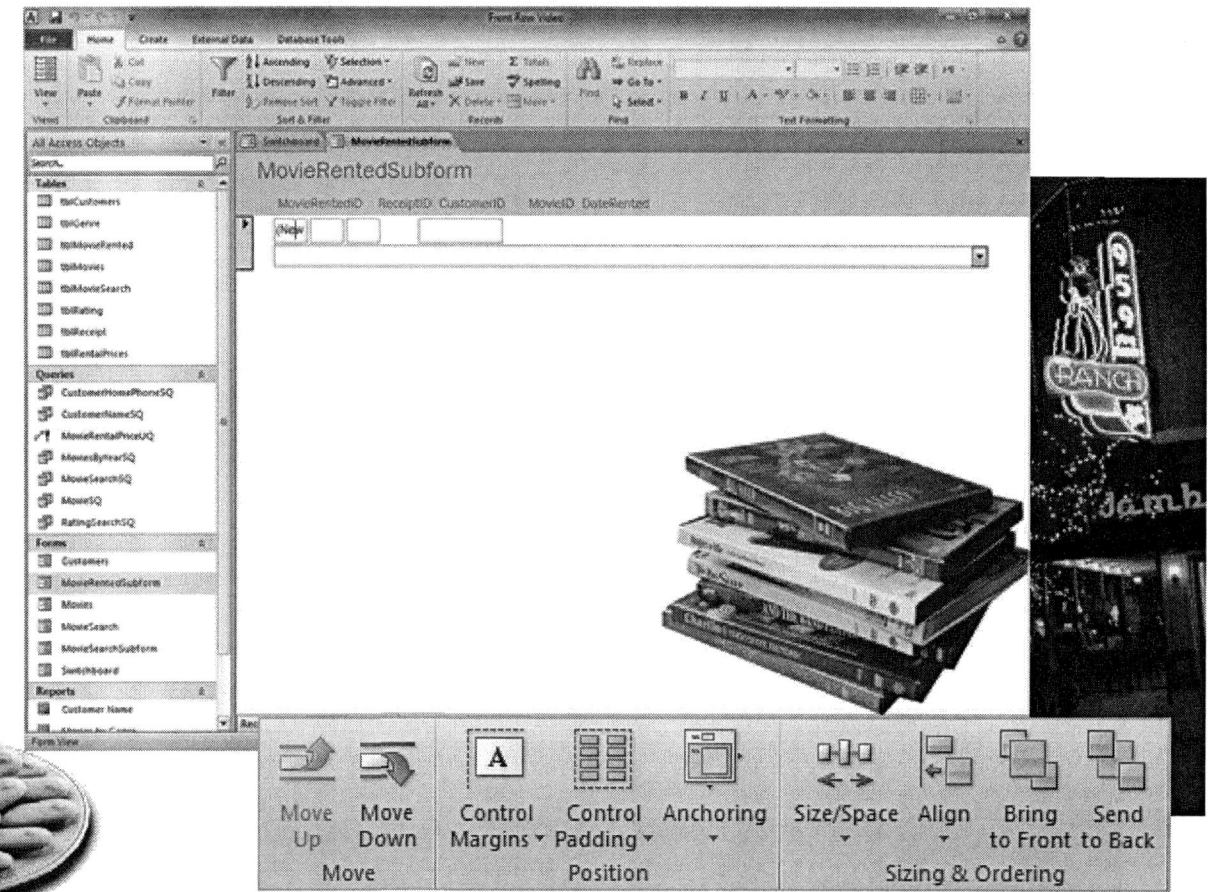

Practice Activities

Lesson 4: Form Design

Try This: Do the following steps

1. Open your Brown Bag Lunch database. Or, you may download **BBL Adv ver4.accdb**

2. Create a Form with the Form Wizard. Use tblReceiptProducts as the Record Source and select all available Fields. Select the Datasheet Layout.

Name the Form: ReceiptProductsSubform.

3. Use the Form Tools in Design View to format the datasheet with alternating Row colors.

4. Select the ProductID Text Field and delete the Control and the Label.

5. Create a Combo Box Control and select tblProducts as the Record Source. Choose ProductId and Item from the available Fields. Sort the Items Ascending. Hide the Key Column (ProductID). Select ProductID to Store in tblReceiptProducts. Enter a Label: Products.

Finish the Wizard.

6. Select the new Combo Box use the Property Sheet to change the name to ProductsCombo.

7. Use the Form Design Tools->Design to change the Tab Order so that the DateReceipt is first, ProductsCombo is second and Memo is third.

8. Save your changes. Test the Form in Datasheet View. Does the Products Combo work?

9. Close the Subform.

10. Close the Brown Bag Lunch database.

Test Yourself

1. Which of the following is true about Tabular Arrangement in Form Design?
(Give all correct answers.)
A. Arranges Fields in a Table
B. Allows the use of the Arrange commands for moving and merging Fields
Tip: Advanced Access, page 101

2. Which is true about Cells in a Table?
(Give all correct answers.)
A. Margin is the space between the Cell border and the Data
B. Default Margin is none
C. Margins can be edited, but Padding cannot
Tip: Advanced Access, page 105

3. Which term refers to the space between Cells in a Table?
A. Margin
B. Padding
C. Anchoring
D. Gap
Tip: Advanced Access, page 105

4. Anchoring locks a Cell into place, keeping it in the same spot, such as Top Left regardless of resizing.
A. True
B. False
Tip: Advanced Access, page 107

5. Which is a method of changing the size of a Cell in Access?
A. Form Design Tools-> Arrange-> Sizing & Ordering-> Size and Space
B. Form Design Tools-> Table Tools-> Sizing
C. Table Tools-> Layout-> Cell Size
D. Edited with the Property Sheet
Tip: Advanced Access, page 108, 109

Access 2010: Advanced Form Design

The Receipt Form, part 2

Advanced Access Objectives

In this lesson, you will learn how to:

1. Create a Select Query that combines (JOINS) several Tables by matching Keys.

2. Create a Blank Form and select a Query as the Record Source in the Form Properties.

3. Add existing Fields to a Form.

4. Add a Subform and Link the Form and Subform by three Key Fields.

5. Test the Receipt Form, see if it works.

© 2012 Comma Productions, LLC

Lesson 5 : The Receipt Form, part 2

1. Readings
Read Lesson 5 in the Advanced Access guide, page 119-148.

Project
Create and format a Receipt Form that uses a Combo Box to look up a customer by their phone number.

Downloads
FrontRowVideo Adv5.accdb
BBL Adv ver5.accdb

2. Practice
Do the Practice Activity on page 149.

3. Assessment
Review the Test questions on page 150.

Create Ribbon

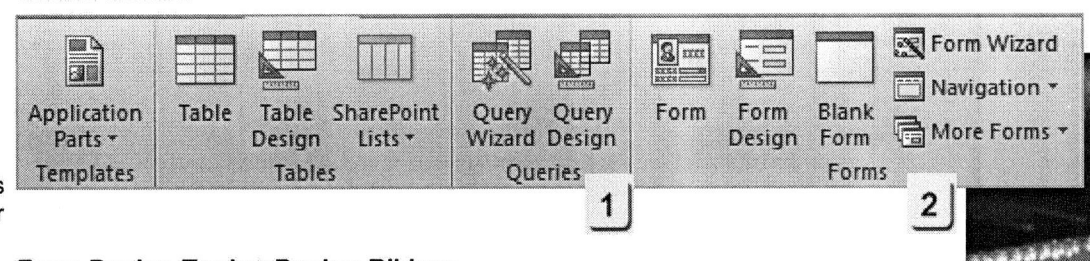

Form Design Tools->Design Ribbon

Menu Maps

From the **Create Ribbon**
1. Create ->Queries->Query Design, page 128
2. Create ->Forms->Blank Form, page 131

From the **Form Design Tools->Design Ribbon**.
3. Form Design Tools->Design->Tools->Property Sheet, page 132
4. Form Design Tools->Design->Header & Footer, page 133
5. Form Design Tools->Design->Tools->Add Existing Fields, page 138
6. Form Design Tools->Design->Controls->Subform/Subreport, page 140

The Receipt Form, part 2

The Receipt Form should work like this: You should be able to type in a customer phone number and have the Form display the name and address. So, this Form needs a Combo Box that will look up the phone number, a Query that will find the name and address that matches that phone number, and a little bit of formatting to make it happen.

Microsoft Office Access 2010: Example of the completed Receipt Form

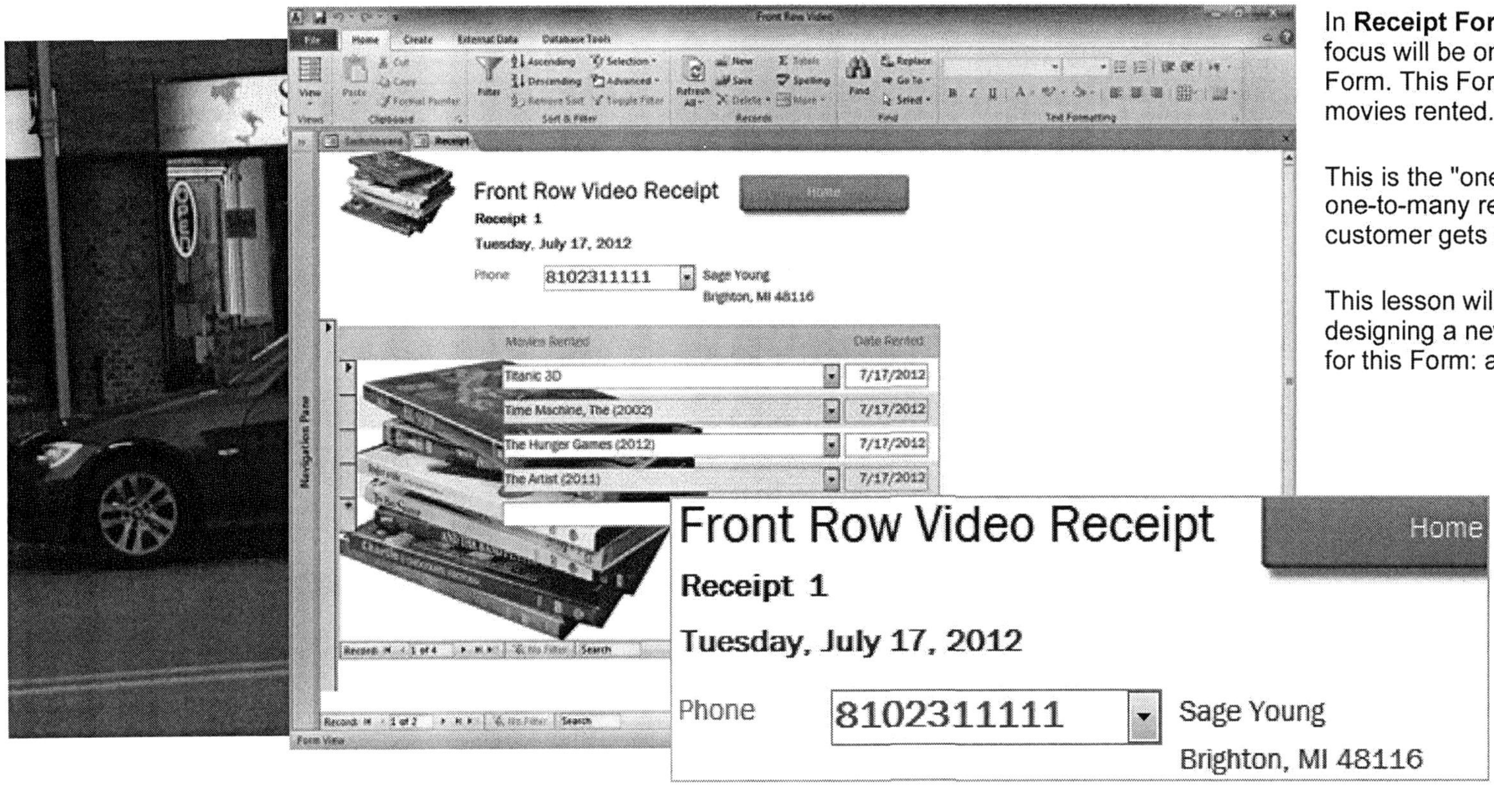

In **Receipt Form, part 2,** the focus will be on the Receipt Form. This Form will list the movies rented.

This is the "one" part of the one-to-many relationship. One customer gets many movies.

This lesson will begin by designing a new Record Source for this Form: a Select Query.

What is the Plan?

One customer may get many movies. So, the Receipt Form will have a Form and Subform. The Receipt Form will also use a Combo box to look up a customer by their phone number. The Subform will list the movies rented.

Create a Record Source for the Form

The **ReceiptSQ** Select Query will JOIN the Receipt Table with a Query, CustomerNameSQ, that combines (concatenates) the name and address fields.

Create the Form: Receipt

The Receipt Form will use a Combo Box to look up the customer's phone number and display their name and address.

That's the plan.

Microsoft Office Access 2010: Example of the completed Receipt Form in Design View

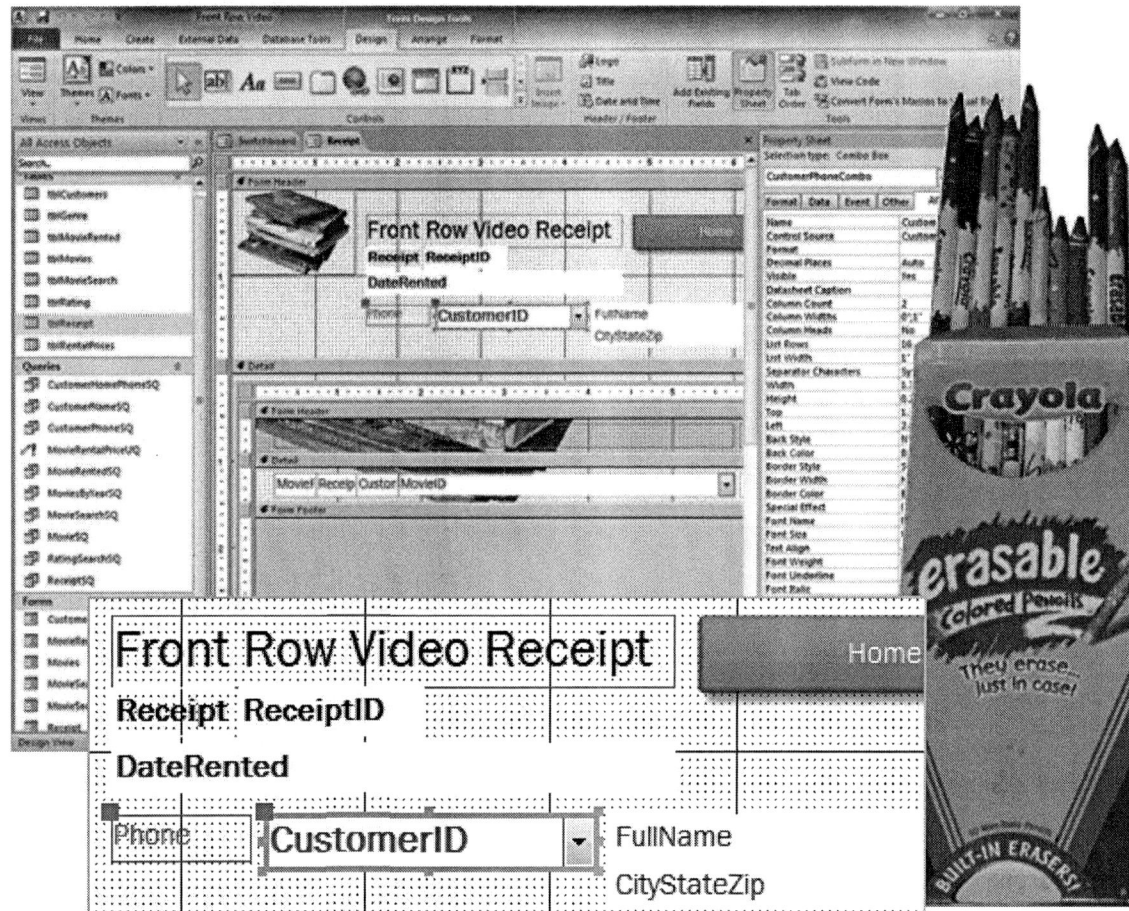

Before You Begin

Before You Begin: Open the Sample Database
Go to **Start -> All Programs ->Microsoft Office**.
Click on **Microsoft Office Access 2010.**
Access will prompt you to open a database.
Select: <u>FrontRowVideo Adv5.accdb</u>

The sample file, <u>**FrontRowVideo Adv5.accdb,**</u>
was developed in the previous lesson. If you did
well in the previous lesson, you can continue with
your own database if you wish. Your Forms
probably look better than the sample ones.

Keep going....

Memo to Self: Databases need to Read and
Write. Click **Enable Content** if you see the
Security Warning.

Start ->All Programs-> Microsoft Office-> Microsoft Access 2010

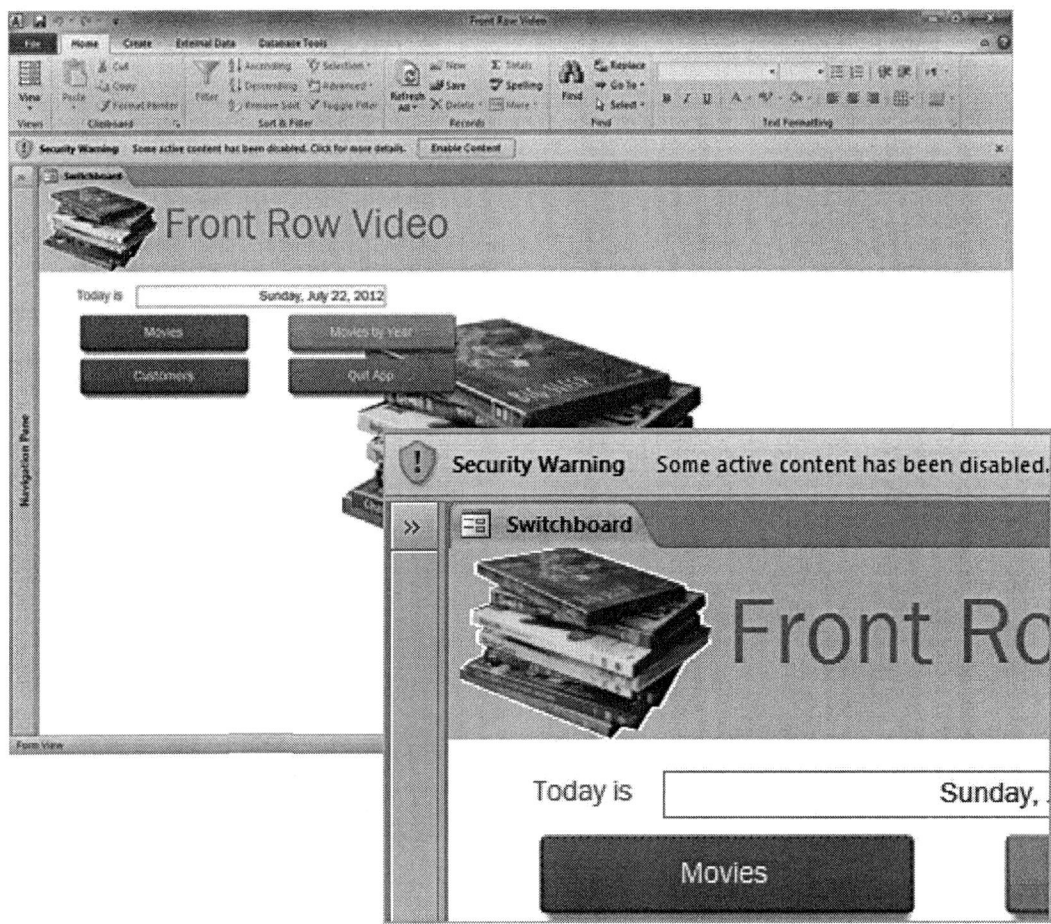

Know Your Data
Try This: Review the Database
Open the **Navigation Pane.**
Go to **All Access Objects.**

The Front Row Video has the following:
Eight Tables: tblCustomers, tblGenre, tblMovieRented, tblMovies, tblMovieSearch, tblRating, tblRecipt and tblRentalPrices.

Seven Queries: CustomerHomePhoneSQ, CustomerNameSQ, MovieRentalPriceUQ, MoviesByYearSQ, MovieSearchSQ, MovieSQ and RatingSearchSQ.

Six Forms: Customers, Movies, MovieSearch, MovieSearchSubform, MoviesRentedSubform and the Switchboard.

Three Reports: Customer Name, Movies by Genre, and Movies by Year.

One Macro: OpenSearchMovie

All Access Objects

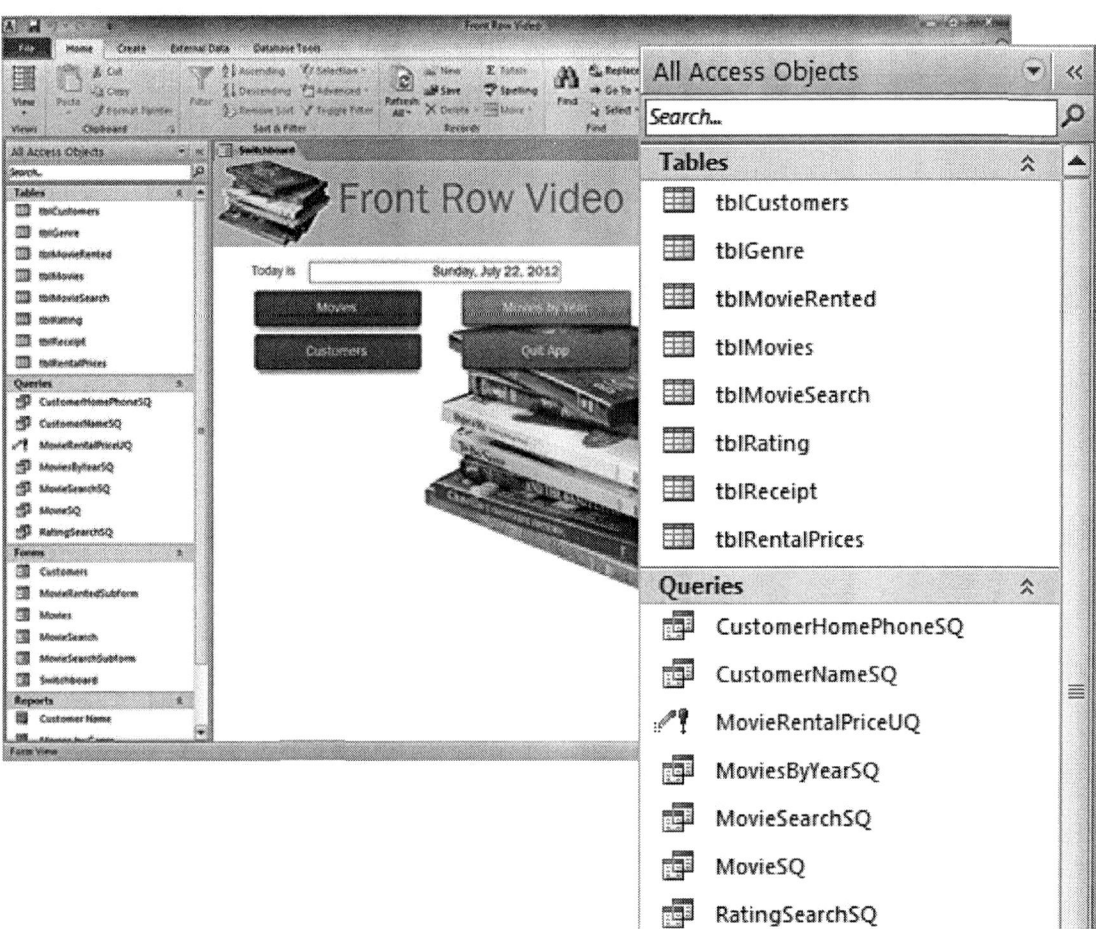

Know Your Data: tblReceipt

The Receipt Form will store data in a simple Table, tblReceipt. Our discussion always begins by reviewing the data.

1. Try it: Review the Receipt Table
Go to **All Access Objects ->Table.**
Open a **Table: tblRecipt.**

Try This, Too: Change the View
Go to Home->Views->View.
Select a **View: Design View.**

What Do You See? This Table, tblReceipt, has numbers only:
ReceiptID (the Primary Key)
CustomerID (a Foreign Key)
DateRented (Date/Time)

This Table is in Third Normal Form: the Key, the whole Key and nothing but the Key.
Please **Close** tblReceipt.

Keep going...

All Access Objects ->Tables

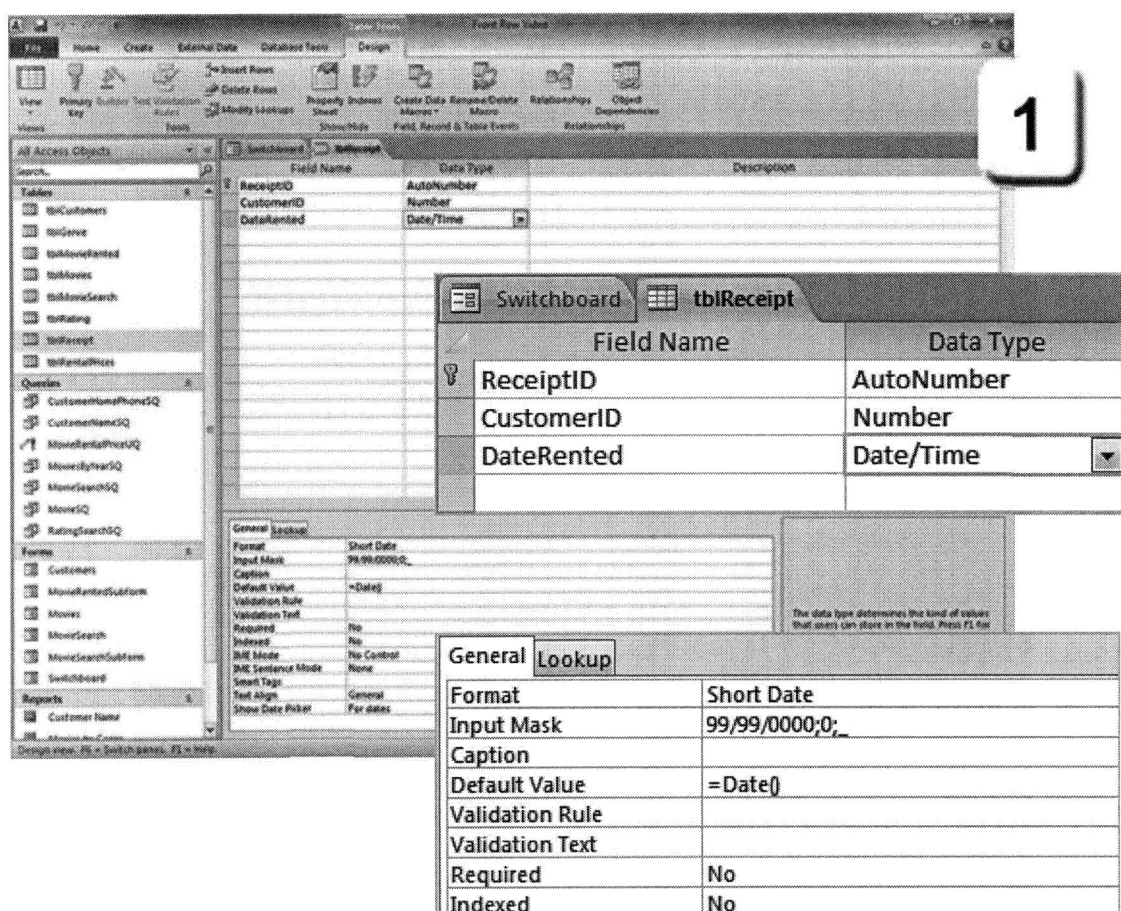

Field Name	Data Type
ReceiptID	AutoNumber
CustomerID	Number
DateRented	Date/Time

General	Lookup	
Format	Short Date	
Input Mask	99/99/0000;0;_	
Caption		
Default Value	=Date()	
Validation Rule		
Validation Text		
Required	No	
Indexed	No	

Take Two

Know Your Data: CustomerNameSQ

We want to display the customer's name and address on the screen after we look up the phone number. We already have a Query that combines (concatenates) these Fields. Let's see if it meets our needs.

2. Try it: Review the Customer Query
Go to **All Access Objects ->Queries.**
Open a Query: CustomerNameSQ.

Try This, Too: Change the View
Go to **Home->Views->View.**
Select a **View: Design View.**

What Do You See? The Query has one Table: tblCustomers. In addition to the CustomerID, FirstName and LastName. there are three Fields which combine (concatenate) the name and address:
FullName
LastNameFirst
CItyStateZip

Keep going...

All Access Objects ->Queries

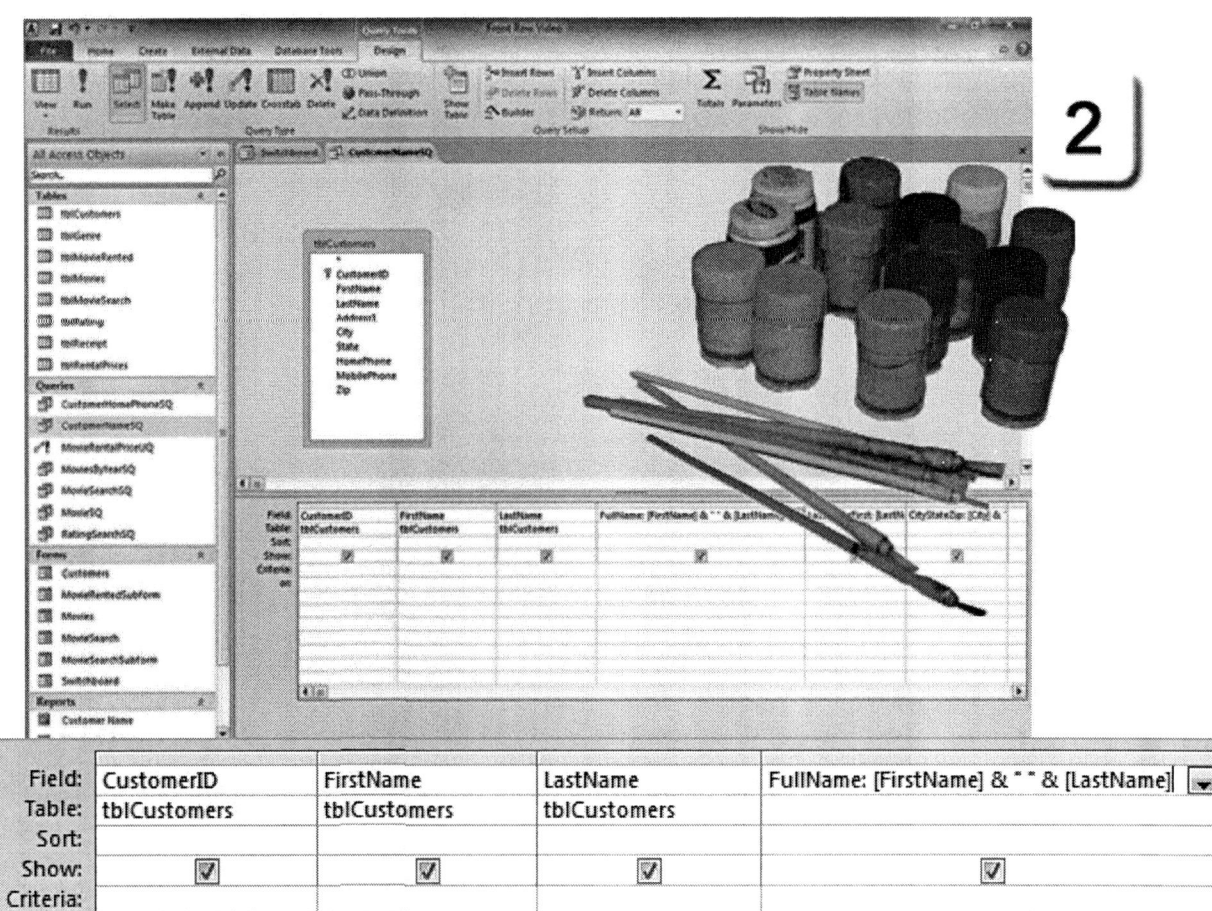

2

Field:	CustomerID	FirstName	LastName	FullName: [FirstName] & " " & [LastName]
Table:	tblCustomers	tblCustomers	tblCustomers	
Sort:				
Show:	☑	☑	☑	☑
Criteria:				

Know Your Data:
Edit the Query

The Receipt Form will look up a customer's phone number. The CustomerNameSQ should include a phone number as well.

3. Try it: Edit the CustomerNameSQ
Go to tblCustomers.
Double-click a Field: HomePhone.

What Do You See? The HomePhone Field should be added to the QBE Grid on the bottom of the Query.

Do This, Now: Save the Query
Go to **File->Save**.

Close the CustomerNameSQ Query.

This Query will be used as the Record Source for the Receipt Form.

Query Tools ->Design

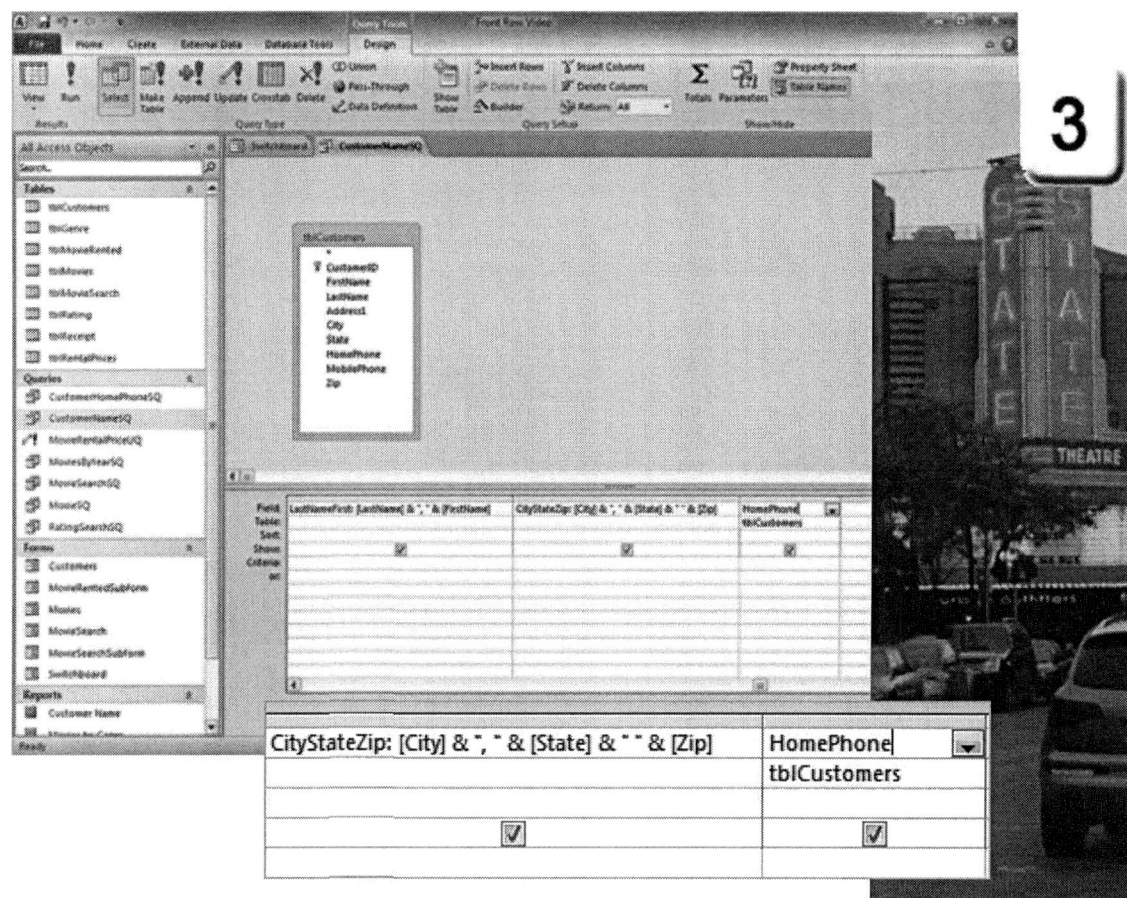

Create a Record Source for the Receipt Form

The Receipt Form will use a new Query that is based on tblReceipt.

However tblReceipt is only numbers, so we need to look up the customer's name and address in a Query, CustomerNameSQ, and link that to tblReceipt by a common Key, CustomerID.

1. Try it: Create a Select Query
Go to **Create ->Queries->Query Design.**

What Do You See? A blank query will open. The **Show Table** window will prompt you to choose a Table or Query for the Record Source.

Select a Table: tblReceipt.
Click **Add**.

Select a Query: CustomerNameSQ.
Click **Add**.
Click **Close**. Keep going...

Create ->Queries->Query Design

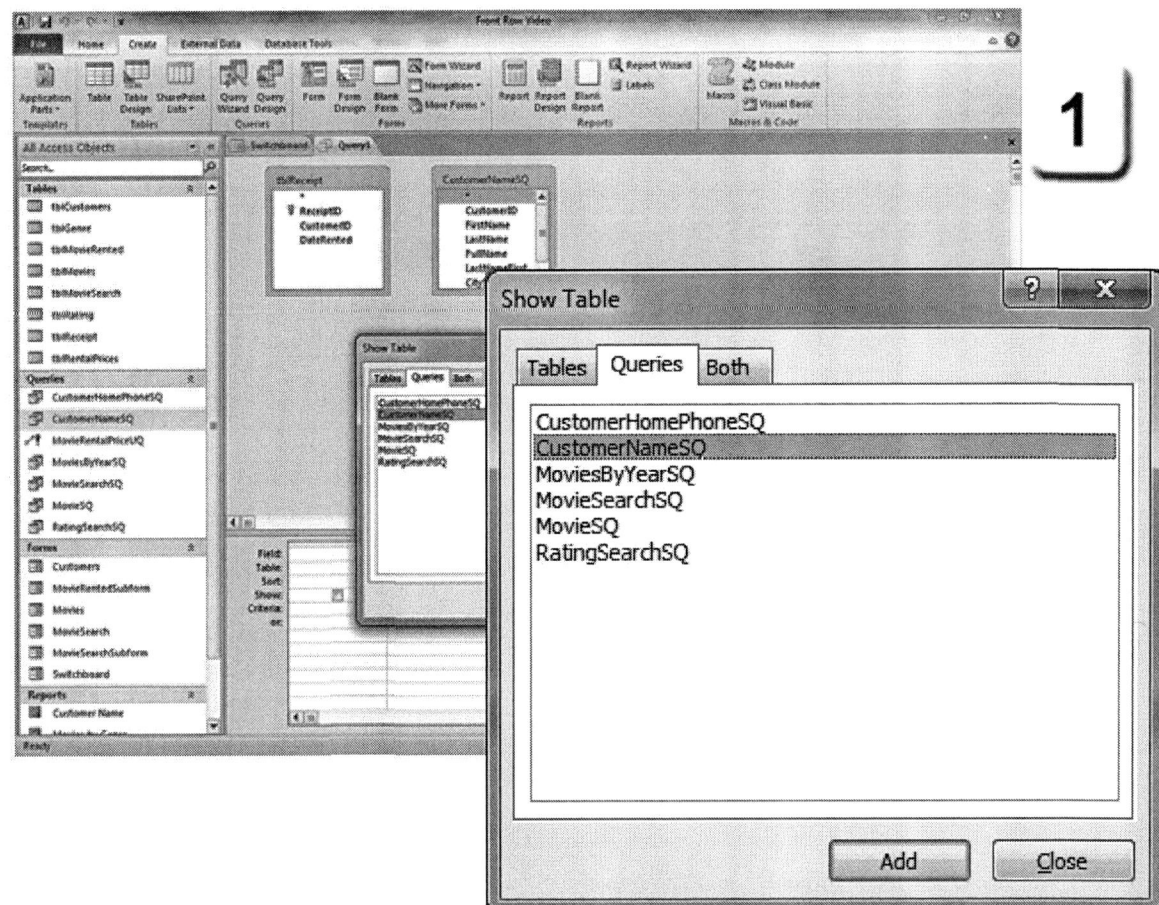

Exam 77-885: Microsoft Access 2010
4. Creating and Managing Queries
4.2. Manage source tables and relationships: Use the Show Table command

Query Tools ->Design->Query Type->Select

Join the Table and Query

Both the Table and Query have the same Key: CustomerID. We can create an ad hoc relationship between the Table and the Query, a JOIN.

2. Try it: Create Ad Hoc Relationships

Go to tblReceipt.
Select a Field: CustomerID.
Drag CustomerID to the Query, CustomerNameSQ and drop it on the matching Key, CustomerID.

What Do You See? There should be a JOIN between the Table and the Query. Now, if we have a CustomerID in tblReceipt we can look up the name, address and phone that goes with that CustomerID.

Keep going...

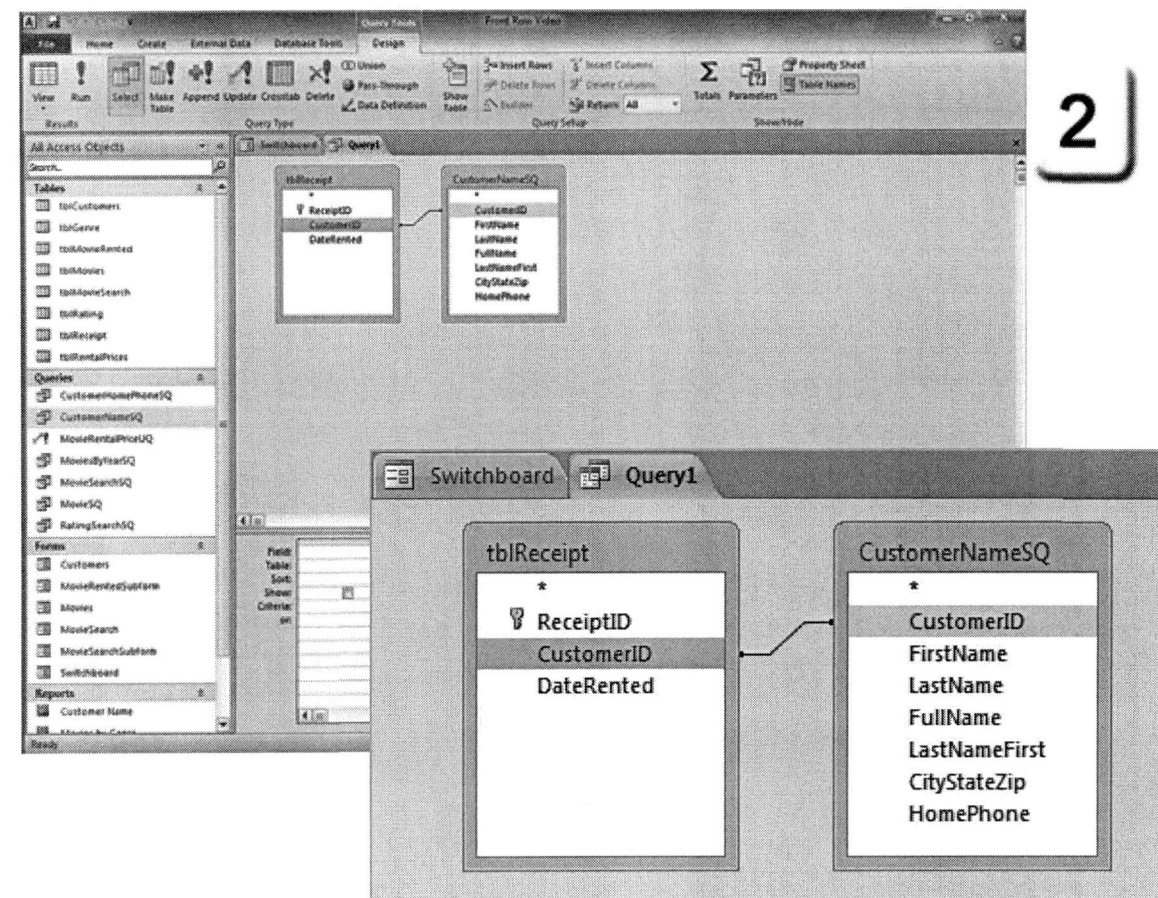

Exam 77-885: Microsoft Access 2010
4. Creating and Managing Queries
4.2. Manage source tables and relationships: Create Ad Hoc Relationships

Query Tools ->Design->Query Type->Select

Add Fields to the Query

3. Try it: Add Fields to the Query

From tblReceipt select the following Fields:
ReceiptID
CustomerID
DateRented

From CustomerNameSQ select these Fields:
FullName
CityStateZip
HomePhone

Do This, Now: Save the Query
Go to **File->Save**.
Enter a name: ReceiptSQ.
Click **OK**.

Close the Query. The Record Source for the Receipt Form is done.

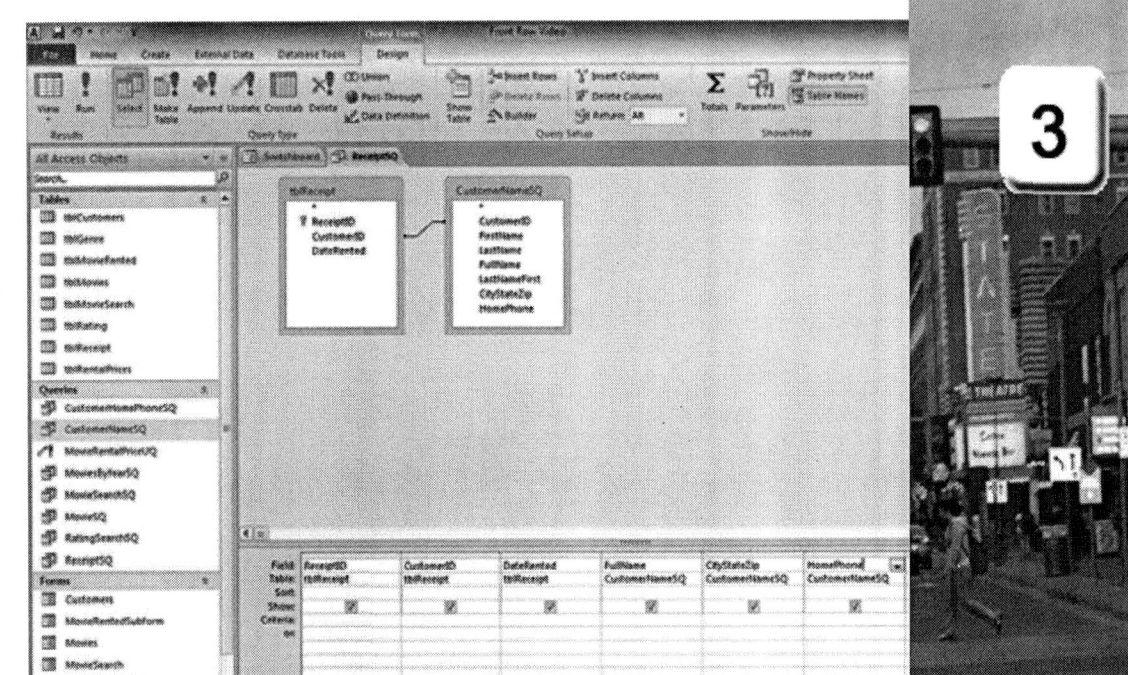

Field:	ReceiptID	CustomerID	DateRented	FullName	CityStateZip	HomePhone
Table:	tblReceipt	tblReceipt	tblReceipt	CustomerNameSQ	CustomerNameSQ	CustomerNameSQ
Sort:						
Show:	☑	☑	☑	☑	☑	☑
Criteria:						
or:						

Exam 77-885: Microsoft Access 2010
4. Creating and Managing Queries
4.3. Manipulate fields: Add Fields to a Query

Create a Receipt Form

We have everything we need to create the
Receipt Form, now. Let's start with a blank
Form and build it together.

1. Try it: Create a Blank Form
Go to **Create ->Forms->Blank Form.**

What Do You See? A new, blank Form will
open in Form View.

Try This, Too: Change the View
Go to **Home->Views->View.**
Select a View: **Design View.**

And Do This, As Well: View the Properties
Go to **Form Design Tools->Design->Tools.**
Click on: **Property Sheet.**

Keep going...

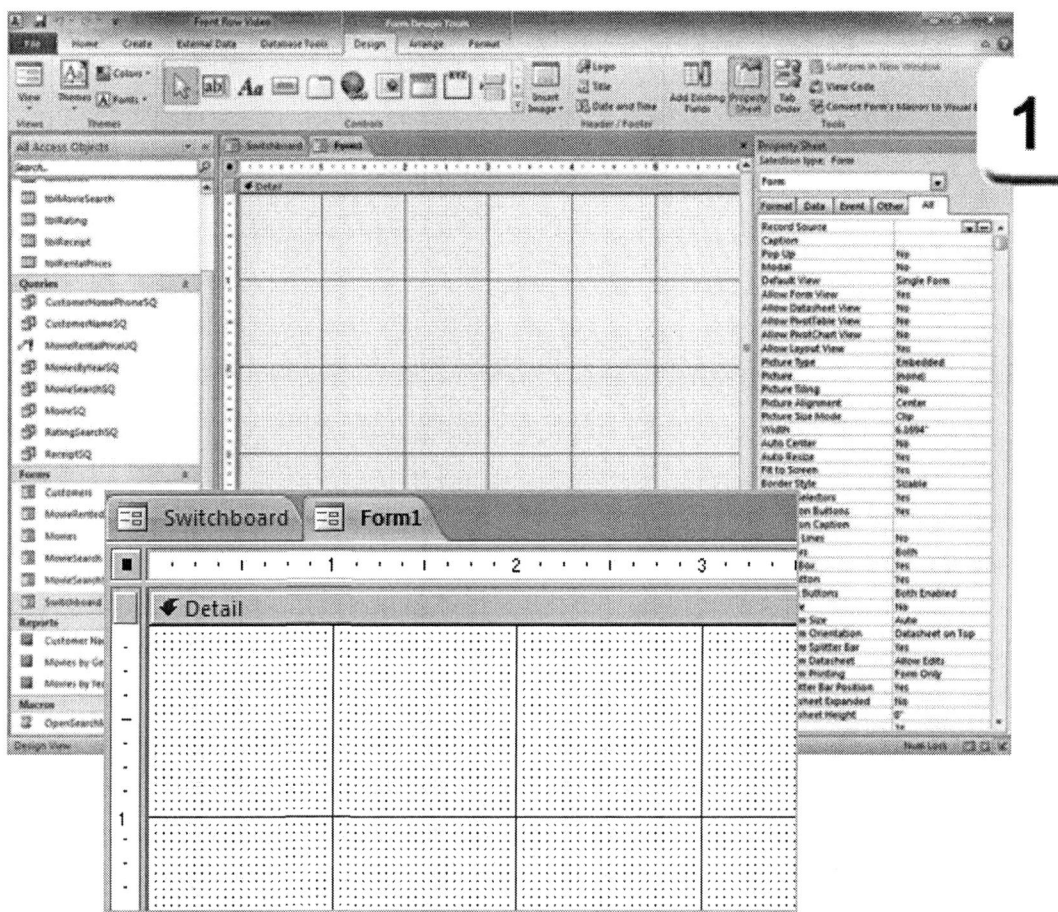

Exam 77-885: Microsoft Access 2010
3. Building Forms
3.1. Create forms: Create a Blank Form

Form Design Tools->Design->Tools->Property Sheet->All

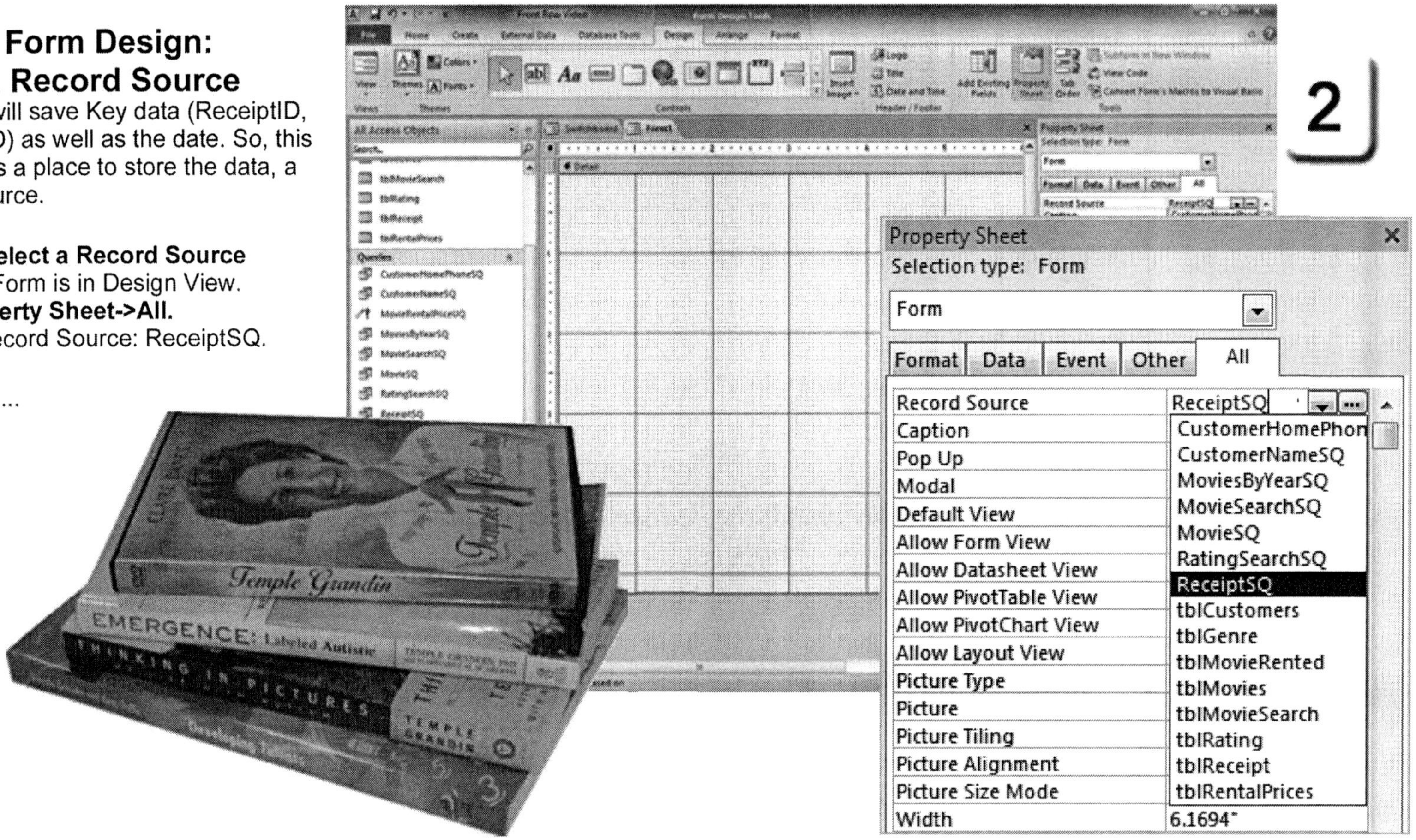

Receipt Form Design:
Select a Record Source

The Form will save Key data (ReceiptID, CustomerID) as well as the date. So, this Form needs a place to store the data, a Record Source.

2. Try it: Select a Record Source
The blank Form is in Design View.
Go to **Property Sheet->All.**
Select a Record Source: ReceiptSQ.

Keep going...

Property Sheet ✕

Selection type: Form

| Form | ▾ |

| Format | Data | Event | Other | All |

Record Source	ReceiptSQ	▾ ...
Caption	CustomerHomePhon
Pop Up	CustomerNameSQ
Modal	MoviesByYearSQ
Default View	MovieSearchSQ
Allow Form View	MovieSQ
Allow Datasheet View	RatingSearchSQ
Allow PivotTable View	ReceiptSQ
Allow PivotChart View	tblCustomers
Allow Layout View	tblGenre
Picture Type	tblMovieRented
Picture	tblMovies
Picture Tiling	tblMovieSearch
Picture Alignment	tblRating
Picture Size Mode	tblReceipt
Width	6.1694" tblRentalPrices

Exam 77-885: Microsoft Access 2010
3. Building Forms
3.2. Apply Form Design options: View the Property Sheet

Receipt Form Design:
Edit the Header

Please take a moment to add a Header and decorate it. We have walked through these steps in other lessons.

3. Try it: Add a Title
Go to **Form Design Tools->Design.**
Go to **Header & Footer->Title.**
Edit the Title: Front Row Video Receipt.

And Try This: Add a Logo
Go to **Form Design Tools->Design.**
Go to **Header & Footer->Logo.**
Browse for an Image: popcorn1.

Please resize and format the Title and Logo as you wish.

Now, Do This: Save the Form
Go to **File->Save.**
Enter a name: Receipt.

That's the Header with all of its business branding. Now, for the User Interface....

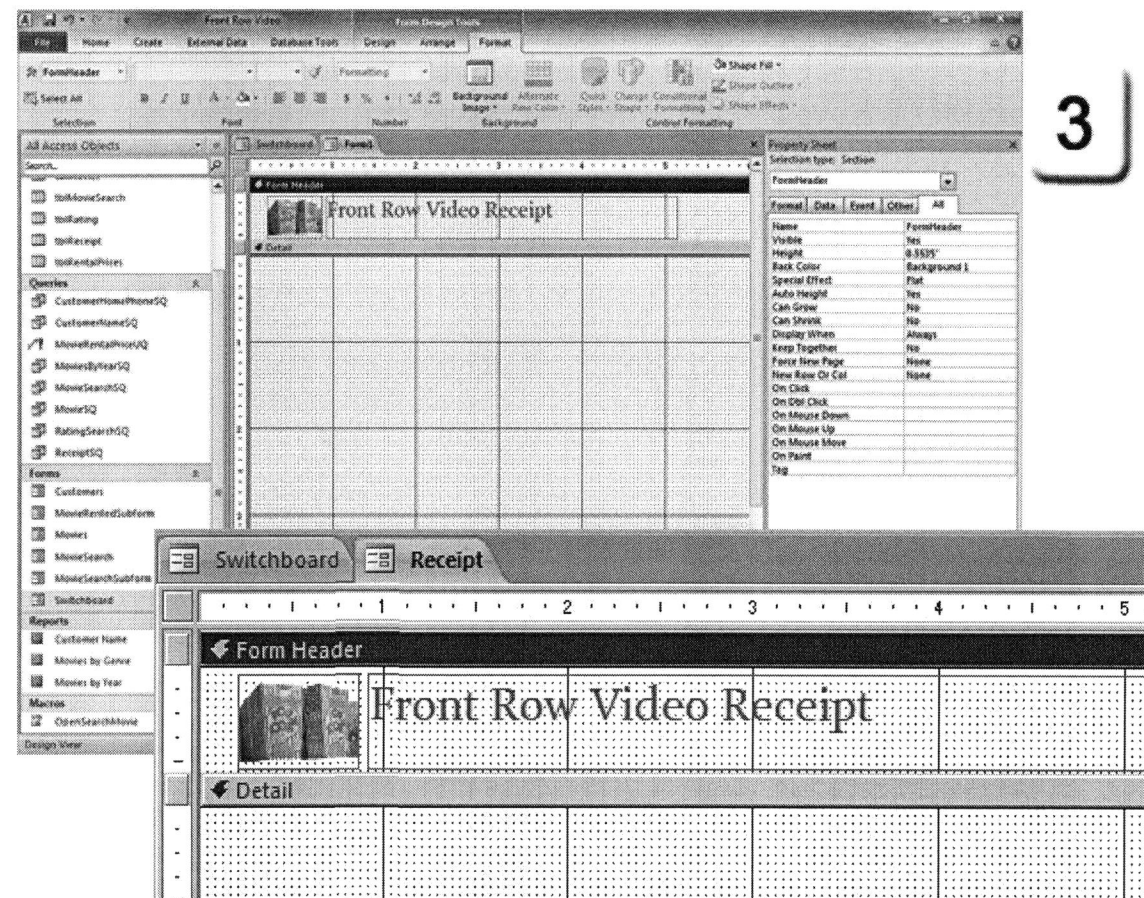

Exam 77-885: Microsoft Access 2010
3. Building Forms
3.2. Apply Form Design options: Format Header/Footer

Receipt Form Design:
Add a Combo Box

We want to be able to look up a customer by their phone number. Here are the steps to create the CustomerPhone Combo.

4. Try it: Add a Combo Box
The Receipt Form is still open in Design View.
Go to **Form Design Tools->Design->Controls.**
Select a Control: **Combo Box.**

Click anywhere in the Detail section of the Form. The Combo Box Wizard will open.

Try This, Too: Walk Through the Wizard
Select a Record Source: Table or Query.
Click **Next.**

Keep going...

Form Design Tools->Design->Controls->Combo Box

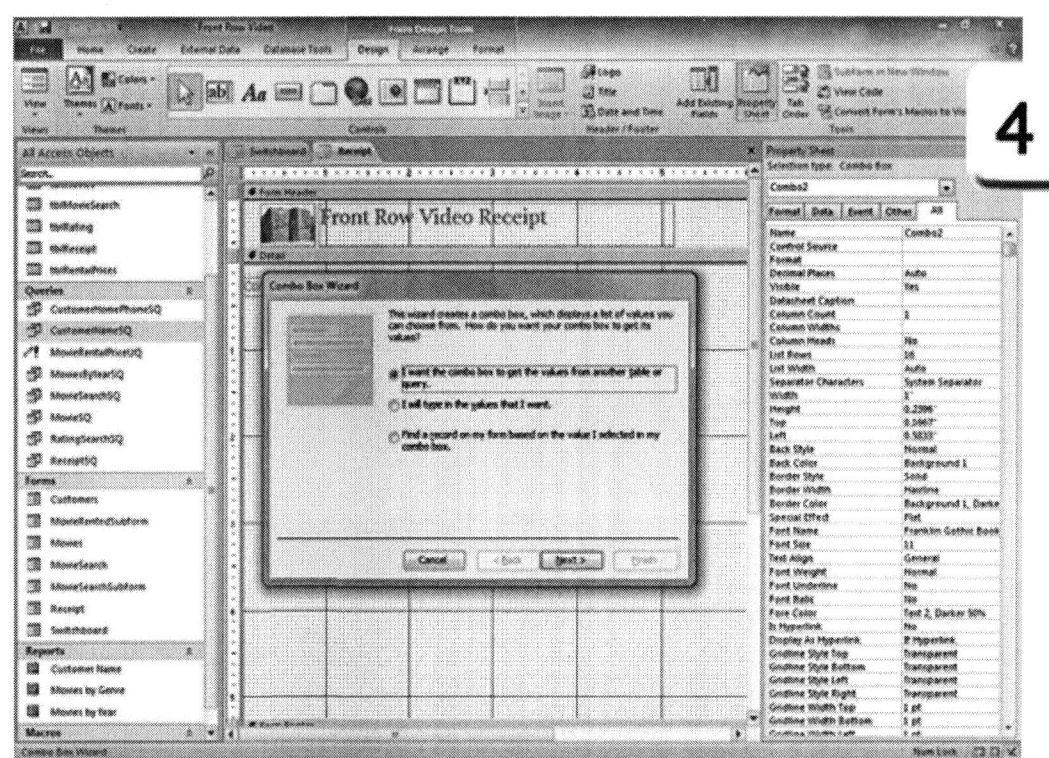

Exam 77-885: Microsoft Access 2010
3. Building Forms
3.2. Apply Form Design options: Add a Drop Down Box

Receipt Form Design: Combo Box Options

Here are the answers to the first steps in the Combo Box Wizard.

5. Try it: Select a Record Source
Select a Query: CustomerNameSQ

Go Next: Select the Fields
Select two available Fields:
CustomerID
HomePhone

Go Next: Sort the Fields
Select HomePhone to Sort (ascending)

Go Next: Keep going...

Form Design Tools->Design->Controls->Combo Box

Exam 77-885: Microsoft Access 2010
3. Building Forms
3.2. Apply Form Design options: Add a Drop Down Box

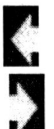

Form Design Tools->Design->Controls->Combo Box

Receipt Form Design:
Combo Box Key Decision
There are two Columns in this Combo Box: CustomerID, which will be stored in the Receipt Table, tblReceipt, and HomePhone, which is what the User should see when they select the Combo Box. If you want the User to see the second Column, you have to hide (resize to zero) the first Column.

6. Try it: Hide the First Column
Select the first Column: CustomerID.
Resize the first Column: 0"

Go **Next**. Keep going...

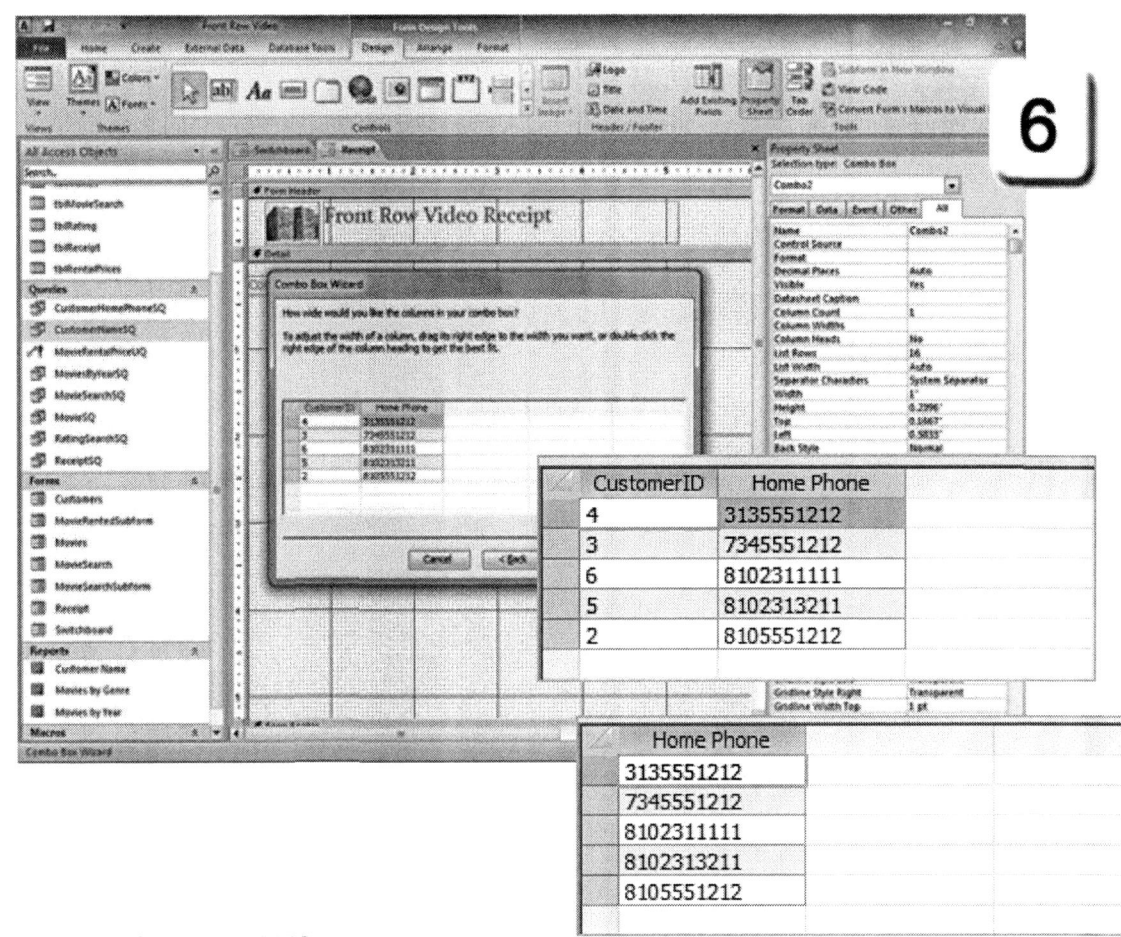

CustomerID	Home Phone
4	3135551212
3	7345551212
6	8102311111
5	8102313211
2	8105551212

Home Phone
3135551212
7345551212
8102311111
8102313211
8105551212

Exam 77-885: Microsoft Access 2010
3. Building Forms
3.2. Apply Form Design options: Add a Drop Down Box

Receipt Form Design:
Combo Box Store Value

7. Try it: Select a Field to Store
There are two Fields available.
Select: CustomerID.

Go Next. Store a Value
Store that value in this field: CustomerID.

Go Next. Enter a Label
Label: Phone Number

Click **Finish**.

Try This, Too: Format the Combo Box
The Combo Box is still selected.
Go to **Property Sheet->All.**
Width: 1.75"
Height: 0.25"
Top: 0.1667"
Left: 1.25"
Font Size: 12
Font Color: Red (#FF0000).

Let's take a look at what we just did.
Keep going

Form Design Tools->Design->Controls->Combo Box

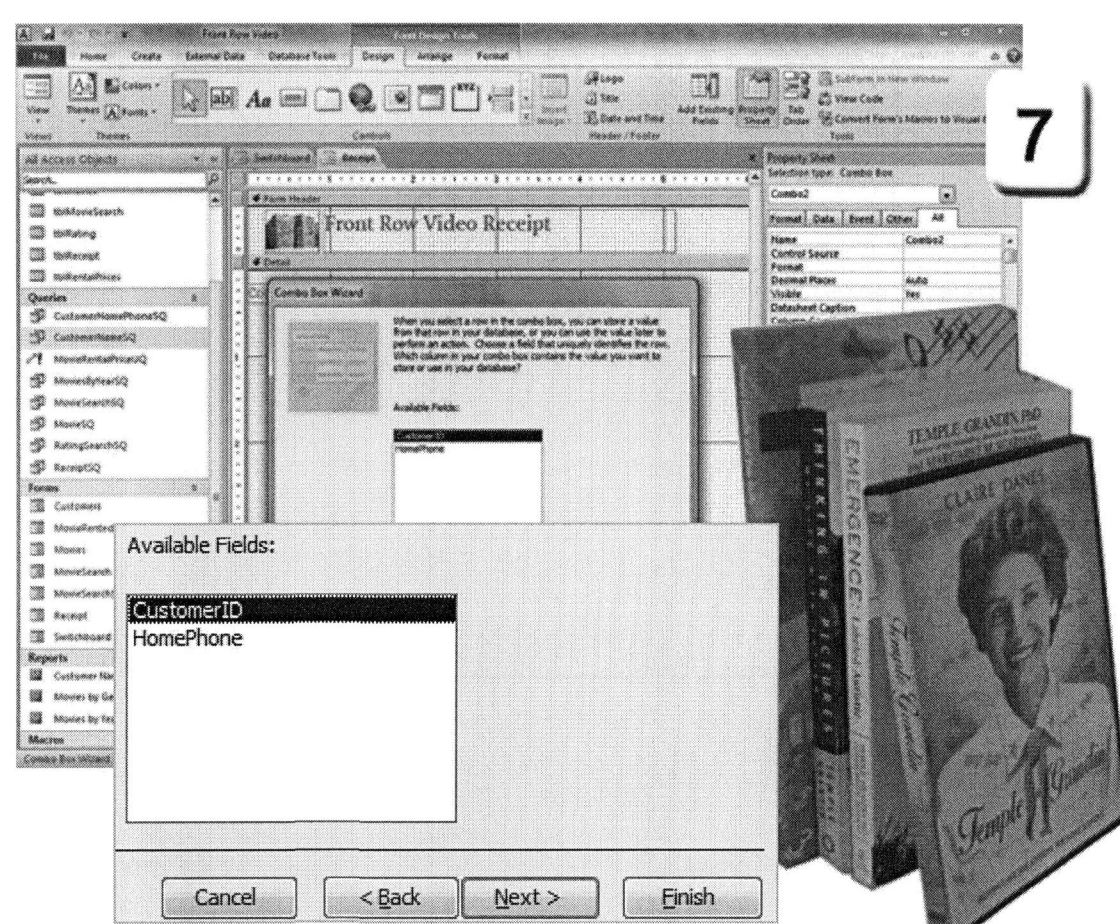

Exam 77-885: Microsoft Access 2010
3. Building Forms
3.2. Apply Form Design options: Add a Drop Down Box

Receipt Form Design:
Add the Customer Data

You can display the customer's name and address in Text Box Controls. The ReceiptSQ Query, the Record Source for the Receipt Form, includes FullName and CityStateZip so they can be added as Existing Fields.

8. Try it: Add Existing Fields
The Receipt Form is still open in Design View. Go to **Form Design Tools->Design->Tools.** Click on: **Add Existing Fields.**

What Do You See? The Available Fields will be shown in the Field List.

Try This, Too: Add Two Fields
Drag two Fields to the Detail Section:
FullName
CityStateZip

In the example on this page, the Control Labels were deleted and the Text Box Controls were resized.

Save. Save. Save!

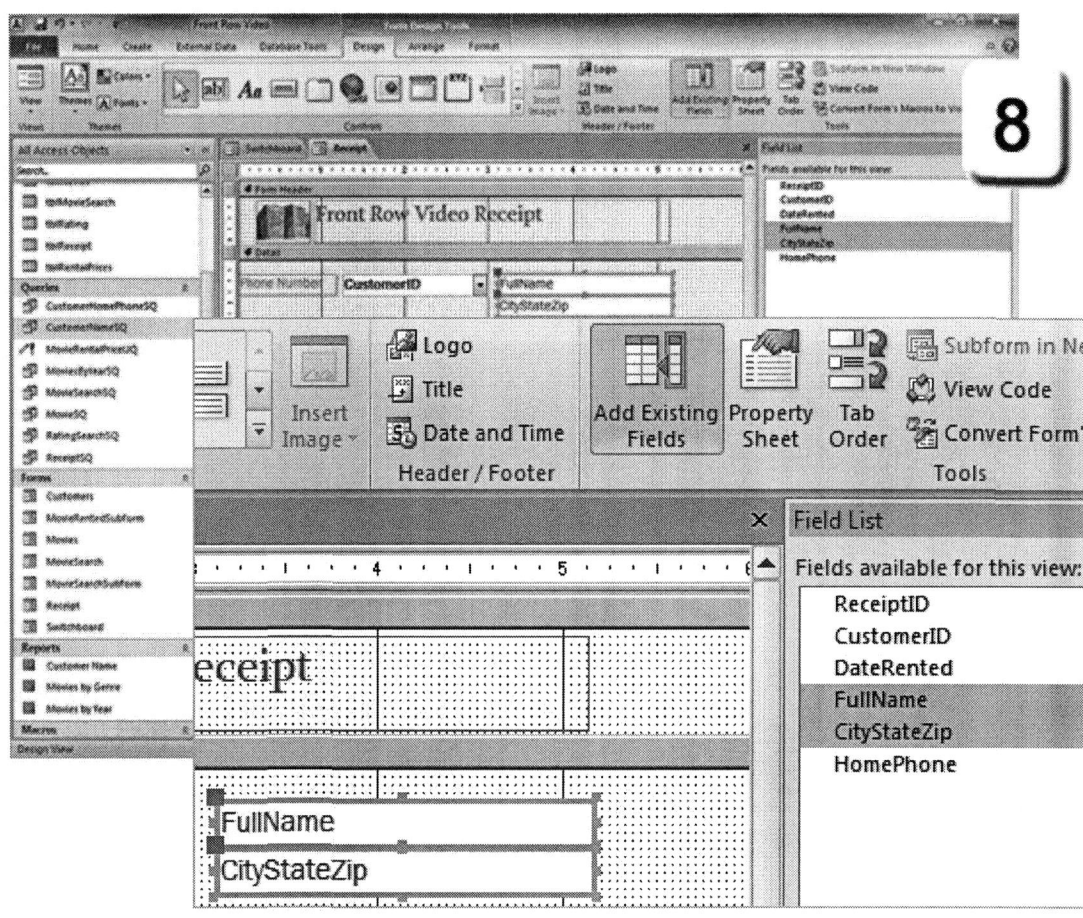

Exam 77-885: Microsoft Access 2010
3. Building Forms
3.2. Apply Form Design options: Add Existing Fields

Test the Form

So, does it work? There's only way to find out: test the Form as a User would.

Before You Begin: Change the View
Go to Form Design Tools->Design->Views.
Select a View: Form View.

9. Try it: Select a Phone Number
Go to the CustomerPhoneCombo.
Select a Phone Number from the Combo Box.

What Do You See? Does the customer's name and address change when you select a phone number from the Combo Box?

Try This, Too: Type a Phone Number
Go to the CustomerPhoneCombo.
Type: 8102313211.
Type ENTER on the keyboard.

Did that work, too?

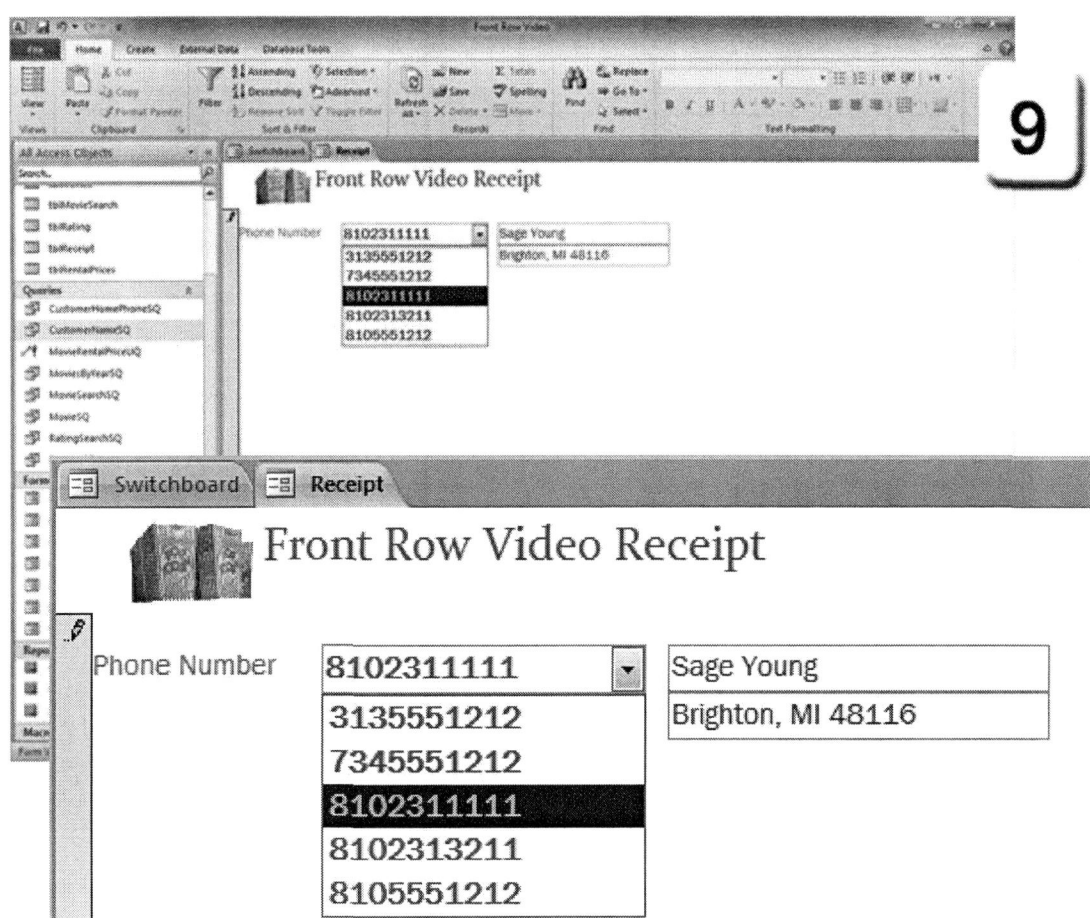

Form Design Tools->Design->Controls->Subform/Subreport

Add the Subform to the Form

The Subform is ready to be added to the MovieSearch Form. First, you need to open the Master Form in Design View. Then you can add the Child Subform as a Control.

Before You Begin: Change the View
Go to **Home ->Views->View->Form Design.** The Form Design Tools should be available. Please turn on the Property Sheet as well.

1. Try This: Add a Subform
Go to **Form Design Tools->Design->Controls.**
Click on **Subform/Subreport.**
Click on the **Detail Section** of the Receipt Form. The **Subform Wizard** should open.

What Do You See? You will be prompted to select an existing Table, Query or Form.

Go to **Use an Existing Form.**
Select MovieRentedSubform.

Click **Next.** Keep going.

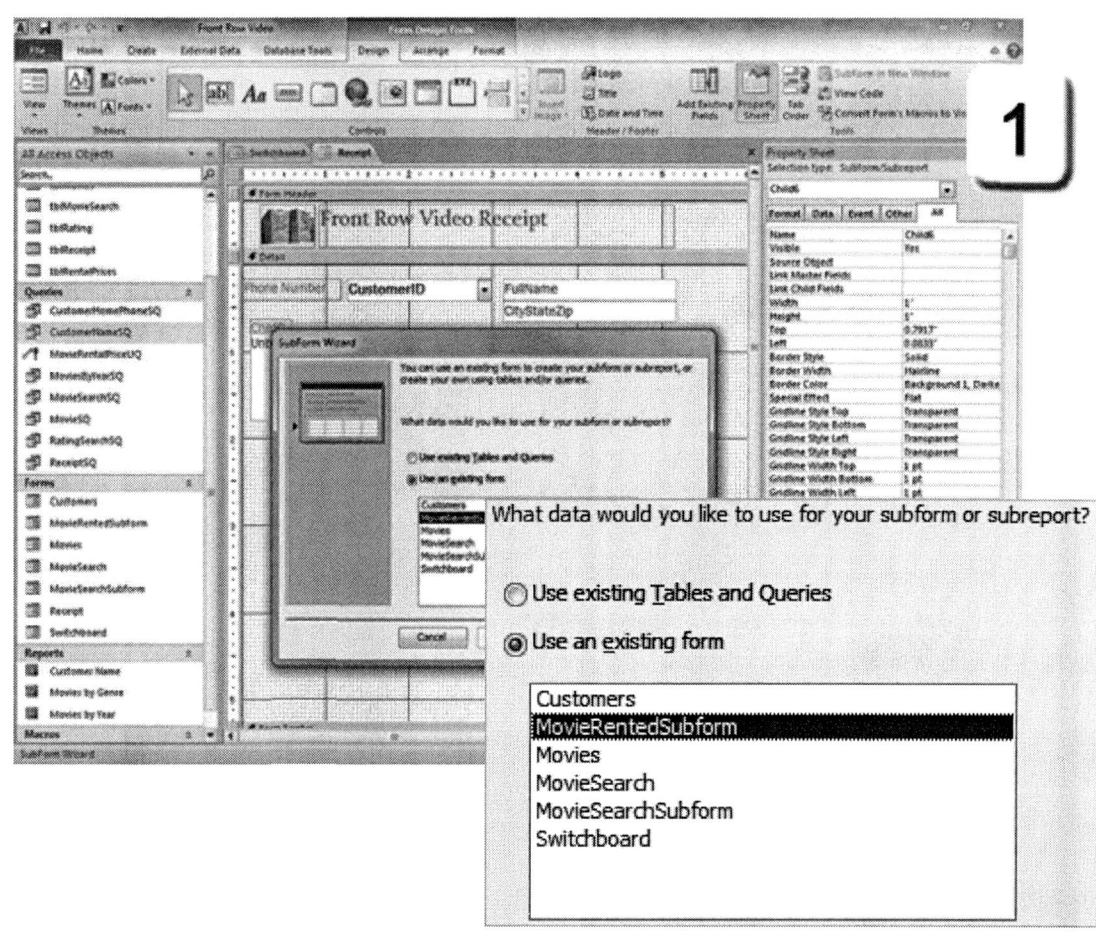

Exam 77-885: Microsoft Access 2010
3. Building Forms
3.2. Apply Form Design options: Add a Subform

Subform: Select the Fields

The next step in the Subform Wizard asks you to choose which Field(s) will be used to link the Master Form to the Child, the Subform.

We will select three Fields which the Subform will inherit. For example, when a CustomerID is selected with the Combo Box on the Parent Form it will be saved to tblMovieRented in the Child, or Subform as well.

2. Try it: Select a Field
The default option is: **Choose from a list.**
Select: **Define my own.**

Select a Form/report Field: ReceiptID
Select a Subform/subreport Field: ReceiptID.

Select a Form/report Field: CustomerID
Select a Subform/subreport Field: CustomerID.

Select a Form/report Field: DateRented
Select a Subform/subreport Field: DateRented.

Click **Next**. Keep going...

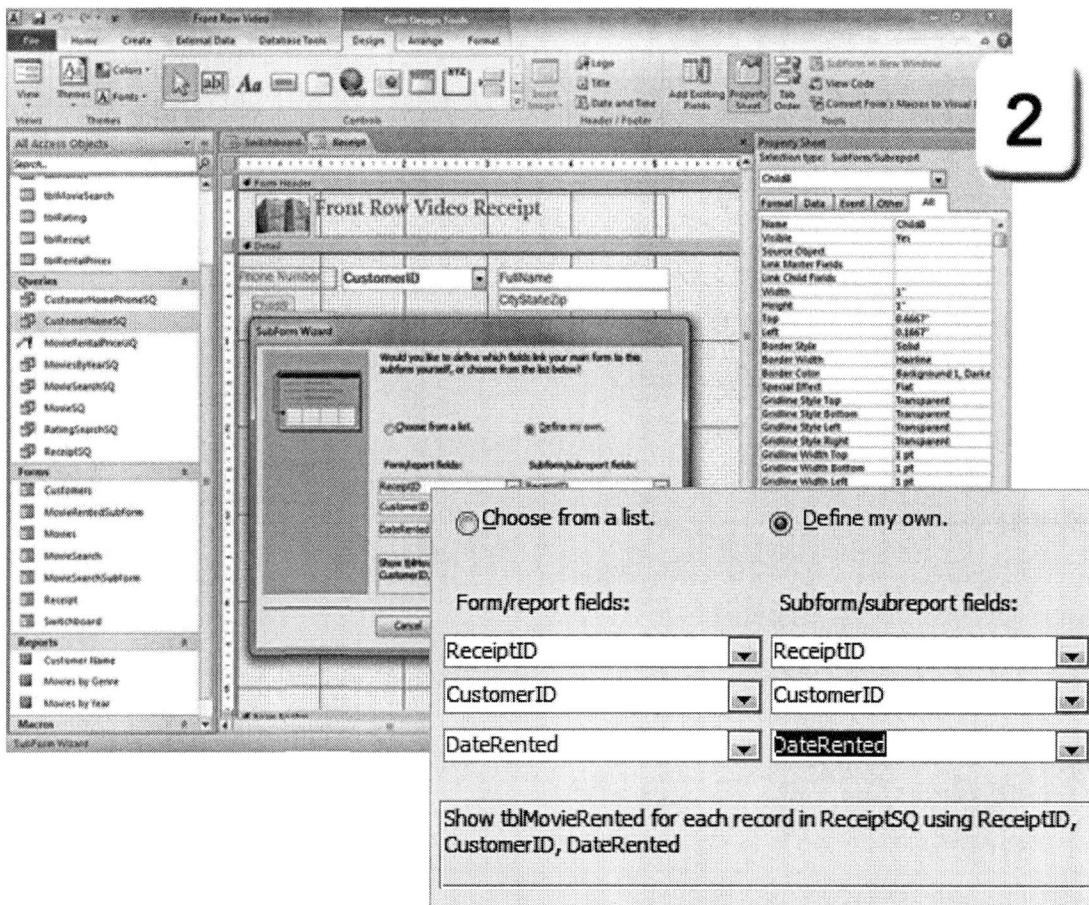

Exam 77-885: Microsoft Access 2010
3. Building Forms
3.2. Apply Form Design options: Add a Subform

Finish the Subform Wizard

3. Try it: Name the Subform
Enter the Name: MovieRentedSubform.
Click Finish to close the Subform Wizard.

What Do You See? There should be a new Subform in the Detail section of the Form.

Try This, Too: Review the Properties
Select the Subform: there should be a yellow border around the Subform when it is selected.
Go to **Property Sheet->All**.

The Name is: MovieRentedSubform.
Link Master Fields:
ReceiptID; CustomerID; DateRented
Link Child Fields:
ReceiptID; CustomerID; DateRented

And Try This: Edit the Subform Properties
Edit the Height: 4"
Left: 0"
(Delete the Subform Label, too.)
Well, does it work? Does it?

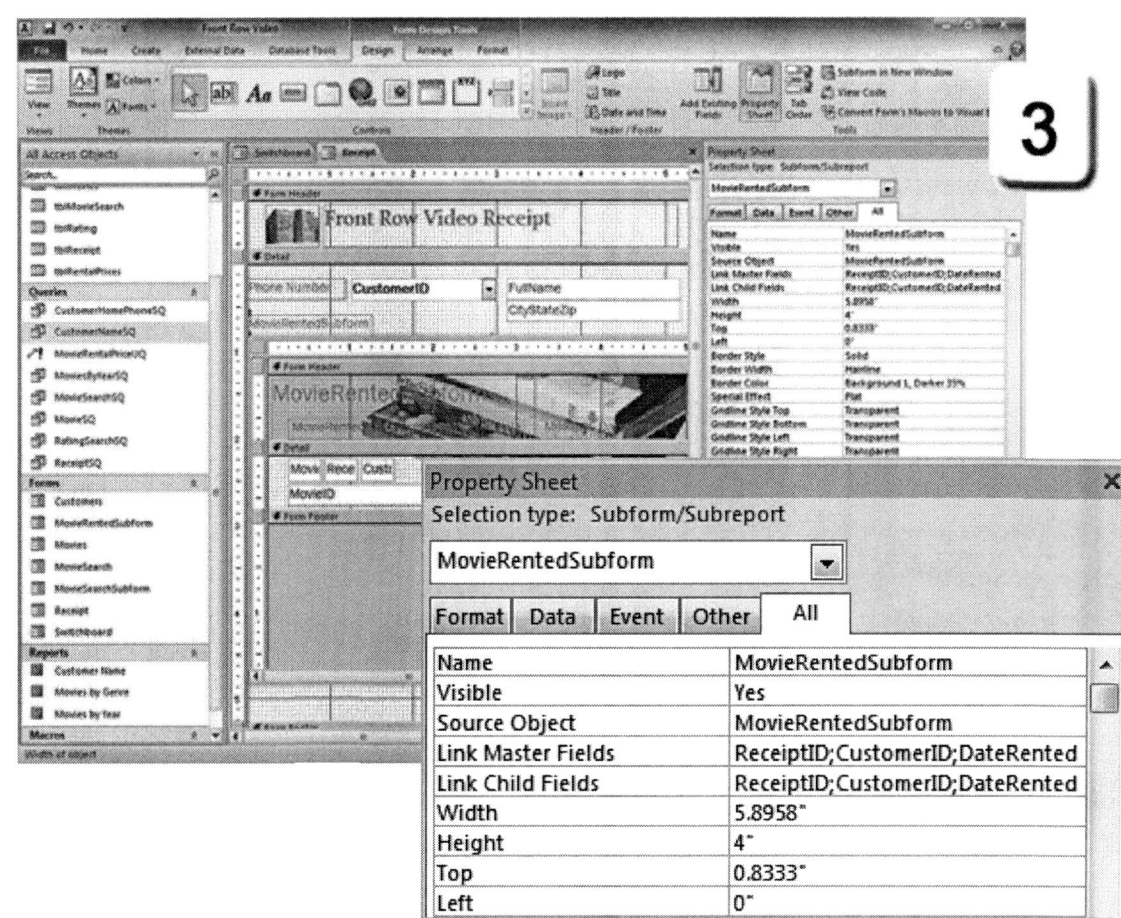

3

Property Sheet	
Selection type: Subform/Subreport	
MovieRentedSubform	

Format	Data	Event	Other	All

Name	MovieRentedSubform
Visible	Yes
Source Object	MovieRentedSubform
Link Master Fields	ReceiptID;CustomerID;DateRented
Link Child Fields	ReceiptID;CustomerID;DateRented
Width	5.8958"
Height	4"
Top	0.8333"
Left	0"

Test the Receipt Form

There is only one way to test this Mighty
Access Form: enter the data like a real User.

Before You Begin: Change the View.
Go to **Design Tools->Design->Views.**
Select a **View: Form View.**

4. Try it: Test the Receipt Form
Enter a phone number: 8105551212
Tab to the next FIeld.
Confirm the name: Deeter Poohbah

Select five movies:
Harry Potter and the Sorcerer's Stone
Harry Potter and the Chamber of Secrets
Harry Potter and the Prisoner of Azkaban
Harry Potter and the Goblet of Fire
Harry Potter and the Deathly Hallows: Part 2

What Do You See? There are two sets of
Record Selectors which can be confusing.
The ones in the MovieRentedSubform
navigate the Movies. The ones at the bottom
of the Receipt Form navigate the Receipts.

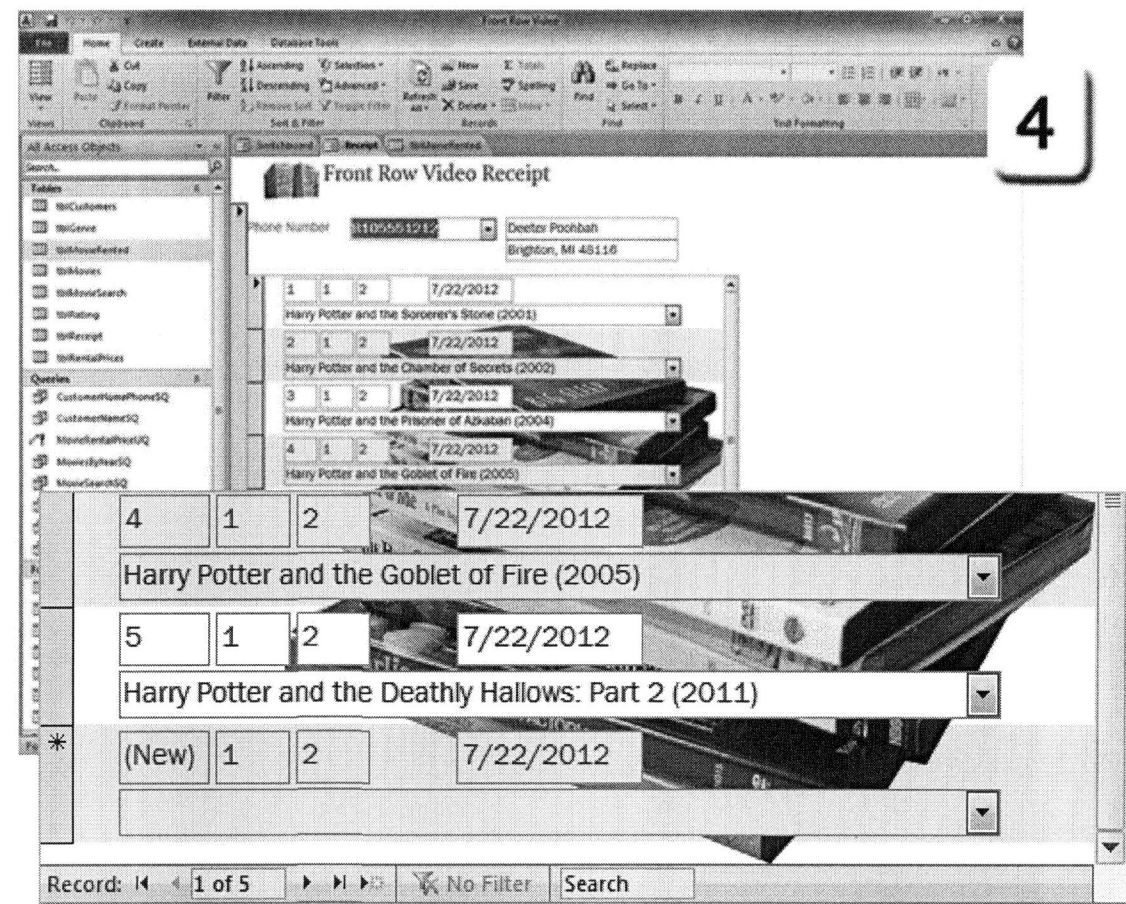

Exam 77-885: Microsoft Access 2010
3. Building Forms
3.2. Apply Form Design options: Add a Subform

A Little More Formatting

This Subform does not need a Form Header. In fact, there are several other Cells that do not have to be displayed. We can hide them.

5. Try it: Format the Header Properties
The Receipt Form is in Design View.
Go to the MovieRentedSubform.
Select the Form Header.

Go to **Property Sheet->All.**
Visible: No.

And Try This: Format the Control Properties
Go to the MovieRentedSubform.
Go to the Table in the Detail Section.
Select the Controls: MovieRentedID,
ReceiptID, CustomerID and DateRented.

Go to **Property Sheet->All.**
Visible: No.

Curious? Save the changes and let's see...

Form Design Tools->Design->Tools->Property Sheet

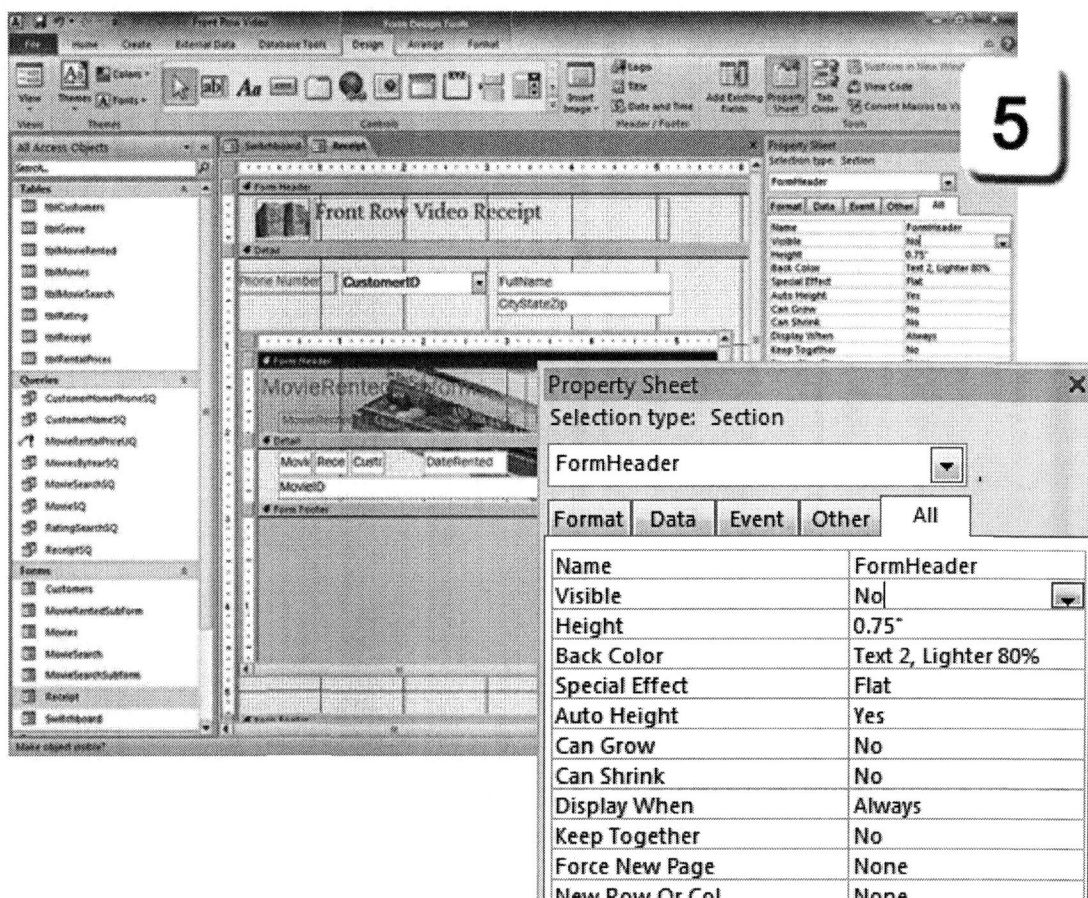

Exam 77-885: Microsoft Access 2010
3. Building Forms
3.2. Apply Form Design options: Format Header and Footer

Test the Receipt Form, Again
Before You Begin: Change the View.
Go to **Design Tools->Design->Views.**
Select a **View: Form View.**

6. Try it: Test the Receipt Form, Again
Create a NEW Receipt with the Record
Selectors at the bottom of the Form.
Confirm that this is a BLANK Receipt.

Add a customer:
Enter a phone number: 7345551212
TAB to the next Field.
Confirm the name: Mary Contrary

Select two movies:
Titanic 3D
The Hunger Games (2012)

What Don't You See? The Key Controls are
not visible.

Did that work? If it did, **Save Save, Save.**

Form Design Tools->Design->Views->View

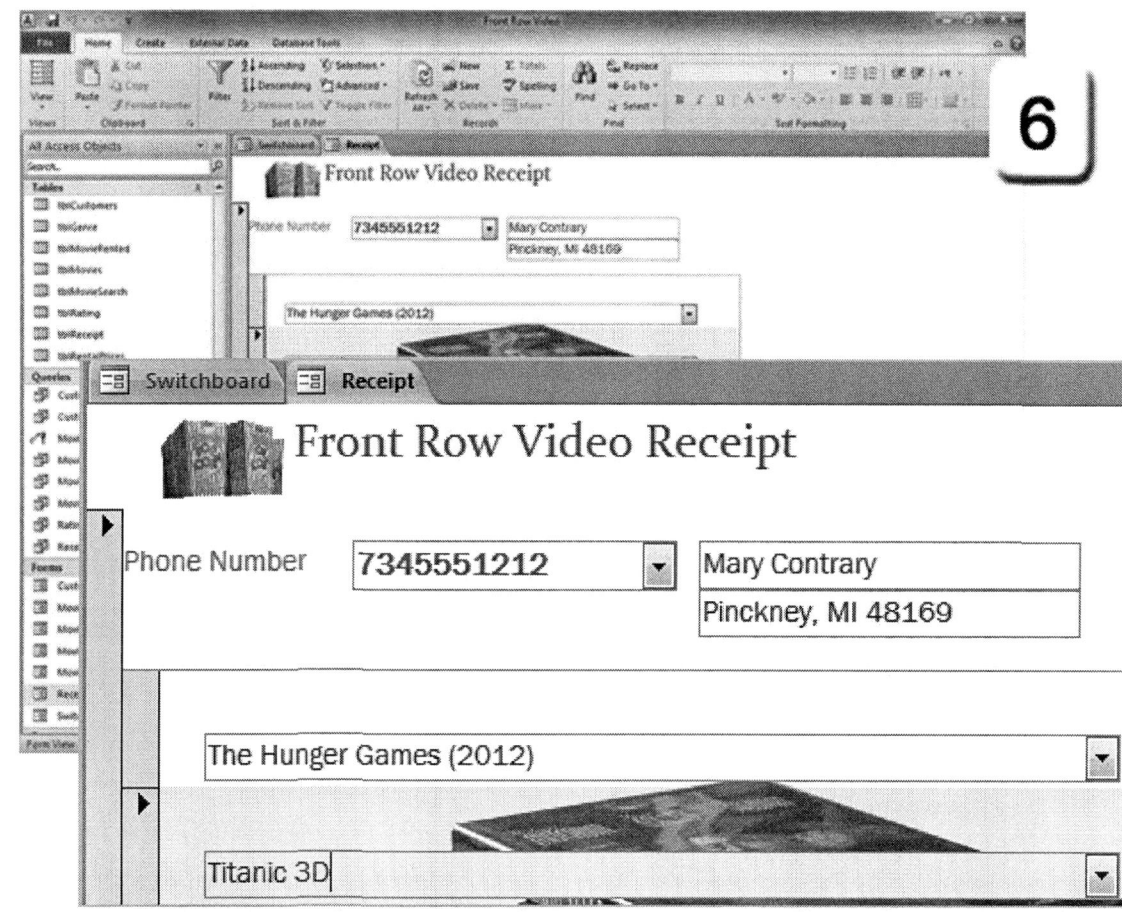

Exam 77-885: Microsoft Access 2010
3. Building Forms
3.2. Apply Form Design options: Format Header and Footer

Review the Data

What Was All That About? Why would someone take the trouble to create a Table and position the Key Controls, then just make them invisible? Follow me to find out...

The data from the Receipt Form and Subform is saved in a Table: tblMovieRented.

7. Try it: Review the Data in the Table
Go to **All Access Objects ->Tables**
Open a Table: tblMovieRented.

What Do You See? This is what you should see if a database is designed well: the Key, the Whole Key, and nothing but the Key.

Try This, Too: Proof the Data in the Table
CustomerID2 has 5 movies.
CustomerID3 has 2 movies.

How does that compare to the data you entered into the Receipt Form?

Keep going...

All Access Objects ->Tables

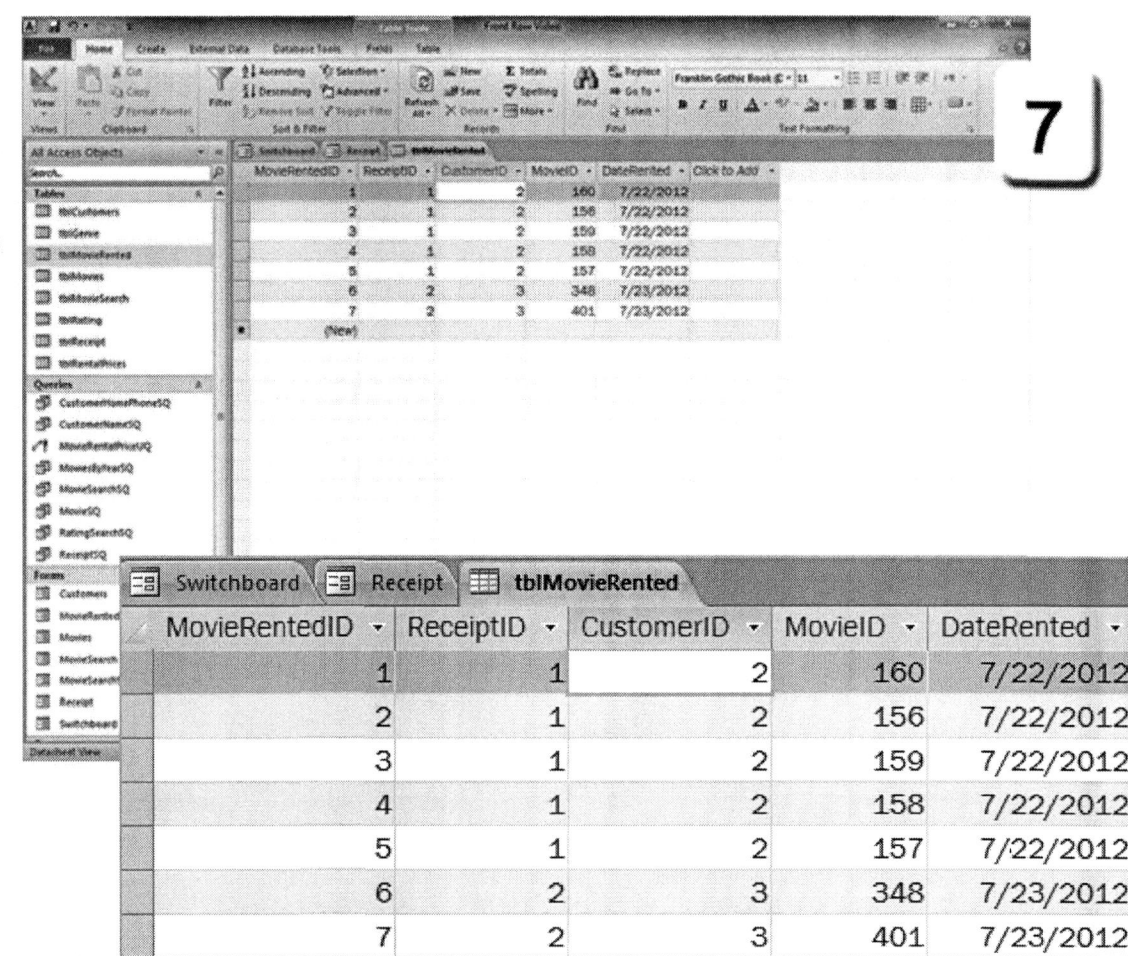

MovieRentedID	ReceiptID	CustomerID	MovieID	DateRented
1	1	2	160	7/22/2012
2	1	2	156	7/22/2012
3	1	2	159	7/22/2012
4	1	2	158	7/22/2012
5	1	2	157	7/22/2012
6	2	3	348	7/23/2012
7	2	3	401	7/23/2012

Views and Reviews

8. What Do You See? Programmers have two different roles. You need to see the Form as a User would. You also need to determine if the Form is saving the right data.

The Computer Mama Sez: When you are proofing a Form, it helps to see the Key data and compare what you see in the Form to what is stored in the Table.

Do they match? Is number matched to number? Text matched to Text?

In the example on this page:
Who: CustomerID 2 (Deeter Poohbah)
Bought: ReceiptID 1
What: MovieID 160, 156 and 159.

A Form is just a pretty, programmable face on a Table. The Table holds the data, the data, the data. The data is everything.

Comparison of the Key data in tblMovieRented and the MovieRentedSubform

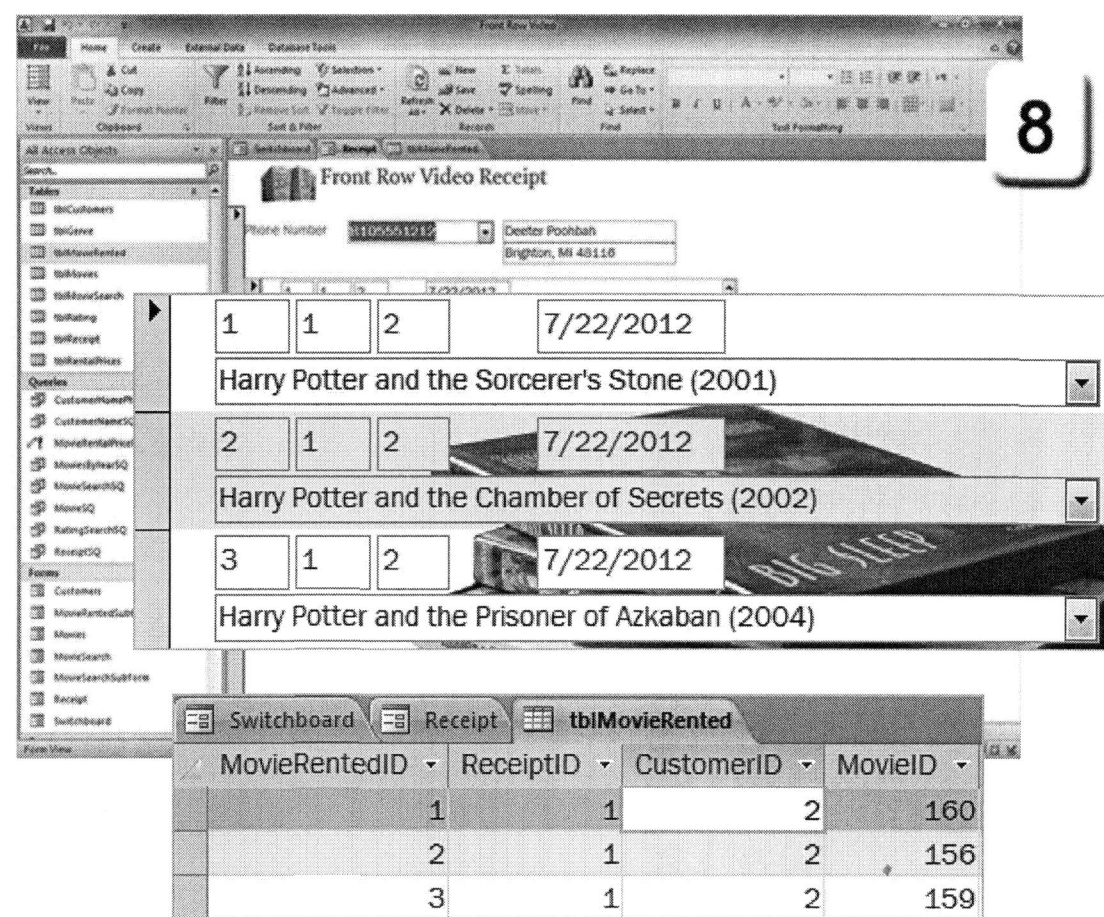

Summary

The goal of these two lessons in Advanced Form Design was to create and format a Receipt Form. It looks like we got there.

In **Receipt Form, part 1**, we designed the ReceiptSubform: the list of the movies rented. This is the "many" part of the one-to-many relationship: many movies.

In **Receipt Form, part 2**, we designed a Receipt Form that uses a Combo Box to find a customer by their phone number. The Form and Subform were linked by common Keys and tested.

Well, you done real good. You can have more than two cookies if you wish.

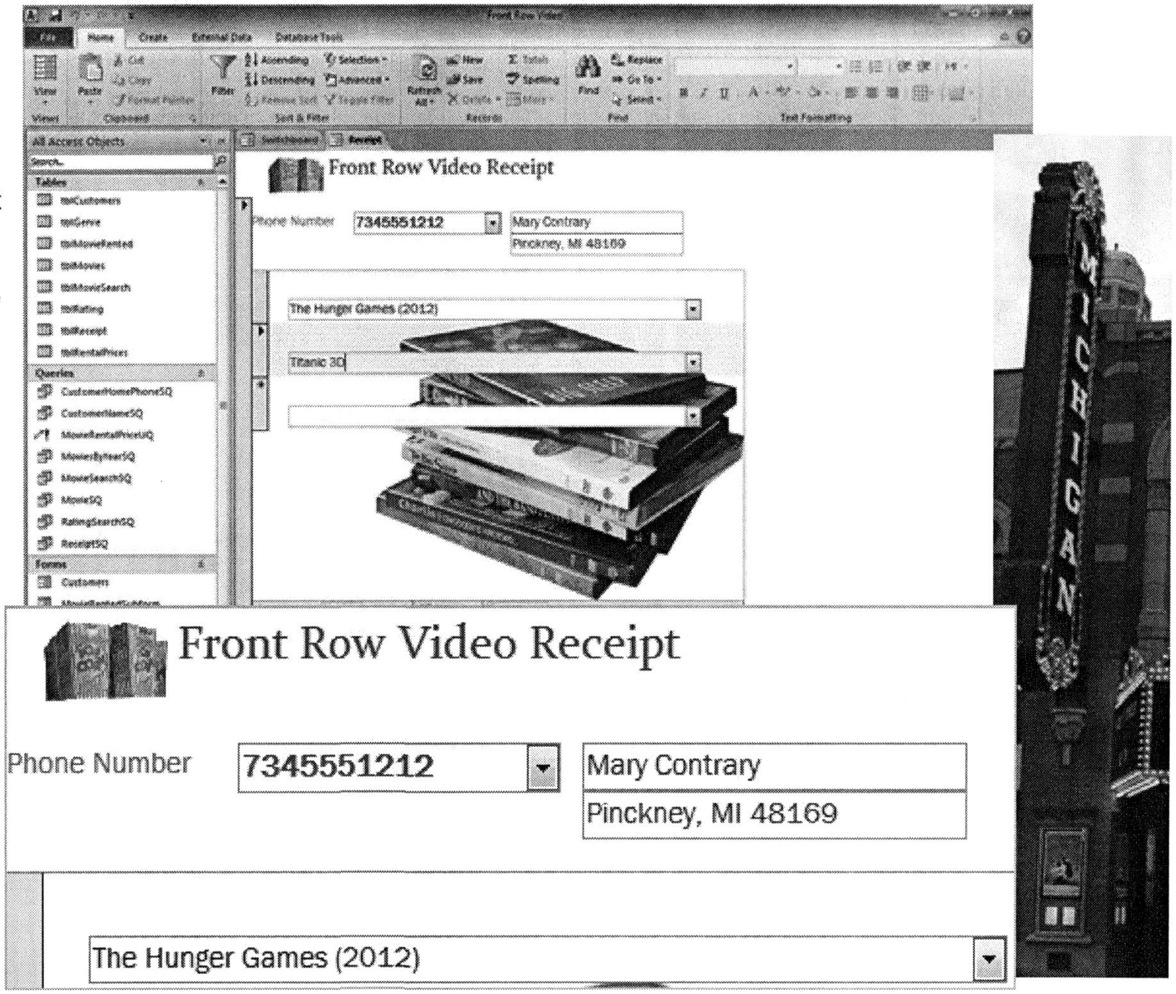

Practice Activities

Lesson 5: Advanced Form Design, part 2

Try This: Do the following steps

1. Open the Brown Bag Lunch database you have been working on. Or, you may download **BBL Adv ver5.accdb**

2. Create a Select Query and choose tblCustomers for the Record Source. Add all of the Fields to the QBE Grid.

3. Add a new Concatenated field as follows:
FullName: [FirstName] &" "& [LastName]

4. Add another Concatenated Field as follows:
CityStateZip: [City]&", "&[State]&" "&[Zip]

5. Save the Query as CustomerNameSQ.

6. Create a Select Query and choose tblCustomers for the Record Source.

7. Add the following Criteria for the Company Field Create a Select Query and Add the following Table: tblReceipt. Add a Query: CompanyNameSQ. Create a JOIN from CustomerID in tblReceipt to Customer ID in CompanyNameSQ.

8. Add the following Fields to the QBE Grid from tblReceipt: ReceiptID, CustomerID, and Date/Time.

9. Add the following Fields to the QBE Grid from CustomerNameSQ: Company', FullName, Phone, and CItyStateZip. Save the Query and name it: ReceiptSQ.

10. Create the Receipt Form in with the Form Wizard and select ReceiptSQ as the Record Source. Choose the Columnar Layout. Enter the label: Customer Receipt.

11. Format the Form Header and include the Brown Bag Logo.JPG. Format the logo 1" x 1"

12. Move the ReceiptID Control and Label to the Form Header.

13. Select the CustomerID Control and delete it. Create a Combo Box Control and select CustomerNameSQ for the Record Source. Select CustomerID and FullName from the available Fields. Sort by Customer (Ascending). Hide (resize) the Key Column for CustomerID to be zero. Select CustomerID from the available Fields and Store CustomerID. Enter the Label: Customers.

14. Save the Form: Receipt. Test the Form in Form View. Does the Customer Combo work?

15. Return to Design View and add the Subform with the Subform/Subreport Control. Use an existing Form: ReceiptProductsSubform. Define your own JOIN:
ReceiptID to ReceiptID
CustomerID to CustomerID
Date/Time to DateReceipt

16. Finish the Wizard and Save the Form.

17. Test the Form in Form View. Select a customer: Andrea Carter. Select two products: Avocado Wrap and Bacon, Egg & Cheese. Save this Record.

18. Go to Receipt 2. Select a customer: Selena Sullivan. Select two products: Breakfast Burrito, Chips and Salsa. Save this Record.

19. Close the Receipt Form. Close the Brown Bag Lunch database.

Test Yourself

1. Only Tables can be Joined.
A. True
B. False
Tip: Advanced Access, page 129

2. Which of the following is true about adding a Subform? (Give all correct answers.)
A. The Master Form must be open
B. The Master Form does not need to be open
C. The Child Form is added as Control to the Master Form
D. Child Form is another name for Subform
Tip: Advanced Access, page 140

3. Where does the command Add Existing Fields get the available Fields from?
A. All available fields in the database
B. The last Query or Table viewed
C. The Table or Query currently open
D. The Record Source for the Form
Tip: Advanced Access, page 138

4. Subforms can use which of the following for Data? (Give all correct answers.)
A. Existing Tables
B. Existing Queries
C. Existing Forms
Tip: Advanced Access, page 140

5. When using the command Create->Forms->Blank Form, what View does the Form open in?
A. Normal
B. Form
C. Layout
D. Design
Tip: Advanced Access, page 131

Access 2010: Advanced Report Design

The Receipt Printout, part 1

Advanced Access Objectives

In this lesson, you will learn how to:

1. Create a Select Query that groups the sales and calculates the Totals for each Receipt.

2. Use the Group By and Totals Row in a Query.

3. Create a Blank Report and select a Query as the Record Source.

4. Edit the Report Page Setup and change the page Size and Orientation.

© 2012 Comma Productions, LLC

Front Row Video

Receipt   1

7/22/2012

Deeter Poohbah

Brighton, MI 48116

No of Movies   5

Total Due $17.50

Lesson 6 : The Receipt Printout

1. Readings

Read Lesson 6 in the Advanced Access guide, page 151-176.

Project

A Receipt Printout Report formatted as a Table and sized for a POS Printer.

Downloads

FrontRowVideo Adv6.accdb
BBL Adv ver6.accdb

2. Practice

Do the Practice Activity on page 177.

3. Assessment

Review the Test questions on page 178.

Query Tools->Design

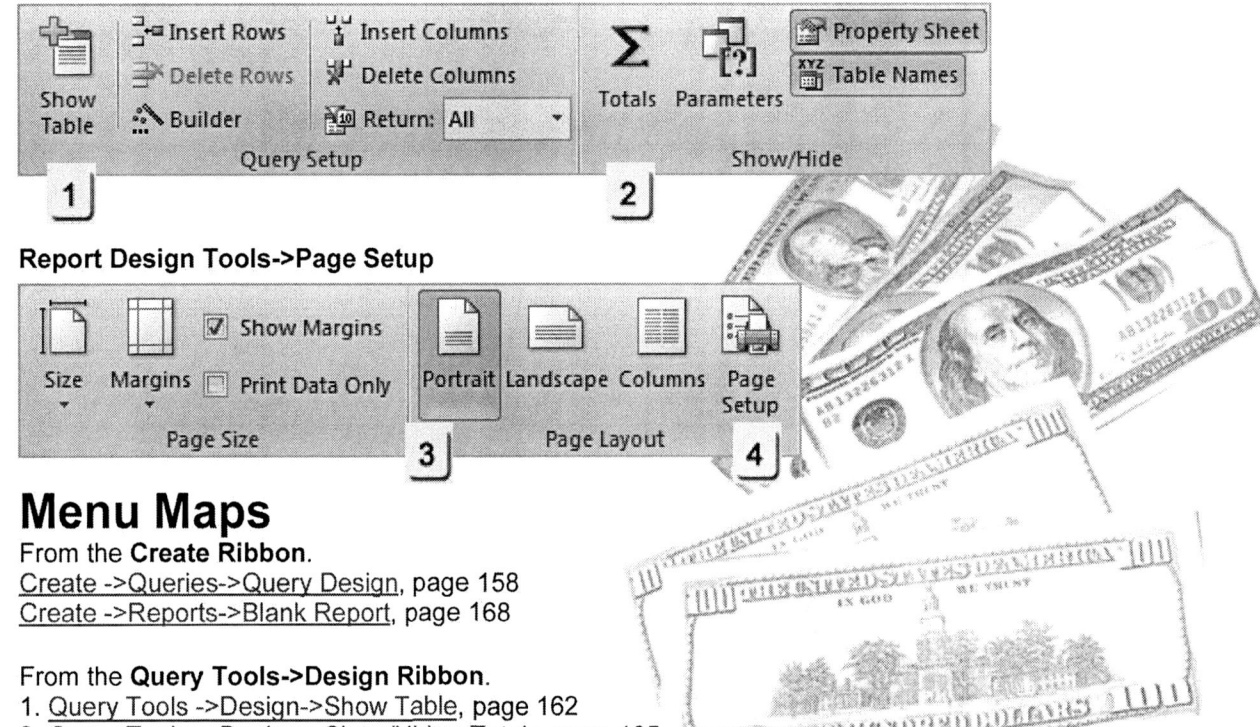

Report Design Tools->Page Setup

Menu Maps

From the **Create Ribbon**.
Create ->Queries->Query Design, page 158
Create ->Reports->Blank Report, page 168

From the **Query Tools->Design Ribbon**.
1. Query Tools ->Design->Show Table, page 162
2. Query Tools ->Design->Show/Hide->Totals, page 165

3. Report Design Tools ->Page Setup, page 170
4. Report Design Tools ->Page Setup->Page Set Up, page 171

The Receipt Printout

The customer rents a couple of movies and the purchase is complete. When he leaves the store he will have a handful of movies and a receipt that lists the movies he rented: who bought what. In the Front Row Video store, our customer would get a small receipt from a Point of Sale (POS) printer. The paper roll is usually 2 inches wide, so the printout will not be a full page Receipt Report.

Microsoft Office Access 2010: Example of the completed Receipt Print Out

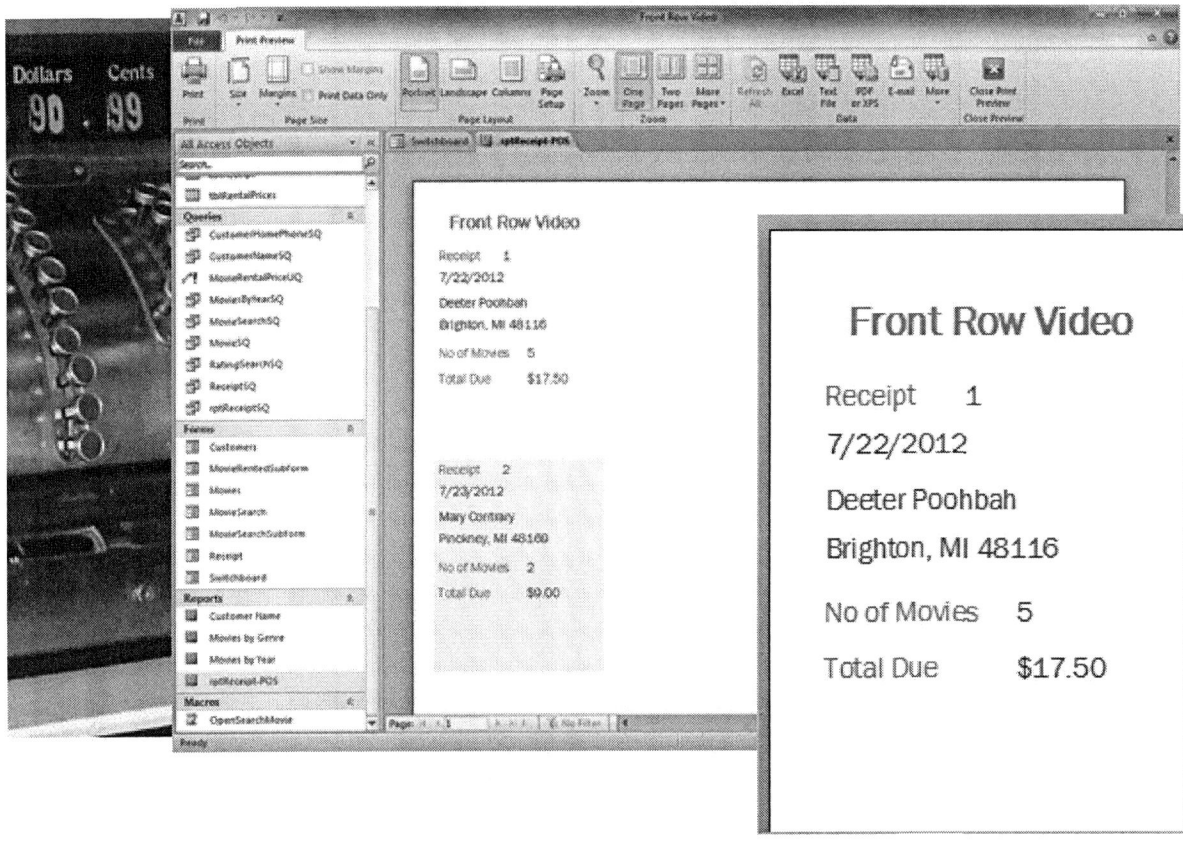

In **Advanced Report Design part 1: The Receipt Printout** the focus will be on creating a Query that calculates the Total for each Receipt. the Receipt will be formatted for a POS printer.

In **Advanced Report Design part 2**, we'll create a Subreport that lists the movies and add the Subreport to the Receipt Printout.

In **Advanced Report Design part 3: The Producers,** we'll look at essential business reports including Mailing Labels and Mail Merges.

What is the Plan?

The Record Source for the Receipt Printout will be a Query, **rtpMovieRentedSQ,** that uses the same Table that was the Record Source for the Receipt Subform, **tblMovieRented**. This Table has Key Data that says who bought what?

Here is the plan:

Review the Record Source: tblMovieRented
Open tblMovieRented in Design View.
Identify the Key Fields.

Create a Query: rtpReceiptSQ
Add tblMovieRented and related Tables.
Create JOINS between the Tables.
Group the Records by Receipt.
Calculate the Amount Due for each Receipt.

Create the Report: rptReceipt-POS
The **rptReceipt-POS** will be a Tabular Form formatted as a Table. The Report will be sized to fit a POS printer.

That's the plan for now.

Example of the Receipt Printout in Design View

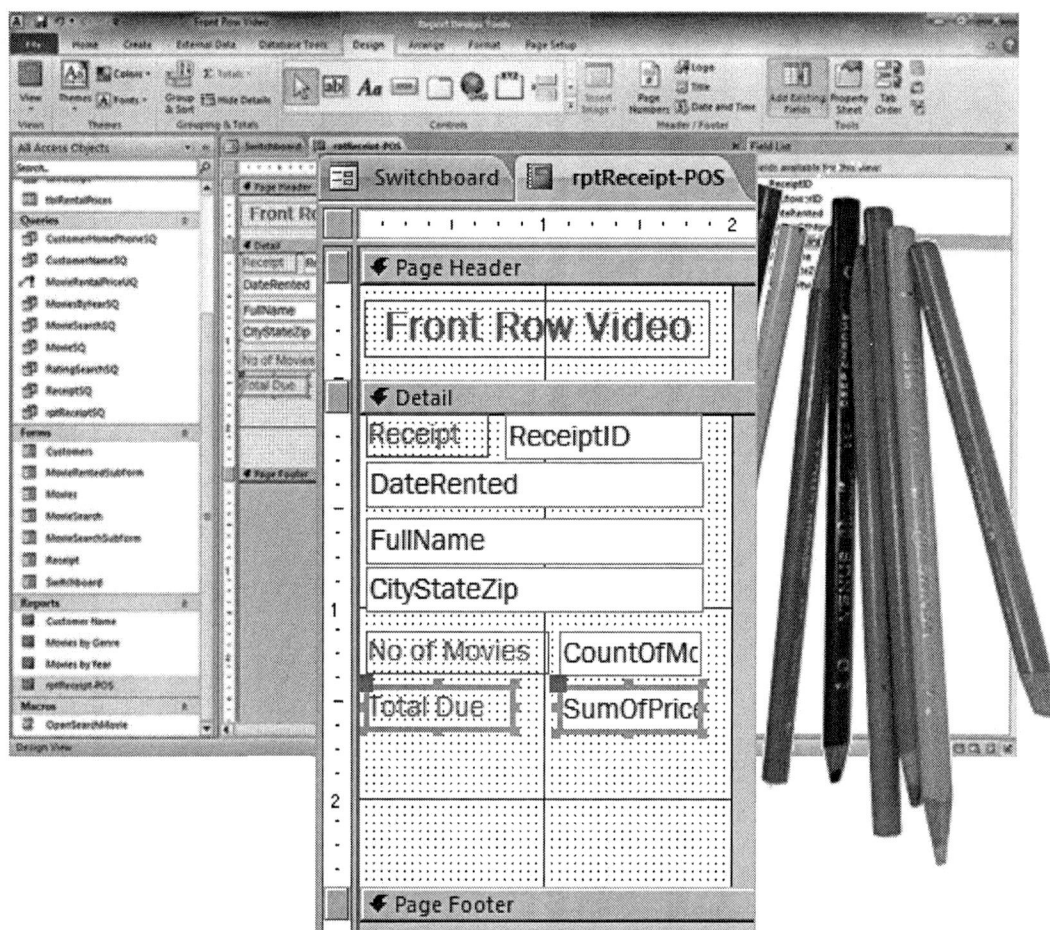

Before You Begin

Before You Begin: Open the Sample Database
Go to **Start -> All Programs ->Microsoft Office**.
Click on **Microsoft Office Access 2010.**
Access will prompt you to open a database.
Select: <u>**FrontRowVideo Adv6.accdb**</u>

The database, <u>**FrontRowVideo Adv6.accdb**</u>, was developed in the previous lesson. You do not have to download a new sample. You can continue with your own database if you wish.

Keep going....

Memo to Self: Databases need to Read and Write. Click **Enable Content** if you see the Security Warning.

Start ->All Programs-> Microsoft Office-> Microsoft Access 2010

Know Your Data
Try This: Review the Database
Open the **Navigation Pane.**
Go to **All Access Objects.**

The Front Row View has the following:
Eight Tables: tblCustomers, tblGenre, tblMovieRented, tblMovies, tblMovieSearch, tblRating, tblRecipt and tblRentalPrices.

Eight Queries: CustomerHomePhoneSQ, CustomerNameSQ, MovieRentalPriceUQ, MoviesByYearSQ, MovieSearchSQ, MovieSQ, RatingSearchSQ and ReceiptSQ.

Seven Forms: Customers, MovieRentedSubform, Movies, MovieSearch, MovieSearchSubform, Receipt and Switchboard.

Three Reports: Customer Name. Movies by Genre, and Movies by Year.

One Macro: OpenSearchMovie

All Access Objects

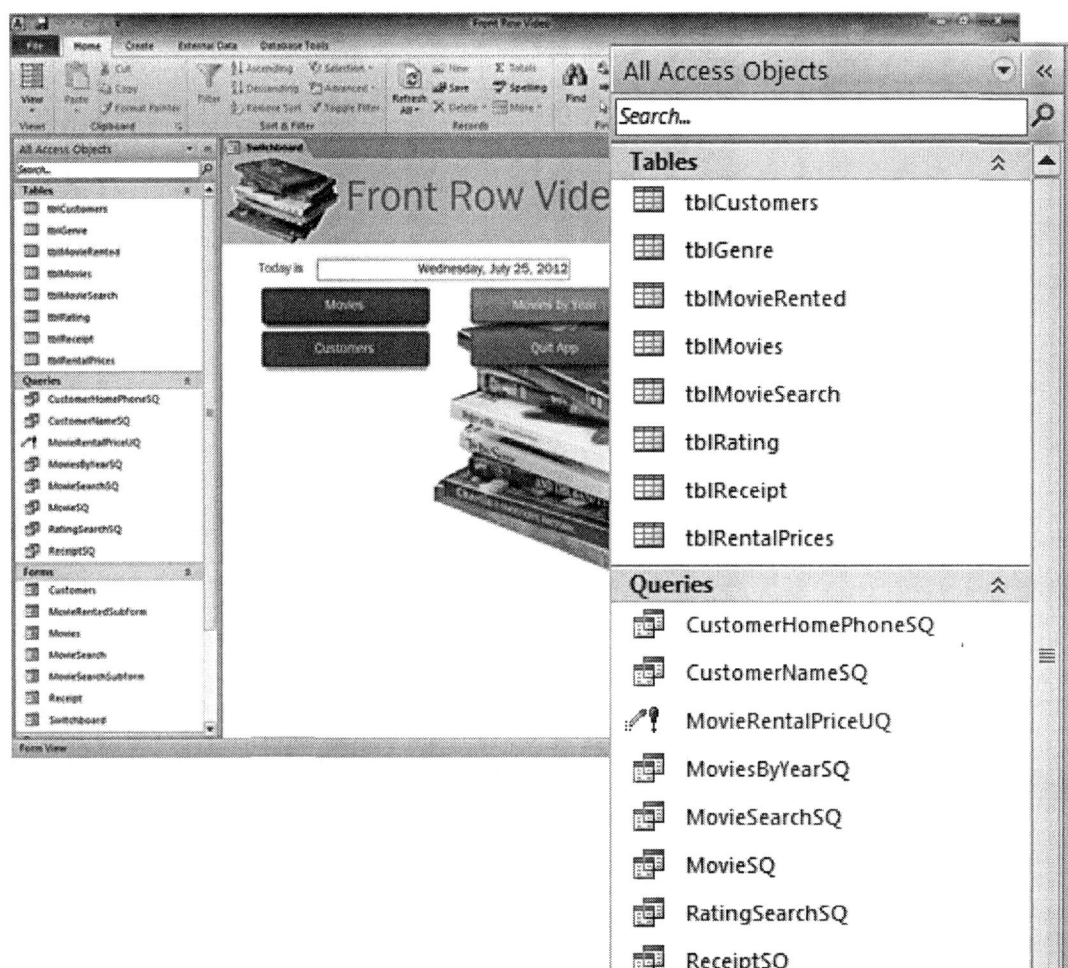

Review the Record Source

The **ReceiptPrintout** will use a Table for the Record Source: tblMovieRented. Please begin this lesson by reviewing the Table Properties.

1. Try it: Review the Record Souce
Go to **All Access Objects->Tables.**
Open a Table: tblMovieRented.
Go to **Home ->Views ->View-> Design View.**

What Do You See? This Table has Keys for:
Who (CustomerID)
Bought (ReceiptID)
What (MovieID)

The **DateRented** is important. Our business model uses the DateRented to calculate how many days since the movie was rented.

Close the Table.
Keep going..

Home ->Views ->View->Design View

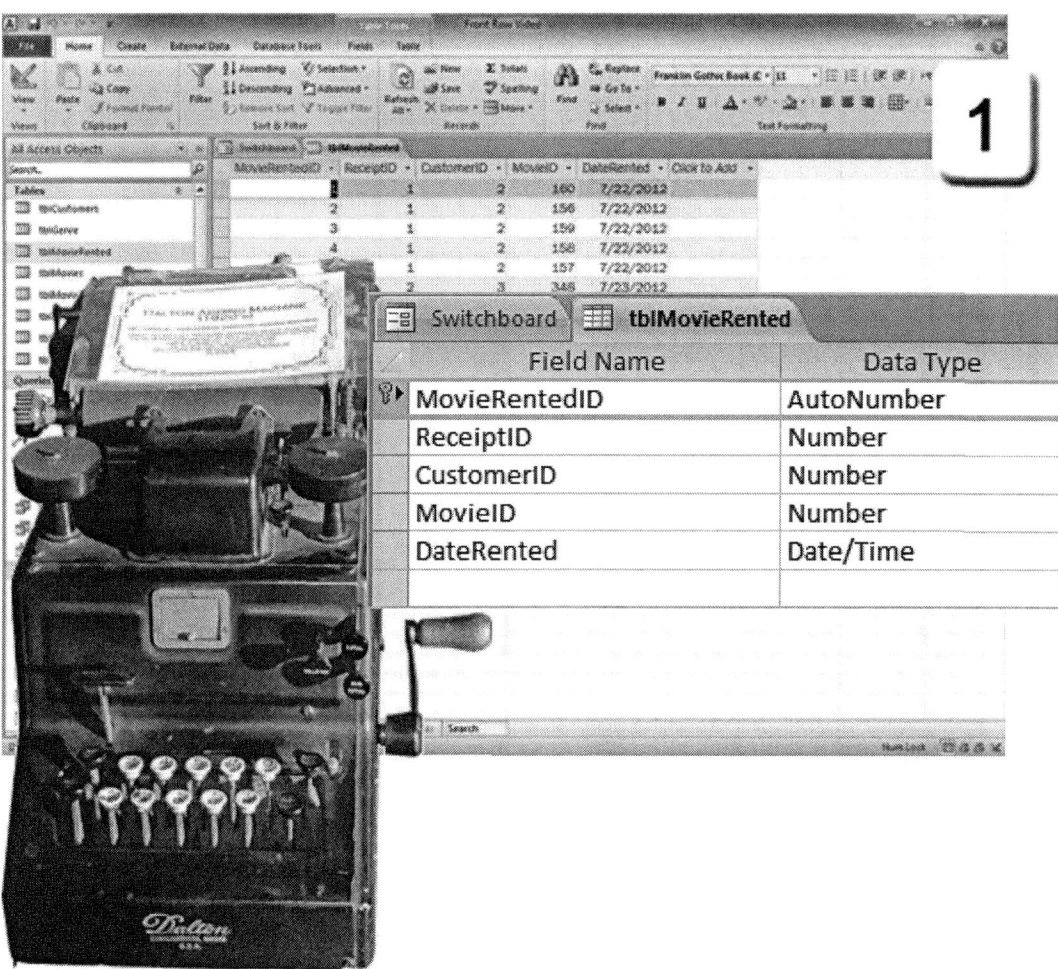

Field Name	Data Type
MovieRentedID	AutoNumber
ReceiptID	Number
CustomerID	Number
MovieID	Number
DateRented	Date/Time

Create a Select Query: MovieRentedSQ

A new Query will calculate the total for each Receipt. So, Queries get their data from Tables. Please add them.

2. Try it: Create a Query
Go to **Create ->Queries ->Query Design**. You will be prompted by the **Show Table**.

Select a Table: tblMovieRented.
Click **Add**.

Select a Table: tblCustomers.
Click **Add**.

Select a Table: tblMovies.
Click **Add**.

Select a Table: tblRentalPrices.
Click **Add**.

Close the Show Table Window.
Keep going...

Create ->Queries->Query Design

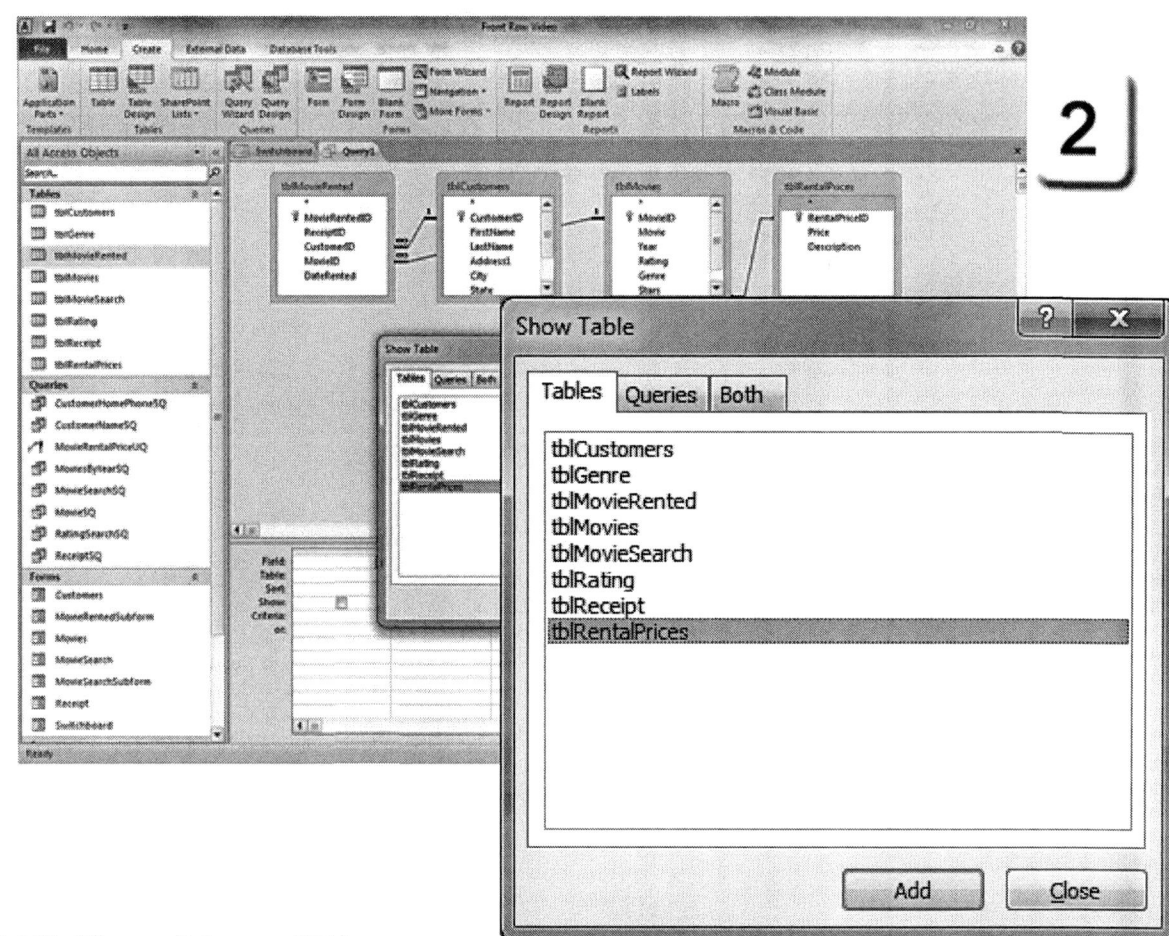

Exam 77-885: Microsoft Access 2010
4. Creating and Managing Queries
4.2. Manage source tables and relationships: Use the Show Table Options

MovieRentedSQ: JOINS

As you added each Table to the Query, the Tables were JOINED by their Keys.

3. Try it: Review the JOINS
tblMovieRented.CustomerID to tblCustomers.CustomerID.

tblMovieRented.MovieID to tblMovies.MovieID.

tblMovies.RentalPriceID to tblRentalPrices.RentalPriceID.

Keep going...

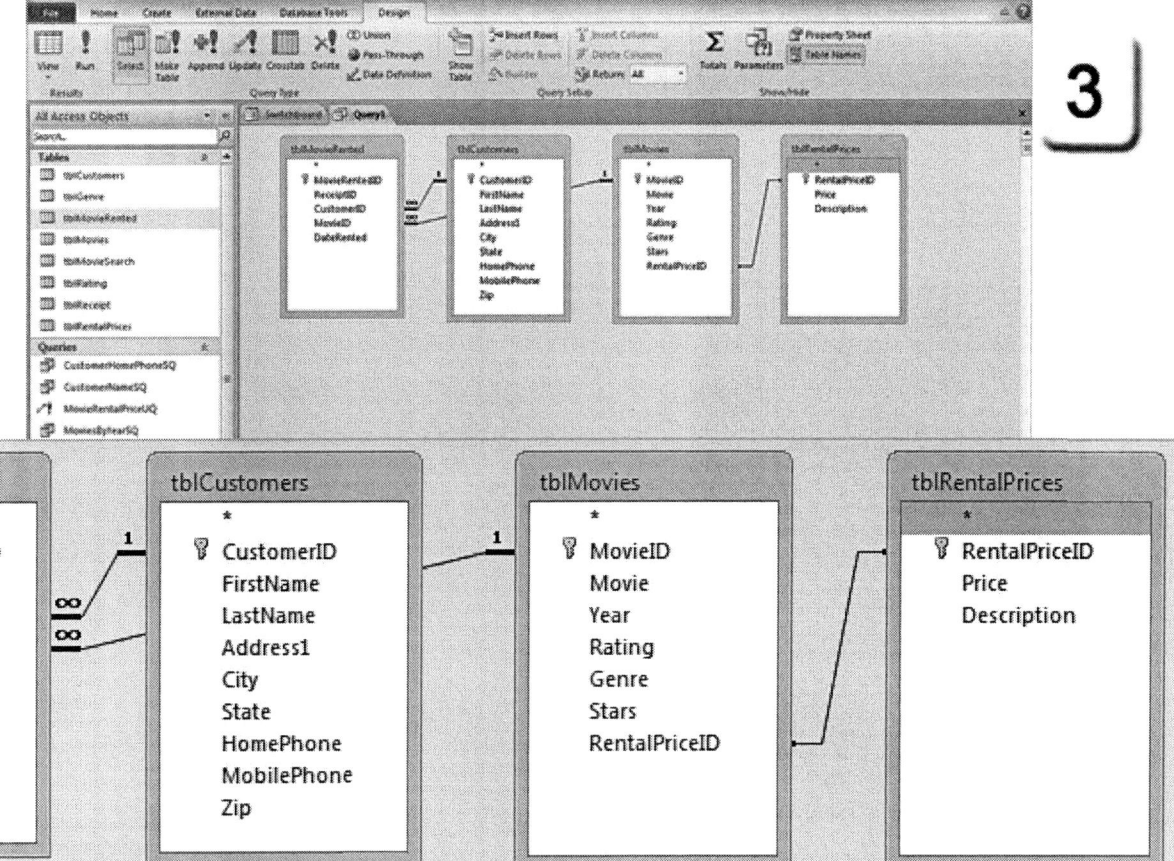

Exam 77-885: Microsoft Access 2010
4. Creating and Managing Queries
4.2. Manage source tables and relationships

MovieRentedSQ: Fields

4. Try it: Add Fields to the Query
Add the following Fields to the QBE Grid:
From tblMovieRented:
ReceiptID
CustomerID
DateRented

From tblMovies:
Movie

From tblRentalPrices:
Price

Do This, Now: Save the Query
Go to **File->Save**.
Enter the name: **rptReceiptSQ**.

Keep going...

Query Tools ->Design

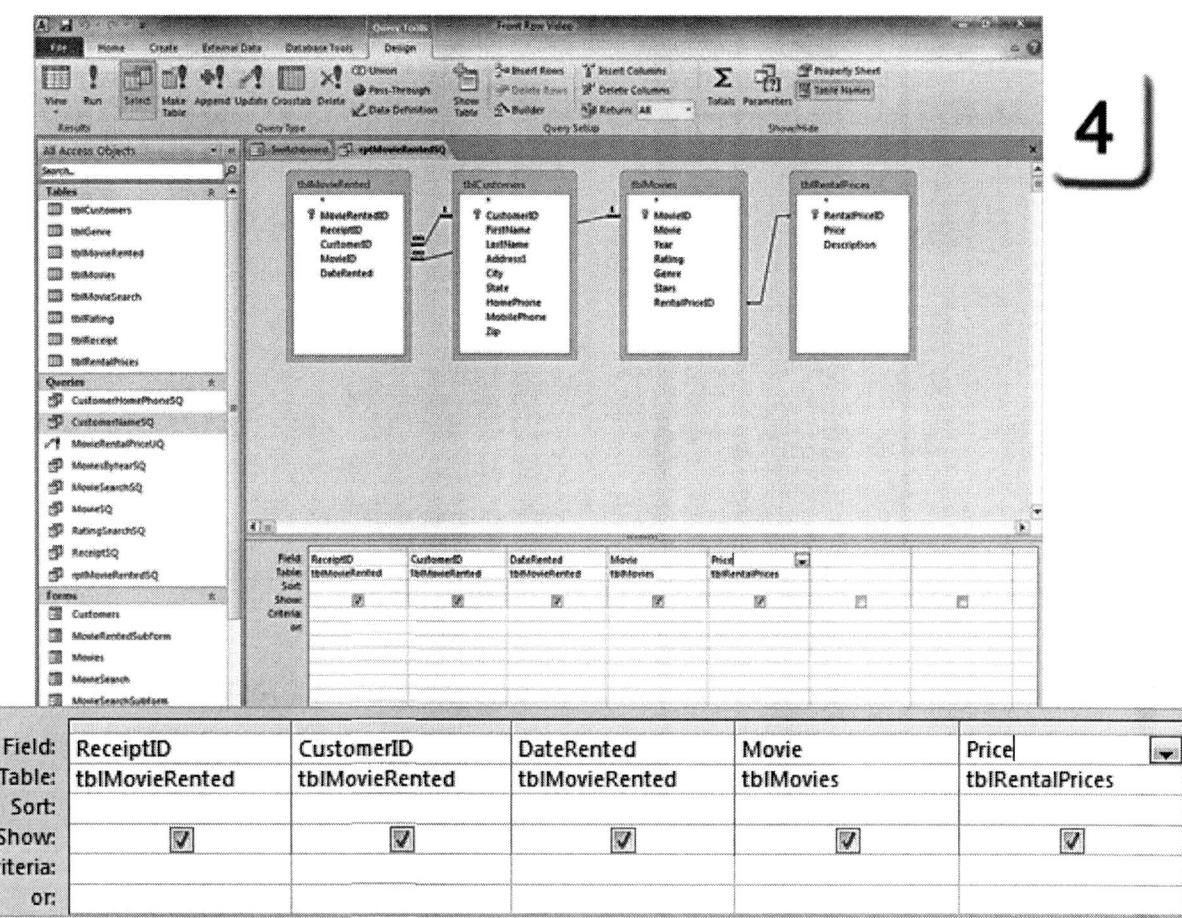

Field:	ReceiptID	CustomerID	DateRented	Movie	Price	
Table:	tblMovieRented	tblMovieRented	tblMovieRented	tblMovies	tblRentalPrices	
Sort:						
Show:	☑	☑	☑	☑	☑	
Criteria:						
or:						

Exam 77-885: Microsoft Access 2010
4. Creating and Managing Queries
4.3. Manipulate fields: Add Fields to a Query

Run the rptReceiptSQ Query

5. Try it: Run the Query
Go to **Query Tools ->Design->Results.**
Click on **Run.**

What Do You See? The **rtpReceiptSQ** Query
returned seven Records.
On Receipt 1 CustomerID 2 has 5 movies.
On Receipt 2, CustomerID 3 has 2 movies.

So far so good. Let's return to the **Design View**. We can make a few improvements.

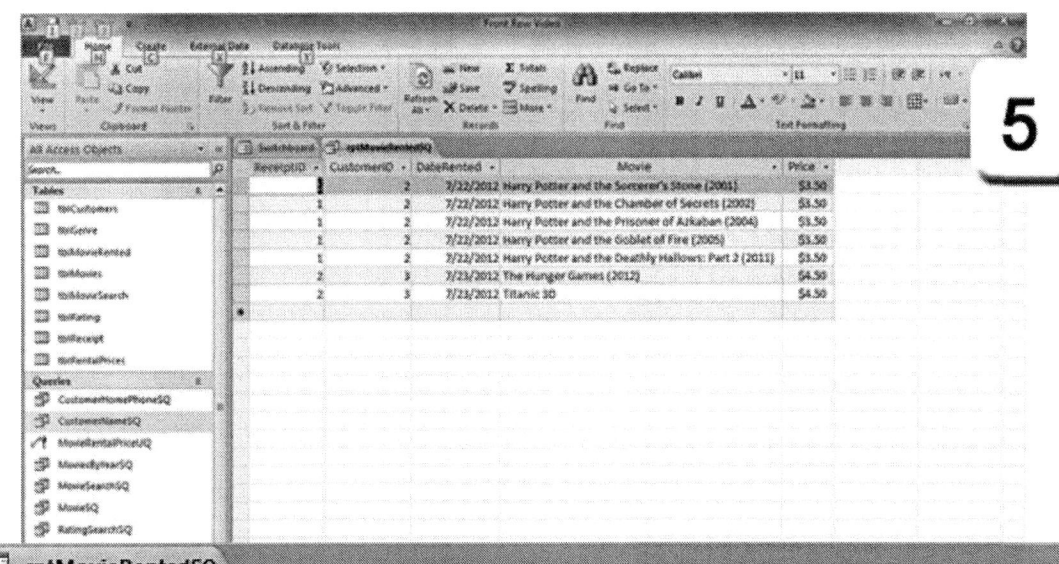

5

ReceiptID ▾	CustomerID ▾	DateRented ▾	Movie ▾	Price ▾
1	2	7/22/2012	Harry Potter and the Sorcerer's Stone (2001)	$3.50
1	2	7/22/2012	Harry Potter and the Chamber of Secrets (2002)	$3.50
1	2	7/22/2012	Harry Potter and the Prisoner of Azkaban (2004)	$3.50
1	2	7/22/2012	Harry Potter and the Goblet of Fire (2005)	$3.50
1	2	7/22/2012	Harry Potter and the Deathly Hallows: Part 2 (2011)	$3.50
2	3	7/23/2012	The Hunger Games (2012)	$4.50
2	3	7/23/2012	Titanic 3D	$4.50

Switchboard rptMovieRentedSQ

Use a Query in a Query
This Query is linked to tblCustomers. We have a Query that already combines the name and address Fields. We can use that Query instead of tblCustomers.

Before You Begin: Delete a Table
Select a Table: tblCustomers.
Click **DELETE** on your keyboard. Bye bye.

6. Try it: Add a Query
Go to **Query Tools ->Design->Show Table.**
Go to **Queries.**
Select a Query: CustomerNameSQ.
Click **Add.**
Close the Show Table Window. Keep going...

Query Tools ->Design->Show Table

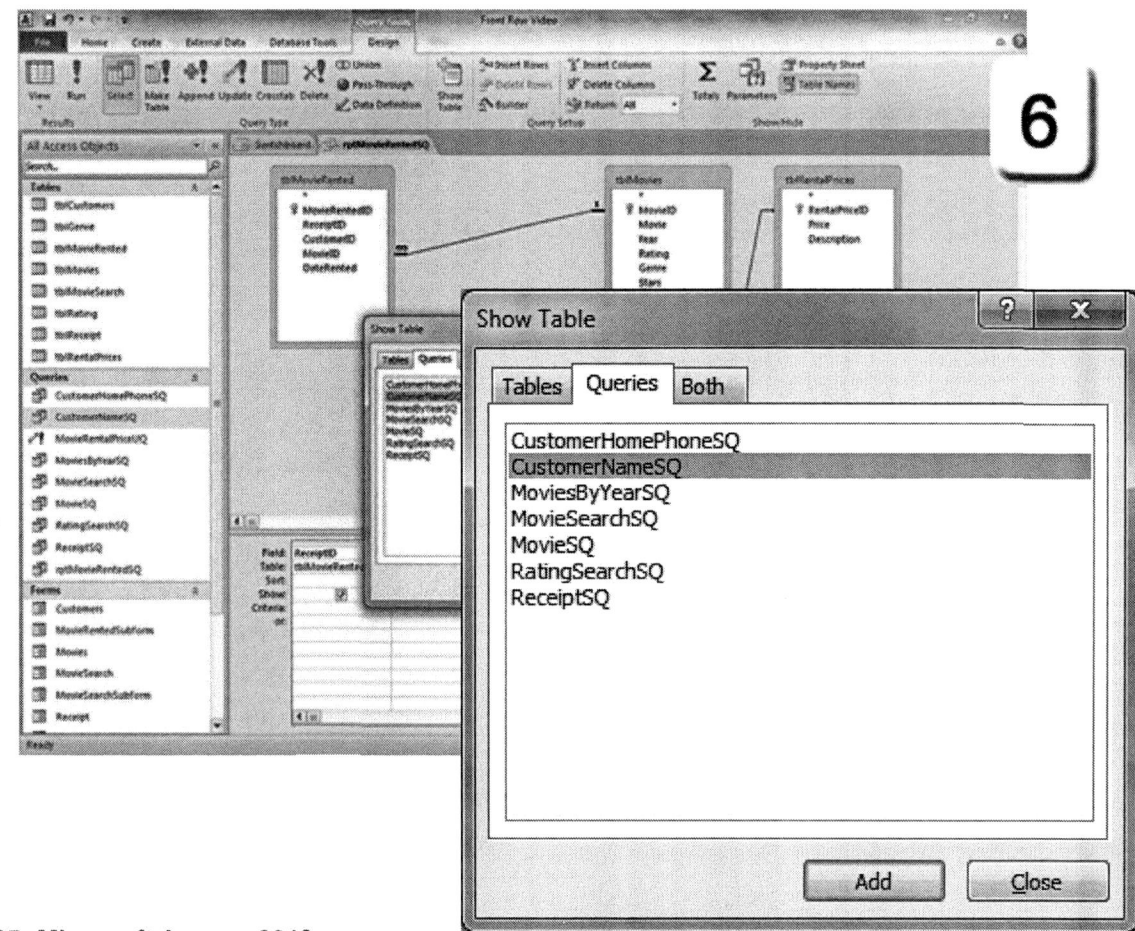

Exam 77-885: Microsoft Access 2010
4. Creating and Managing Queries
4.2. Manage source tables and relationships: Remove a Table

Create a Relationship with a JOIN Between Key Fields

The CustomerNameSQ Query can be JOINED to tblMovieRented by a common Key: CustomerID.

7. Try This: Create an Ad Hoc Relationship
Drag CustomerID from tblMovieRented to CustomerID in CustomerNameSQ.

And Try This, Too: Add More Fields
Add the following Fields to the QBE Grid:
From CustomerNameSQ:
FullName
CityStateZip
HomePhone

Save, Save, Save.
Keep going, please.

Query Tools ->Design

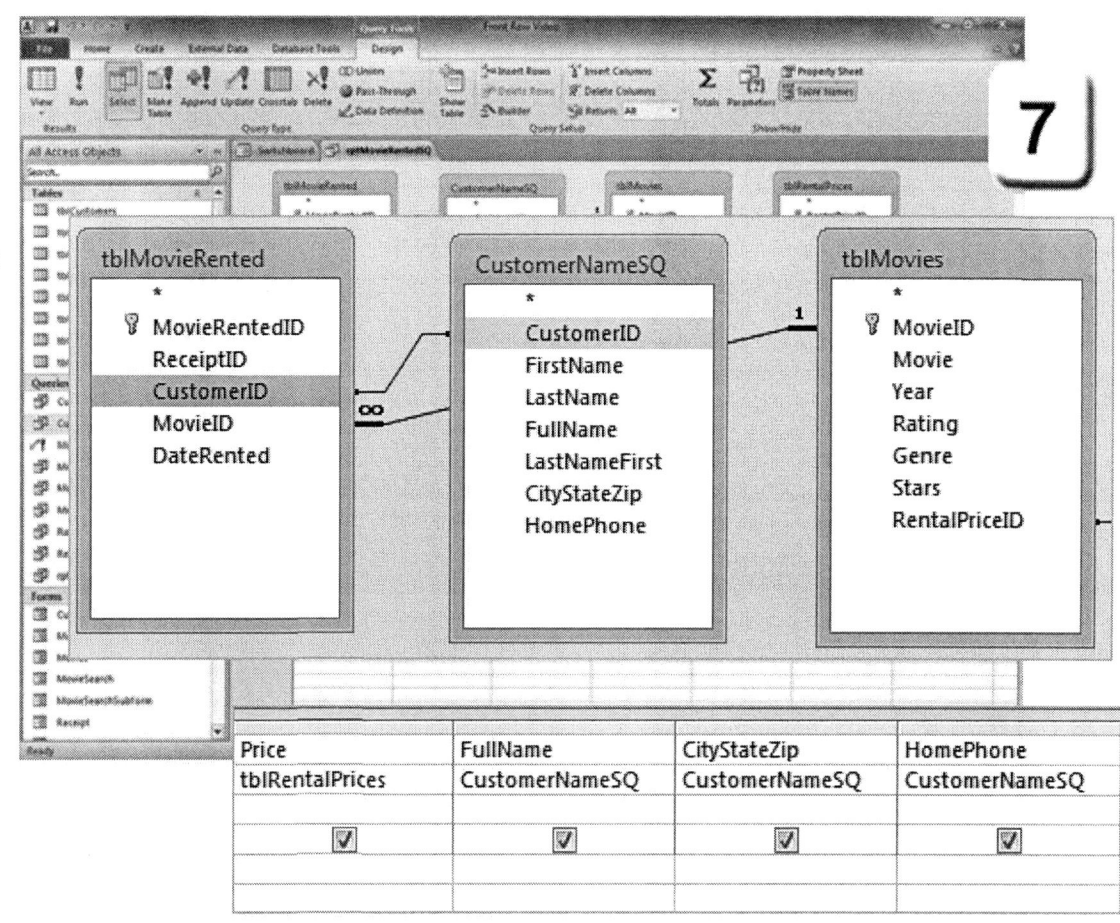

Exam 77-885: Microsoft Access 2010
4. Creating and Managing Queries
4.3. Manipulate fields: Add Fields to a Query

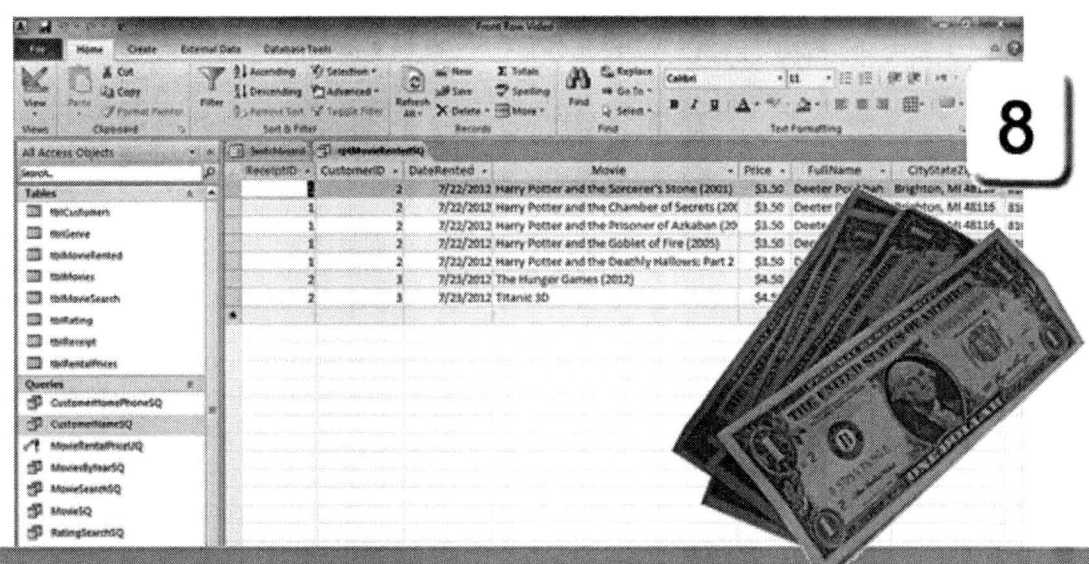

Query Tools ->Design->Results-> Run.

Run the Query, Again
8. Try it: Run the Query
Go to **Query Tools ->Design->Results->
Run.**

What Do You See? The **rptReceiptSQ** Query
returned seven Records, again. This Query
includes data we need on the Receipt Printout:
the customer's name, address and phone
number.

Please return to the **Design View**.

ReceiptID ▾	CustomerID ▾	DateRented ▾	Movie ▾	Price ▾	FullName ▾
1	2	7/22/2012	Harry Potter and the Sorcerer's Stone (2001)	$3.50	Deeter Poohbah
1	2	7/22/2012	Harry Potter and the Chamber of Secrets (2002)	$3.50	Deeter Poohbah
1	2	7/22/2012	Harry Potter and the Prisoner of Azkaban (2004	$3.50	Deeter Poohbah
1	2	7/22/2012	Harry Potter and the Goblet of Fire (2005)	$3.50	Deeter Poohbah
1	2	7/22/2012	Harry Potter and the Deathly Hallows: Part 2 (2(	$3.50	Deeter Poohbah
2	3	7/23/2012	The Hunger Games (2012)	$4.50	Mary Contrary
2	3	7/23/2012	Titanic 3D	$4.50	Mary Contrary

Calculate Totals in a Query

You can use this Query to calculate the Total for each Receipt. The first step in calculating the Totals is to **Group** the data. The Records will be **Grouped By** ReceiptID first so that each Receipt can be totaled separately.

1. Try it: Show the Total Row
The **rptReceiptSQ** is open in Design View.
Go to **Query Tools ->Design->Show/Hide**
Click on **Totals.**

What Do You See? There should be a new **Total Row** in the QBE Grid. The Totals Row has **Group By** as the value for each Field.

OK, the Total Row is shown and ready to go. Keep going...

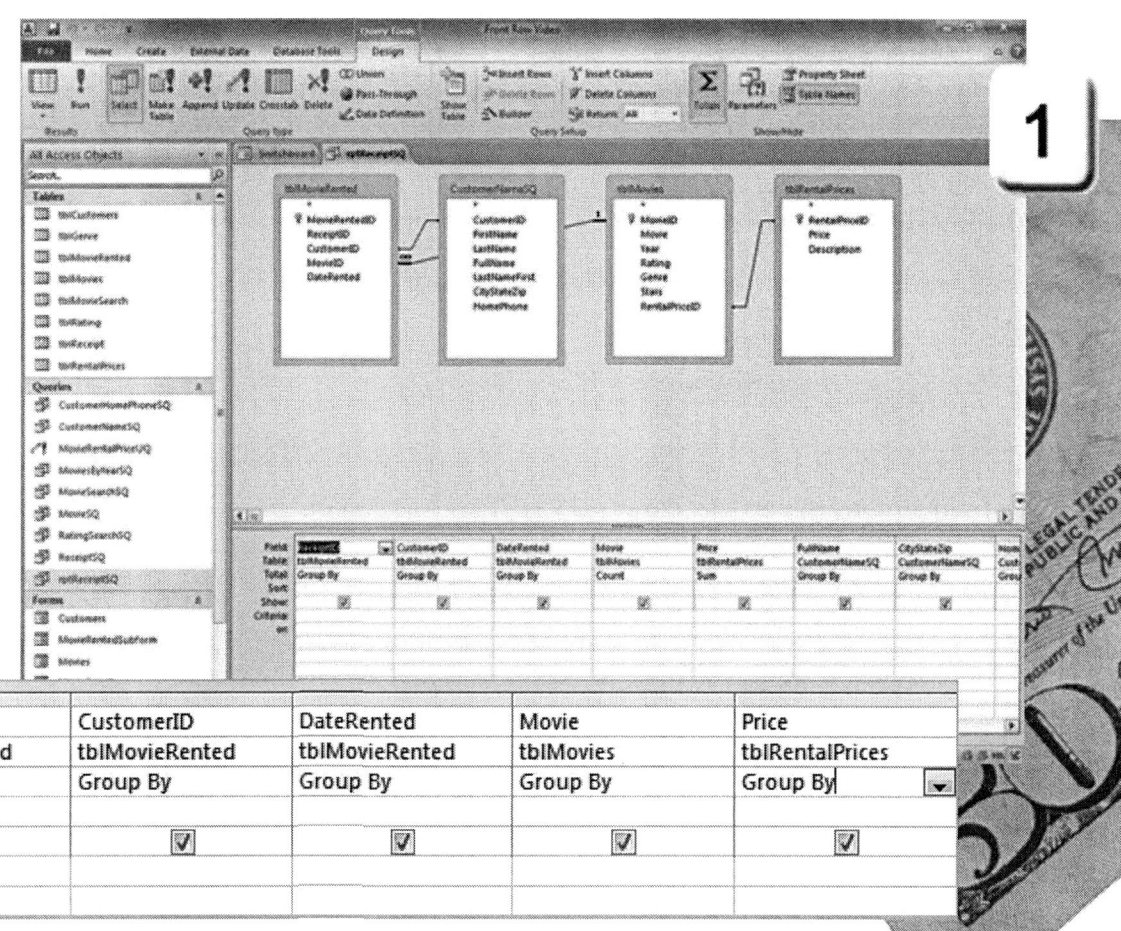

Field:	ReceiptID	CustomerID	DateRented	Movie	Price	
Table:	tblMovieRented	tblMovieRented	tblMovieRented	tblMovies	tblRentalPrices	
Total:	Group By	Group By	Group By	Group By	Group By	▼
Sort:						
Show:	☑	☑	☑	☑	☑	
Criteria:						
or:						

Exam 77-885: Microsoft Access 2010
4. Creating and Managing Queries
4.3. Manipulate fields: Calculate Totals

Take One

Use the Total Row

By default, the Total Row uses Group By for each Field. The other options include:
Sum
Avg
Min
Max
Count
SDev
Var
First
Last
Expression
Where

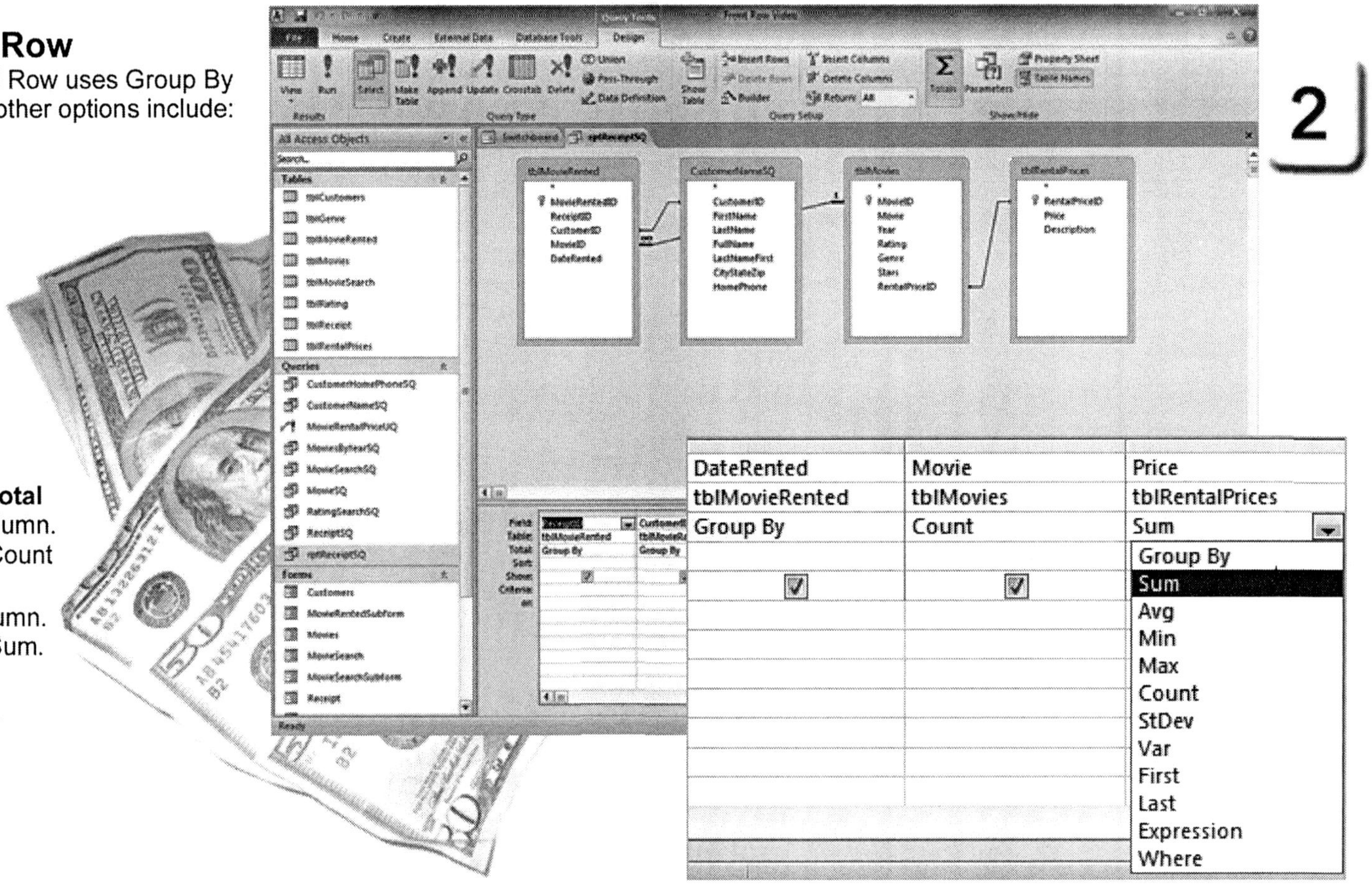

2. Try it: Edit the Total
Go to the Movie Column.
Change the Total: Count

Go to the Price Column.
Change the Total: Sum.

Keep going, please.

DateRented	Movie	Price
tblMovieRented	tblMovies	tblRentalPrices
Group By	Count	Sum
		Group By
✓	✓	Sum
		Avg
		Min
		Max
		Count
		StDev
		Var
		First
		Last
		Expression
		Where

Exam 77-885: Microsoft Access 2010
4. Creating and Managing Queries
4.3. Manipulate fields: Use the Totals Row

Run the Query

When you Run the Query you should see how many movies (CountOfMovie) and how much they cost (SumOfPrice) are on each Receipt.

3. Try it: Run the Query
Go to **Query Tools ->Design->Results-> Run.**

What Do You See? The **rptReceiptSQ** Query returned two Records this time:
ReceiptID 1 has 7 movies for $17.50.
ReceiptID 2 has 2 movies for $9.00.

Not bad.

Save and **Close** the Query. We have the Record Source for the Receipt Printout, now.

Query Tools ->Design->Results-> Run.

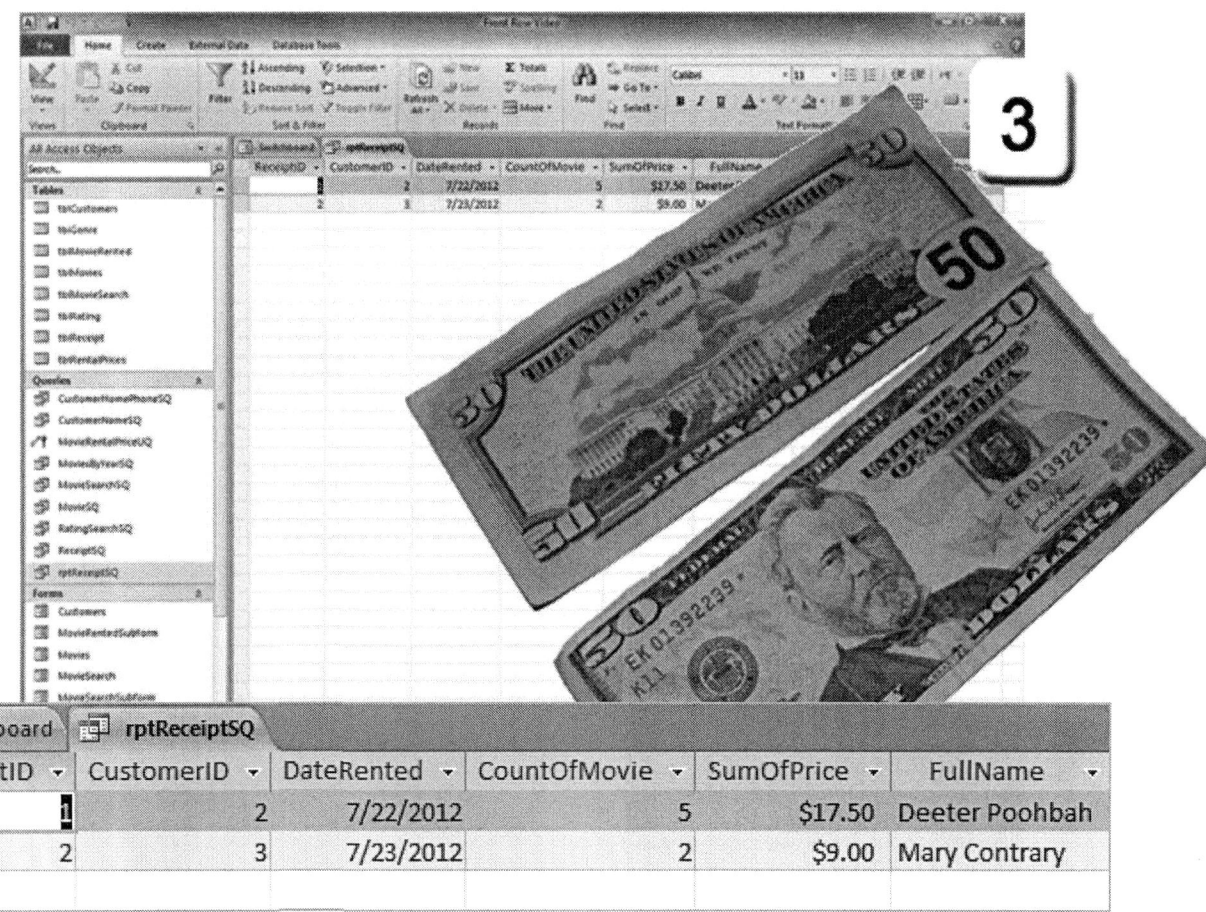

ReceiptID	CustomerID	DateRented	CountOfMovie	SumOfPrice	FullName
1	2	7/22/2012	5	$17.50	Deeter Poohbah
2	3	7/23/2012	2	$9.00	Mary Contrary

Exam 77-885: Microsoft Access 2010
4. Creating and Managing Queries
4.3. Manipulate fields: Calculate Totals

The Receipt Printout

The Receipt Printout will be very small: only 2 inches wide. For this example, we will begin with a Blank Report and format the Page Layout before we add the Fields.

1. Try it: Create a Blank Report
Go to **Create ->Reports->Blank Report.**

What Do You See? A new, blank Report should open in **Layout View.**

Do This, Now: View the Properties
Go to **Report Layout Tools->Tools.**
Click on **Property Sheet.**

And Do This: Select a Record Source
Go to **Properties->All.**
Select a **Record Source**: rptReceiptSQ.

OK, Save the Report
Go to **File->Save.**
Enter the name: rptReceipt-POS.

Keep going..

Create ->Reports->Blank Report

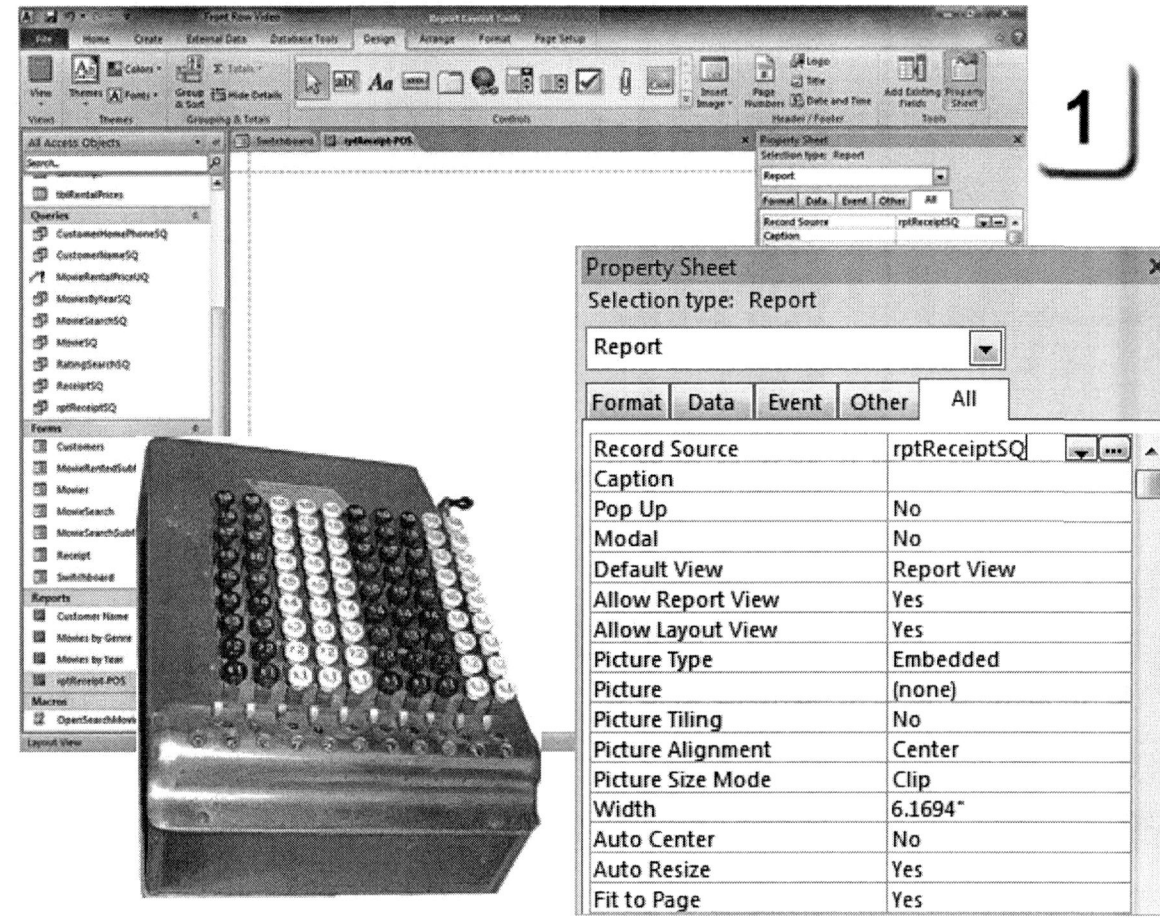

Exam 77-885: Microsoft Access 2010
5. Designing Reports
5.1. Create reports: Create a Blank Report

Report Page Layout

The Report Layout has be edited to fit a POS printer. We need to change the width of this Report. We can also edit the height of the Page Header and Detail Section.

Before You Begin: Change the View
Go to **Report Layout Tools->Views**.
Choose a **View: Design View**.
The Property Sheet should be open.

2. Try it: Edit the Report Properties
Select the Report.
Go to **Property Sheet->All**.
Edit the Width: 2"

And Try This: Edit the Page Header
Select the Page Header.
Go to **Property Sheet->All**.
Edit the Height: 0.5"

Yep, Try This: Edit the Detail Section
Select the Detail Section.
Go to **Property Sheet->All**.
Edit the Height: 2"
Keep going...

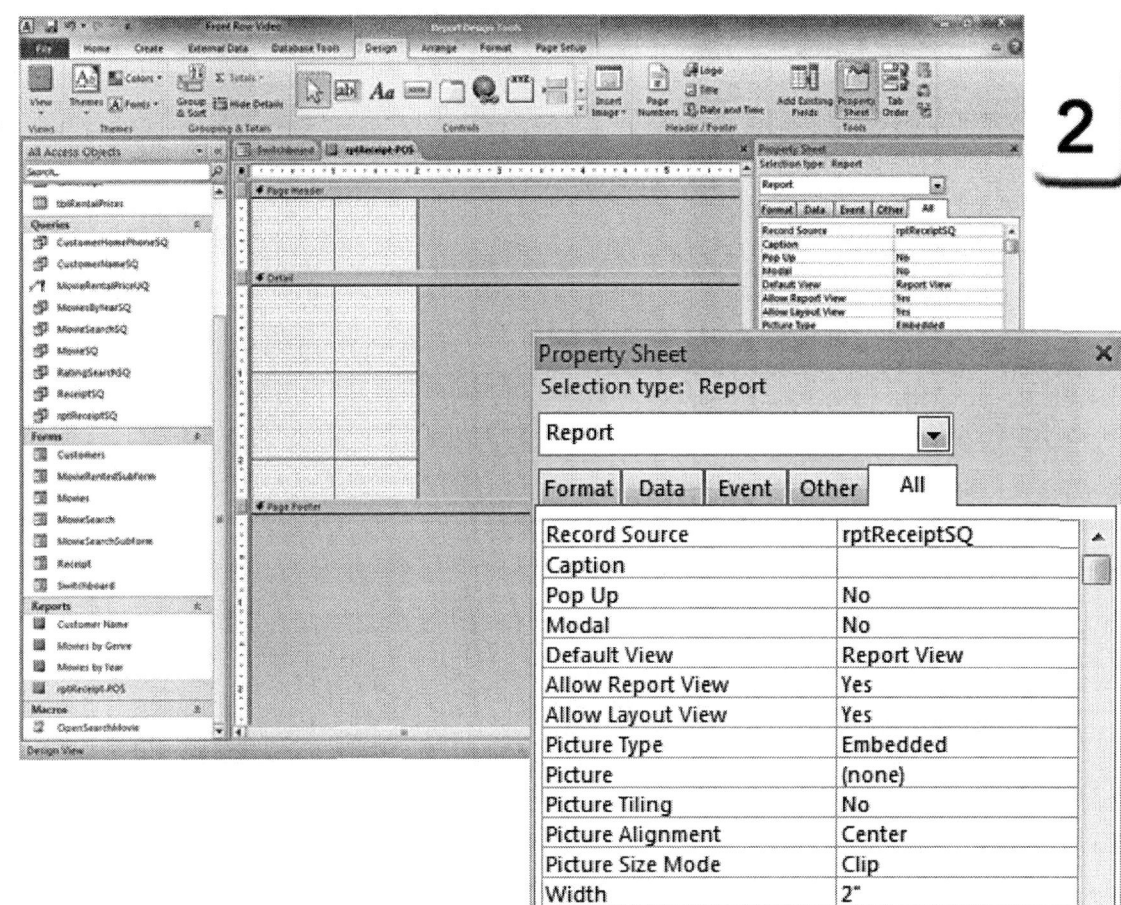

Property Sheet	
Selection type: Report	
Report	
Format	Data	Event	Other	All

Record Source	rptReceiptSQ
Caption	
Pop Up	No
Modal	No
Default View	Report View
Allow Report View	Yes
Allow Layout View	Yes
Picture Type	Embedded
Picture	(none)
Picture Tiling	No
Picture Alignment	Center
Picture Size Mode	Clip
Width	2"

Exam 77-885: Microsoft Access 2010
5. Designing Reports
5.5. Apply Report Page Setup options: Change Size

Page Setup Options

3. Try it: Review the Page Setup Ribbon
The **Page Setup Ribbon** has two Groups:
Page Size and Page Layout.

Review the Page Size Group
The **Size** templates include many of the
same page and envelope dimensions that
you have seen in Microsoft Word. The
Margin options are Normal, Wide and
Narrow.

Review the Page Layout Group
There are two Orientations: **Portrait** and
Landscape. Our Report will be Portrait. By
default, this Report has one **Column**.

Keep going...

Report Design Tools ->Page Setup

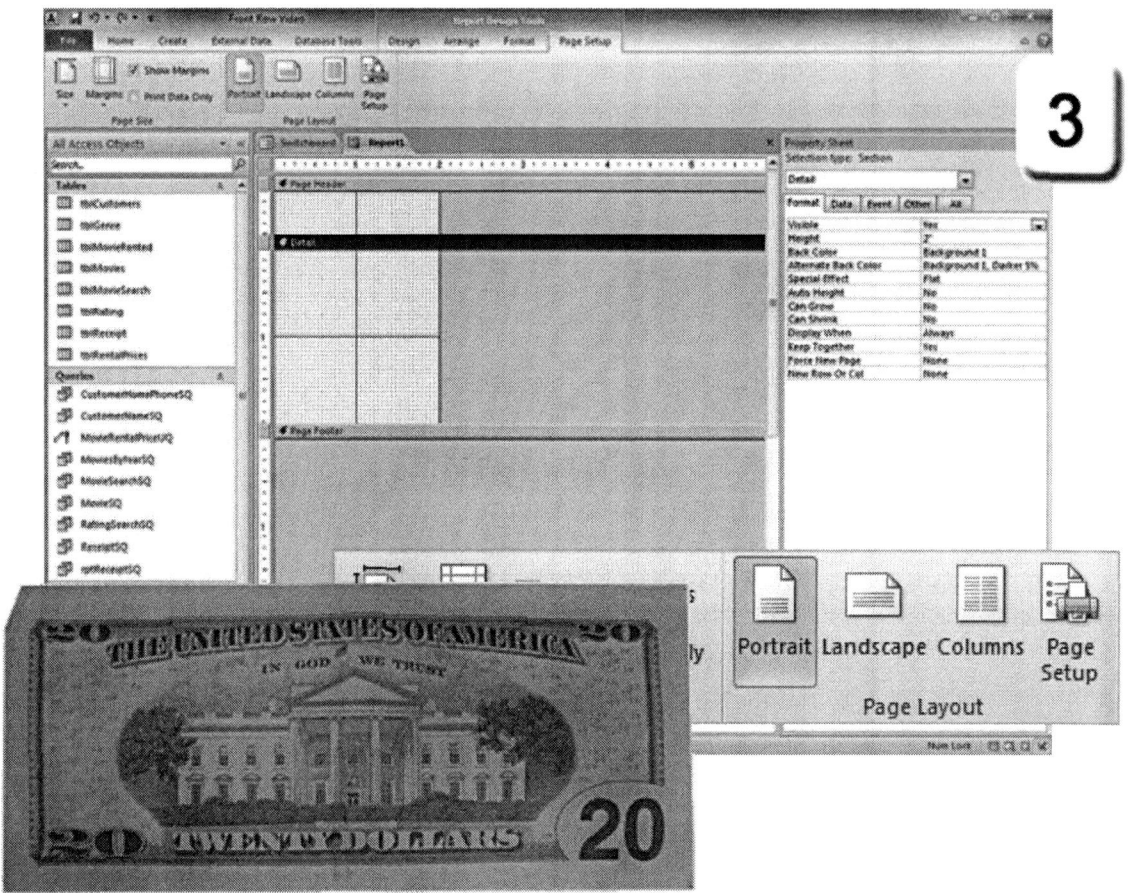

Exam 77-885: Microsoft Access 2010
5. Designing Reports
5.5. Apply Report Page Setup options: Size and Orientation

More Page Setup Options

4. Sure, Try This: Review the Page Setup
Page Setup is a summary of the options that you can edit. Please take a look.
Go to **Report Design Tools ->Page Setup**.
Go to **Page Layout->Page Setup**.

There are three Tabs for Print Options (margins), Page (size) and Columns.

Try This, Too: Edit the Columns
Go to the **Columns** Tab.

What Do You See? There is 1 Column in this Report. The Column Size is 2" wide: the **Same as Detail**.

Click **Ok** to **Close** the Page Setup.

Keep going...

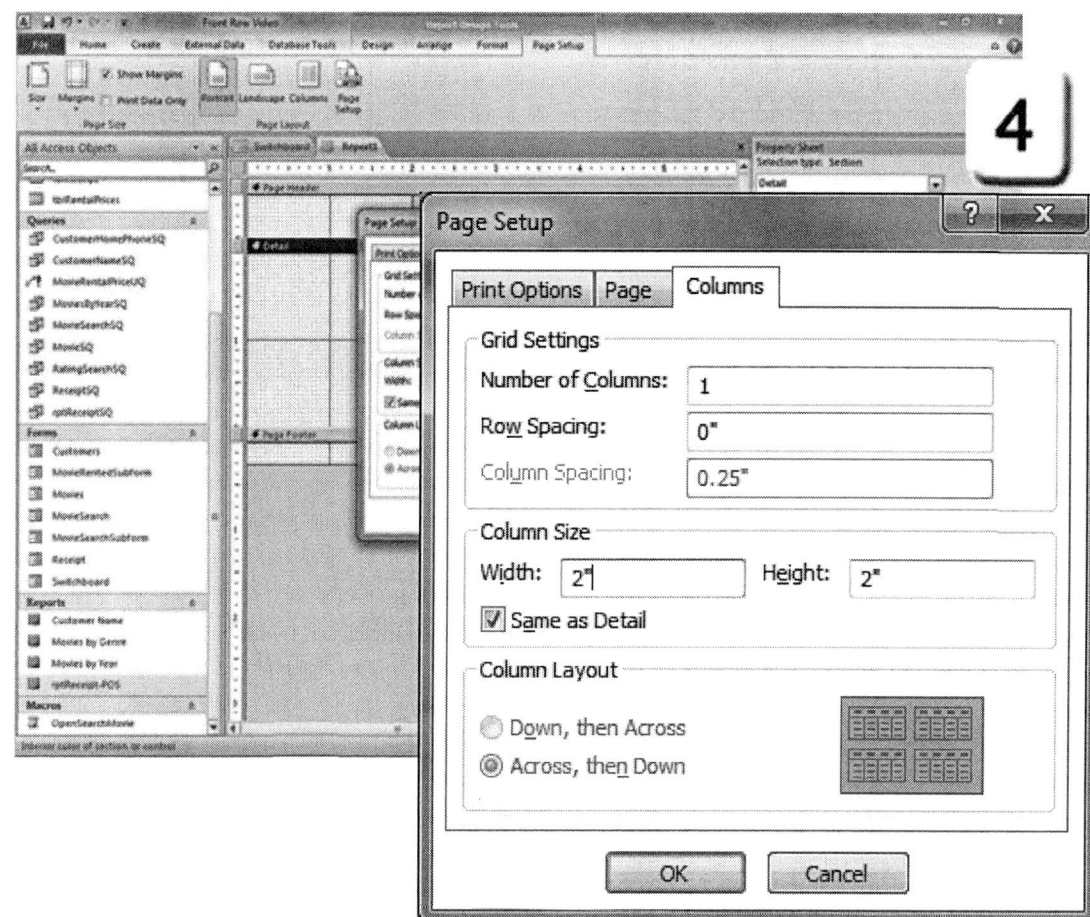

Exam 77-885: Microsoft Access 2010
5. Designing Reports
5.5. Apply Report Page Setup options: Columns

Edit the Page Header

If it's going to be in your customer's hand then it needs to have your company name at the top...spelled right, too.

5. Try it: Edit the Page Header
The Report is open in Design View.
Go to **Report Design Tools ->Design.**
Select a **Control**: Label.

Add the Label to the Page Header.
Edit the Label: Front Row Video.

You can format the text size in the Label larger to make the company name more noticeable if you wish.

Keep going...

Report Design Tools ->Design->Controls->Label

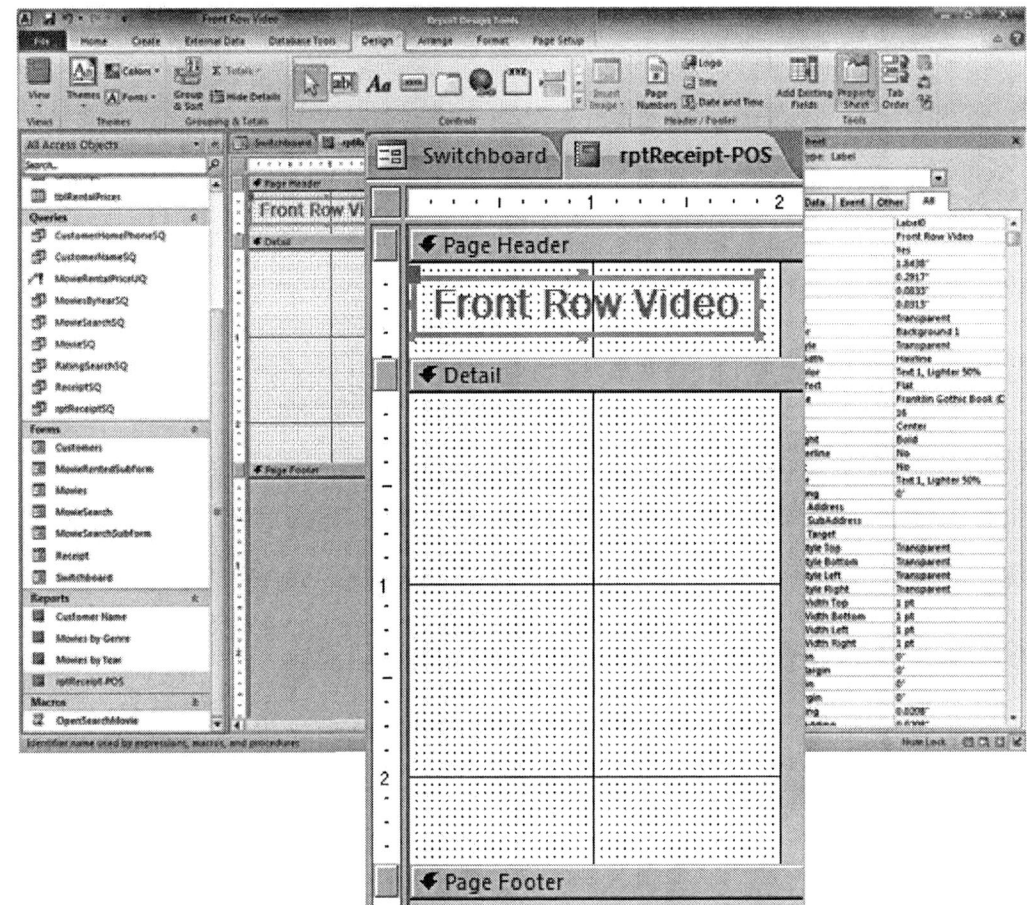

Exam 77-885: Microsoft Access 2010
5. Designing Reports
5.2. Apply Report Design options: Add Bound and Unbound Controls

Add Existing Fields to a Report

6. Try it: View the Field List
The Report is still open in Design View.
Go to **Report Design Tools ->Design->Tools.**
Click on: **Add Existing Fields**

What Do You See? The **Field List** should be available on the right side of the database.

Try This, Too: Add Existing Fields
Drag the following Fields to the Report:
DateRented
FullName
CityStateZip

Do This: Delete the Field Labels
This is a simple, narrow printout and does not need a label to explain.

Try This, as Well: Edit the Field Properties
Go to **Report Design Tools ->Design->Tools.**
Click on **Property Sheet.**
Move the Fields first, <u>then</u> resize them.
Left:0.0417"
Width: 1.80"
Keep going...

Report Design Tools ->Design->Tools->Add Existing Fields

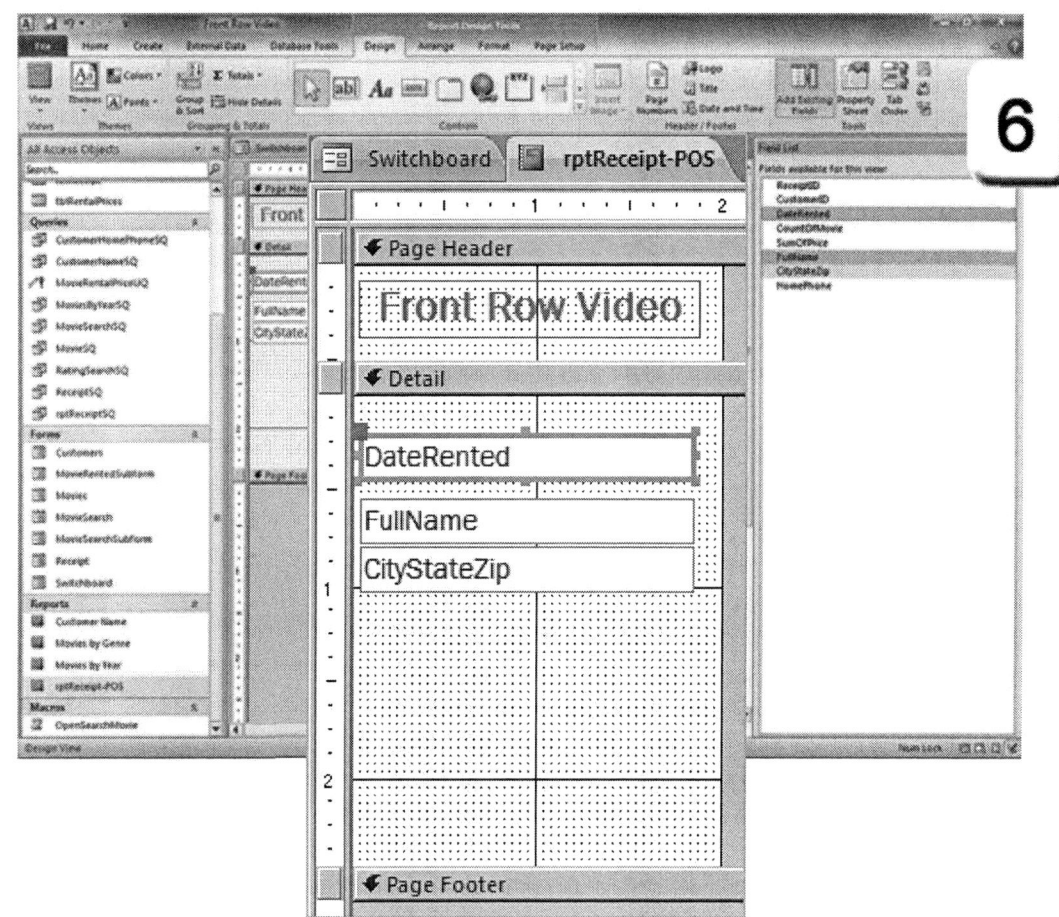

Exam 77-885: Microsoft Access 2010
5. Designing Reports
5.2. Apply Report Design options: Add Bound and Unbound Controls

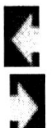

Add the Calculated Controls

7. Try it: Add the Calculated Controls
Go to **Report Design Tools ->Design->Tools.**
Click on **Add Existing Fields,** again.
Drag the following Fields to the Report:
ReceiptID
CountofMovies
SumofPrice

Try This, as Well: Edit the Fields
Select a Field: ReceiptID.
Edit the label: Receipt.

Select another Field: CountofMovies.
Edit the label: No of Movies.

Select a Field: SumOfPrice.
Edit the label: Total Due.

Try This, Too: Format the Field Outline
Select all of the Fields in the Detail Section.
Go to **Report Design Tools ->Format.**
Go to **Control Formatting-> Shape Outline.**
Choose an Outline Color: Transparent.
Please resize and position the Fields as needed.
Keep going..

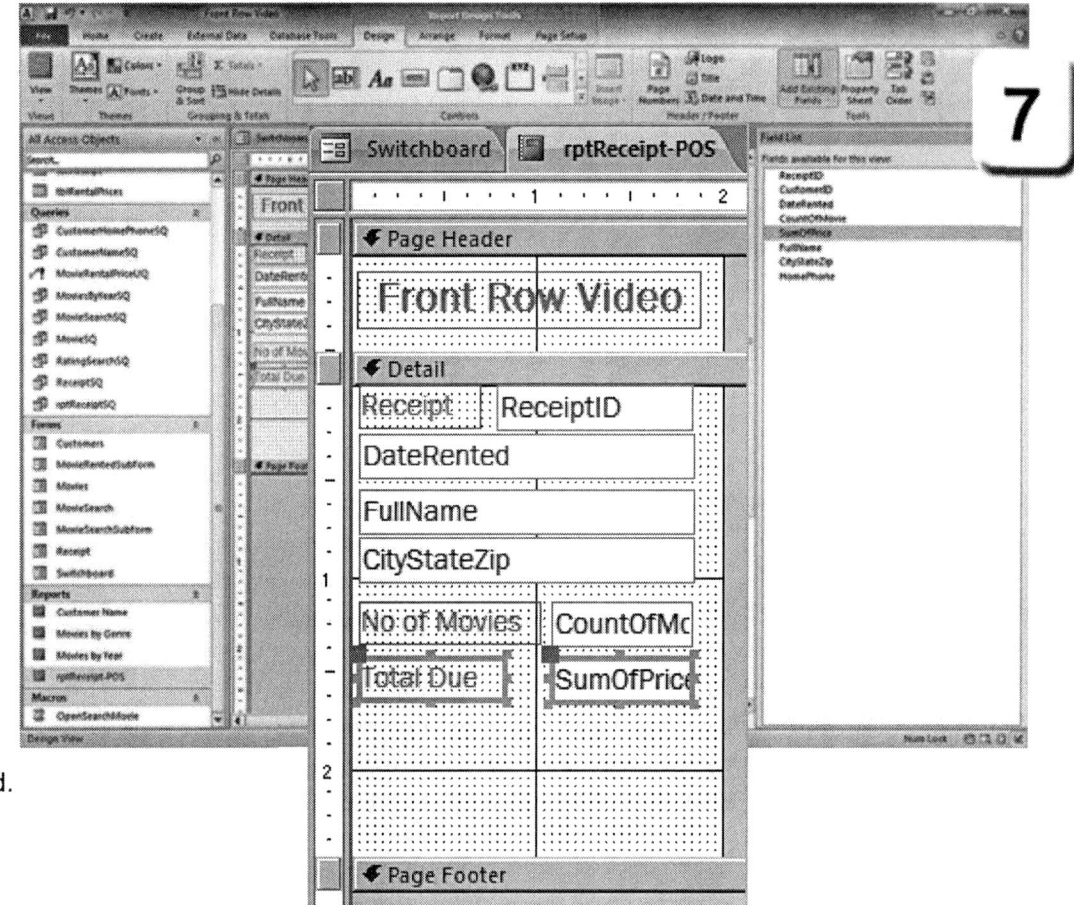

Exam 77-885: Microsoft Access 2010
5. Designing Reports
5.2. Apply Report Design options: Add Calculated Controls

Print Preview the Report

8. Try it: Preview the Report
Go to **Report Design Tools->Design->Views.**
Choose a **View: Print Preview.**

What Do You See? There are two Records in this Print Preview: Receipt 1 and Receipt 2.

Each Receipt calculates the number of movies rented and sums the Total Due.

This looks good...very good.
Definitely, **Save, Save, Save.**

Close the Print Preview.
Close the Report.

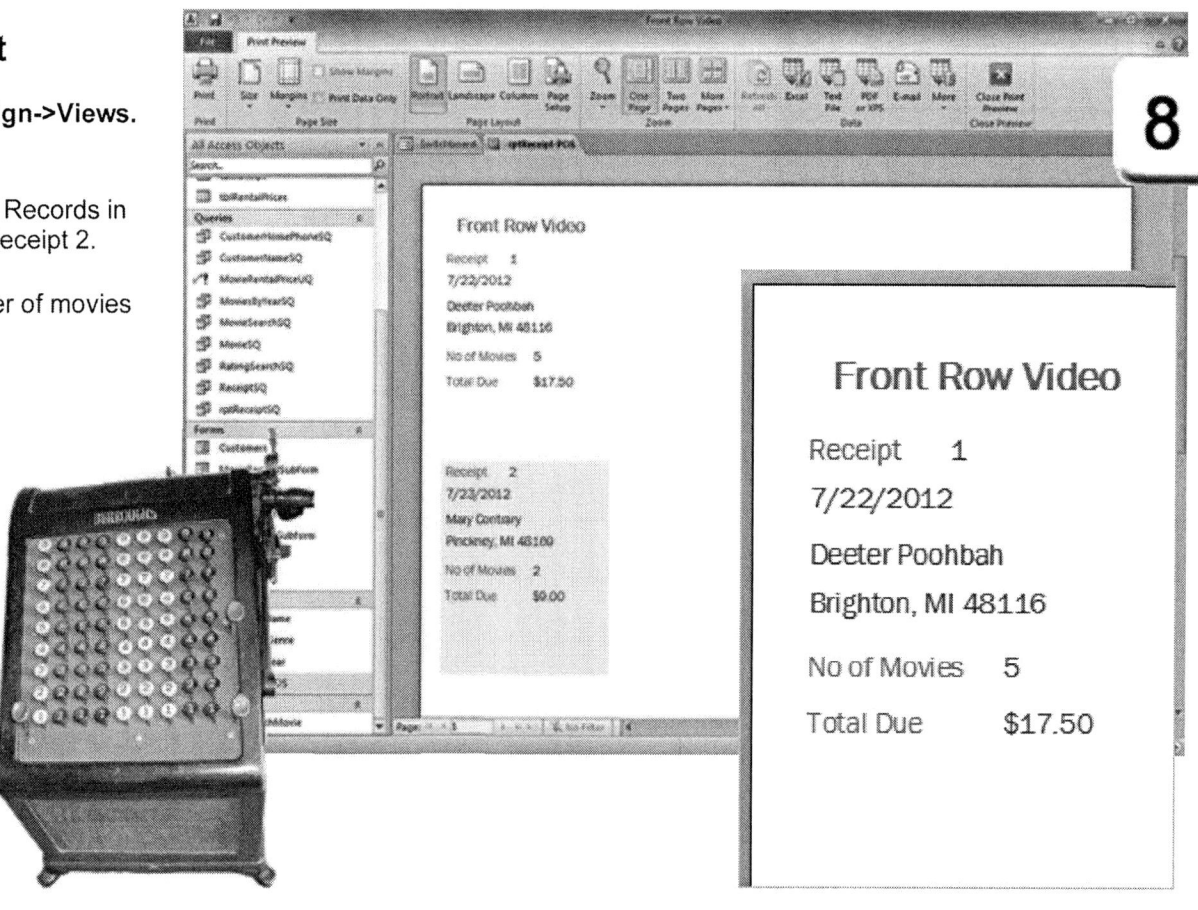

Exam 77-885: Microsoft Access 2010
5. Designing Reports
5.2. Apply Report Design options: Add Calculated Controls

What's the Next Step?

This lesson, **Advanced Report Design part 1,** began by creating a Query that calculates the Total for each Receipt. We used the Group By and Total Row to calculate the Sum of the rental prices and Count the movies on this Receipt.

The Report Page Layout was edited to make a small, 2" wide printout for a Point of Sale (POS) printer.

In the next lesson, **Advanced Report Design part 2,** we will create e Subreport that lists the movies and add the Subreport to the Receipt.

OK, one cookie. Then, back to work!

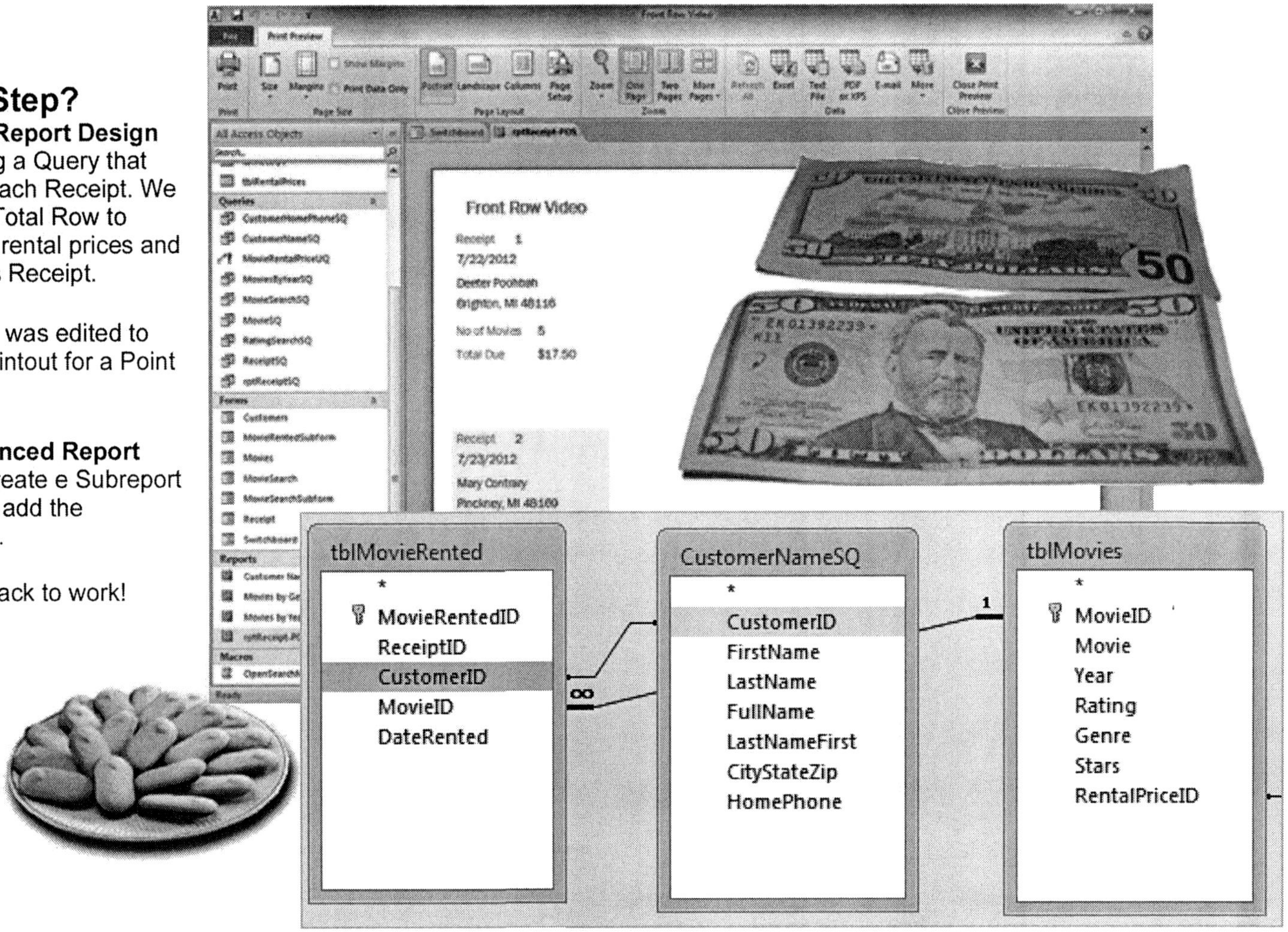

Practice Activities

Lesson 6: Advanced Report Design, part 1

Try This: Do the following steps

1. Open the Brown Bag Lunch database you have been working on.

Or, you may download **BBL Adv ver6.accdb**

2. Create a Select Query and add the following Record Sources: tblReceiptProducts, CustomerNameSQ, tblProducts.

JOIN the Tables by Key data:
From CustomerID in tblReceiptProducts to

Customer ID in CompanyNameSQ

From ProductID in tblReceiptProducts to

ProductID in tblProducts.

3. Add the following Fields to the QBE Grid:
From tblReceiptProducts:

ReceiptID, DateReceipt

From CompanyNameSQ:

Company, Fullname, Address, CityStateZip, Phone

From tblProducts: Price

4. Save the Query as rptReceiptSQ. Run the Query to test it.

5. Return to the Design View and select the Totals in the Query Tools. Change the Price from Group BY to Sum. Save the Query and Run it again. This Query should calculate the SUM of the Prices for each customer. Close the Query.

6. Create a new Report with the Report Wizard. Select rptReceiptSQ as the Record Source. Select all available Fields. Group by ReceiptID. Choose the Stepped Layout. Enter the Title: Brown Bag Lunch Co.

Select to Preview the Report and Finish the Wizard.

7. Close the Print Preview. Edit the Report in Design View.

Delete the Labels in the Page Header.

8. Arrange the Controls so that they look like a business address.

9. Select and edit the following Controls: DateReceipt , Fullname, Address, CityStateZip, Phone
Width: 3"
Left: 0.25"

Text Align: Left

10. Move the Price Control to the Report Header. Format the Price Control so that the data is aligned right. Add a Label: Total this Receipt.

11. Format the Properties for the DateReceipt: Medium Date.

12. Save the Brown Bag Lunch Co Report. Go to Print Preview and see the print out. Return to Design View and adjust the Controls as needed,

13. Close the Brown Bag Lunch Co Report..

14. Close the Brown Bag Lunch database. Get a cookie, if you wish.

Test Yourself

1. A Query can use another Query as a Record Source.
A. True
B. False
Tip: Advanced Access, page 162

2. Which are options in the Total Row?
(Give all correct answers.)
A. Group By
B. Count
C. Sum
Tip: Advanced Access, page 166

3. Which are Page Layout options for a Report?
(Give all correct answers.)
A. Portrait
B. Landscape
C. Columns (Number of)
Tip: Advanced Access, page 170

4. You cannot delete Field Labels.
A. True
B. False
Tip: Advanced Access, page 173

5. Which are Groups on the Page Setup Ribbon?
A. Page Size
B. Page Layout
C. Themes
D. Print Options
Tip: Advanced Access, page 170

Access 2010: Advanced Report Design

The Receipt Printout, part 2

Advanced Access Objectives

In this lesson, you will learn how to:

1. Create a Select Query that combines (JOINS) several Tables by matching Keys.

2. Create a Tabular Report and use the Report Arrange options to Insert Rows, Merge Cells and Move Fields into different Rows.

3. Resize the SubReport and format the Headers.

4. Add a SubReport and Link the Form and Subform by a Key Field.

5. Test the Receipt Report in Print Preview.

© 2012 Comma Productions, LLC

Lesson 7 : The Receipt Printout, part 2

1. Readings
Read Lesson 7 in the Advanced Access guide, page 179-208.

Project
A Receipt Subreport that will be added to the Receipt Report from the prior lesson.

Downloads
FrontRowVideo Adv7.accdb
BBL Adv ver7.accdb

2. Practice
Do the Practice Activity on page 209.

3. Assessment
Review the Test questions on page 210.

Report Design Tools->Arrange Ribbon

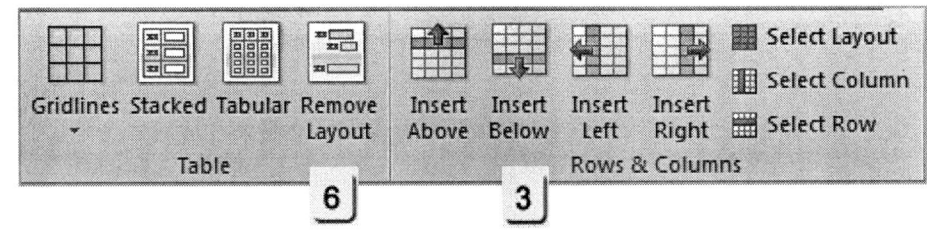

Report Design Tools->Arrange Ribbon, continued

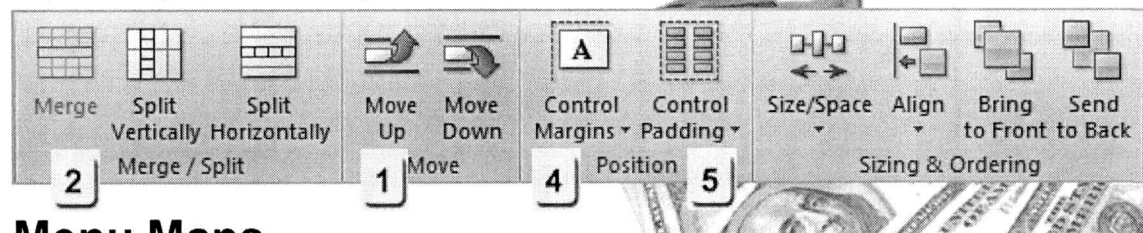

Menu Maps
From the **Create Ribbon**
Create ->Queries->Query Design, page 186
Create ->Reports-> Report Design, page 190

From the **Report Design Tools->Arrange Ribbon**.
1. Report Layout Tools ->Arrange->Move, page 192
2. Report Design Tools ->Arrange->Merge/Split, page 193
3. Report Design Tools ->Arrange->Rows & Columns, page 194
4. Report Design Tools ->Arrange->Position->Control Margins, page 196
5. Report Design Tools ->Arrange->Position->Padding, page 197
6. Report Design Tools ->Arrange->Table->Remove Layout, page 198

The Receipt Printout, part 2

The Receipt Subreport is very similar to the Receipt Subform. The steps to create and format the list of movies in a Table are the same. The challenge with the Receipt Subreport is size: 2" is a very small page when compared to a Form that is as big as a monitor. In this case, we will use the Table options to minimize the Cell padding and Spacing.

Microsoft Office Access 2010: Example of the completed Receipt Printout

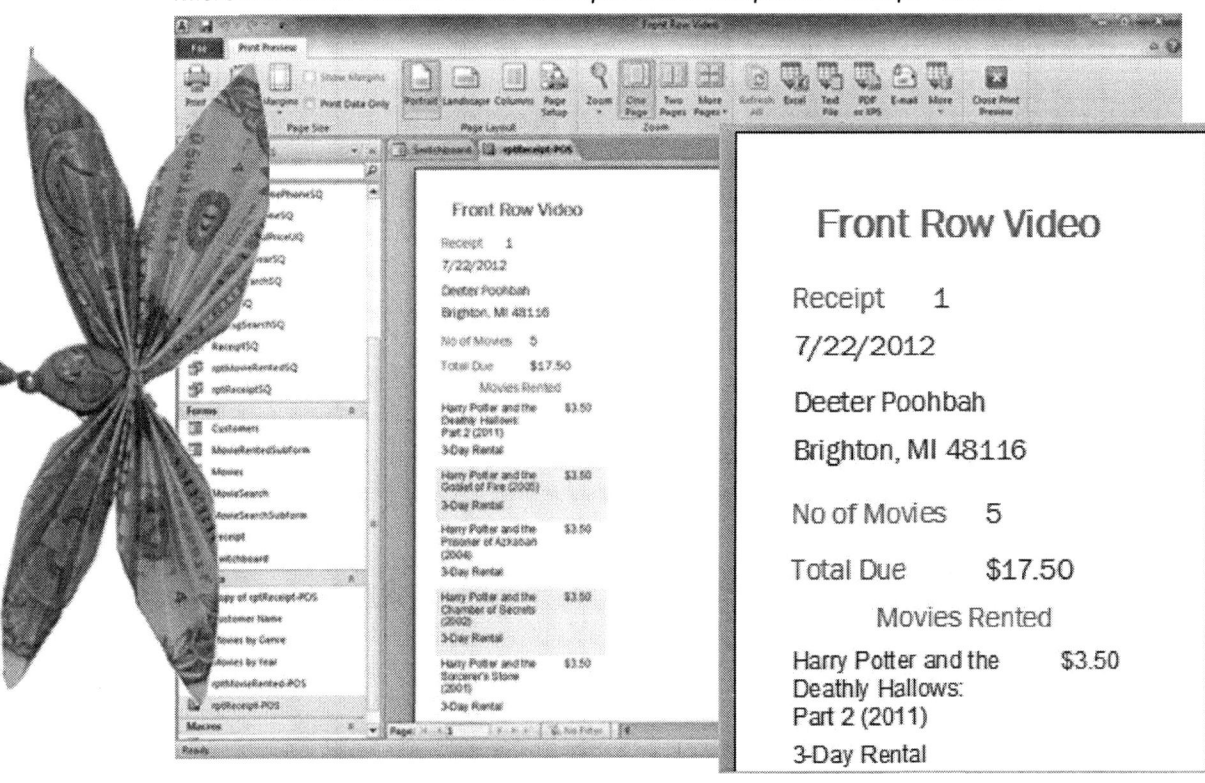

In Advanced Report Design part 1:
The Receipt Printout was based on a Query that calculates the Total for each Receipt. The Receipt, rptReceipt-POS, was formatted for a 2" wide POS printer.

In Advanced Report Design part 2,
we'll create a Subreport that lists the movies and add the Subreport to the Receipt Printout.

In Advanced Report Design part 3:
The Producers, we'll look at several tasks including calculating overdue movies and notifying our customers.

What is the Plan?

One customer may get many movies. So, the Receipt will have a Report and Subreport. The Subreport will list the movies rented.

The **rptMovieRented-POS** Subreport will use a Query, rptMovieRentedSQ with 3 Tables: tblMovieRented, tblMovies and tblRentalPrice.

Create the Query Source: rptMovieRentedSQ
Open tblMovieRented in Design View
Identify the Key Fields
Create a Select Query: rptMovieRentedSQ.

Create the Subreport: rptMovieRented-POS
The **rptMovieRented-POS** Subreport will be a Tabular Report formatted as a Table. The Controls and Headers have to be edited before the Report can be resized for the narrow 2" POS printer.

That's the plan.

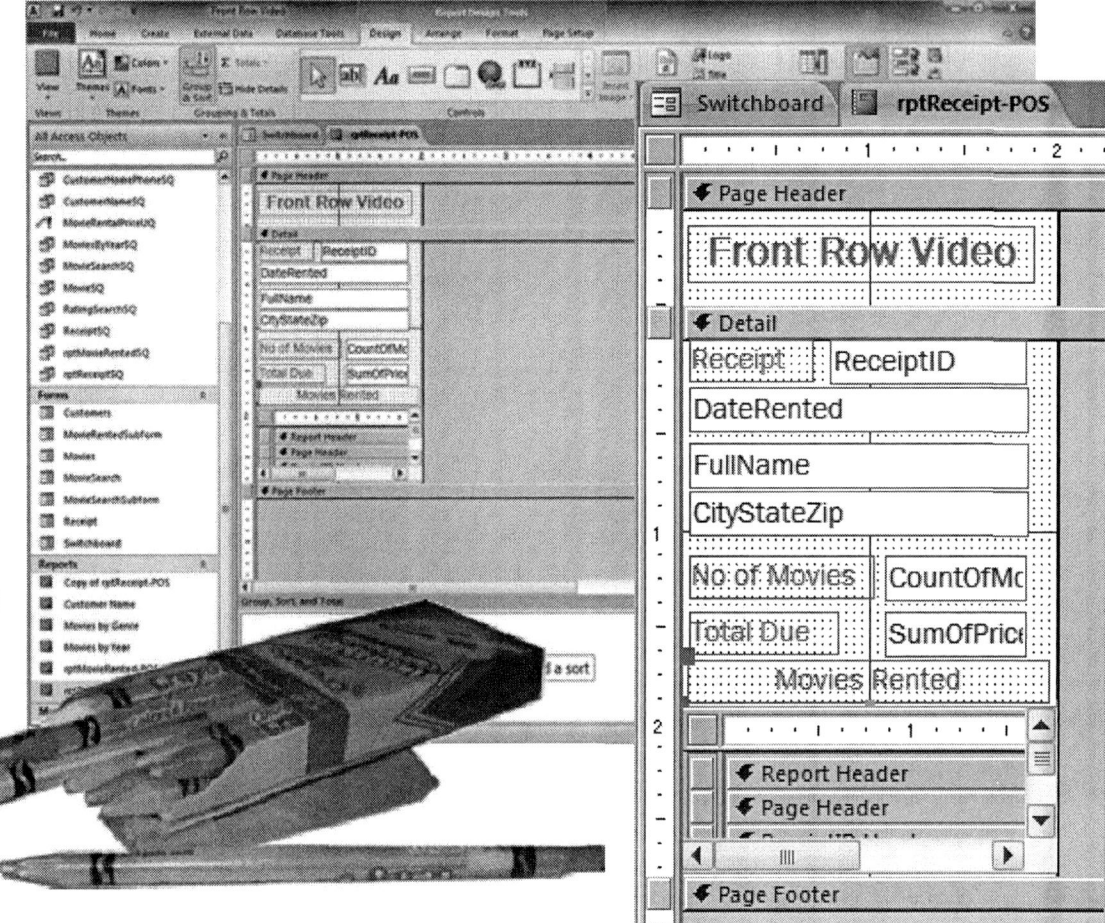

Before You Begin

Before You Begin: Open the Sample Database
Go to **Start -> All Programs ->Microsoft Office**.
Click on **Microsoft Office Access 2010.**
Access will prompt you to open a database.
Select: <u>FrontRowVideo Adv7.accdb</u>

The sample file, **FrontRowVideo Adv7.accdb,**
includes the Receipt Report that was developed in
the previous lesson. If your Report works you can
continue with your own database if you wish.

Keep going....

Memo to Self: Databases need to Read and
Write. Click **Enable Content** if you see the
Security Warning.

Start ->All Programs-> Microsoft Office-> Microsoft Access 2010

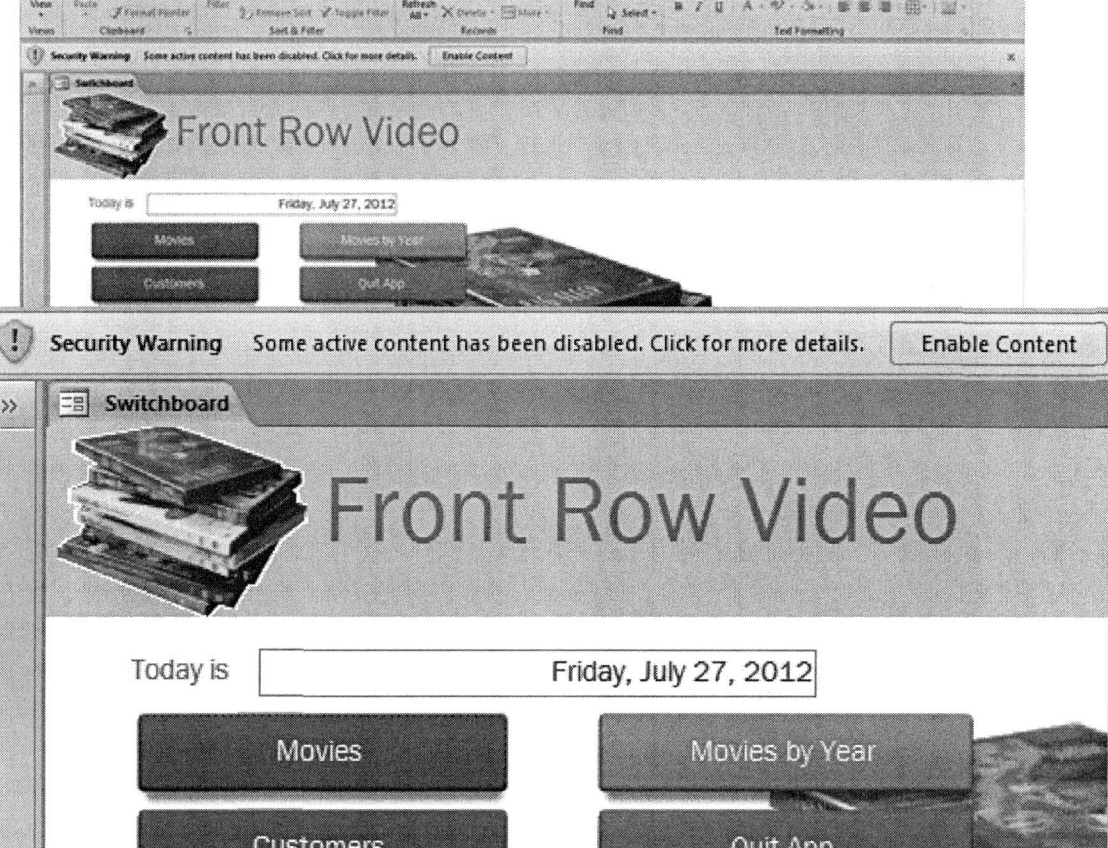

Know Your Data
Try This: Review the Database
Open the **Navigation Pane.**
Go to **All Access Objects.**

The Front Row View has the following:
Eight Tables: tblCustomers, tblGenre, tblMovieRented, tblMovies, tblMovieSearch, tblRating, tblRecipt and tblRentalPrices.

Nine Queries: CustomerHomePhoneSQ, CustomerNameSQ, MovieRentalPriceUQ, MoviesByYearSQ, MovieSearchSQ, MovieSQ, RatingSearchSQ, ReceiptSQ and rptReceiptSQ.

Seven Forms: Customers, Movies, MovieSearch, MovieSearchSubform, Receipt and MoviesRentedSubform.

Four Reports: Customer Name. Movies by Genre, Movies by Year, rptReceipt-POS.

One Macro: OpenSearchMovie

All Access Objects

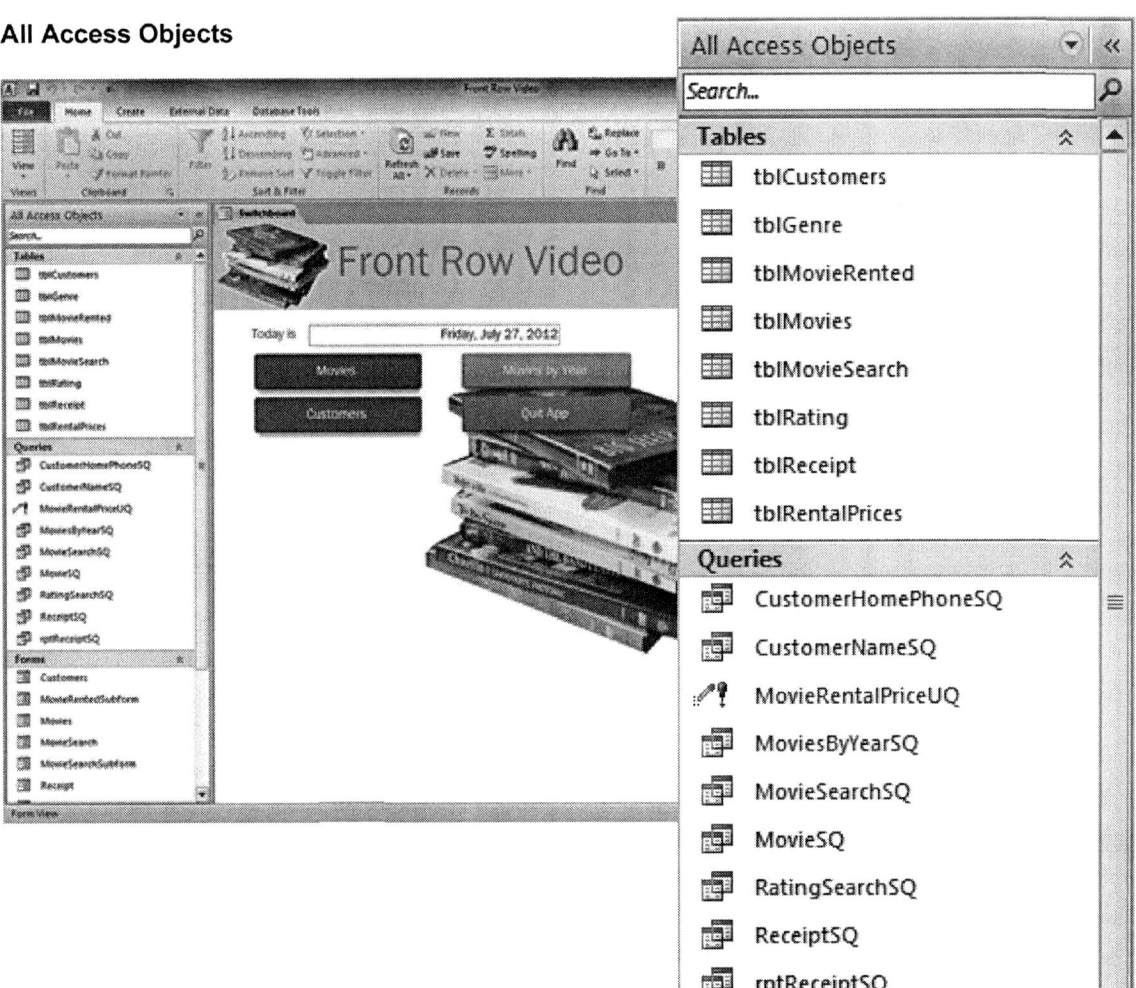

Review the Record Source

The Receipt Subform will look up the data in a Table, tblMovieRented. Our discussion always begins by reviewing the data.

1. Try This: Review the Record Source
Go to **All Access Objects ->Tables.**
Open a **Table: tblMovieRented.**

Do This, Too: Change the View
Go to **Home->Views->View.**
Select a **View: Design View.**

What Do You See? This Table, tblMovieRented, has numbers only:
MovieRentedID (the Primary Key)
ReceiptID (a Foriegn Key)
CustomerID (a Foreign Key)
MovieID (a Foreign Key)
DateRented (Date/Time)

This Table is in Third Normal Form: the Key, the whole Key and nothing but the Key.

Please **Close** tblMovieRented. Keep going.

All Access Objects ->Tables

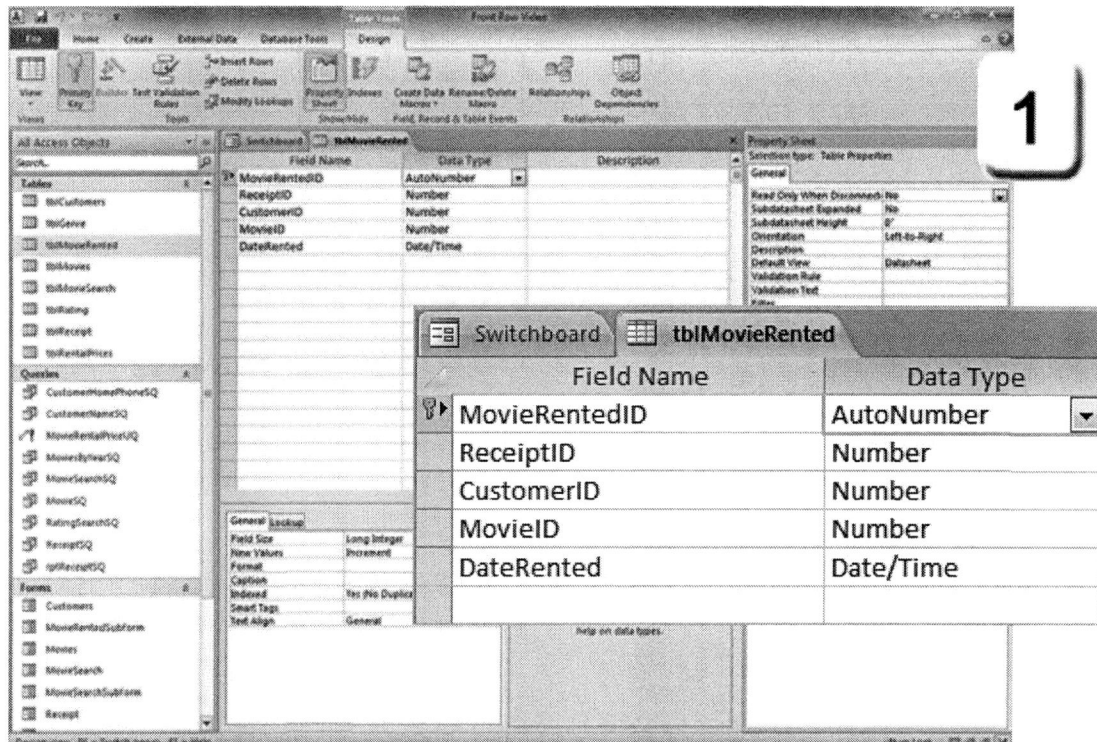

Field Name	Data Type
MovieRentedID	AutoNumber
ReceiptID	Number
CustomerID	Number
MovieID	Number
DateRented	Date/Time

Create a Select Query: rptMovieRentedSQ

Queries look up the Key and return the data: This new Query will list the movies for each Receipt.

2. Try it: Create a Query
Go to **Create ->Queries ->Query Design**. You will be prompted by the **Show Table**.

Select a Table: tblMovieRented.
Click **Add**.

Select a Table: tblMovies.
Click **Add**.

Select a Table: tblRentalPrices.
Click **Add**.

Close the Show Table Window.
Keep going...

Create ->Queries ->Query Design

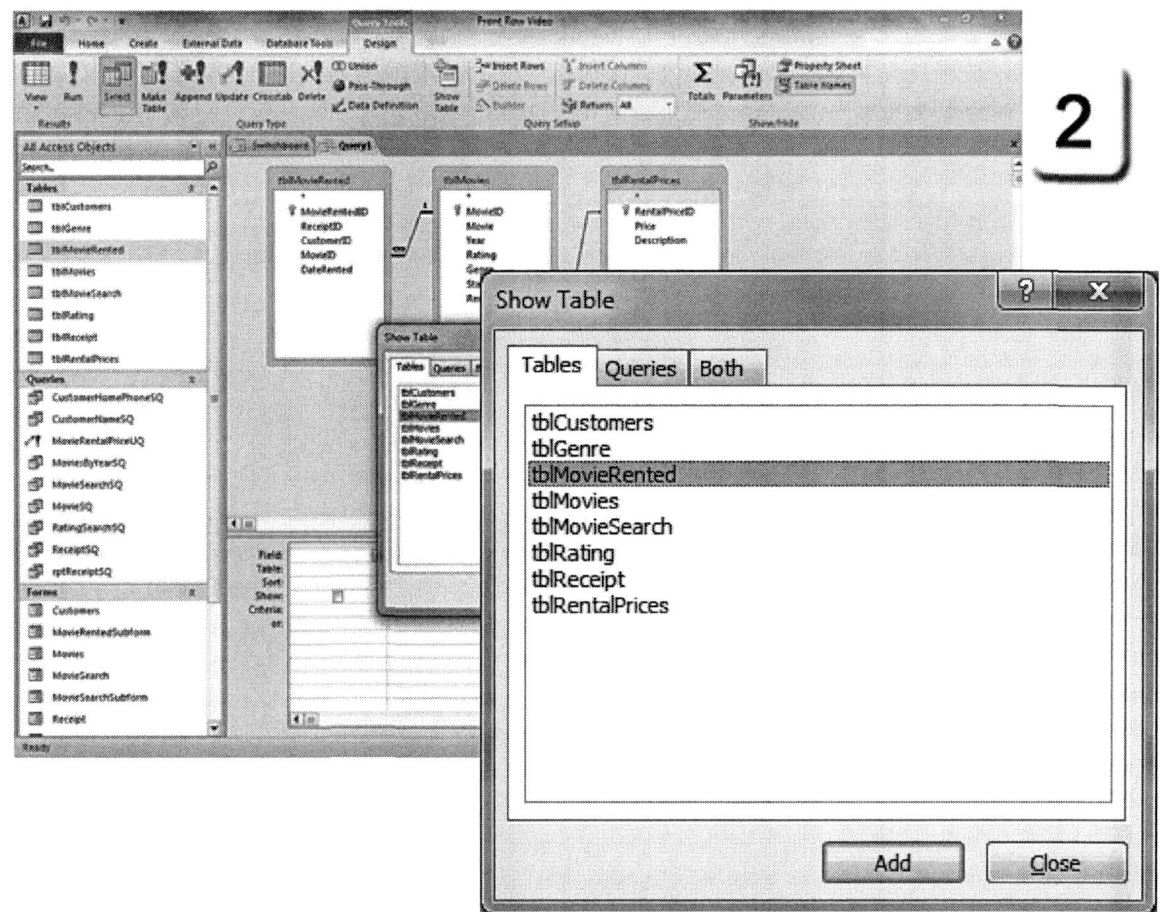

2

Exam 77-885: Microsoft Access 2010
4. Creating and Managing Queries
4.2. **Manage source tables and relationships: Use the Show Table Options**

rptMovieRentedSQ:JOINS

As you added each Table to the Query, the Tables were JOINED by their Keys.

3. Try it: Review the JOINS

tblMovieRented.MovieID to tblMovies.MovieID.

tblMovies.RentalPriceID to tblRentalPrices.RentalPriceID.

Keep going...

Query Tools ->Design

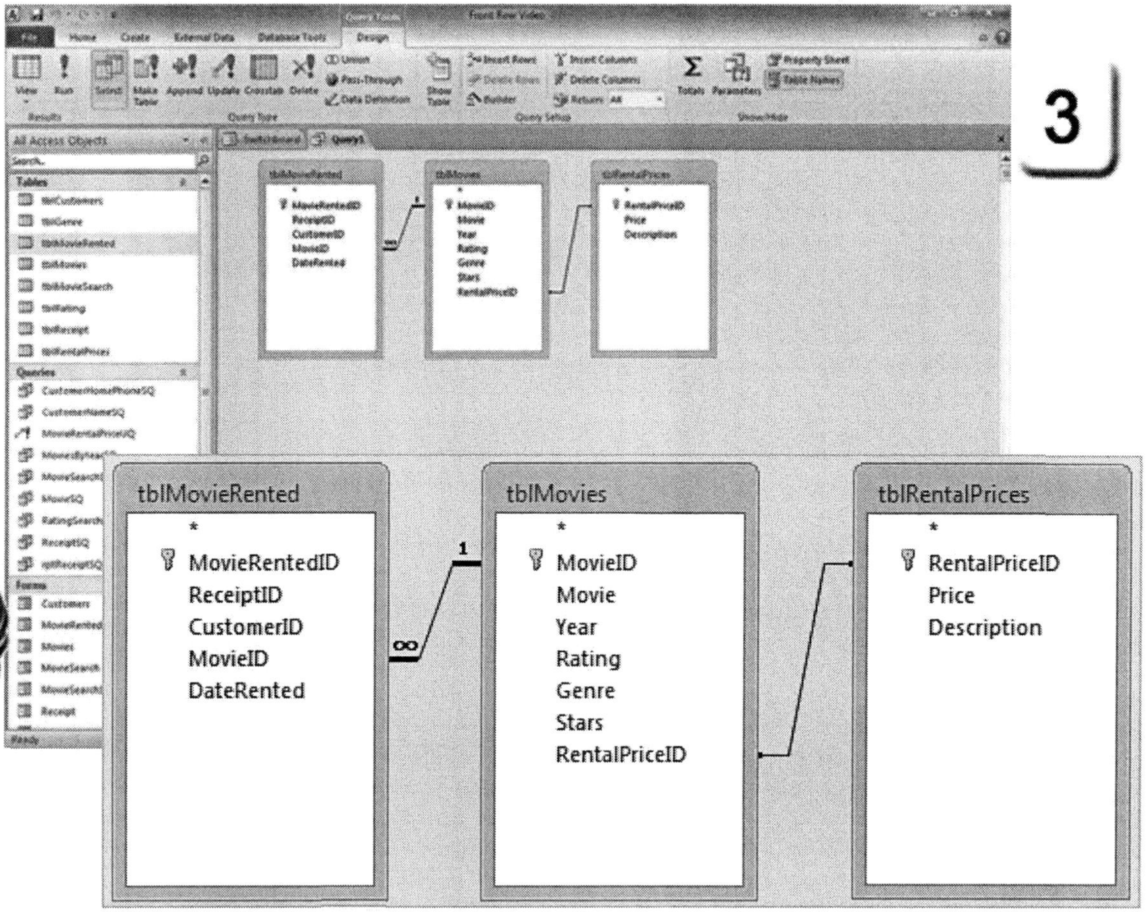

tblMovieRented		tblMovies		tblRentalPrices
*		*		*
🔑 MovieRentedID		🔑 MovieID		🔑 RentalPriceID
ReceiptID	1	Movie		Price
CustomerID		Year		Description
MovieID		Rating		
DateRented	∞	Genre		
		Stars		
		RentalPriceID		

Exam 77-885: Microsoft Access 2010
4. Creating and Managing Queries
4.2. Manage source tables and relationships

Take Two

Query Tools ->Design

rptMovieRentedSQ: Fields
4. Try it: Add Fields to the Query
Add the following Fields to the QBE Grid:
From tblMovieRented:
ReceiptID
DateRented

From tblMovies:
Movie

From tblRentalPrices:
Price
Description

Do This, Now: Save the Query
Go to **File->Save**.
Enter the name: **rptMovieRentedSQ**.

Keep going...

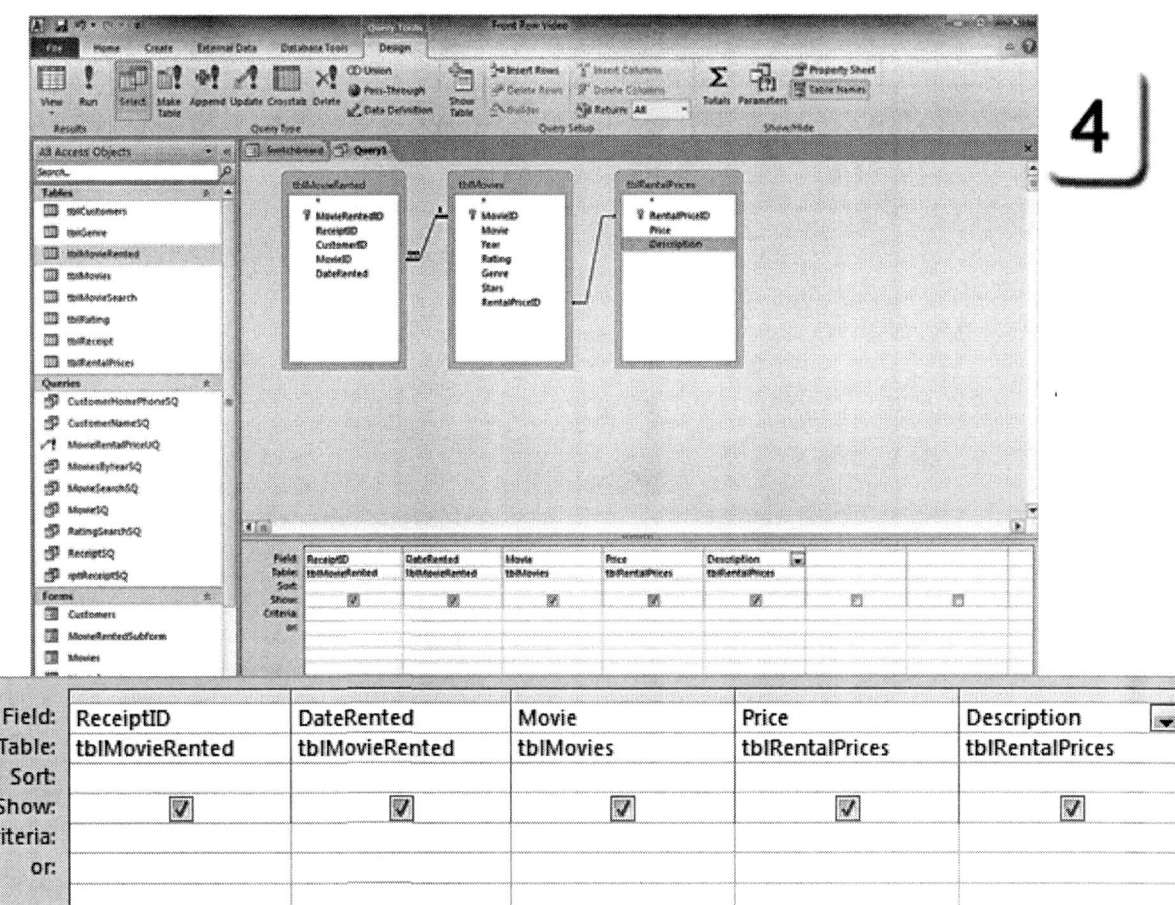

Field:	ReceiptID	DateRented	Movie	Price	Description	▼
Table:	tblMovieRented	tblMovieRented	tblMovies	tblRentalPrices	tblRentalPrices	
Sort:						
Show:	☑	☑	☑	☑	☑	
Criteria:						
or:						

Exam 77-885: Microsoft Access 2010
4. Creating and Managing Queries
4.3. Manipulate fields: Add Fields to a Query

rptMovieRentedSQ: Run!

5. Try it: Run the Query
Go to **Query Tools ->Design->Results.**
Click on **Run**.

What Do You See? The **rptMovieRentedSQ**
Query returned seven Records.
Receipt 1 has 5 movies.
Receipt 2 has 2 movies.
That's what we wanted to see.

This Query is the Record Source for the
Subreport, **rptMovieRented-POS.**

Done and Done. **Close** the Query.

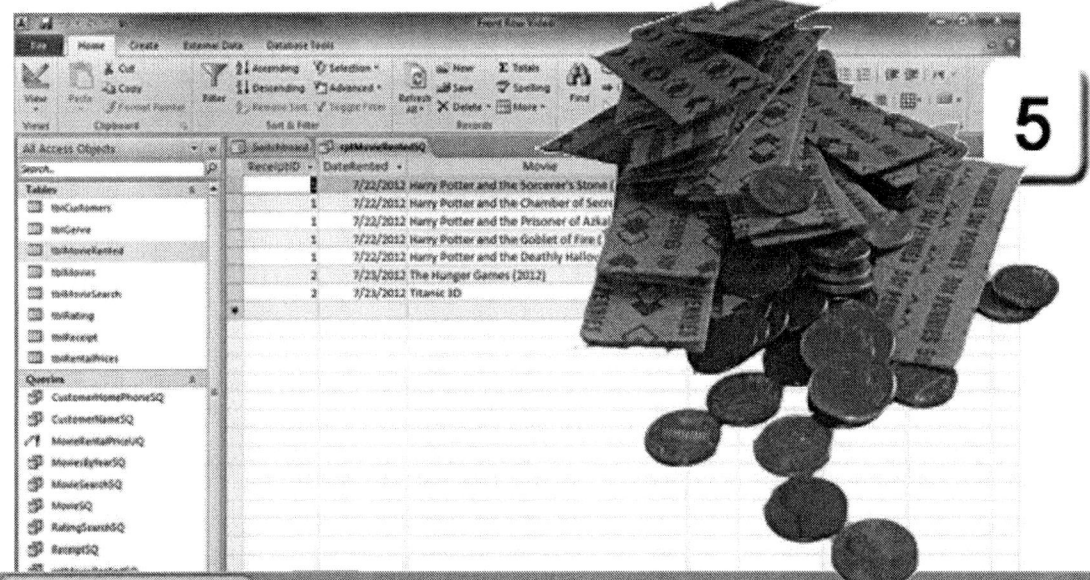

ReceiptID ▾	DateRented ▾	Movie ▾	Price ▾	Description ▾
1	7/22/2012	Harry Potter and the Sorcerer's Stone (2001)	$3.50	3-Day Rental
1	7/22/2012	Harry Potter and the Chamber of Secrets (2002)	$3.50	3-Day Rental
1	7/22/2012	Harry Potter and the Prisoner of Azkaban (2004)	$3.50	3-Day Rental
1	7/22/2012	Harry Potter and the Goblet of Fire (2005)	$3.50	3-Day Rental
1	7/22/2012	Harry Potter and the Deathly Hallows: Part 2 (2011)	$3.50	3-Day Rental
2	7/23/2012	The Hunger Games (2012)	$4.50	1-Day Rental
2	7/23/2012	Titanic 3D	$4.50	1-Day Rental

Create the Subreport

The Receipt Subreport will be less than 2"
wide. So, we will begin with a Report Design
and format the Fields in the Table. Then, we'll
change the width of the Report.

1. Try it: Create the Subreport
Go to **All Access Objects->Queries**.
Select a Query: rptMovieRentedSQ.
Go to **Create ->Reports-> Report.**

What Do You See? A new Report should open
in **Layout View.**

OK, Save the Report
Go to **File->Save**.
Enter the name: rptMovieRented-POS.

Keep going..

Create ->Reports-> Report

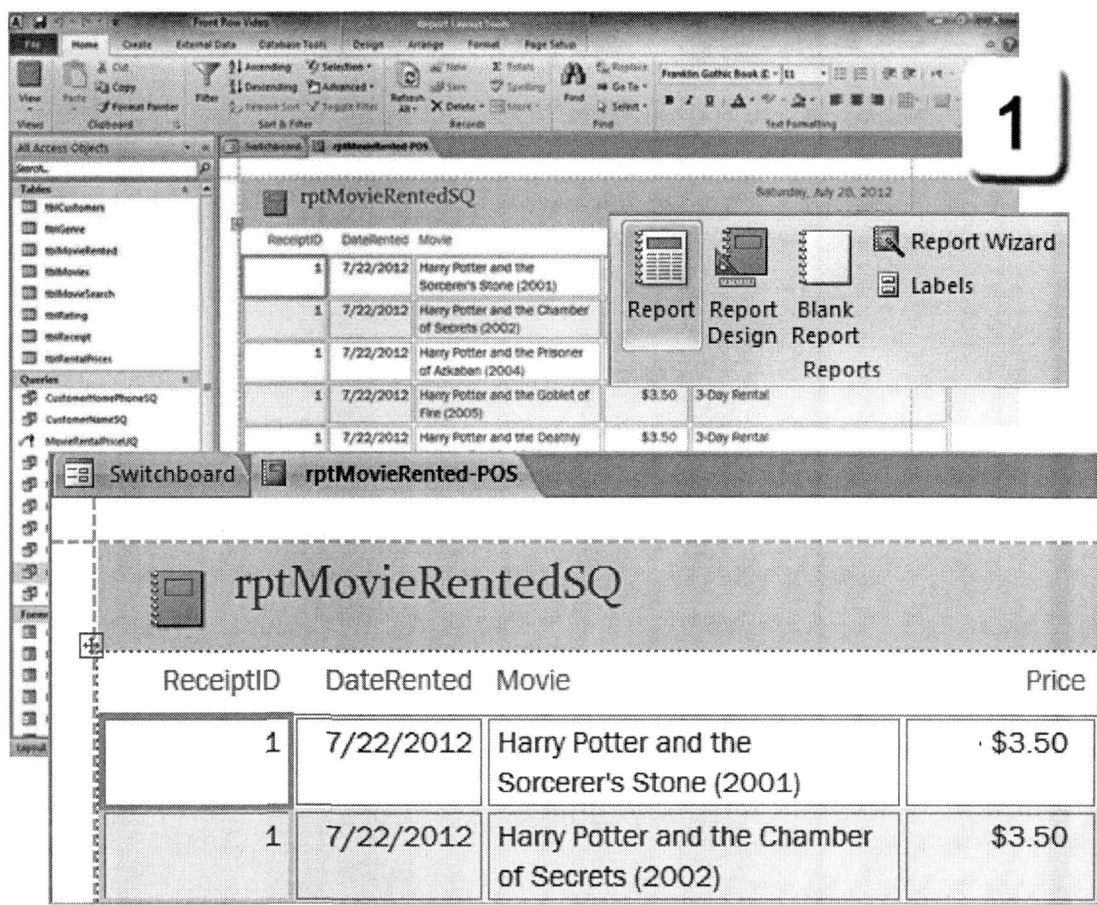

Exam 77-885: Microsoft Access 2010
5. Designing Reports
5.1. Create reports

Group and Sort

All of the movies that belong on the same Receipt will be Grouped together. When you select a Field to Group and Sort, you are creating a Group Header for that Field.

2. Try it: Group By
Go to **Report Layout Tools ->Design.**
Go to **Grouping and Totals.**
Select **Group & Sort.**

What Do You See? The Group, Sort and Total options should be available on the bottom of the Report.

Try This, Too: Add a Group
Click on **Add a Group**.
Select a Field: ReceiptID.

Keep going...

Report Layout Tools ->Design->Grouping and Totals->Group & Sort

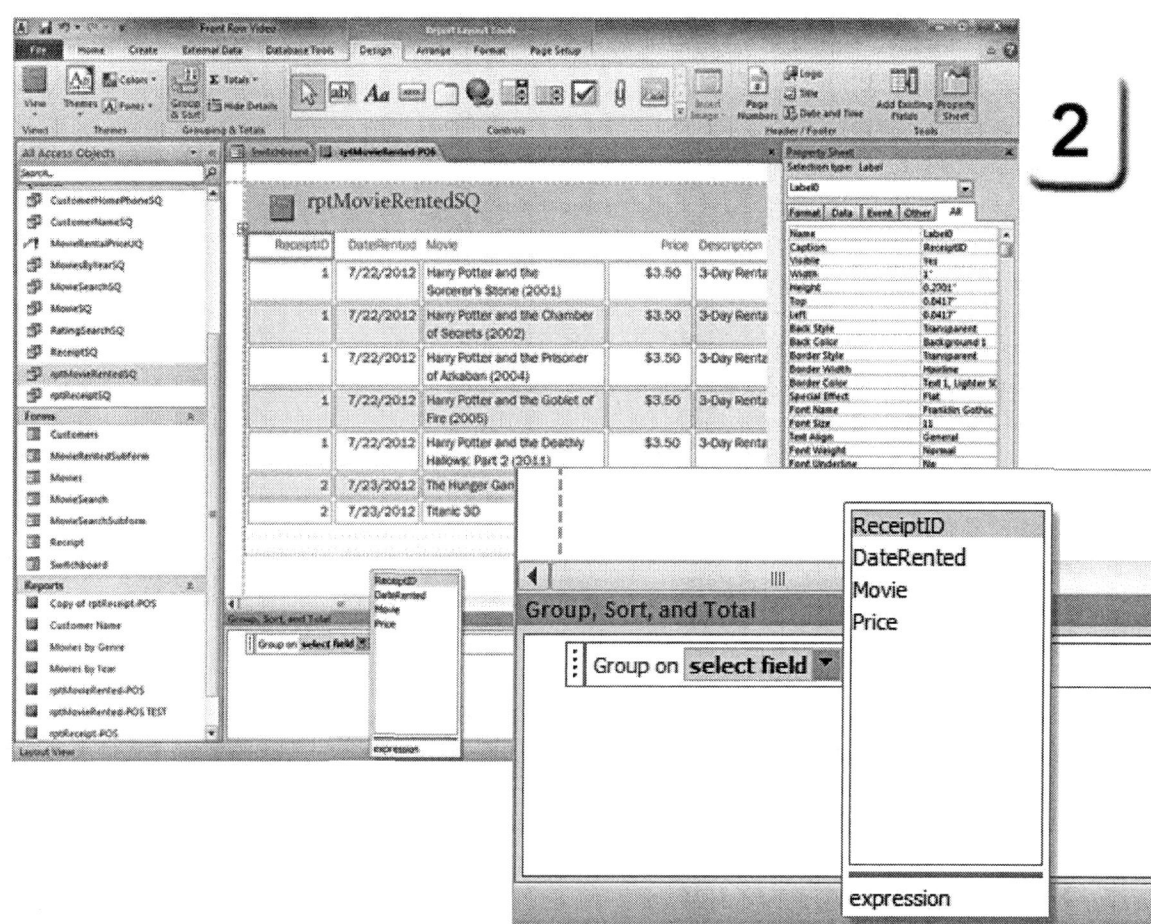

Exam 77-885: Microsoft Access 2010
5. Designing Reports
5.3. Apply Report Arrange options: Move

Move a Field

Adding a Group created a new Group Header for this Field, ReceiptID. A new Row was created in this Table as well. We can move other Fields to that Row.

3. Try it: Add Another Group
The Report is still in Report Layout View.
Select a Field: DateRented.
Go to **Report Layout Tools ->Arrange**.
Go to **Move->Move Up**.

What Do You See? There should be two Fields in the same Row in this Table:
ReceiptID and DateRented.

Keep going...

What If It Doesn't Work? Confirm that you selected the Field, not the Label, OK?

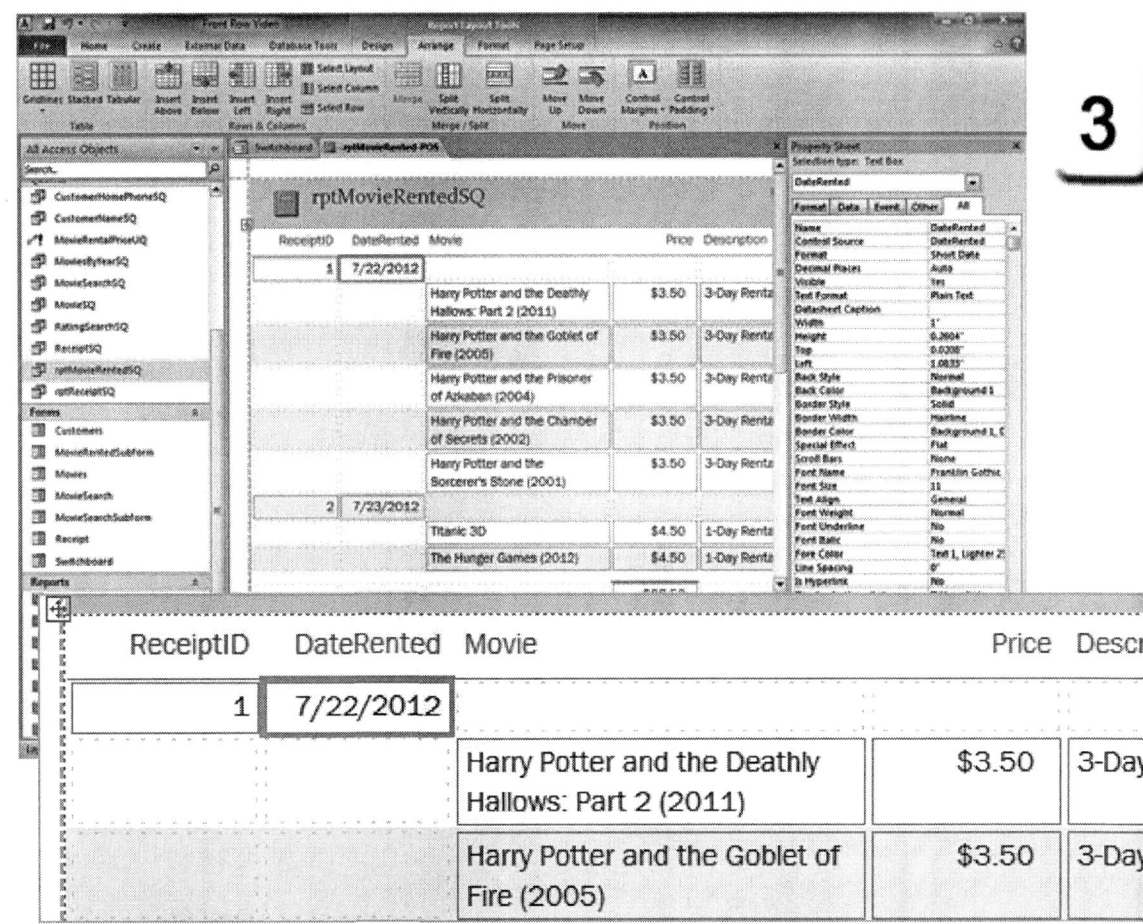

Exam 77-885: Microsoft Access 2010
5. Designing Reports
5.3. Apply Report Arrange options: Move

Do More in Design View
The goal is to resize and edit the Table so that it will fit a narrow printout. The next steps are easier to do in Design View.

Before You Begin: Change the View
Go to **Report Layout Tools ->Design->Views.**
Select a **View: Design View.**

4. Try it: Merge Several Fields
There are several blank Cells to the left of the Movie Field. The blank Cells are in the ReceiptID and DateRented Columns. Our goal is to **merge** those Cells together.

Select those blank Cells as well as the Movies Field by holding the Control key on your Keyboard.
Go to **Report Design Tools ->Arrange.**
Go to **Merge/Split->Merge.**

What Do You See? The Movies Field should fill the merged Cell.

Keep going, please.

Report Design Tools ->Arrange->Merge/Split->Merge

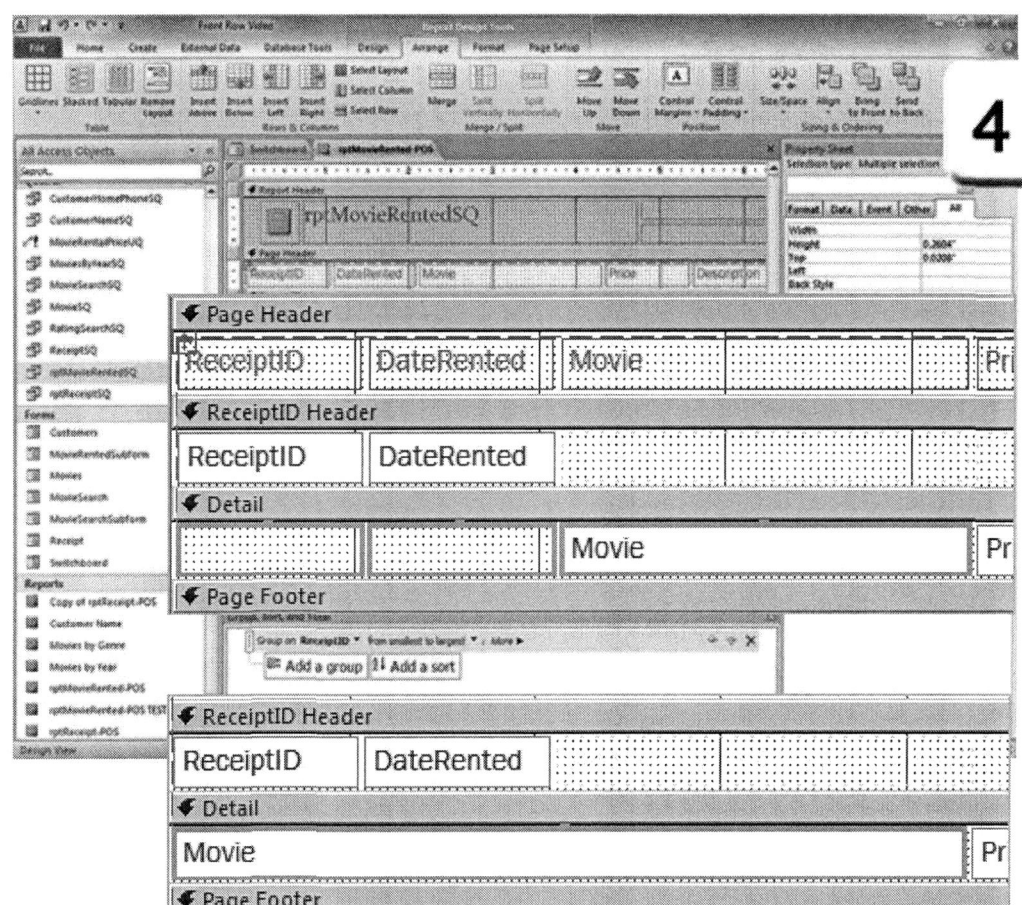

Exam 77-885: Microsoft Access 2010
5. Designing Reports
5.3. Apply Report Arrange options: Merge

Insert a Row in a Table

This step is like a monkey puzzle. We'll add a new Row so that we can move the description below the name of the movie. Adding a Row is the best way to make this fit on a 2" printout.

5. Try it: Insert a Row
Go to the Detail Section.
Select the Row that includes the Fields for the Movie, Price and Description.
Go to **Report Design Tools ->Arrange**.
Go to **Rows & Columns->Insert Below**.

What Do You See? There will be a new Row. The Columns should match the width of the Movie, Price and Description Fields.

Keep going...

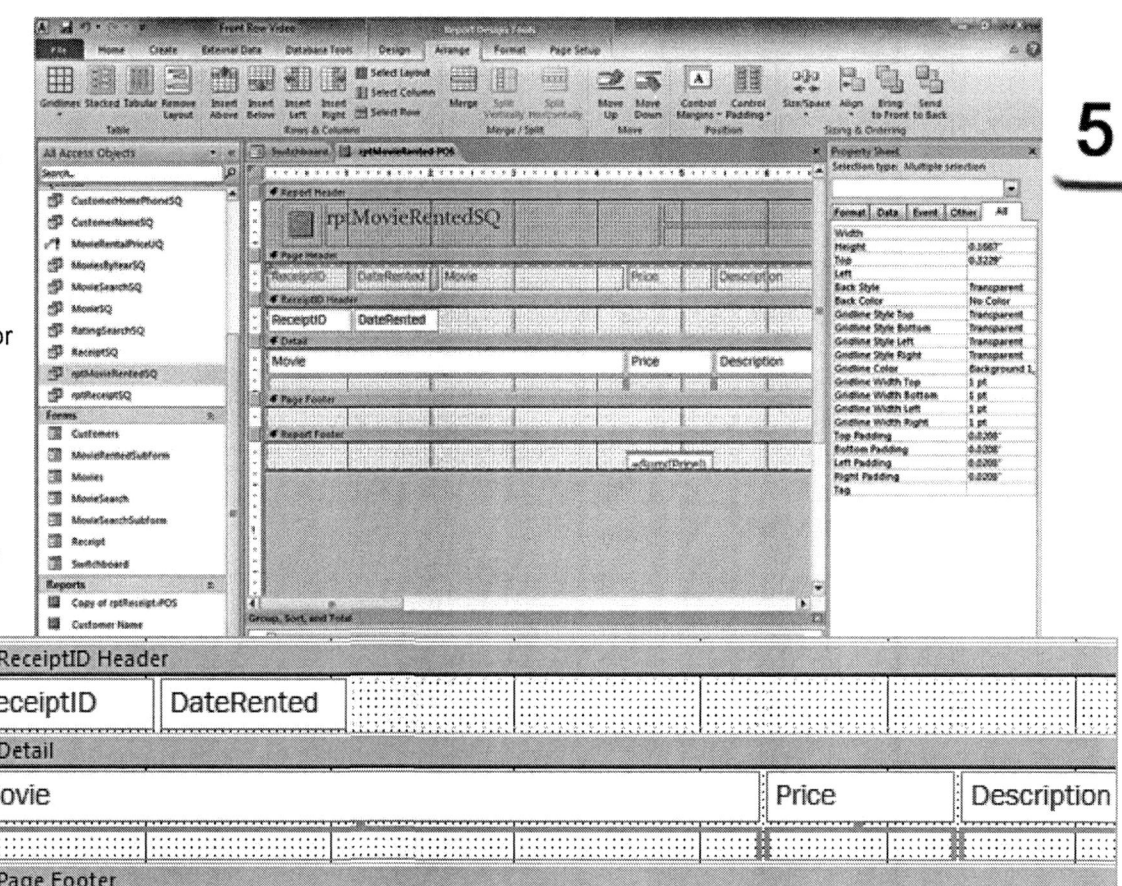

5

Exam 77-885: Microsoft Access 2010
5. Designing Reports
5.3. Apply Report Arrange options: Insert a Row

Move and Merge

6. Try it: Move a Field Down
The Report is still in Design View.
Select a Field: Description.
Go to **Report Layout Tools ->Arrange.**
Go to **Move->Move Down.**

Try This, Too: Select the Row
Select any Cell in Row 2.
Go to **Report Layout Tools ->Arrange.**
Go to **Rows & Columns->Select Row.**
All of the Cells in that Row should be
selected.

And Try This, Too: Merge the Fields
Go to **Report Design Tools ->Arrange.**
Go to **Merge/Split->Merge.**

Keep going...

Report Design Tools ->Arrange->Merge/Split->Merge

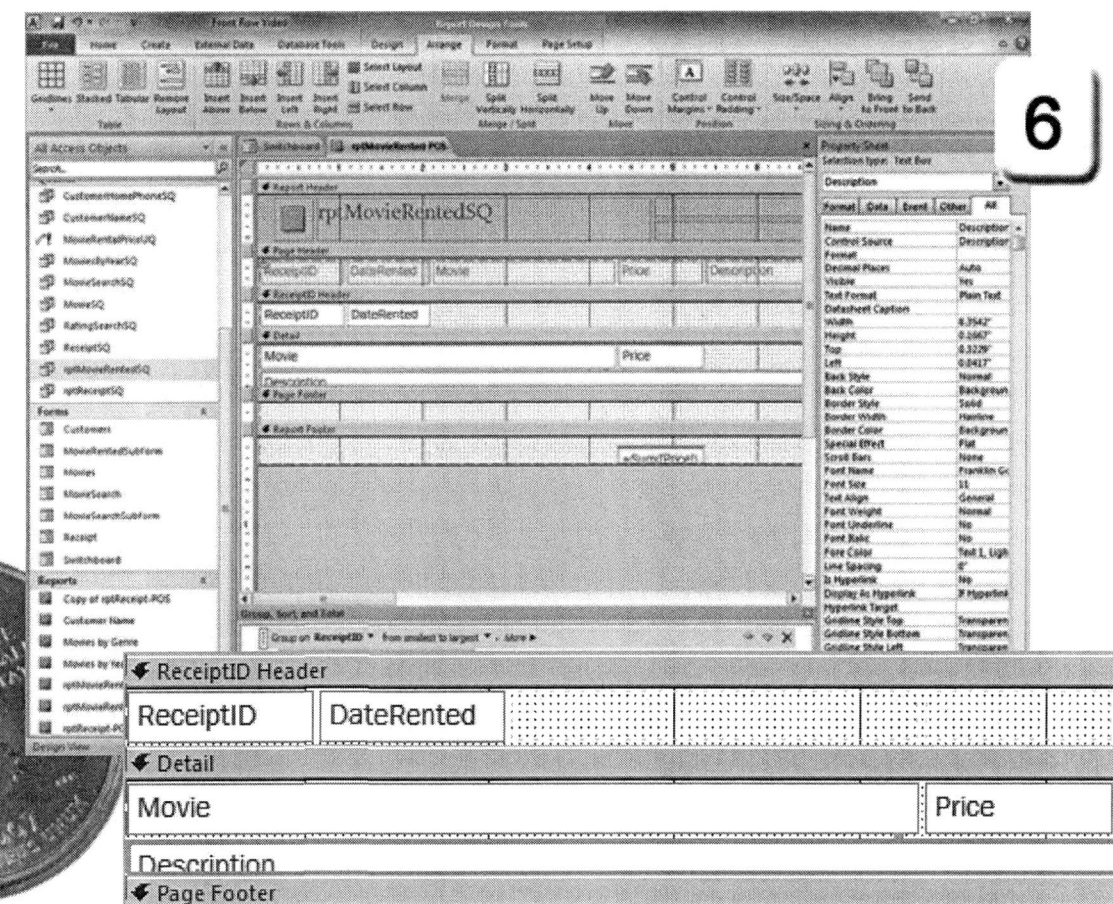

Exam 77-885: Microsoft Access 2010
5. Designing Reports
5.3. Apply Report Arrange options: Merge

Report Design Tools ->Arrange->Position->Control Margins

Arrange: Control Margins

The space between the Cell border and the Field is the Margin. The default Margin is None. The other options include Narrow, Medium and Wide.

Before You Begin: Select the Table.
Go to **Report Design Tools ->Arrange**.
Go to **Rows & Columns->Select Layout**.

7. Try This: Control the Cell Margins
Go to **Report Design Tools ->Arrange**.
Go to **Position->Control Margins**.
Select a Margin size: None.
Keep going...

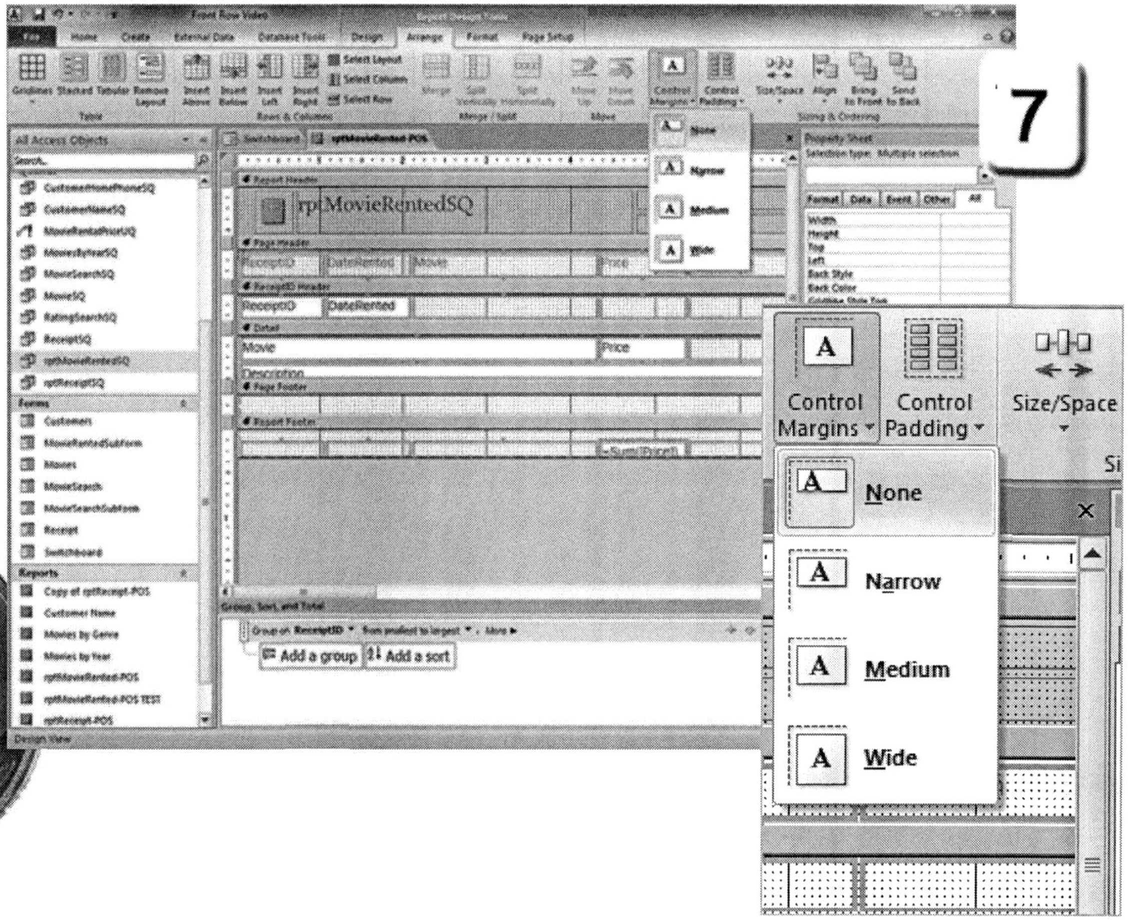

Exam 77-885: Microsoft Access 2010
5. Designing Reports
5.3. Apply Report Arrange options: Control Margins

Arrange: Padding

The **Padding** is the space between the Cells.

8. Try it: Edit the Cell Padding
The Report is still in Design View.
The Layout is selected.
Go to **Form Design Tools->Arrange.**
Go to **Position->Padding.**
Select a Padding size: None.

Those are the best choices in the Arrange Ribbon, given our goals.

Do This Now: Save. Save Save.

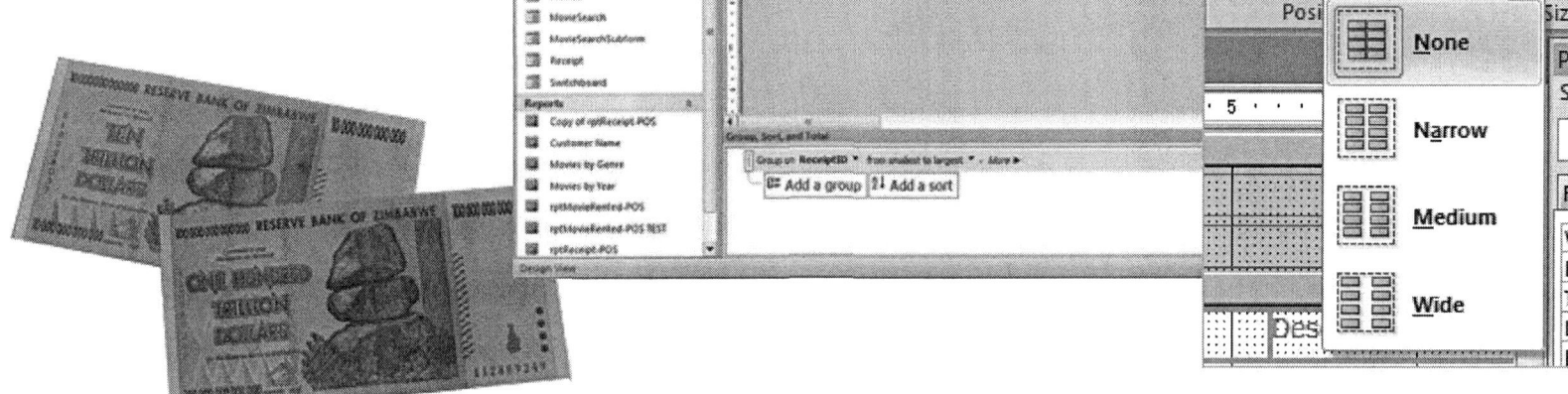

Exam 77-885: Microsoft Access 2010
5. Designing Reports
5.3. Apply Report Arrange options: Padding

Remove the Layout...

Tables offer excellent tools for arranging data. They also have constraints. The fastest way to finish this Report is to **Remove the Layout** and resize the Controls.

1. Try it: Remove the Layout
The Report is open in Design View.
Go to **Report Design Tools ->Arrange**
Go to **Table->Remove Layout**.

What Do You See? The Controls are still in the same position however the Table has been removed: there are no empty Cells.

Keep going...

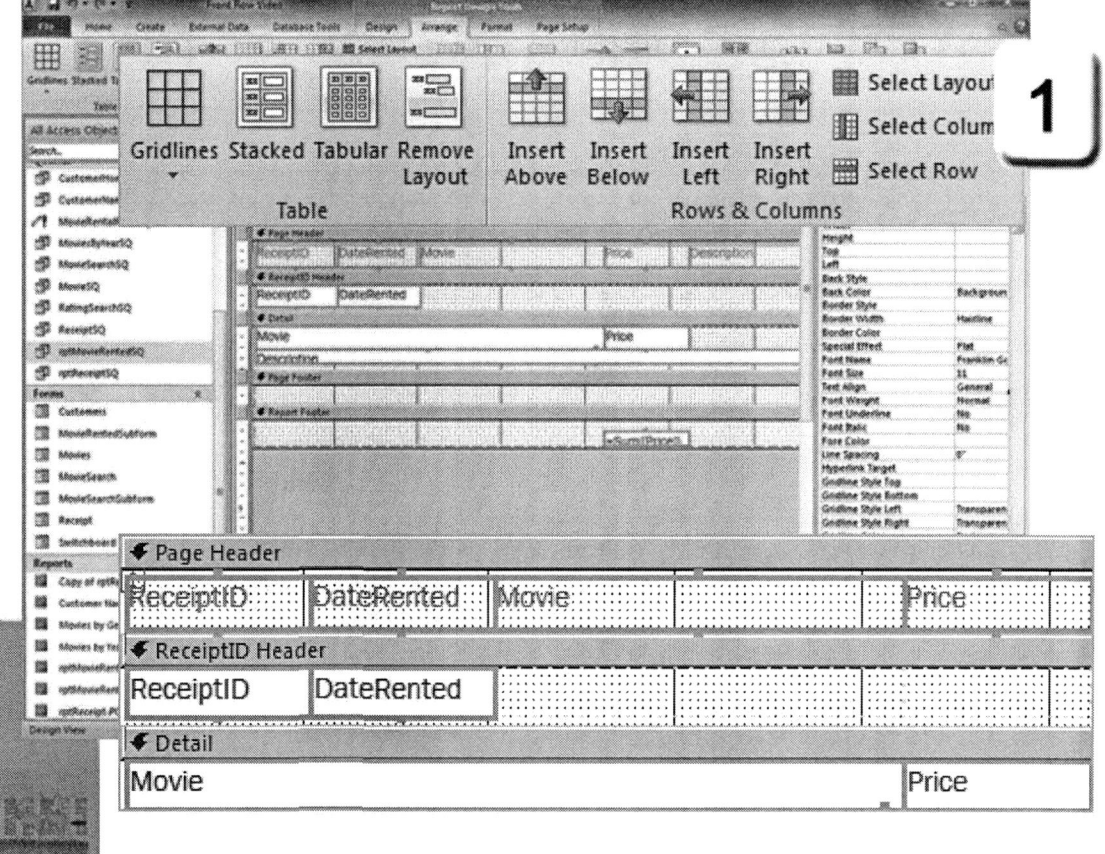

Exam 77-885: Microsoft Access 2010
5. Designing Reports
5.3. Apply Report Arrange options: Remove Layout

...and Resize the Controls

Please select each Control and edit the Properties as follows:

2. Try it: Edit the Control Properties
Select a Control: ReceiptID
Width: 0.5"

Select a Control: DateRented
Width: 1"
Left: 0.8"

Select a Control: Movie
Width:1.25"

Select a Control: Price
Width: 0.55"
Left: 1.375"

Select a Control: Description
Width:1.9"

Select a Control: SumPrice
Left:0.8"

Keep going...

Report Design Tools ->Design->Tools->Property Sheet

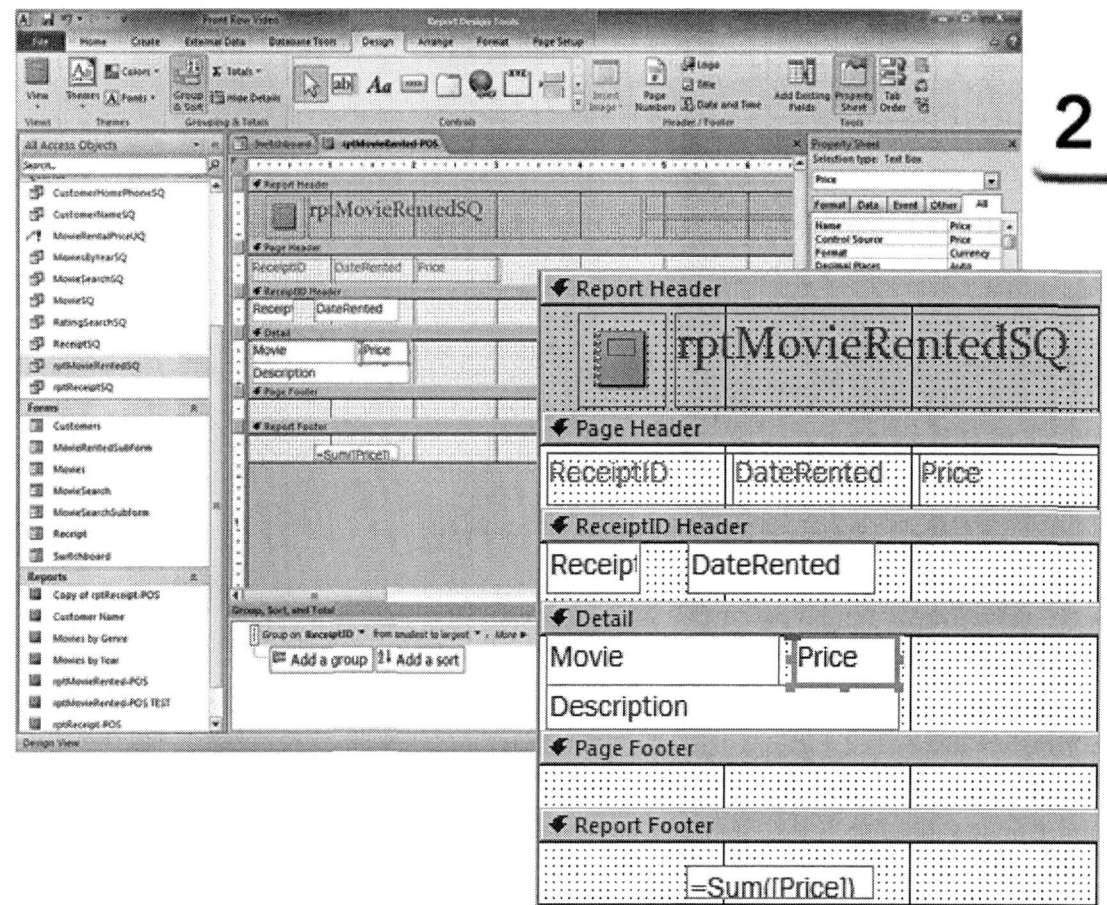

Exam 77-885: Microsoft Access 2010
5. Designing Reports
5.3. Apply Report Arrange options: Reposition and Format Records

Report Design Tools ->Design->Tools->Property Sheet

Modify the Headers
The Report Header and Page Header are not needed in a Subreport. Please remove the Labels and format the Headers.

3. Try it: Modify the Headers
Select the Report Header.
Delete all of the Labels in the Report Header.
Edit the Report Header Height: 0"

Select the Page Header.
Delete all of the Labels in the Page Header.
Edit the Page Header Height: 0"

Select the Page Footer.
Delete everything in the Page Footer.
Edit the Page Footer Height: 0"

Keep going...

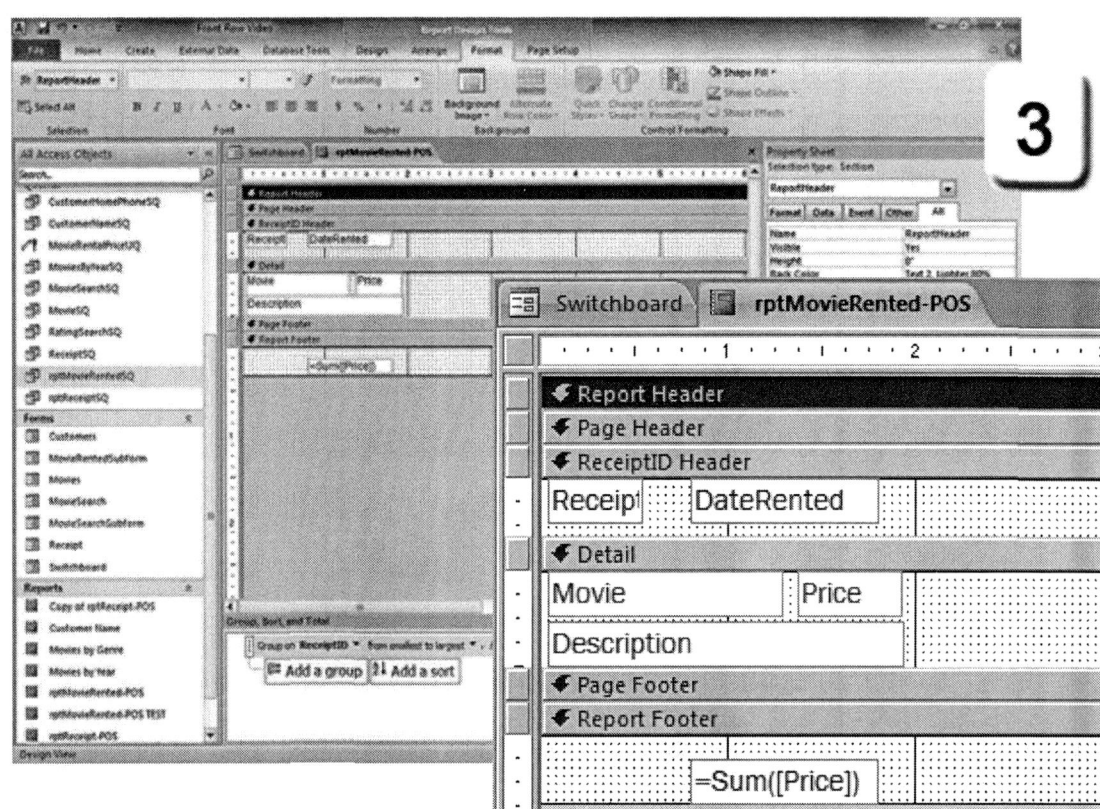

3

Exam 77-885: Microsoft Access 2010
5. Designing Reports
5.2. Apply Report Design options: Modify the Header/Footer

Format the Report

By default, the Text size in a Report is 11pt. We need a smaller Font Size to fit a POS Printout.

Before You Begin: Select All Controls
Go to **Report Design Tools ->Format->Selection.**
Click on Select All.

4. Try it: Format the Report
Go to **Report Design Tools ->Format->Font.**
Select a Font: Arial.
Select a Size: 9

Go to **Report Design Tools->Format.**
Go to **Conditional Formatting->Shape Outline.**
Select an Outline: Transparent.

Keep going...

Report Design Tools ->Format->Font

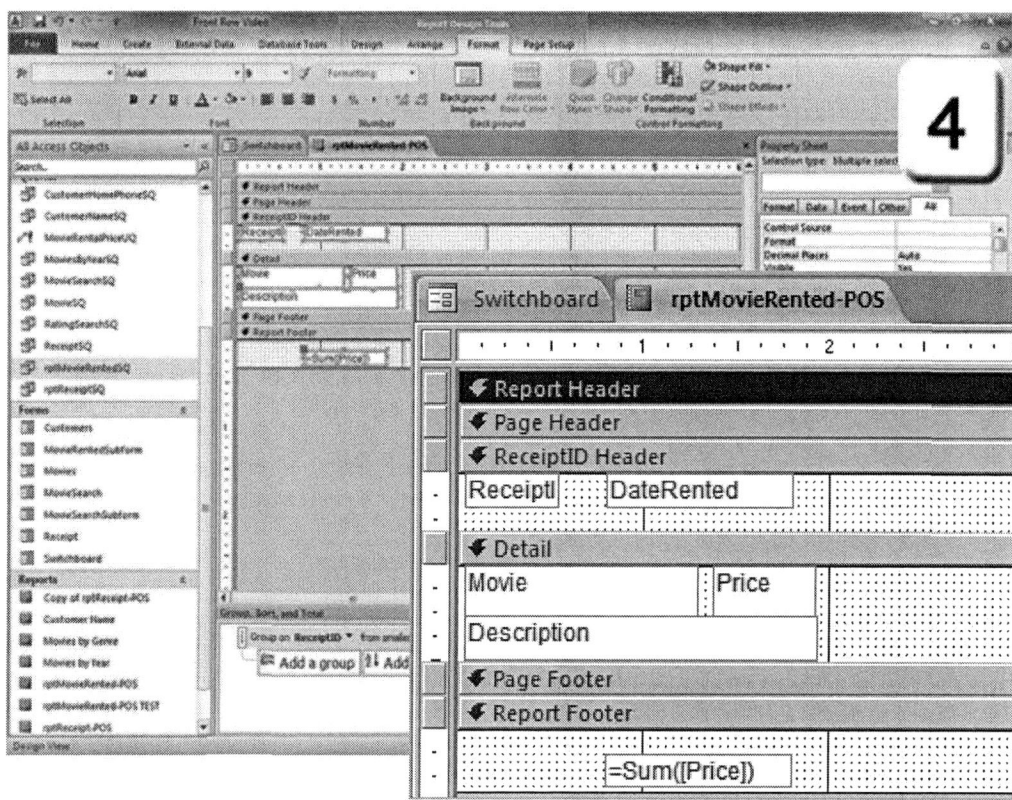

Exam 77-885: Microsoft Access 2010
5. Designing Reports
5.3. Apply Report Arrange options: Reposition and Format Records

Advanced Microsoft Access 2010   Page 201 of 347

Resize the Subreport

Finally, everything has been resized and placed in the right position. We can resize the little Subreport.

5. Try it: Resize the Subreport
Select the Report.
Go to **Property Sheet->All.**
Width: 2"

Save. Save. Save like you mean it.
So...what does the Report look like?

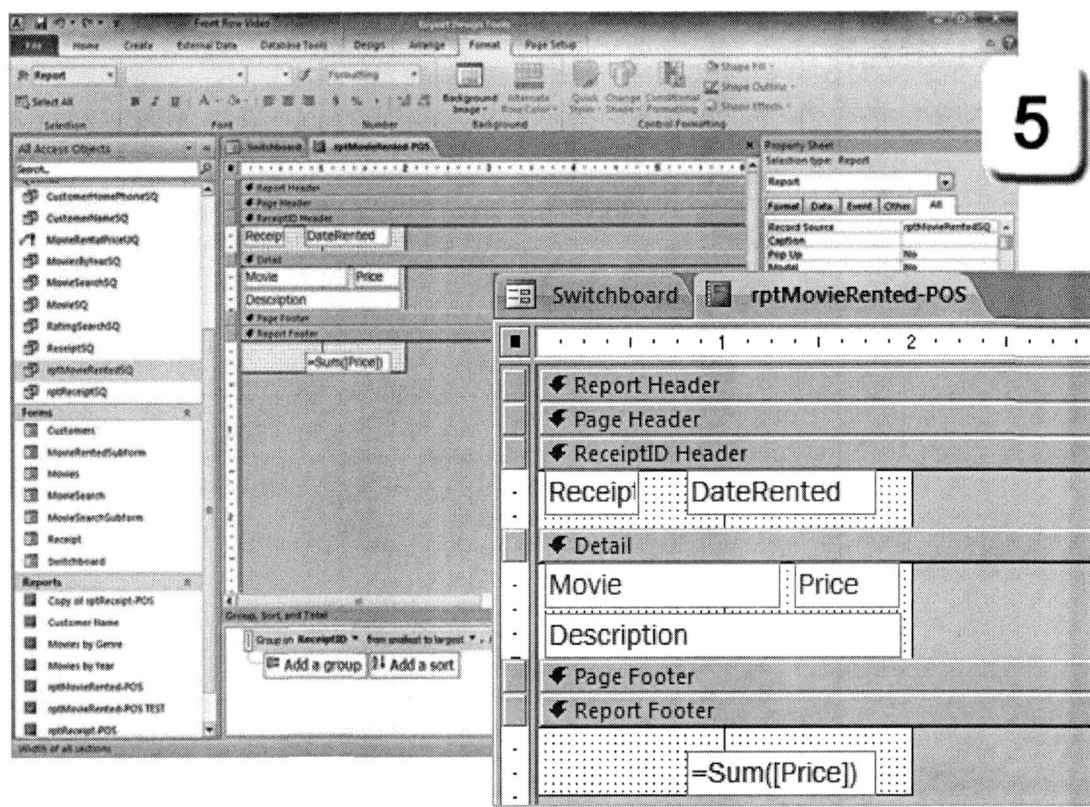

Exam 77-885: Microsoft Access 2010
5. Designing Reports
5.3. Apply Report Arrange options: Reposition and Format Records

Preview the Report!

6. Try it: Change the View
Go to **Report Design Tools ->Design->Views.**
Select a **View: Print Preview.**

What Do You See? The rptMovieRented is Grouped by the ReceiptID. Each movie is listed by name, price and the rental description. The Subreport works. Please hide the Report Header.

Try This, Too: Hide the Report Header.
Go to the **Design View.**
Select the **Report Header.**
Go to **Properties->All.**
Visible: No

Preview the Report, Again
Go to **Report Design Tools ->Design->Views.**
Select a **View: Print Preview.**

The Report Header is hidden. Done and Done.
Close the Print Preview.
Save and **Close** the Report.

Only one more step to finish the Receipt printout. We're ready to add the Subreport to the Receipt.

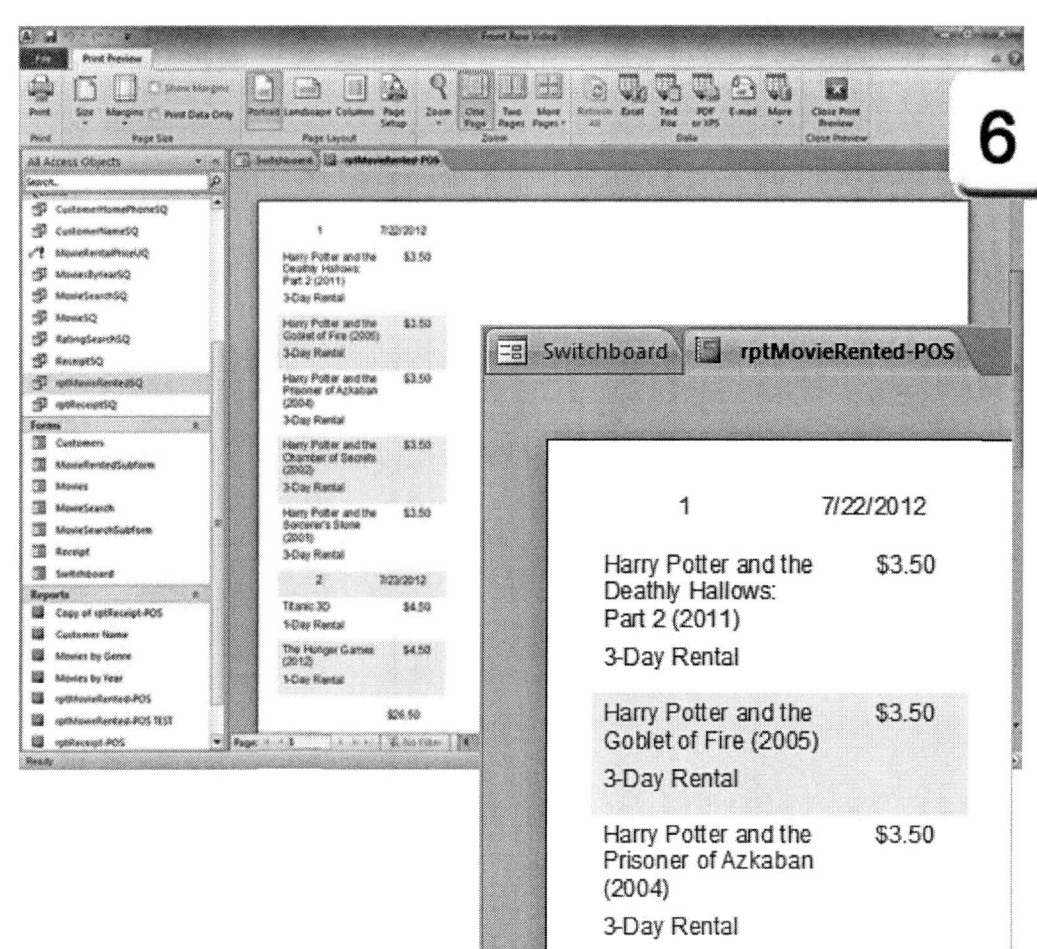

Add a Subreport

Before You Begin: Open a Report
Go to all **Access Objects->Reports**.
Open a Report: rptReceipt-POS.
Go to **Home->Views->View->Design View**.
The Report Design Tools should be available.

1. Try it: Add a Subreport
Go to **Report Design Tools ->Design->Controls**.
Select a Control: Subform/Subreport.
Click in the Detail Section.

What Do You See? The SubReport Wizard should open and guide you through the process.

Try This, Too: Select the Data
Choose: Use existing report or form.
Select a Report: rptMovieRented-POS

Click **Next**. Keep going...

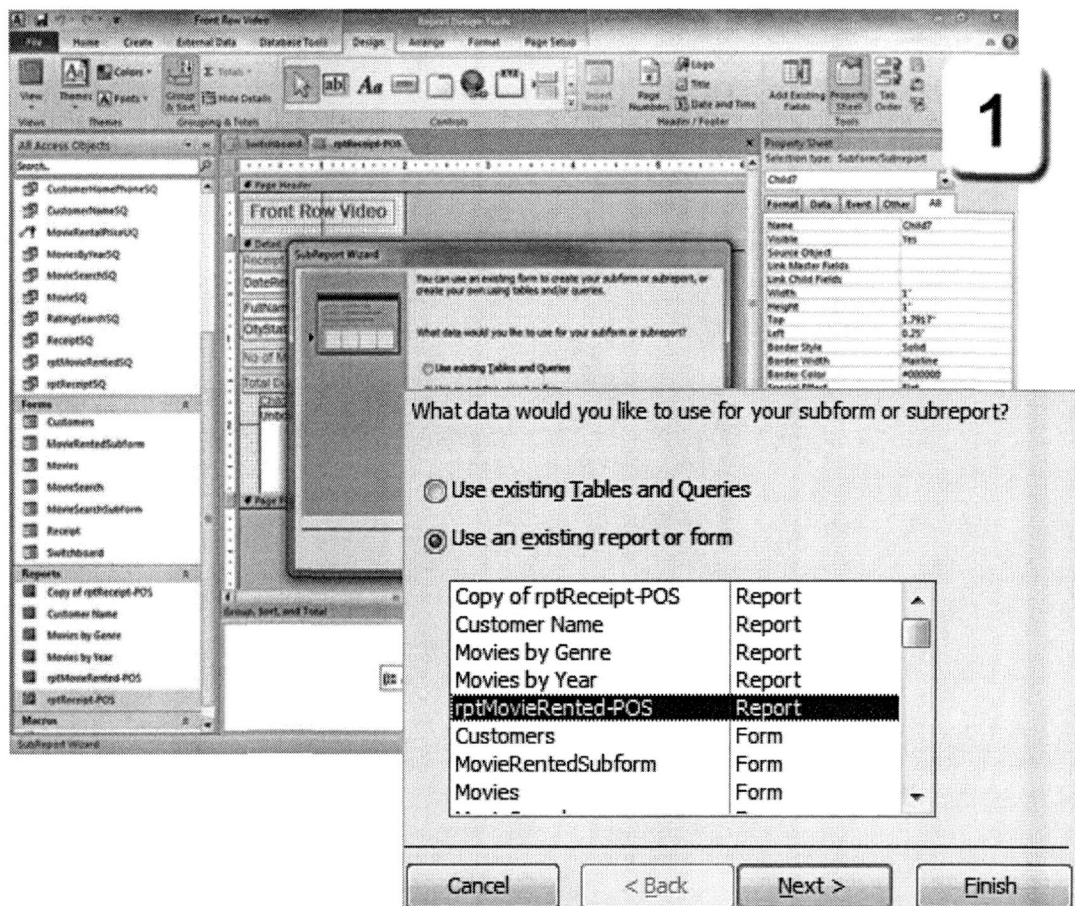

Exam 77-885: Microsoft Access 2010
5. Designing Reports
5.2. Apply Report Design options: Add Bound and Unbound Controls

Take Two

The SubReport Wizard

2. Try it: Define your own relationship.
Select ReceiptID for Report and the Subreport.
Click **Next**.

Try This, Too: Enter a Name
Enter a name: Movies Rented.
Click **Finish**.

Well? Keep going.

Report Design Tools ->Design->Controls

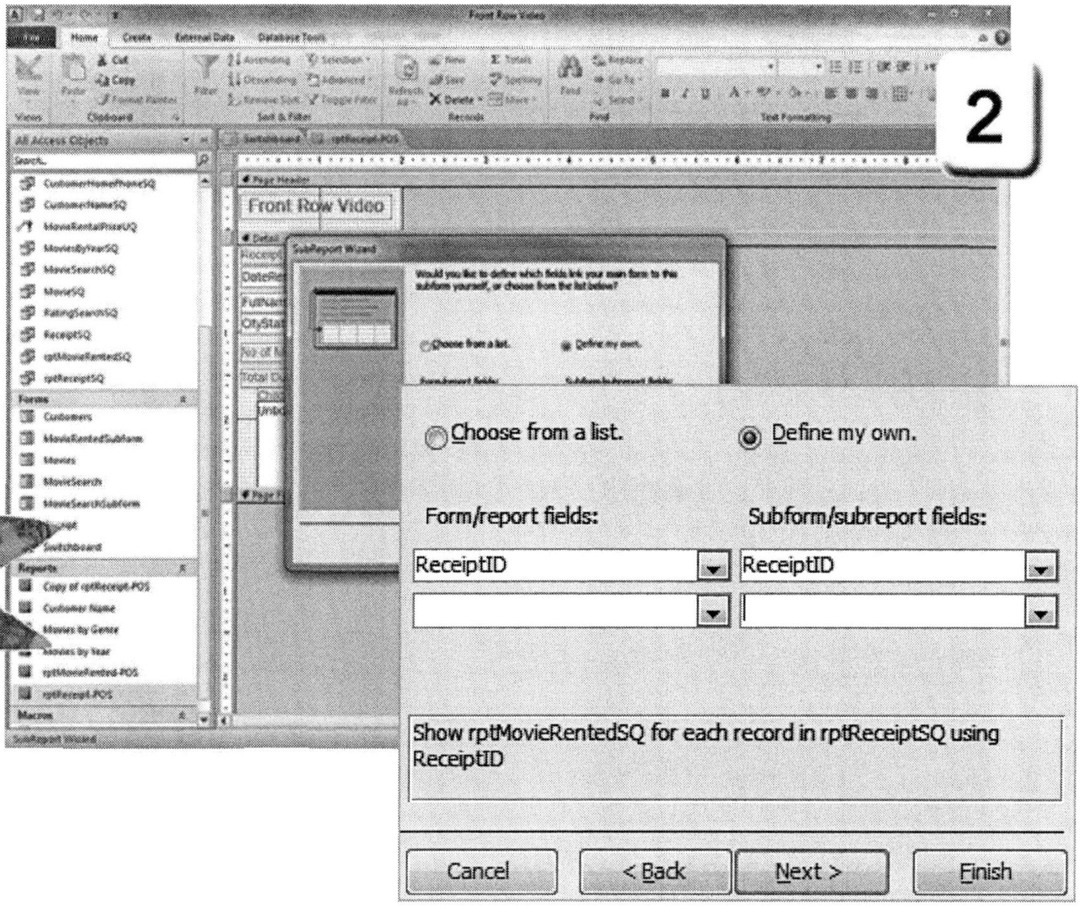

2
Front Row Video
Choose from a list.
Define my own.
Form/report fields:
Subform/subreport fields:
ReceiptID
ReceiptID
Show rptMovieRentedSQ for each record in rptReceiptSQ using ReceiptID
Cancel
< Back
Next >
Finish

Exam 77-885: Microsoft Access 2010
5. Designing Reports
5.2. Apply Report Design options: Add Bound and Unbound Controls

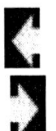

Review the Finished Report
3. Try it: Review the Report
rptMovieRented has a SubReport that is linked to the Report by the ReceiptID.

In the example on this page, the Subreport is aligned Left (0" in the Property Sheet.)

Try This, Too: Format the SubReport Border.
Select the SubReport.
Go to **Report Design Tools ->Format.**
Go to **Conditional Formatting.->Shape Outline.**
Select an **Outline: Transparent.**

What does it look like in Print Preview?

Report Design Tools ->Design->Views->View

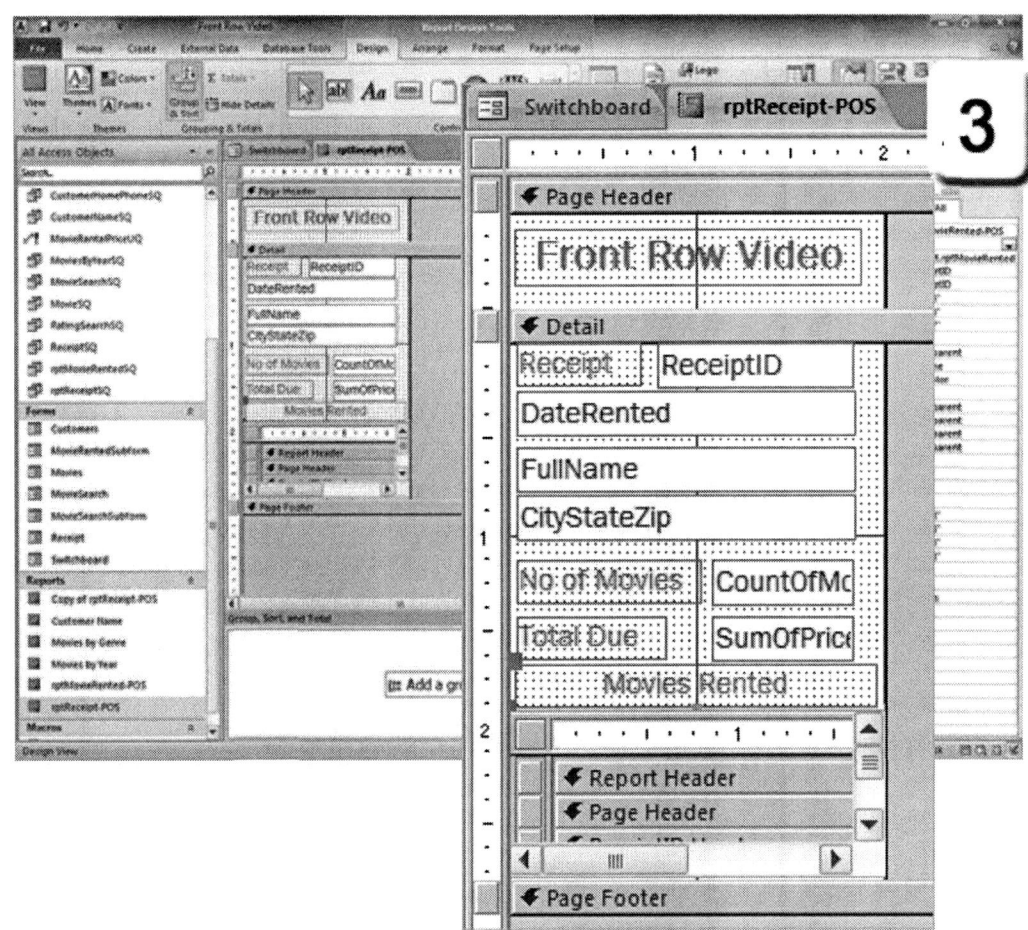

Exam 77-885: Microsoft Access 2010
5. Designing Reports
5.2. Apply Report Design options: Add Bound and Unbound Controls

Preview the Receipt Printout

4. Try it: Preview the Report
Go to **Report Design Tools ->Design->Views.**
Select a **View: Print Preview.**

What Do You See? The Receipt printout shows who bought what. The Report lists the customer, the movies rented and the price. The Report also calculates the Total Price for each Receipt.

That's good. **Save** and **Close** the Report.

Report Design Tools ->Design->Views->View

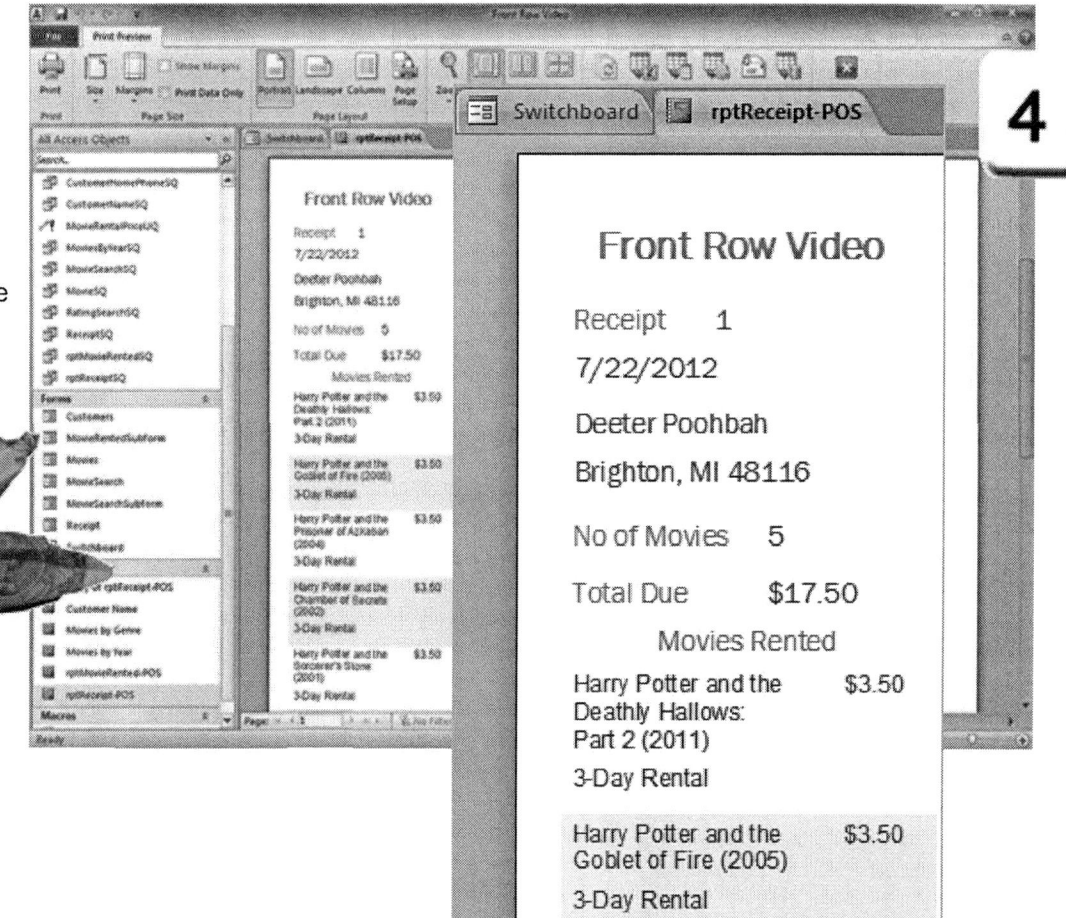

Summary

This discussion began by creating a Select Query that combined several Tables by matching their Keys. We used that Query as the Record Source for the Subreport.

The Subreport was designed as a Table. We used the Report Arrange options to Insert Rows, Merge Cells and Move Fields into different Rows.

We had to Resize the Subreport and format the Headers to fit a 2" layout. Finally, we linked the Form and Subform by a Key Field, ReceiptID.

You done real good. Go get the cookies!

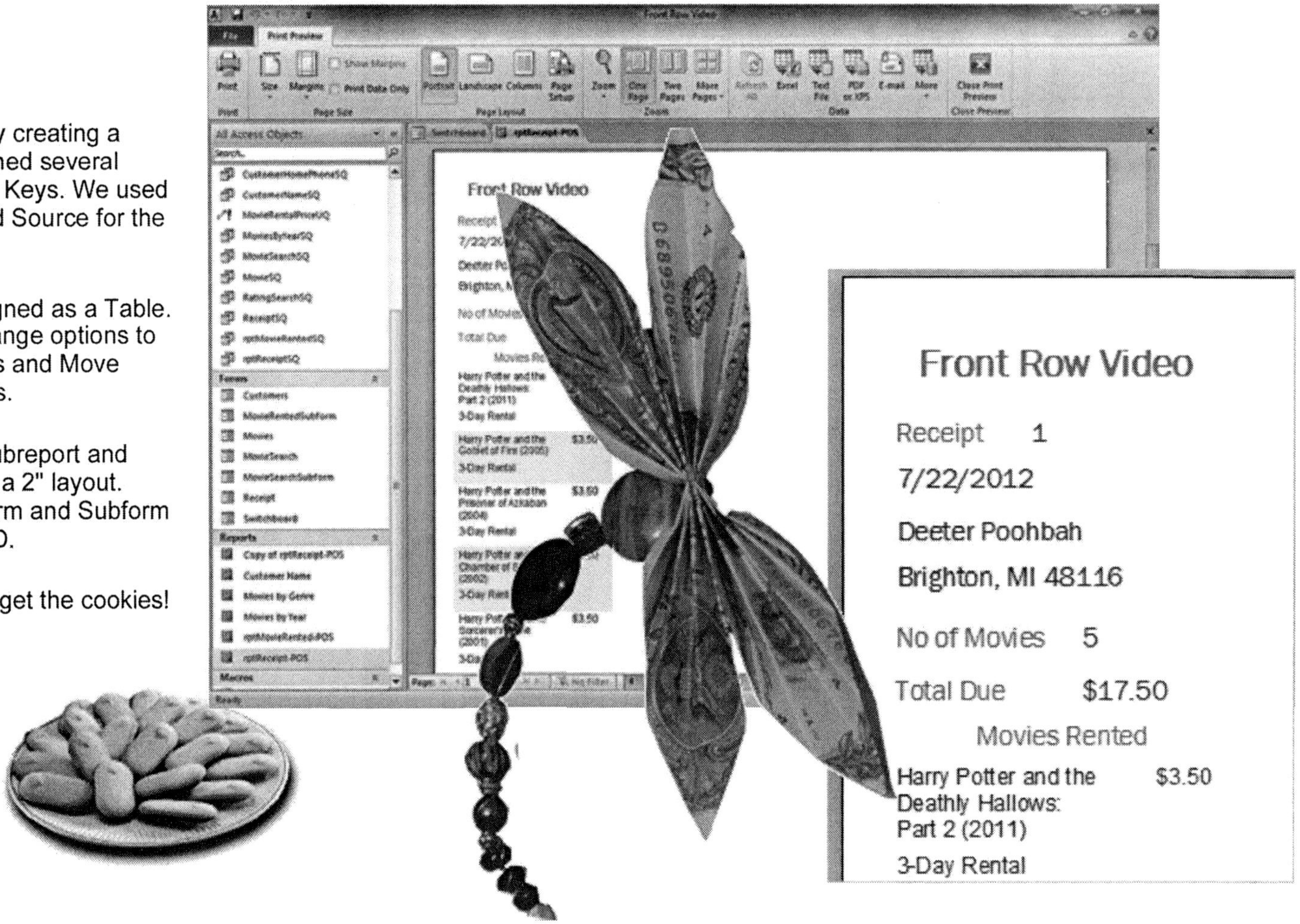

Front Row Video

Receipt   1

7/22/2012

Deeter Poohbah

Brighton, MI 48116

No of Movies   5

Total Due $17.50

Movies Rented

Harry Potter and the $3.50
Deathly Hallows:
Part 2 (2011)

3-Day Rental

Practice Activities

Lesson 7: Advanced Report Design, part 2

Try This: Do the following steps

1. Open the Brown Bag Lunch database you have been working on. Or, you may download **BBL Adv ver7.accdb**.

2. Create a Select Query and add the following Record Sources: tblReceiptProducts, tblProducts. JOIN the Tables by Key data:

From ProductID in tblReceiptProducts to ProductID in CompanyNameSQ

3. Add the following Fields to the QBE Grid:
From tblReceiptProducts: ReceiptID, DateReceipt
From tblProducts: Specialty, Type, Description, Price

Sort by Specialty (ascending)

4. Save the Query as rptReceiptProductsSQ. Run the Query to test it.

5. Return to the Design View and select the Totals in the Query Tools. Change the Price from Group BY to Sum. Save the Query and Run it again. This Query should calculate the SUM of the Prices for each customer. Close the Query.

6. Create a new Report with the Report Wizard.

Select rptReceiptProductsSQ as the Record Source.
Select all available Fields.
View this Report by tblReceiptProduct. Group by ReceiptID.
Sort by Specialty then by Description.

Select to Summary and SUM the Price.
Choose the Stepped Layout. Enter the Title: ReceiptProductsSubform.
Check to Preview the Report and Finish the Wizard.

7. Review this Report in Print Preview. Close the Print Preview. Edit the Report in Design View.

Delete the Labels in the Page Header. Resize the Page Header so that the Height is 0".

8. Select the Report Header and edit the Property for Visible: No.

9. Select the ReceiptID Header and edit the Property for Visible: No.

10. Select the ReceiptID and edit the Property for Visible: No.

11. Select all of the Controls the Detail Section and edit the Property for Can Grow: Yes.

12. Save and close the ReceiptProductsSubform.

13. Open the Brown Bag Lunch Co Report in Design View.

14. Use the Subform/Subreport Wizard to add a Subreport to the Detail Section. Start the Wizard by clicking under the Name and Address Controls in the Detail Section. Use these answers for the Wizard: Use an existing Report: ReceiptProductsSubform. Define your own link: ReceiptID. Edit the Label: ReceiptProductsSubform and finish the Wizard.

15. Select the Subreport and use the Report Design Tools to Format the Shape Outline Color: Transparent.

16. Save the Brown Bag Lunch Co Report. Go to Print Preview and see the print out. Not bad?

17. Close the Brown Bag Lunch Co Report.

18. Close the Brown Bag Lunch database.

Test Yourself

1. A SubReport needs to match the page size of the Report it will be added to.
A. True
B. False
Tip: Advanced Access, page 190

2. Which Report tool would be used to print all movies rented by a single customer on the same receipt?
A. Totals
B. Grouping
C. Group and Sort
D. Foot Options
Tip: Advanced Access, page 191

3. What tools are used to rearrange the Cells in a Table? (Give all correct answers.)
A. Merge & Split
B. Insert Rows and Columns
C. Move Up and Down
Tip: Advanced Access, page 193, 194, 195

4. Which are Cell Margin options?
(Give all correct answers.)
A. None
B. Narrow
C. Minimum
D. Medium
E. Wide
Tip: Advanced Access, page 196

5. Remove Layout Command does which of the following?
A. Removes the Table Layout, leaving just the cells
B. Removes any empty Cells from the layout
C. Leaves the Cells in their current position
D. Returns the Cells to their original positions
Tip: Advanced Access, page 198

Access 2010: Sharing and Collaboration
The Producers

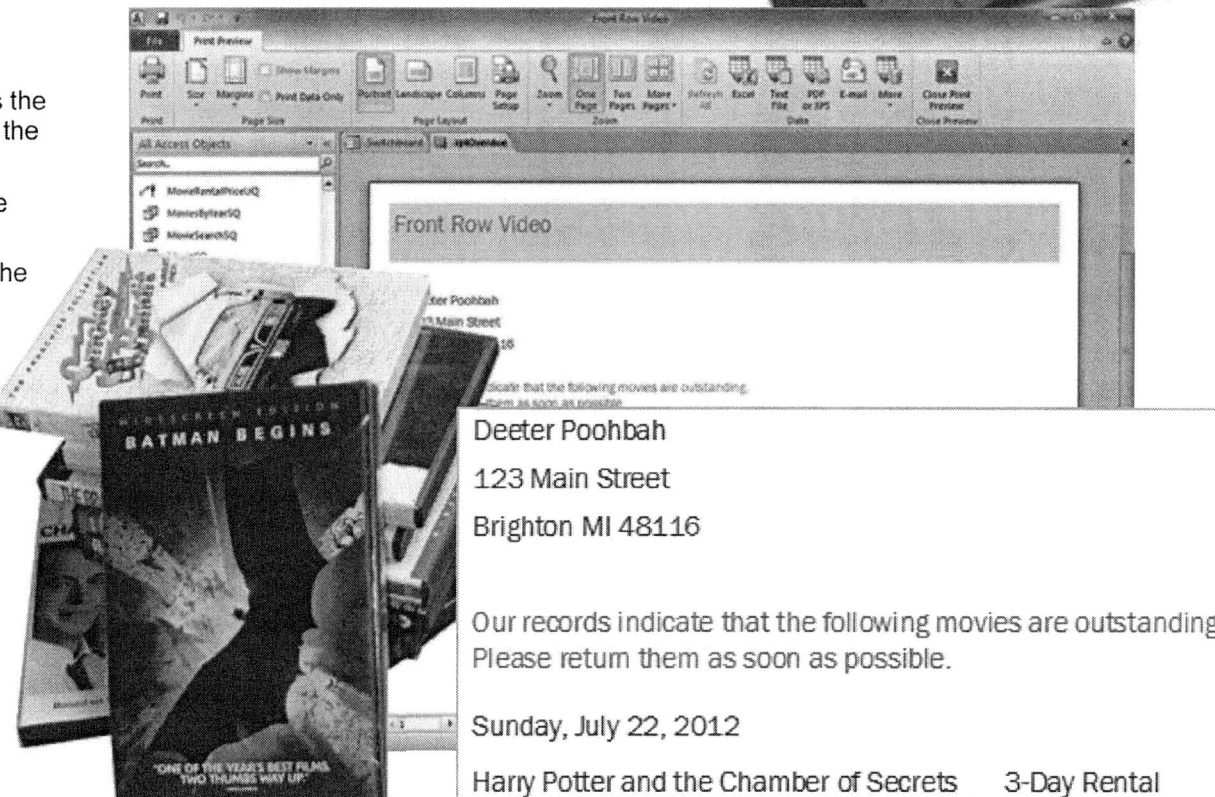

Advanced Access Objectives
In this lesson, you will learn how to:

1. Create a Select Query that calculates the overdue movies for each customer with the DateDiff() function.

2. Format the Report Headers to include Bound and Unbound Controls.

3. Edit the Report Tab Order and align the Controls to the grid.

© 2012 Comma Productions, LLC

Lesson 8 : The Producers

1. Readings

Read Lesson 8 in the Advanced Access guide, page 211-238.

Project

A Report that uses a Query to calculate which movies are overdue.

Downloads

FrontRowVideo Adv8.accdb
BBL Adv ver8.accdb

2. Practice

Do the Practice Activity on page 239.

3. Assessment

Review the Test questions on page 240.

Query Tools->Design

Report Design Tools->Arrange

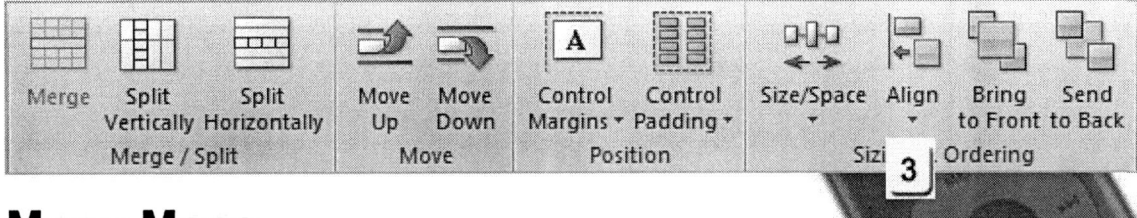

Menu Maps

From the **Create Ribbon**.
1. Create ->Queries->Query Design, page 217
2. Create ->Reports->Report Wizard, page 226

From the **Report Design Tools->Arrange Ribbon**.
3. Report Design Tools ->Arrange->Sizing and Ordering->Align, page 229

From the **Report Design Ribbons**.
4. Report Design Tools ->Design-> Grouping and Totals ->Group & Sort, page 233
5. Report Design Tools ->Design->Tools->Tab Order, page 235

The Producers

Most businesses are date driven. For example, these movies are rented for 1, 3, or 5 days. If the movies are not returned as agreed, the customer could be notified which movies are overdue. These business rules can be programmed into our Mighty Access database. A Query can calculate the difference between the date the movie was rented and the current date.

Microsoft Office Access 2010: Example of the completed Overdue Movie Letter

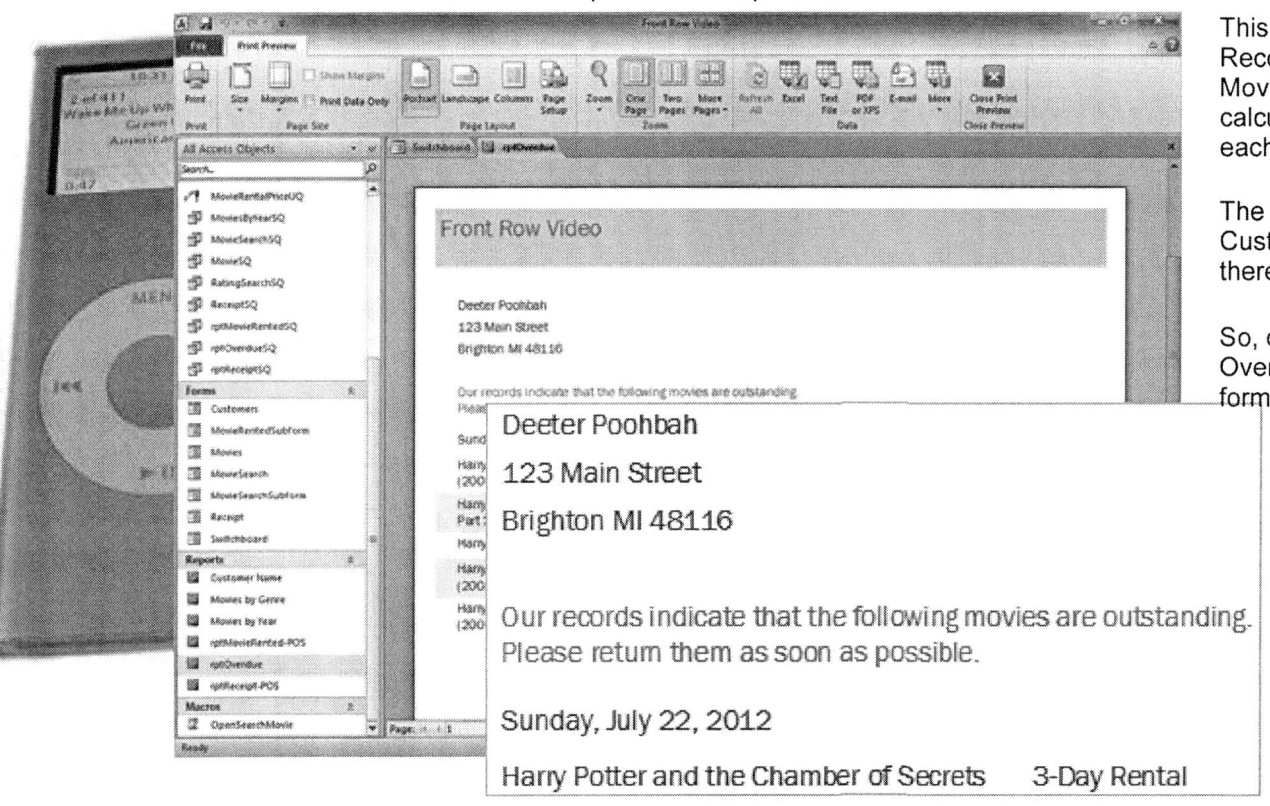

This lesson begins by creating the Record Source for the Overdue Movie Report, a Query that calculates the numbers of days that each movie is overdue.

The Report will be Grouped by Customer and formatted so that there is only one customer per page.

So, our tardy customers get an Overdue Movie Report that is formatted like a letter.

What is the Plan?

The Record Source for the Overdue Movie Letter will be a Query, **rtpOverdueSQ,** that will calculate the number of days from the date the movie was rented. Here is the plan:

Create a Query: rtpOverdueSQ
Add tblMovieRented and related Tables.
Create JOINS between the Tables.
Group the Records by Customer.
Calculate the Amount Due for each Customer.

Create the Report: rptOverdueMovie
rptOverdueMovie will be formatted as a business letter: one page per customer.

That's the plan for now.

Example of the Overdue Movie Letter in Design View

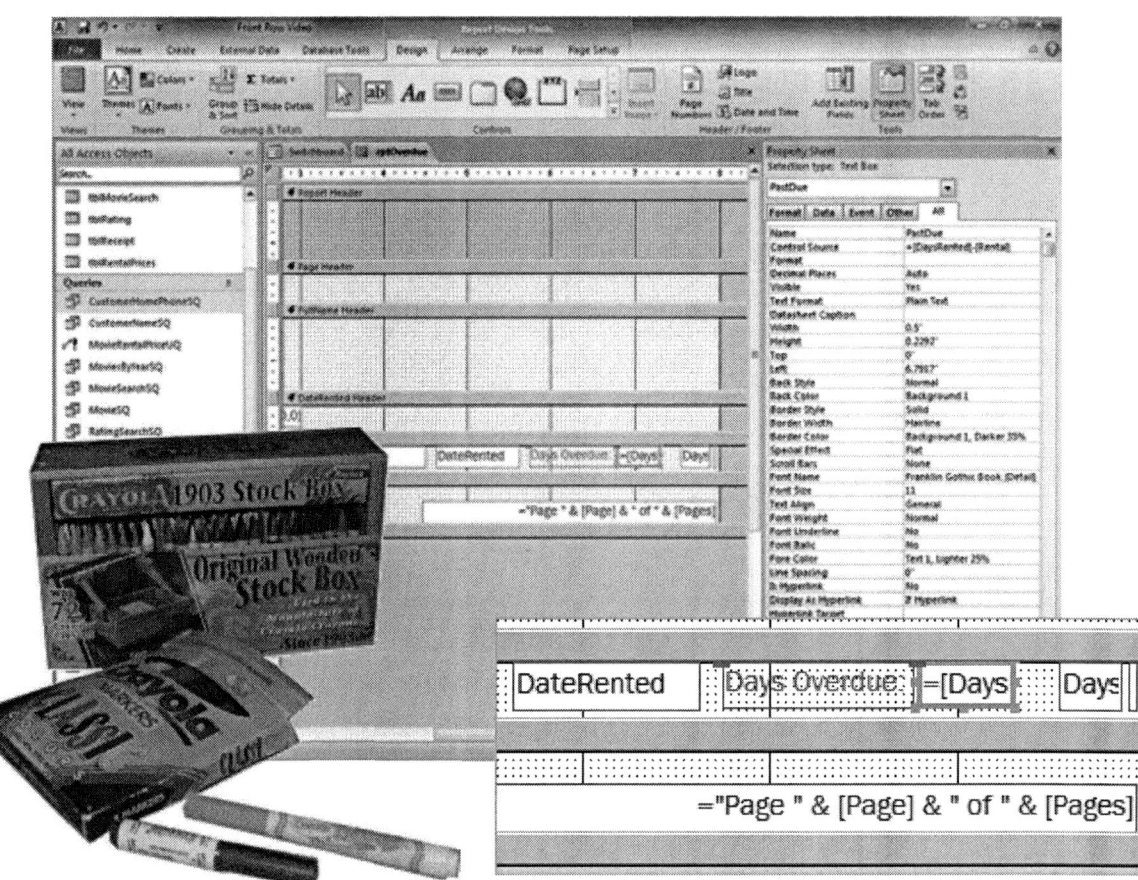

Before You Begin

Before You Begin: Open the Sample Database
Go to **Start -> All Programs ->Microsoft Office**.
Click on **Microsoft Office Access 2010.**
Access will prompt you to open a database.
Select: **FrontRowVideo Adv8.accdb**

The database, **FrontRowVideo Adv8.accdb,** was
developed in the previous lessons. You do not have
to download a new sample. You can continue with
your own database if you wish.

Keep going....

Memo to Self: Databases need to Read and Write.
Click **Enable Content** if you see the Security
Warning.

Start ->All Programs-> Microsoft Office-> Microsoft Access 2010

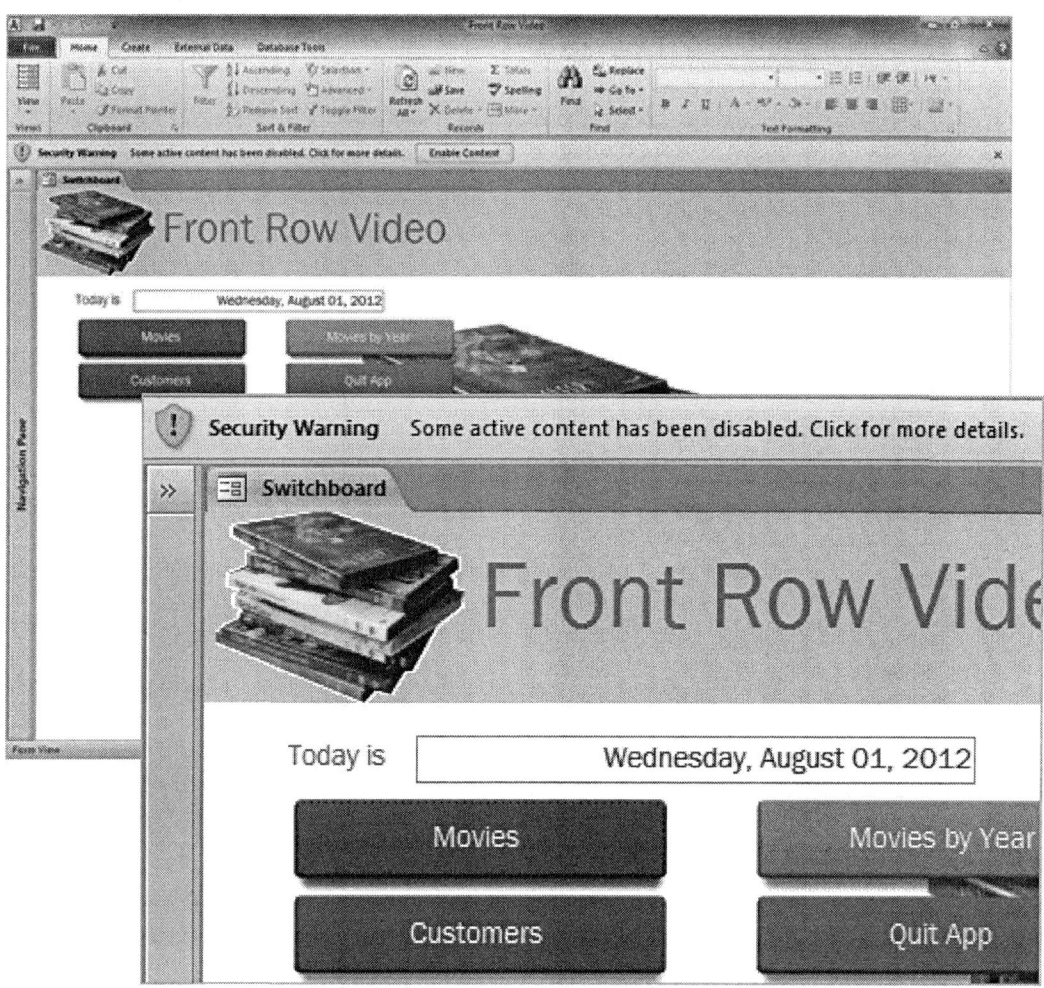

Know Your Data
Try This: Review the Database
Open the **Navigation Pane.**
Go to **All Access Objects.**

The Front Row Video has the following:
Eight Tables: tblCustomers, tblGenre,
tblMovieRented, tblMovies, tblMovieSearch,
tblRating, tblReceipt and tblRentalPrices.

Ten Queries: CustomerHomePhoneSQ,
CustomerNameSQ, MovieRentalPriceUQ,
MoviesByYearSQ, MovieSearchSQ, MovieSQ,
RatingSearchSQ, ReceiptSQ,
rptMovieRentedSQ and rptReceiptSQ.

Seven Forms: Customers,
MovieRentedSubform, Movies, MovieSearch,
MovieSearchSubform, Receipt and Switchboard.

Five Reports: Customer Name. Movies by
Genre, Movies by Year, rptMovieRented-POS
and rptReceipt-POS.

One Macro: OpenSearchMovie

All Access Objects

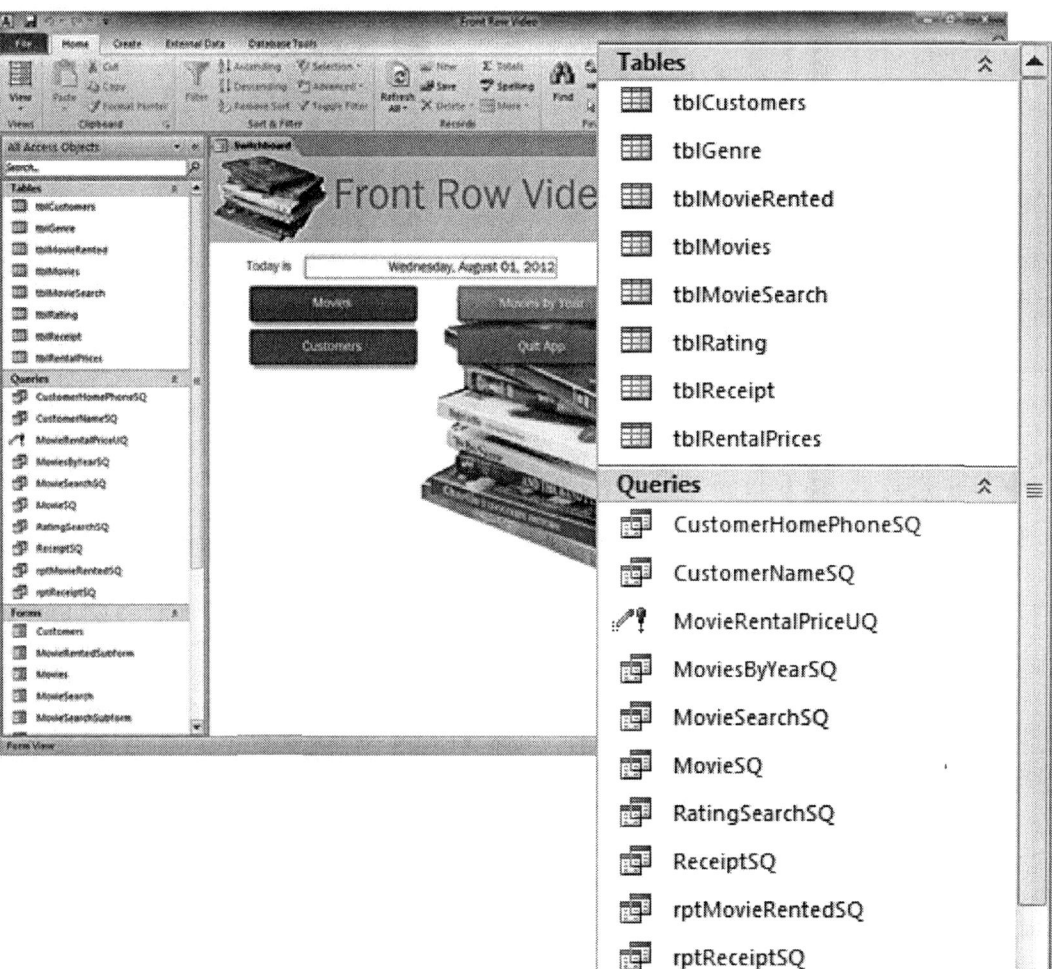

Create a New Select Query: rptOverdueSQ

A new Query will calculate the difference between the DateRented and the current date. Please create a new Select Query and add the following Tables.

2. Try it: Create a Query

Go to **Create ->Queries ->Query Design**. You will be prompted by the Show Table.

Select a Table: tblMovieRented. Click **Add**.

Select a Table: tblMovies. Click **Add**.

Select a Table: tblRentalPrices. Click **Add**.

Close the Show Table Window. Keep going...

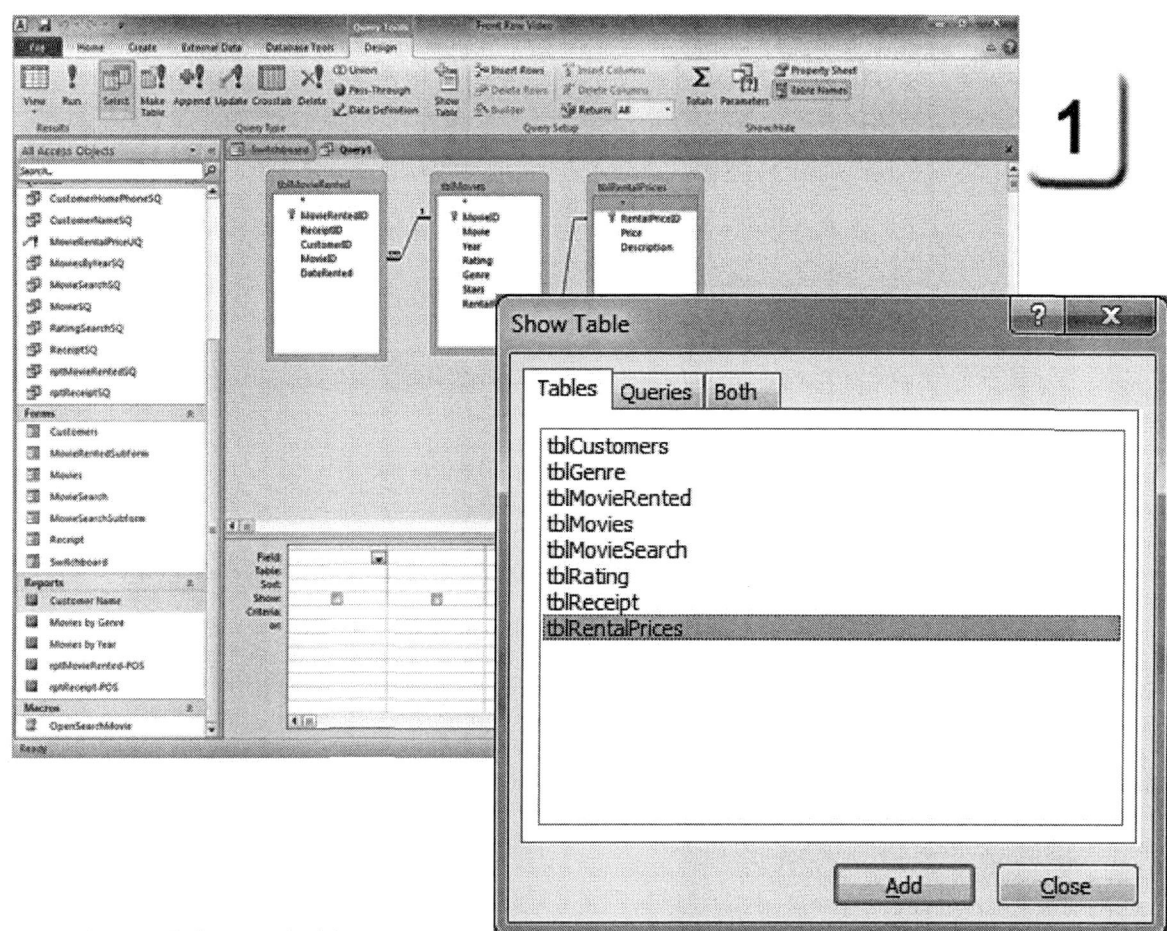

Exam 77-885: Microsoft Access 2010
4. Creating and Managing Queries
4.2. Manage source tables and relationships: Use the Show Table Options

rptOverdueSQ: JOINS

As you added each Table to the Query, the Tables were JOINED by their Keys.

2. Try it: Review the JOINS
tblMovieRented.MovieID to tblMovies.MovieID.

tblMovies.RentalPriceID to tblRentalPrices.RentalPriceID.

Keep going...

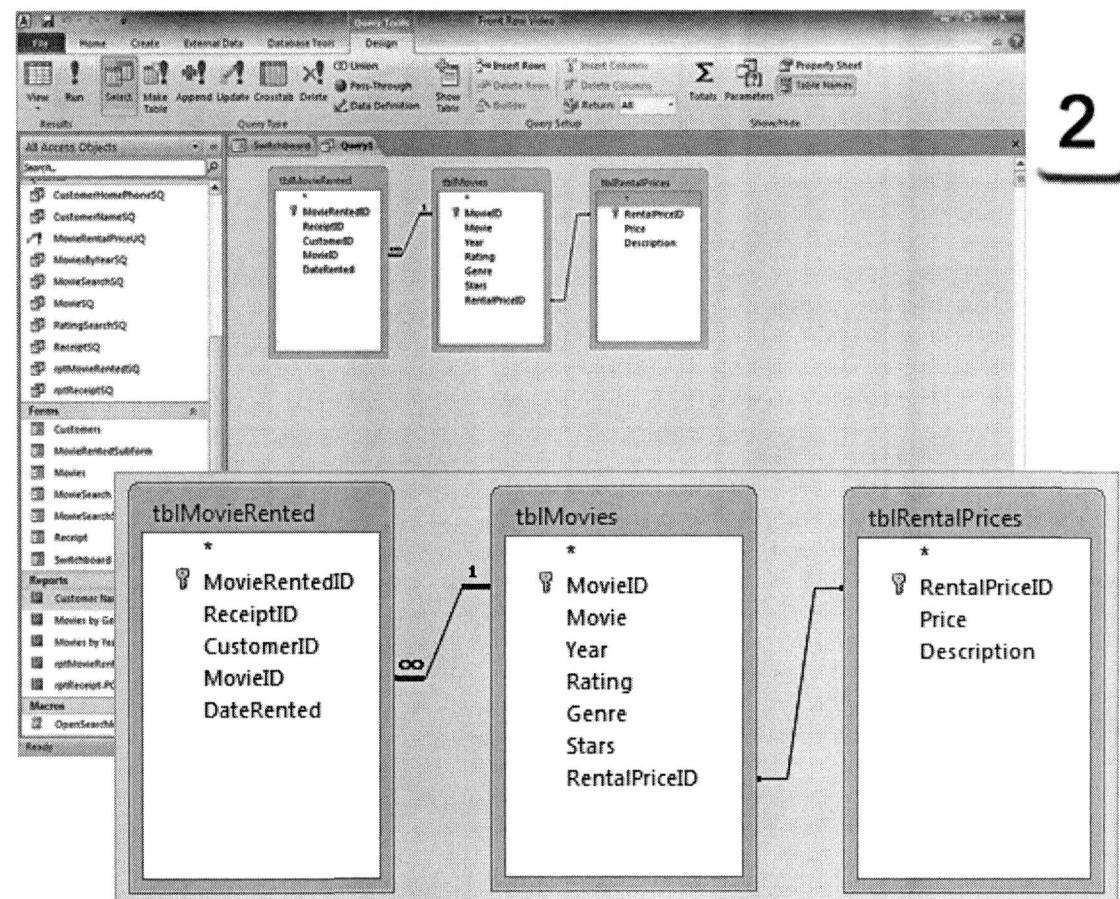

Exam 77-885: Microsoft Access 2010
4. Creating and Managing Queries
4.2. Manage source tables and relationships

rptOverdueSQ: Fields
3. Try it: Add Fields to the Query
Add the following Fields to the QBE Grid:

From tblMovieRented:
ReceiptID
CustomerID
DateRented

From tblMovies:
Movie

From tblRentalPrices:
Price
Description

Do This, Now: Save the Query
Go to **File->Save**.
Enter the name: **rptOverdueSQ**.

Keep going...

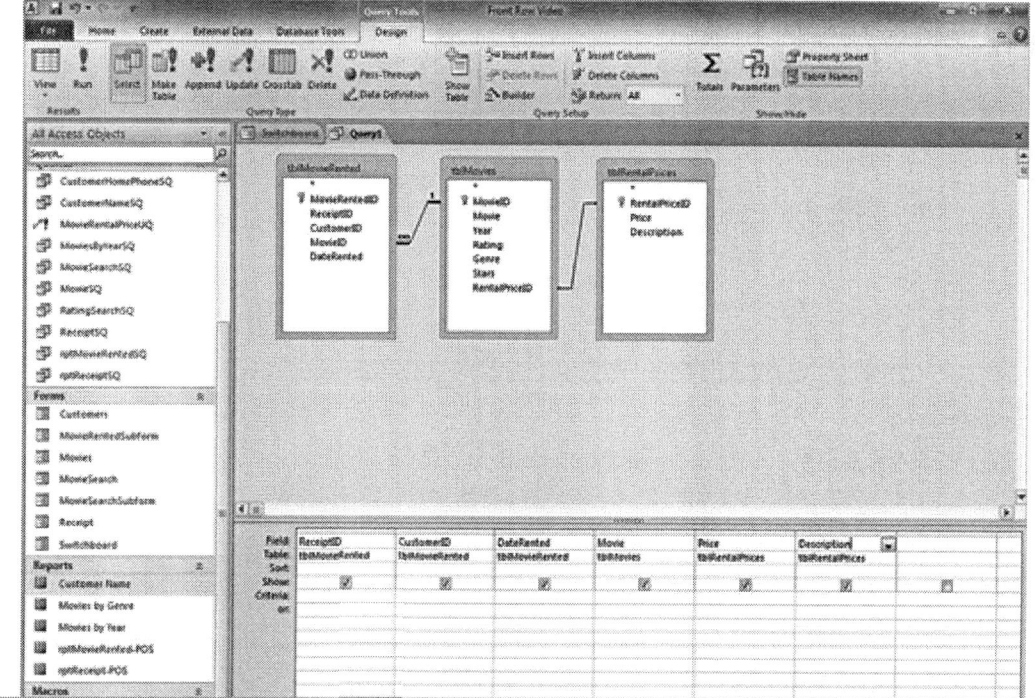

Field:	ReceiptID	CustomerID	DateRented	Movie	Price	Description
Table:	tblMovieRented	tblMovieRented	tblMovieRented	tblMovies	tblRentalPrices	tblRentalPrices
Sort:						
Show:	☑	☑	☑	☑	☑	☑
Criteria:						
or:						

Exam 77-885: Microsoft Access 2010
4. Creating and Managing Queries
4.2. Manage source tables and relationships

Calculate the Date Difference

Many businesses need to calculate the difference between two dates. Microsoft Access uses a **DateDiff()** function. It goes like this:

DaysRented: DateDiff("d",[DateRented],Now ())

Where DaysRented is the Alias,
DateDiff() is the function,
"d" is the time interval,
[DateRented] is a field in tblMovieRented.

Other DateDiff intervals are:

Month	"m"
Year	"yyyy"
Week	"ww"
Hour	"h"
Minutes	"n"

4. Try it: Create a Calculated Field
Click on a blank Field in the QBE Grid.
Right click to **Zoom**. Enter the Expression:

DaysRented: DateDiff("d",[DateRented],Now ())

Click **OK.** Keep going, please.

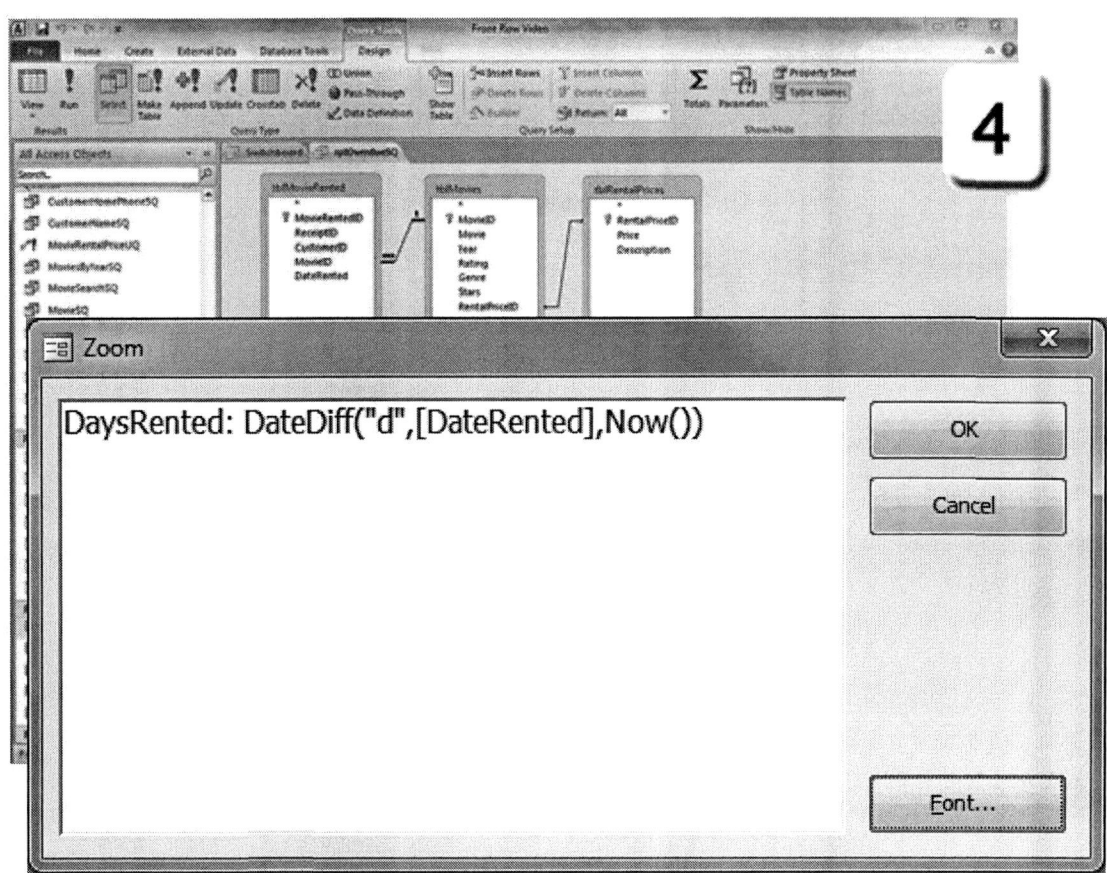

Exam 77-885: Microsoft Access 2010
4. Creating and Managing Queries
4.3. Manipulate fields: Create a Calculated Control

Determine the Number of Days

This query has to determine if the DaysRented is greater than the rental agreement. The Description Field in tblRentalPrices is "3-day rental."

Microsoft Access uses the Left() function to remove the text and just leave the first number.

Rental: (Left([Description],1))

Where Rental is the Alias,
Left() is the function,
1 is the first character in the data,
[Description] is the field in tblRental.

5. Try it: Use the Left Function
Click on a blank Field in the QBE Grid.
Right click to Zoom. Enter the Expression:

Rental: (Left([Description],1))

Click **OK**. Keep going...

Memo to Self: Yes, there is a Right() function that you can use to trim everything but the number of characters you want on the right.

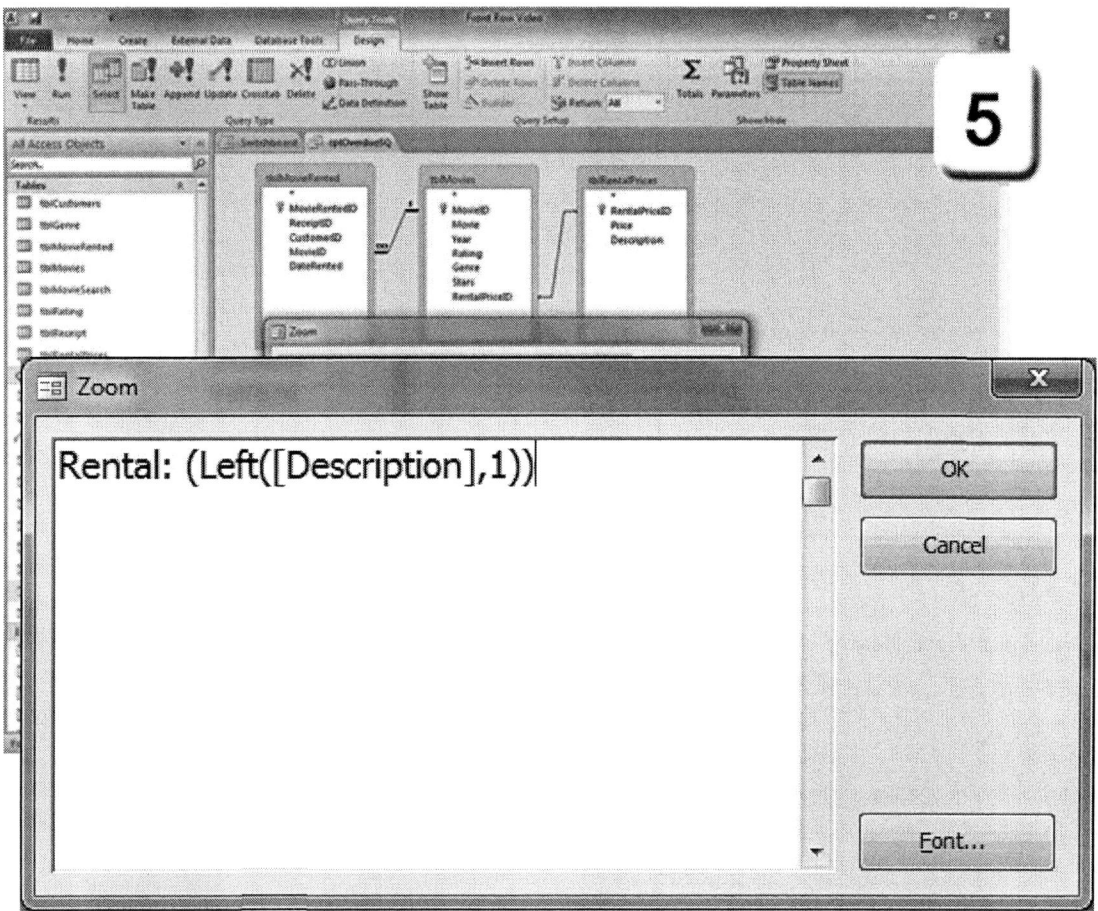

Exam 77-885: Microsoft Access 2010
4. Creating and Managing Queries
4.3. Manipulate fields: Create a Calculated Control

Create a Logical Expression

In Microsoft Access a Logical function compares two statements and chooses one answer. The Logical function in Access begins with IIF.

If you subtract the movie rental:
(Left([Description],1)

from the days rented
DateDiff("d",[DateRented],Now())

and that amount is greater than the days rented, then it's, "Not Overdue."

If the amount is not greater, then it's, "Overdue."

6. Try it: Create a Logical Expression
Click on a blank Field in the QBE Grid.
Right click to Zoom. Enter the Expression:

Overdue: IIf(Left([Description],1)-DateDiff("d", [DateRented],Now())>DateDiff("d", [DateRented],Now()),"Not Overdue","Overdue")

Click OK. Keep going..

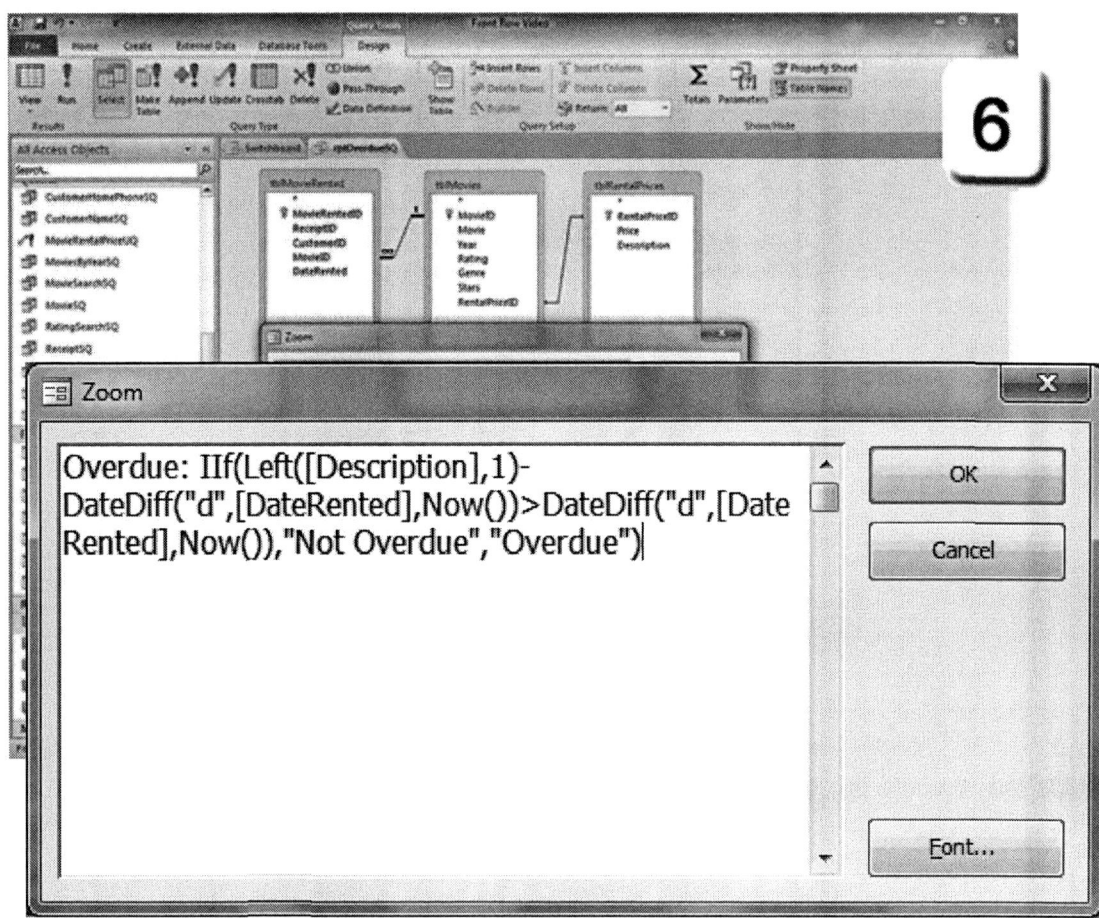

Zoom

Overdue: IIf(Left([Description],1)-DateDiff("d",[DateRented],Now())>DateDiff("d",[Date Rented],Now()),"Not Overdue","Overdue")

Exam 77-885: Microsoft Access 2010
4. Creating and Managing Queries
4.3. Manipulate fields: Create a Calculated Control

Query Tools ->Design->Results->Run

Test the Query

Well, there are several Expressions in this Query. The only way to know if it works is to Run it and review the results. Let's run.

7. Try it: Run the Query
Go to **Query Tools ->Design->Results->Run.**

What Do You See? The rptOverdueSQ Query calculated the following:
DaysRented
Rental
Overdue

Save. Save. Save.

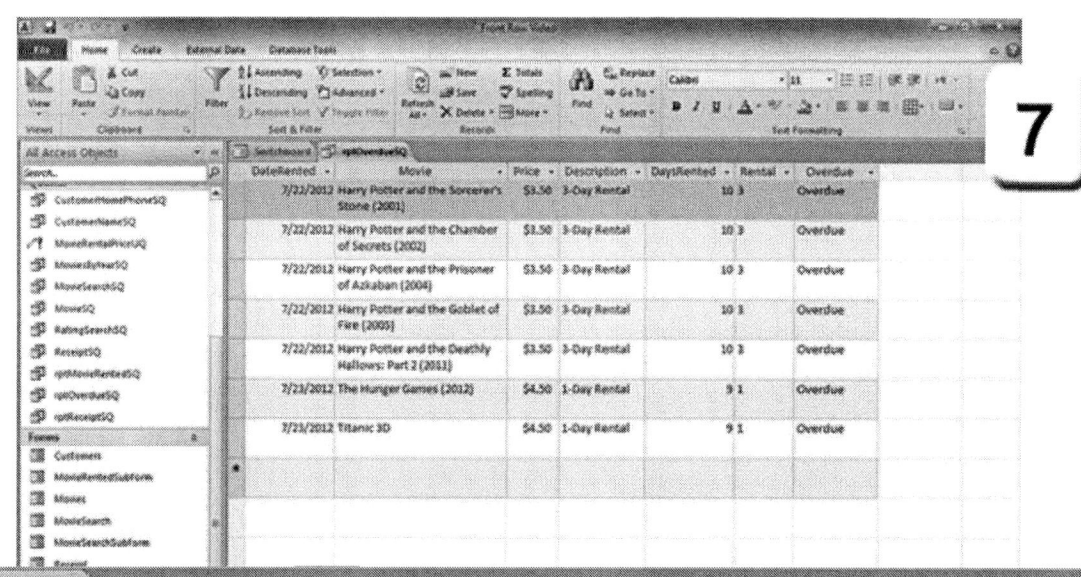

	DateRented ▾	Movie ▾	Price ▾	Description ▾	DaysRented ▾	Rental ▾	Overdue ▾
	7/22/2012	Harry Potter and the Sorcerer's Stone (2001)	$3.50	3-Day Rental	10	3	Overdue
	7/22/2012	Harry Potter and the Chamber of Secrets (2002)	$3.50	3-Day Rental	10	3	Overdue
	7/22/2012	Harry Potter and the Prisoner of Azkaban (2004)	$3.50	3-Day Rental	10	3	Overdue

Exam 77-885: Microsoft Access 2010
4. Creating and Managing Queries
4.3. Manipulate fields: Create a Calculated Control

Query Tools ->Design->Query Setup->Show/Table

Add the Customer Data

We need to add the Customer Table and create the name and address Fields that are needed in a Mail Label or Mail Merge.

Before You Begin: Change the View
Go to **Home->Views->View->Design View**.

8. Try it: Add a Table
Go to **Query Tools ->Design->Query Setup.**
Click on **Show/Table.**

What Do You See? The **Show Table** window will prompt you to choose a Record Source.
Select a Table: tblCustomers.
Click **Add**.
Click **Close**. Keep going...

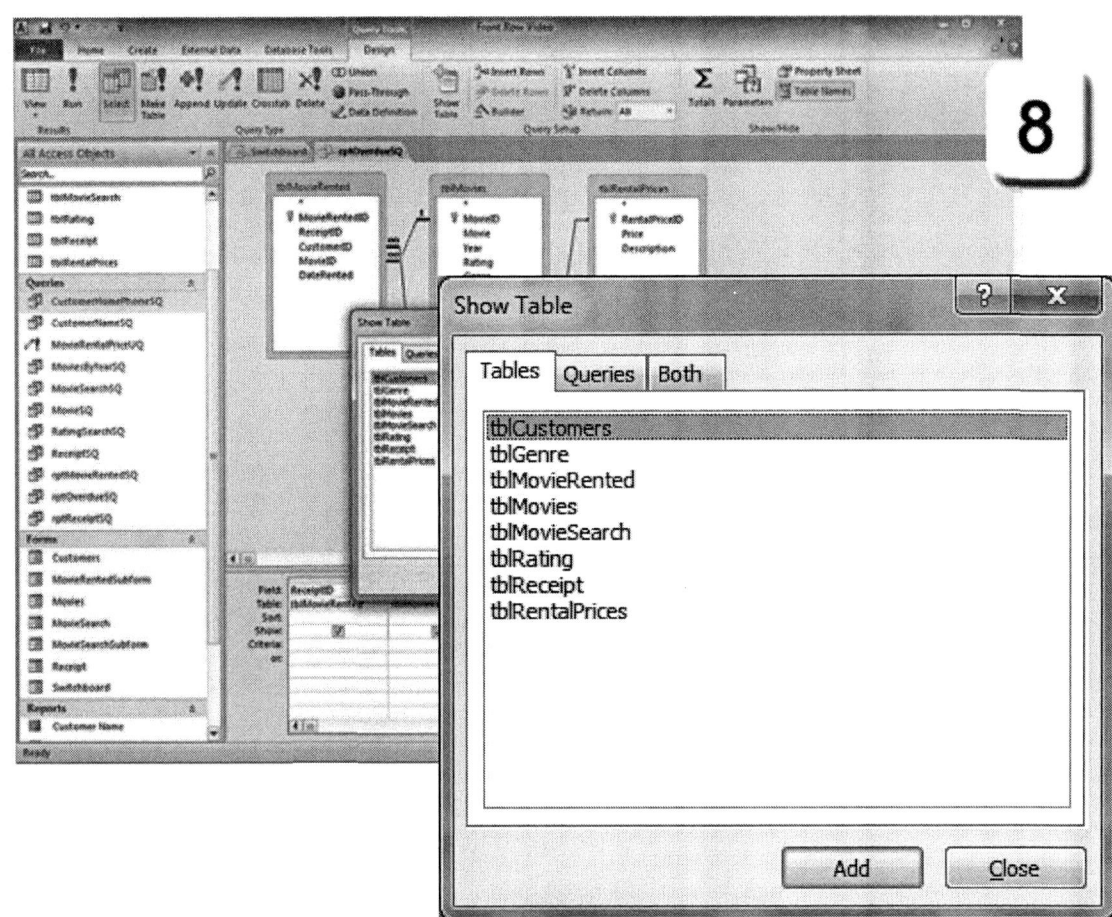

Exam 77-885: Microsoft Access 2010
4. Creating and Managing Queries
4.2. Manage source tables and relationships: Use the Show/Table option

rptOverdueSQ: Finish and Run
Do This: Confirm the JOIN
CustomerID from tblMovieRented
CustomerID in tblCustomers.

9. Try This: Add Fields to the Query
Add the following Fields to the QBE Grid:
FullName: [FirstName]&" "& [LastName]
Address1
CityStateZip: [City] & " " & [State] & " " & [Zip]

Now, Try This: Run the Query
Go to **Query Tools ->Design->Results->Run.**

What Do You See? The rptOverdueSQ Query
includes the name and address.

Save and Save, again.
Close the Query.

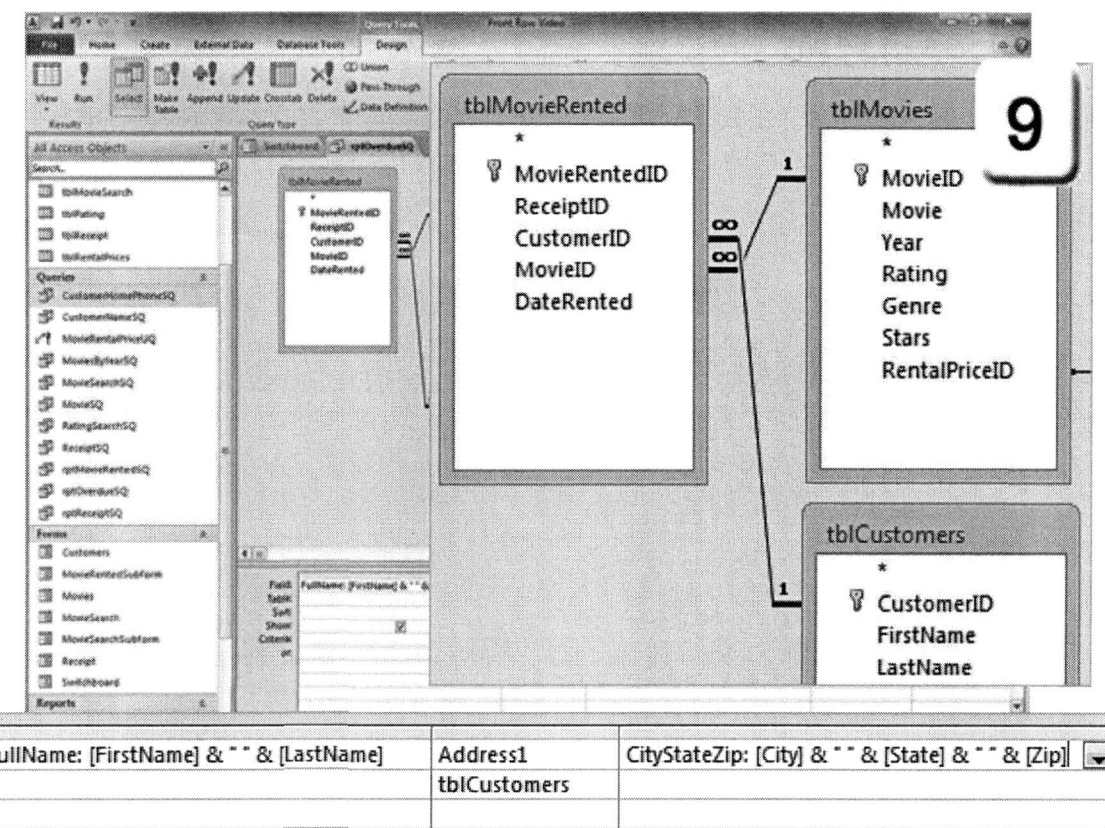

Field:	FullName: [FirstName] & " " & [LastName]	Address1	CityStateZip: [City] & " " & [State] & " " & [Zip]	
Table:		tblCustomers		
Sort:				
Show:	☑	☑	☑	
Criteria:				
or:				

Exam 77-885: Microsoft Access 2010
4. Creating and Managing Queries
4.3. Manipulate fields: Add Fields

The Overdue Letter

Let's walk through the Report Wizard to create the Overdue Letter. We will use rptOverdueSQ as the Record Source.

1. Try it: Use the Report Wizard
Go to **Create ->Reports->Report Wizard.**

Select a Record Source: rptOverdueSQ.
Select these available Fields:
FullName
Address1
CityStateZip
Movie
Description
DateRented
DaysRented
Rental

View the Report By: tblCustomers.
Group By: DateRented.
Sort By: Movie.
Orientation: Portrait.

Save this Report as rptOverdue.

Create ->Reports->Report Wizard

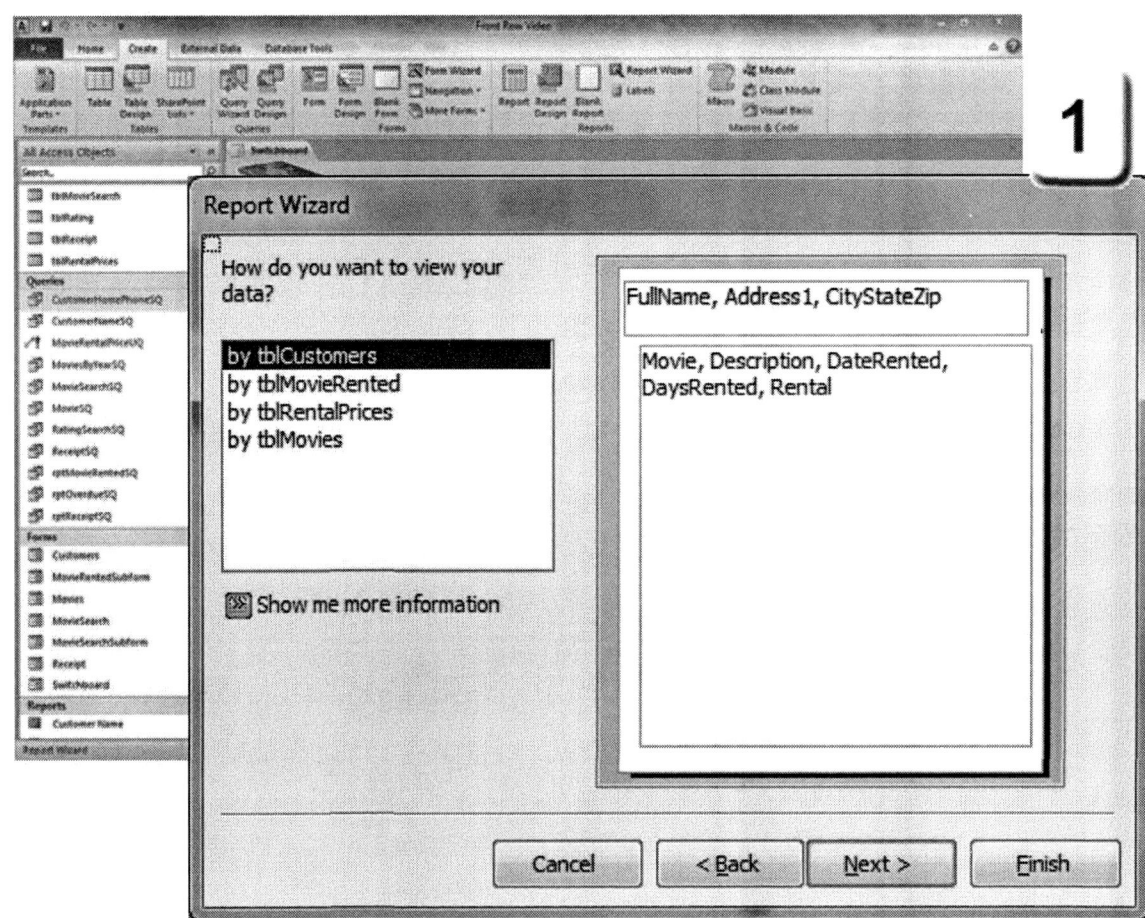

Exam 77-885: Microsoft Access 2010
5. Designing Reports
5.1. Create reports: Use the Report Wizard

Print Preview
2. Try it: Review the Print Preview
The Wizard concludes by opening the Report in Print Preview.

What Do You See? The Report Wizard does a good job getting all of the Controls on a page. However, this Report will be formatted to look like a business letter.

The customer information will be arranged into an Address Block. A new Text Field will be added for the letter.

That's the plan for the next couple of pages.

OK, Do This: Close the Print Preview
Go to **Print Preview->Close Print Preview.**

You should see the Report in Design View.

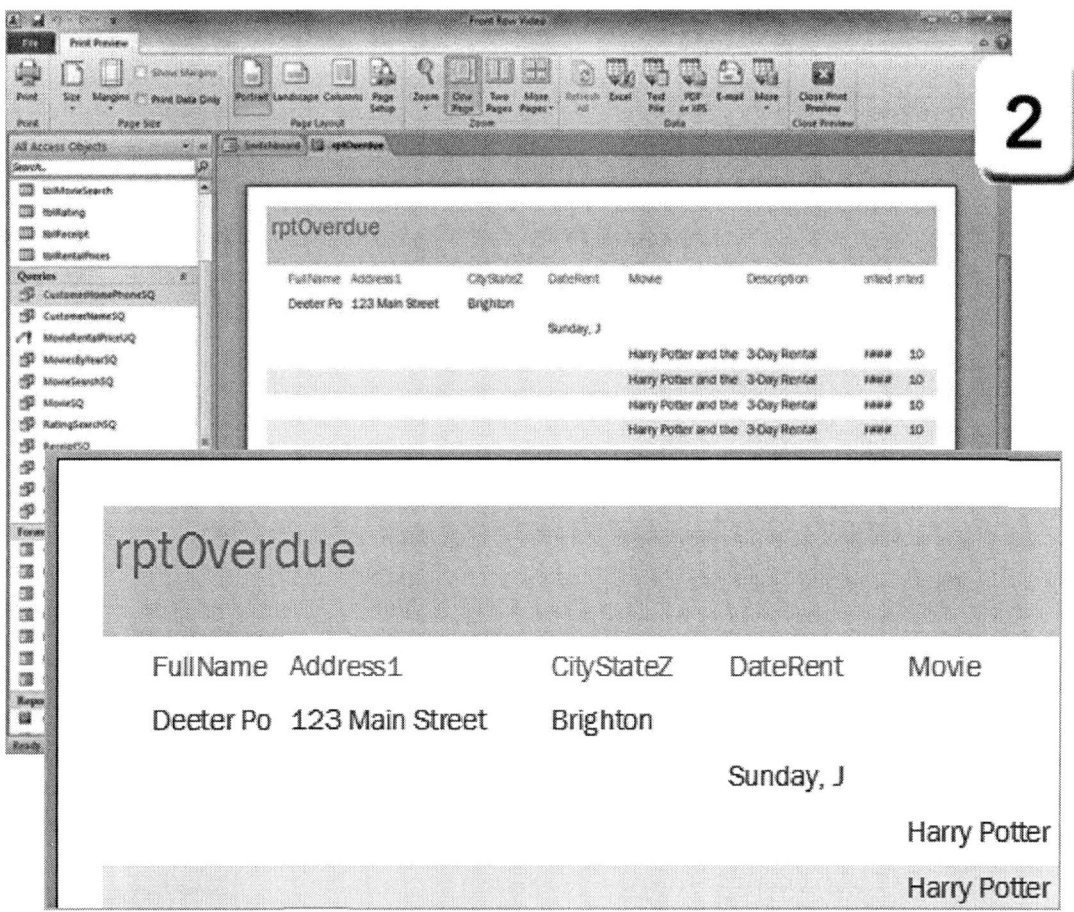

Exam 77-885: Microsoft Access 2010
5. Designing Reports
5.1. Create reports: Use the Report Wizard

Edit the Report Headers

3. Try it: Edit the Report Headers
The rptOverdue is open in Design View.
The Property Sheet is available.

Edit the following Properties:

Select: Report Header.
Edit the Caption: Front Row Video

Select: Page Header.
Delete all of the Labels.

In the FullName Header
Select: FullName, Address1 and
CityStateZip.
Align them as shown on this page, first.
Width: 1.75"
Left: 0.25"

In the DateRented Header
Select: DateRented
Width: 2.75"
Left: 0.25"

Please keep going.

Report Design Tools ->Design ->Tools->Property Sheet

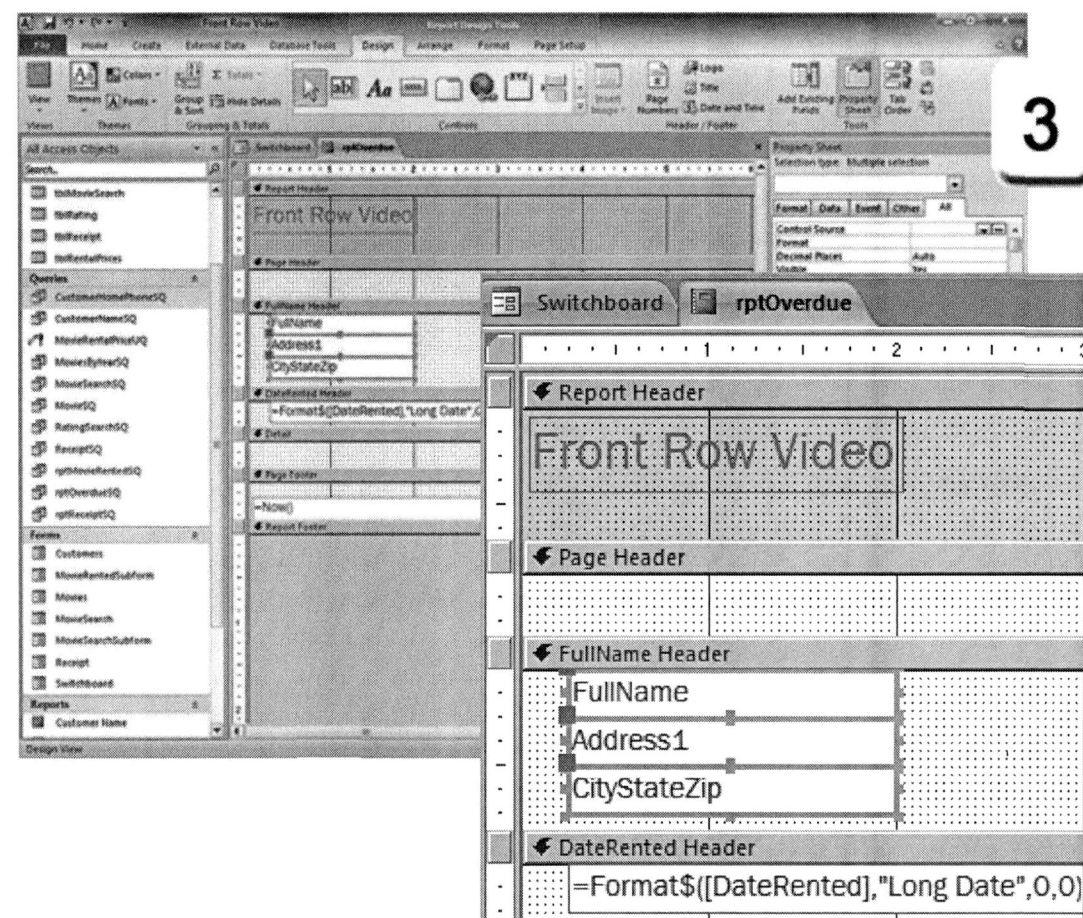

Exam 77-885: Microsoft Access 2010
5. Designing Reports
5.3. Apply Report Arrange options: Reposition and Format Fields

Align Controls to the Grid

There is another way to line up the Fields. The dots that you see in the background whenever a Form or Report is in Design View mark the Grid. You can use the Grid to align Controls precisely.

4. Try it: Align Controls to the Grid
Go to the FullName Header
Select: FullName, Address1 and CityStateZip.
Go to **Report Design Tools ->Arrange.**
Go to **Sizing and Ordering->Align.**

What Do You See? There are several options for aligning the Controls including:
To Grid
Left
Right
Top
Bottom

Select an Alignment: To Grid.
Keep going...

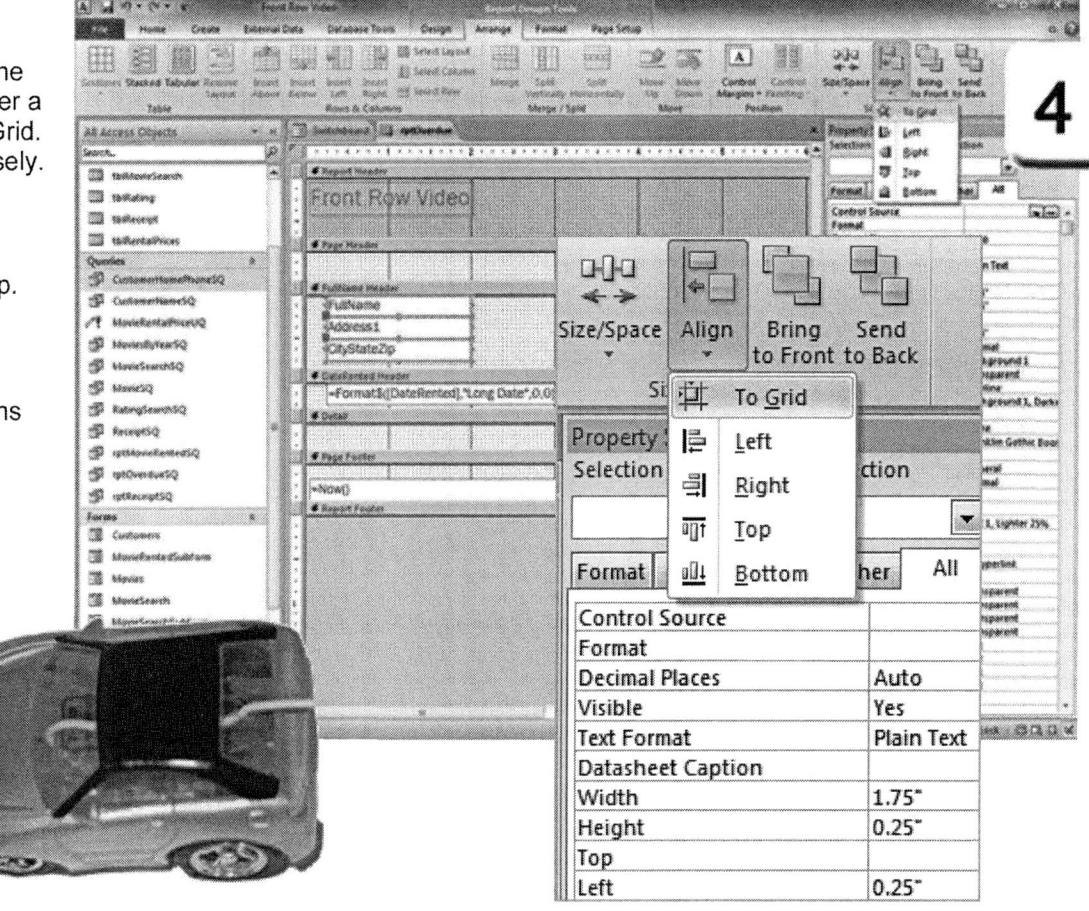

Exam 77-885: Microsoft Access 2010
5. Designing Reports
5.3. Apply Report Arrange options: Align Report Controls to Grid

Edit the Detail Section Controls

Before You Begin: Move the Fields Left
Please drag all of the Fields to the left side of the Report. Otherwise, the Report itself may be resized depending on where the Fields are when you make them wider.

5. Now, Try it: Edit the Detail Section Controls
Go to the **Detail Section** and edit the following:

Select: Movie
Width: 2.75"
Left: 0.25"

Select: Description
Width: 1.375"
Left: 3.125"

Select: DateRented
Width: 1.0"
Left: 4.625"

Select: DaysRented and Rental
Visible: No
Keep going...

Report Design Tools ->Design-> Tools->Property Sheet

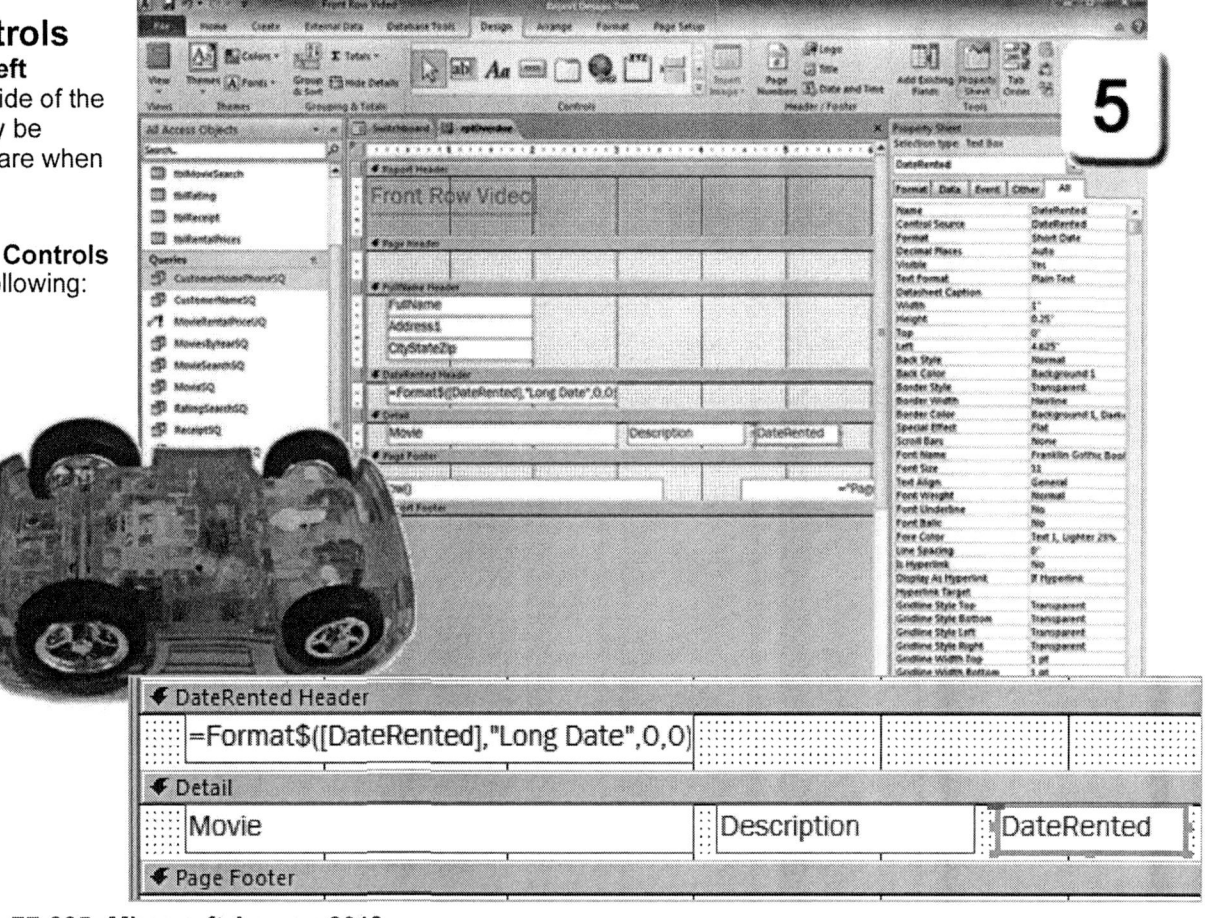

Exam 77-885: Microsoft Access 2010
5. Designing Reports
5.2. Apply Report Design options: Reorder Tab Function

Add a Calculated Control

This Report can calculate the number of days each movie is past due. Here are the steps.

6. Try it: Add a Calculated Control
Go to **Report Design Tools ->Design->Controls.**
Select a Control: Text Box.
Click on the Detail Section to create the Control.

Now, Do This: Edit the Properties
The Unbound Text Box is selected.
Go to **Property Sheet->All.**
Edit the Name: PastDue

Try This, Too: Edit the Control Source:
Click on the Control Source (It is blank).
Click on the three-dot builder to open the Expression Builder.

Select an Expression Element: rptOverdue.
Select the Categories to create the expression:
=[DaysRented]-[Rental]

Click **OK**. So...what did that do?

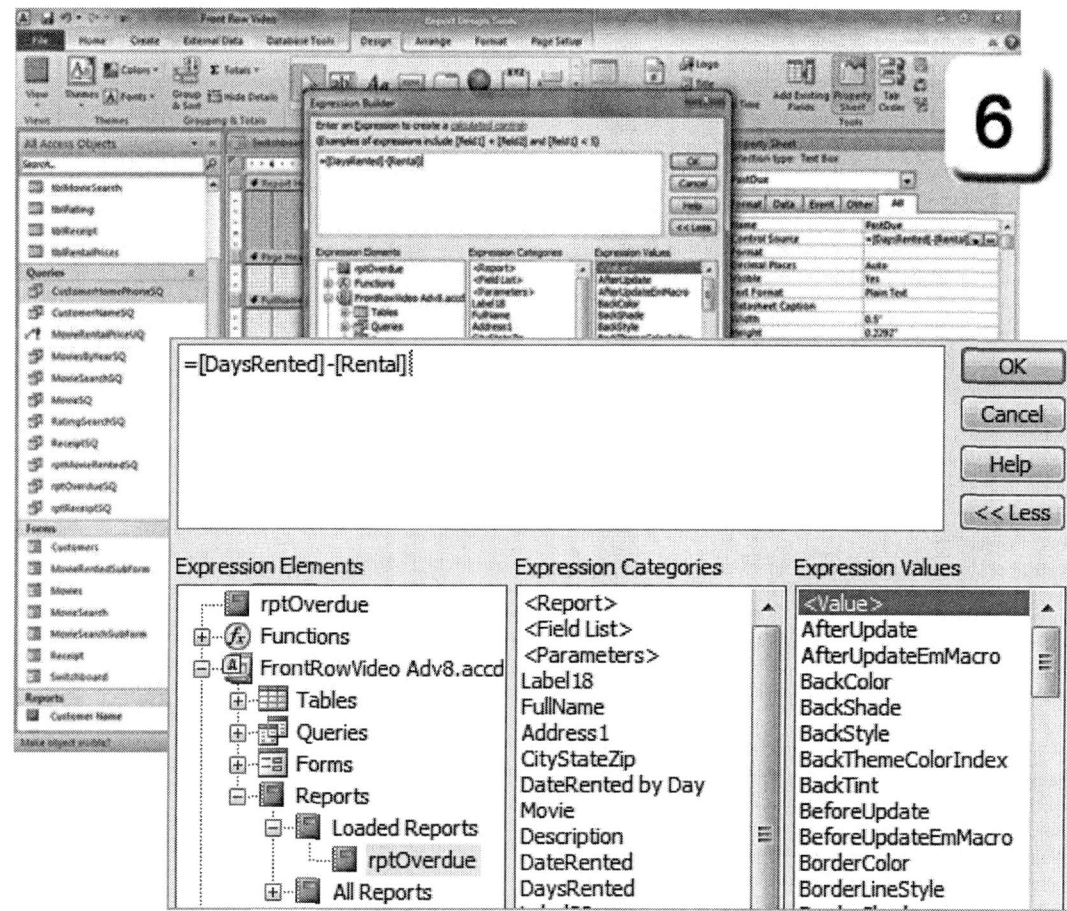

Exam 77-885: Microsoft Access 2010
5. Designing Reports
5.2. Apply Report Design options: Add Bound and Unbound Controls

HOME

Review the Properties

7. Try it: Review the Properties

The PastDue Text Box is an Unbound Control. It looks up the values on two other Controls and calculates the difference. The formula subtracts the [DaysRented] from the number of days in the [Rental] Field.

The [DaysRented] and the [Rental] Fields are not visible when the Report is in Print Preview or Layout View.

OK, Try This: Edit the Properties

Name: PastDue
Width: 0.5"
Top: 0"
Left: 6.79"

Edit the Label: Days Overdue.

Keep going, please.

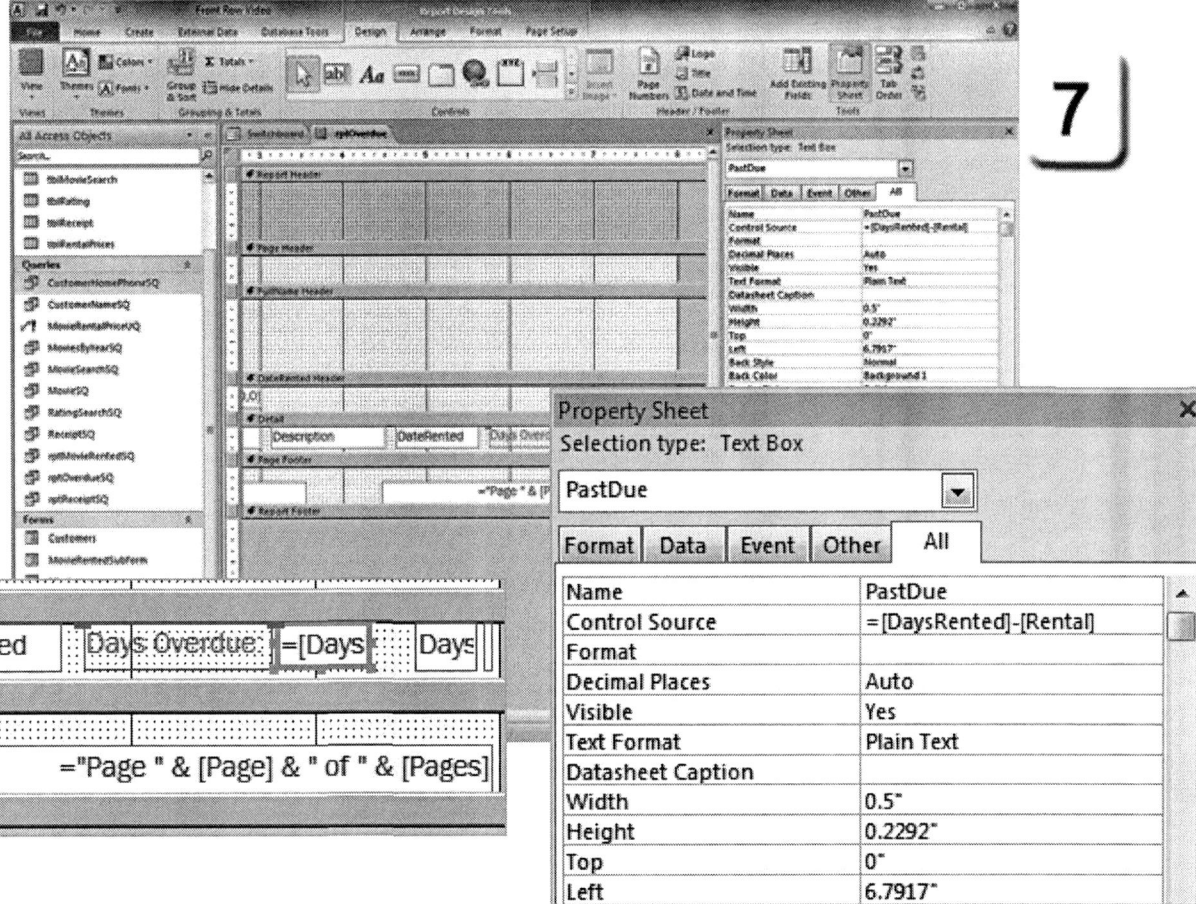

DateRented	Days Overdue: =[Days	Days

="Page " & [Page] & " of " & [Pages]

Property Sheet

Selection type: Text Box

PastDue

Format	Data	Event	Other	All

Name	PastDue
Control Source	=[DaysRented]-[Rental]
Format	
Decimal Places	Auto
Visible	Yes
Text Format	Plain Text
Datasheet Caption	
Width	0.5"
Height	0.2292"
Top	0"
Left	6.7917"

Exam 77-885: Microsoft Access 2010
5. Designing Reports
5.2. Apply Report Design options: Add Bound and Unbound Controls

Force a New Page

Each customer should have their own letter. So, we need to Force a New Page. The Page Break will be added to the FullName Footer.

Before You Begin: Show the Footer
Go to **Report Design Tools ->Design**.
Go to **Grouping and Totals ->Group & Sort**.

In the Group, Sort and Total pane:
Select: Group on **FullName**.
Click on **More**.
Select: with a footer section.

What Do You See? There should be a new FullName Footer in the Report.

8. Try it: Force a New Page
Select the FullName Footer.
Go to **Property Sheet->All**.
Force New Page: After Section.

Report Design Tools ->Design-> Grouping and Totals ->Group & Sort

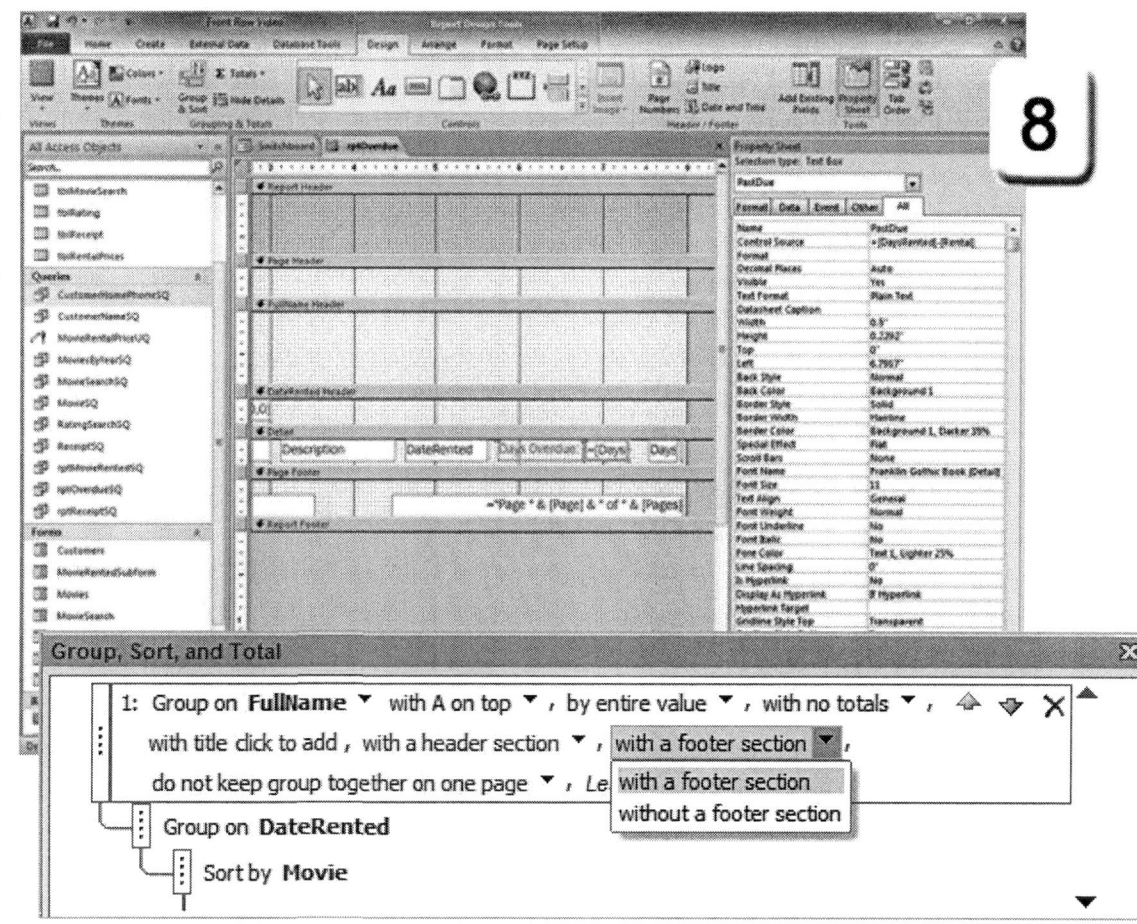

Exam 77-885: Microsoft Access 2010
5. Designing Reports
5.2. Apply Report Design options: Insert a Page Break

Add an Unbound Control

This letter will use a Label, an Unbound Control, to display the text that tells customers they have overdue movies. The Label will be added to the FullName Header.

Before You Begin: Edit the Header
Select the FullName Header.
Go to **Property Sheet->All**.
Height: 1.5"

9. Try it: Add an Unbound Control
Go to **Report Design Tools ->Design->Controls.**
Select a Control: Label.
Click on the **FullName Header** to create the Control.
Type: Our records indicate that the following movies are outstanding. Please return them as soon as possible.

Now, Do This: Edit the Properties
The Unbound Label is selected.
Go to **Property Sheet->All.**
Name: OverdueLetter.
Height: 0.4479"
Width" 4.5"
Top: 1".
Left: 0.25"
Font Size: 11

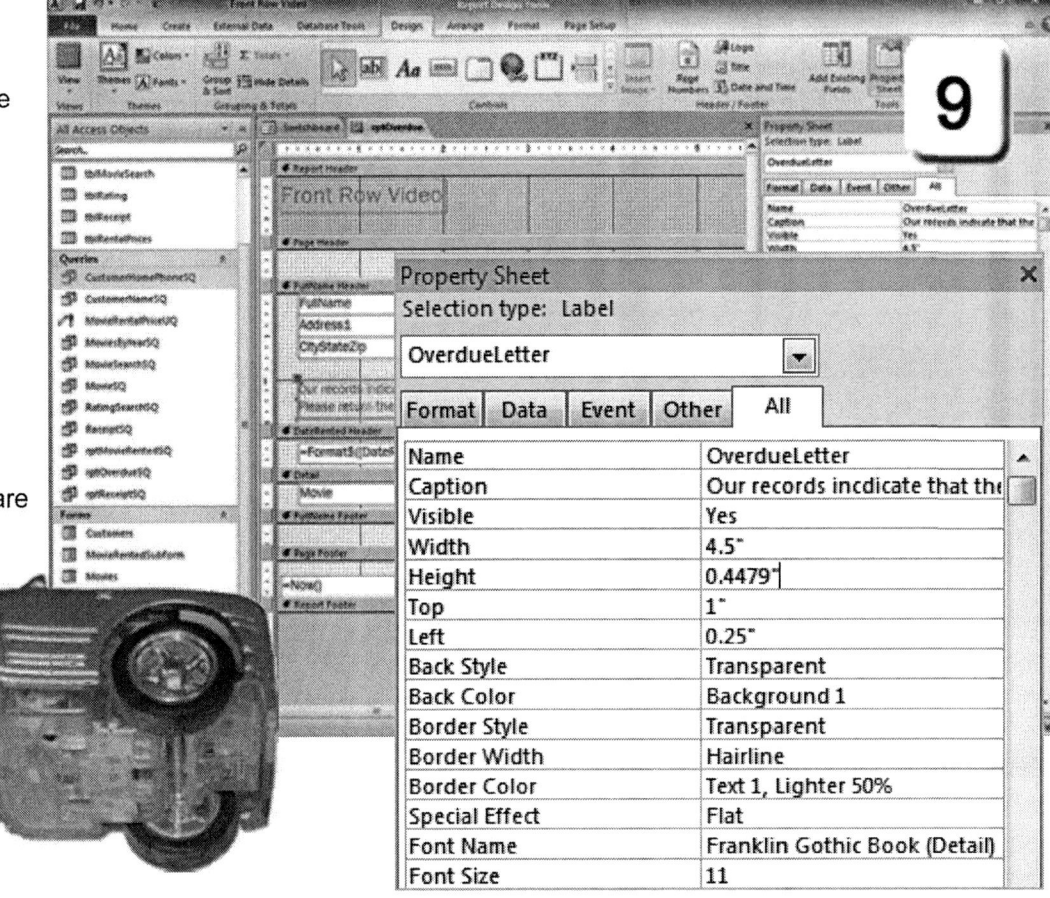

Exam 77-885: Microsoft Access 2010
5. Designing Reports
5.2. Apply Report Design options: Add Bound and Unbound Controls

Edit the Tab Order

Some of the Controls were added after we walked through the Report Wizard It may be useful to edit the Tab Order.

Try it: Review the Tab Order
The rptOverdue is still open in Design View. The Property Sheet is available.

Select the Report.
Go to **Report Design Tools ->Design->Tools**.
Click on **Tab Oder**.

What Do You See? The Tab Order Window lists the Controls in each Section.

Select a Section: Detail.
Click on: **Auto Order.**

Now, What? Microsoft Access will reorder the Tabs in the Detail Section so that they Tab logically from left to right.

Click **OK** to close the Tab Order Window.

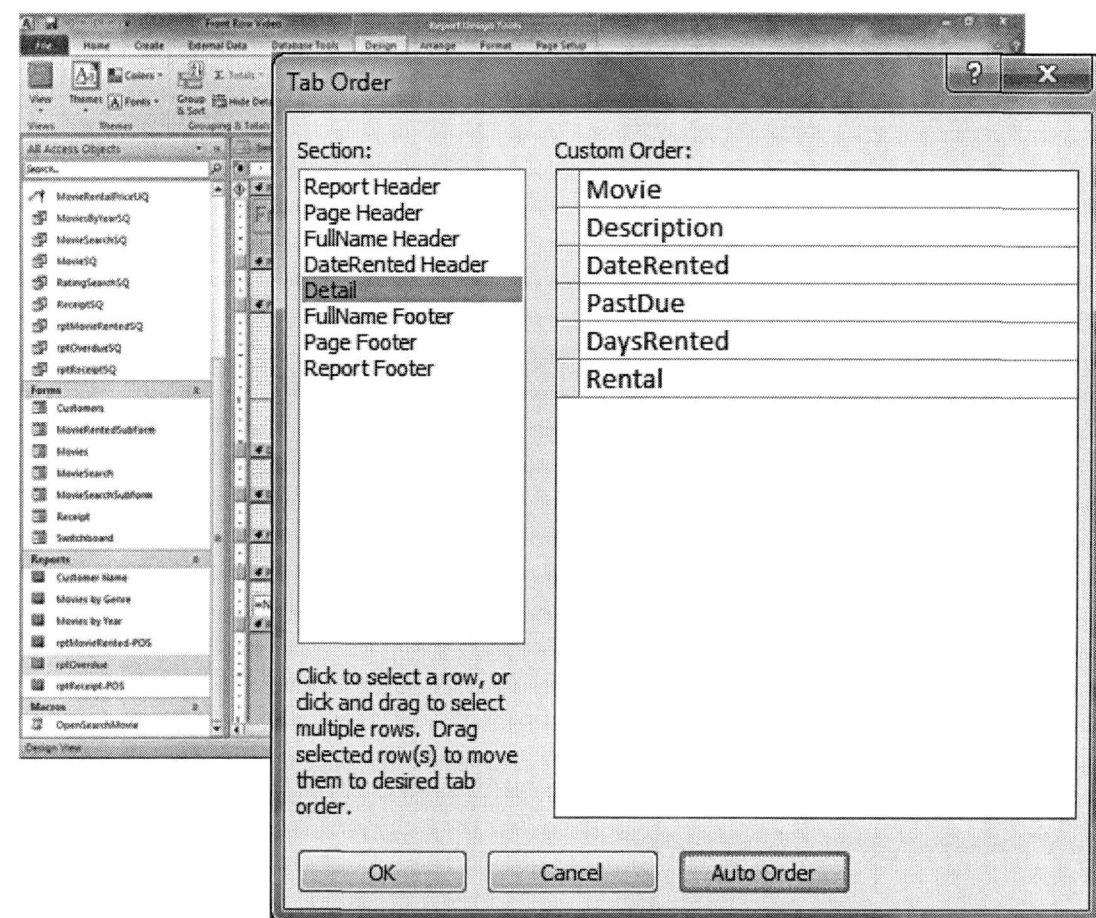

Exam 77-885: Microsoft Access 2010
5. Designing Reports
5.2. Apply Report Design options: Reorder Tab Order

Cool Properties: Grow/Shrink

The Computer Mama sez that the best gems in the Property Sheet are Grow and Shrink. These options allow the Control to fit the data.

Try it: Edit the Control Property

The rptOverdue is still open in Design View. The Property Sheet is available.

Go the Detail Section.
Select a Control: Movie.
Edit the following on the Property Sheet:
Can Grow: Yes.
Can Shrink: Yes.

Do This, Now: Save.

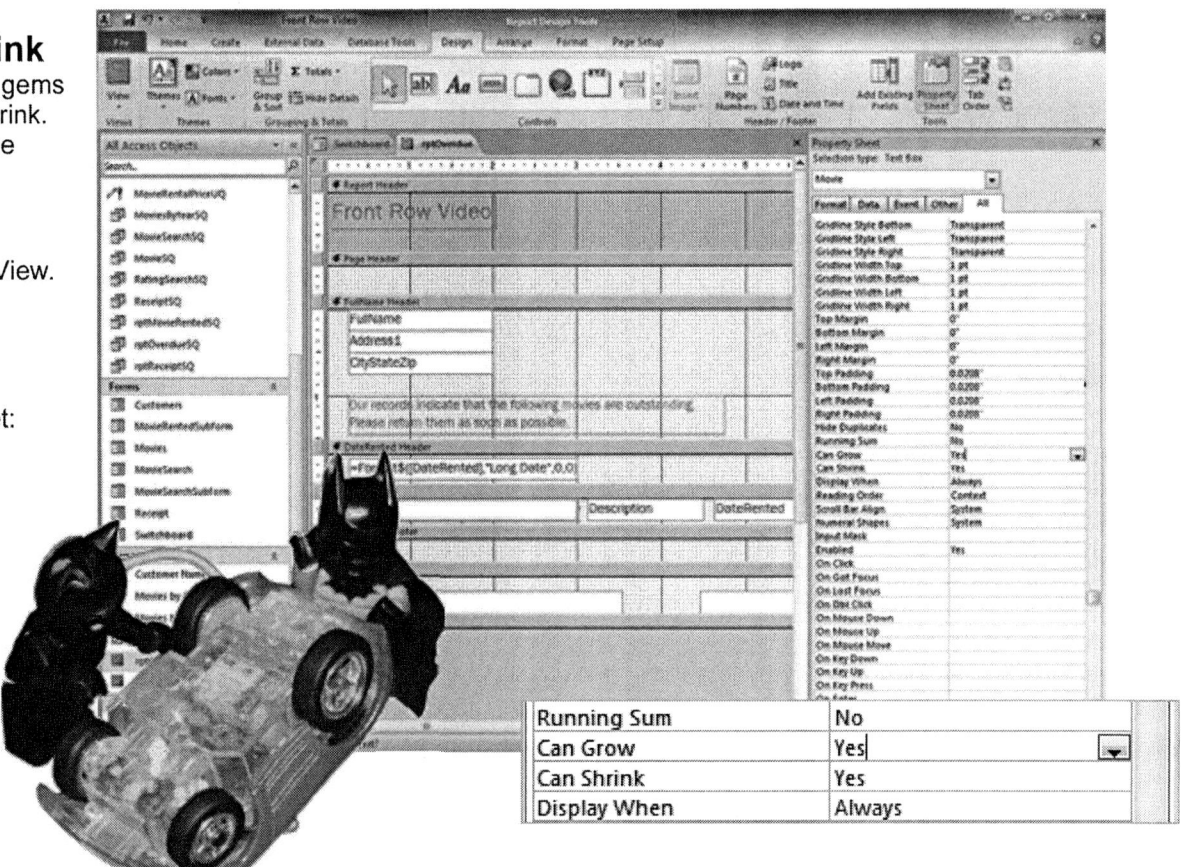

Running Sum	No
Can Grow	Yes
Can Shrink	Yes
Display When	Always

Exam 77-885: Microsoft Access 2010
5. Designing Reports
5.2. Apply Report Design options: Can Grow/ Can Shrink Properties

Preview the Report
Try it: Change the View
Go to **Report Design Tools ->Design->**
Views.
Select a View: Print Preview.

What Do You See? The Report looks like a business letter. There is one customer per page. The customer's name and address are displayed at the top. The overdue movies are listed.

Not bad. This Report could include the Front Row Video address and phone number, as well as the company logo.

Save and **Close** the Report.

Memo to Self: There is a Report Wizard to create the Mailing Labels that go with this letter if you wish to notify your customers by mail.

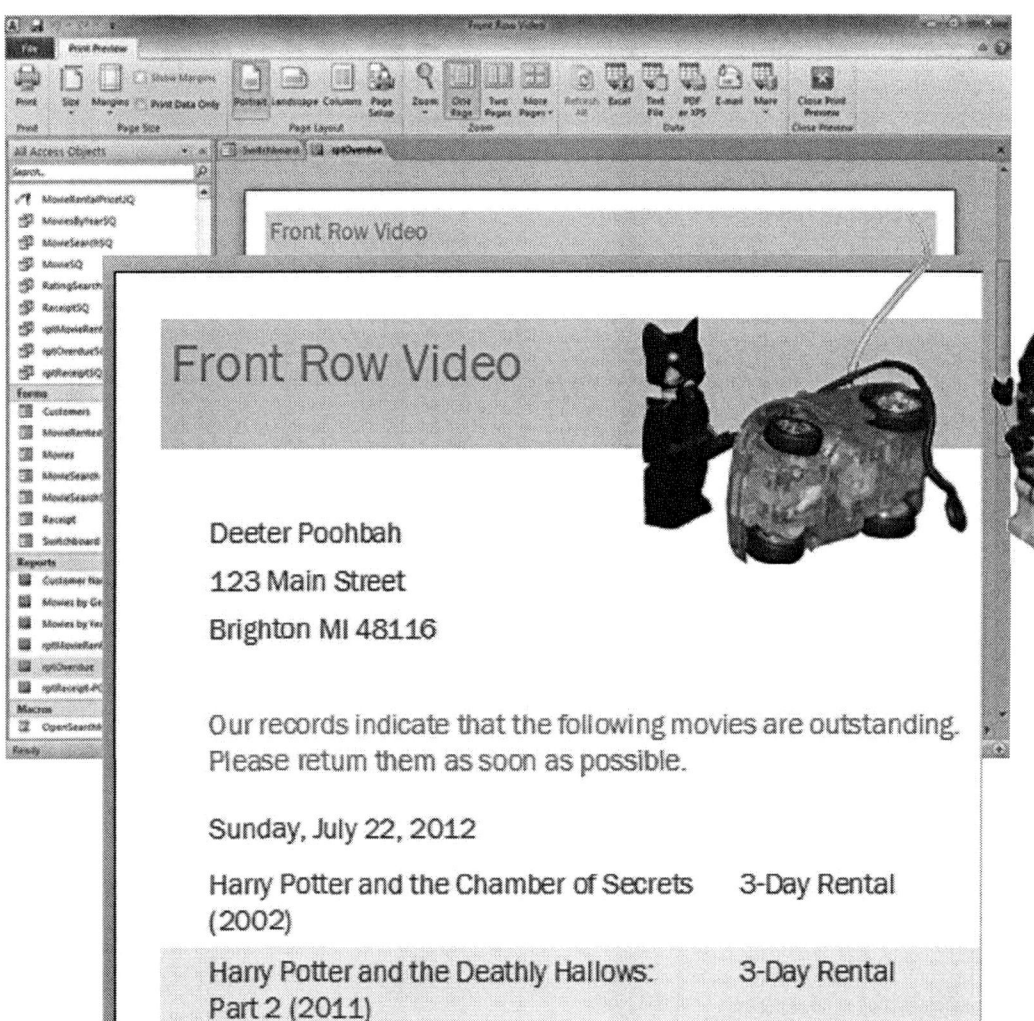

Summary

So, our customers who forget to return their movies will get an Overdue Movie Report that is formatted like a letter.

We began by creating the Record Source for the Overdue Movie Report, a Query that calculates the numbers of days that each movie is overdue. We also spent some time editing the Report so that there is only one customer per page.

This lesson is called the Producers because of the tremendous productivity that a company gets with a Mighty Access database.

Well, you done good,
You get the cookies.

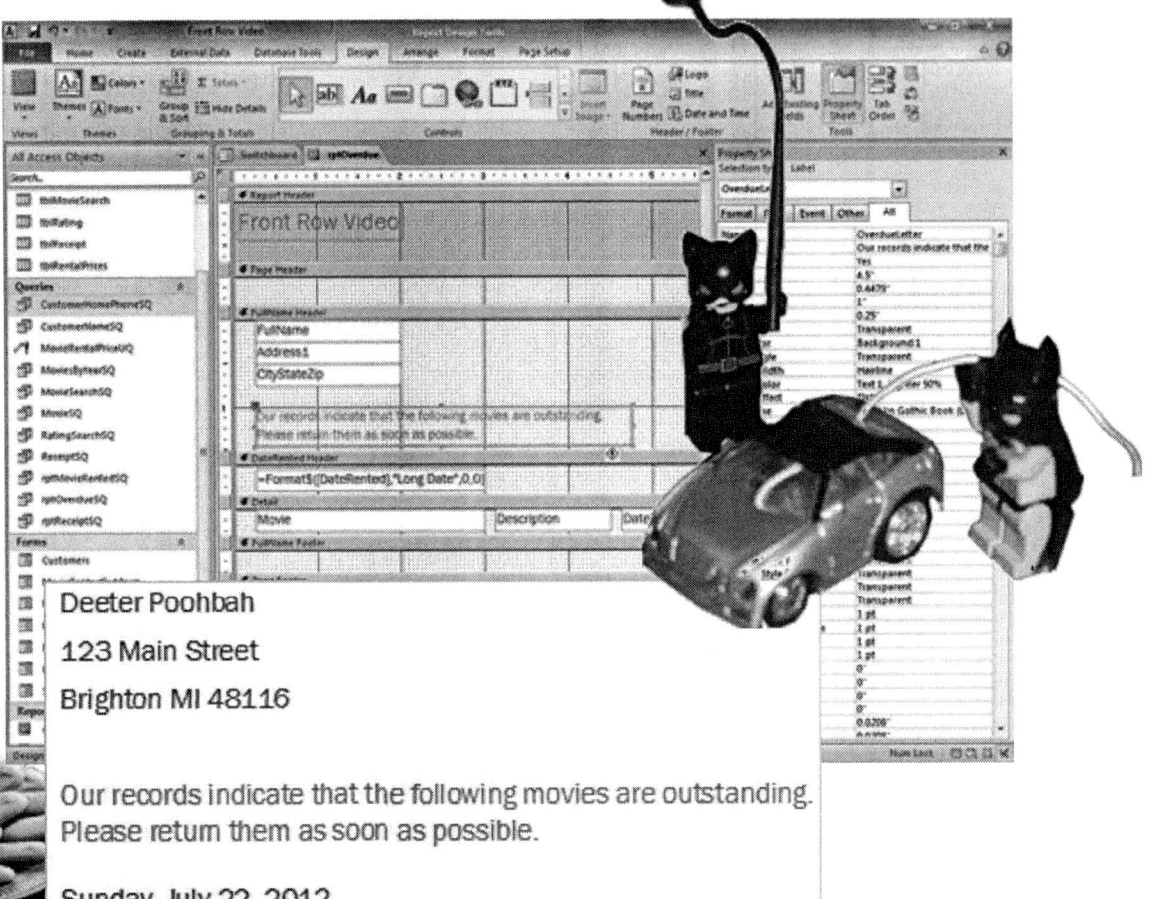

Practice Activities

Lesson 8: The Producers

Try This: Do the following steps

1. Open the Brown Bag Lunch database you have been working on.

Or, you may download **BBL Adv ver8.accdb**.

2. Create a Select Query and add the following Record Sources: tblReceiptProducts, tblProducts. JOIN the Tables by Key data:

From ProductID in tblReceiptProducts to ProductID in CompanyNameSQ

3. Add the following Fields to the QBE Grid:
From tblReceiptProducts: ReceiptID, DateReceipt, CustomerID.
From tblProducts: Specialty, Type, Description, Price

Sort by Specialty (ascending)

4. Save the Query as rptLastProductOrdered. Run the Query to test it.

5. Return to the Design View and create a Control that calculates the difference between the date on the Receipt and today's date.

DaysSinceLastOrder: DateDiff("d",[DateReceipt],Now())

6. Save the Query and Run it again. This Query should calculate the days from today to the date on the Receipt.

7. Close the Query. You can use this as a Subreport if you wish.

8. Close the Brown Bag Lunch database.

Test Yourself

1. Which Date Differences can Access calculate?
(Give all correct answers.)
A. Day
B. Month
C. Year
D. Week
E. Hour
F. Minute
Tip: Advanced Access, page 220

2. Which of the following is true?
(Give all correct answers.)
A. The Left() Function leaves only the number on the left of a string of text
B. The Left() Function removes the text to the left of a number
C. The Right() Function leaves only the number on the right of a string of text
D. The Right() Function removes the text to the right of a number
Tip: Advanced Access, page 221

3. Access uses the IF function for Logical functions, the same as Excel.
A. True
B. False
Tip: Advanced Access, page 222

4. Which of the following is true about the Grid?
(Give all correct answers.)
A. Visible in Design Mode
B. Can be used to align items
Tip: Advanced Access, page 229

5. A Control can use Fields that are not visible in the Report Print Preview
A. True
B. False
Tip: Advanced Access, page 232

Access 2010: Sharing and Collaboration

Prepare to Share

Advanced Access Objectives
In this lesson, you will learn how to:

1. Analyze the data as a Crosstab Query.

2. Visualize the data as a PivotChart and filter the Records with a Combo Box on the Report.

3. Save a Report as an XPS or PDF file format.

4. Send a Report by E-mail.

5. Export the Report data into different formats including Microsoft Word and Excel.

© 2012 Comma Productions, LLC

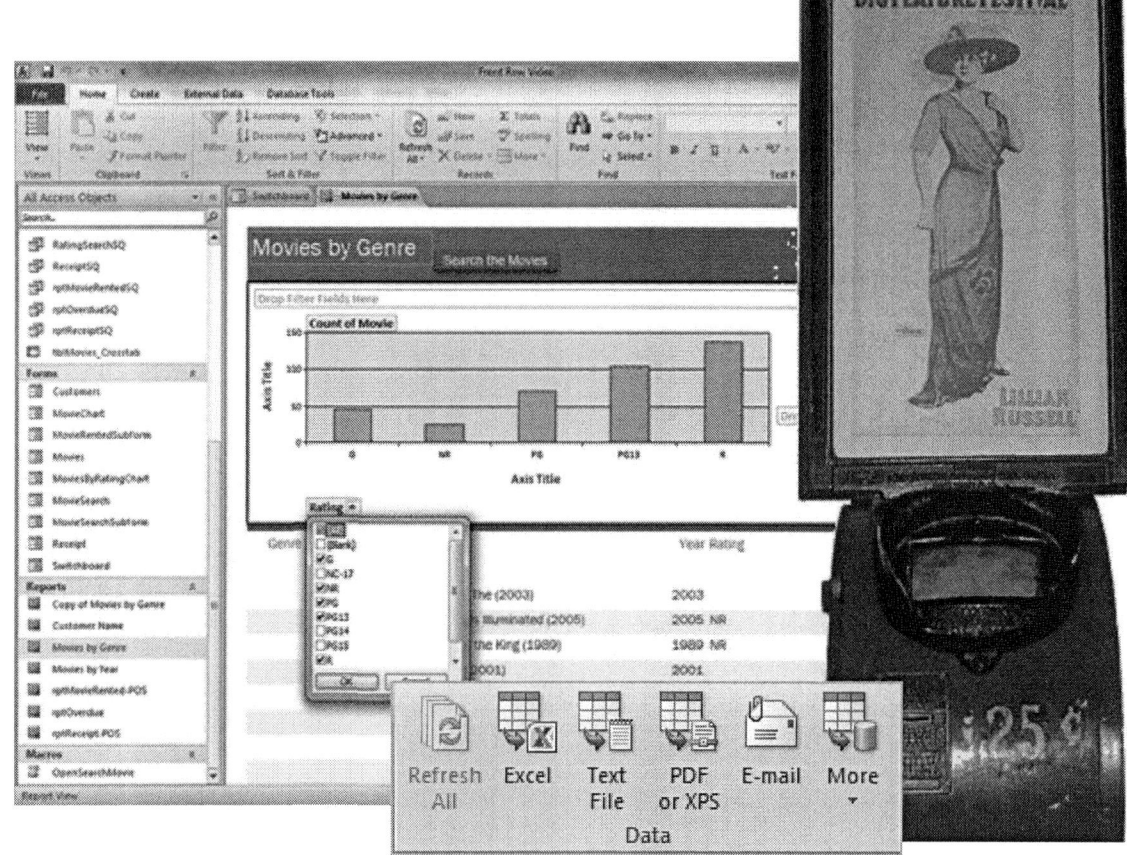

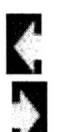

Lesson 9 : Prepare to Share

1. Readings

Read Lesson 9 in the Advanced Access guide, page 241-273.

Project

Create a Crosstab Query and a PivotChart to analyze the data. Export and print the Report in several formats.

Downloads

FrontRowVideo Adv9.accdb
BBL Adv ver9.accdb

2. Practice

Do the Practice Activity on page 274.

3. Assessment

Review the Test questions on page 274.

Create Ribbon

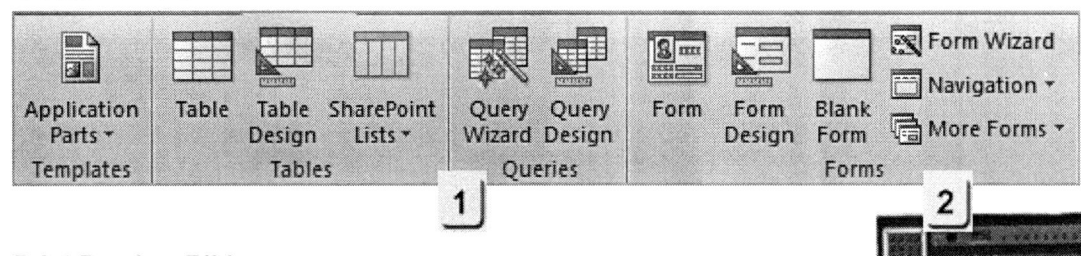

Print Preview Ribbon

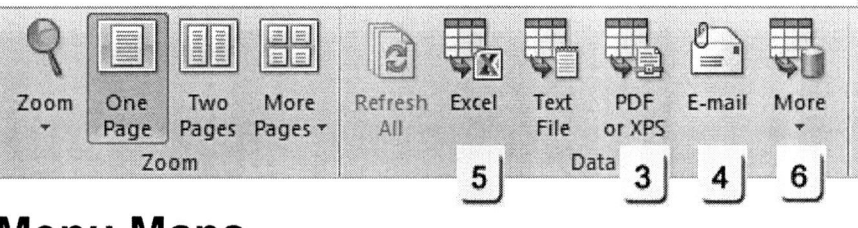

Menu Maps

From the **Create Ribbon**
1. Create ->Queries ->Query Wizard->Crosstab Query Wizard, page 248
2. Create ->Forms->More Forms->PivotChart, page 255

From the **Print Preview Ribbon**.
3. Print Preview ->Data->PDF or XPS, page 266
4. Print Preview ->Data->E-mail, page 268
5. Print Preview ->Data->Excel, page 269
4. Print Preview ->Data->More->Word, page 271

Prepare to Share

Microsoft Access is a wonderful program for gathering and tracking data. Once we mastered Forms and Queries for data entry, we spent a lot of time formatting the output from our database as receipts, reports and even customer letters. How can we share this information with customers and businesses who do not have a copy of our Mighty Access database?

Example of the completed PivotChart Report

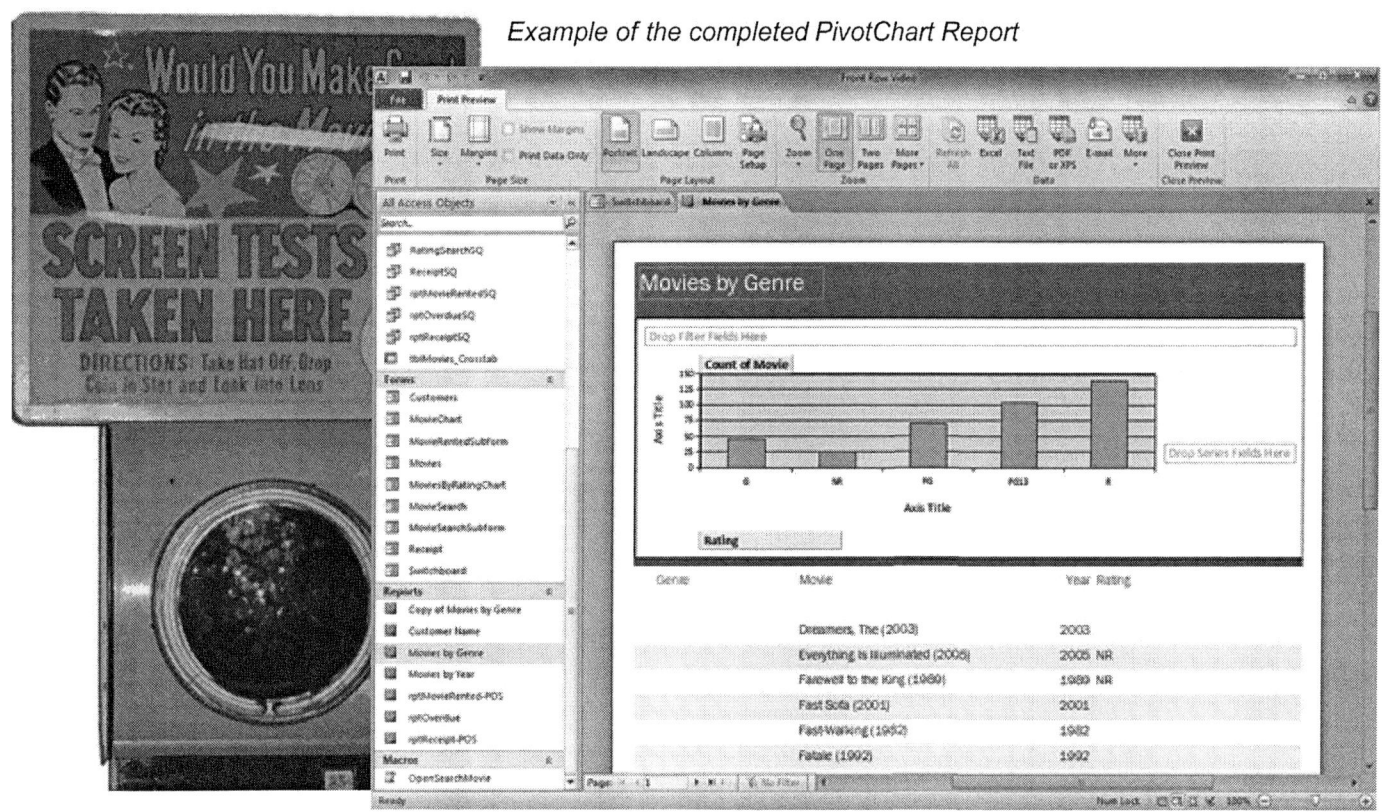

This lesson looks at ways to export the data out of Microsoft Access.

First, we'll analyze the data with two different methods: a Crosstab Query and a PivotChart. The Crosstab Query presents the data in a Table. The PivotChart analyzes data visually.

Then, we'll export the data into formats that we can share and send by E-mail: Word, Excel, XPS and PDF files.

What is the Plan?

The data analysis will be done with two different approaches: a Crosstab Query that creates a Table array of numbers and a PivotChart that visualizes the same information as a graph.

Create a Crosstab Query: tblMovies_Crosstab

Review the Record Source: tblMovies.
Create a Crosstab Query with the Wizard.

Select Genre for the Row Headings.
Select Rating for the Column Headings.

Create a PivotChart Form: MoviesByRatingChart

Create aPivotChart based on tblMovies.

Add a PivotChart to the Movies by Genre Report

Modify the Report Header of an existing Report, .
Add the PivotChart to the Report Header as an Unbound Subform/Subreport.

When the Report is in Print Preview, we will practice exporting the data into several file formats that can be shared and sent by E-mail.

So, will that work? Let's find out.

Microsoft Office Access 2010: Example of the completed Report in Design View

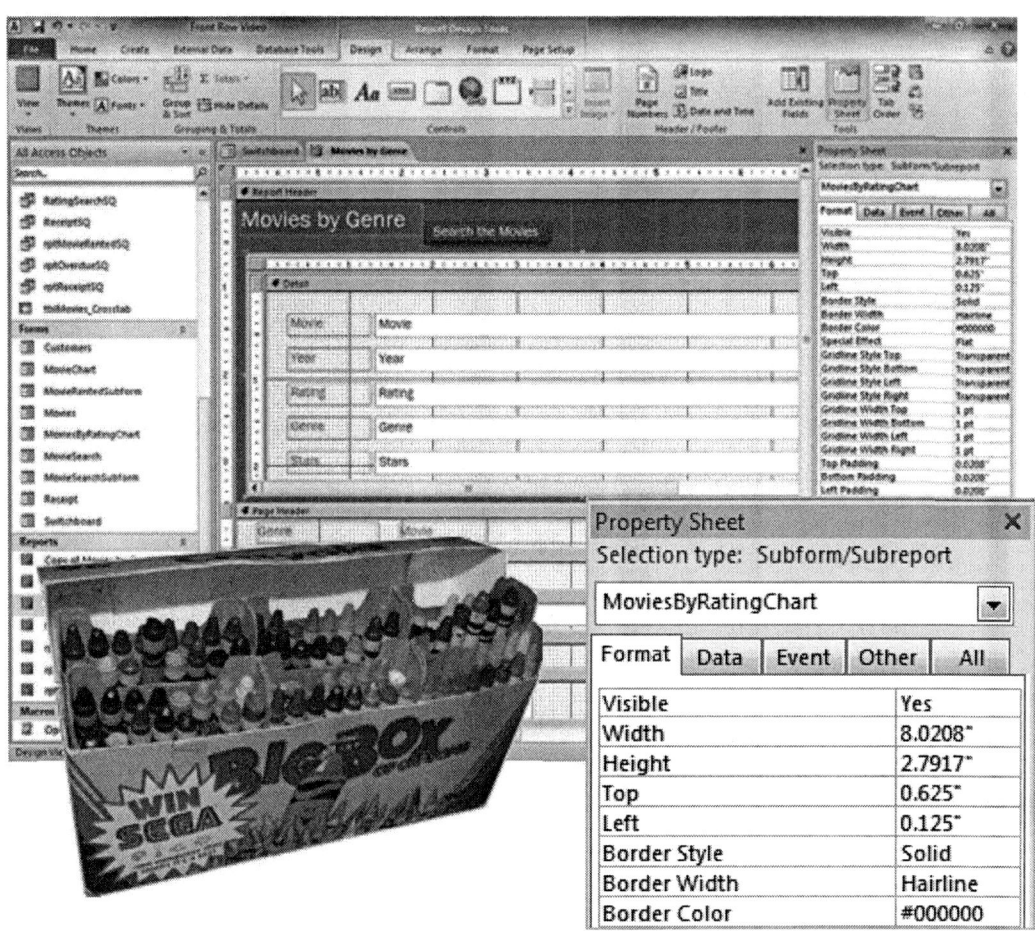

Before You Begin

Before You Begin: Open the Sample Database
Go to **Start -> All Programs ->Microsoft Office**.
Click on **Microsoft Office Access 2010.**
Access will prompt you to open a database.
Select: <u>FrontRowVideo Adv9.accdb</u>

The sample file, <u>**FrontRowVideo Adv9.accdb,**</u>
includes the Forms, Queries and Reports that
were developed in the previous lessons. If your
programming works you can continue with your
own database if you wish.

Keep going....

Memo to Self: Databases need to Read and
Write. Click **Enable Content** if you see the
Security Warning.

Start ->All Programs-> Microsoft Office-> Microsoft Access 2010

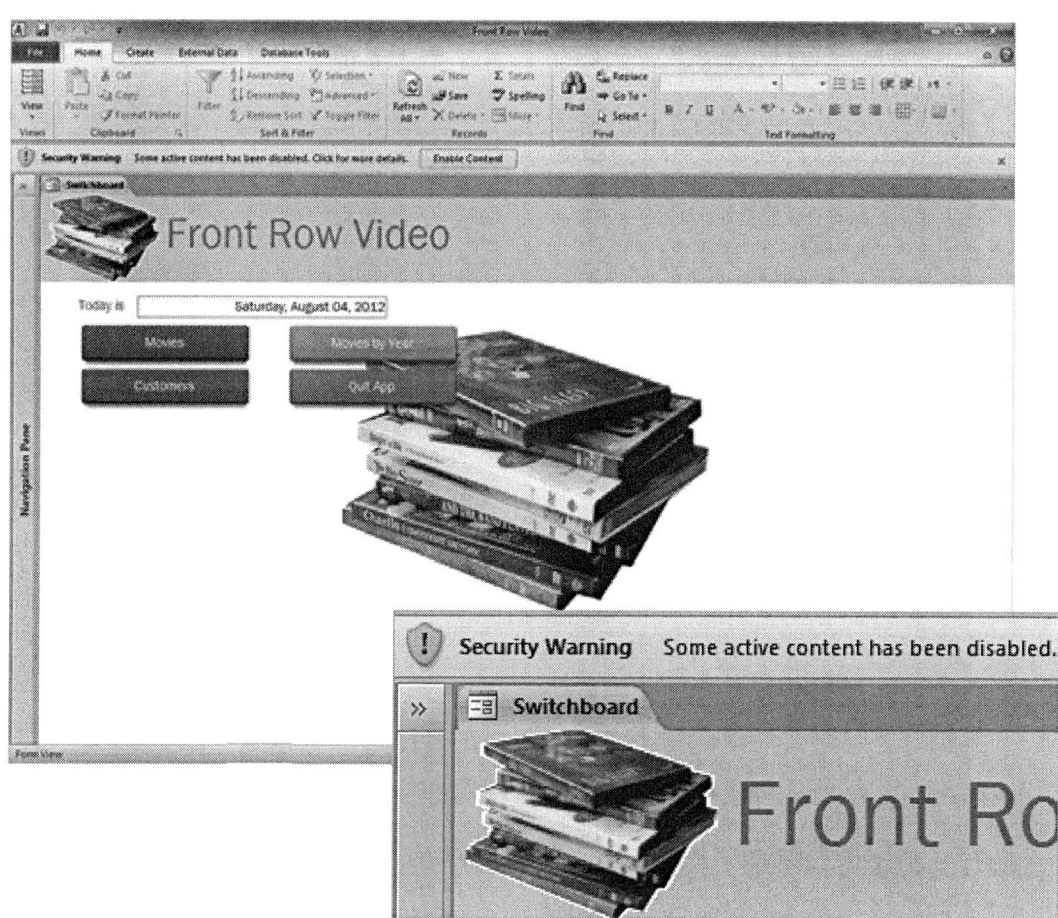

Know Your Database
Try This: Review the Database
Open the **Navigation Pane.**
Go to **All Access Objects.**

The Front Row View has the following:
Eight Tables: tblCustomers, tblGenre,
tblMovieRented, tblMovies,
tblMovieSearch, tblRating, tblRecipt and
tblRentalPrices.

Eleven Queries:
CustomerHomePhoneSQ,
CustomerNameSQ, MovieRentalPriceUQ,
MoviesByYearSQ, MovieSearchSQ,
MovieSQ, RatingSearchSQ, ReceiptSQ,
rptMovieRentedSQ, rptOverduSQ and
rptReceiptSQ.

Seven Forms: Customers, Movies,
MovieSearch, MovieSearchSubform,
Receipt and MoviesRentedSubform.

Six Reports: Customer Name. Movies by
Genre, Movies by Year, rptReceipt-POS,
rptOverdue and rptReceipt-POS.

One Macro: OpenSearchMovie

All Access Objects

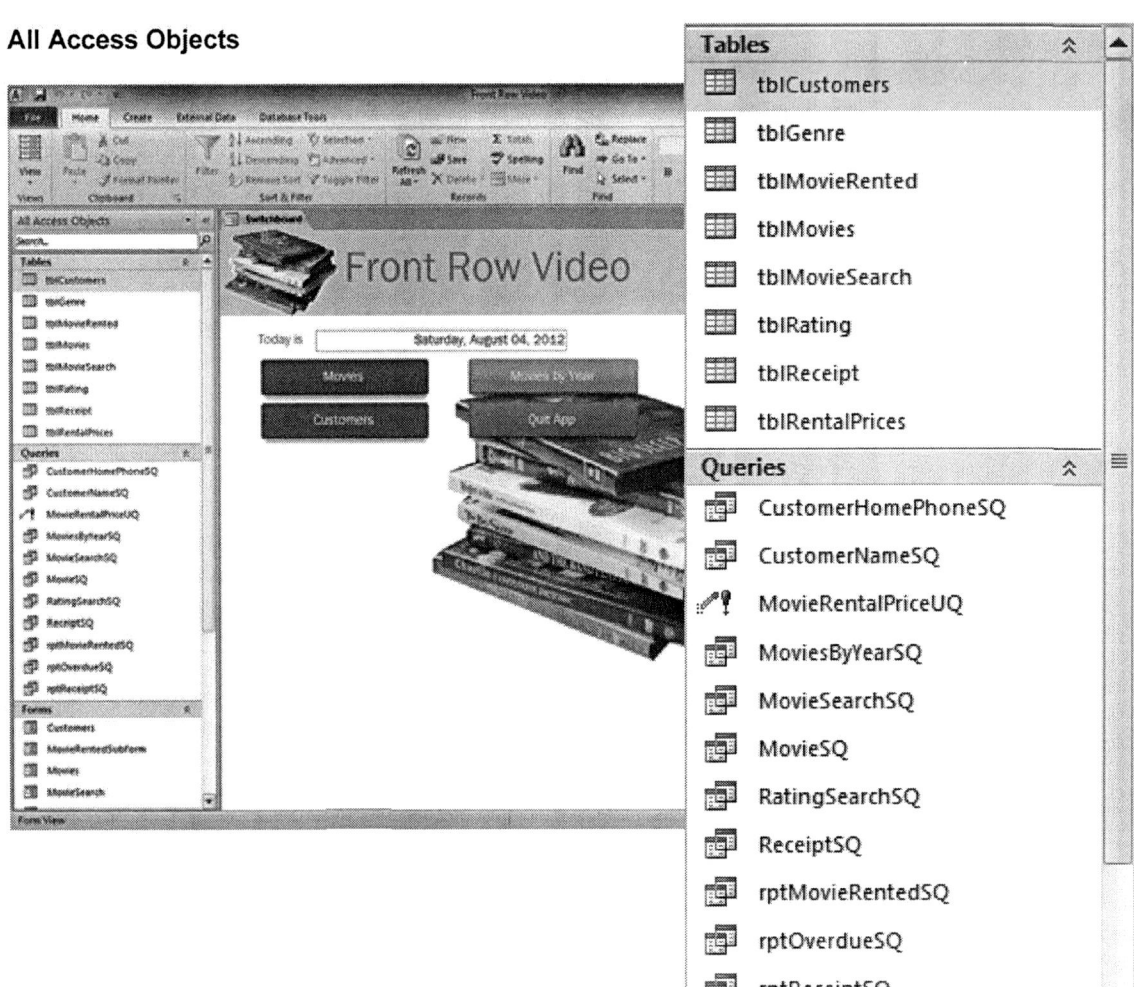

Tables	⋀
▦ tblCustomers	
▦ tblGenre	
▦ tblMovieRented	
▦ tblMovies	
▦ tblMovieSearch	
▦ tblRating	
▦ tblReceipt	
▦ tblRentalPrices	

Queries	⋀
▤ CustomerHomePhoneSQ	
▤ CustomerNameSQ	
✐ MovieRentalPriceUQ	
▤ MoviesByYearSQ	
▤ MovieSearchSQ	
▤ MovieSQ	
▤ RatingSearchSQ	
▤ ReceiptSQ	
▤ rptMovieRentedSQ	
▤ rptOverdueSQ	
▤ rptReceiptSQ	

Review the Record Source

1. Try This: Review the Record Source
Go to **All Access Objects ->Tables**.
Open a **Table: tblMovies**.

What Do You See? There are 401 Records.
Each Record includes:
Movie
Year
Rating
Genre
Stars
RentalPriceID

How many Comedies have a PG13 Rating?
How many Comedies have an R Rating?
How many PG13 Movies are Action flix?

A Table is a collection of Records. Queries and Reports can analyze those Records. This lesson will use a Crosstab Query to look at the Ratings by Genre. Then, we'll use a PivotChart to visualize the data.

Please **Close** tblMovies. Let's get started.

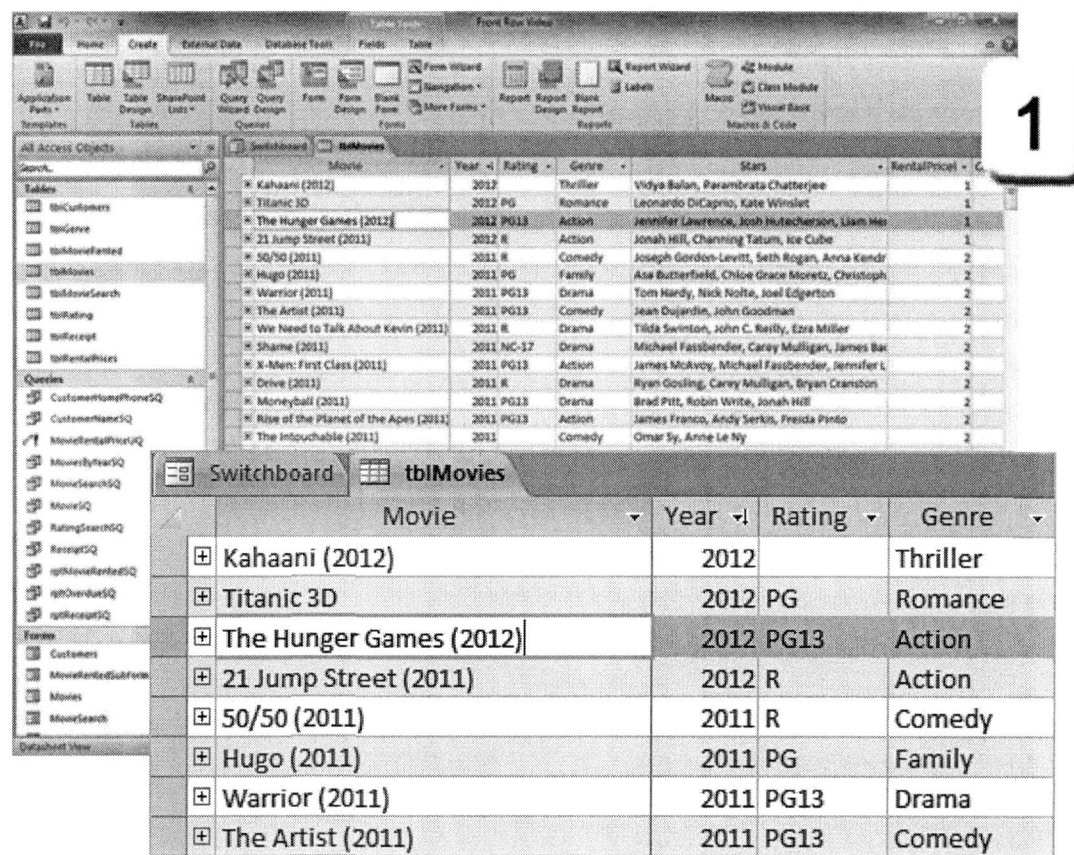

Movie		Year	Rating	Genre
⊞	Kahaani (2012)	2012		Thriller
⊞	Titanic 3D	2012	PG	Romance
⊞	The Hunger Games (2012)	2012	PG13	Action
⊞	21 Jump Street (2011)	2012	R	Action
⊞	50/50 (2011)	2011	R	Comedy
⊞	Hugo (2011)	2011	PG	Family
⊞	Warrior (2011)	2011	PG13	Drama
⊞	The Artist (2011)	2011	PG13	Comedy

Create a Crosstab Query: tblMovies_Crosstab

A Crosstab Query creates a Table that compares the data. In this example, we can use the Crosstab Query to count how many movies we have in each Rating.

2. Try it: Create a Query
Go to **Create ->Queries ->Query Wizard.** You will be prompted to select which Query Wizard you would like to launch.

There are four Query Wizards:
Simple Query Wizard
Crosstab Query Wizard
Find Duplicates Query Wizard
Find Unmatched Query Wizard

Select a Wizard: Crosstab Query Wizard. Click **OK**. The Query Wizard should start.

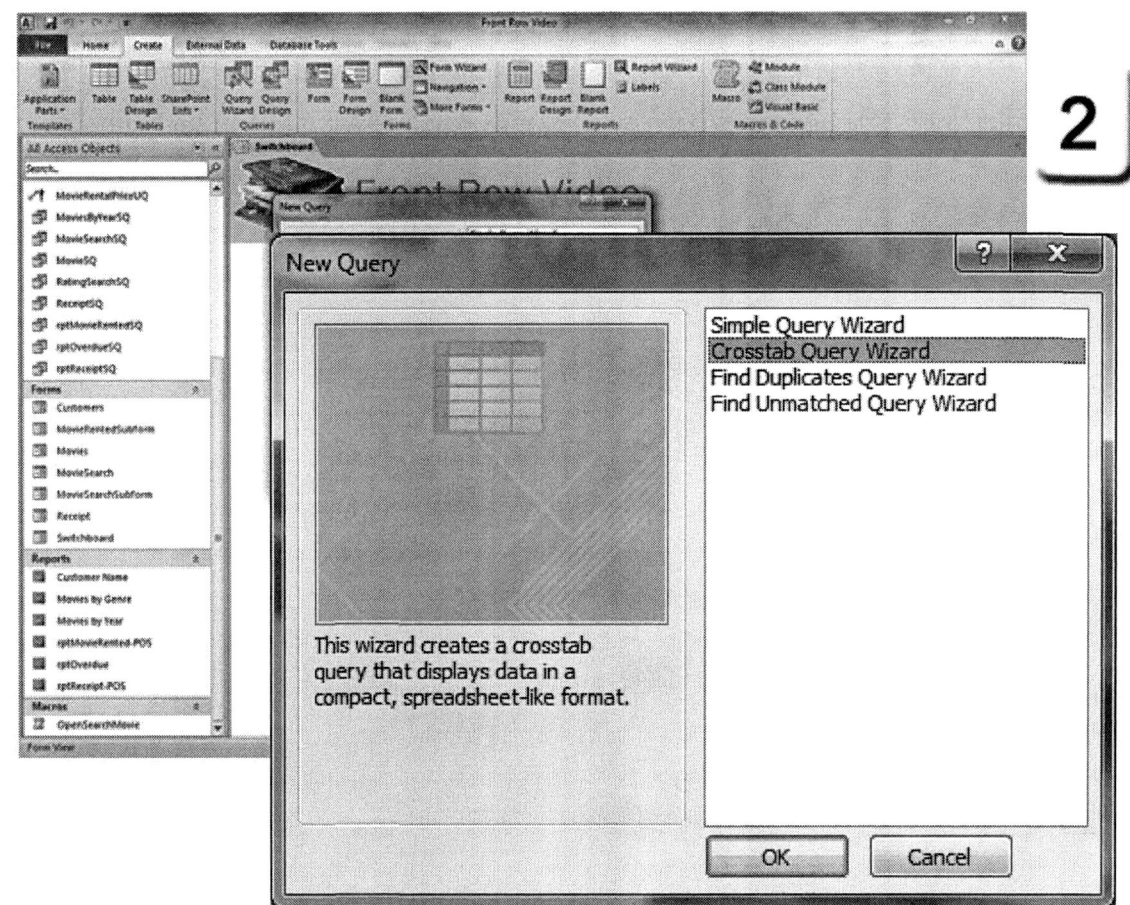

2

Exam 77-885: Microsoft Access 2010
4. Creating and Managing Queries
4.1. Construct queries: Create a Crosstab Query

Crosstab Query Wizard:
Select the Record Source
The Crosstab Query can use a Table or Query for the Record Source.

3. Try it: Select the Record Source
Select a Table: tblMovies.

Click **Next**. Keep going..

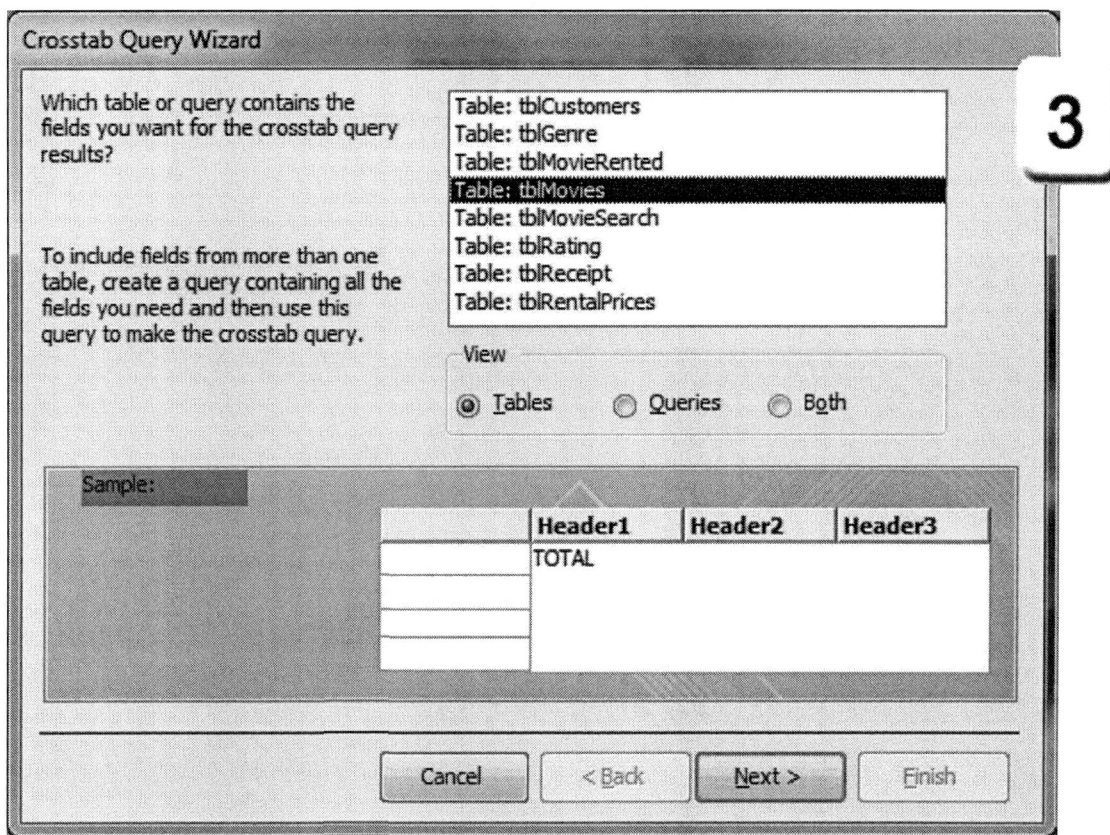

3

Crosstab Query Wizard

Which table or query contains the fields you want for the crosstab query results?

To include fields from more than one table, create a query containing all the fields you need and then use this query to make the crosstab query.

Table: tblCustomers
Table: tblGenre
Table: tblMovieRented
Table: tblMovies
Table: tblMovieSearch
Table: tblRating
Table: tblReceipt
Table: tblRentalPrices

View
◉ Tables   ○ Queries   ○ Both

Sample:

	Header1	Header2	Header3
	TOTAL		

Cancel   < Back   Next >   Finish

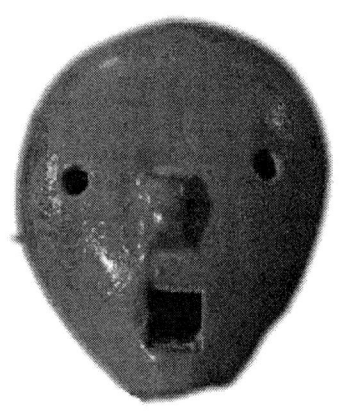

Exam 77-885: Microsoft Access 2010
4. Creating and Managing Queries
4.1. Construct queries: Create a Crosstab Query

Crosstab Query Wizard:
Select the Row Headings

The Row Headings will be shown on the left side of the Crosstab layout. All of the Fields in the Table are available. You can select more than one Field if you wish.

4. Try it: Select the Row Headings
Select a Field: Genre.

What Do You See? The sample layout shows the position of the Genre data.

Click **Next**. Keep going...

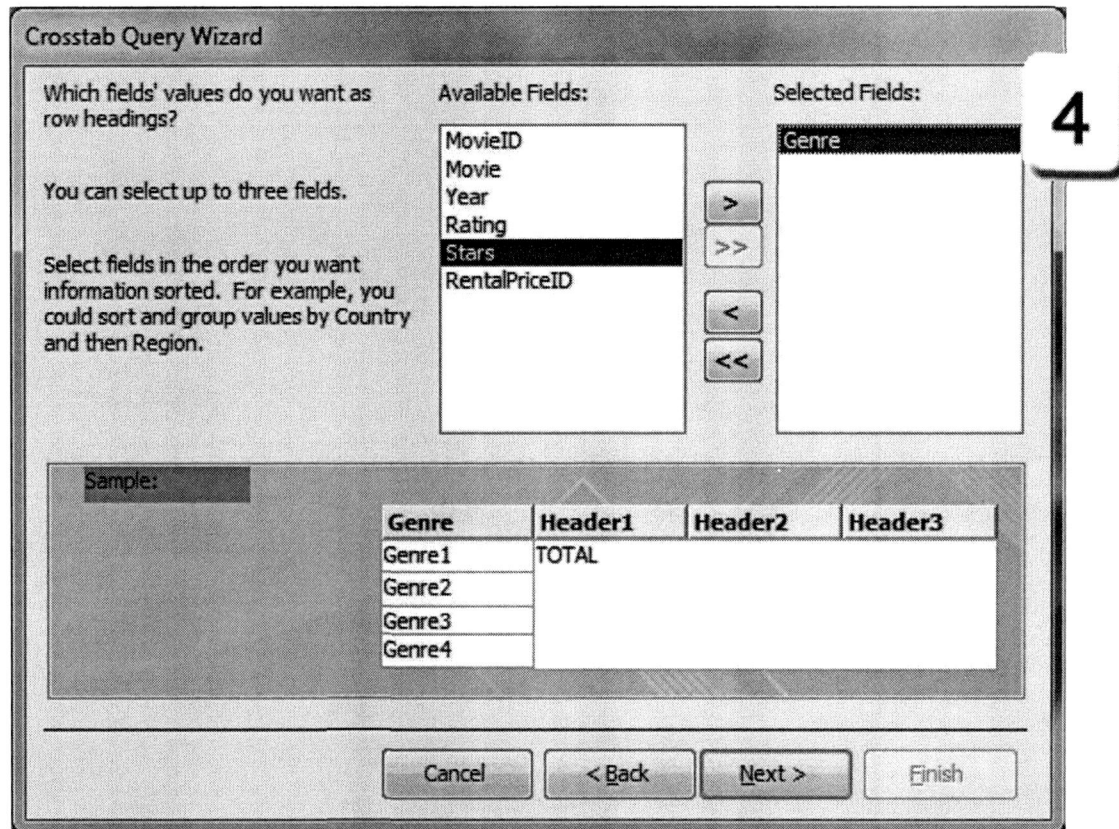

Exam 77-885: Microsoft Access 2010
4. Creating and Managing Queries
4.1. Construct queries: Create a Crosstab Query

Crosstab Query Wizard:
Select the Row Headings

The Column Headings will be shown on the top of the Crosstab layout. The remaining Fields in the Table are available. You can select one Field for the Column Heading.

5. Try it: Select the Column Headings
Select a Field: Rating.

What Do You See? The sample layout shows the position of the Rating data.

Click **Next**. Keep going...

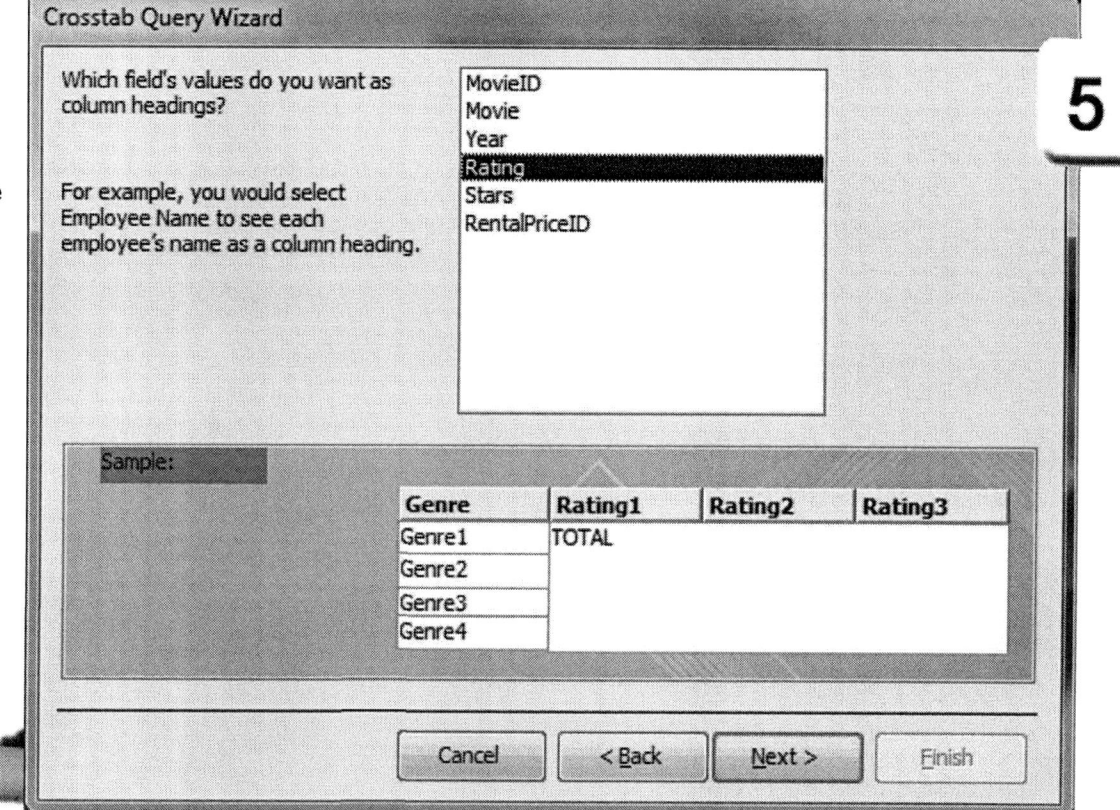

Exam 77-885: Microsoft Access 2010
4. Creating and Managing Queries
4.1. Construct queries: Create a Crosstab Query

Create ->Queries ->Query Wizard->Crosstab Query Wizard

Crosstab Query Wizard: Select a Function

A Crosstab Query can use many math functions including: Avg, Count, First, Last, Max, Min, StDev, Sum, Var.

6. Try it: Select a Function
Select a Field: MovieID.
Select a Function: Count.

What Do You See? By default, there is a check mark to include **row sums**.

Click **Next**. Keep going...

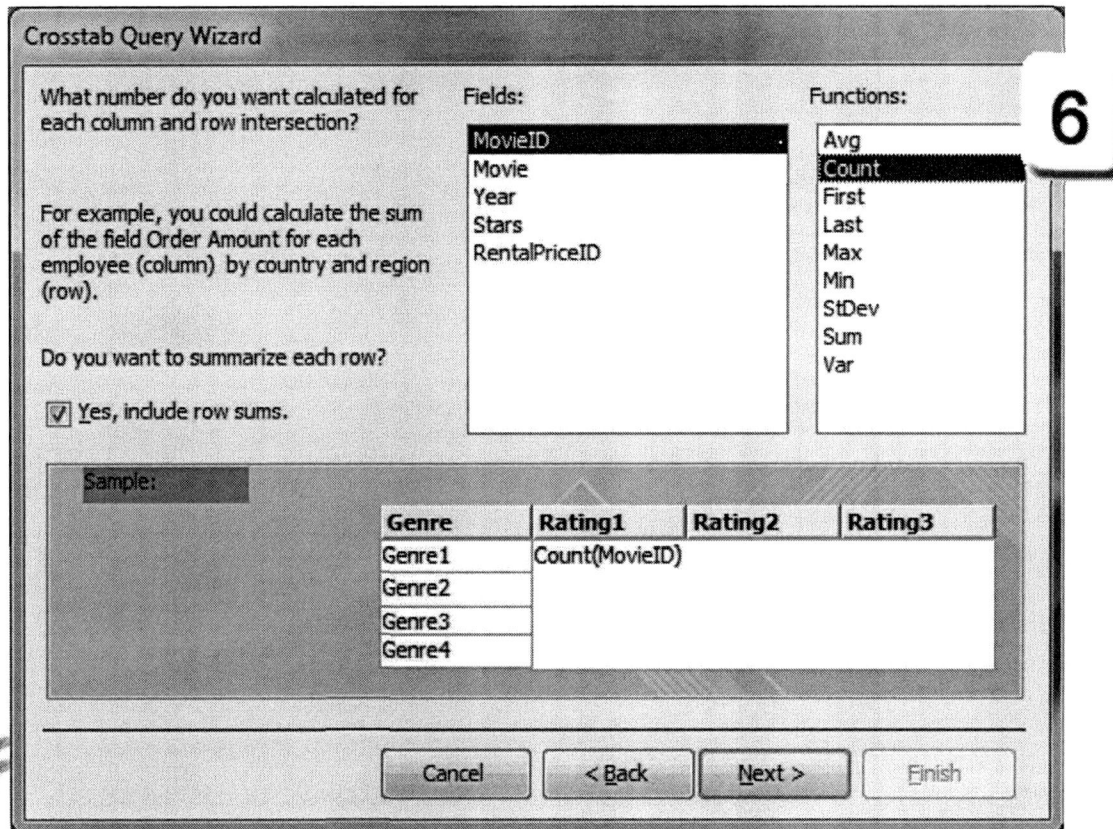

Crosstab Query Wizard

What number do you want calculated for each column and row intersection?

For example, you could calculate the sum of the field Order Amount for each employee (column) by country and region (row).

Do you want to summarize each row?

☑ Yes, include row sums.

Fields:

MovieID
Movie
Year
Stars
RentalPriceID

Functions:

Avg
Count
First
Last
Max
Min
StDev
Sum
Var

6

Sample:

Genre	Rating1	Rating2	Rating3
Genre1	Count(MovieID)		
Genre2			
Genre3			
Genre4			

Cancel   < Back   Next >   Finish

Exam 77-885: Microsoft Access 2010
4. Creating and Managing Queries
4.1. Construct queries: Create a Crosstab Query

Crosstab Query Wizard:
Name the Query

7. Try it: Name the Crosstab Query
The Crosstab Query created a name that include the Record Source: tblMovies.

That works. We'll accept the default name.

What Else Do You See? The Wizard will run the Query so that you can **View** the results when you are finished.

If you are ready, click **Finish**.

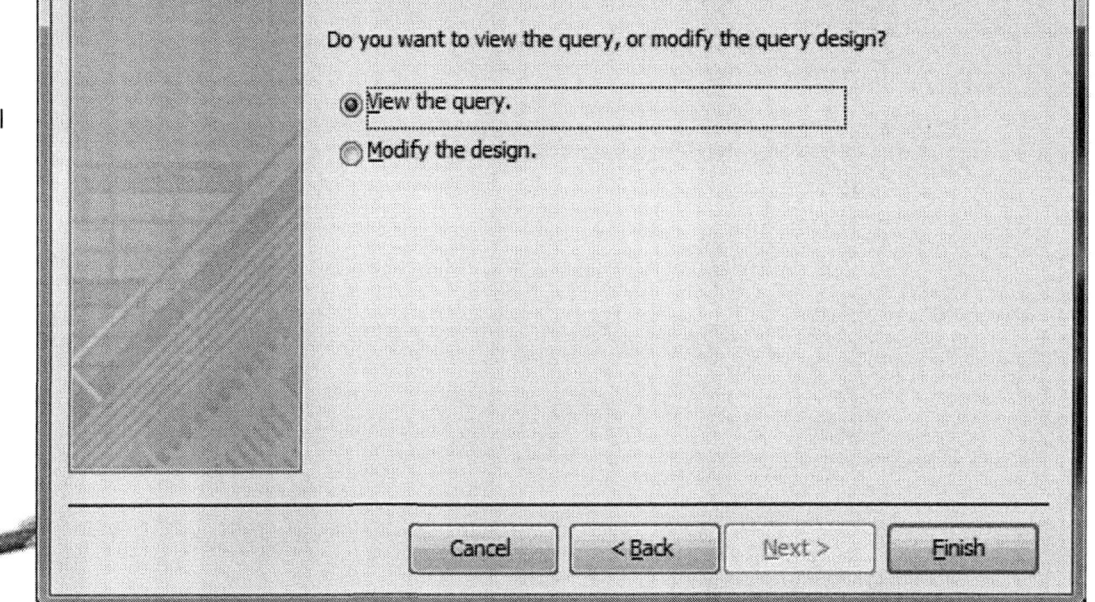

HOME

Take Two

Crosstab Query Wizard: View the Results

8. Try it: View the Results

The Crosstab Query shows the Genre in the Rows and the Ratings in the Columns.

There is a Column that Counts the Total for each Genre. In this example, there are 13 Action movies in tblMovies.

The Crosstab Query Counts the number of movies in each Rating, as well. In this example there is one G Rated Comedy and 35 G Rated Family films.

What Do You See? The Row Header, Genre, has a Filter. You can use the drop down to select one, some or all of the Genres if you wish.

OK, **Close** the Crosstab Query. If you are prompted to **Save** the Query, click **Yes**.

Create ->Queries ->Query Wizard->Crosstab Query Wizard

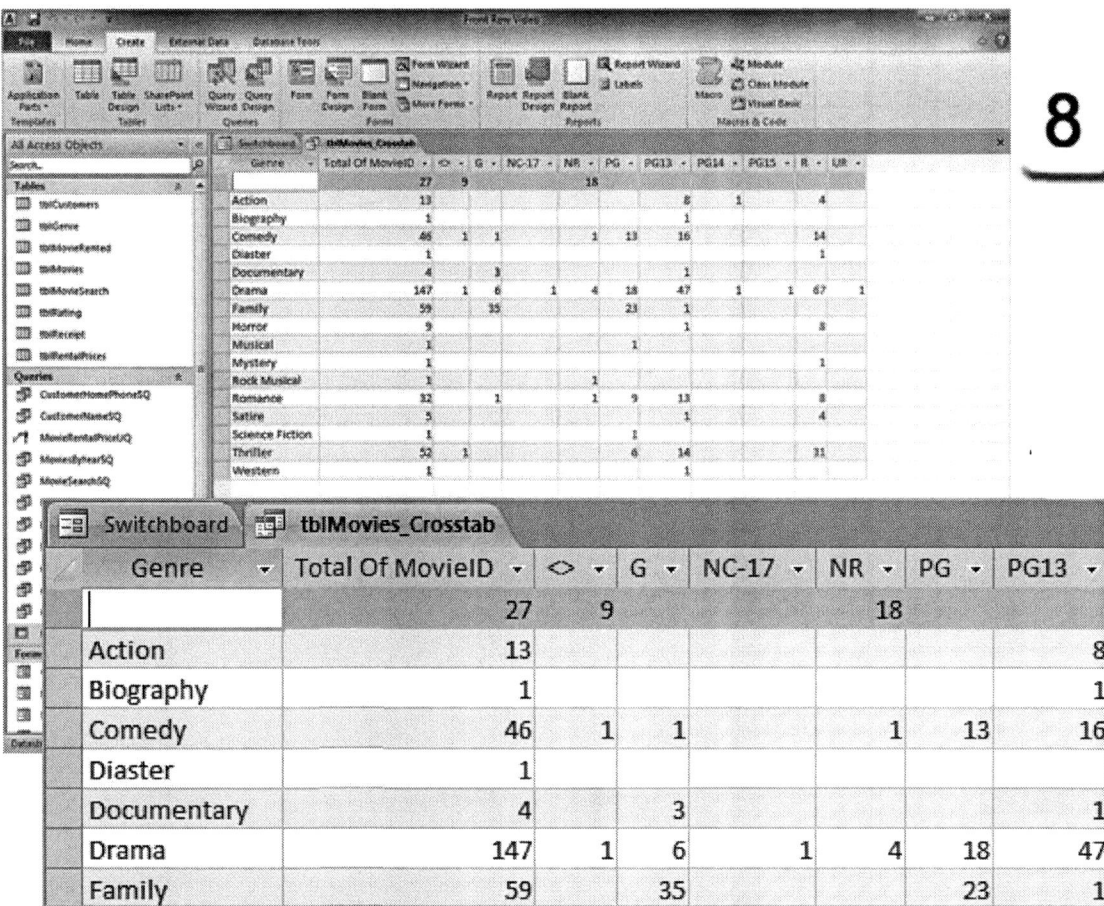

8

Genre	Total Of MovieID	<>	G	NC-17	NR	PG	PG13
	27	9			18		
Action	13						8
Biography	1						1
Comedy	46	1	1		1	13	16
Diaster	1						
Documentary	4		3				1
Drama	147	1	6	1	4	18	47
Family	59		35			23	1

Exam 77-885: Microsoft Access 2010
4. Creating and Managing Queries
4.1. Construct queries: Create a Crosstab Query

Visualize the Data:
Create a PivotChart

A Crosstab Query can be packed with information, but many people find it helpful to see that data in a Chart. The following pages show how to create a PivotChart.

Everything in Access starts with the data. PivotCharts do, too. This lesson will use the Movie table as the Record Source.

The PivotChart will be a Form that is added to a Report. It really works well!

1. Try it: Create a PivotChart
Go to **All Access Objects->Tables.**
Open a Table: tblMovies.
Go to **Create ->Forms->More Forms.**
Click on **PivotChart.**

Keep going...

Create ->Forms->More Forms->PivotChart

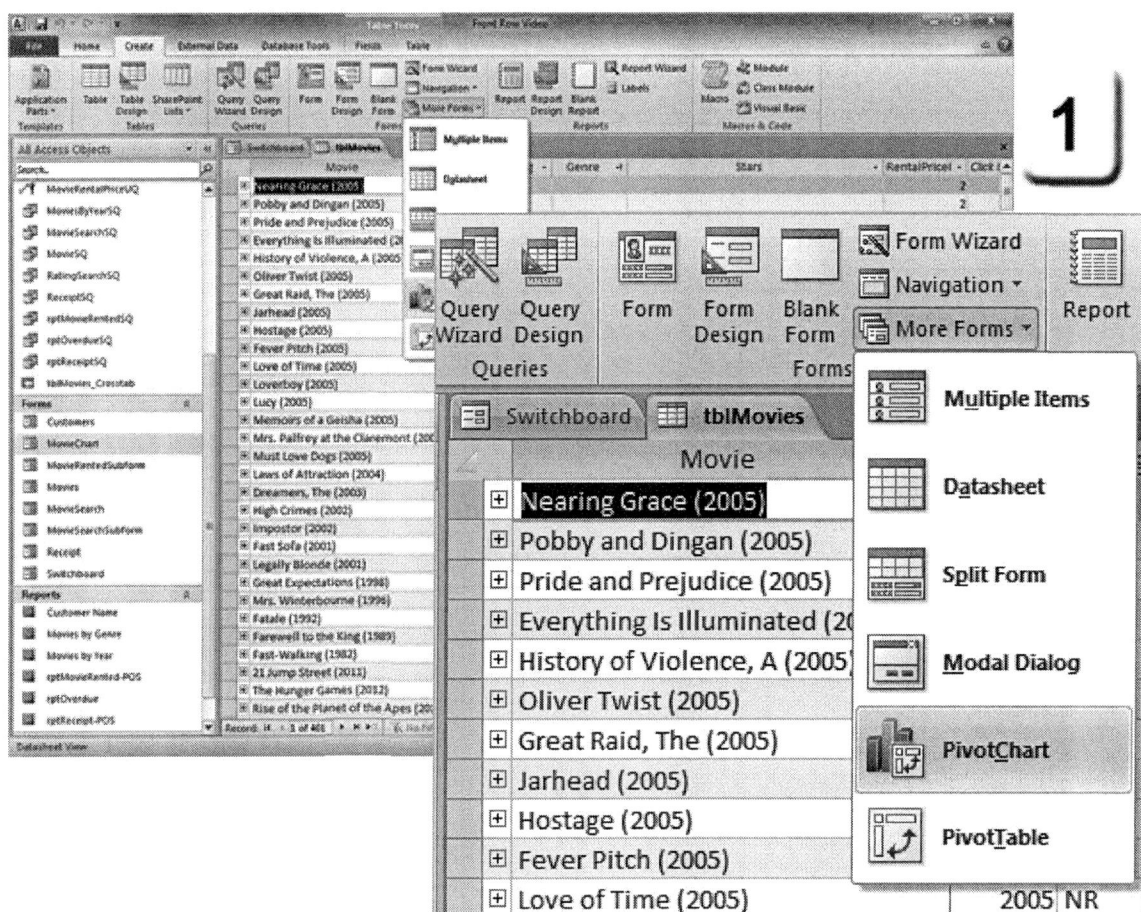

Exam 77-885: Microsoft Access 2010
5. Designing Reports
5.2. Apply Report Design options: Create a Graph

Hello, PivotChart!
A new, blank PivotChart should open. The Chart Field List should be available on the right side. The Chart Field List shows all of the Fields you can select from tblMovies.

If You Do Not See the Chart Field List:
Go to **PivotChart Tools ->Design->Show/Hide.** Click on **Field List.**

2. Try it: Add a Data Field
Go to the Chart Field List.
Select a Field: Movie.
Drag the Movie Field to Data Field Drop Zone: Drop Data Fields Here.

What Do You See? The Data Drop Zone now has a Data Field: Count of Movie.

There should be a Chart as well.
Keep going...

Where Have You Seen This, Before? Microsoft Excel 2010 has many excellent Tools for formatting PivotTables and PivotCharts.

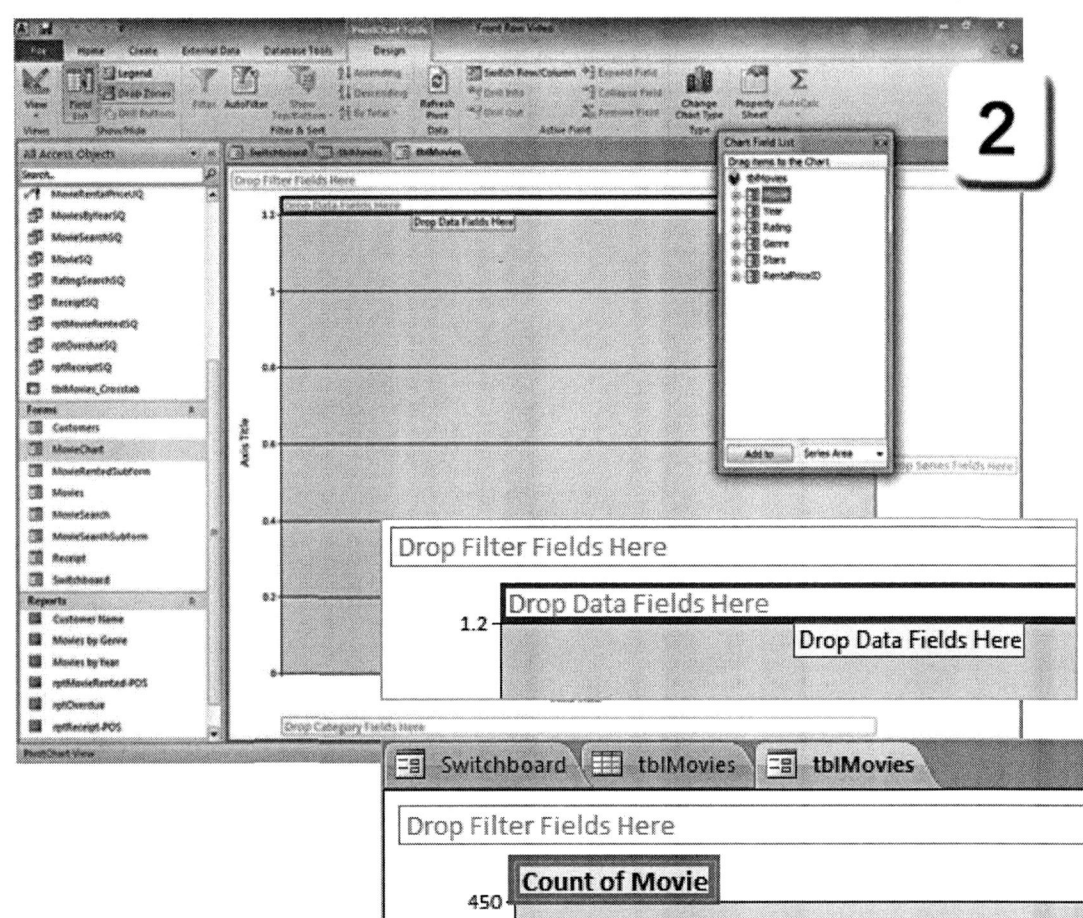

Exam 77-885: Microsoft Access 2010
5. Designing Reports
5.2. Apply Report Design options: Create a Graph

PivotChart: Add a Category

Our new PivotChart has one Column, representing 100% of the Movies. This PivotChart needs a Category to Group the data. Let's use Rating.

3. Try it: Add a Category

Go to the Chart Field List.
Select a Field: Rating.
Drag the Rating Field to the Category Drop Zone: Drop Category Fields Here.

What Do You See? The Category Drop Zone now has a Data Field: Rating. The PivotChart now has a Column for each Rating.

Alright, this looks good.

Do This, Now: Save the Form
Go to **File->Save**.
Enter a name: MoviesByRatingChart.

Where tblMovies is the Record Source,
Rating is the Field,
and the data is displayed as a Chart.

Keep going...

PivotChart Tools ->Design->Show/Hide->Field List

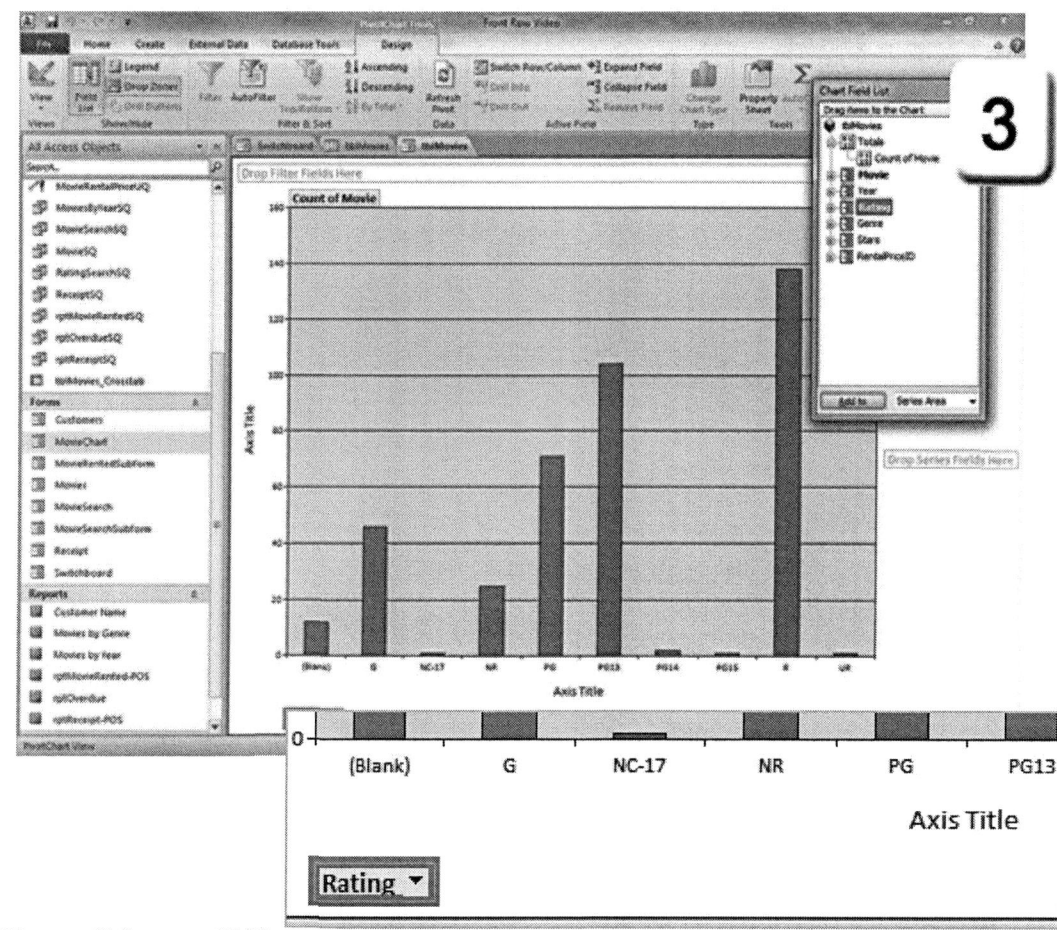

Exam 77-885: Microsoft Access 2010
5. Designing Reports
5.2. Apply Report Design options: Create a Graph

PivotChart Tools ->Design->Show/Hide->Field List

PivotChart: Filter the Data

You can **Filter** the PivotChart and show specific Ratings if you wish.

In this example, instead of showing all Ratings, this PivotChart will display only four Ratings.

4. Try it: Add a Subform/Subreport
Click on the Rating Category at the bottom of the PivotChart.

First, uncheck All.
(None of the Ratings are selected.)
Select (check) the following Ratings:
G
PG
PG13
R

Click **OK**.

How did that change the PivotChart?
There should be four columns in this graph- no blanks.

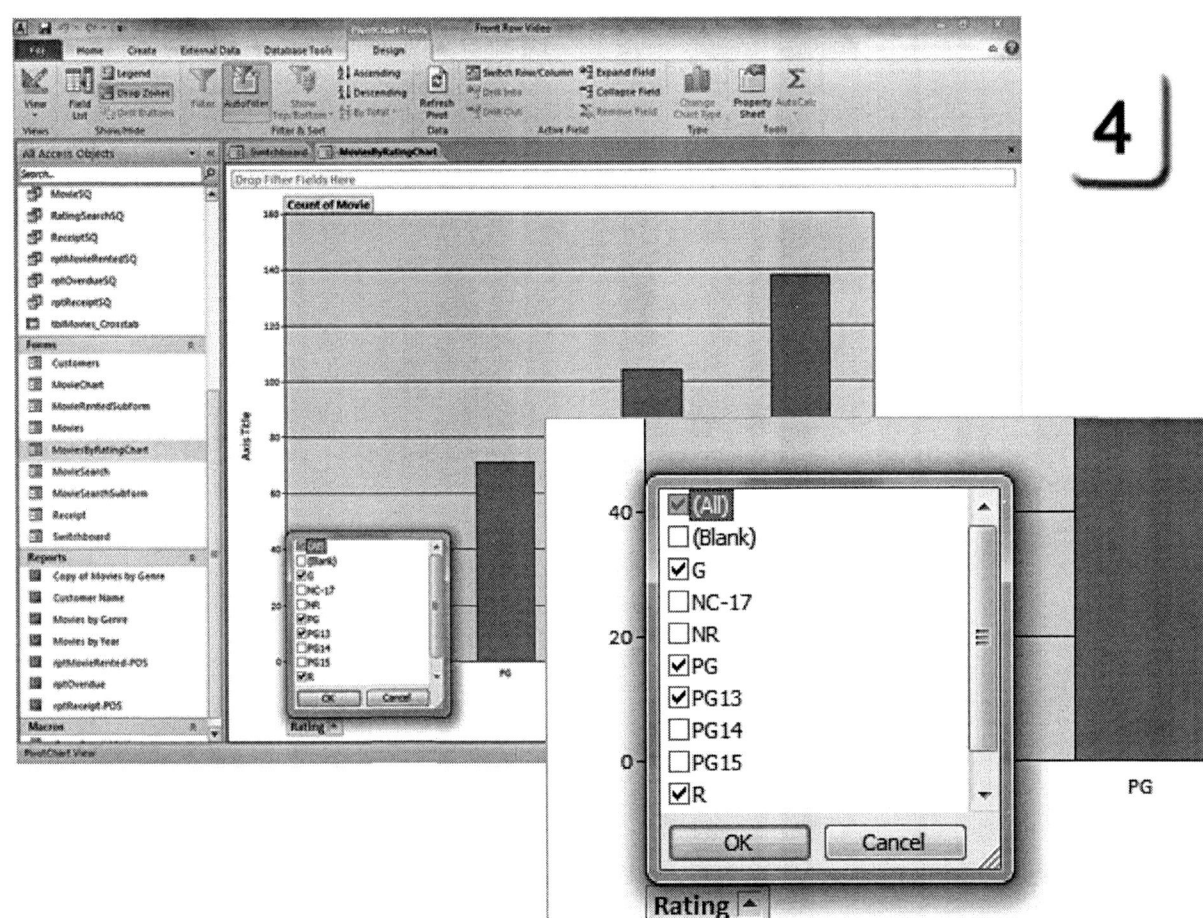

4

Exam 77-885: Microsoft Access 2010
5. Designing Reports
5.2. Apply Report Design options: Create a Graph

Extra for Experts:
Format the PivotChart

This PivotChart can be formatted just like a Chart in Microsoft Excel. The formatting options can be found in the PivotChart Properties in Microsoft Access.

5. Try it: Format the PivotChart
The PivotChart is still open in Layout View.
Select a Column.
Go to **PivotChart Tools ->Design->Tools.**
Click on **Property Sheet.**

What Do You See? There are five Tabs in the PivotChart Properties.
Go to **Border/Fill.**
Select a Fill Color: Orange.

Save and **Close** the MoviesByRatingChart.

The Computer Mama Sez: You should bookmark this page if you want to remember something cool.

PivotChart Tools ->Design->Tools->Property Sheet

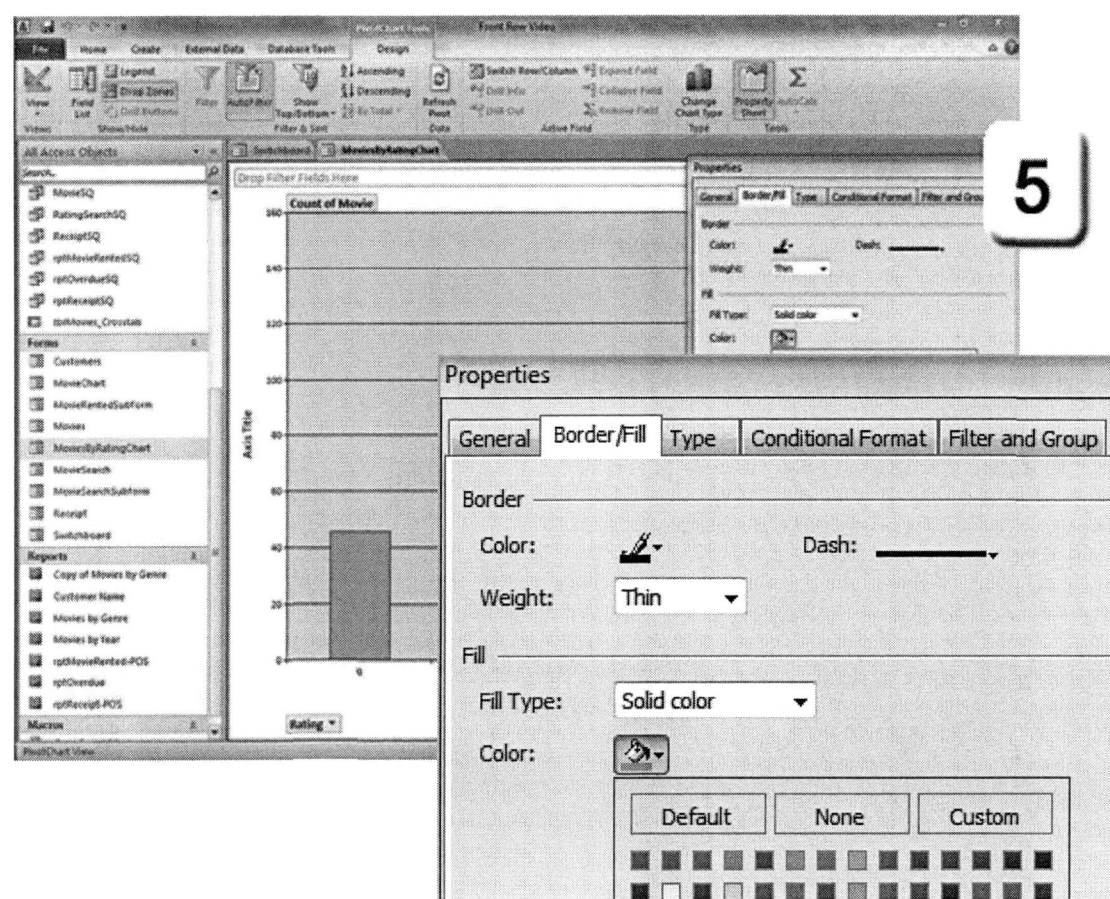

5

Exam 77-885: Microsoft Access 2010
5. Designing Reports
5.2. Apply Report Design options: Create a Graph

Add the Chart to a Report

In our earlier examples, we added a Subform to a Form and a Subreport to a Report. You can actually add a Form to a Report as well. Here are the steps.

This example will use a Report that was created in a previous lesson. If you do not have this Report, you can begin with a blank Report if you wish.

1. Try it: Review the Report
Go to All Access Objects->Reports.
Open a Report: Movies by Genre.

What Do You See? The Report opened in Layout View. The Report Header includes a Label and a Command button that opens the Movie Search Form.

Say, did we do that programming? Really?

Keep going...

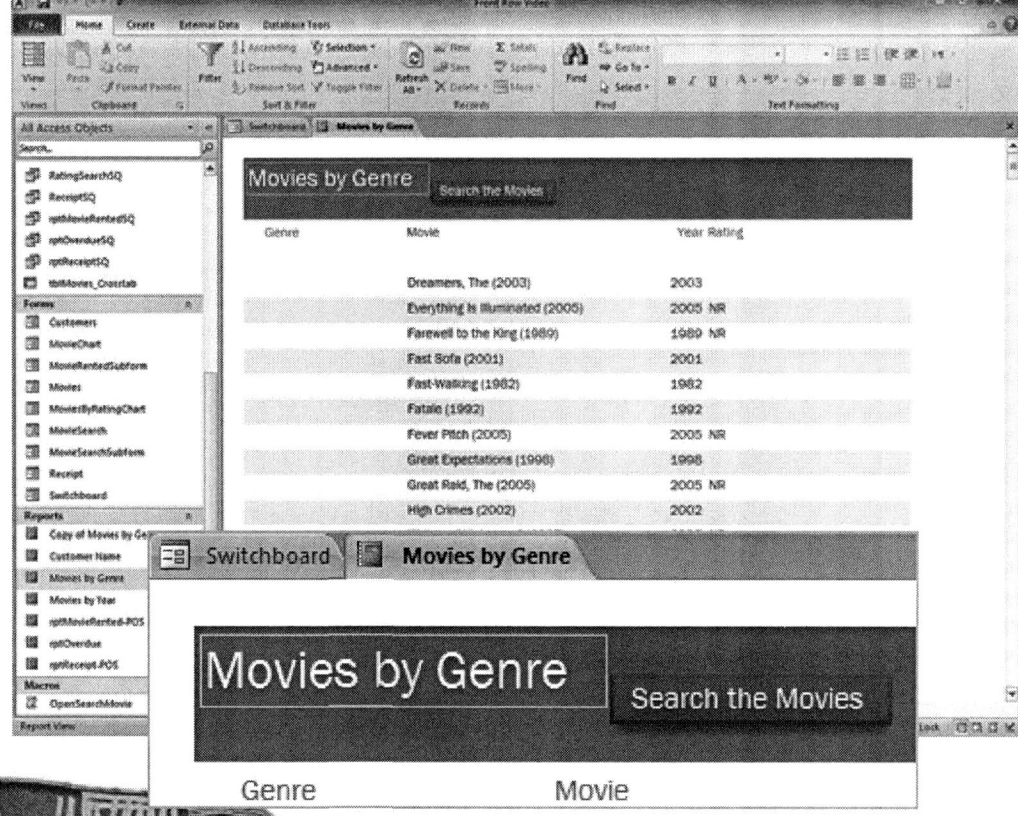

Format the Report Header

This PivotChart will be added to the Report Header. Before that, we need to edit the height of the Header to make room.

Before You Begin: Change the View
Go to **Home->Views->View.**
Select a **View: Design View**.
The Property Sheet should be available.

2. Try it: Format the Header Properties
Select the Report Header.
Go to **Property Sheet->Format.**
Height: 3.5"

That definitely made it bigger. Keep going...

Report Layout Tools->Design->Tools->Property Sheet

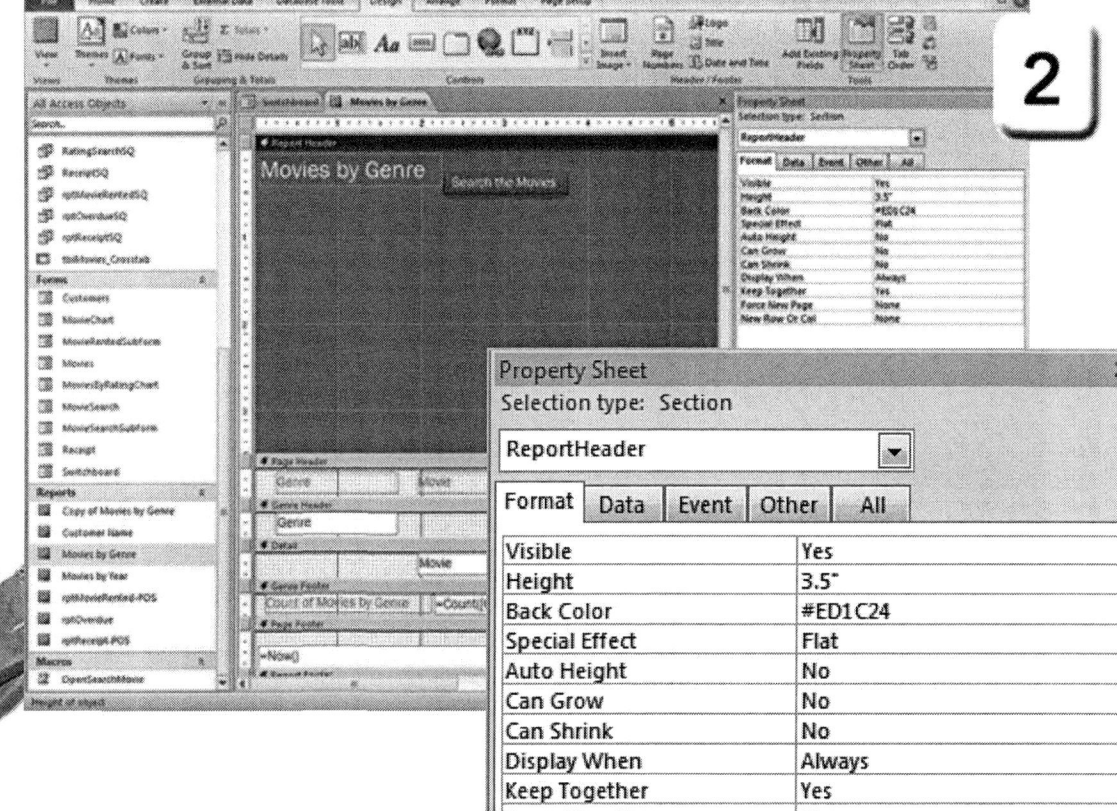

Property Sheet

Selection type: Section

ReportHeader

Format	Data	Event	Other	All

Visible	Yes
Height	3.5"
Back Color	#ED1C24
Special Effect	Flat
Auto Height	No
Can Grow	No
Can Shrink	No
Display When	Always
Keep Together	Yes
Force New Page	None
New Row Or Col	None

Exam 77-885: Microsoft Access 2010
5. Designing Reports
5.2. Apply Report Design options: Format the Header/Footer

Add a Chart to a Report

Subforms and Subreports are added as an Unbound Control. You will be asked which Form or Report you want and how the Report or Form is Bound. Here are the answers.

3. Try it: Add a Subform/Subreport
The Movies by Genre Report is in Design View. The Report Header is selected.

Go to **Report Design Tools->Controls.**
Select a Control: **Subform/Subreport.**
Click on the Report Header to start the SubReport Wizard.

The Subreport Wizard will prompt you:
Use an Existing Form: MoviesByRatingChart.
Define the Links: None. (Bottom of the list.)
Name: MoviesByRatingChart.

Click **Finish**. Keep going...

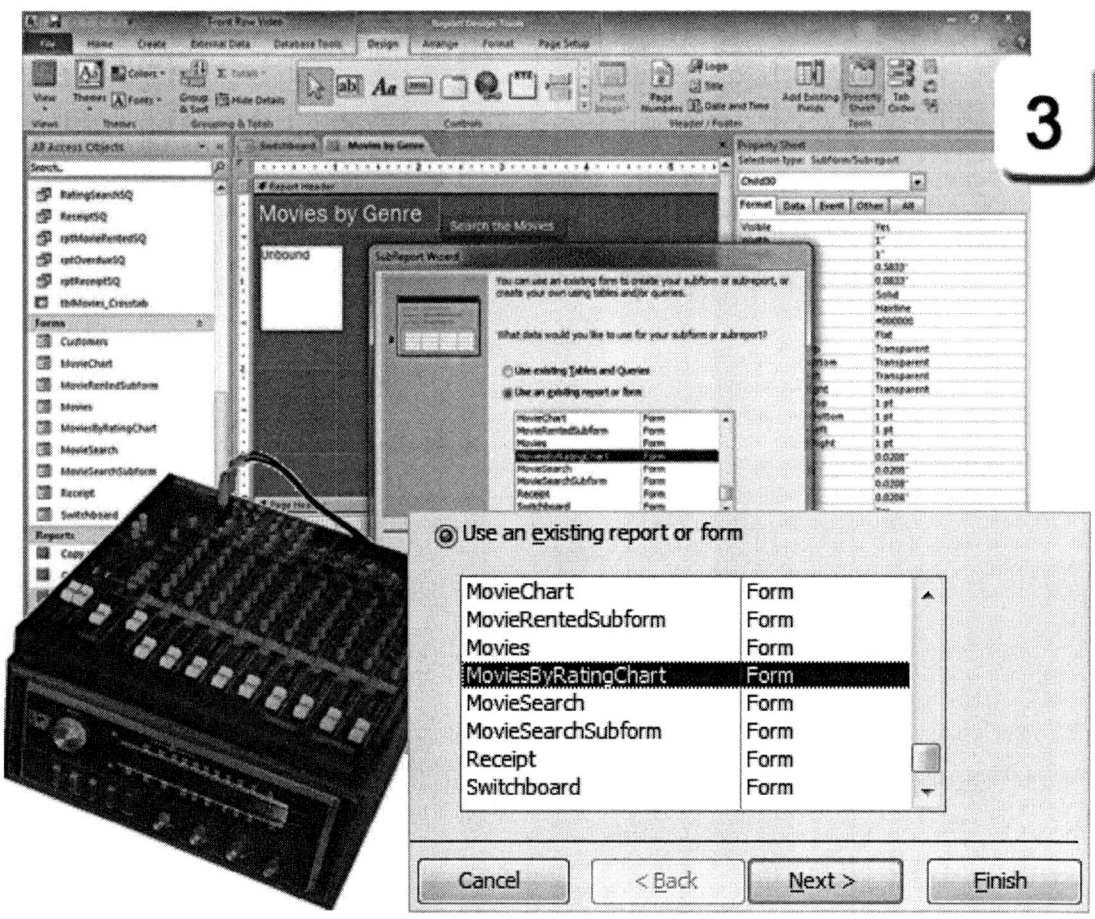

Exam 77-885: Microsoft Access 2010
5. Designing Reports
5.2. Apply Report Design options: Add Bound and Unbound Controls

Edit the Subreport Properties

You can use the Property Sheet to place the Subform precisely if you wish.

Before You Begin: Delete the Label
The Movies by Genre Report is in Design View. The Subform is selected. There is a Subform Label that you should delete before you format the SubReport.

4. Try it: Edit the Subreport Properties
Go to **Property Sheet->Format**.
Top: 0.625"
Left: 0.125"
Border Stye: Solid.
Border Width: Hairline.
Border Color: #000000 (black).

Keep going...

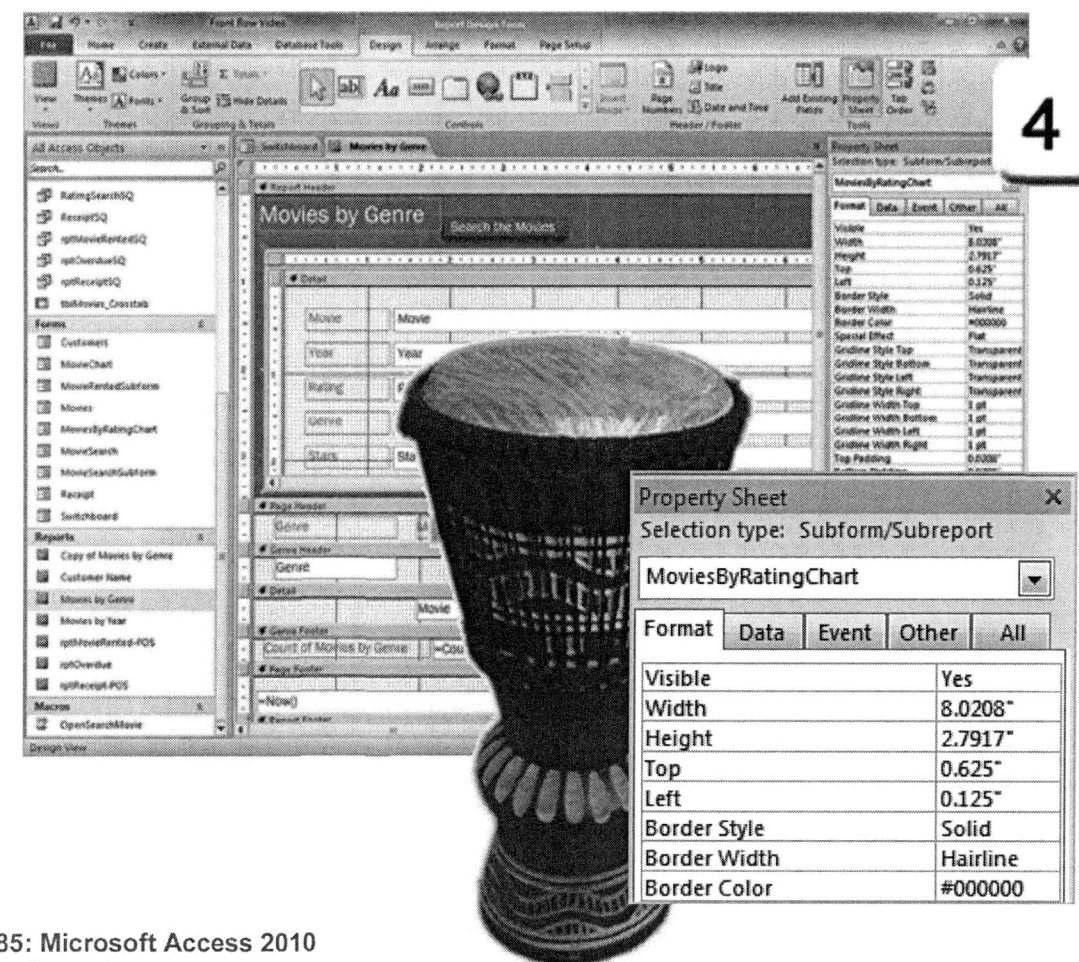

Property Sheet

Selection type: Subform/Subreport

MoviesByRatingChart

Format	Data	Event	Other	All

Visible	Yes
Width	8.0208"
Height	2.7917"
Top	0.625"
Left	0.125"
Border Style	Solid
Border Width	Hairline
Border Color	#000000

Exam 77-885: Microsoft Access 2010
5. Designing Reports
5.2. Apply Report Design options: Add Bound and Unbound Controls

Use the PivotChart

You can use the Rating Drop Down Box to filter the PivotChart. This functionality is available when the Report is in Layout View.

Before You Begin: Change the View
Go to **Report Design Tools->Views->View.**
Select a **View: Layout View.**

What Do You See? The PivotChart is displayed at the top of this Report.

5. Try This: Change the PivotChart.
Click on the Rating Category at the bottom.
Select (check) an additional Rating: NR
Click **OK**.

So, What Do You See? There should be five Columns in the Pivot Chart now.

Memo to Self: The PivotCharts filters are not available when the Report is in Print Preview. The Control is visible but it is like clicking on a drawing-nothing happens.

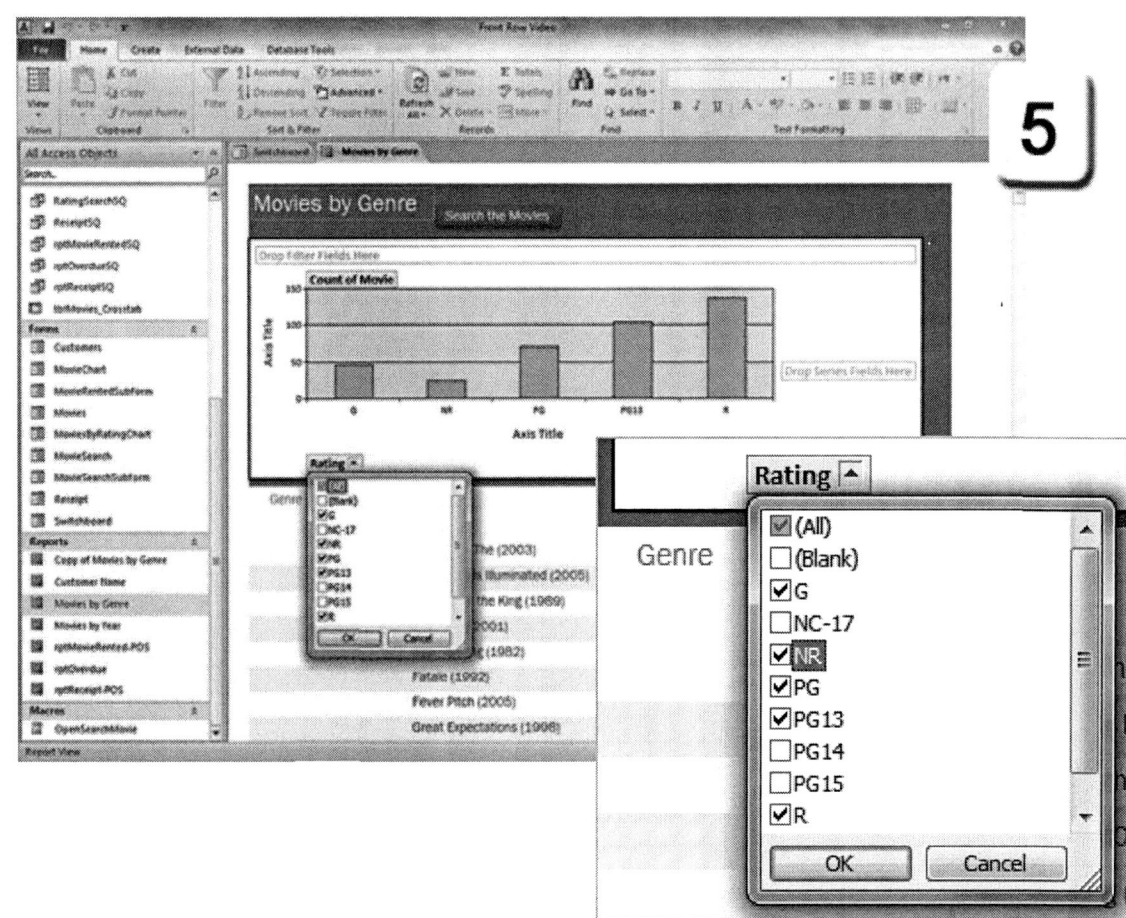

Exam 77-885: Microsoft Access 2010
5. Designing Reports
5.2. Apply Report Design options: Use a Drop Down Box on a Report

Print Preview: Data Options

This Mighty Microsoft Access Report is ready to print. What are the options?

6. Try This: Print Preview the Report
Go to **Report Design Tools->Views->View.**
Select a **View: Print Preview.**

What Do You See? In addition to Page Size and Page Layout, you can share the **Data** as Excel, Word, PDF/XPS, E-mail and more.

Keeeeeep going.

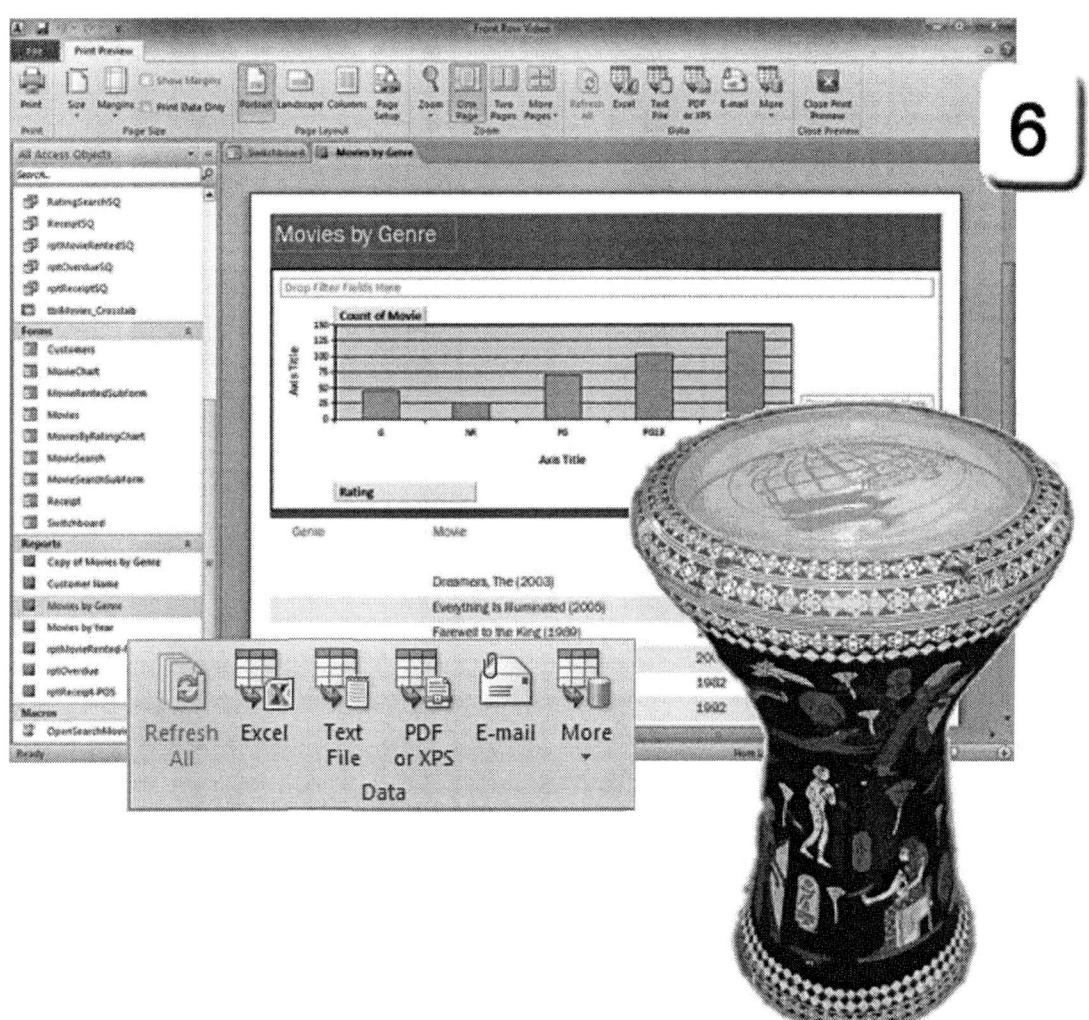

Publish as PDF or XPS

PDF means Portable Document File.
Adobe Systems developed the PDF format in 1993 as a way to view files if someone did not have the program that created that file.

XPS means XML Paper Specification.
Microsoft developed the XPS format in 2009. XPS is open source code. It is also independent of software or operating system.

So, we can send this Report as a PDF, even if the recipient does not have Microsoft Access.

1. Try This: Send the Data to PDF or XPS
Go to **Print Preview->Data->PDF or XPS.**

Publish a PDF or XPS: Please browse to your Documents folder and fill in the blanks.
File Name: Movies by Genre.xps
Save as Type: XPS Document.

Optimize for: Standard (publish online or print)

Click on **Publish**. Keep going...

Print Preview ->Data->PDF or XPS

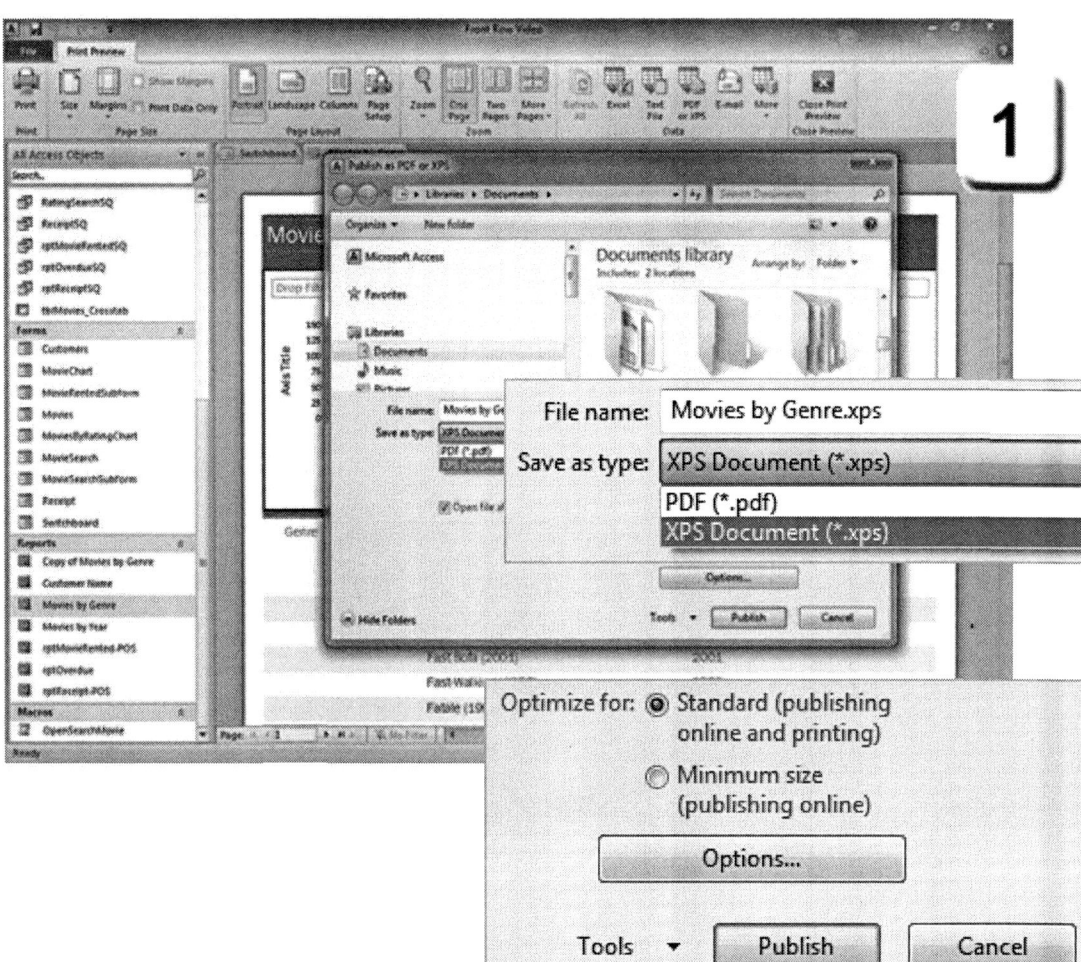

Review the XPS File

2. Try it: Review the XPS File

When the Save as XPS is complete, the Report should open in the XPS Viewer, which is free. The Report formatting and layout are the same as they looked in Print Preview in Access.

What Else Do You See? When you export to a different format-XPS, PDF, Word or Excel-Microsoft Access asks if you would like to save these steps in case this task will be done again.

For these lessons, you can simply **Close** the window that asks you to Save Export Steps.

Memo to Self: A Report that was saved as a PDF or XPS file will NOT open in Microsoft Access, again.

Print Preview ->Data->PDF or XPS

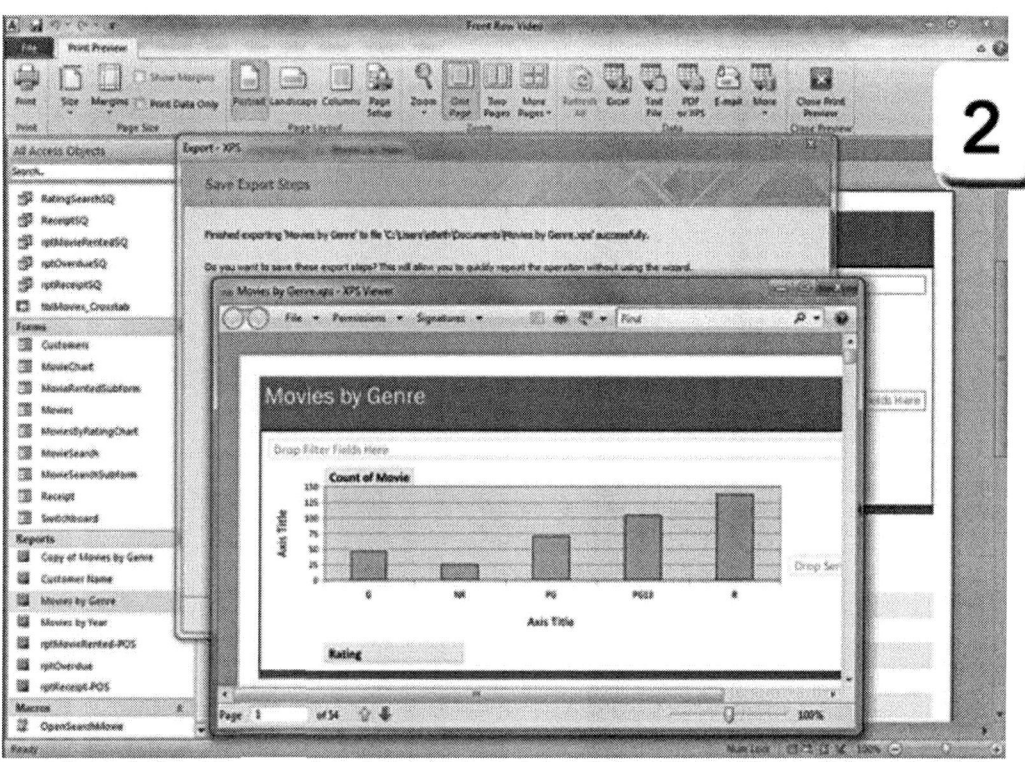

Send as an E-mail attachment

You can send an Access Report by E-mail. The E-mail option lets you pick how you would like the data formatted.

3. Try it: Send as E-mail
The Movies by Genre Report is in Print Preview.
The Print Preview Ribbon is available.

Go to **Print Preview ->Data->E-mail.**

Send Object As: You will be prompted to select a output format. The format options include:
Excel 97-Excel 2003 Workbook (*.xls)
HTML (*.htm; *.htlm)
Microsoft Excel 5.0/95 Workbook (*.xls)
PDF Format (*.pdf)
Rich Text Format (*.rtf)
Snapshot Format (*.snp)
Text Files (*.txt)
XPS Format (*.xps)

If you would like to test this option, choose PDF Format and send an e-mail to yourself.

If not, please click **Cancel**. Done and done.

Print Preview ->Data->E-mail

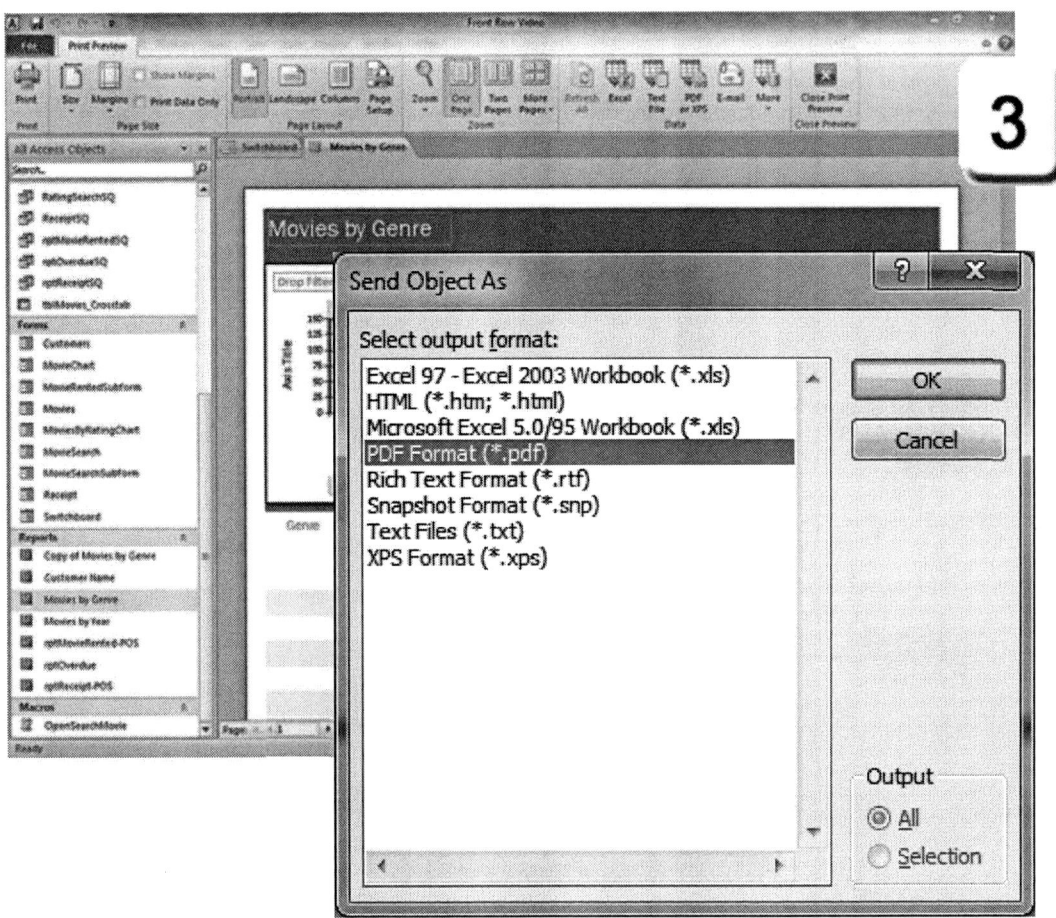

Data: Export to Excel

Tables, Reports and Queries can be exported to Microsoft Excel so that you can analyze it with a powerful set of Formula and Data Tools.

For this example, please Save and Close the Movies by Genre Report. We'll choose a different Report: Movies by Year.

Before You Begin: Open a Different Report
Go to **All Access Objects->Reports**.
Open a Report: Movies by Year.
The Report should open in Layout View.
Change the View to **Print Preview**.

4. Try it: Export to Excel
Go to **Print Preview ->Data->Excel**.

Export-Excel Spreadsheet: You will be prompted to **Browse** for a Folder. The default name for the spreadsheet is the name of the Report in Access. The File format is Excel 97-Excel 2003 Workbook (*.xls).

Click **OK** to create a spreadsheet. Keep going.

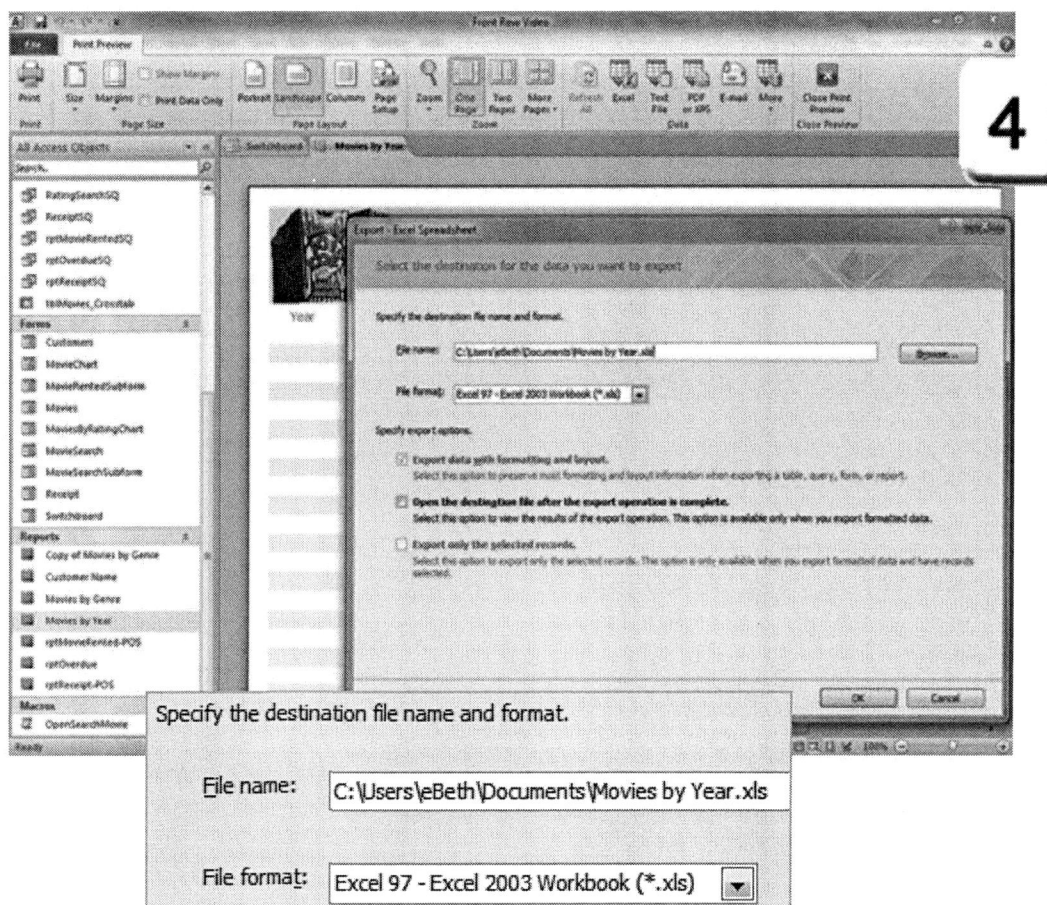

Specify the destination file name and format.

File name: C:\Users\eBeth\Documents\Movies by Year.xls

File format: Excel 97 - Excel 2003 Workbook (*.xls)

Hello, Microsoft Excel

5. Try it: Review the Spreadsheet
Go to the Documents Folder.
Open a File: Movies by Year.xls.

What Do You See? The movies have been grouped by Year: 2012, 2011, 2010.
All of the Fields from tblMovies have been exported: Year, Movie, MovieID, Rating, Genre, Stars and RentalID.

What Else Do You See? This spreadsheet does not include any formulas or formatting-just numbers and text.

Are We There, Yet? Yes, the goal was to get data out of Access and into Excel. That worked. Now you can use an impressive array of Data Tools in Excel to analyze that exported information.

When you are ready, Close the spreadsheet and return to Microsoft Access.

Microsoft Excel->Home

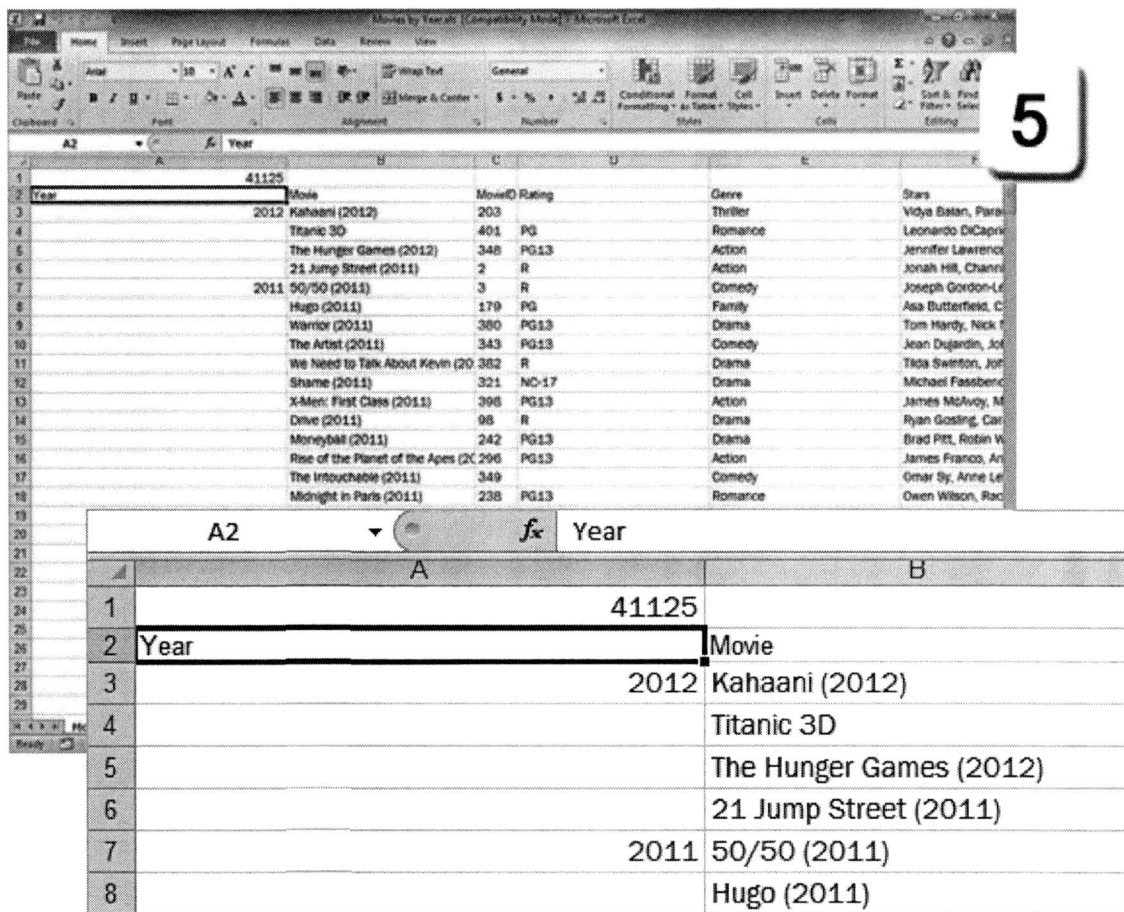

Data: Export to Word

The previous pages demonstrated how to export a Report to Excel. The Print Preview also has a way to export data to Word.

Where Are We Now? The movie data in Excel is closed and we are back in Access.

The Movies by Year Report is still open in **Print Preview.** If the **Save Export Steps** window is open you can simply close it.

6. Try it: Export to Word
Go to **Print Preview ->Data->More.**
Click on **Word.**

Export-RTF: You will be prompted to Browse for a Folder. The default name for the RTF file is the name of the Report in Access. The File format is Rich Text Format (RFT) which can be opened in Word and most editing software.

Click **OK** to create an RTF file.
Did that work? Let's find out.

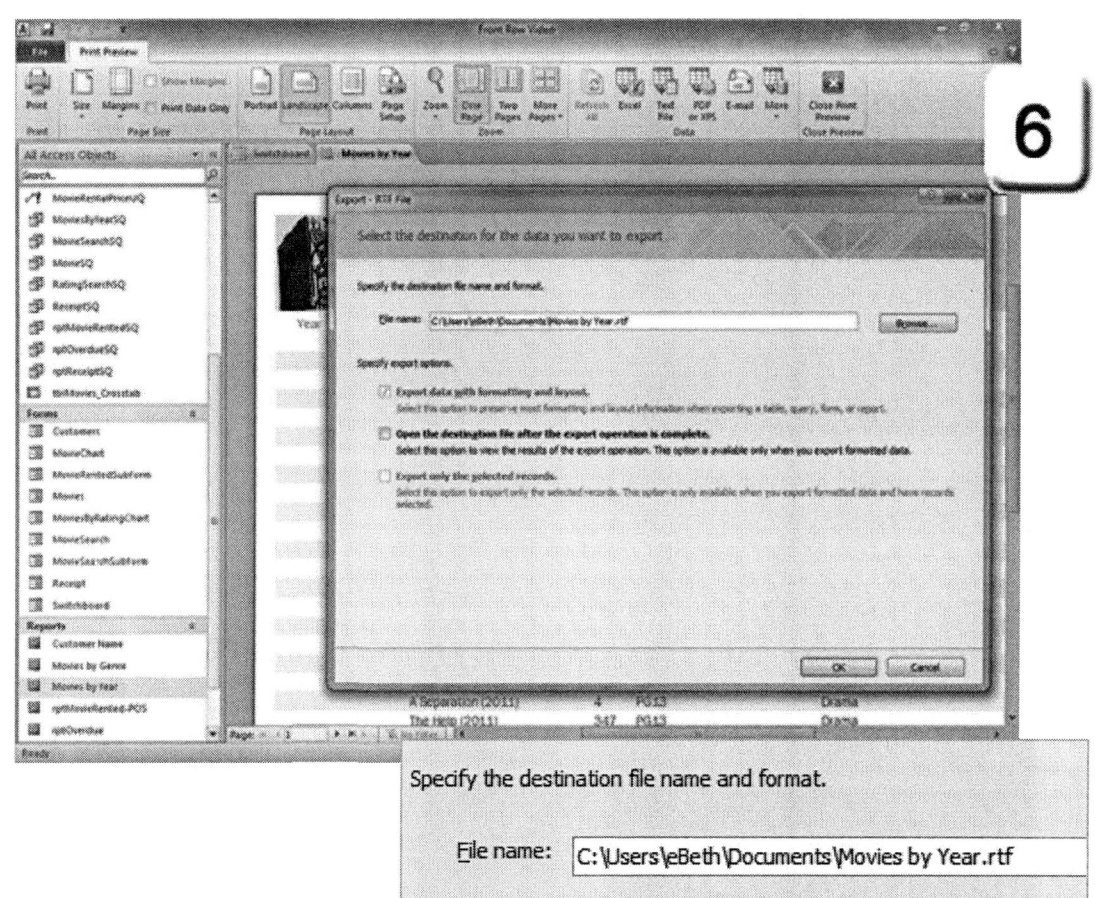

Specify the destination file name and format.

File name: C:\Users\eBeth\Documents\Movies by Year.rtf

Hello, Microsoft Word

7. Try it: Review the Document
Go to the Documents Folder.
Open a File: Movies by Year.rtf

What Do You See? The movies have been grouped by Year: 2012, 2011, 2010.
All of the Fields from tblMovies have been exported: Year, Movie, MovieID, Rating, Genre, Stars and RentalID.

What Else Do You See? Like the Excel spreadsheet, this is a simple data output. The file is in Rich Text Format. It does not have all of the formatting that is in a Word Document.

For example, this output looks like it is a Table with Rows and Columns. However, if you click in the data you will see it is just Text with spaces between Text- no Tables.

Where Are We? The goal was to export the data into Microsoft Word so that we could format the report. That we have done. Please **Close** the Rich Text Format (rft) file. Back in Access, **Close** the Report in Print Preview.

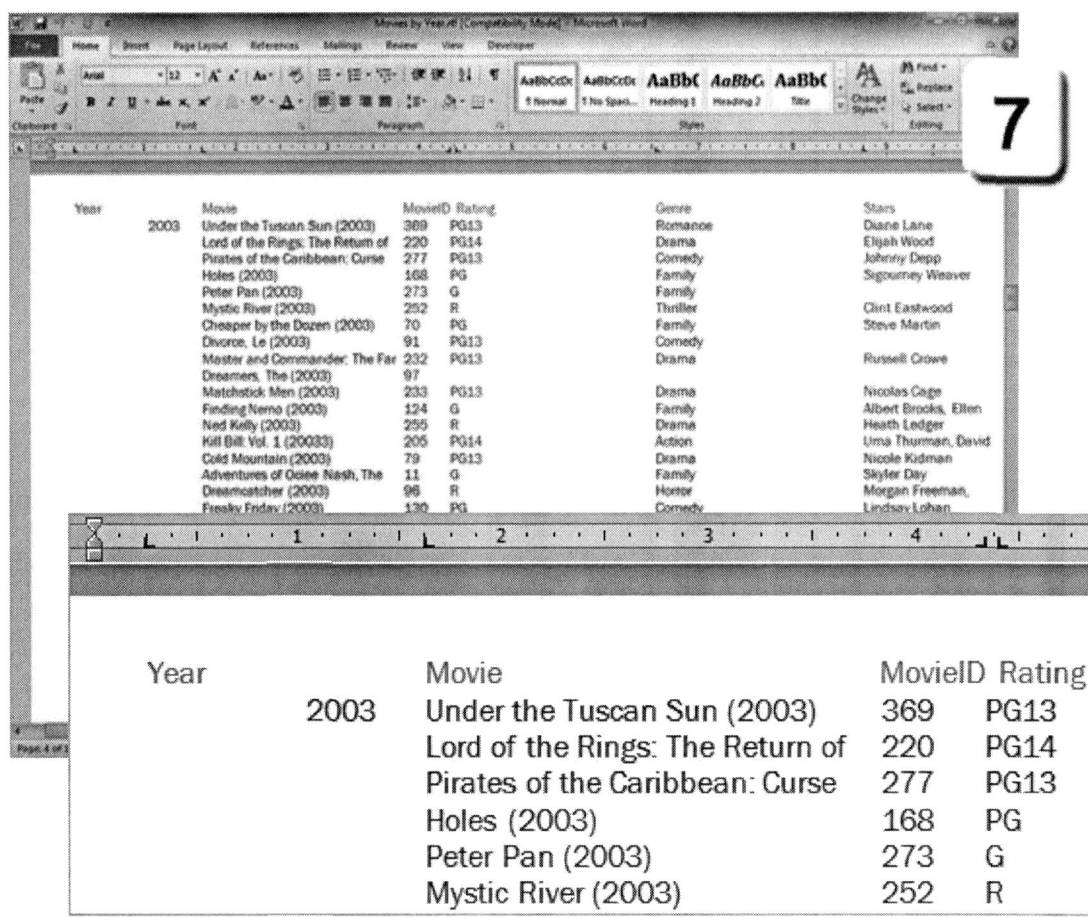

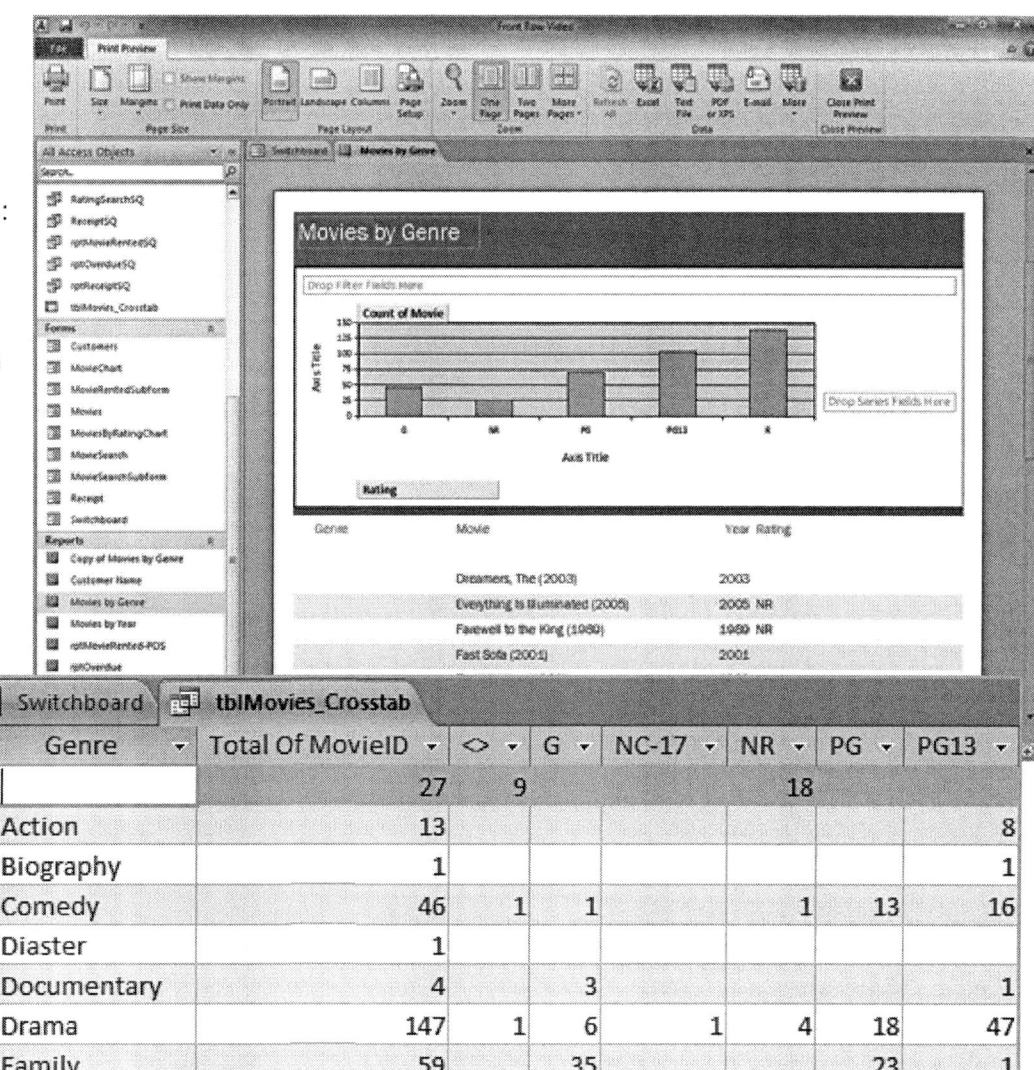

Summary
This lesson set out to accomplish the following:
-Analyze the data as a Crosstab Query.
-Visualize the data as a PivotChart and filter the Records with a Combo Box.

We also practiced exporting the Report data in different formats including Word (Rich Text Format), Excel, XPS or PDF file formats.

Well, you done good.
There's cookies in the kitchen. Take two!

Genre	Total Of MovieID	<>	G	NC-17	NR	PG	PG13
	27	9			18		
Action	13						8
Biography	1						1
Comedy	46	1	1		1	13	16
Diaster	1						
Documentary	4		3				1
Drama	147	1	6	1	4	18	47
Family	59		35			23	1

Practice Activities

Lesson 9: Prepare to Share
Try This: Do the following steps

1. Open your Brown Bag Lunch database.

Or, you may download **BBL Adv ver9.accdb**

2. Create a CrossTab Query and with the Query Wizard.

Use the following answers:
Record Source: ItemSQ.
Row Headings: Type
Column Headings: Specialty
Select Item for the Calculated Field and use COUNT for the

Function. Save the Query: ItemSQ_Crosstab.

3. Export the ItemSQ_Crosstab to Microsoft Excel. Save it in your Documents Folder.

4. Go to the Documents Folder, open the spreadsheet in Excel and review the data. Did this spreadsheet include any

Formulas? Close this file and return to Access.

5. Save and Close the Query.

6. Go to Access and open a Report: Products by Specialty.

7. Export the Report as a Text File. Save it to your Documents Folder as Products by Specialty-rtf. Go to the Documents Folder, open the document in Word and review the formatting.

Close this file and return to Access.

8. Export the Report as a PDF File. Save it to your Documents Folder as Products by Specialty-pdf. Go to the Documents Folder, open the document in Adobe Acrobat. Close this file

and return to Access.

9. Close the Report. Close the Brown Bag Lunch database.

Test Yourself

1. Which is true about a CrossTab Query? (Give all correct answers.)
A. Creates a Table that compares data
B. Can use a Table or Query as a Record Source
C. Can use many math functions, such as Count and Sum
Tip: Advanced Access, page 248, 252

2. A PivotChart in Access 2010 is created as a Report.
A. True
B. False
Tip: Advanced Access, page 255

3. A PivotChart in Access can be formatted like a Chart in Excel.
A. True
B. False
Tip: Advanced Access, page 259

4. Which of the following is true about PivotChart Filters?
(Give all correct answers.)
A. Can Filter data on the Chart by adding or removing Fields
B. Controls are available in Layout View
C. Controls are not available in Print Preview
Tip: Advanced Access, page 264

5. Which are options for sharing Access data? (Give all correct answers.)
A. Excel
B. Word
C. PDF/ XPS
D. E-mail
E. Text File
Tip: Advanced Access, page 264, 271

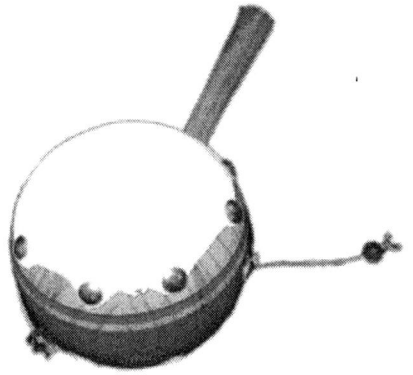

Access 2010: The Administrator
Strategies for Archiving

Advanced Access Objectives
In this lesson, you will learn how to:

1. Append new Records to an existing Table.

2. Create an Action Query to Update the data for selected Records in a Table.

3. Use an Action Query to Make a new Table and copy selected Records to that new Table.

4. Create a Delete Query and practice with a copy of an existing Table.

© 2012 Comma Productions, LLC

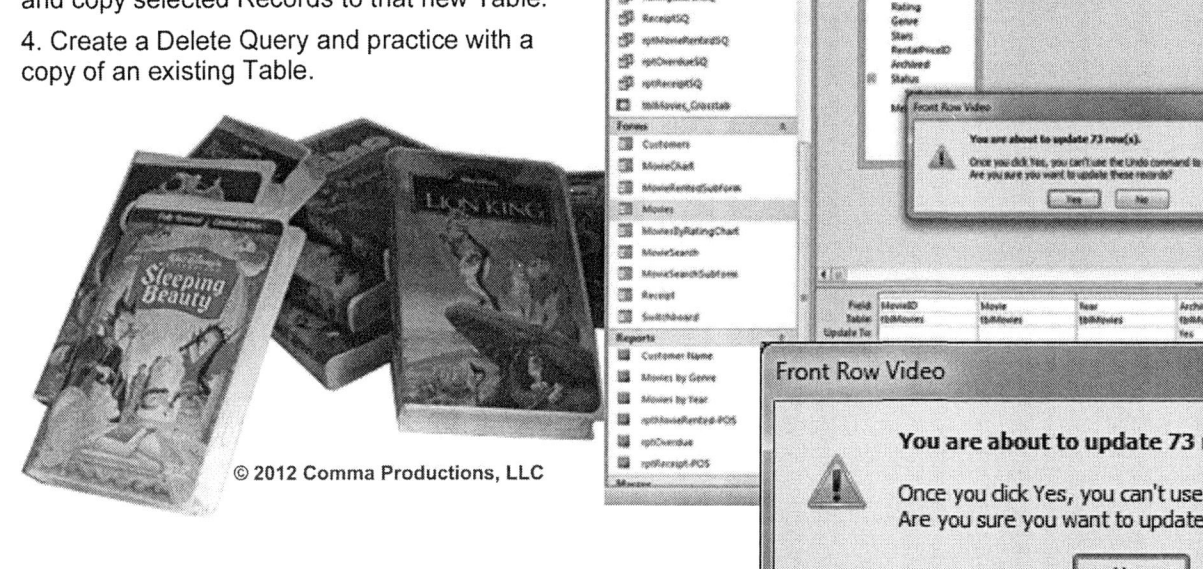

Front Row Video

You are about to update 73 row(s).

Once you click Yes, you can't use the Undo command to reverse the changes. Are you sure you want to update these records?

Yes   No

Lesson 10 : Strategies for Archiving

1. Readings

Read Lesson 10 in the Advanced Access guide, page 275-307.

Project

Several Action Queries that Append, Update and move the data in the Tables.

Downloads

FrontRowVideo Adv10.accdb
tblMoviesNEW.xlsx
BBL Adv ver10.accdb

2. Practice

Do the Practice Activity on page 308.

3. Assessment

Review the Test questions on page 308.

External Data Ribbon

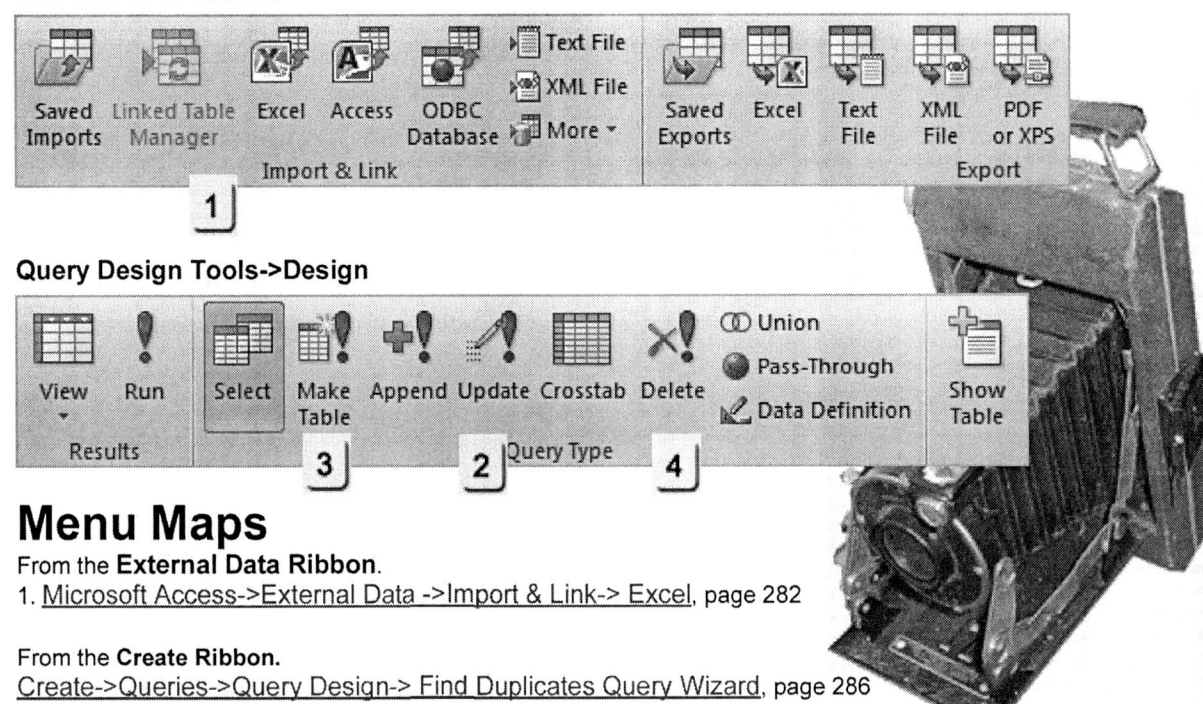

Menu Maps

From the **External Data Ribbon**.
1. Microsoft Access->External Data ->Import & Link-> Excel, page 282

From the **Create Ribbon.**
Create->Queries->Query Design-> Find Duplicates Query Wizard, page 286

From the **Report Design Ribbons.**
2. Query Tools ->Design->Query Type-> Update, page 300
3. Query Tools ->Design->Query Type-> Make Table, page 302
4. Query Tools ->Design->Query Type->Delete, page 305

Lights, Camera, Action!

Action Queries can change the data in the Tables. For example, we created an **Update** Query to find any movie released before the year 2000 and set the rental price (RentalPriceID). The other Action Queries include **Append** (add more Records), **Delete** (subtract Records), and **Make Table** (Copy the Records from a Query into a new Table.)

Microsoft Office Access 2010: Example of an Action Query

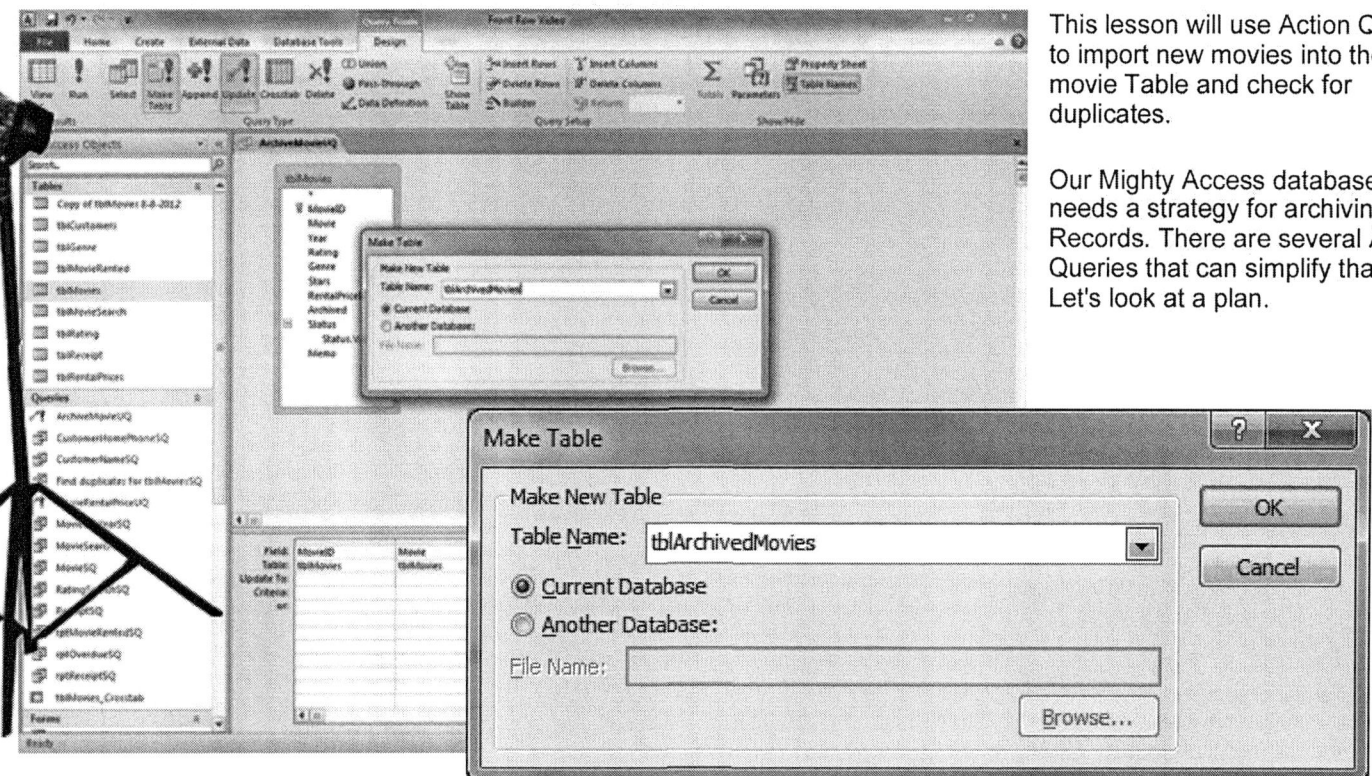

This lesson will use Action Queries to import new movies into the movie Table and check for duplicates.

Our Mighty Access database needs a strategy for archiving the Records. There are several Action Queries that can simplify that task. Let's look at a plan.

What is the Plan?

The first goal is to import the new movie titles into the movie Table with an Append Query. The archive strategy has several steps as well.

Import New Records into Access
Import a spreadsheet into Access
Append the new Records to tblMovies.

Revise the Table: tblMovieTitles
Add new Fields: Archived, Status, Memo.
Add the Fields to the Movies Form.

Create a Update Query: ArchiveMovieUQ
Add tblMovies as the Record Source.
UPDATE the Archive Field to Yes.

Run a Make Table Query: ArchiveMovieMT
Save the UPDATE Query as a MAKE TABLE.
Create a new Table: tblArchiveMovies.

Use Action Queries to Test the Data
Create an UNMATCHED Query.
Create a FIND DUPLICATES Query.
Create a DELETE Query.
That's a good plan.

Example of an Action Query in Design View

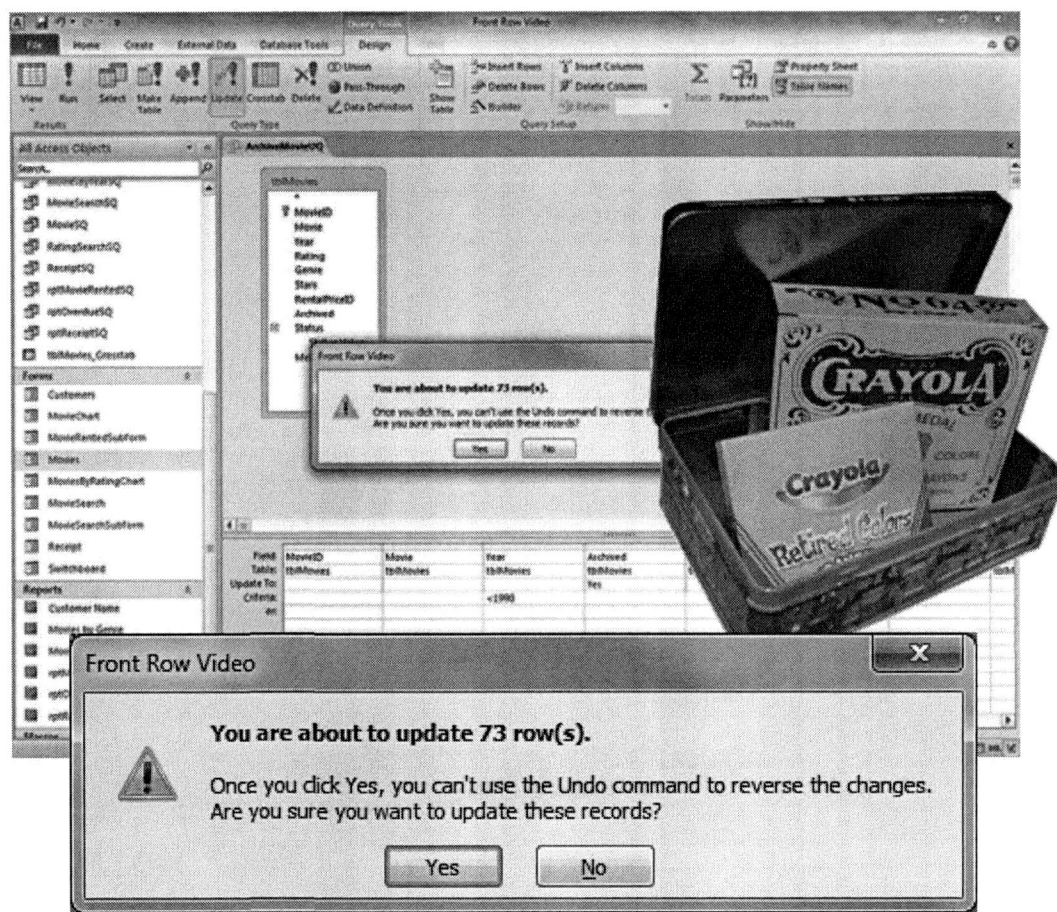

Before You Begin

Before You Begin: Open the Sample Database
Go to **Start -> All Programs ->Microsoft Office**.
Click on **Microsoft Office Access 2010.**
Access will prompt you to open a database.
Select: <u>FrontRowVideo Adv10.accdb</u>

The database, **FrontRowVideo Adv10.accdb,** was developed in the previous lessons. You do not have to download a new sample. You can continue with your own database if you wish.

This lesson uses an Action Query to import new movies into the movie Table. There is a sample spreadsheet with the additional movie titles that you should download before you begin, too.
Download the spreadsheet: **tblMoviesNEW.xlsx**

Keep going....

Memo to Self: Databases need to Read and Write. Click **Enable Content** if you see the Security Warning.

Start ->All Programs-> Microsoft Office-> Microsoft Access 2010

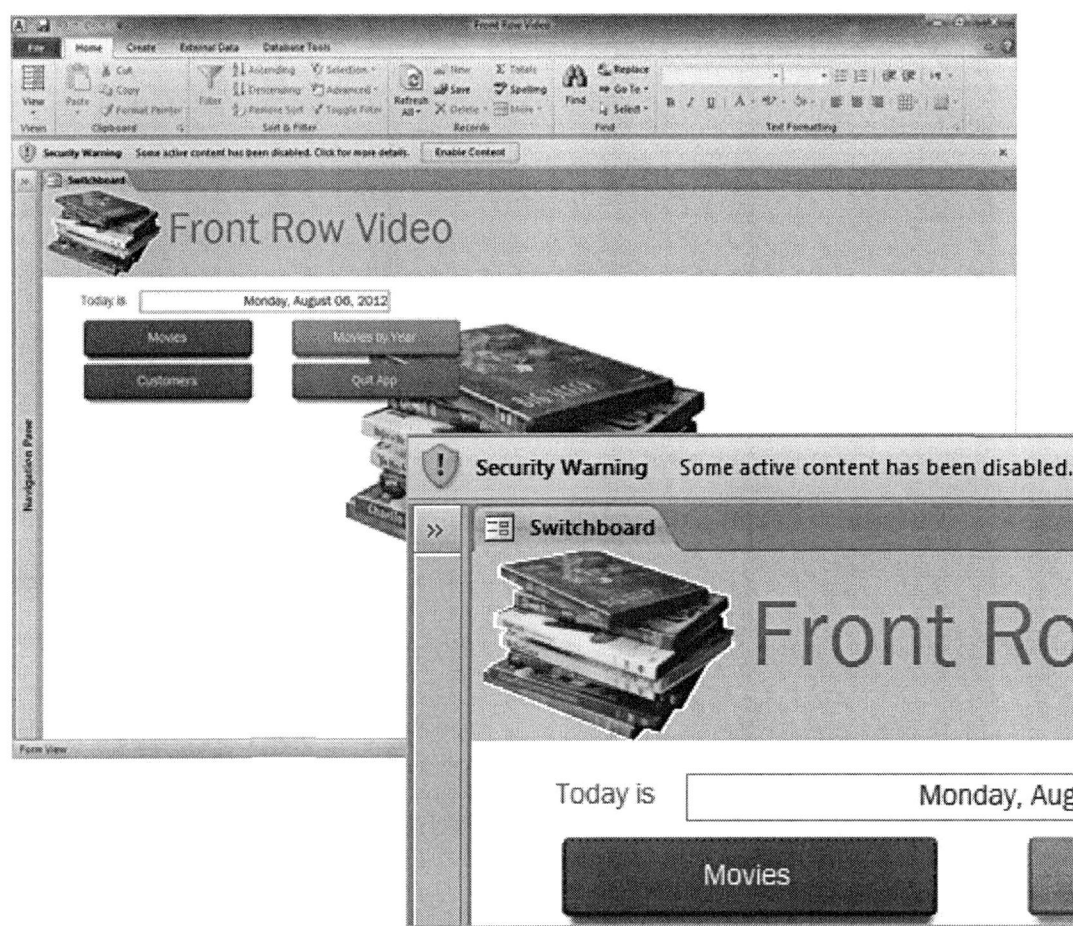

Know Your Data
Try This: Review the Database
Open the **Navigation Pane.**
Go to **All Access Objects.**

The Front Row Video database has the following:
Eight Tables: tblCustomers, tblGenre, tblMovieRented, tblMovies, tblMovieSearch, tblRating, tblRecipt and tblRentalPrices.

Twelve Queries: CustomerHomePhoneSQ, CustomerNameSQ, MovieRentalPriceUQ, MoviesByYearSQ, MovieSearchSQ, MovieSQ, RatingSearchSQ, ReceiptSQ, rptMovieRentedSQ, rptOverdueSQ rptReceiptSQ and tblMovies_Crosstab.

Eight Forms: Customers, MovieRentedSubform, Movies, MoviesbyRatingChart, MovieSearch, MovieSearchSubform, Receipt and Switchboard.

Six Reports: Customer Name. Movies by Genre, Movies by Year, rptMovieRented-POS, rptOverdue, and rptReceipt-POS.

One Macro: OpenSearchMovie

All Access Objects

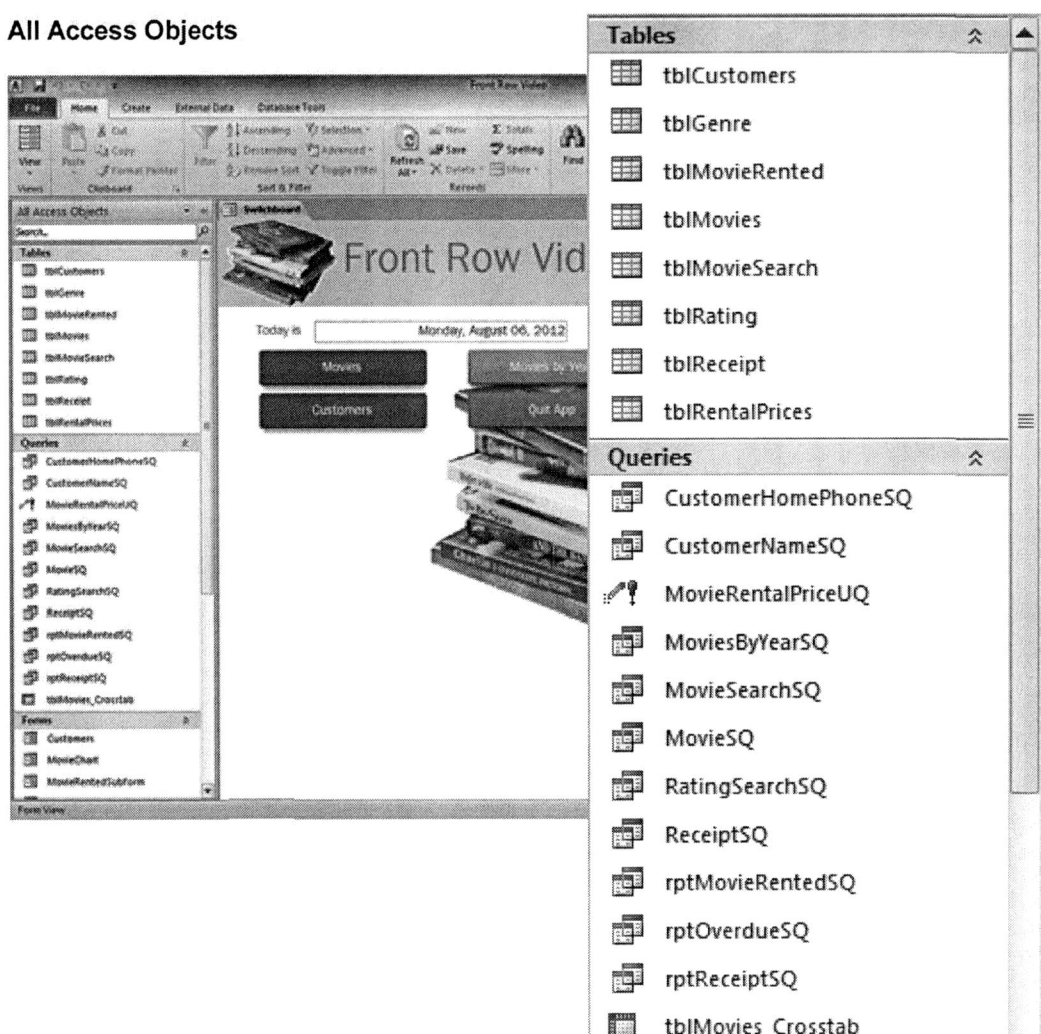

Import Data into Access:
Review the New Information
Look before you leap. Many companies send spreadsheets with updated product information. Before you import any data in Microsoft Access, you should review it.

1. Try it: Review the New Data
Start Microsoft Excel 2010.
Go to **File->Open**.
Browse for the file: **tblMoviesNEW.xlsx**.
Please open the spreadsheet.

What Do You See? There are 10 new movies in this spreadsheet. The first Row is the Header Row. It includes the following Fields: Movie, Year, Rating, Genre and Stars.

What Should You Be Looking For? These Field names MATCH the ones in the Access Table, tblMovies.

Close the spreadsheet.
The next step is in Access.

Microsoft Excel->Home

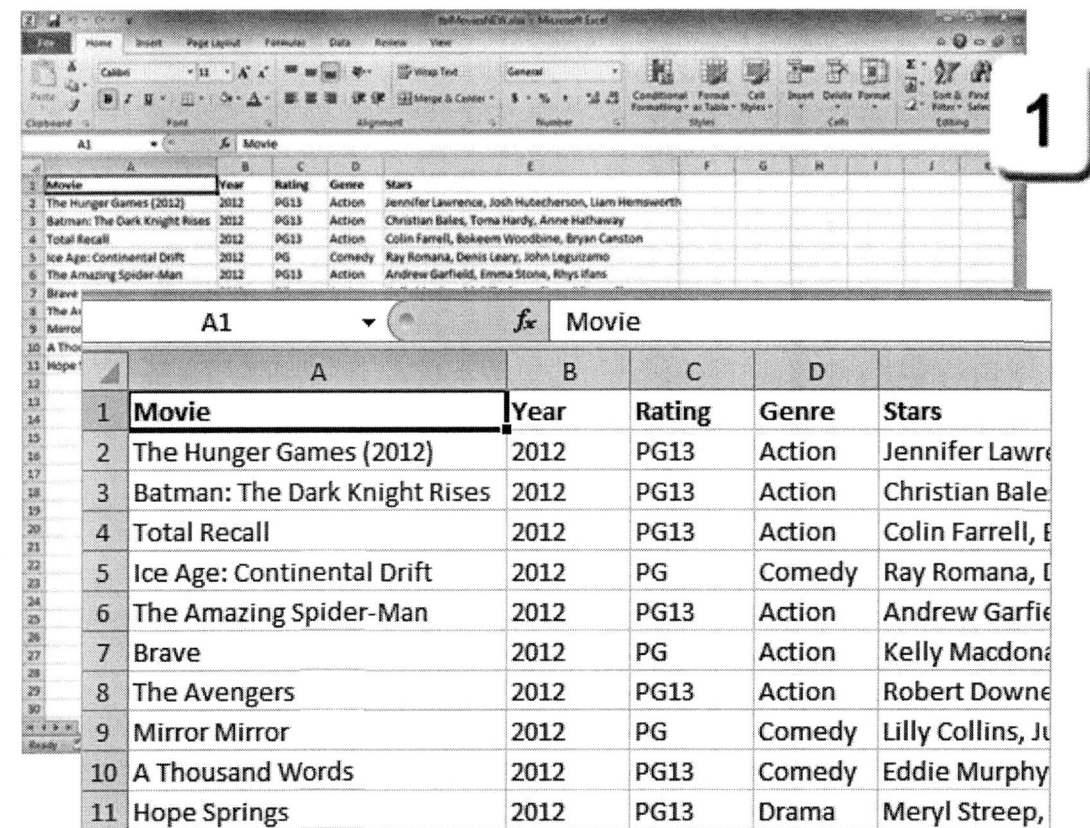

	A	B	C	D	
1	Movie	Year	Rating	Genre	Stars
2	The Hunger Games (2012)	2012	PG13	Action	Jennifer Lawre
3	Batman: The Dark Knight Rises	2012	PG13	Action	Christian Bale
4	Total Recall	2012	PG13	Action	Colin Farrell, E
5	Ice Age: Continental Drift	2012	PG	Comedy	Ray Romana, [
6	The Amazing Spider-Man	2012	PG13	Action	Andrew Garfie
7	Brave	2012	PG	Action	Kelly Macdona
8	The Avengers	2012	PG13	Action	Robert Downe
9	Mirror Mirror	2012	PG	Comedy	Lilly Collins, Ju
10	A Thousand Words	2012	PG13	Comedy	Eddie Murphy
11	Hope Springs	2012	PG13	Drama	Meryl Streep,

Exam 77-885: Microsoft Access 2010
2. Building Tables
2.5. Import data from a single data file: Append Data into an Existing Table

HOME

Import Data into Access:
Get External Data

There is an **Import Spreadsheet Wizard** that walks you through the process of importing data into Access. The steps ask to find the data and identify the Header Row

2. Try it: Get External Data
The Front Row Video database is open.
Go to **External Data ->Import & Link-> Excel.**

Try This, Too: Browse for the Data Source
Select: **tblMoviesNEW.xlsx**

Try This, Too: Specify How to Store the Data
The three import options include:
Import into a new table
Append (add) records to a table
Link to an external table
Select: **Append** and choose a Table: tblMovies.

Click **OK**. Keep going...

Microsoft Access->External Data ->Import & Link-> Excel

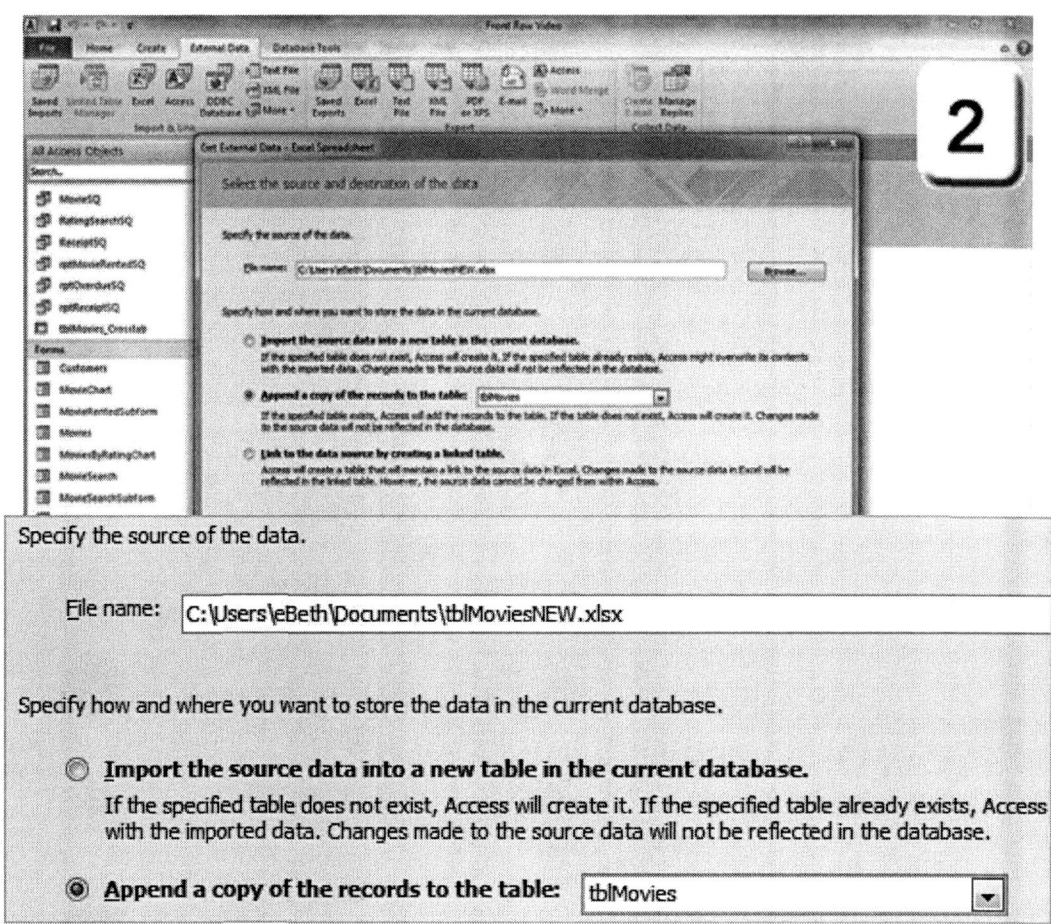

Specify the source of the data.

File name: C:\Users\eBeth\Documents\tblMoviesNEW.xlsx

Specify how and where you want to store the data in the current database.

◎   **Import the source data into a new table in the current database.**

If the specified table does not exist, Access will create it. If the specified table already exists, Access with the imported data. Changes made to the source data will not be reflected in the database.

◉   **Append a copy of the records to the table:**   tblMovies

Exam 77-885: Microsoft Access 2010
2. Building Tables
2.5. Import data from a single data file: Append Data into an Existing Table

Append Data to a Table: Select a Worksheet

3. Try it: Select a Worksheet or Range
An Excel workbook can have more than one spreadsheet or Named Range.

The Import Spreadsheet Wizard will ask you to confirm which Worksheet has the data. You can select a Worksheet or a Named Range.

Select a worksheet: New Movies.

What Do You See? The sample data for tblMovieTitles looks like the spreadsheet we just reviewed. So, we are good to go.

Click **Next**. Keep going...

Microsoft Access->External Data ->Import & Link-> Excel

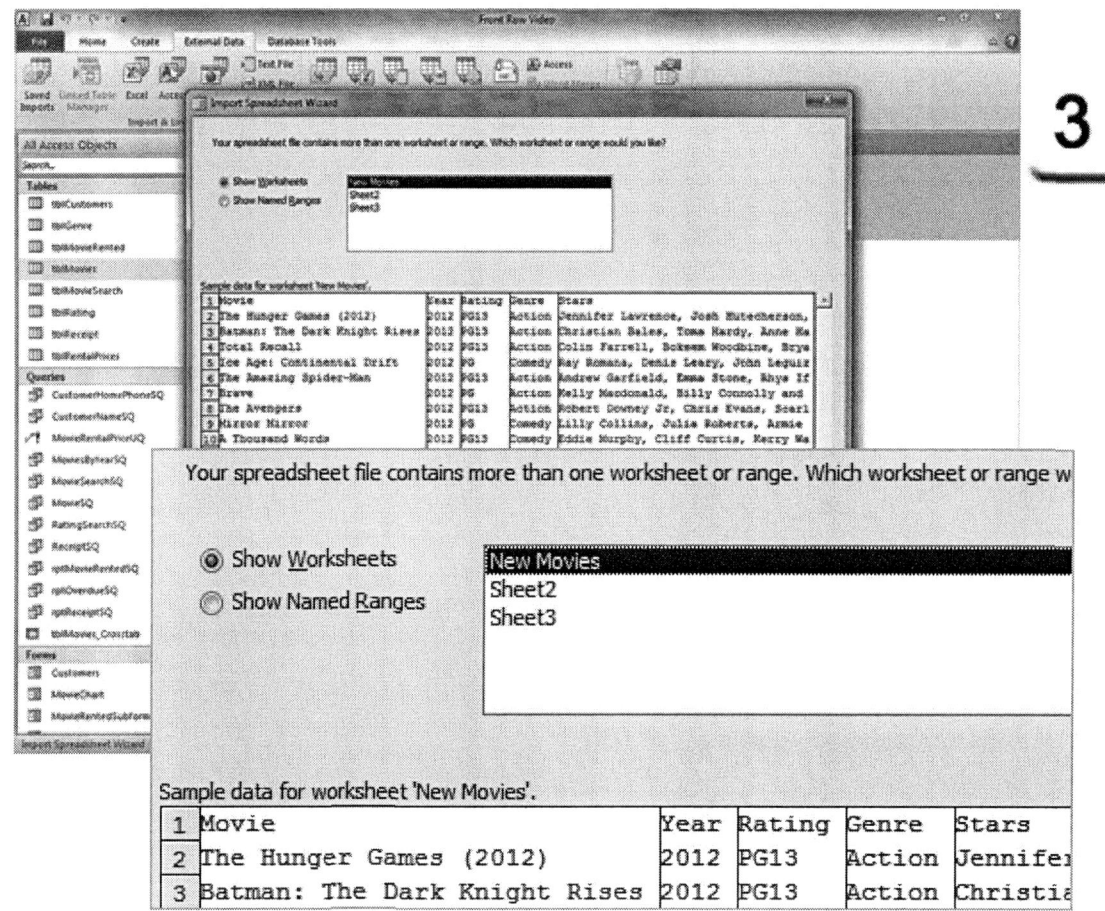

Exam 77-885: Microsoft Access 2010
2. Building Tables
2.5. Import data from a single data file: Append Data into an Existing Table

Microsoft Access->External Data ->Import & Link-> Excel

Append Data to a Table: Identify the Header Row

This step compares the Fields in the External Data to the Fields in the existing Table. The Field Names AND Data Types need to MATCH. Text goes with Text. Numbers go with Numbers.

4. Try it: Confirm the Header Row

This sample spreadsheet has a Header Row. The Header Row contains all of the Field Names: Movie, Year, Rating, etc.

Everything looks good.
Click **Next**.

Try This, Too: Import to Table

Confirm the Table: tblMovies.
Click **Finish** to close the Import Wizard.
If the **Save Import Steps** window is open you can simply close it

So, did the Wizard append (add) these movies to the right Table?

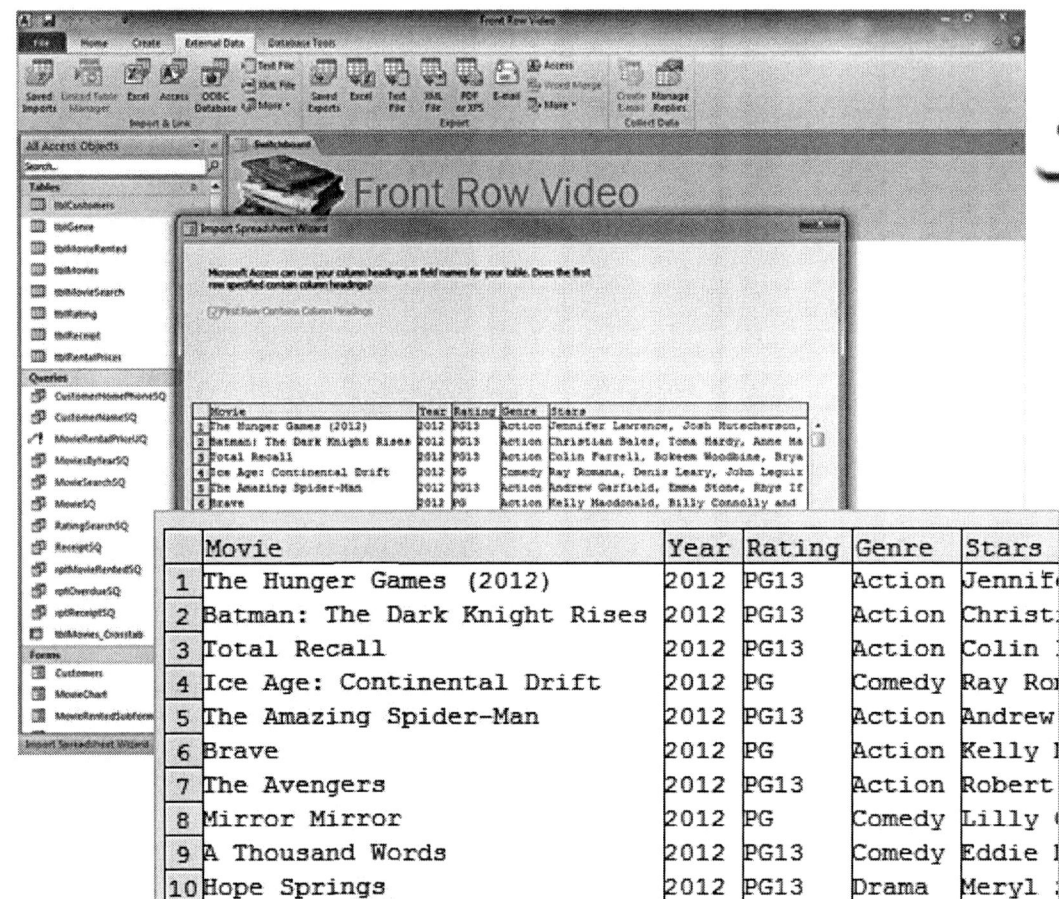

4

	Movie	Year	Rating	Genre	Stars
1	The Hunger Games (2012)	2012	PG13	Action	Jennif
2	Batman: The Dark Knight Rises	2012	PG13	Action	Christ
3	Total Recall	2012	PG13	Action	Colin
4	Ice Age: Continental Drift	2012	PG	Comedy	Ray Ro
5	The Amazing Spider-Man	2012	PG13	Action	Andrew
6	Brave	2012	PG	Action	Kelly
7	The Avengers	2012	PG13	Action	Robert
8	Mirror Mirror	2012	PG	Comedy	Lilly
9	A Thousand Words	2012	PG13	Comedy	Eddie
10	Hope Springs	2012	PG13	Drama	Meryl

Exam 77-885: Microsoft Access 2010
2. Building Tables
2.5. Import data from a single data file: Append Data into an Existing Table

Append Data to a Table: Review the Data

5. Try it: Review the Table Records
Go to **All Access Objects->Tables**.
Open a Table: tblMovies.
The Table should open in Datasheet View.

Know Your Numbers! This Table began with 401 Records. There are now 411 Records, so all 10 new movies were imported from the Excel spreadsheet.

What Do You See? There are two copies of the same movie, *The Hunger Games (2012.)* Apparently, there are duplicates in this Table.

Yeah, there's always more work to do, isn't there? Luckily, there is a Query Wizard that will help you find the repeats.

Close the Table. Let's create the Find Duplicates Query.

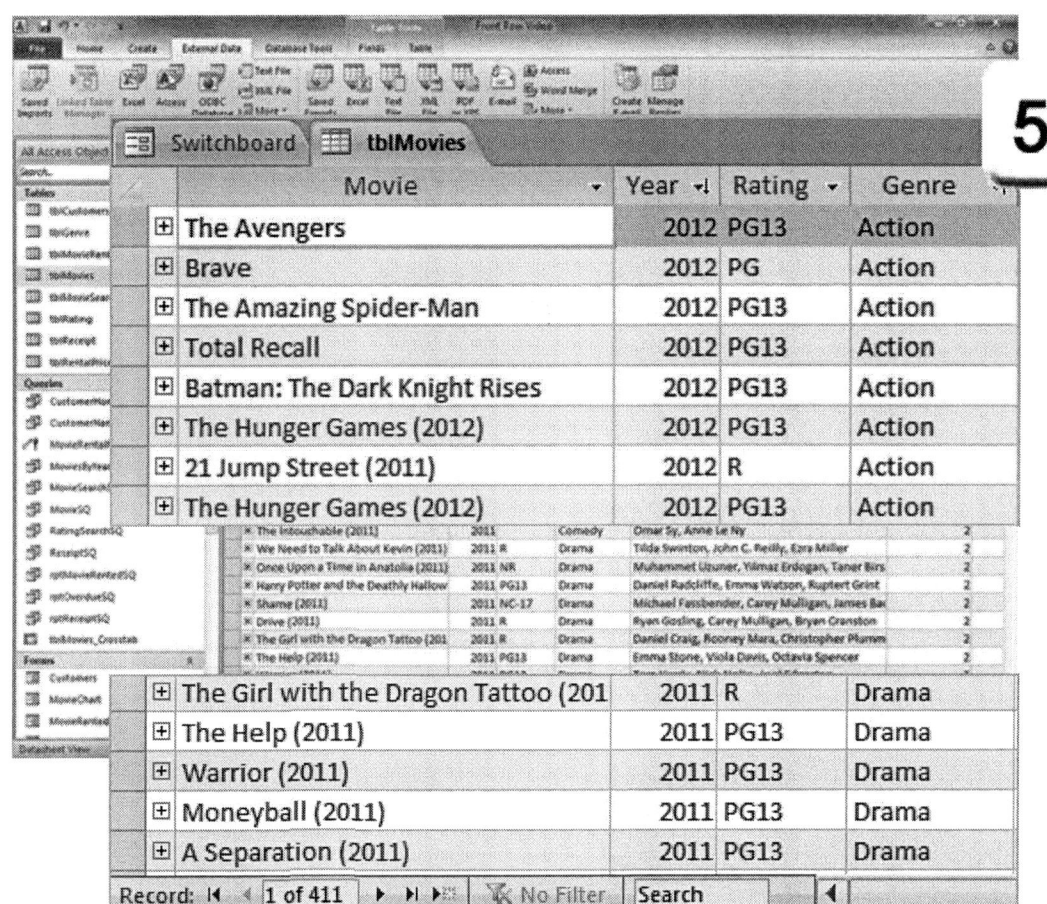

Exam 77-885: Microsoft Access 2010
2. Building Tables
2.5. Import data from a single data file: Append Data into an Existing Table

Append Data to a Table: Find Duplicates Query

"There's a Query for that!" Access has a Find Duplicates Query Wizard that will walk you through the steps.

6. Try it: Find Duplicates Wizard
Go to **Create->Queries->Query Design.**
Click on **Find Duplicates Wizard**

Click **OK**. The Query Wizard should begin.

Create->Queries->Query Design-> Find Duplicates Query Wizard

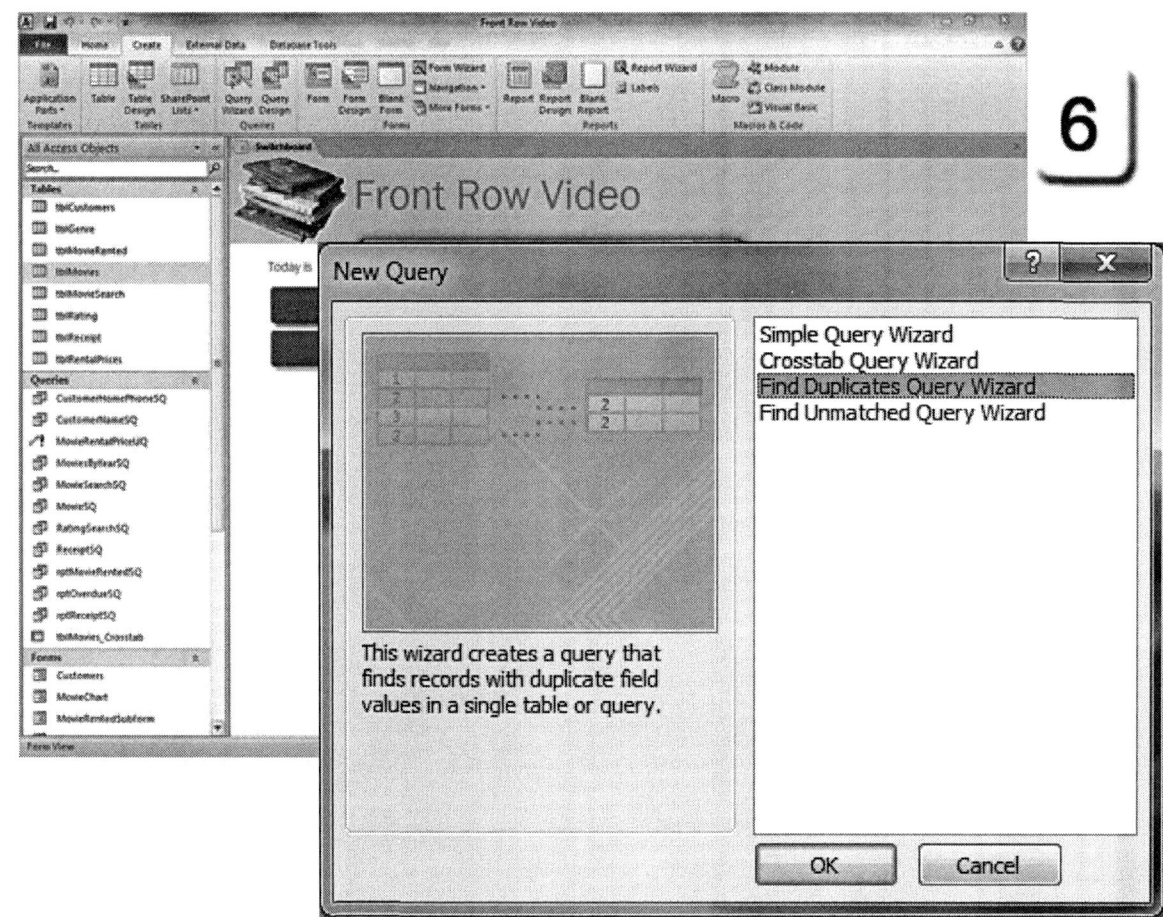

New Query

Simple Query Wizard
Crosstab Query Wizard
Find Duplicates Query Wizard
Find Unmatched Query Wizard

This wizard creates a query that finds records with duplicate field values in a single table or query.

OK   Cancel

Exam 77-885: Microsoft Access 2010
4. Creating and Managing Queries
4.1. Construct queries: Find Duplicates

Find Duplicates Query Wizard

7. Try it: Select a Record Source
Table or Query: tblMovies.
Click **Next**.

Try This: Select the Field with Duplicates
Select an Available Field: Movie.
Click **Next**.

Skip This: Select Another Field

Now, Do This: Name the Query
Enter a name: Find duplicates for tblMoviesSQ.

Click **Finish**.

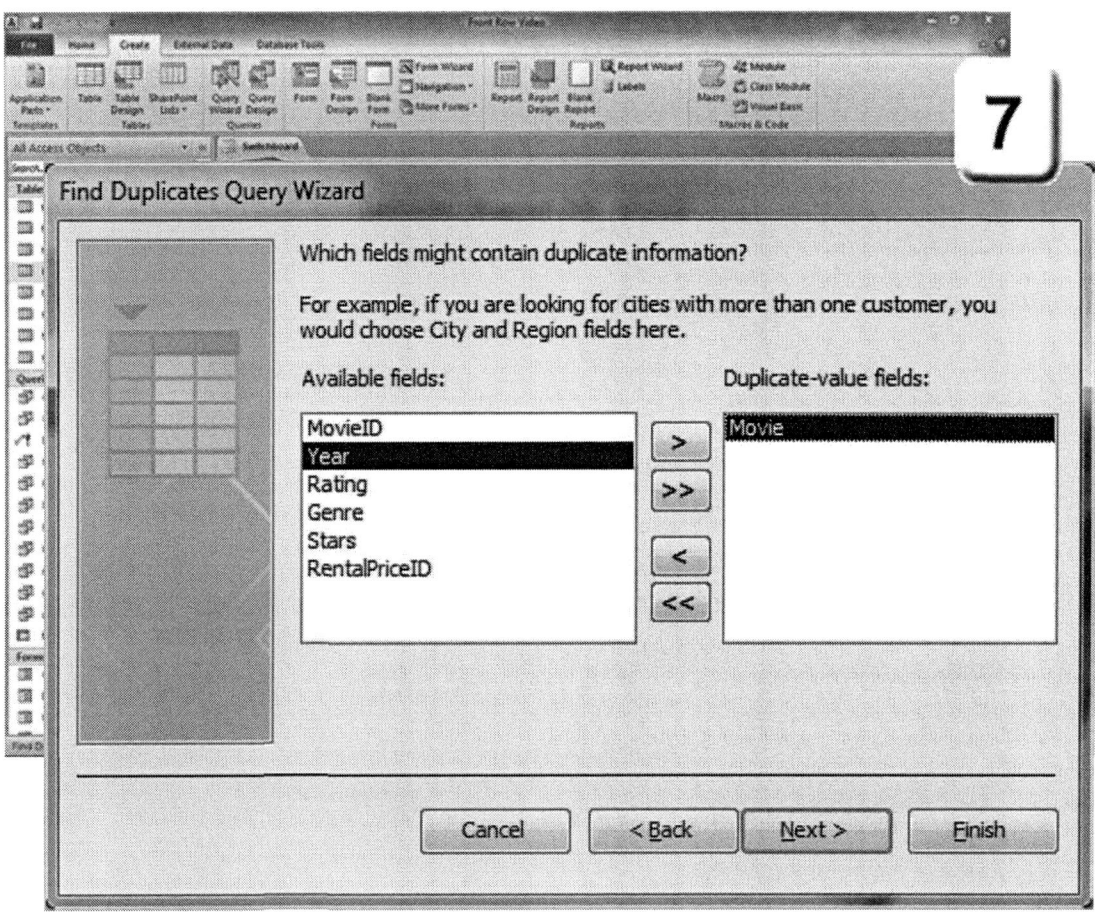

Exam 77-885: Microsoft Access 2010
4. Creating and Managing Queries
4.1. Construct queries: Find Duplicates

HOME

Create->Queries->Query Design-> Find Duplicates Query Wizard

Find Duplicates Results

8. Try it: Review the Query Results
The **Find duplicates for tblMoviesSQ** Query found two copies of one movie, "The Hunger Games."

What Else Did You Notice? This Query does not allow you to expand the Rows to see both movies. If you could see both you would delete one.

So, how do you handle duplicates? If the duplicate is a new Record that hasn't been used in any Receipts, you can go to tblMovies and delete it.

If the duplicate was already used in a Receipt, you need to edit the Receipt to use to correct movie before you delete the duplicate movie.

Still, this little Query searched through the Movie Field and found two that matched. How did it do that?

Let's see for ourselves.

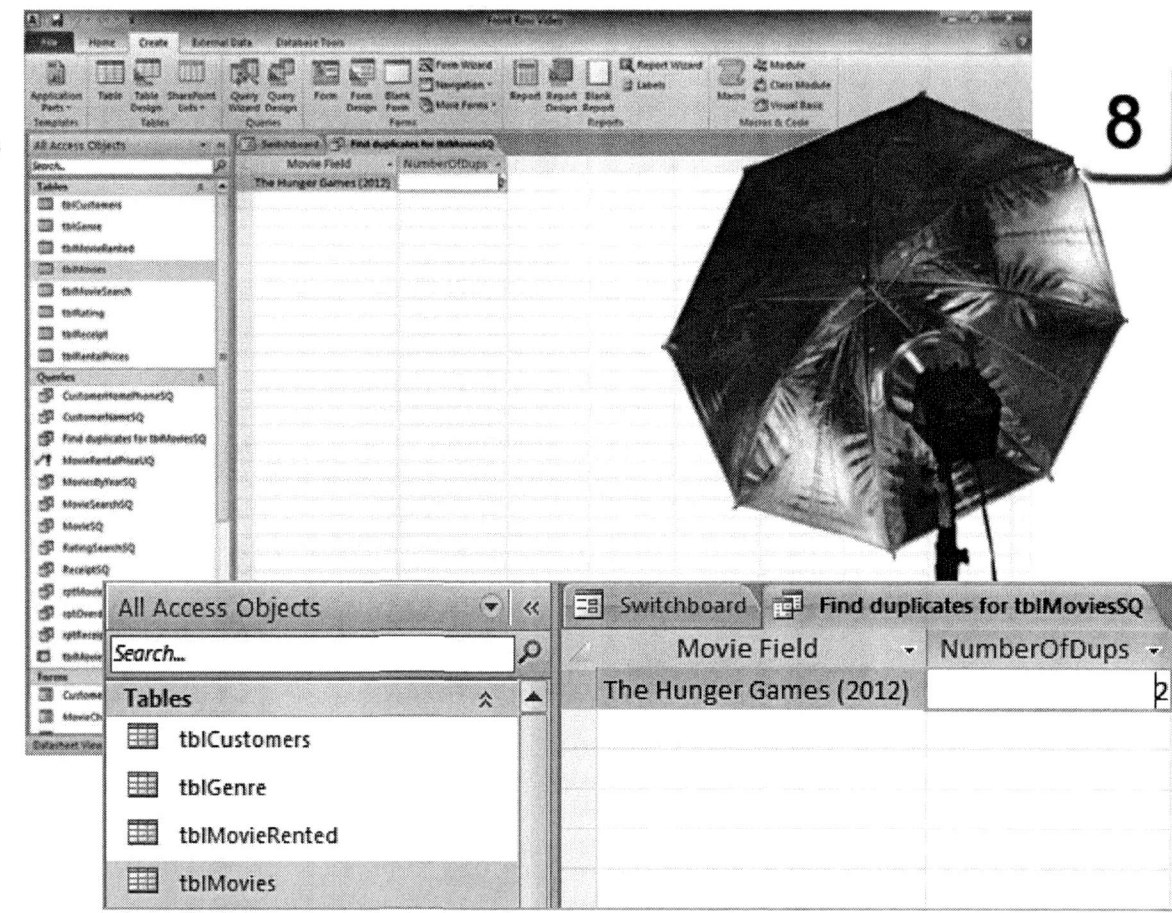

8

Exam 77-885: Microsoft Access 2010
4. Creating and Managing Queries
4.1. Construct queries: Find Duplicates

Find Duplicates Query Design

The Query Design is fascinating. Once you see how it works, one can only marvel at the simplicity.

9. Try it: Review the Query in Design View
The **Find duplicates for tblMoviesSQ** Query is open.
Go to **Home->Views->View->Design View**.

What Do You See? This Query has one Table: tblMovies. There are only three Fields in the QBE Grid. The Totals Row is available. Queries read from left to right. So this Query is asking three questions.

Movie Field: Movie asks "Which movie? Is this the first time we've seen this movie in the list?" This Field looks in tblMovies for the **First** time a movie appears.

NumberofDups: Movie asks "Is there more than one copy of this movie?" This Field looks in tblMovies and **Counts** the Records. The Criteria is (Greater than) >1.

Movie asks "Are we the same? Ok, let's Group!" This Field **Groups** the movies that match.

Way cool. Please **Close** this Query.

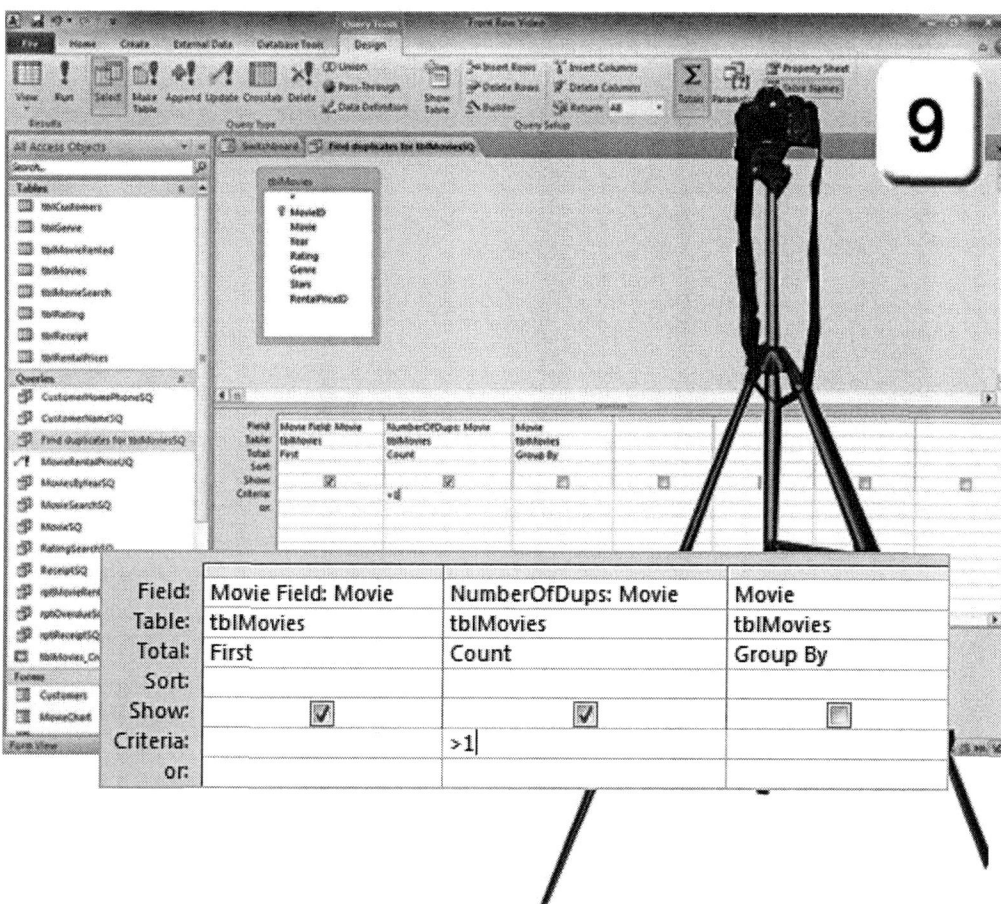

Field:	Movie Field: Movie	NumberOfDups: Movie	Movie
Table:	tblMovies	tblMovies	tblMovies
Total:	First	Count	Group By
Sort:			
Show:	☑	☑	☐
Criteria:		>1	
or:			

Exam 77-885: Microsoft Access 2010
2. Building Tables
2.1.1. Create tables in Design View

Deleting Data: Consider This!

1. Consider This: Should You Delete Data?
Deleting data is not a good idea in a relational database. When you create a Receipt in our database, you need information from five Tables. Consider this scenario.

Say you deleted the Movie, "Brave" from tblMovies. Say the Primary Key, MovieID, for this Movie was 407.

Now, you want to run a Report that looks up all of the Receipts. Any Receipt that had MovieID 407 will be incomplete. There is no data because that Key is missing.

This is not good.

The preferred method is to Archive a Record by marking it as Archived, Done or Obsolete.

Microsoft Access: Example of the warning message when a Record is deleted

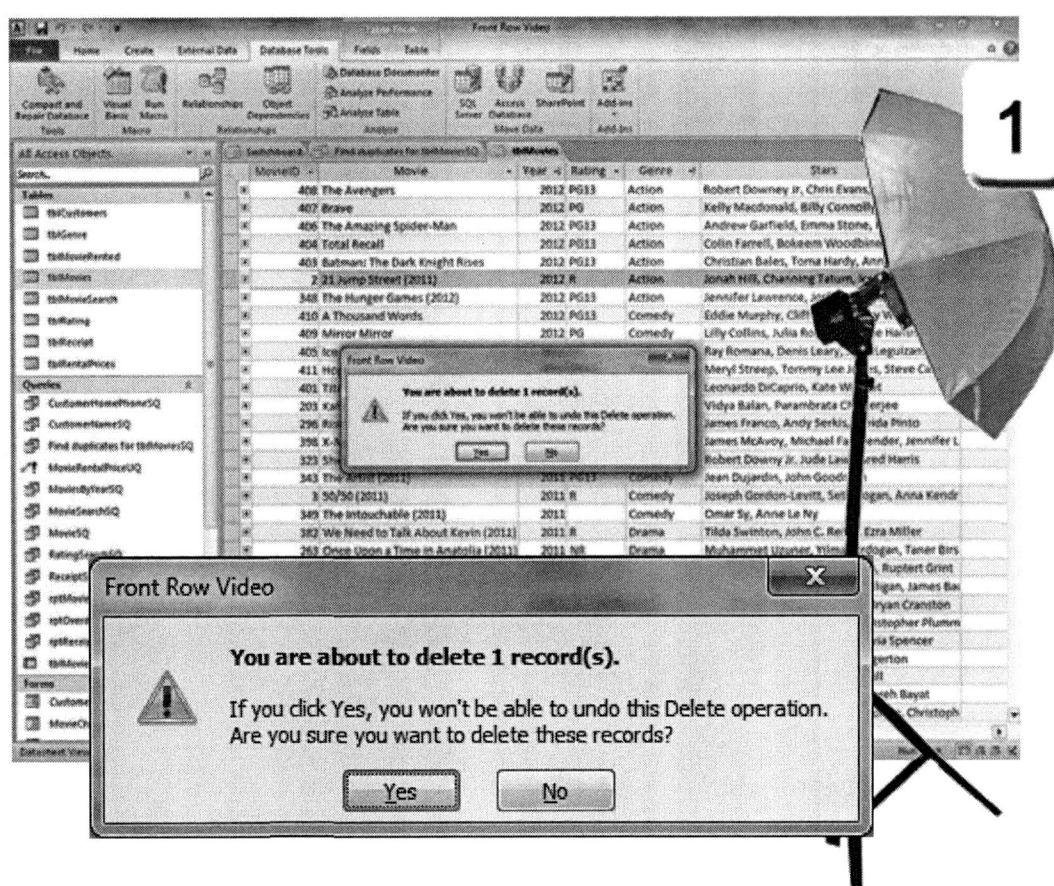

Create a Archive Program

2. An Alternative Approach: Archive the Data

The following pages will look at ways to archive old data. Here is a overview.

Revise the Movie Table: tblMovies

There are three Fields that should be added to the Movie Table make this a really useful database.

First, there will be a Yes/No Field that indicates if the Movie is Archived.

Second, there will be a Multi-Value Field that documents the status.

Third, we'll add a Memo Field.

Create a Make Table Query

The Archived Movies will be selected and copied into a new Table.

Create a Delete Query

The last Action Query deletes the Archived Movies from tblMovies.

So, when you are ready...

Microsoft Access: Example of the completed Make Table Query

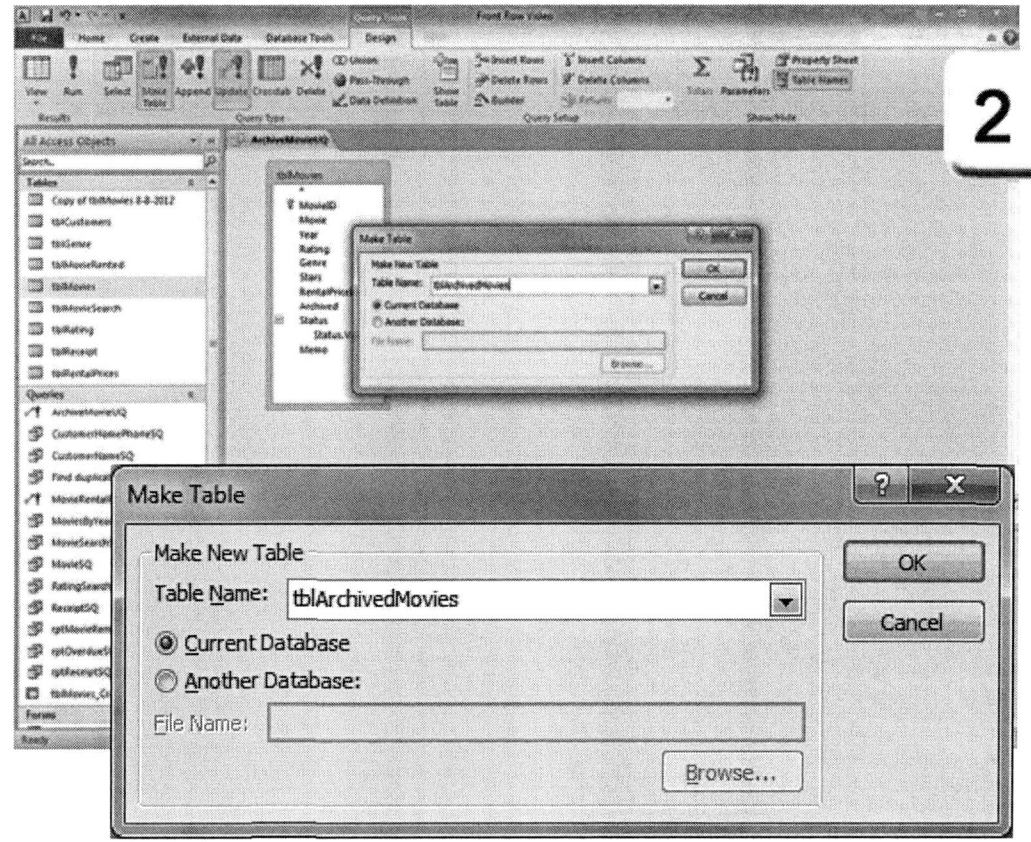

Exam 77-885: Microsoft Access 2010
2. Building Tables
2.1.1. Create tables in Design View

Save a Copy of the Table

Good database administrators do not lose data. Before editing a Table in any working database, it is a wise precaution to create a backup copy of that Table.

3. Try it: Save a Copy of the Table
The Movie Table may still be open, if not..
Go to **All Access Objects->Tables**.
Open a Table: tblMovies.

Try This, Too: Save a Copy
Go to **File->Object As**.
Enter a name: Copy of tblMovies 8-8-2012, where 8-8-2012 is the current date of the backup copy.

Click **OK**. Now, click on the **Home** Ribbon to see the database Objects.
Close the Copy of tblMovies 8-8-2012 Table..

There is a current backup copy of the data. Now...we can keep going...

File ->Save Object As

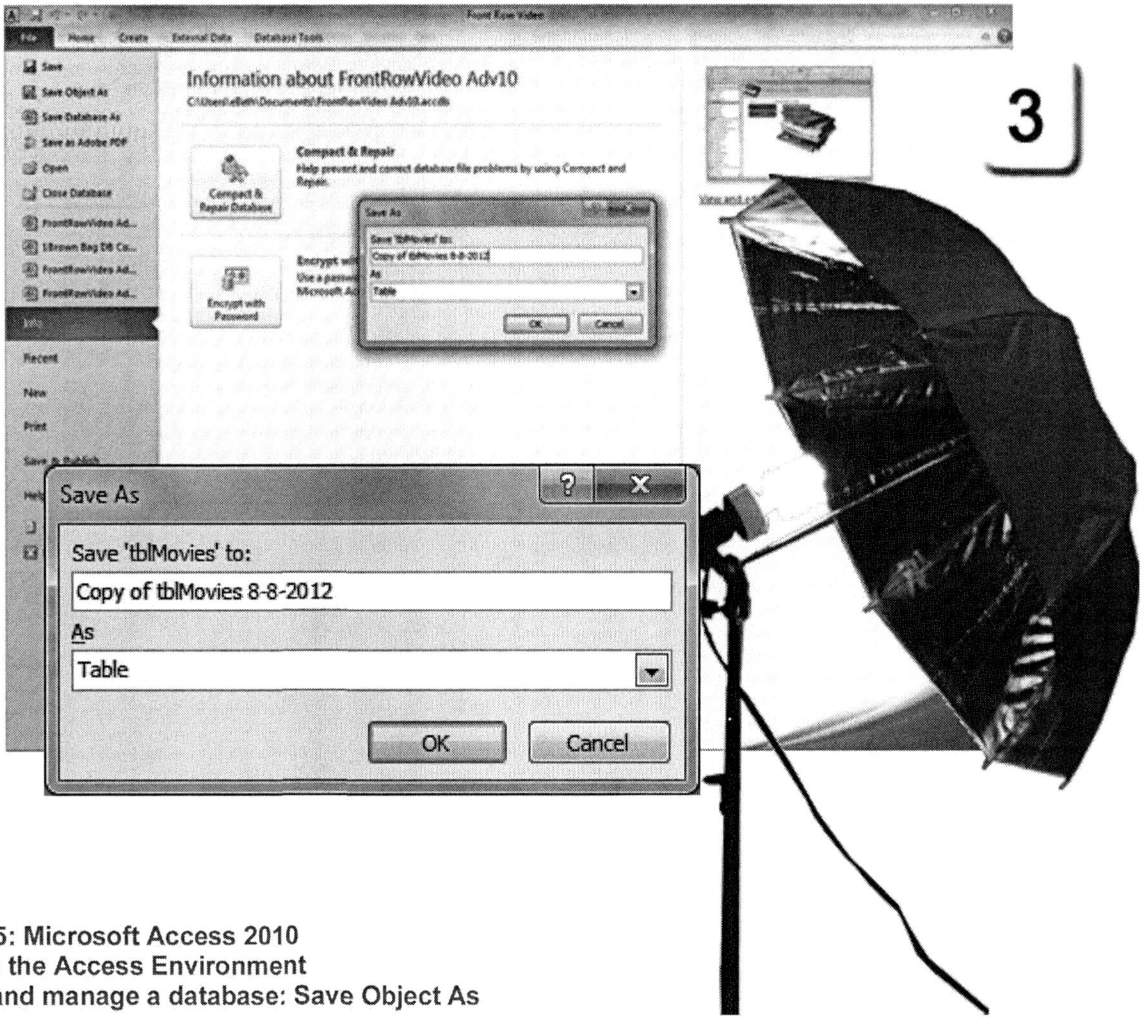

Exam 77-885: Microsoft Access 2010
1. Managing the Access Environment
1.1. Create and manage a database: Save Object As

Add New Fields to the Table

The Movie Table needs a Field that indicates a Record should be archived and marked as no longer part of the daily rentals. The Archived Field can be as simple as **Yes/No**.

Before You Begin: Open the Table
Go to **All Access Objects->Tables**.
Select a Table: tblMovies.
Go to **Home ->Views->View->Design View**.
The **Table Tools** should be available.

4. Try This: Add a New Field
Field Name: Archived
Data Type: Yes/No

What Do You See? By default Microsoft Access uses a check box for this Control. A "Yes" answer means True or On. A "No" answer means False or Off.

Keep going...

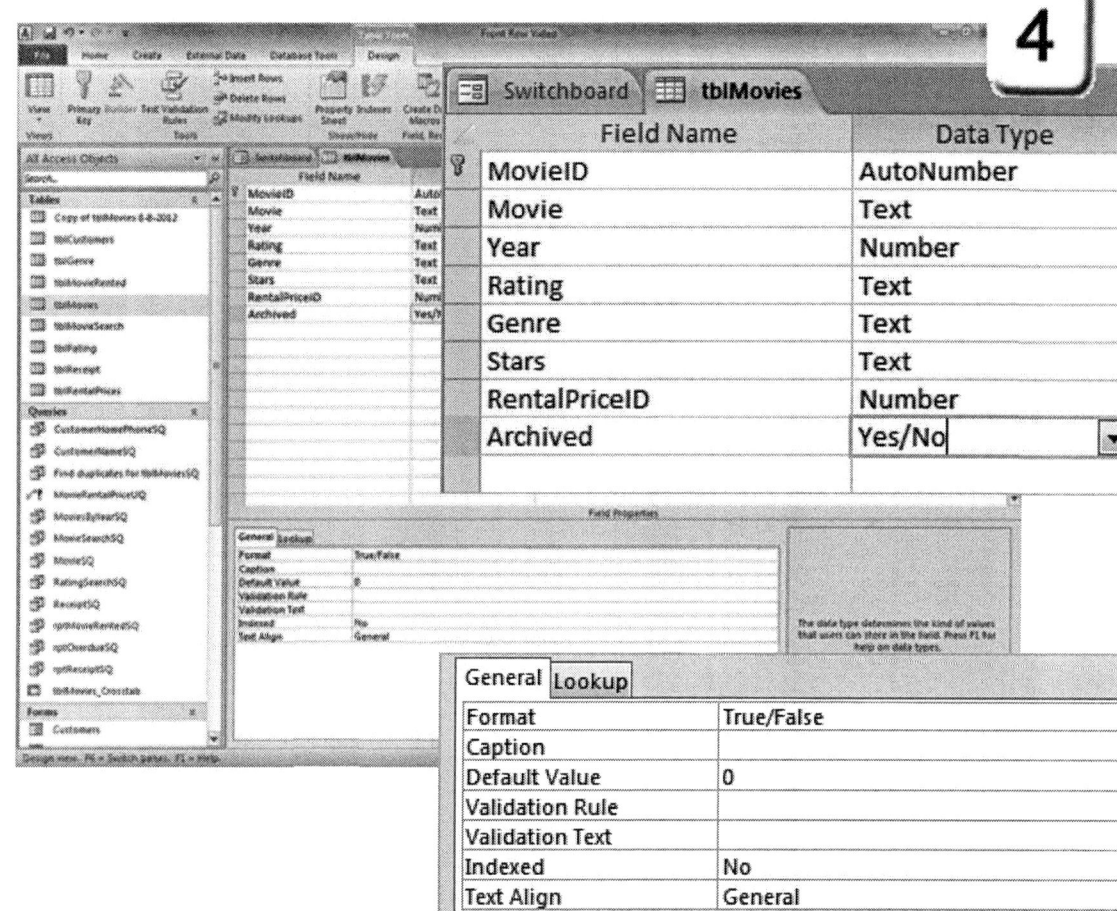

Field Name	Data Type
MovieID	AutoNumber
Movie	Text
Year	Number
Rating	Text
Genre	Text
Stars	Text
RentalPriceID	Number
Archived	Yes/No

General Lookup	
Format	True/False
Caption	
Default Value	0
Validation Rule	
Validation Text	
Indexed	No
Text Align	General

Exam 77-885: Microsoft Access 2010
2. Building Tables
2.2. Create and Modify Fields: Modify the Field Properties Yes/No

Add a MultiValue Field

A **MultiValue Field** lets Users select more than one answer to a question. You can use a MultiValue Field to document why a movie was Archived.

5. Try it: Add a MultiValue Field
Field Name: Status.
Data Type: Lookup Wizard.

What Do You See? The Lookup WIzard will prompt you for the following:

Record Source: I will type in the values that I want. Click **Next**.

Type in the Values:
Damaged
Lost
No Sale
Do Not Reimage.
Click **Next**.

Label: Status.

Click **Finish**. Keep going...

Table Tools ->Design

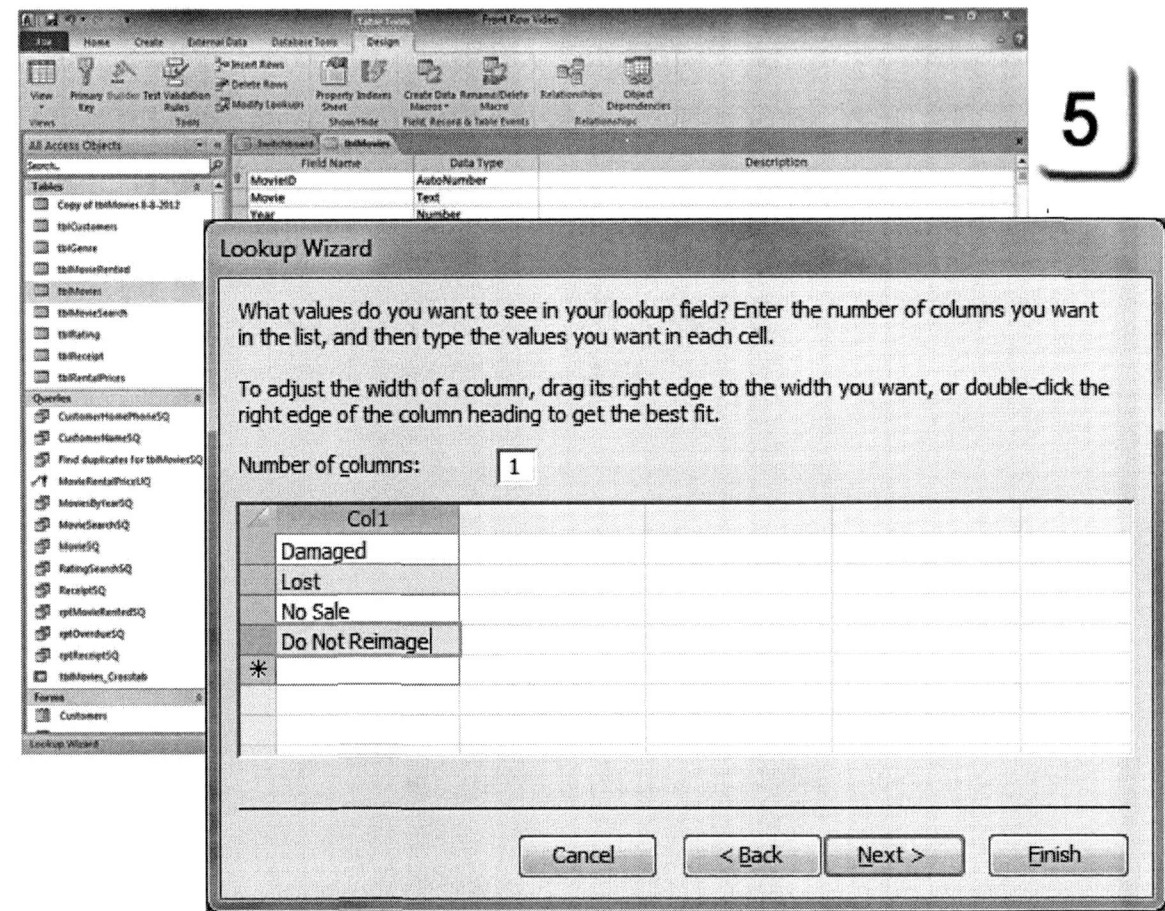

Exam 77-885: Microsoft Access 2010
2. Building Tables
2.1.1. Create tables in Design View: Create and modify MultiValue Fields

Review the MultiValue Field

The Lookup Wizard walked us through the task of creating a Lookup List. There are two additional choices in the last step of the Wizard: Limit to List and Allow Multiple Edits. By default, these options are not selected.

Where would you change them? Look in the Field Properties: there are two Tabs! We usually edit the General Properties. There is also a Lookup Tab. Well, let's look.

6. Try it: Review the Field Properties
Select a Field: Status.
Go to **Field Properties-> Lookup.**

What Do You See? The Properties are:
Display Control: Combo Box
Row Source Type: Value List.
Row Source:
Limit to List: Yes (Users can't add to the list).
Allow Multiple Values: Yes (Pick more than 1).
Allow Value List Edits: No.

Field Properties-> Lookup

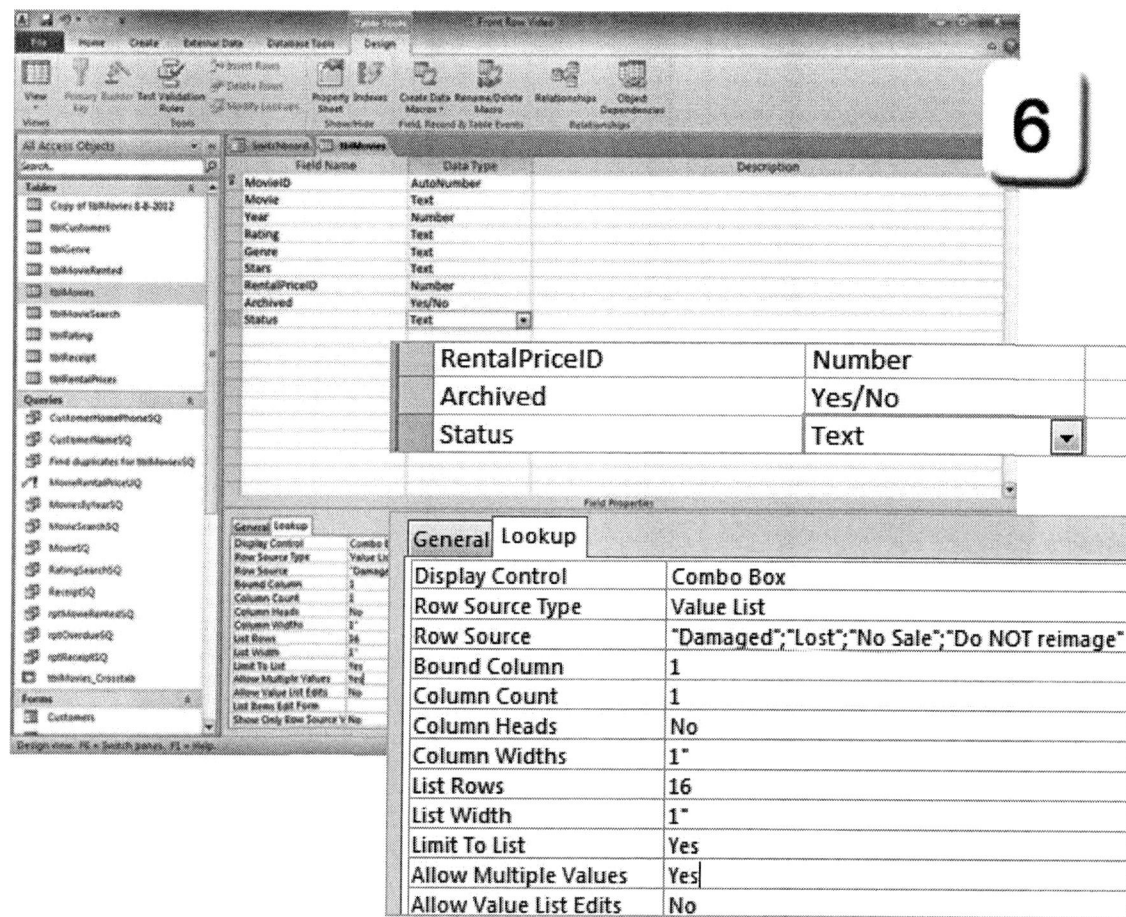

RentalPriceID	Number
Archived	Yes/No
Status	Text

General	Lookup
Display Control	Combo Box
Row Source Type	Value List
Row Source	"Damaged";"Lost";"No Sale";"Do NOT reimage"
Bound Column	1
Column Count	1
Column Heads	No
Column Widths	1"
List Rows	16
List Width	1"
Limit To List	Yes
Allow Multiple Values	Yes
Allow Value List Edits	No

Exam 77-885: Microsoft Access 2010
2. Building Tables
2.1.1. Create tables in Design View: Create and modify MultiValue Fields

Add a Memo Field

Another useful Field is the **Memo Field**. Memo Fields can hold a lot. In fact, Memo Fields can store 2GB of data. There are two Memo Field Properties worth considering: Text Format and Append Only. By marking the Memo Field Append Only, Users can ADD to the Memo, but they cannot DELETE the previous entries.

7. Try it: Add a Memo Field
Field Name: Memo.
Data Type: Memo.

Try This, Too: Edit the Field Properties
Go to **Field Properties->General.**
Text Format: Rich Text.
Append Only: Yes

Save and **Close** the Table, please.

Memo to Self: Selecting "Yes" for the Append option also **Tracks** the history. The history is available when you add this Field to a Form. You can right-click the Memo Field in Form View to see the tracking.

Table Tools ->Design

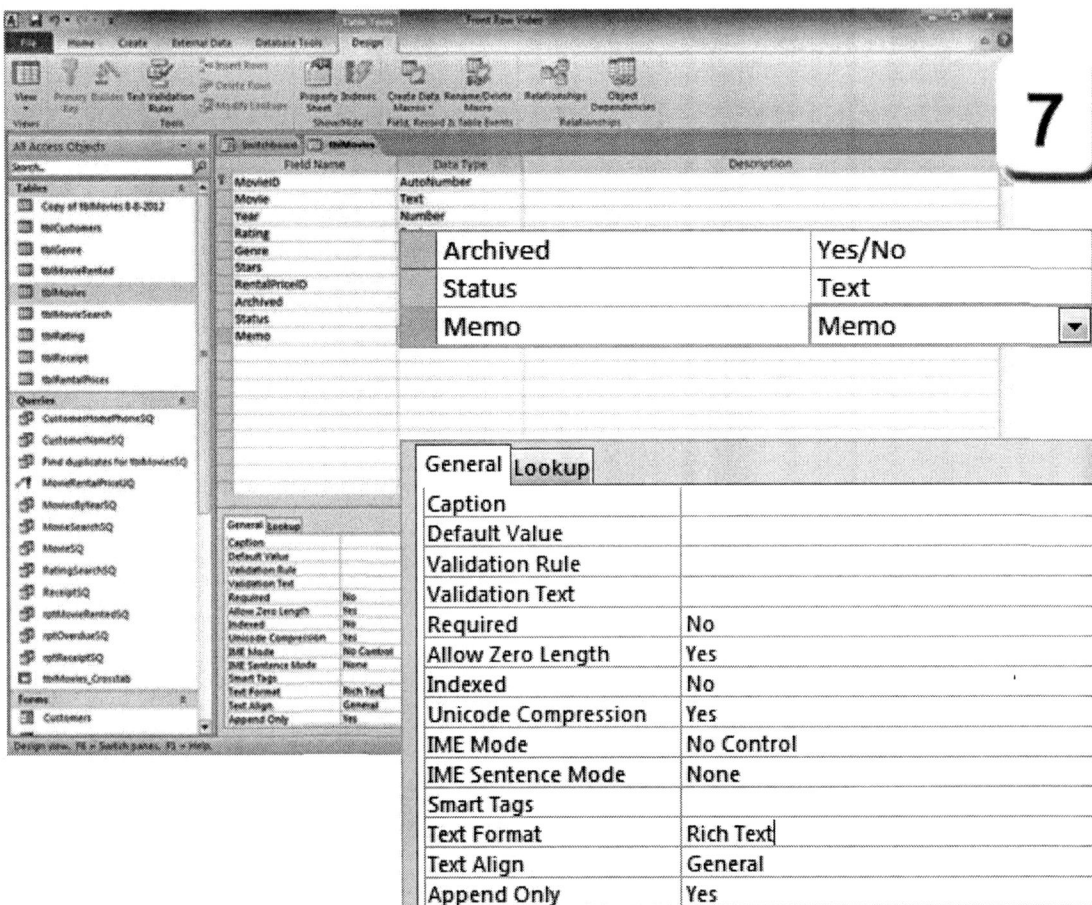

Archived	Yes/No
Status	Text
Memo	Memo

General	Lookup
Caption	
Default Value	
Validation Rule	
Validation Text	
Required	No
Allow Zero Length	Yes
Indexed	No
Unicode Compression	Yes
IME Mode	No Control
IME Sentence Mode	None
Smart Tags	
Text Format	Rich Text
Text Align	General
Append Only	Yes

Exam 77-885: Microsoft Access 2010
2. Building Tables
2.1.1. Create tables in Design View: Create and modify Memo Fields

Add the Fields to the Form

The Movie Table is updated. Done and done. We can add the new Fields to the Movie Form, now. You can also improve the layout and placement of the Controls if you wish.

8. Try it: Add the Field to a Form
Open the Movie Form in Design View.
Go to **Form Design Tools ->Design->Tools.**
Click on **Add Existing Fields.**
Add three Fields to the Form:
Archive
Status
Memo

Go ahead, make the Form Header purple.
Save your changes and keep going.

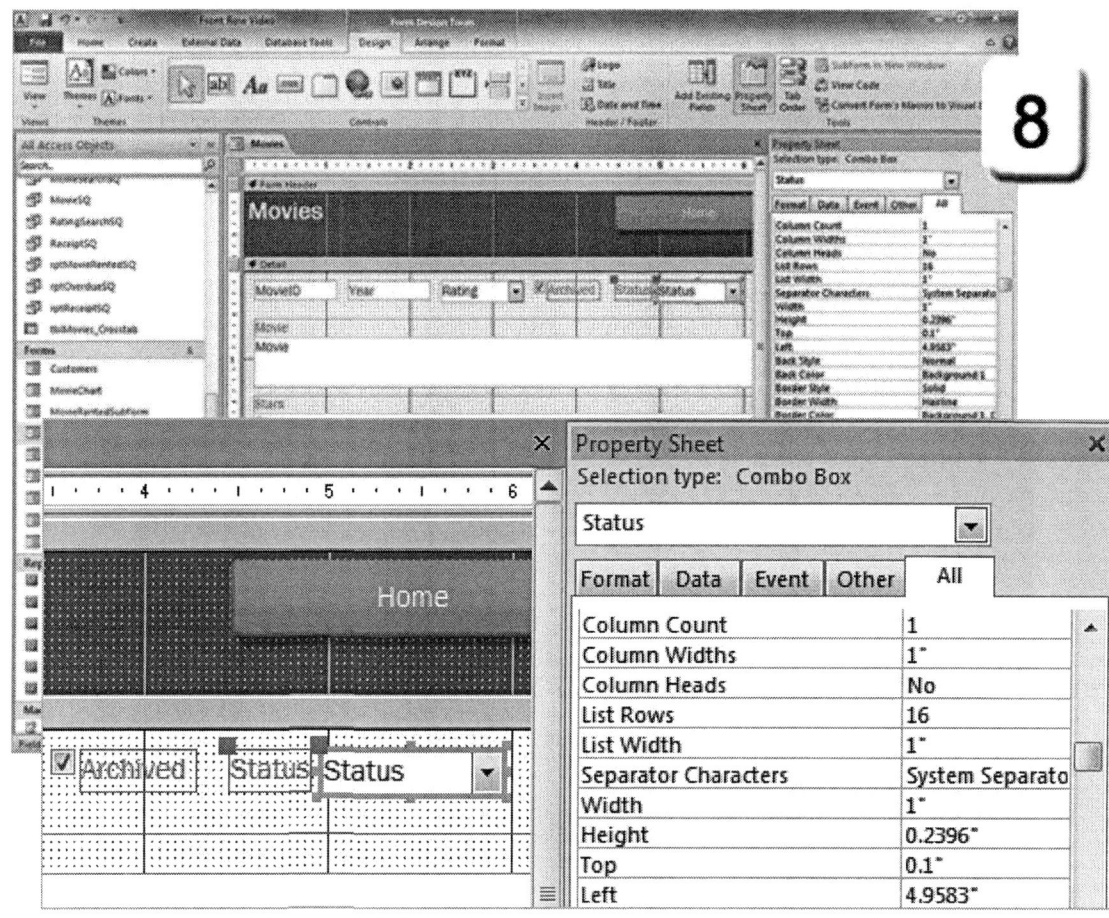

Exam 77-885: Microsoft Access 2010
3. Building Forms
3.2. Apply Form Design options: Add Existing Fields to a Form

Form Design Tools ->Views->View->Form View

Test the New Form Fields
Before You Begin: Change the View
Go to **Form Design Tools ->Views->View.**
Select a View: Form View.

Still Before You Begin: Find a Movie
Click on the Movie Field.
Go to **Home->Find->Find.**
Find What: Amityville II: The Possession.
Match: Any part of Find.
Click **Find Next** to go to that movie.

9. Try it: Test the New Form Fields
Check: Archived.
Change the Status: No Sale, Do Not reimage.
You can add some sample text to the Memo Field.
Please **Close** the Movies Form.

The data should be updated in tblMovies. You
could find all of the movies that were released
before 1990 and mark them as Archived.

Or...you can use an Action Query to update them
all at once. Let's go for the Action Query.

Exam 77-885: Microsoft Access 2010
3. Building Forms
3.2. Apply Form Design options: Add Existing Fields to a Form

Select the Oldies

The goal in this next step is to create an Update Query that will mark all of the Movies released before 1990 as "Archived." The best place to start is to make a Select Query and see if it finds the right Movies. When it works we'll save the Select Query as an Update Query.

1. Try it: Create a Select Query
Go to **Create ->Queries ->Query Design.**
You will be prompted by the **Show Table**.
Select a Table: tblMovies.
Click **Add** and **Close** the Show/Table Window.

Try This, Too: Add Fields
Add these Fields to the QBE Grid:
MovieID, Movie, Year, Archived, Rating, Genre, Stars and RentalPriceID.

Yep, And This: Add a Criteria
Select a Field: Year.
Enter a Criteria: <1990

When you **Run** this Query you should find 73 movies that have this Criteria. Keep going...

Create ->Queries->Query Design

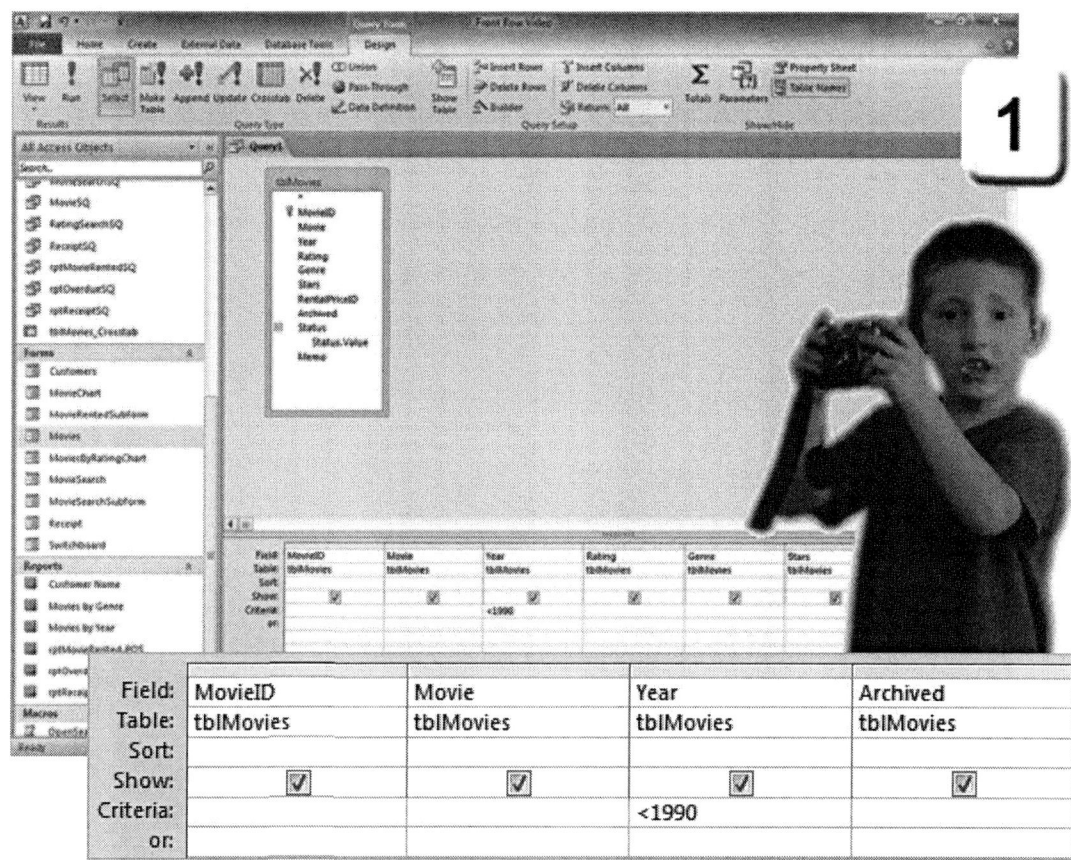

Field:	MovieID	Movie	Year	Archived
Table:	tblMovies	tblMovies	tblMovies	tblMovies
Sort:				
Show:	☑	☑	☑	☑
Criteria:			<1990	
or:				

Exam 77-885: Microsoft Access 2010
4. Creating and Managing Queries
4.1. Construct queries: Create a Select Query

Update the Oldies

The same Query that selected the Movies can be changed into an Action Query and **Update** the Archive Field to "Yes." Here are the steps.

Before You Begin: Change the View
Go to **Home->Views-View->Design View.**

2. Try it: Create an Update Query
Go to **Query Tools ->Design->Query Type.**
Select a Query Type: **Update**.

What Do You See? There will be a new Row in the QBE grid: Update to.

Try This, Too: Enter the Update Value
Go to a Field: Archived.
Update to: Yes.

Better Do This, Now: Save the Query
Go to **File->Save**.
Enter a name: **ArchiveMovieUQ**,
where UQ means Update Query.

Keep going...

Query Tools ->Design->Query Type-> Update

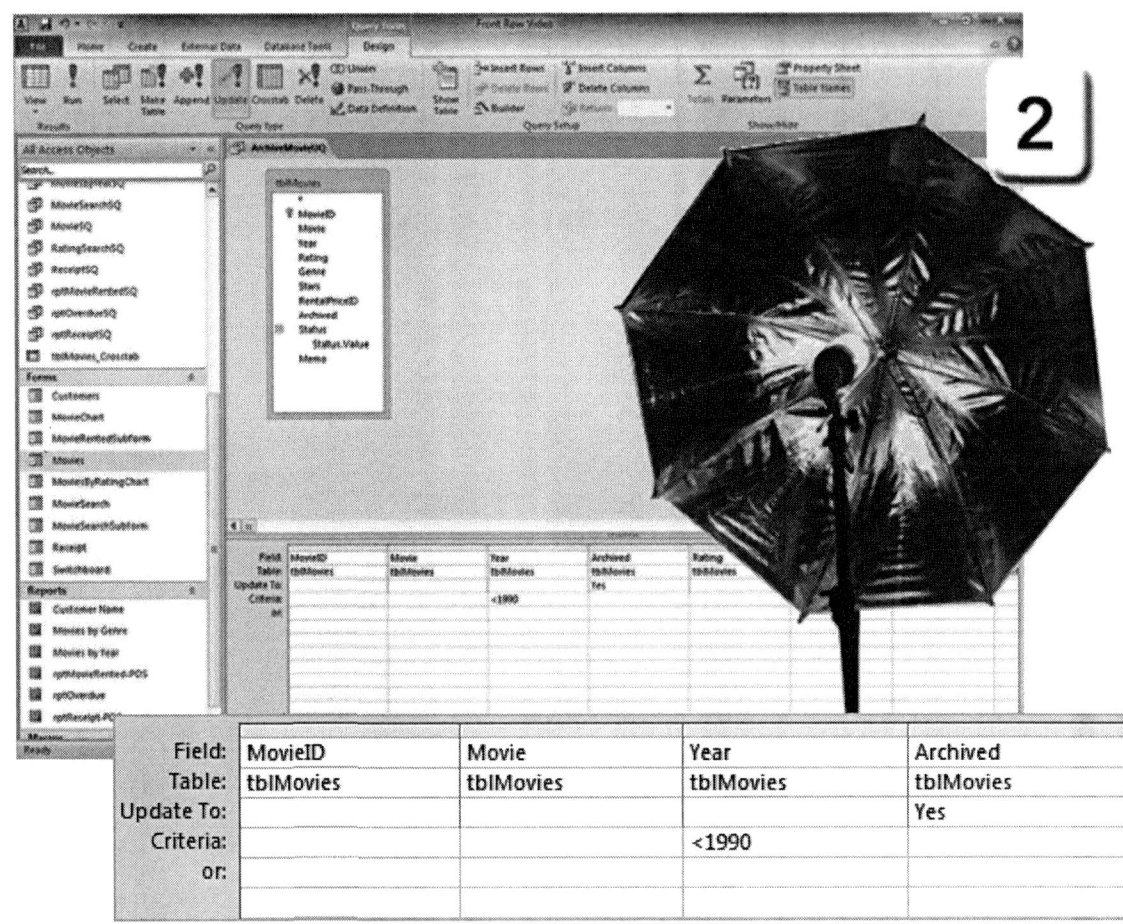

Field:	MovieID	Movie	Year	Archived
Table:	tblMovies	tblMovies	tblMovies	tblMovies
Update To:				Yes
Criteria:			<1990	
or:				

Exam 77-885: Microsoft Access 2010
4. Creating and Managing Queries
4.1. Construct queries: Create an Update Query

Run the Update Query

An Update Query is an Action Query. When you run the Update Query, you will be notified that this Action will change the Records and that there is No UNDO.

3. Try it: Run the Update Query
Go to **Query Tools ->Design->Results-> Run.**

What Do You See? This Query will update 73 Rows in tblMovies. That number matches the one we saw when we tested the Query as a Select Query. Click **Yes** to Run the Update.

Trust But Verify: Confirm the Updated Rows
Go to **All Access Objects->Table**.
Open a Table: tblMovies.

What Do You See, Now? Did the Update Query change the Archived Field to Yes for the Movies released before 1990?

Please **Close** tblMovies and return to the ArchiveMovieUQ Query.

Query Tools ->Design->Results-> Run

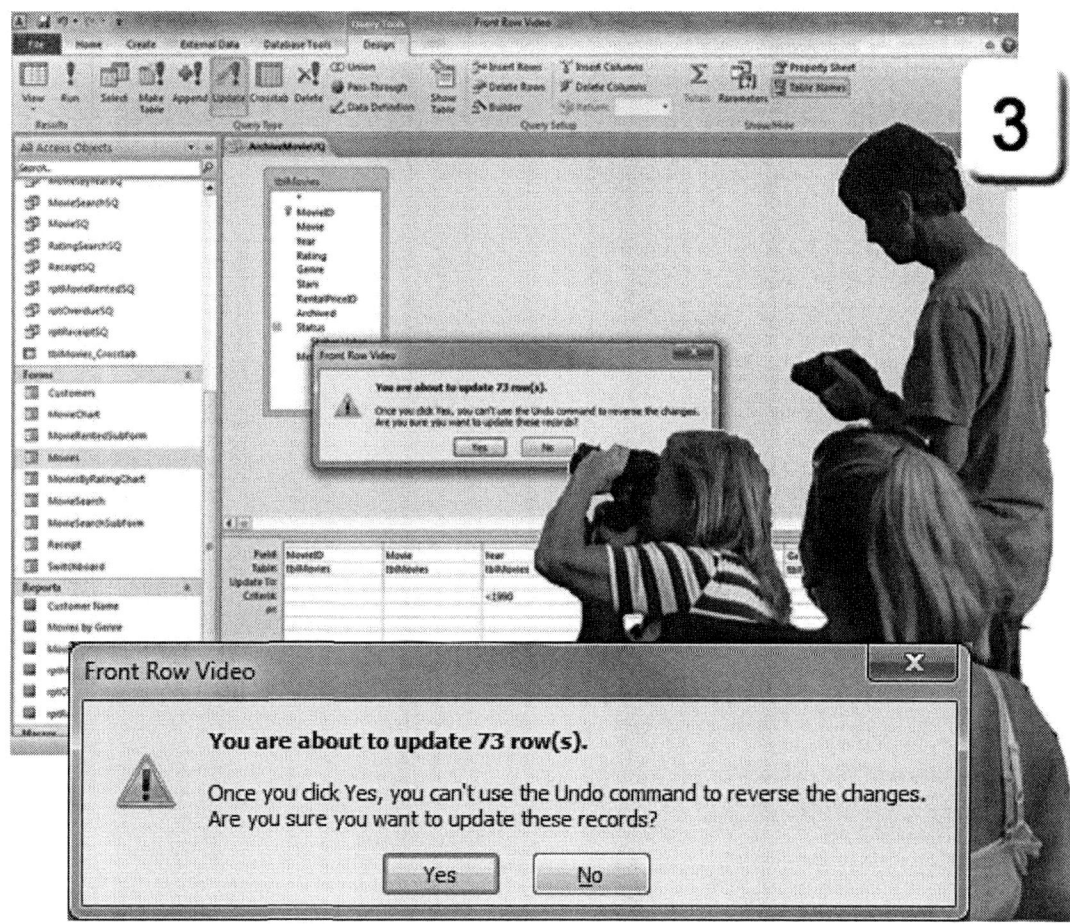

Exam 77-885: Microsoft Access 2010
4. Creating and Managing Queries
4.1. Construct queries: Create an Update Query

HOME

Query Tools ->Design->Query Type-> Make Table

Copy to a New Table

The Update Query, **ArchiveMovieUQ**, will also work as another type of Action Query: a Make Table Query. The Make Table Query selects the Records that match the Criteria and copies those Records into a new Table.

4. Try it: Create a Make Table Query
Go to **Query Tools ->Design->Query Type.**
Select a Query Type: **Make Table.**

What Do You See? You will be prompted to name the new Table.
Enter the Table Name: tblArchiveMovies.
Click **OK** to Run the Make Table Query.

Do This, Now: Save the Make Table Query
Go to **File->Save Object As.**
Enter the name: **ArchiveMovieMT,**
where MT means this is a Make Table Query.

Keep going...

Memo to Self: By default, this new Table will be made in the Current Database.

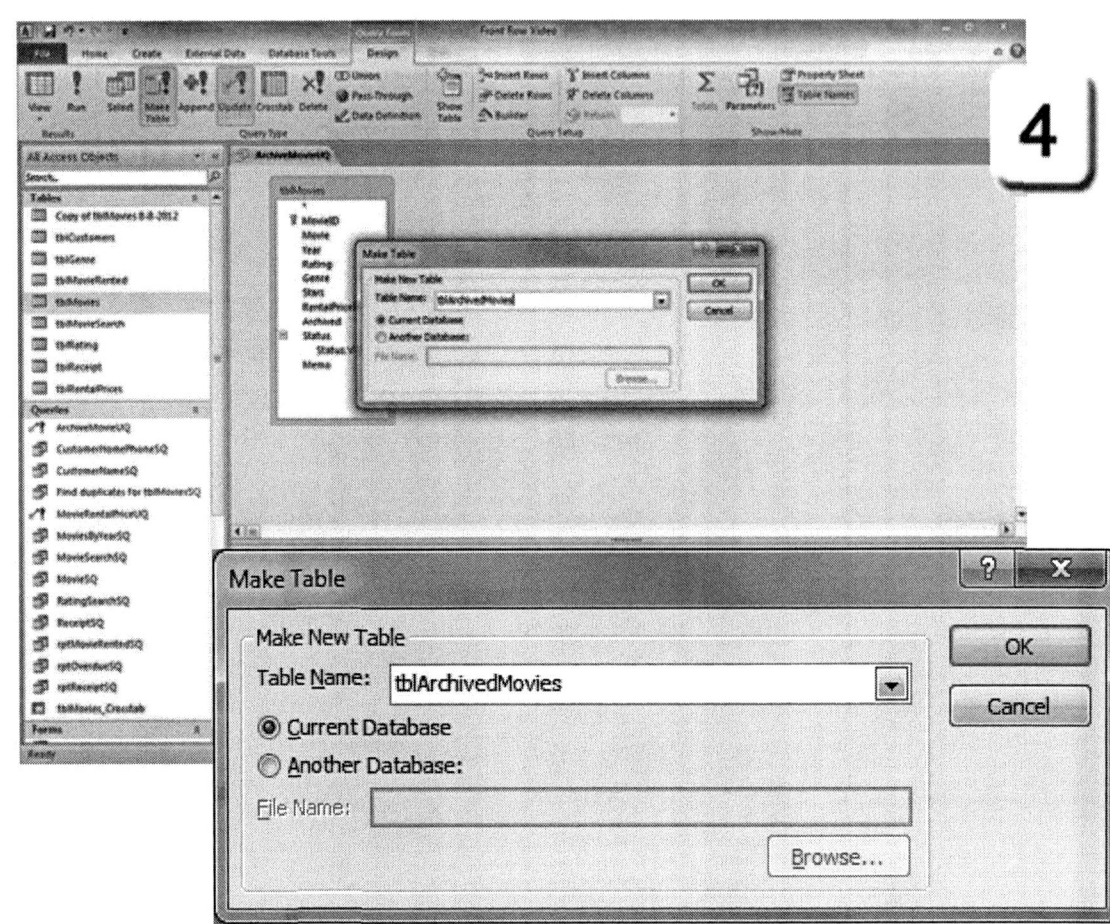

Exam 77-885: Microsoft Access 2010
4. Creating and Managing Queries
4.1. Construct queries: Create an Action Query Make Table

Review the Data

Did all of the Records get copied to the new Table when we ran the Make Table Query?

5. Try it: Review the Data
Go to **All Access Objects->Tables**.
Open a Table: tblArchivedMovies.

What Do You See? There should be 73 Records in tblArchivedMovies.
Close tblArchivedMovies.
OK. Save and Close ArchiveMovieMT.

Little Summary: There are two Queries that can be modified and reused for archiving.

ArchiveMovieUQ: This Query uses a Criteria to Filter the Records by Year. It is an Update Query that will change the Archived Field to "Yes" for all of the selected Records.

ArchiveMovieMT: This Query uses the same Criteria to Filter the Records by Year. The Records that match the Criteria are copied into a Table named tblArchivedMovies.

Query Tools ->Design->Query Type-> Make Table

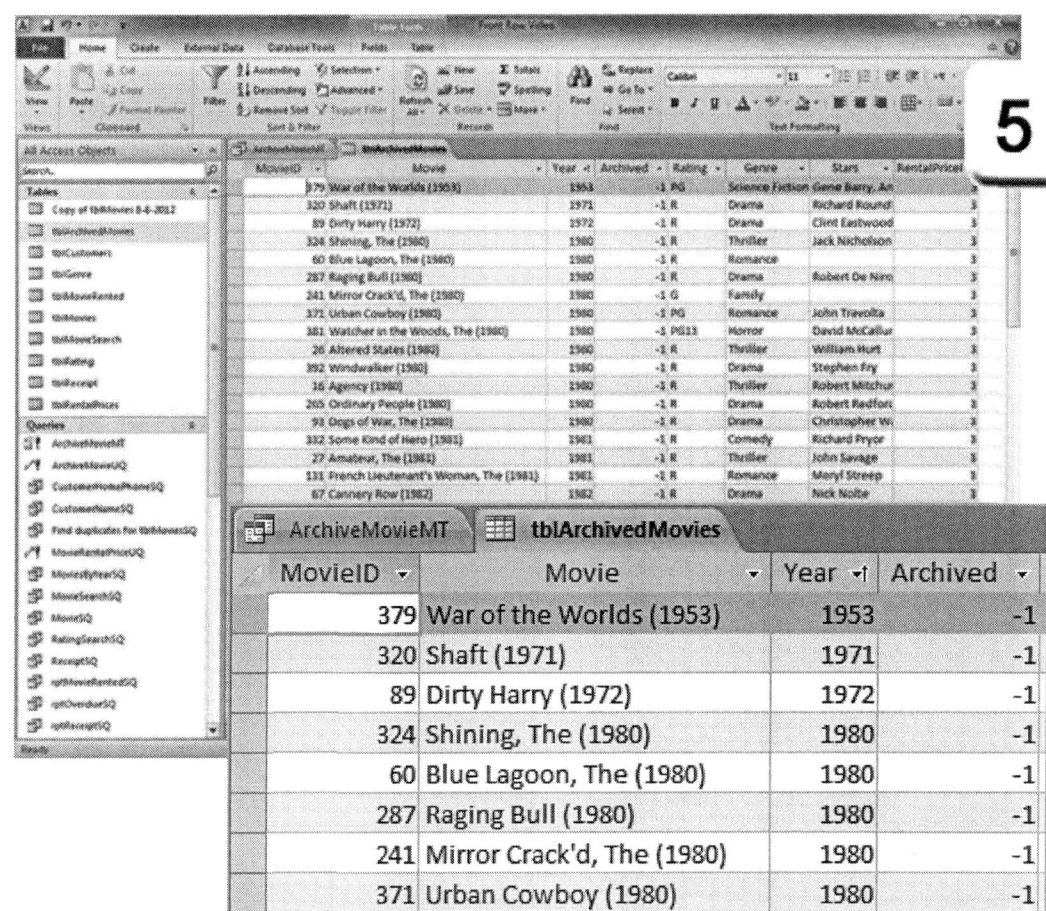

Exam 77-885: Microsoft Access 2010
4. Creating and Managing Queries
4.1. Construct queries: Create an Action Query Make Table

The Last Action Query

A **Delete Query** does exactly what the name spells out: it deletes data. As mentioned earlier, deleting data is not the best practice for a database administrator. However, this option may be better than marking bad records as archived.

The following example will use a copy of the Movie Table to test the Delete Query.

1. Try it: Create a New Query
Go to **Create ->Queries ->Query Design**.
You will be prompted by the Show Table.
Select a Table: Copy of tblMovies 8-8-2012.
Click **Add** and **Close** the Show/Table Window.

Try This, Too: Add Fields
Add these Fields to the QBE Grid: MovieID, Movie, Year, Rating, Genre, Stars and RentalPriceID.

And Try This: Add a Criteria
Select a Field: Year.
Enter a Criteria: <1990

Do This, Now: Run the Select Query
Did this Query select 73 Records?

Create->Queries->Query Design

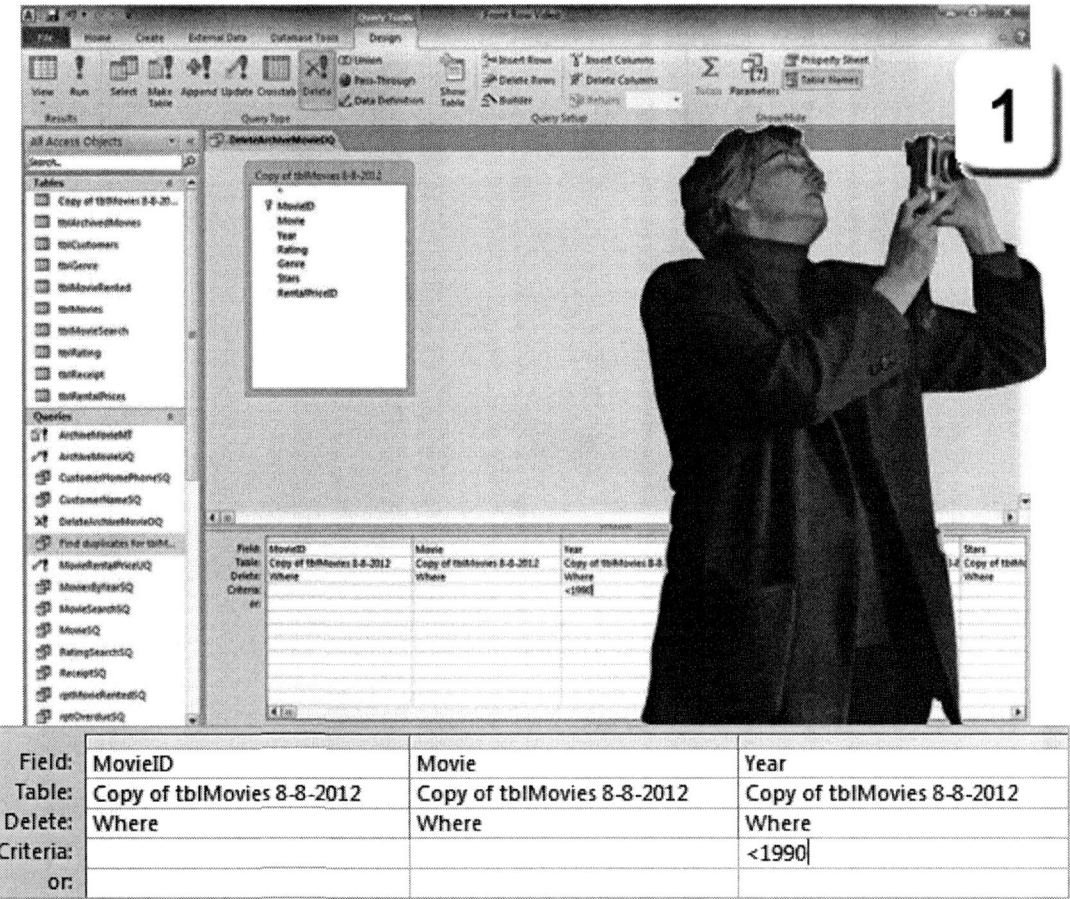

Field:	MovieID	Movie	Year
Table:	Copy of tblMovies 8-8-2012	Copy of tblMovies 8-8-2012	Copy of tblMovies 8-8-2012
Delete:	Where	Where	Where
Criteria:			<1990
or:			

Exam 77-885: Microsoft Access 2010
4. Creating and Managing Queries
4.1. Construct queries: Create a Delete Query

Run the Delete Query

So the Select Query works. Now, you can change it into a Delete Query.

Before You Begin: Change the View
Go to **Home ->Views->View.**
Select a View: Design View.

2. Try it: Create a Delete Query
Go to **Query Tools ->Design->Query Type.**
Select a Query Type: **Delete.**

Try This, Too: Run the Delete Query
Go to **Query Tools ->Design->Results-> Run.**

What Do You See? You will be prompted that you are about to delete 73 Rows. You are also reminded that there is no UNDO. This is permanent data heaven.

Click Yes to delete the data from the **Copy of tblMovies 8-8-2012** Table.

So, let's go see what's left in this Table.

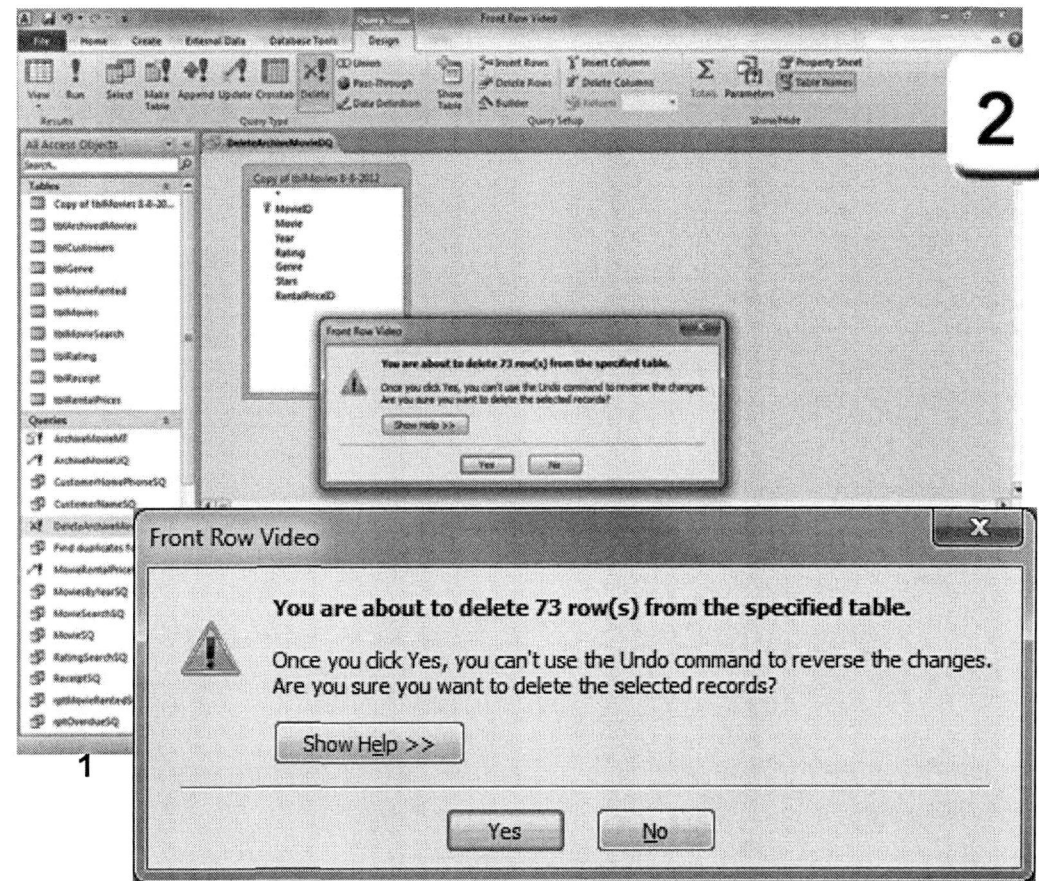

Exam 77-885: Microsoft Access 2010
4. Creating and Managing Queries
4.1. Construct queries: Create a Delete Quer

Review the Data

3. Try it: Review the Data
Go to **All Access Objects->Tables**.
Open a Table:**Copy of tblMovies 8-8-2012**.

Try This, Too: Sort the Records
Select a Field: Year.
Go to **Home ->Sort & Filter->Ascending**.

What Do You See? There were 411 Records in Copy of tblMovies 8-8-2012. The Delete Query deleted 73 movies, leaving 338.

Well, for what it is worth, the movies were effectively deleted as promised.
Close the Copy of the Movies Table.

Do This, Now" Save the Delete Query
Go to **File->Save**.
Enter a name: DeleteArchiveMoviesDQ.
Close the Delete Query.

Home ->Sort & Filter->Ascending

Exam 77-885: Microsoft Access 2010
4. Creating and Managing Queries
4.1. Construct queries: Create a Delete Query

Summary

This discussion began by importing the new movies into the Movie Table and checking for duplicates.

We also created several Action Queries to simplify the task of archiving the old movies. The steps included adding new Fields to the Movie Table: Archived, Status and and Memo. We also added those Fields to the Movies Form.

The Action Queries included:
An Update Query, **ArchiveMovieUQ** to UPDATE the Archive Field to Yes for the old movies.

A Make Table Query, **ArchiveMovieMT,** to copy the Archived Records into a new Table: tblArchiveMovies.

Two new Action Queries to Test the Data:
Find duplicates for tblMoviesSQ
ArchiveMovieMT

Now that was a very good lesson. You done good! Go get the cookies!

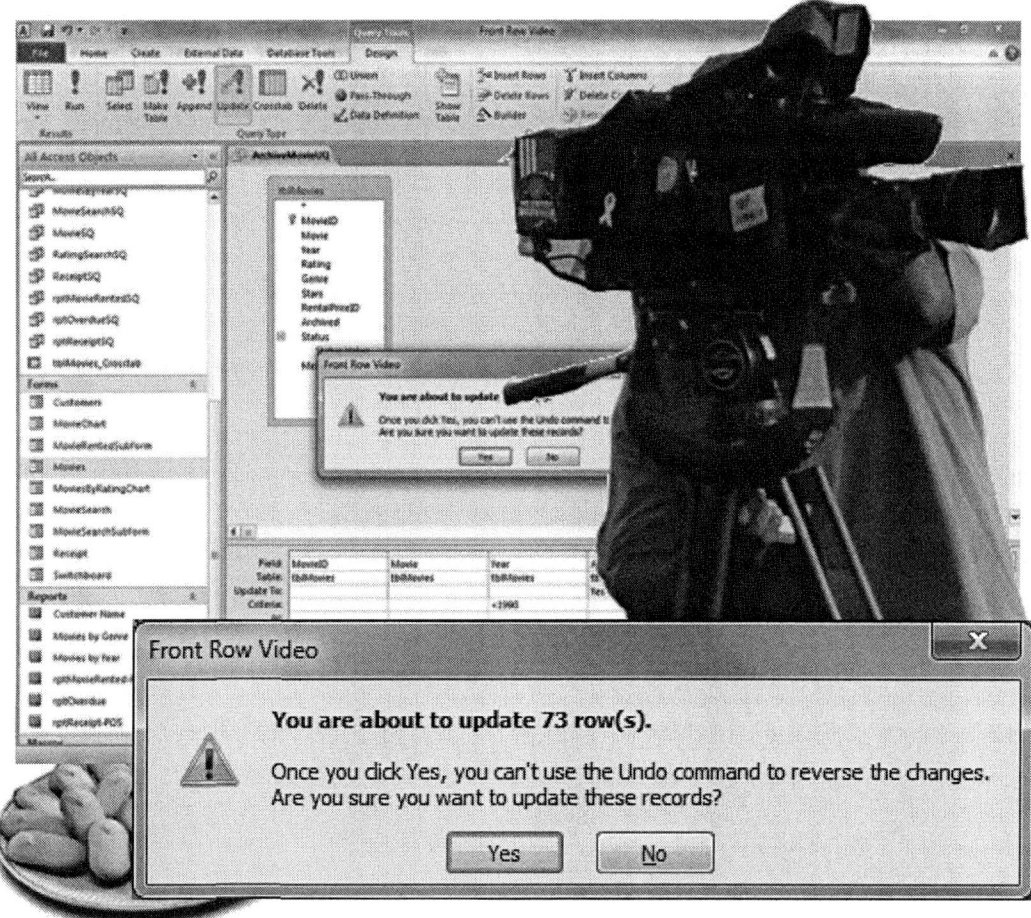

Practice Activities

Lesson 10: Strategies for Archiving

Try This: Do the following steps

1. Open your Brown Bag Lunch database

Or, you may download **BBL Adv ver10.accdb**

2. Edit the Products Table, tblProducts, in Design View. Add the following Fields:
Field Name: Discontinued, Data Type: Yes/No
Field Name: Reason, Data Type: Memo

Save the changes and close the Table.

3. Create a Select Query in Design View. Select tblProducts as the Record Source. Add all of the Fields to the QBE Grid. Run the Query to test it. Return to the Design View.

4. Add a Criteria to the Type Field: "Snacks" Run the Query to test it. Return to the Design View.

5. Change this Select Query to an Update Query.

Update Discontinued to Yes.

Update Memo to: "Not interested in this product."

6. Save the Query as ProductDiscontinedUQ.

7. Run the ProductDiscontinedUQ Update Query and confirm that the data in the Products Table was changed.

8. Close the Update Query.

9. Close the Brown Bag Lunch database.

Test Yourself

1. Which are options for importing External Data? (Give all correct answers.)
A. Import into a new Table
B. Link to an external Table
C. Append (add) Records to a Table
Tip: Advanced Access, page 282

2. Access has a Query specifically for finding duplicate records.
A. True
B. False
Tip: Advanced Access, page 286

3. Which of the following is true about Records? (Give all correct answers.)
A. Deleting is not recommended because it removes a Primary Key number
B. Preferred method of removing Records is to Archive it
Tip: Advanced Access, page 290

4. Which of the following is true about a Multi-Value Field?
(Give all correct answers.)
A. Lets users select more than one answer
B. The creator types a list of values to be chosen from
C. Users can be allowed to add new items to the list
D. Users are always limited to the items in the list
Tip: Advanced Access, page 294, 295

5. Which of the following is true about the Memo Field?
A. It can only hold 40 characters
B. It can hold 2 GB of data
C. Users can only add to the existing data
D. Users can be allowed to delete the existing data
E. When the Memo is set to Append only, users can add to but cannot delete existing data
Tip: Advanced Access, page 296

Access 2010: The Administrator
The Performance Network

Advanced Access Objectives
In this lesson, you will learn how to:

1. Split an Access database into two databases-Tables and User Interface-to deploy the database in a multi-user network.

2. Link the two databases and refresh the links with the Linked Table Manager.

3. Manage the Access Environment and set the Access Options for the General, Datasheet, Object Designers, Client Settings, and the Quick Access Toolbar.

4. Open a database Exclusively and Encrypt it with a Password.

5. Compact and Repair a database.

© 2012 Comma Productions, LLC

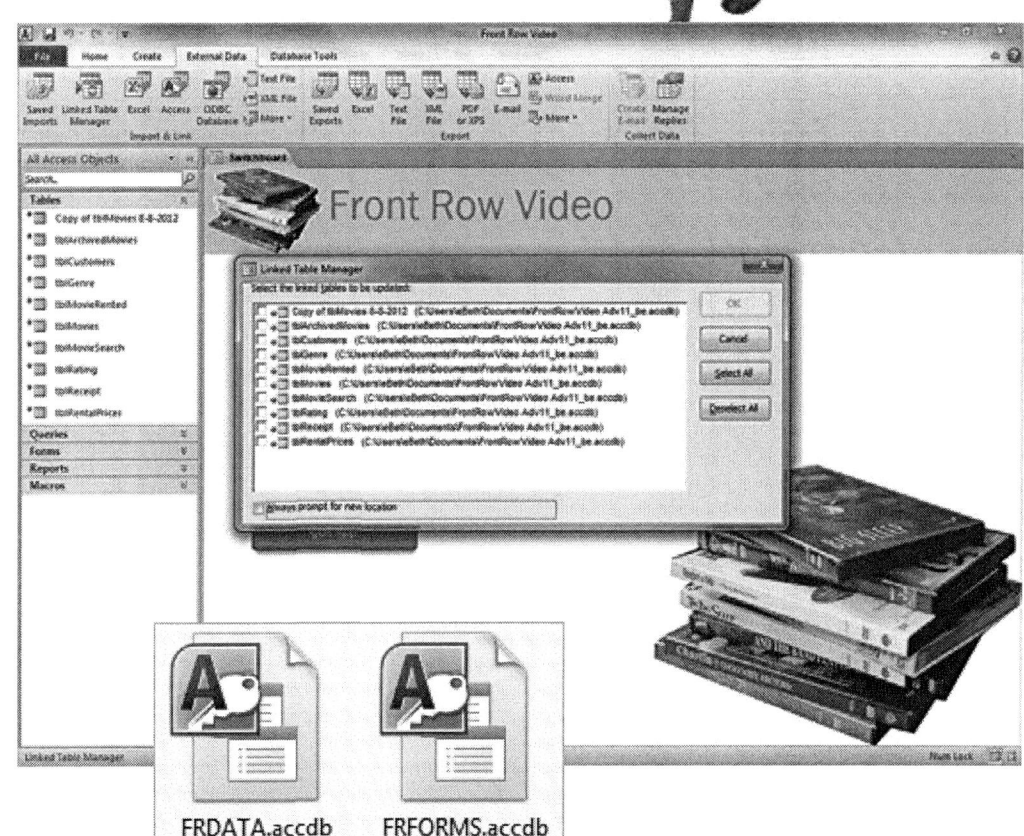

Lesson 11 : The Performance Network

1. Readings

Read Lesson 11 in the Advanced Access guide, page 309-342.

Project

Split a database into two databases and link them together.

Downloads

FrontRowVideo Adv11.accdb
BBL Adv ver10.accdb

2. Practice

Do the Practice Activity on page 343.

3. Assessment

Review the Test questions on page 344.

Get External Data Ribbon

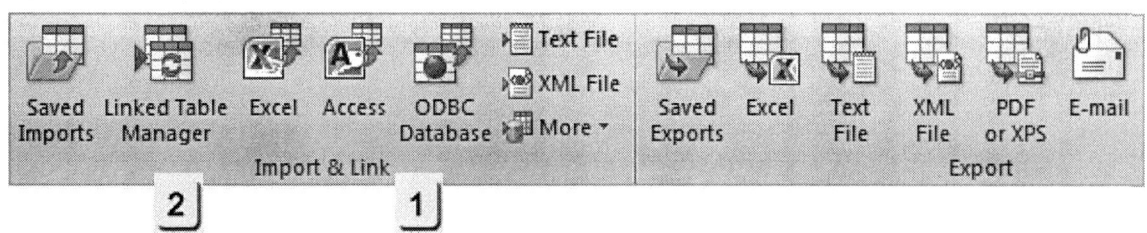

Database Tools Ribbon

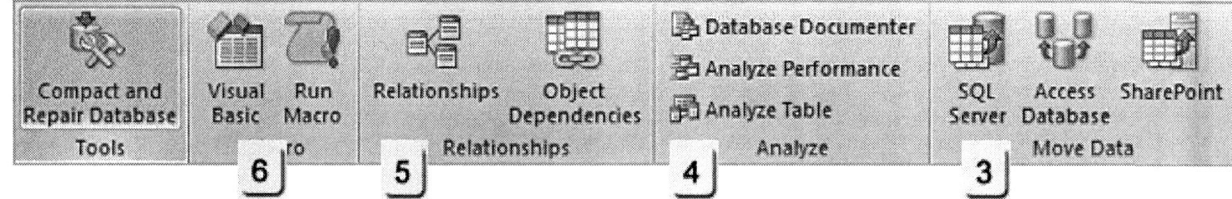

Menu Maps

From the **Get External Data Ribbon**
1. Get External Data ->Import and Link->Access, pg 322
2. Import and Link->Linked Table Manager, pg 325

From the **Database Tools Ribbon**.
3. Database Tools ->Move Data->Access Database, pg 326
4. Database Tools->Analyze->Database Documenter, pg 336
5. Database Tools ->Relationships->Relationships, pg 338
6. Database Tools->Tools->Compact and Repair, pg 341

More Menu Maps

From the **File Menus**
File->Options, pg 329
File ->Open->Open Exclusively, pg 334
File ->Info->Encrypt with Password, pg 335

Standing Room Only

The Mighty Access database you have been programming is alllllmost ready to be released to Real Users. This database works well on one computer. However, the Front Row Video store has several Point of Sale (POS) computers so that many customers can pay quickly. Is there a way that all of the POS computers can share the same database? **Yes!**

Microsoft Office Access 2010: Example of the Linked Tables

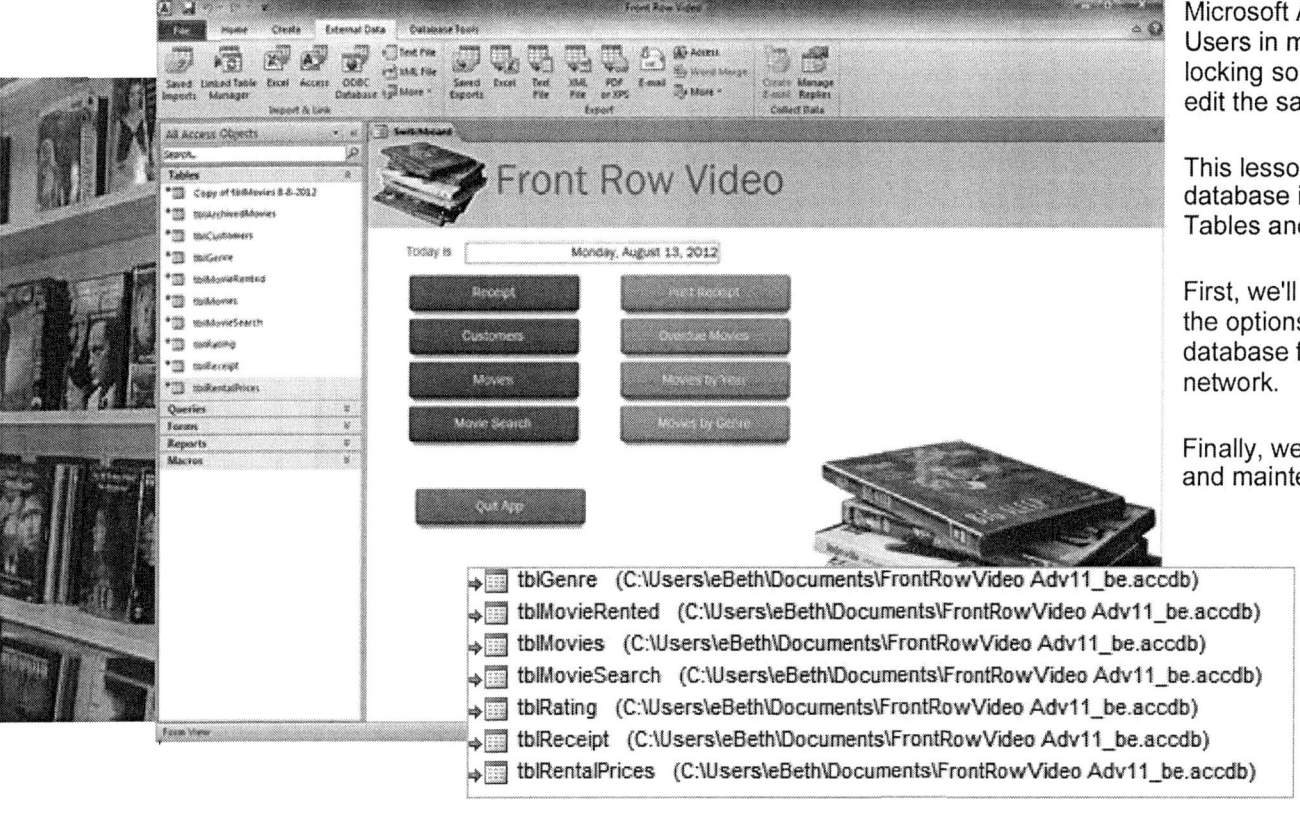

Microsoft Access can support hundreds of Users in many locations. Access has record locking so that two Users don't accidently edit the same record at the same time.

This lesson looks at ways to split the database into two databases: one with the Tables and the other with everything else.

First, we'll analyze the Tables and discuss the options. Then, we'll optimize the database for performance in a multiuser network.

Finally, we'll look at the database security and maintenance.

The Performance Network

Running a database over a network brings up the question of speed and implementation. Previous versions of Microsoft Access (97-2003) were very slow on a LAN. How slow? In some offices, it would take up to 45 seconds for a report to come up in print preview.

What is the slowest part of the database?
Forms and reports. The forms are slow because they are big fat elephants stomping on the network. Forms and Reports make up 90% of the size of a database. In a 20 MB database, the Tables use only use 1 or 2 MB.

A new database structure
Microsoft Access is built on the XML source code. XML means Extended Markup Language. It is an Internet programming language. As a result of the new file structure, Microsoft Access 2007 and 2010 databases are much, much smaller and more responsive than older databases.

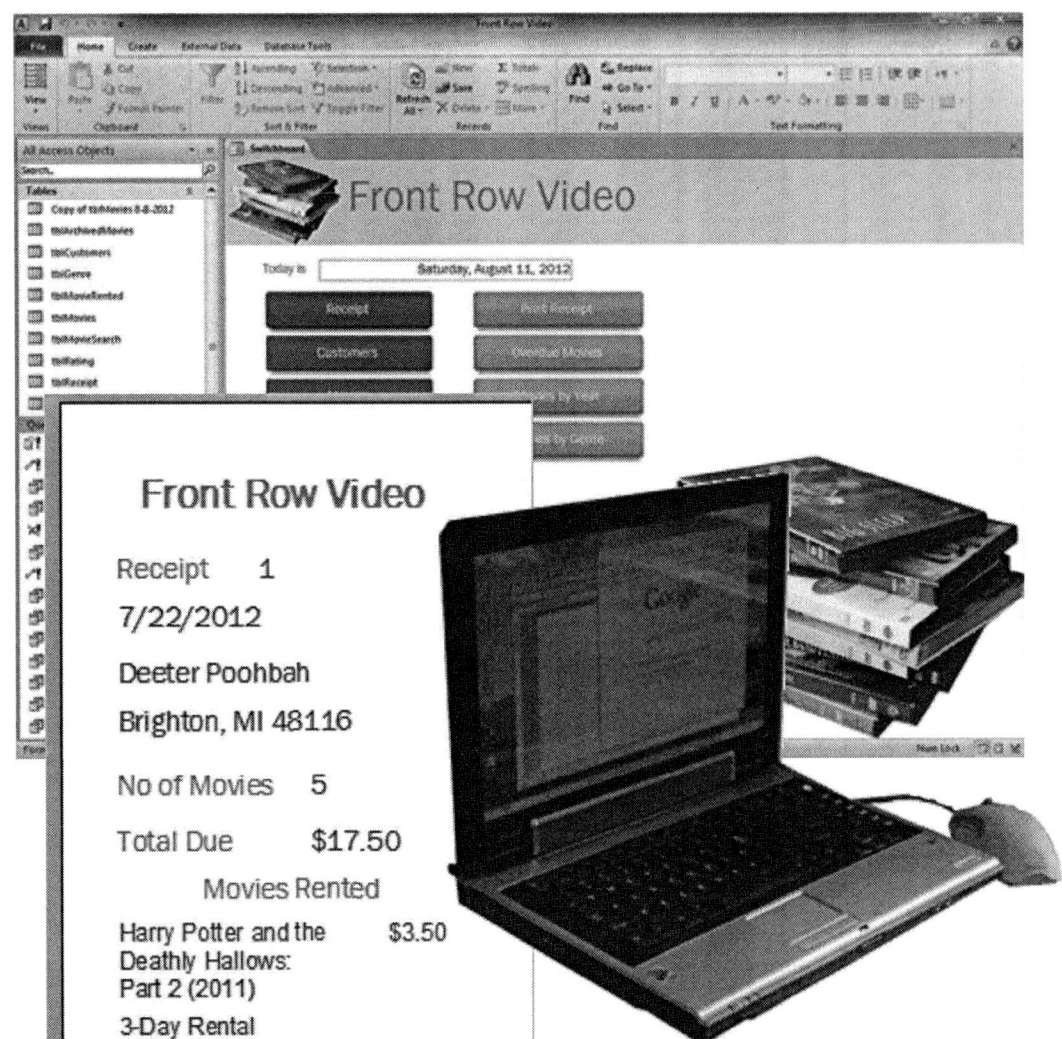

Database Optimization

If you separate the **Forms** from the **Tables** you can work with the elephants on the workstation, and link to the Tables on the server. This is one more step in **Normalizing** the database.

When you began with the Table definitions, you separated like with like. Each Table was a unique collection. The Movie Table contains movie data, not customer phone numbers.

The goal is to create two databases that are **linked** together. One database will contain **nothing but** Tables. This database will be placed on the Server.

The other database will have **everything but** the tables. This can be your user's application and it can run on their own hard drive.

Where should you put the Tables?

The best location would be a Server. All of the computers would connect to the Server to run the database. The Server's job is network storage, backups, and user management, so your database would be in good hands.

Example of a database that has been split into two files: Data and Forms

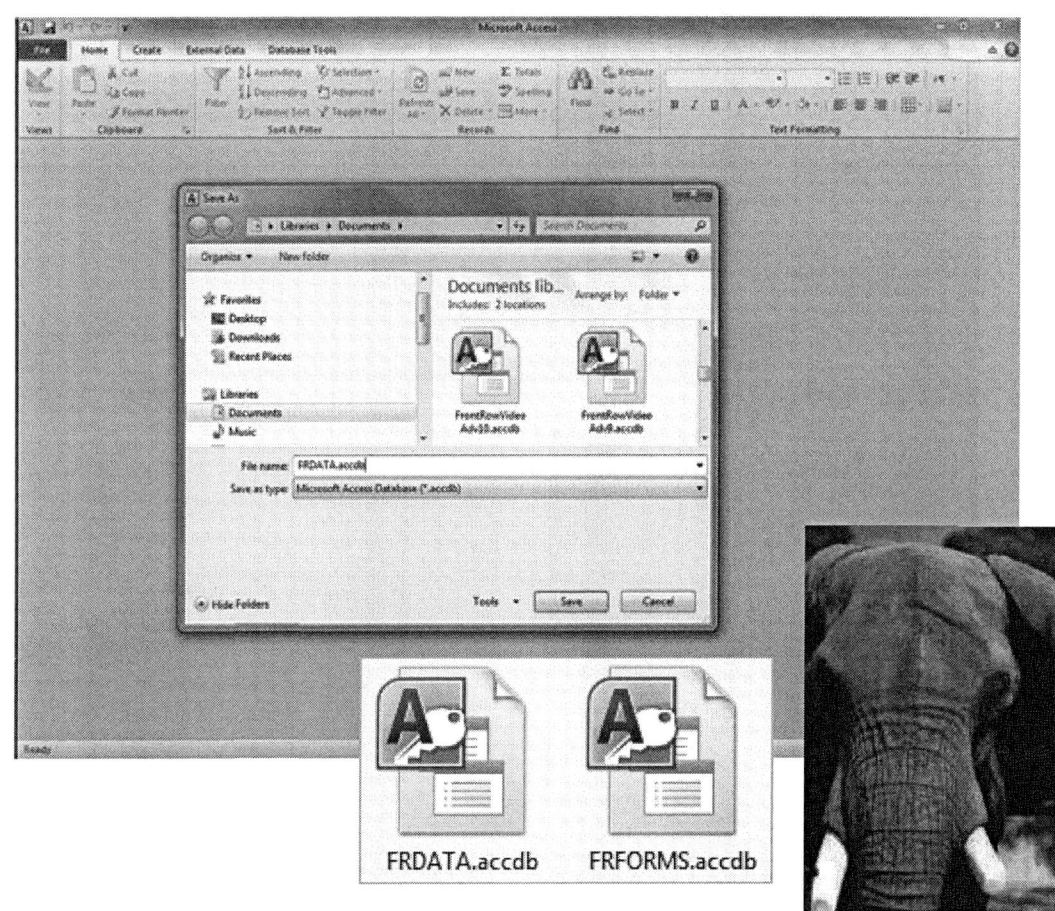

FRDATA.accdb   FRFORMS.accdb

Why Split the Database?

Performance is one reason for splitting a database. The Forms and Reports run locally. Hence, the only information that passes across the network is the data.

Archiving is very useful if you want to filter and backup old Records. Splitting the database is not the same as archiving, or moving old Records into another database. One method for archiving records was discussed in the previous lesson.

There are several steps required to split a database into Linked Table. We'll begin by creating a Backup Copy of the database.

In the first example we'll split the database by hand and consider the options. The Tables will be Linked as External Data, so we'll use the Linked Table Manager. We'll review the Database Splitter, an automated process that's available in Access.

Finally, we'll prepare to release the database. We'll set the Security and print out the Database Documentation. So, that's about it.

Microsoft Office Access 2010: Example of a database with Linked Tables

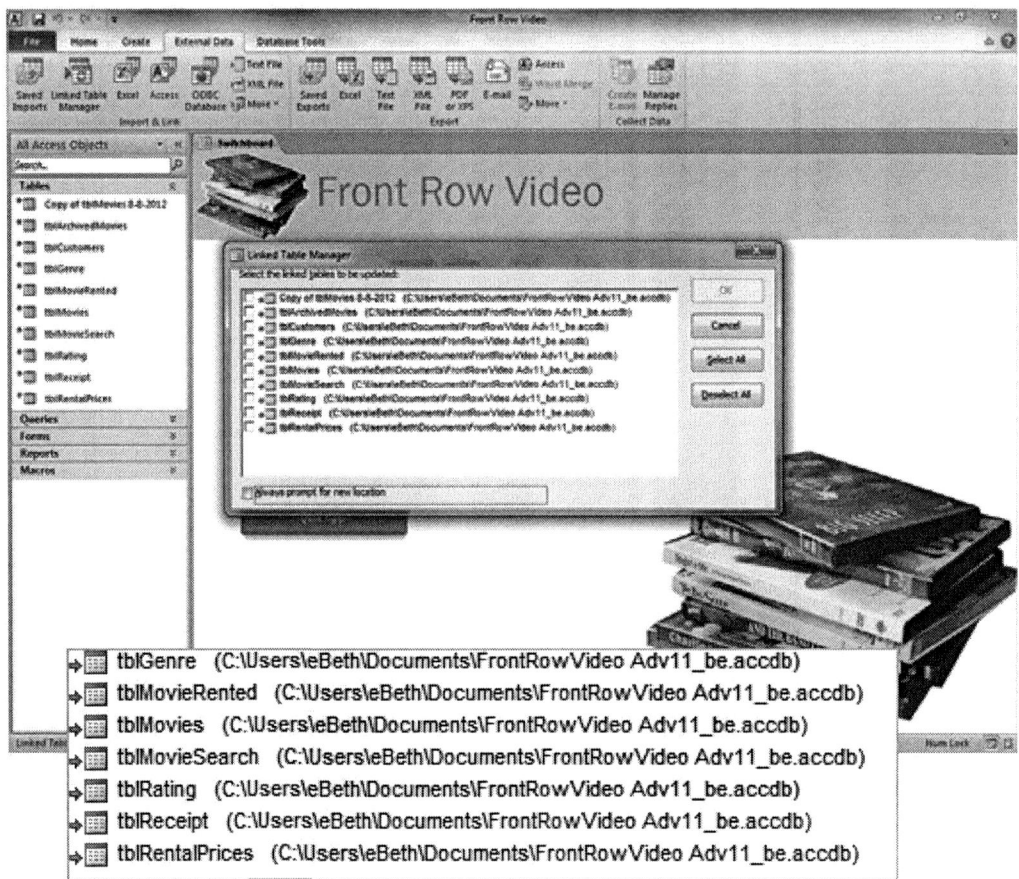

tblGenre   (C:\Users\eBeth\Documents\FrontRowVideo Adv11_be.accdb)

tblMovieRented   (C:\Users\eBeth\Documents\FrontRowVideo Adv11_be.accdb)

tblMovies   (C:\Users\eBeth\Documents\FrontRowVideo Adv11_be.accdb)

tblMovieSearch   (C:\Users\eBeth\Documents\FrontRowVideo Adv11_be.accdb)

tblRating   (C:\Users\eBeth\Documents\FrontRowVideo Adv11_be.accdb)

tblReceipt   (C:\Users\eBeth\Documents\FrontRowVideo Adv11_be.accdb)

tblRentalPrices   (C:\Users\eBeth\Documents\FrontRowVideo Adv11_be.accdb)

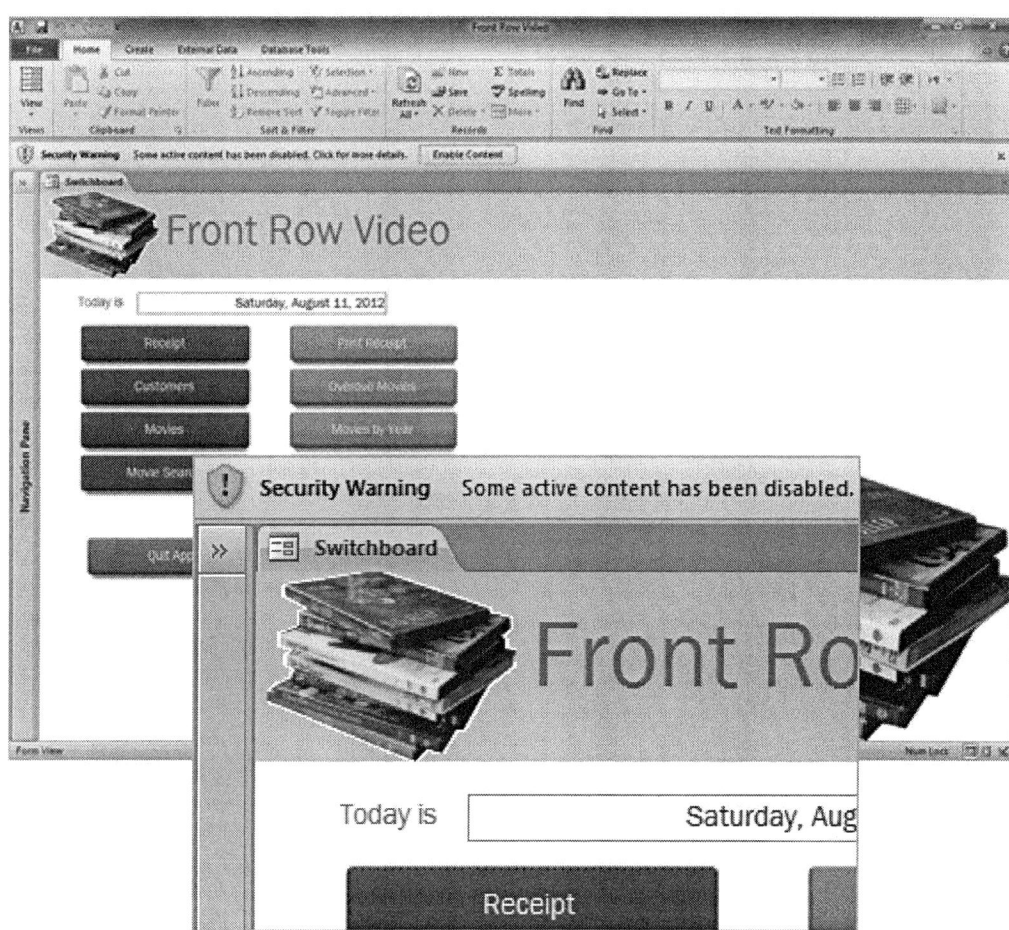

Start ->All Programs-> Microsoft Office-> Microsoft Access 2010

Before You Begin

Before You Begin: Open the Sample Database Go to **Start -> All Programs ->Microsoft Office**.
Click on **Microsoft Office Access 2010**.

Access will prompt you to open a database.
Select: <u>FrontRowVideo Adv11.accdb</u>

The sample file, <u>FrontRowVideo Adv11.accdb,</u> was developed in the previous lesson. If you have been following along in this book, you can continue with your own database if you wish.

Did You Notice? The final database has an updated Switchboard Form. There is a Command Button for every Form and Report that the User needs. You can add the buttons to your Switchboard Form if you wish.

Keep going...

Memo to Self: Databases need to Read and Write. Click **Enable Content** if you see the Security Warning.

Make COPIES of the Database

Begin by making TWO copies of the database: one for the Tables and another one for everything else. Here are the steps.

Before You Begin: Copy the Database
Close and **Save** all Access Objects. If a Table, Form, Query or Report is open, Access will close all open objects before creating the Save As.

Go to **File ->Save Database As.**
Browse to your Documents folder.
Enter the **name:** FRFORMS,
Where FR means Front Row Video and FORMS indicates that this database has the User Interface.
Click **Save**

And Try This: Create a Second Copy
Go to **File ->Save Database As.**
Browse to your Documents folder.
Enter the **name:** FRDATA.
Click **Save**

What Do You See? There should be two new databases in your Documents folder.

File->Save Database As

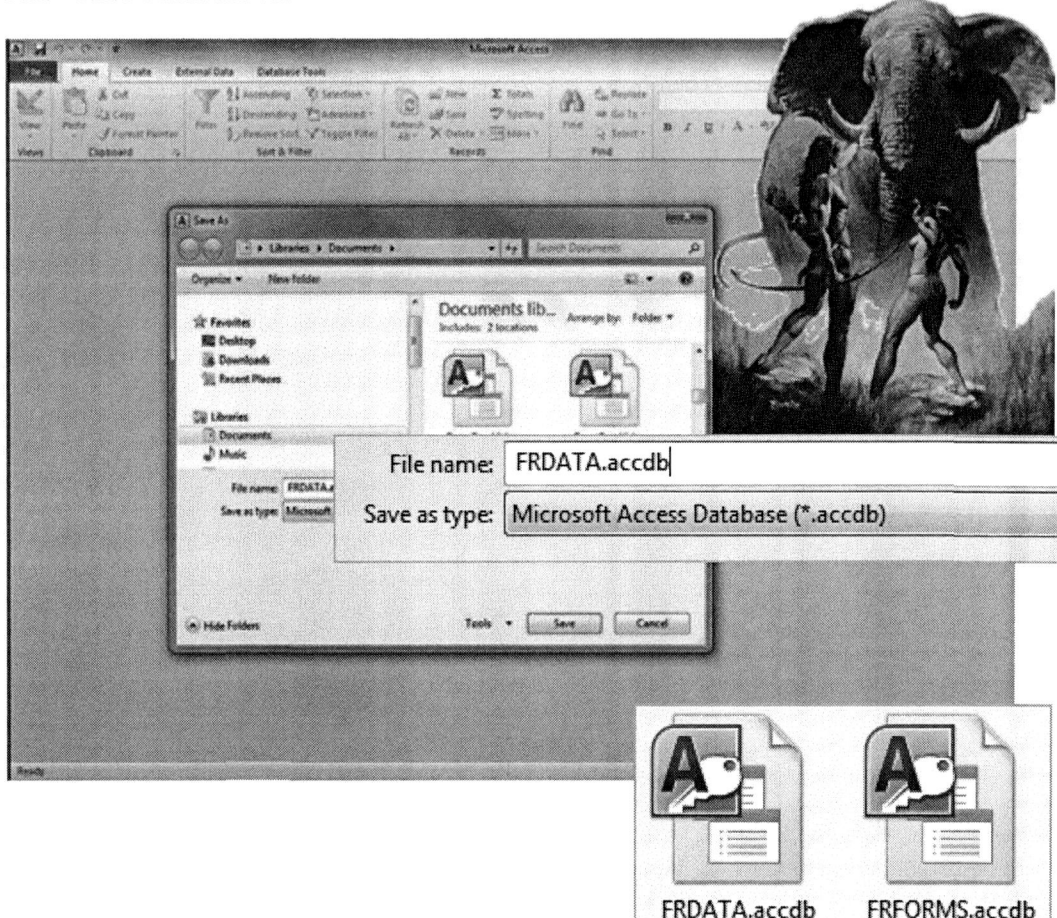

FRDATA.accdb   FRFORMS.accdb

Review the FRDATA Database

1. Try This: Review the Data Database
The FRDATA database is open.

The FRDATA database has the following:
Ten Tables: Copy of tblMovies 8-8-2012, tblArchivedMovies, tblCustomers, tblGenre, tblMovieRented, tblMovies, tblMovieSearch, tblRating, tblReceipt and tblRentalPrices.

Sixteen Queries: ARchiveMovieMT, ArchiveMovieUQ, CustomerHomePhoneSQ, CustomerNameSQ, DeleteArchiveMovieDQ, Find duplicate for tblMoviesSQ, MovieRentalPriceUQ, MoviesByYearSQ, MovieSearchSQ, MovieSQ, RatingSearchSQ, ReceiptSQ, rptMovieRentedSQ, rptOverdueSQ and rptReceiptSQ.

Eight Forms: Customers, Movies, MoviesRentedSubform, MoviesByRatingChart, MovieSearch, MovieSearchSubform, Receipt and MoviesRentedSubform.

Six Reports: Customer Name. Movies by Genre, Movies by Year, rptReceipt-POS, rptOverdue and rptReceipt-POS.

One Macro: OpenSearchMovie

We will delete everything BUT the Tables.

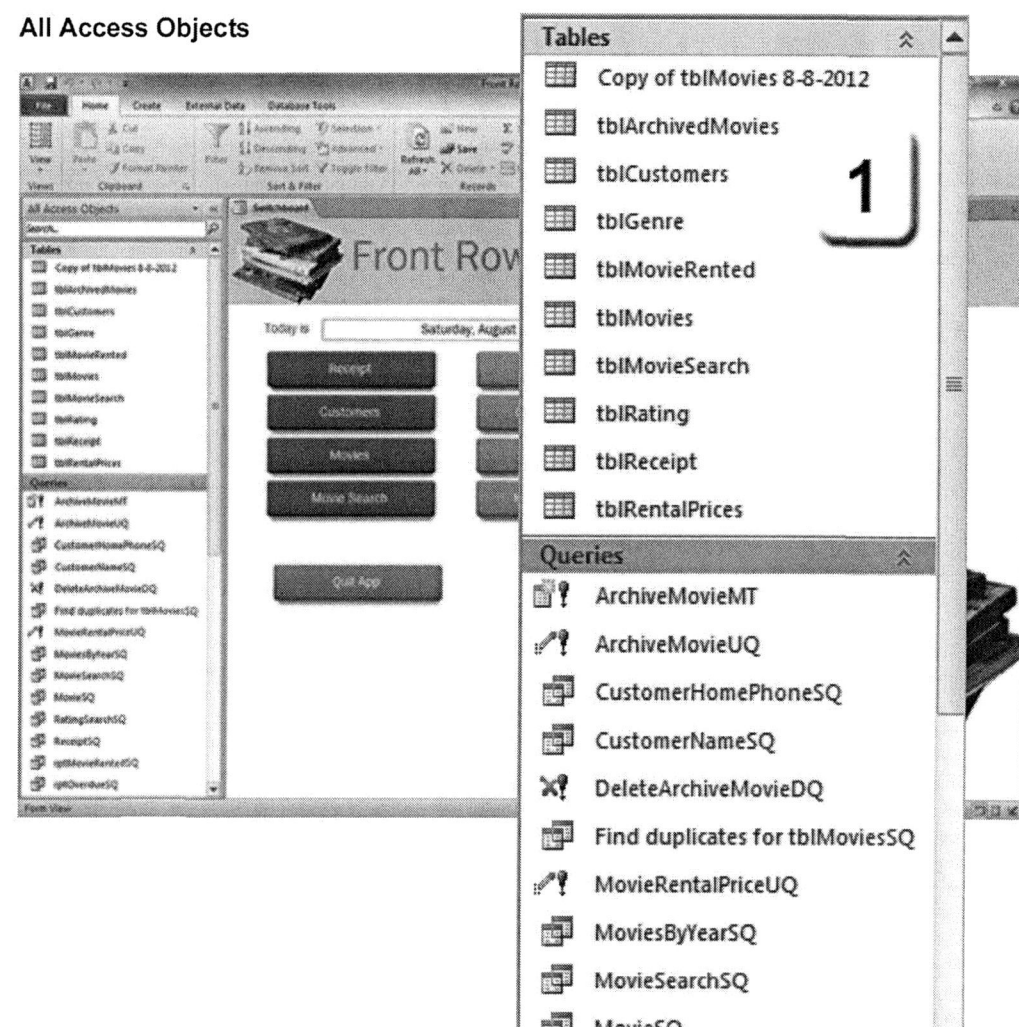

All Access Objects

Tables	
Copy of tblMovies 8-8-2012	
tblArchivedMovies	
tblCustomers	
tblGenre	
tblMovieRented	
tblMovies	
tblMovieSearch	
tblRating	
tblReceipt	
tblRentalPrices	

Queries	
ArchiveMovieMT	
ArchiveMovieUQ	
CustomerHomePhoneSQ	
CustomerNameSQ	
DeleteArchiveMovieDQ	
Find duplicates for tblMoviesSQ	
MovieRentalPriceUQ	
MoviesByYearSQ	
MovieSearchSQ	
MovieSQ	

Delete Everything But the Tables
2. Try This: Delete the Access Objects
Go to **All Access Objects ->Forms.**
Delete a **Form: Customer.**

What Do You See? You will be prompted that this action is permanent: there is no Undo.
Click OK to delete the Form.

Try This: Delete Everything by the Tables
Select and delete the following:
8 Forms
16 Queries
6 Reports
1 Macro

Keep going...

Memo to Self: You have to close the Switchboard Form before you can delete it.

The Computer Mama sez: Remember, this is a COPY of the original database!

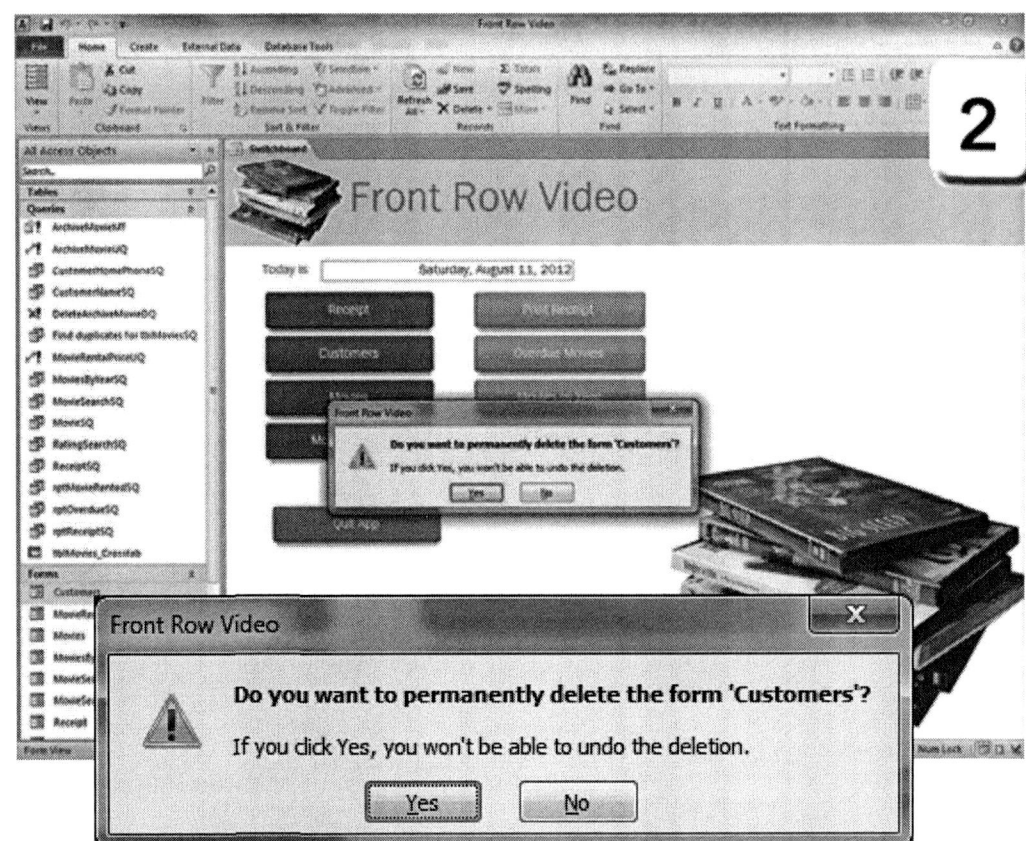

Exam 77-885: Microsoft Access 2010
1. Managing the Access Environment
1.2. Configure the Navigation Pane: Delete Objects

Just Tables, Nothing Else

The Switchboard Form was programmed to open when the database is launched. However, the Switchboard Form has been deleted. Please edit the Access Options.

3. Try it: Edit the Access Options
Go to **File-Options->Current Database**.
Display Form: none.
Click **OK**.

Done and Done,
Close the FRDATA database. It is ready.

File ->Options ->Current Database

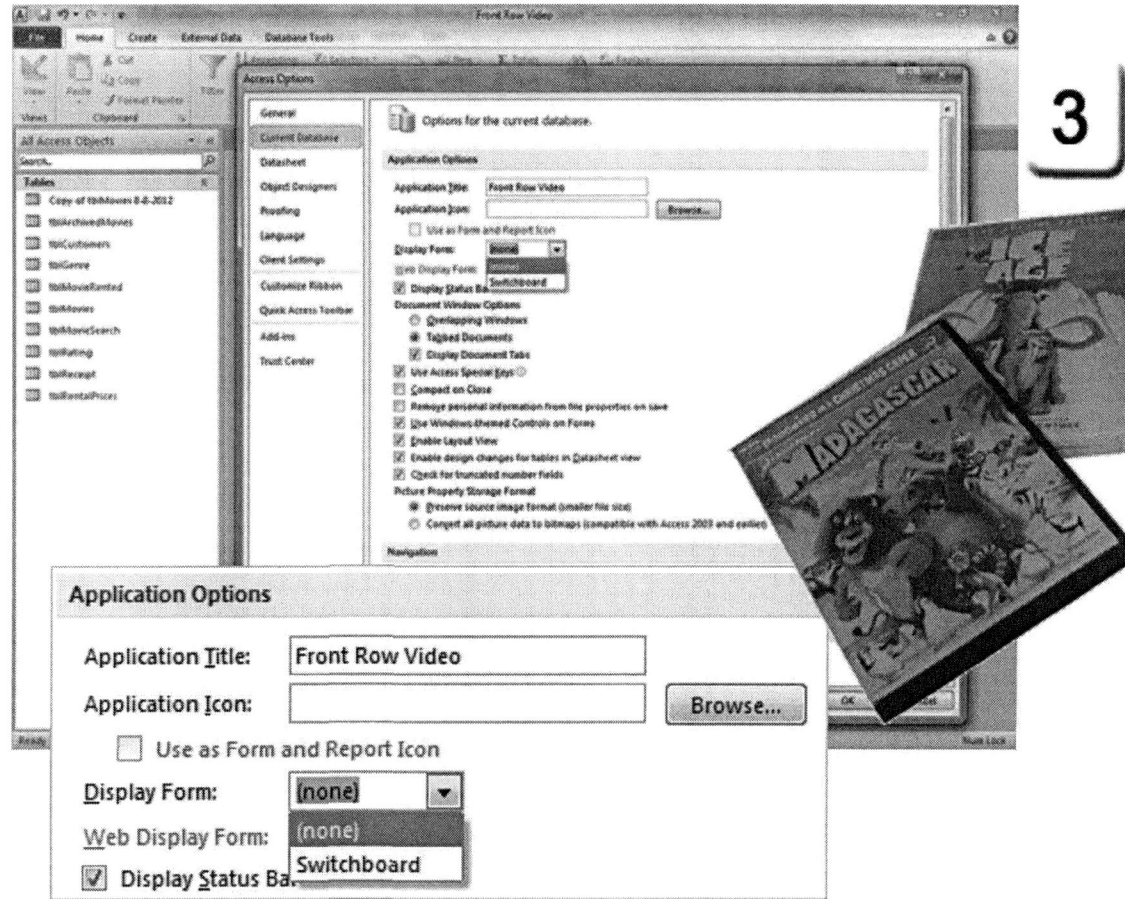

Exam 77-885: Microsoft Access 2010
1. Managing the Access Environment
1.1. Create and manage a database: Set Access Options

Prepare the Forms Database

We just created and reviewed a Data database that only has Tables. The next step is to prepare the Forms database.

The FRFORMS database has everything the User works with: Forms, Queries, Reports and Macros. The Forms database will be installed on the User's computer so it will run very quickly. The Tables will be deleted and then this database will be LINKED to the FRDATA database.

4. Try it: Open the Forms Database
Go to **Start -> All Programs ->Microsoft Office.**
Click on **Microsoft Office Access 2010.**
Access will prompt you to open a database.
Select: **FRFORMS.accb.** If there is a security banner, please Enable the database.

Try This, Too: Delete the Tables
Go to **All Access Objects->Tables.**
Delete the Tables.

Better keep going...

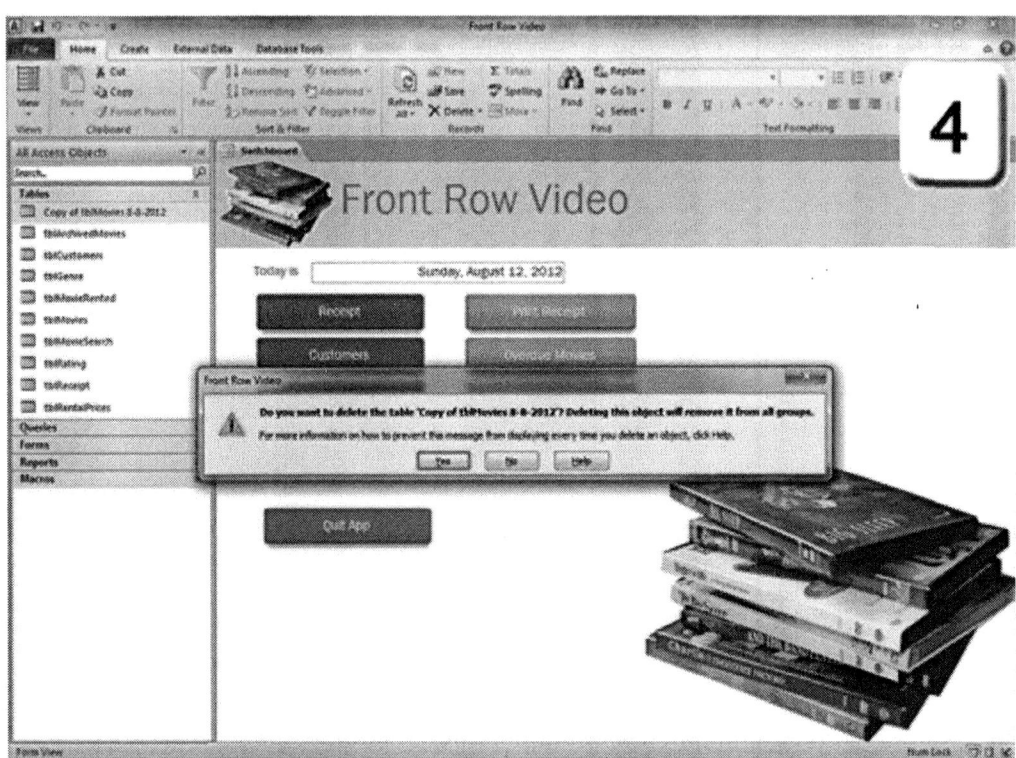

Exam 77-885: Microsoft Access 2010
1. Managing the Access Environment
1.2. Configure the Navigation Pane: Delete Objects

Delete the Relationships

5 .What Do You See? The Tables are linked to one another by the Key Data. You will be asked to delete the relationships before you can delete the Tables.

Click **Yes.** Keep going...

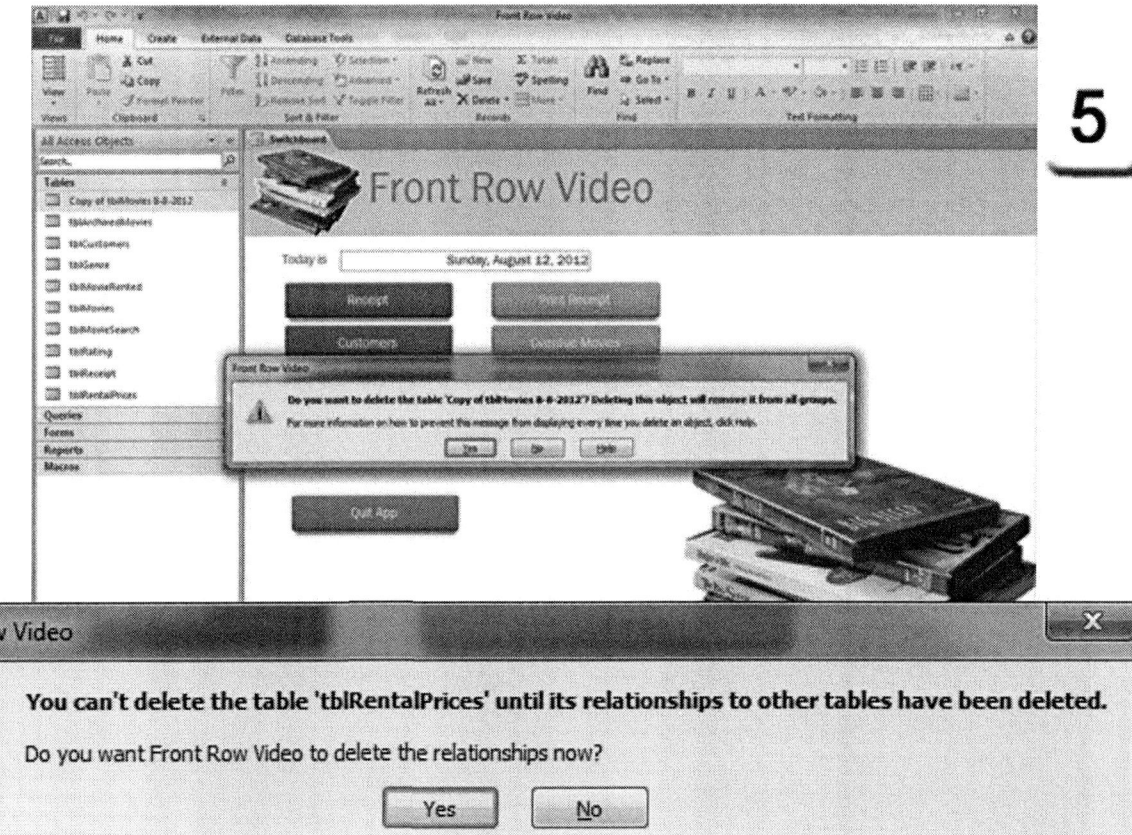

You can't delete the table 'tblRentalPrices' until its relationships to other tables have been deleted.

Do you want Front Row Video to delete the relationships now?

Yes   No

Exam 77-885: Microsoft Access 2010
1. Managing the Access Environment
1.2. Configure the Navigation Pane: Delete Objects

Get External Data

The Forms database needs to **link** to the Tables in the Data database. (Nothing works without the Tables!) The data is imported as **External Data**.

6. Try it: Get External Data
Go to **Get External Data ->Import and Link.**
Click on: **Access**.

What Do You See? The **Get External Data Wizard** will prompt you to **Browse** to the folder that has the FRDATA database and select it.

Try This, Too: Select a Destination
Specify: Link to the data source by creating a linked table.

Click **OK**. Keep going...

Get External Data ->Import and Link->Access

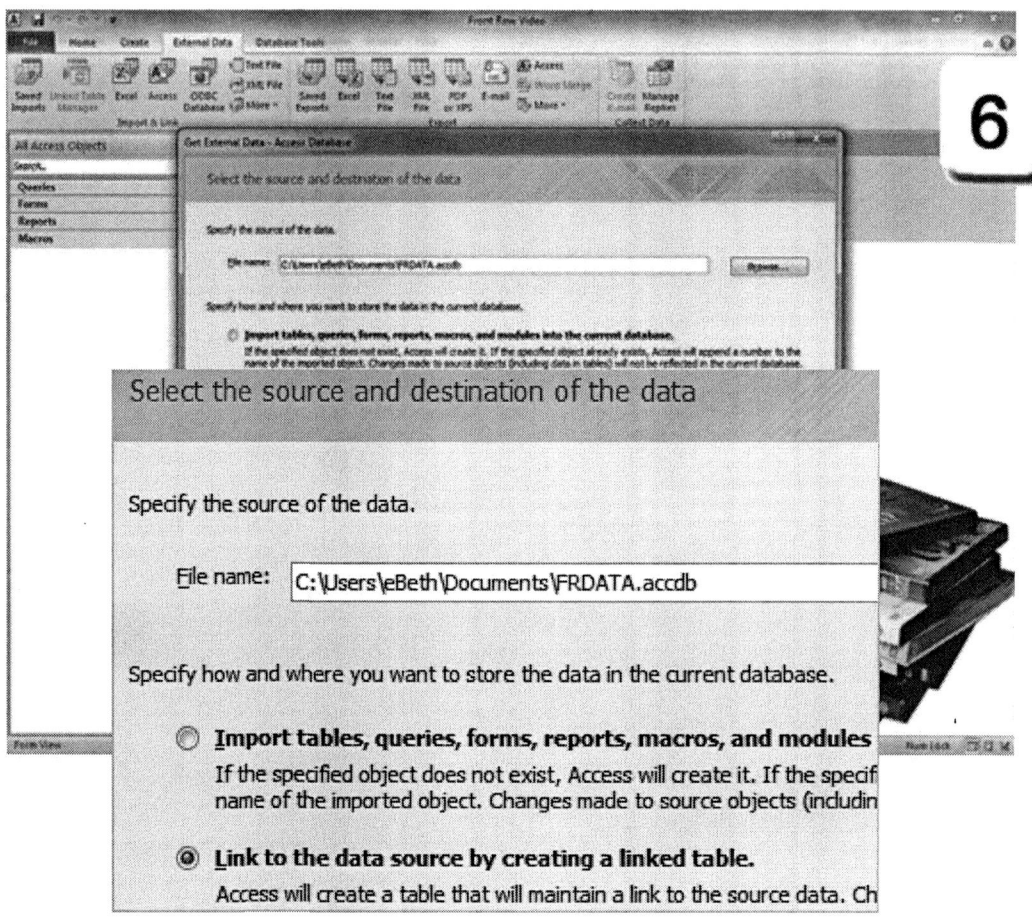

Exam 77-885: Microsoft Access 2010
2. Building Tables
2.5. Import data from a single data file: Import data as Linked Tables

Select and Link the Tables

7. Try it: Link Tables

The Wizard will list the Tables in the FRDATA database. You can select one, some or all depending on the purpose of the application. For instance, the Receipt Tables could be linked to a different financial reports database. In our example we want all of them.

Click **Select All**.
Click **OK**. Keep going...

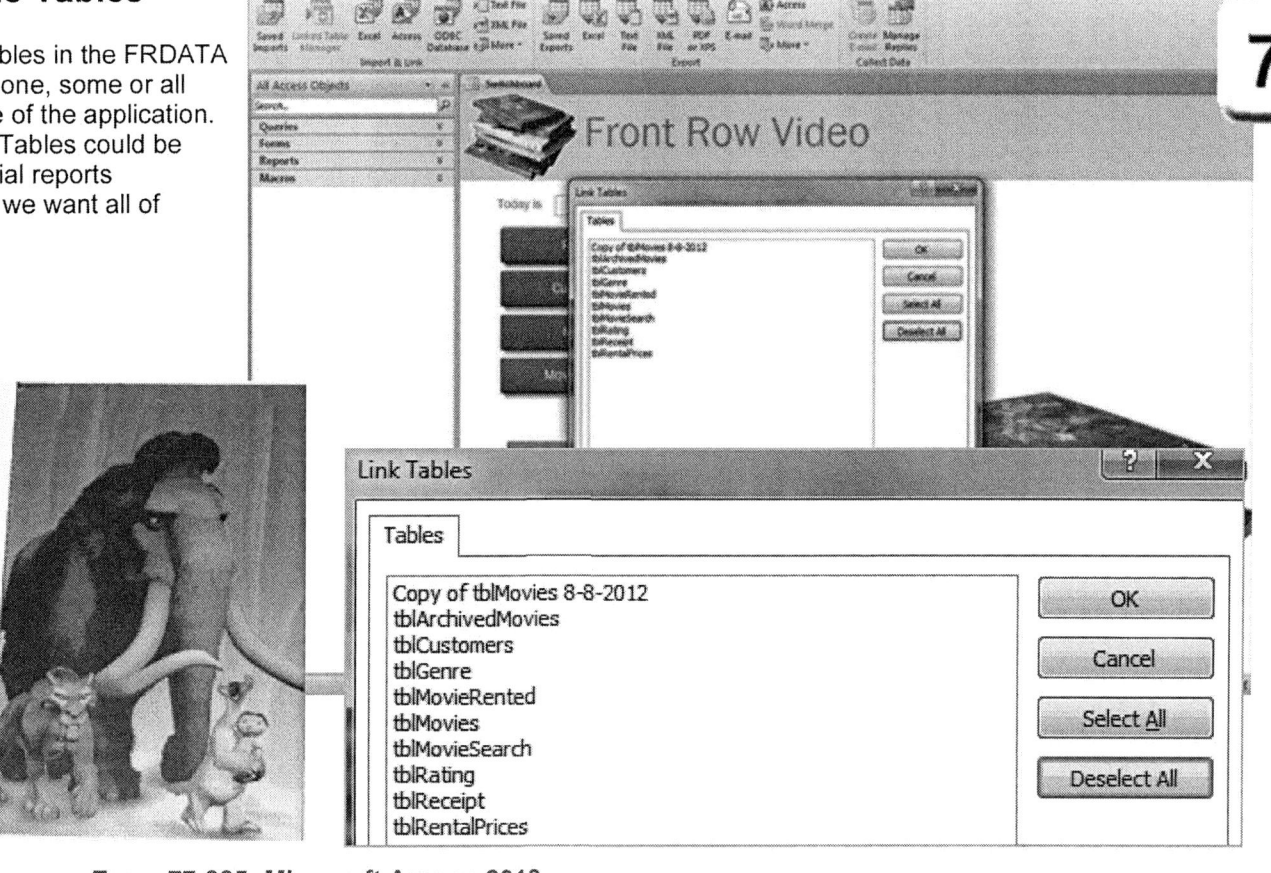

Exam 77-885: Microsoft Access 2010
2. Building Tables
2.5. Import data from a single data file: Import data as Linked Tables

Get External Data ->Import and Link->Access

Hello, Linked Tables!

The Linked Tables have a different icon than the Tables that were created in this Database.

8. Try it: Review the Linked Tables
Go to **All Access Objects->Tables**.
Open any Table and review the data.

These are "live" connections. Whatever you edit in a Form will change the information in these linked Tables.

Each Point of Sale computer in the Front Row Video Store would have a copy of the User interface (Forms, Queries and Reports), FRFORMS.accdb.

All of the FRFORMS databases are linked to the same Tables: FRDATA.accdb.

This works!!

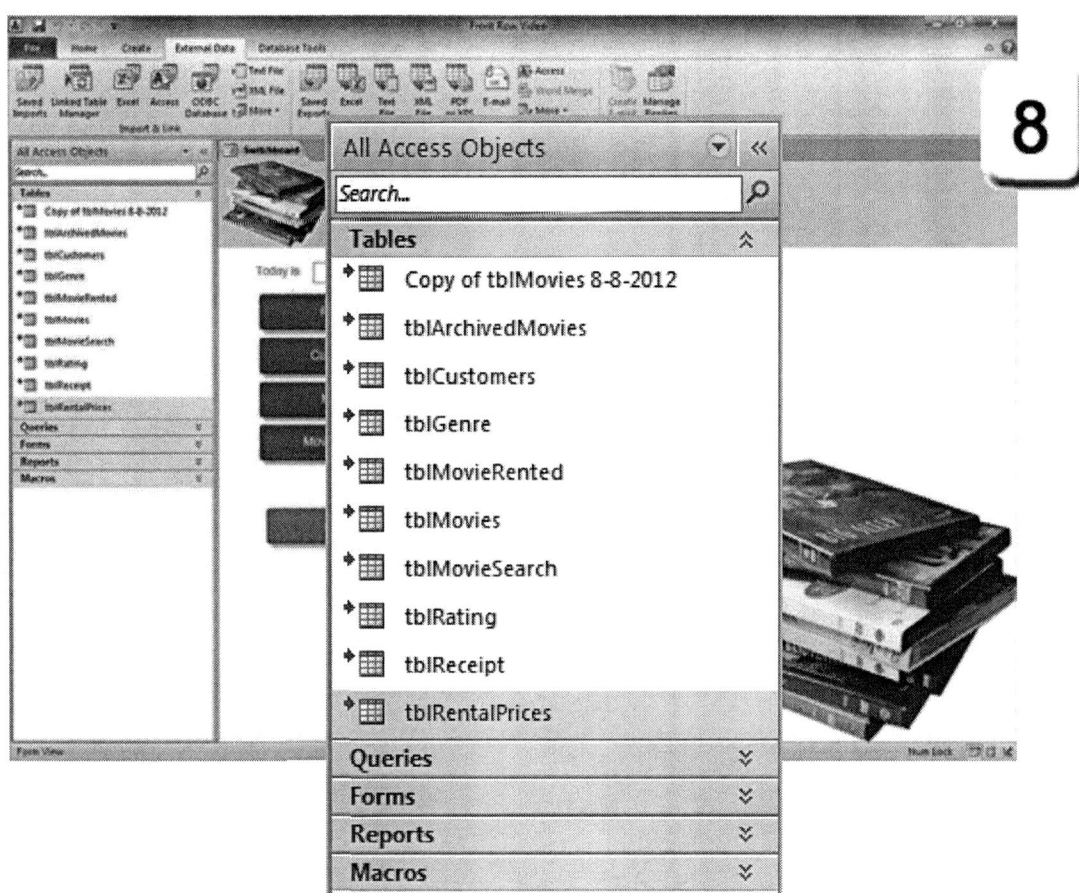

8

Exam 77-885: Microsoft Access 2010
2. Building Tables
2.5. Import data from a single data file: Import data as Linked Tables

Linked Table Manager

What happens to the Linked Tables if the FRDATA database is moved to a different server? Microsoft Access has a way to refresh the links: the **Linked Table Manager**.

9. Try it: Manage the Linked Tables
Go to **Get External Data ->Import and Link**. Select **Linked Table Manager**.

What Do You See? The Linked Table Manager lists the Tables that are linked to this database.

Try This, Too: Prompt for a New Location
When you select this option, Access will bring up a Browser window so that you can seek the new location. Select the FRDATA database.

Click **OK**. The Linked Table Manager will confirm that the linked Tables were successfully refreshed. **Close** the Linked Table Manager.

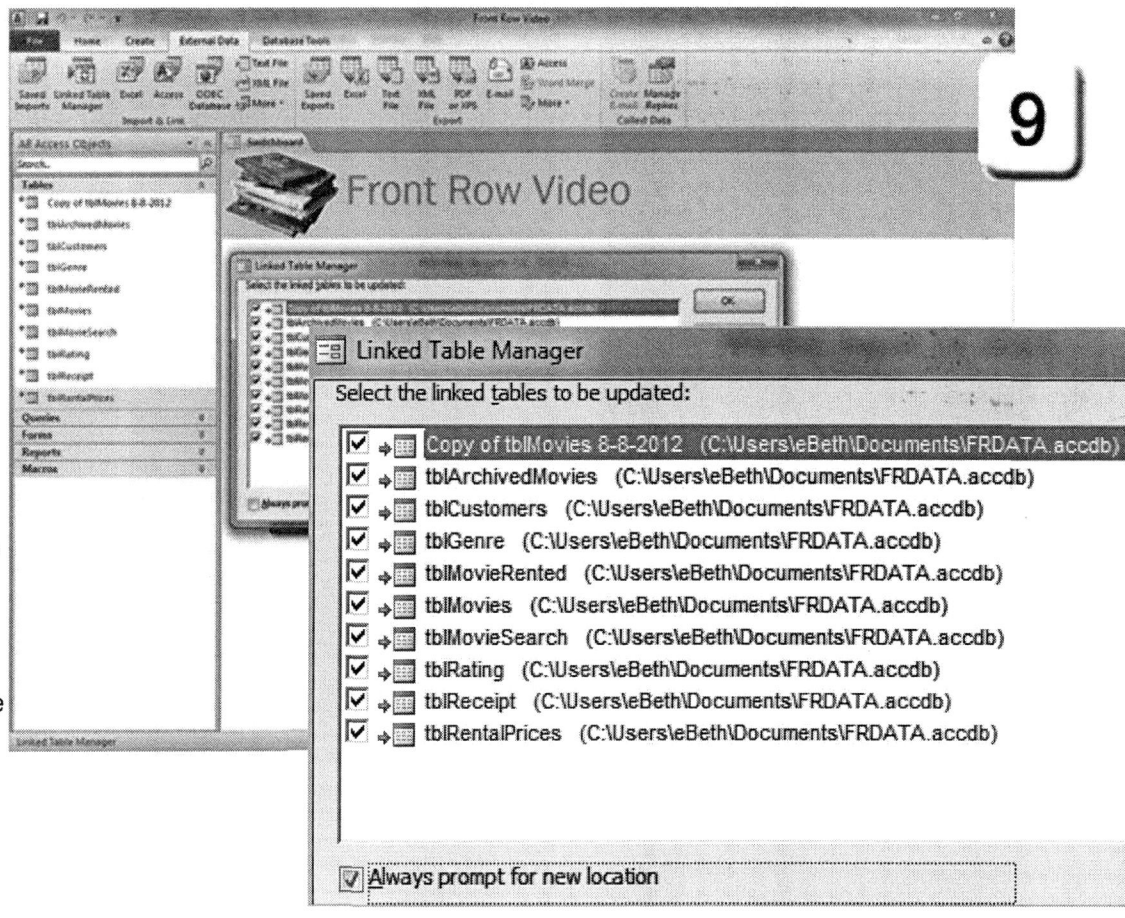

Exam 77-885: Microsoft Access 2010
2. Building Tables
2.5. Import data from a single data file: Import data as Linked Tables

Database Tools ->Move Data->Access Database

The Database Splitter

Microsoft Access has a database tool that will accomplish the same steps that we just completed, manually.

Now that you know the process and the end results, you can try the Wizard if you wish.

1. Try it: Split a Database
Open a COPY of the sample **database, FrontRowVideo Adv11.accdb. This** one has all of the tables, queries, forms and reports.

Go to **Database Tools-> Move Data.**
Select **Access Database.**

What Do You See? The **Database Splitter Wizard** will open with an administrative warning about the security on your Tables.

Click on **Split Database.** Keep going...!

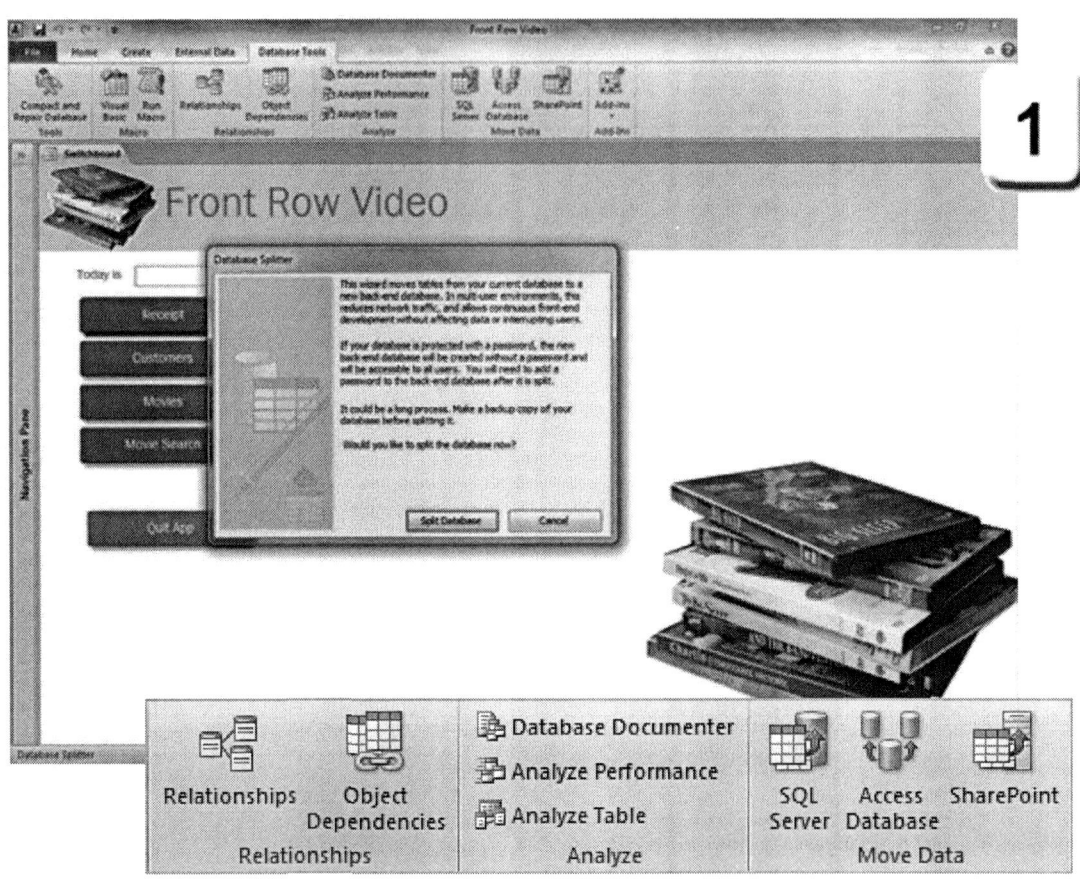

Exam 77-885: Microsoft Access 2010
2. Building Tables
2.5. Import data from a single data file: The Database Splitter

Database Splitter Options

2. Try This: Save the Splits

The Wizard will prompt you to **browse** to a folder and select a location to save your new databases.

Click on **Split**.

The Database Splitter Wizard will confirm when the process is done.

So....what happened?

The original database, FrontRowVideo Adv11.accdb, now has linked Tables. The FrontRowVideo Adv11_be.accdb is a separate database. It has all of the Tables. only Tables.

Keep going...

Database Tools ->Move Data->Access Database

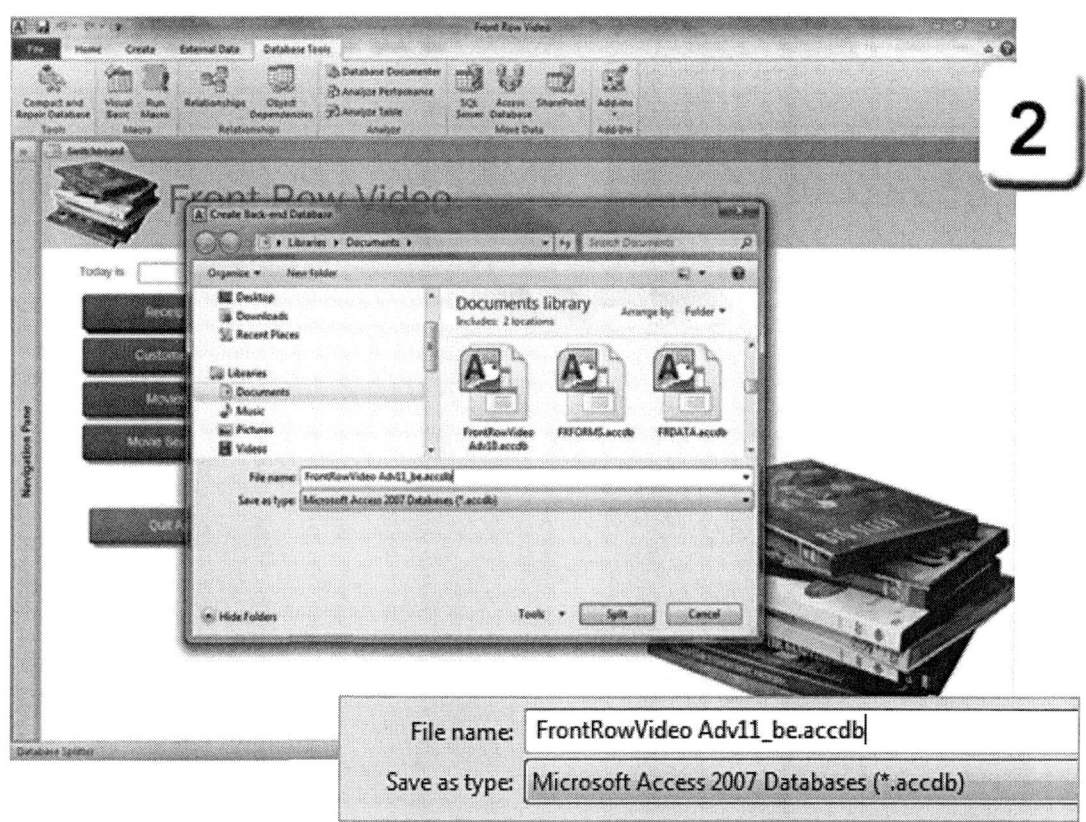

Exam 77-885: Microsoft Access 2010
2. Building Tables
2.5. Import data from a single data file: The Database Splitter

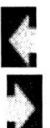

Database Splitter Results

The Database Splitter created a new database just for the Tables. The Forms, Queries, Reports and Macros are still in the database you opened. The linked Tables were saved to a new database.

3. Try it: Review the Linked Tables
FrontRowVideo11.accb. is still open.
Go to **External Data ->Import and Link**.
Click on **Linked Table Manager**.

What Do You See? Review the location for the linked Tables. In this example, the Tables can be found in FrontRowVideo11_be.accb. Access appended "_be" to the name of the Tables database when it was saved.

Click **Cancel** to close the Linked Table Manager.

External Data ->Import and Link->Linked Table Manager

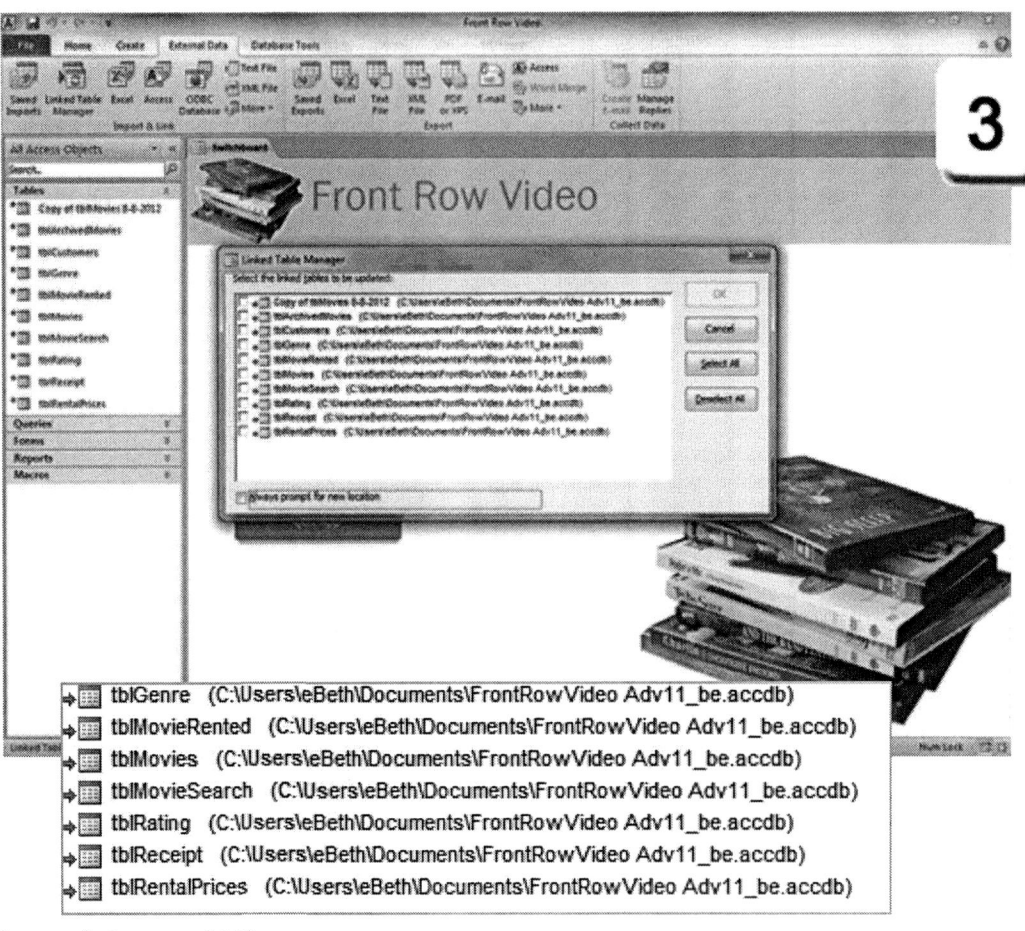

Exam 77-885: Microsoft Access 2010
2. Building Tables
2.5. Import data from a single data file: The Database Splitter

Access Options: General
Our Access database has **Options**.
These Options include:
General
Current Database
Datasheet
Object Designers
Proofing
Language
Customize Ribbon
Quick Access Toolbar
Add-Ins
Trust Center

1. Try it: Review the Access Options
Go to **File-> Options->General**

What Do You See? The **General** options include options for the **User Interface**. For example, the default choice is ClearType fonts for Text. ClearType is a Microsoft option that is very easy to read even if it is small.

You can also specify the default file type and location for a new Access database.
Keep going...

File->Options->General

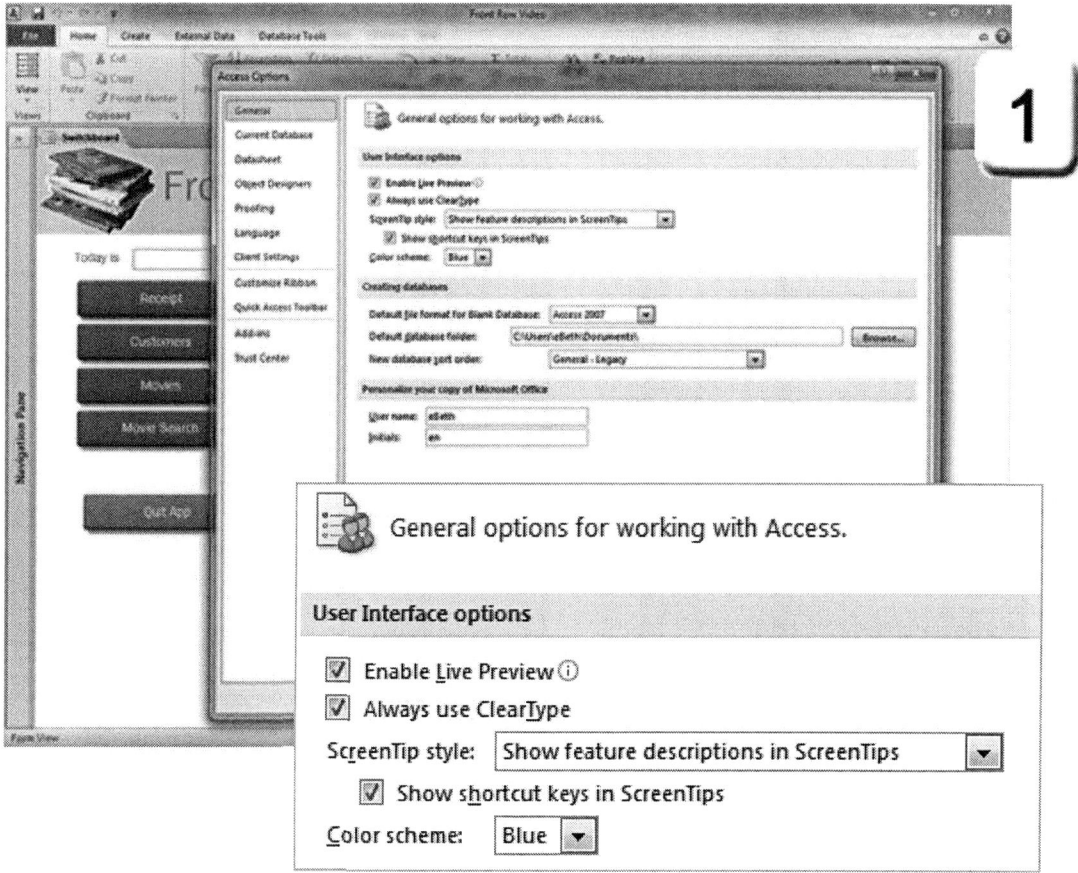

Exam 77-885: Microsoft Access 2010
1. Managing the Access Environment
1.1. Create and manage a database

File->Options->Datasheet

Options: Datasheet

2. Try it: Review the Access Options
Go to **File-> Options->Datasheet.**

What Do You See? The Datasheet options include Gridlines and Cell effects.

You can also select the Default font size, weight (Normal or Bold) and whether it is underlined or italic.

Keep going...

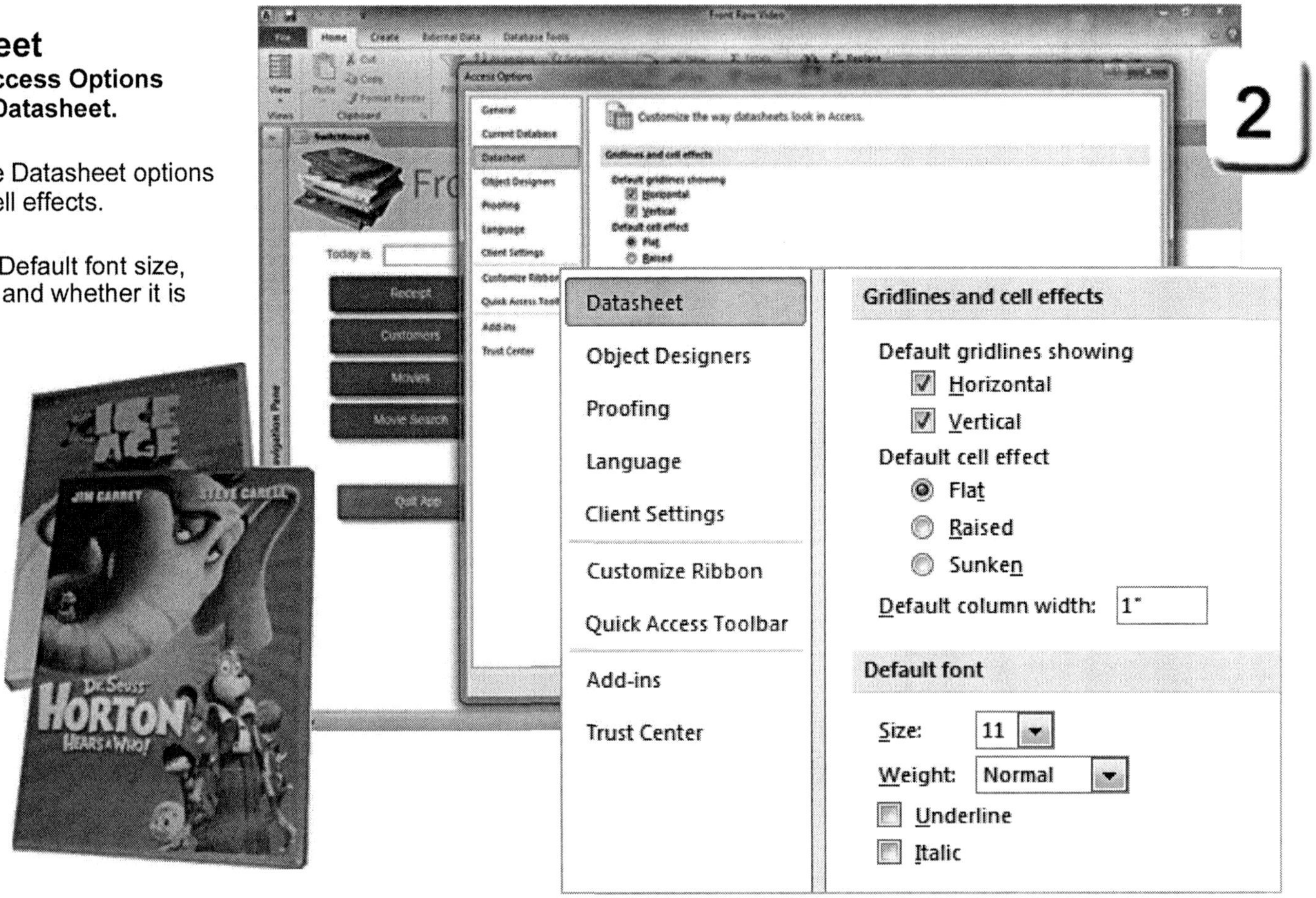

Datasheet

Object Designers

Proofing

Language

Client Settings

Customize Ribbon

Quick Access Toolbar

Add-ins

Trust Center

Gridlines and cell effects

Default gridlines showing
☑ Horizontal
☑ Vertical

Default cell effect
◉ Flat
○ Raised
○ Sunken

Default column width: 1"

Default font

Size: 11 ▾

Weight: Normal ▾

☐ Underline

☐ Italic

Exam 77-885: Microsoft Access 2010
1. Managing the Access Environment
1.1. Create and manage a database: Set Access Options Datasheet

Options: Object Designers

While you were designing this database, Microsoft Access proofed your queries and reviewed your code. Where does Access keep those settings?

3. Try it: Enable Error Checking
Go to **File->Options->Object Designers**.

What Do You See? At the top of the Object Designer list are the default specifications for Tables, Queries, Forms and Reports.

Scroll to the bottom and you will find the **Error Checking** shown on this page.

Keep going...

File->Options->Object Designers

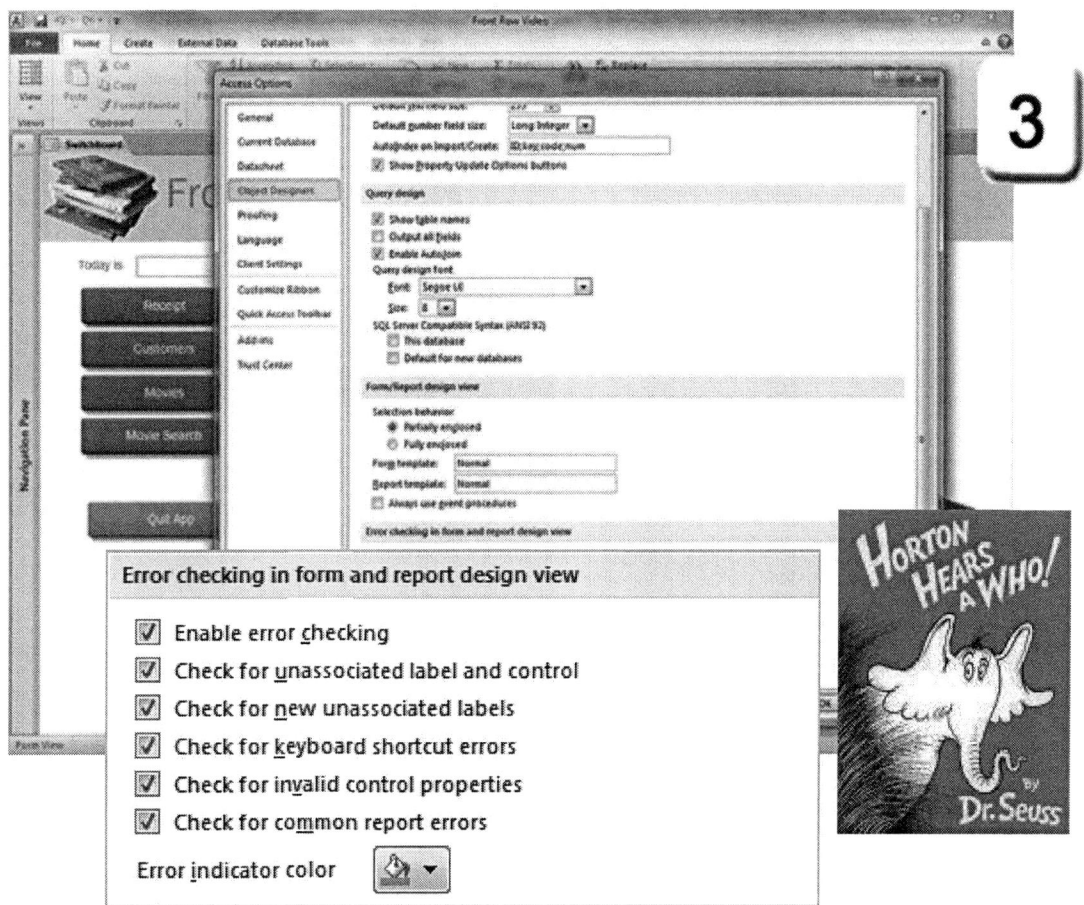

Exam 77-885: Microsoft Access 2010
1. Managing the Access Environment
1.1. Create and manage a database: Set Access Options Object Designers

Options: Client Settings

You can program what Users can do with your Microsoft Access database. Before sharing this mighty database, you should review the options in the **Client Settings**. These settings include:
Editing
Display
Printing
General
Advanced

4. Try it: Edit the Advanced Options
Go to **File->Options->Client Settings.**
Scroll down to **Advanced.**

Default open mode: Shared.
Shared allows many users to open the database. Exclusive restricts the database to one user.

Default record locking: No locks.
If you lock All Records, then the data cannot be updated, only reviewed.

Record-Level Locking
By default, Microsoft Access locks the record someone is editing so that two users cannot change the same record at the same time.

File->Options->Client Settings->Advanced

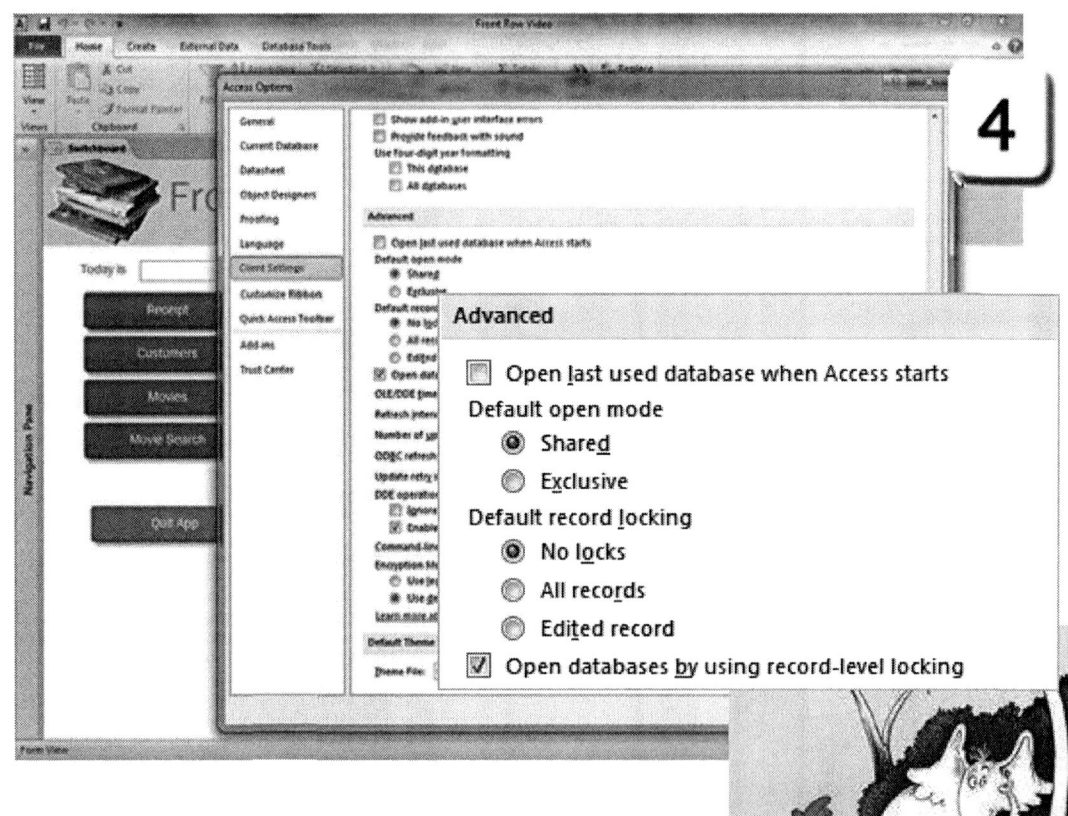

Exam 77-885: Microsoft Access 2010
1. Managing the Access Environment
1.1. Create and manage a database: Set Access Options Advanced

Options: Quick Access Toolbar

The Quick Access Toolbar is at the top of the Access database window. There are three tools built into the Toolbar: Save, Undo and Redo.

You can add any button if you wish, especially if you use it all the time. Here are the steps.

5. Try it: Customize the Quick Access Toolbar
Go to **File->Options->Quick Access Toolbar.**

What Do You See? You can choose from a list of **Popular Commands** or select a button from any Ribbon including the Form, Report and Query Design Ribbons. When you select a command, it will appear next to Save, Undo and Redo.

Click **OK** to close the Options.
Keep going...

File->Options->Quick Access Toolbar

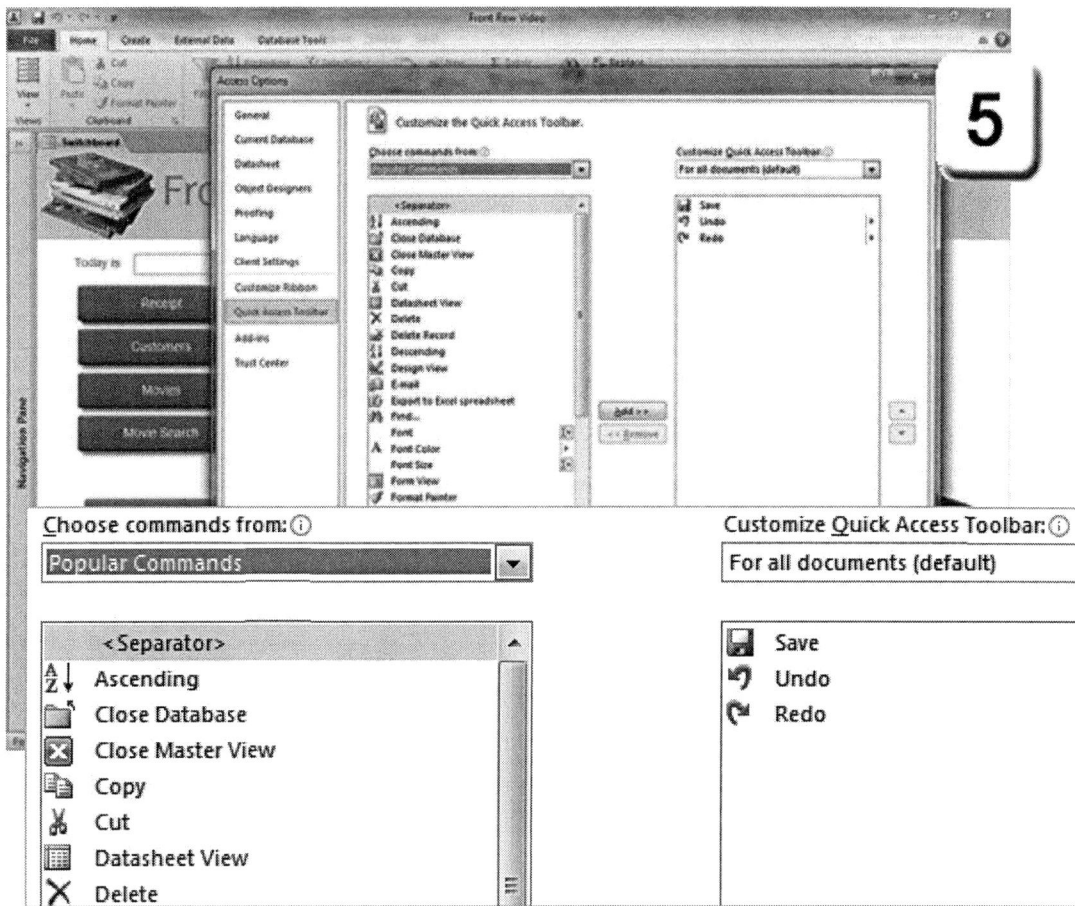

Exam 77-885: Microsoft Access 2010
1. Managing the Access Environment
1.1. Create and manage a database: Set Access Options Quick Access Tool Bar

Advanced Microsoft Access 2010   Page 333 of 347

File Level Security

Password Encryption and simple file level security can be managed with the Microsoft Access Database Tools.

This demonstration begins with a discussion on how to open the database **exclusively** so that you can set the security.

1. Try This: Open the Database Exclusively
Go to **File->Open**.
Browse for any sample database.
Look for the **Open** button. It is in the bottom right corner of the Browse window.

Click the arrow on the Open button.
Select: **Open Exclusive**.

When the database opens, click to **Enable** the database if there is a security banner.

Keep going, please.

File ->Open->Open Exclusively

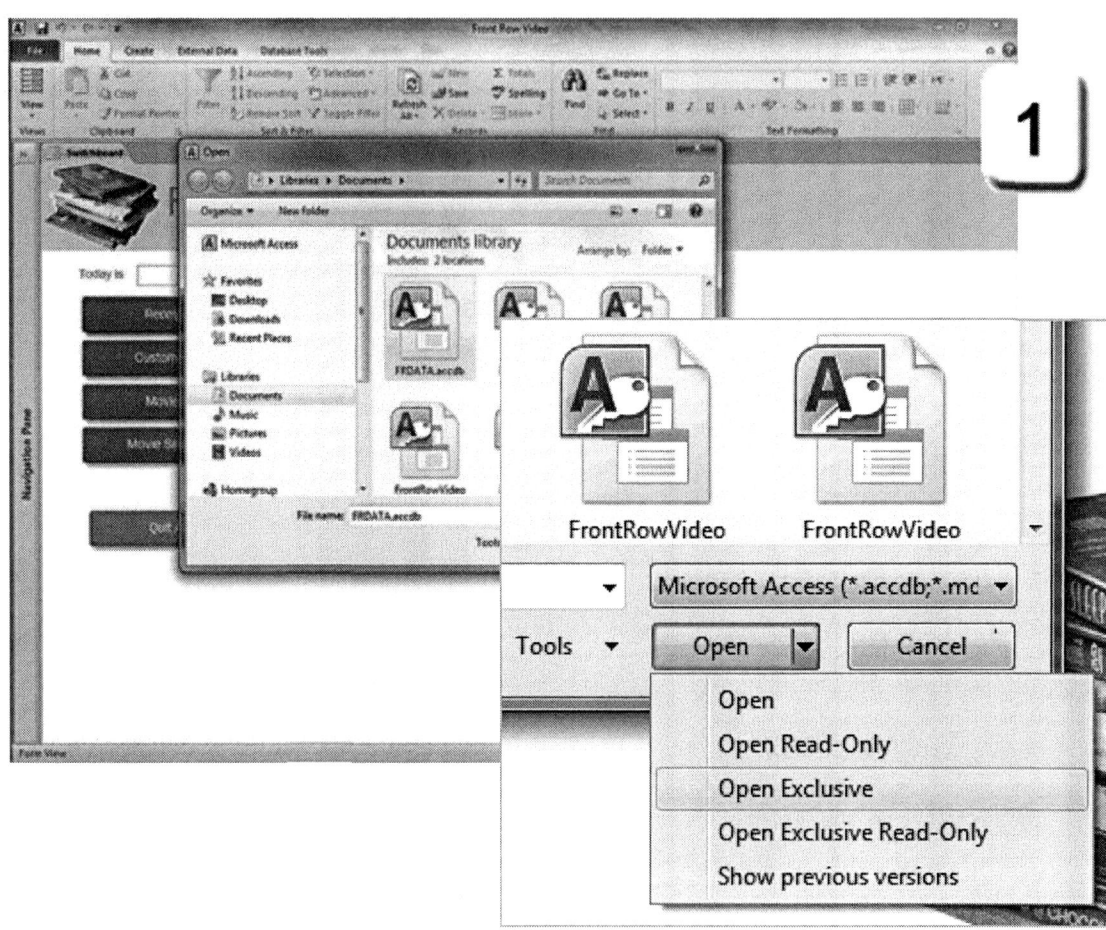

Exam 77-885: Microsoft Access 2010
1. Managing the Access Environment
1.1. Create and manage a database: Open Exclusively

Encrypt with a Password

2. Try it: Encrypt with a Password
Go to **File ->Info->Encrypt with Password**.

What Do You See? You will be asked to enter a password, then retype it to verify it.

Try This, Too: Remove the Password
Go to **File ->Info->Decrypt Database**.

This step will remove the password.

File ->Info->Encrypt with Password

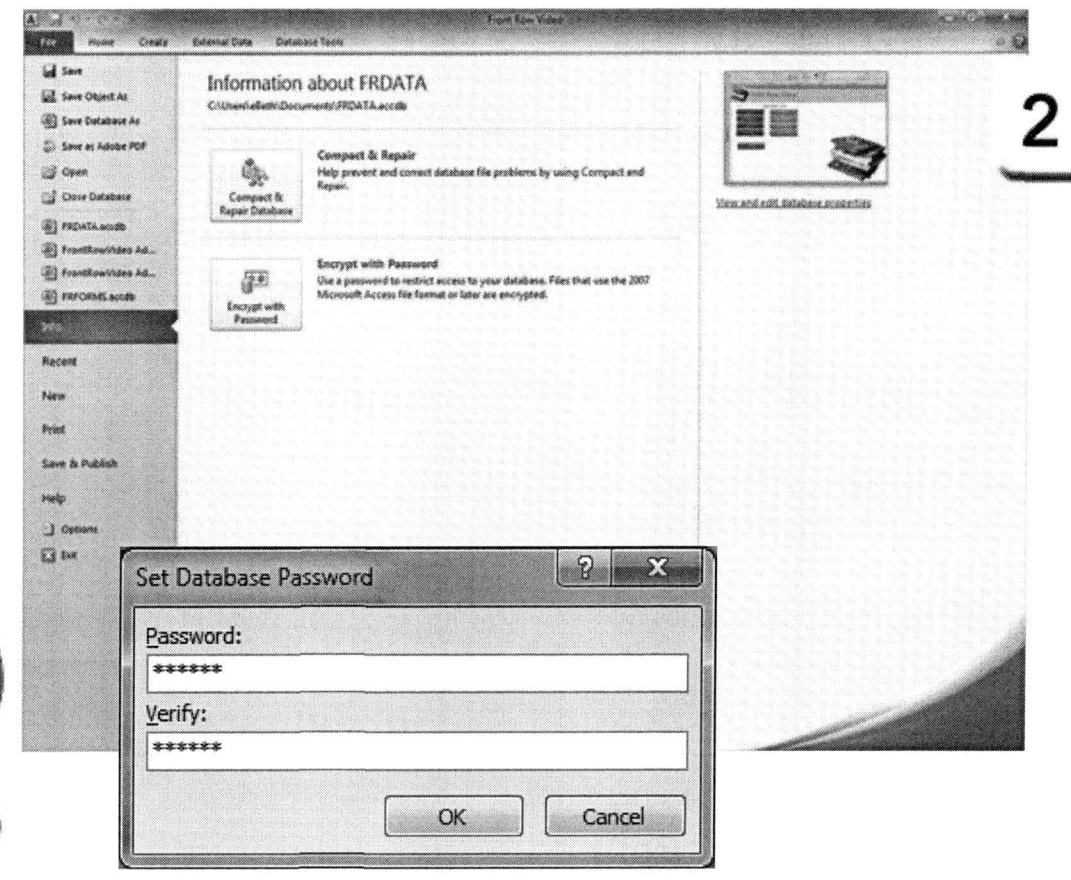

Exam 77-885: Microsoft Access 2010
1. Managing the Access Environment
1.1. Create and manage a database: Encrypt with a Password

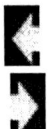

Database Tools->Analyze->Database Documenter

Document the Database

Before you release any database into production, there's one more task that you should do: document the database.

Before You Begin: Open a COPY of the sample database, FrontRowVideo Adv11.accdb. This one has all of the Tables, Queries, Forms and Reports.

1, Try it: Database Documenter
Go to **Database Tools->Analyze**.
Select **Database Documenter**.
Go to **Forms**.
Select All Forms.

Click on **Options**. (lower right corner)
Include for Forms: Code, Permissions
Include for Controls: Nothing

Click **OK**. to close the Options.
Click **OK**, once again, to close the Documentor.

Keep going.

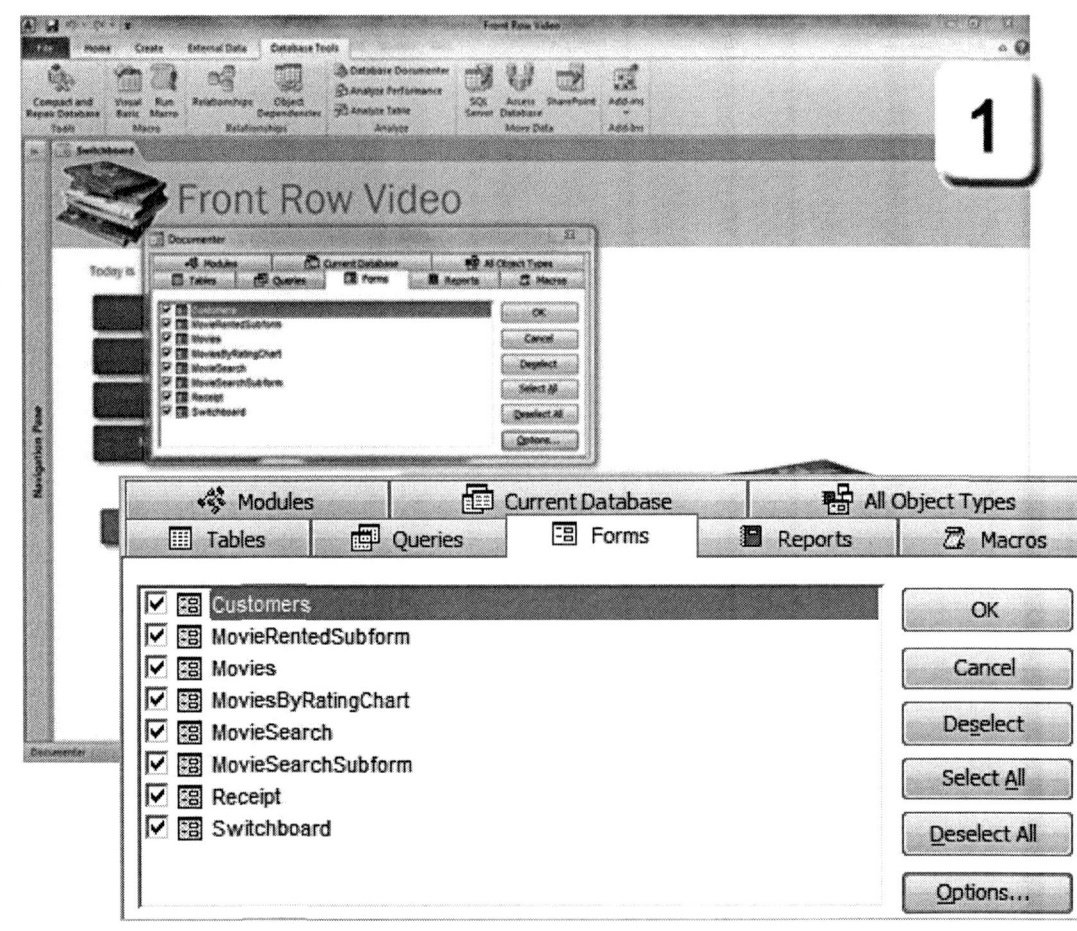

Exam 77-885: Microsoft Access 2010
1. Managing the Access Environment
1.1. Create and manage a database: Database Documenter

Review the Report

2. Try it: Review the Report

These options will generate a small, manageable report that prints out the Code and Permissions for the Forms.

If you selected all of the objects, and all of the documentation, the entire report would be about 200 pages long. And it would be complete!

Close the Print Preview.

Database Tools->Analyze->Database Documenter

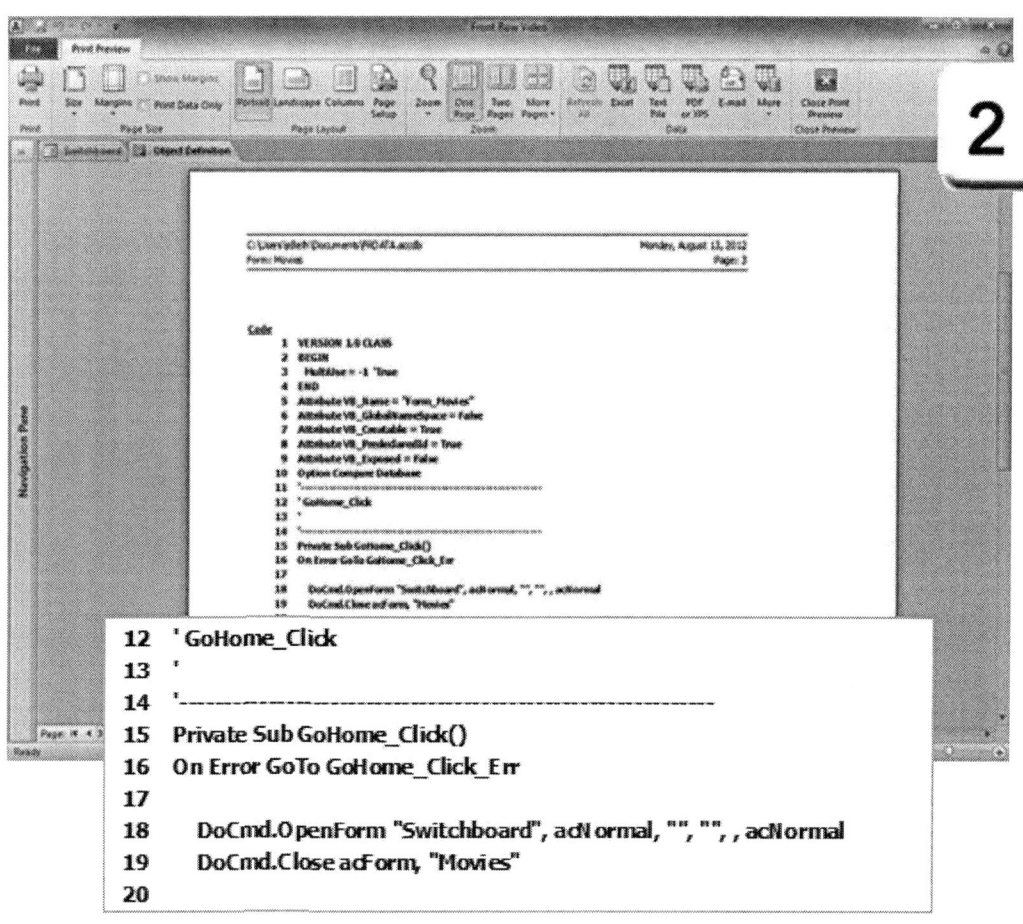

```
12  ' GoHome_Click
13  '
14  '----------------------------------------------
15  Private Sub GoHome_Click()
16  On Error GoTo GoHome_Click_Err
17
18     DoCmd.OpenForm "Switchboard", acNormal, "", "", , acNormal
19     DoCmd.Close acForm, "Movies"
20
```

Exam 77-885: Microsoft Access 2010
1. Managing the Access Environment
1.1. Create and manage a database: Database Documenter

The Relationship Report

You can generate a report of the Relationships in your database.

3. Try it: Make a Relationship Report
Go to **Database Tools ->Relationships.**
Select **Relationships.**
The Relationship diagram should open.

Try This, Too: Make a Relationship Report
Click on **Relationship Report.**

Keeeep going...

Database Tools ->Relationships->Relationships

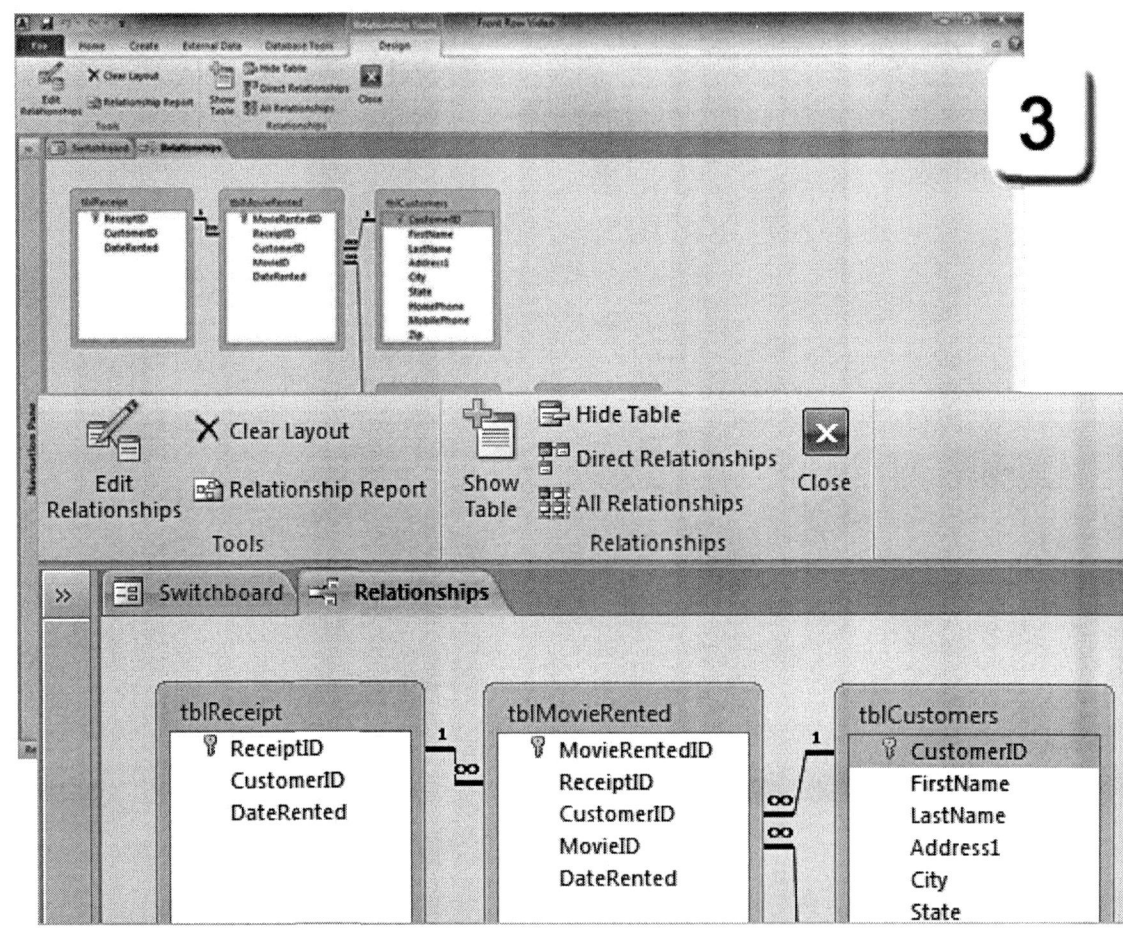

Exam 77-885: Microsoft Access 2010
1. Managing the Access Environment
1.1. Create and manage a database: Database Documenter

Preview the Report

4. Try it: Preview the Relationship Report
Microsoft Access will create a Relationship report and display it in Print Preview.

When you close the Print Preview, you will see the Report Design Tools. You can edit the default text and formatting with the Print Preview options if you wish.

Close the Relationship Report. You do not have to save it for this lesson. In fact, close everything, please. Done and done.

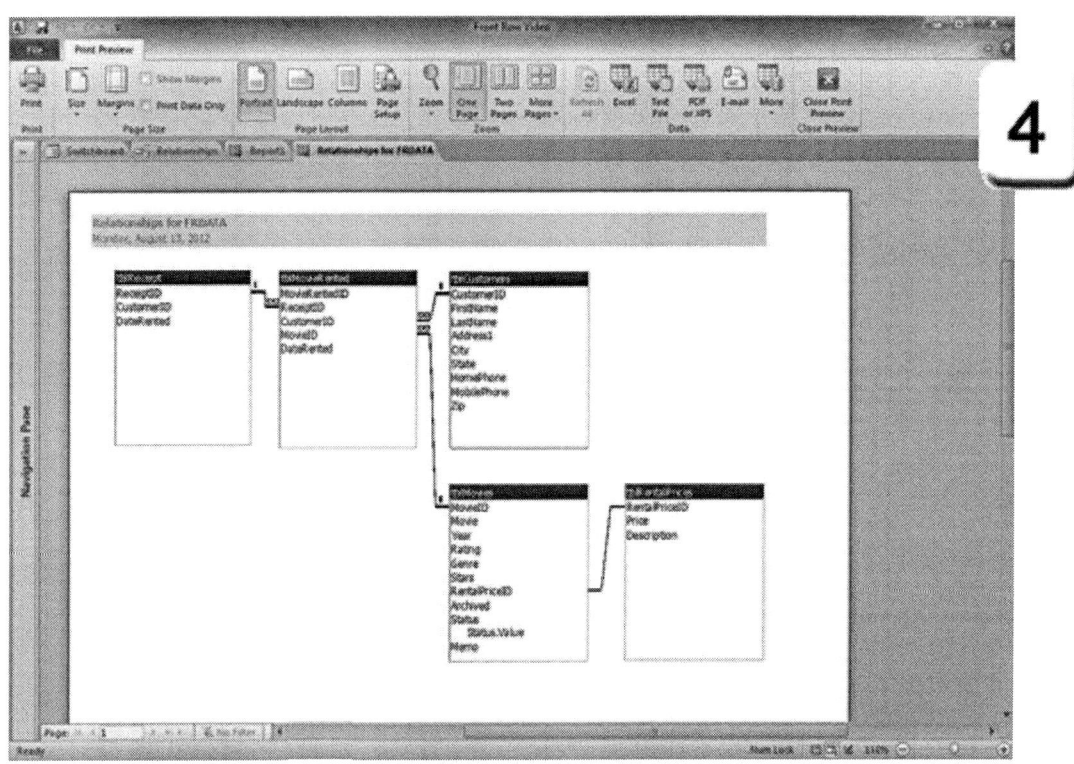

Exam 77-885: Microsoft Access 2010
1. Managing the Access Environment
1.1. Create and manage a database: Relationship Report

Database Maintenance

How does the table create an Auto number and distinguish it from a text field? What makes a Query run? Microsoft Access uses the **Access Jet Database Engine**. This engine is installed when you load the Microsoft Access software. The Jet Database Engine reads and saves the data. The engine also allows users to import and export information into other programs, such as Microsoft Excel.

All databases need routine maintenance. When you add and delete objects in a database, the files may become fragmented. This can happen when you add or delete records in a table. It also occurs when you add and delete Form Fields, Combo Boxes, or Labels.

In Microsoft Access, the command is called: **Compact and Repair**. When you compact an Access database, this utility will copy your file and arrange the database bits more efficiently on your hard drive. Compacting makes the database run faster.

Why does a database need to be repaired? Databases can become corrupted if they are shut down unexpectedly: e.g. the power goes out when you are editing a record. Network problems can also trash a database. Sometimes, switching back and forth from Design to Form View can make a database act goofy.

Exam 77-885: Microsoft Access 2010
1. Managing the Access Environment
1.1. Create and manage a database: Compact and Repair

Compact and Repair

Before You Begin: Save and Close anything that may be open. As with the other File commands, Access will close all Objects before you start.

Try it: Compact and Repair
Go to **Database Tools->Tools.**
Select **Compact and Repair Database**.

What Do You See? It happens so quickly you may wonder if it worked. If you have a large, fragmented database, you may see a progress bar on the bottom of your Window as the process moves along. Be patient: a big database may take several minutes to Compact and Repair.

When the maintenance is done, your database will open again.

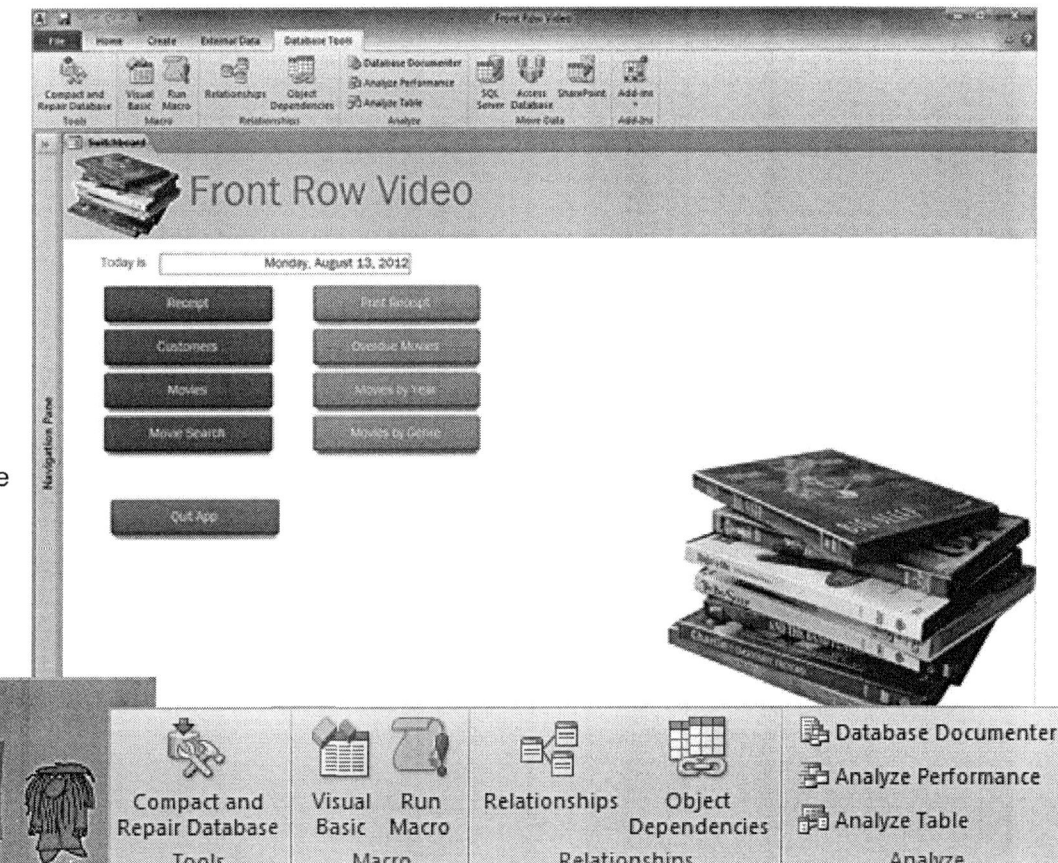

Exam 77-885: Microsoft Access 2010
1. Managing the Access Environment
1.1. Create and manage a database: Compact and Repair

Done and Done!

The goal of this lesson was to split an Access database into two databases-Tables and User Interface-to deploy the database for multi-users.

We used two methods to achieve the same results: by hand, and with the Database Splitter. In both examples, the databases were linked and the Linked Table Manager was used to refresh the links.

We also reviewed the Access Options for the General, Datasheet, Object Designers, Client Settings, and the Quick Access Toolbar.

Security was addressed. There was a discussion on how to open a database Exclusively and Encrypt it with a Password.

Finally, a little database maintenance. We walked through the steps to Compact and Repair a database.

Done and done. really. It's done.

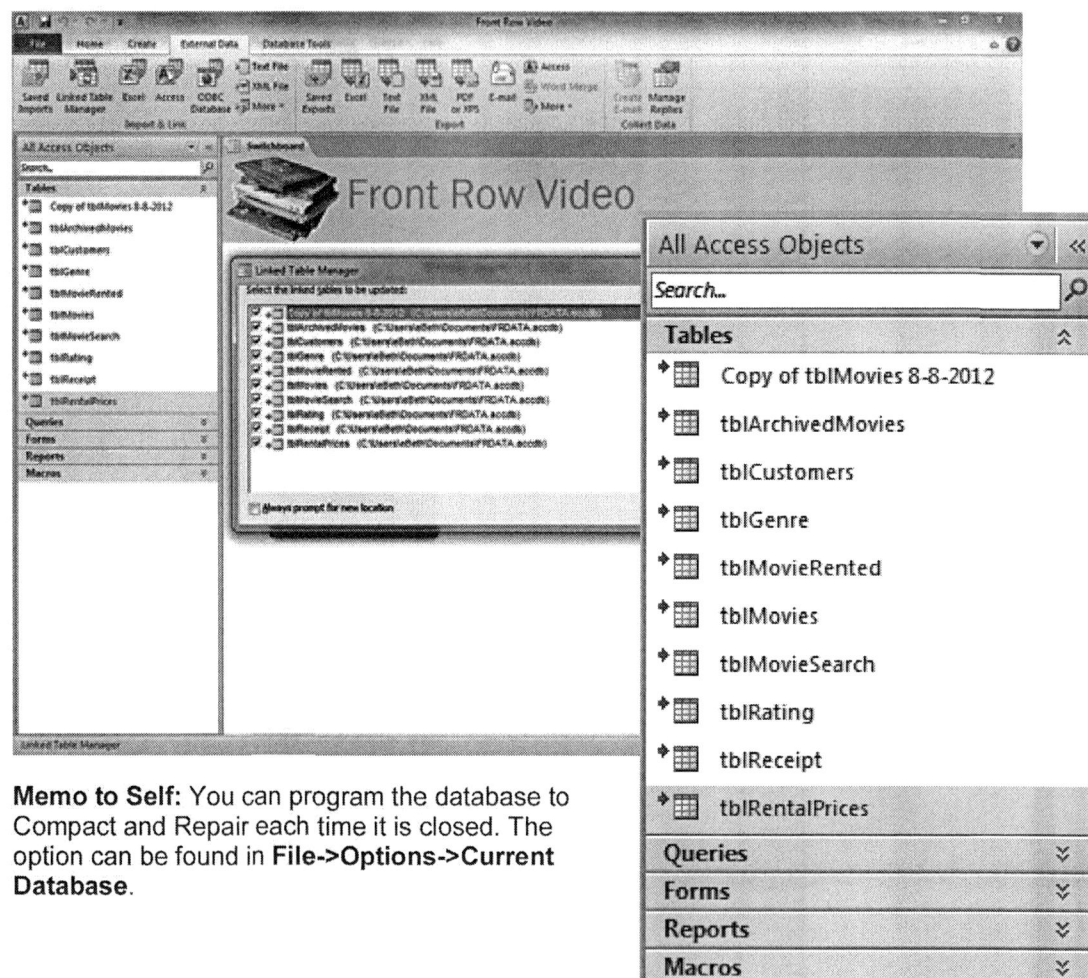

Memo to Self: You can program the database to Compact and Repair each time it is closed. The option can be found in **File->Options->Current Database**.

Practice Activities

Lesson 11: The Performance Network

Try This: Do the following steps

1. Open the Brown Bag Lunch database you have been working on.

Or, you may download **BBL Adv ver10.accdb**

2. Open the database and review the Tables.

3. Use the Database Tools to review the Relationships.

4. Create a Relationship Report.

5. Export the Relationship Report as a PDF File. Save it to your Documents Folder as Relationships for BBL Adv ver11-pdf. Go to the Documents Folder, open the document in Adobe Acrobat. Close this file.

Return to Access and Close the Relationship Tools.

6. Save the Relationship Report as rpt BBL Adv ver11 Relationships.

7. Optimize the database by moving the data into a separate database. Use to the command: Database Tools->Move Data->Access. Spit the database and save the Tables in your Documents Folder. The default name is: BBL Adv ver12_be.accdb.

8. Go to the Access Objects and review the Tables. All of the Tables should be linked, now.

9. Close the Brown Bag Lunch database.

Test Yourself

1. Which are the slowest parts of a Database?
(Give all correct answers.)
A. Forms
B. Tables
C. Macros
D. Report
E. Queries
Tip: Advanced Access, page 312

2. When deleting Forms and other Access objects, there is no option to Undo.
A. True
B. False
Tip: Advanced Access, page 318

3. When deleting Tables that are joined by Key data, you will be asked to delete the relationship before you can delete the Table.
A. True
B. False
Tip: Advanced Access, page 321

4. Which of the following is true about Linked Tables?
(Give all correct answers.)
A. They have a different icon than Tables created in the current database
B. Data edited in a Form will change the data in the linked Tables
Tip: Advanced Access, page 324

5. The Database Splitter Tool does which of the following?
A. Creates two new databases, one for the Tables and the other for the Forms and other objects
B. Creates a new database for the Forms and other objects, leaving the Tables in the current database
C. Creates a new database for the Tables, leaving the Forms and other objects in the current database
D. Creates a new database that includes half of the objects
Tip: Advanced Access, page 328

Advanced Access Skill Test

Before You Begin: Open the sample database
Advanced Access Skill Test.accdb

1.Create a Select Query and add the following Record Sources:
tblReceiptProducts, CustomerNameSQ, tblProducts.
JOIN the Tables by Key data:
From CustomerID in tblReceiptProducts to Customer ID in
CompanyNameSQ
From ProductID in tblReceiptProducts to ProductID in tblProducts.

2. Add the following Fields to the QBE Grid:
From tblReceiptProducts: ReceiptID, DateReceipt
From CompanyNameSQ: Company, Fullname, Address, CityStateZip,
Phone
From tblProducts: Type, Item, Specialty, Description, Price.

3. Save the Query as rptReceiptSQ.
Run the Query to test it. Close the Query.

4.Create a new Report with the Report Wizard.
Select rptReceiptSQ as the Record Source. Select all available Fields.
Group by ReceiptID, then by Company.
Choose the Stepped Layout.
Enter the Title: Brown Bag Lunch Co.
Select to Preview the Report and Finish the Wizard.

5. Create a new Report with the Report Wizard.
Select rptReceiptSQ as the Record Source. Select all available Fields.
Group by ReceiptID, then by Company.
Sort by Type, then by Item.
Choose the Stepped Layout.
Enter the Title: Brown Bag Lunch Co.
Select to Preview the Report and Finish the Wizard.

6. Close the Print Preview and edit the Report in Design View.
Move these Controls to the Company Header:
Company, FullName, Address, CItyStateZip, Phone.
Arrange the Controls stacked, like a return address on an envelope.
Edit the Properties for these Controls: Width: 3", Height: 0.2292", Left:0.3
Edit the Properties on the Detail Section so that they Can Grow.

7. Move the Controls in the Detail Section Left so there are no gaps.

8. Select all of the Labels in the Page Header and Delete them.
Select the Page Number Control and move it next to the Date Control.
Resize the Report so that it is 10" Wide.
Save the Report and test it in Print Preview.
Return to Design View and resize the Controls as needed t
Save the Report and test it in Print Preview.

9. Go to Print Preview and Save the Report as a PDF File.
Name the File: Advanced Access Skill Test EAN, where EAN is your initials.

10. Close the Advanced Access Skill Test EAN.PDF.
Submit this file online.

Microsoft Access 2010 Study Guide
Microsoft Office Specialist (MOS): Exam 77-885 for Access 2010

Advanced Microsoft Access 2010: Index
Microsoft Office Specialist (MOS): Exam 77-885 for Access 2010